A History of
Modern Europe

A History of Modern Europe

Volume 1
From the Renaissance to the Age of Napoleon

JOHN MERRIMAN
Yale University

W. W. Norton & Company
New York · London

For Laura Merriman and
Christopher Merriman

Copyright © 1996 by John Merriman

All rights reserved
Printed in the United States of America
First Edition

The text of this book is composed in Adobe Fairfield Medium
with the display set in Weiss Titling.
Composition by Compset Inc.
Manufacturing by Courier, Westford. Four-color illustrations printed by NEBC.
Book design by Charlotte Staub.
Cover illustration: *Ommeganck in Brussels—Triumph of Isabella* (detail),
early 17th century, by Denis van Alsloot. Victoria and Albert Museum/
Art Resource.
Frontispiece: Vittore Carpaccio, detail from *The Legend of St. Ursula*. Accade-
mia, Venice. Scala/Art Resource, New York.
The Library of Congress has catalogued the one-volume edition as follows:
Merriman, John M.
    A history of modern Europe : from the Renaissance to the present/
John Merriman
        p.   cm.
    Includes bibliographical references and index.
    ISBN 0-393-96885-5
    1. Europe—History—1492–   I. Title.
D228.M485   1996
940.2—dc20   95-50028
                                                                  CIP
Acknowledgments and copyrights appear on pp. 597–602, which constitute a
continuation of the copyright page.

ISBN 0-393-96888-X(pbk.)

W. W. Norton & Company, Inc., 500 Fifth Avenue, New York, N.Y. 10110
                                    http://web.wwnorton.com
W. W. Norton & Company Ltd., 10 Coptic Street, London WC1A 1PU

1 2 3 4 5 6 7 8 9 0

CONTENTS

MAPS

PREFACE

Why a new history of modern Europe? The collapse of communism in 1989–1990 and the break-up of the Soviet Union have redrawn the map of Central and Eastern Europe. A reconfigured Europe calls for a new history. This survey of modern European history explores the roots of the economic and political problems that continue to beset Western and Eastern Europe. For example, it shows how the simmering ethnic tensions that burst into bloody civil war in Bosnia after the disintegration of Yugoslavia echoed the quarrels that eroded the stately Habsburg monarchy a century earlier. To convey an understanding of the complex tensions that still exist in Europe, this survey offers balanced coverage of Russia and Eastern Europe, as well as of the West.

Not only recent events but recent scholarly initiatives suggest that this is the time for a new synthesis. For example, the text draws on the exciting studies in the social history of ideas, approaches that stand at the intersection of intellectual, social, and cultural history. It explains how artistic patronage during the Renaissance and the Golden Age of Dutch culture reveals some of the social foundations of art. Recent studies on the family economy, village and neighborhood life, and the changing structure of work have all enriched this book's account of the transformation of European society from an overwhelmingly peasant society into an increasingly urban and industrial world. The account of the emergence of mass politics in the nineteenth century draws on recent studies of popular culture and the symbolism and power of language.

I have adopted a narrative framework with the goals of both telling a story and analyzing the central themes of the European experience. Each chapter of A History of Modern Europe can be read as part of a larger, interconnected story. Moreover, this book stresses the dynamics of economic, social, and political change.

The story of the emergence of modern Europe and its influence in the world is first of all peopled with extraordinary characters, well known and unknown. The text brings the past to life, presenting portraits of men and women who have played major roles in European history: religious reformers such as Martin Luther and Jean Calvin; Queen Elizabeth I, who solidified the English throne, and Maria Theresa, who preserved the Habsburg monarchy; King Louis XIV of France and Tsar Peter the Great, two monarchs whose reigns exemplified the absolute state; great thinkers like Kepler and Voltaire; Napoleon, both heir to the French Revolution and despot in the tradition of absolute rulers; and the monstrous Adolf Hitler and Joseph Stalin. But ordinary men and women have also played a significant role in Europe's story, and they are in this book as well, making their own history. These chapters thus evoke the lives of both leaders and ordinary people in periods of rapid economic and political change, revolution, and war.

Of the central themes in our story, the politics of states and of peoples is the first important one. The growth of strong, centralized states helped shape modern Europe. Medieval Europe was a maze of overlapping political and judicial authorities. In 1500, virtually all Europeans defined themselves in terms of family, village, town, neighborhood, and religious solidarities. Dynastic states consolidated and extended their territories while increasing the reach of their effective authority over their own people. Great Powers emerged. Then, with the rise of nationalism in the wake of the French Revolution and the Napoleonic era, demands of ethnic groups for national states encouraged the unification of Italy and Germany and stirred unrest among Croats, Hungarians, and Romanians, who were anxious for their own national states. Ordinary people demanded freedom and political sovereignty, with revolution both a reflection of and a motor for political change. The emergence of liberalism in the nineteenth century and then the quest for democratic political structures and mass politics have transformed Europe, beginning in Western Europe. Even the autocracies of Russia and Central and Eastern Europe were not immune to change, and there the quest for democracy still continues.

While discussing dynastic rivalries and then nationalism, the book also considers how wars themselves have often generated political and social change. French financial and military contributions to the American War of Independence further accentuated the financial crisis of the monarchy of France, helping spark the French Revolution. French armies of military conscripts, replacing the professional armies of the age of aristocracy, contributed to the emergence of nationalism. The defeat of the Russian army by the Japanese in 1905 brought political concessions that helped prepare the way for the Russian Revolution of 1917. The German, Austro-Hungarian, Ottoman, and Russian empires disappeared in the wake of the bloodbath of World War I; the economic and social impact of that war generated political instability, facilitating the emergence of fascism and communism.

Like politics, religion has also been a significant factor in the lives of Europeans and in the quest for freedom in the modern world. Catholicism was a unifying force in the Middle Ages; European popular culture for centuries was based on religious belief. However, religion has also been a frequently divisive force in modern European history; after the Reformation in the sixteenth century, states extended their authority over religion, while religious minorities demanded the right to practice their own religion. Religious (as well as racial and cultural) intolerance has scarred the European experience, ranging from the expulsion of Jews and Muslims from Spain at the end of the fifteenth century, to Louis XIV's abrogation of religious toleration for Protestants during the seventeenth century, to the horror of the Nazi Holocaust during World War II. While religion has become less politically divisive in modern Europe, endemic religious conflict in Northern Ireland and the bloody civil war in Bosnia recall the ravaging of Central Europe during the Thirty Years' War.

The causes and effects of economic change are a third thread that weaves through the history of modern Europe. The expansion of commerce in the early modern period, which owed much to the development of means of raising investment capital and obtaining credit, transformed life in both Western and Eastern Europe. The Industrial Revolution, which began in England in the eighteenth century and spread to continental Europe in the nineteenth, was related to a rise in population and agricultural production but also manifested significant continuities with the past, and drew on technology that had been in place for centuries. It ultimately changed the ways Europeans worked and lived.

Europe's interaction with the rest of the world is a fourth major theme that runs through this history. Europe cannot be studied in isolation. Europeans, to be sure, have learned from Muslim, Asian, and African cultures. Through commercial contact, conquest, intellectual, religious, and political influence, and, finally, decolonization, the European powers and cultures have affected the histories of non-Western peoples.

European history remains crucial to understanding the contemporary world. The political, religious, economic, and global concerns that affect Europe and the world today can best be addressed by examining their roots and development. At the same time, the study of European history in itself can enrich our lives, as we contemplate not only the distressing failures and appalling tragedies of the past, but also the exhilarating triumphs that have been part of the European experience.

ACKNOWLEDGMENTS

When I was about ten or eleven in Portland, Oregon, I decided to write a history of the world, country by country, beginning with Albania. Surrounding myself with books, I reached the F's or G's, five or ten pages for each country, before giving up. Lawrence Robinson of Jesuit High School in Portland, Oregon, rekindled my interest in history, at a time when my passionate devotion to basketball and baseball overwhelmed everything else. I also owe a debt of thanks to Albert Feuerwerker and Gerhard Weinberg, in whose courses I learned a great deal when I was a somewhat floundering undergraduate at the University of Michigan. In graduate school, still at Michigan, Charles Tilly, now at the New School for Social Research, first encouraged me to keep my eye on the dynamics of economic, social, and political change, and their effect on ordinary people. This I have tried to do. And I have also always believed that meaningful detail and color reveal the rich texture of the past, and that history can be vivid and compelling. I have tried to write this history with that in mind. Bertolt Brecht's poem "A Worker Reads History" poses questions that I still think are important to answer:

Who built the seven gates of Thebes?
The books are filled with the names of kings.
Was it kings who hauled the craggy blocks of stone?
And Babylon, so many times destroyed,
Who built the city up each time? In which of Lima's houses,
The city glittering with gold, lived those who built it?
In the evening, when the Chinese wall was finished
Where did the masons go? Imperial Rome
Is full of arcs of triumph. Who reared them up? Over whom
Did the Caesars triumph? Byzantium lives in song,
Were all her dwellings palaces? And even in Atlantis of the legend
The night the sea rushed in,
The drowning men still bellowed for their slaves.

Young Alexander conquered India.
He alone?

Caesar beat the Gauls,
Was there not even a cook in his army?
Philip of Spain wept as his fleet
Was sunk and destroyed. Were there no other tears?
Frederick the Great triumphed in the Seven Years War. Who
Triumphed with him?

Each page a victory,
At whose expense the victory ball?
Every ten years a great man,
Who paid the piper?

So many particulars.
So many questions.

   While writing this book, I have necessarily accumulated a good many
debts to colleagues and friends. At Yale, Roberto González-Echevarria, Ivo
Banac, Mark Micale, Lee Wandel, Henry Hyder, Vincent Moncrief, Linda
Colley, Robin Winks, Geoffrey Parker, David Underdown, David Marshall,
Richard Brodhead, Piotr Wandycz, Laura King, and, above all, Mark
Steinberg and David Bell, shared their knowledge and expertise. I also
want to thank Jeffrey Burds of the University of Rochester, Harold Selesky
of the University of Alabama, Laura Englestein of Princeton University,
Leslie Page Moch of Michigan State University, John Lynn of the Univer-
sity of Illinois, Richard Stites of Georgetown University, David Cannadine
of Columbia University, Jim Boyden of Tulane University, Paul Hanson of
Butler University, Michael Burns and Robert Schwartz of Mount Holyoke
College, Thomas Kaiser of the University of Arkansas, Christopher John-
son of Wayne State University, Louise Tilly of the New School for Social
Research, Paul Monod of Middlebury College, Peter McPhee of the Uni-
versity of Melbourne, Judy Coffin of the University of Texas, Austin, John
Sweets of the University of Kansas, General (ret.) Harold Nelson, David
Large of Montana State University, Kathleen Nilan of Arizona State Uni-
versity, Elinor Accampo of the University of Southern California, Jim Mc-
Clain of Brown University, Alan Forrest of York University, George
Behlmer of the University of Washington, Mary Jo Maynes of the Univer-
sity of Minnesota, Thomas Head of Washington University, Jonathan De-
wald of the University of Buffalo, Johan Åhr of Muhlenberg College, as
well as Margaret McLane, Jan Albers, Martha Hoffman-Strock, Daryl Lee,
Tom Maulucci and Michael Levin. I would also like to thank Daniel
Orlovsky of Southern Methodist University, and Max Oberfus of Washing-
ton University, Mary O'Neal of the University of Washington, and a number of anonymous readers.
   For much of the time I have been working on this book, I was Master of
Branford College at Yale. At Branford, my former assistant and long-time
friend Larue Brion made it possible for me to do both. I also want to thank
Betsy McCauley and Jerri Cummings in the Department of History at Yale.

My colleague Jonathan Spence completed his splendid history of modern China, also with W.W. Norton and Co., in remarkably good time, showing me that a long survey could not only be started, but finished.

I want to thank Christopher and Lois Johnson, Ted and Joby Margadant, Roberto and Isabel González-Echevarria, Bob Schwartz and Marietta Clement, Dick and Cindy Brodhead, Steven Kaplan, Edward Rohrbach, David Bushnell and Karla Klarin, Jeanne Innes and John Innes, Yves and Colette Lequin, Maurice and Marie-Claude Garden, and Victoria Johnson, all good friends who have wondered politely when these two volumes would finally be finished. I hope they will enjoy the result. Many of these chapters were written and revised in Balazuc in the Ardèche in France. To Guy Larochette and Marie-Elyse Hilaire, Thierry and Carole Lacharay, Jacques and Catherine Imbertèche, Max and Doris Brioude, Huguette Laroche, Pierre Soares, Lucien and Catherine Mollier, and Hervé and Françoise Parain, among others, and in Collioure, to Jean and Gila Serreau and Philippe Calmus and Corinne Mouchard, *amitiés*.

I have nothing but the greatest admiration for W.W. Norton and Co., very special publishers to whom I am indebted. At Norton, Ruth Mandel resourcefully and imaginatively suggested illustrations and relentlessly tracked down those on which we decided. Bonnie Hall, Adam Dunn, Claire Acher, and Neil Hoos helped with photo research; Roberta Flechner did an excellent job laying out the book; Tim Holahan took care of many details that made production-time work sessions at Norton both useful and enjoyable. David Lynch and Joan Rosenblatt read the galleys and caught a number of errors.

Donald Lamm, chairman of the board and former president of Norton, embodies the best in publishing. He has helped make Norton a very special place. Don first proposed this project to me. As preliminary discussions moved along, Steve Forman took up editorial responsibility. He has not only been a wonderful editor, but also a friend. Sandy Lifland's deft, skillful, and patient work as developmental editor has contributed greatly to the book. It has also been a great privilege and pleasure to work with her.

Peter Gay read chapters with his usual care and skill; as always, we lunched and laughed, debated and discussed. For more than two decades, I have valued his friendship, and that of Ruth Gay.

Carol Merriman has also read and edited every chapter with a keen eye. She has tolerated with patience and good humor the almost constant presence of this book, along with other projects, in our lives for a decade, as well as my usual quirks and growing obsessiveness. The writing of these volumes has been part of the young lives of Laura Merriman and Christopher Merriman, certainly more than each might have preferred as they grew older. I dedicate this book to them in appreciation and with much love.

Balazuc (Ardèche), France
December 1995

PART ONE

FOUNDATIONS

As Europe emerged from the Middle Ages, the foundations for a dynamic era of trading, global discovery, and state-building developed that would affect the lives of both rich and poor alike for centuries. During the Italian Renaissance, which lasted from about 1330 to 1530, humanists rediscovered texts from classical Greece and Rome. Renaissance artists and scholars celebrated the beauty of nature and the dignity of mankind, helping shape the intellectual and cultural history of the modern world. Moreover, after a period when almost all of Western Europe adhered to one religion, abuses in the Church would lead to cries for reform that would not be stilled until most of Europe was divided between Protestants and Catholics. Religious conflict and wars would tear Europe apart, leading to reform in the Church but leaving permanent religious divisions where once there had been near-uniformity of belief and worship.

CHAPTER 1

MEDIEVAL LEGACIES AND TRANSFORMING DISCOVERIES

Jacob Fugger (1455–1525) was one of the sons of a weaver who settled in the southern German town of Augsburg late in the fourteenth century. At age fourteen, he joined his brothers as a trader in spices, silks, and woolen goods. He traded, above all, with the Adriatic port of Venice, where Fugger learned double-entry bookkeeping (keeping track of business credits and debits), which was then unknown in the German states. Jacob Fugger soon proclaimed himself "merchant by the grace of God" and amassed a vast fortune, which he used to loan sizable sums to various rulers in Central Europe. At times he counted an annual return of 50 percent or more. Someone wrote of Fugger that "his name is known in every kingdom and every region, even among the heathens. Emperors, kings, princes, and lords sent emissaries to him; the pope hailed him and embraced him as his own dear son; the cardinals stood up when he appeared." When asked if he wanted to retire, Jacob Fugger replied that he intended to go on making money until he dropped dead.

The family history of the Fuggers intersected with economic growth and statemaking in Central Europe. The Fuggers emerged as the wealthiest and most influential of the international banking families that financed warring states, answering the call of the highest bidder. In 1519, the Fuggers helped Charles V become Holy Roman emperor by providing funds with which the ambitious Habsburg could bribe electors. The Fuggers raised and transported the money that made possible imperial foreign policy. Loaning money to ambitious rulers, as well as popes and military entrepreneurs, the Fugger family rose to princely status and facilitated the consolidation of territorial states and the emergence of a dynamic economy not only in the Mediterranean region but also in the German states and Northwestern Europe by helping merchants and manufacturers find credit for their enterprises.

(Left) Jacob Fugger, merchant-banker and creditor of rulers and popes, traded *(right)* with the port of Seville, stepping-off point for colonization of the New World.

Both the emergence of stronger sovereign states and the growth of trade and manufacturing ultimately changed the face of Europe. The stronger states, as well as the expanding economy, contributed to a sense that many Europeans had in 1500 of living in a period of rebirth and revitalization. In Italy, the cultural movement we know as the Renaissance was still in bloom, and was beginning to reach across the Alps into Northern Europe. The Genoese explorer Christopher Columbus' voyages to the New World were causing a great stir in Spain and the Mediterranean region. A chorus of criticism of abuses within the Catholic Church could be heard in some places, particularly in the German states.

Although famine, disease, and war (horsemen of the apocalypse) still trampled their victims across Europe, there were other significant changes as well. Substantial population growth occurred in the late fifteenth and sixteenth centuries. Europe's population stood at about 70 million in 1500 and perhaps 90 million in 1600 (well less than a third of that today). These gains overcame the horrific loss of one-third of the European population caused by the Black Death (the bubonic plague) in the mid-fourteenth century. The expansion of the population brought a recovery in European commerce, particularly in the Mediterranean region and in England and Northwestern Europe, where the Fuggers and other merchant-bankers were financing new industry and trade. Towns multiplied and their merchants grew more prosperous, building elegant houses near markets.

The emergence of sovereign monarchical states also had its roots in the late medieval period (1350–1500). England and France were two precocious states that stood as exceptions amid the territorial fragmentation that characterized medieval Europe. They foreshadowed the emergence of even stronger states during the sixteenth and particularly the seventeenth centuries and the European state system itself in the early modern period.

Finally, the pace of change was quickened by several inventions that would help shape the emergence of the modern world. Gunpowder, first used in China and adopted by Europeans in the fourteenth century, made warfare more deadly, gradually eliminating the heavily armed knight. The invention of printing in the mid-fifteenth century engendered a cultural revolution first felt in religious life, with the Bible and other religious texts now more widely available to be read and debated. And the compass, first used to determine direction by Chinese and Mediterranean navigators in the eleventh or twelfth century, now helped guide European exploration across the oceans.

CONTINUITIES FROM THE MEDIEVAL PERIOD

During the medieval period, England and France emerged as sovereign states. Furthermore, smaller territories also began to coalesce into larger units and rulers began to consolidate and extend their authority. European society took on the shape it would exhibit through 1789, with three orders—clergy, nobles, and peasants—standing in relationships of mutual obligation to each other. Material well-being would remain at a subsistence level for most peasants but would start to improve as commercial trade across greater distances began to rise in the eleventh century. Moreover, small-scale textile manufacturing would grow, as would towns, particularly in Italy and Northwestern Europe during the twelfth and thirteenth centuries.

The Fragmentation of Europe

With the collapse of the Roman Empire in the fifth century, Europe experienced an influx of new peoples. From the east came the Magyars (Hungarians), who settled in Central Europe, where they were converted to Christianity. From Scandinavia came the so-called Northmen (or Norse or Vikings), who reached Ukraine, and who for the most part became Christians. The Arabs invaded Europe in the eighth century, subsequently expanding their influence into North Africa and Spain. The Mongols poured into what is now Russia and Ukraine, sacking Kiev in the 1230s, before their empire began to collapse in the fifteenth century. This multitude of influences contributed to both the political and cultural fragmentation of Europe.

In 1500, Europe was a maze of about 1,500 fragmented states. Economic, political, and judicial institutions were overwhelmingly local. Territories and cities were subject to a confused array of overlapping jurisdictions. Paris, one of five cities in Europe with more than 100,000 inhabitants, was dotted with enclaves of ecclesiastical authority. The city-states of Italy and trading towns of northern Germany were among cities that managed to preserve their independence from territorial rulers. Town residents hoped that town walls would protect them against bandits and disease (during times of plague and epidemics) and would preserve their autonomy.

Villages or, within towns, parishes, formed the universe for most Europeans. Local loyalties, and those to churches, took precedence over those to the state, the effective reach of which in many places remained quite limited. For example, in the late fifteenth century, an entire Balkan village claimed responsibility for the murder of its lord. Many villages were, for all intents and purposes, virtually self-governing; village councils, for example, established which crops would be planted on common land and set the date plowing was to begin. Such councils coexisted with seigneurial authority (that of lords). England, for example, consisted of thousands of relatively small rural communities, interspersed with towns and a handful of major cities.

Europe stood at the crossroads between civilizations and religions. After the collapse of the Roman Empire, Christendom itself had been split between the Roman Catholic Church and the Eastern Orthodox Church following the Great Schism between the two churches in 1054. The claim by the bishop of Rome—the pope—to authority over all Eastern Christians (as well as a festering doctrinal dispute over the nature of the Holy Trinity) led to the break, culminating in the pope's excommunication of the patriarch of Constantinople. By 1500, the Eastern Orthodox Church held the allegiance of most of the people of Russia and the Balkans. The Roman Catholic and Orthodox worlds met in the eastern part of Central Europe, with Poland, Bohemia, and Hungary looking to the West.

The Catholic Church, as an alternate source of allegiance and power claiming to be a universal state (with its own language, Latin), presented a potential impediment to state authority. As both the Church and the monarchies became more centralized, conflict between them became inevitable. The Church itself had been a centralized religious authority since the Roman Empire, the collapse of which left the papacy in Rome independent of secular rule. After the middle of the eleventh century, the popes were elected by the cardinals, each of whom had been appointed by previous popes. Bishops and abbots pledged obedience to the pope in return for tenure over abbey lands and ecclesiastical revenues.

In the Ottoman Empire, religious and political sovereignty rested in the same person, the sultan. In contrast, rulers of territorial states in Europe had succeeded in making themselves largely autonomous from Church authority. Although the Church was wealthy and powerful (owning about 25 percent of the land of Catalonia and Castile, about 33 percent in Bohemia, and perhaps 65 percent in southern Italy), princes were unwilling to let the Church impinge on their secular authority, even though ecclesiastical leaders in many cases crowned them. During the fourteenth and fifteenth centuries, rulers refused to allow ecclesiastical tribunals in their territories. The pope also commanded his bishops and other clergy to be loyal to the rulers of secular states.

Muslims continued to challenge both Roman and Eastern Orthodox Christendom. During the medieval period, Western Christians had attempted to win back lands conquered by Muslims, especially seeking to recapture and hold Jerusalem in the Crusades. In 1204, believing the Eastern Orthodox religion to be heresy, the Crusaders conquered the Eastern Orthodox Byzantine Empire, which had extended from eastern Italy to the Black Sea's eastern end. In doing so, Western Christians eliminated the most effective barrier against Islam. In the fourteenth century, the Ottoman Turks (who were Muslims) conquered two-thirds of Anatolia, much of the Balkan peninsula, and Greece. During the fourteenth and early fifteenth centuries, the Byzantine Empire (which was Greek in culture and Eastern Orthodox Christian in religion) was reduced to a small area straddling the straits between Asia and Europe, which included its capital, Constantinople (modern Istanbul), and some surrounding areas. Finally, the Ottoman Turks captured Constantinople after a lengthy siege in 1453, and by 1481, the Ottoman Turkish Empire extended to the Danube River in Central Europe. Roman Catholic Europe for the next several centuries would view Islam as a perpetual threat to its religion and culture.

Europe thus confronted a huge semicircle of states under direct or indirect Turkish control. The Western powers, which had launched Christian crusades against the Muslims, now were forced into a series of defensive wars against the threat of Islam, which Christians believed represented the "scourge of God." The Venetians constructed fortifications along the Adriatic coast against the Turks in the fifteenth and sixteenth centuries.

Part of Europe's fragmentation was due to its three systems of law. The legal concepts, principles, and procedures of civil law evolved from Roman law, which was based on the rational interpretation of written law applied to human affairs. Civil laws were decreed and thereby sanctioned by rulers, whose authority stemmed in part from their right to make or impose laws. The development of civil law, then, was conducive to the development of sovereign states by closely associating the power of rulers of states with the force of law. Canon law, established by the pope for the Western Church, codified in Latin the canons of Church councils and the revealed authorities of the Bible and Church fathers. As in civil law, canon law helped affirm the authority of rulers, that is, the pope, by closely linking the law to the authority of the ruler, whose subjects owed him personal allegiance.

Customary, or common law, was a codification of established custom, implying a constant reference to decisions taken earlier by judges. It was the usual mode of law in all areas where Roman law was not used. In Western Europe, customary law developed out of the customs of feudalism, a set of reciprocal economic, social, and political relationships that encouraged decentralized power structures.

In England, where common law unified the customary law for the whole land, laws were overseen by local courts, which contributed to the decentralization of royal authority. Unlike Roman law, which helped shape the sense that the ruler was a sovereign lawgiver who could override custom, customary law helped corporate groups (such as guilds) or individuals assert their interests and rights by establishing precedents that, at least in principle, could override the ruler's intervention in the legal process.

Although French customary law also evolved from feudal laws, French kings exploited differences in laws in their kingdom as they gradually increased their influence and authority. In this way, the Parlement of Paris emerged as a royal court to arbitrate among local laws, while in much of southern France, a unified (if not always written) code based on Roman law existed.

Europe's political fragmentation was accompanied by cultural fragmentation, reinforced by the many languages spoken. Latin, the language of culture, was still spoken in university towns (thus the "Latin Quarter" in Paris). Distances and difficulties in travel and communication were also imposing. It sometimes took months for mail to arrive. Yet, upon receiving a letter from another town, a Spanish scholar enthused, "If it had been a trout it would still have been fresh." The fastest galleys, which were rowed by slaves (slavery had been wiped out in Northern Europe, but still existed in some of the Mediterranean countries), could travel more than 100 miles per day. Nonetheless, the shortest time from Madrid to Venice was twenty-two days, and the longest, in bad weather, was four times that.

Slaves rowing a galley in the Mediterranean.

The poor man, the artisan, and the lord in late fifteenth-century miniatures.

Some merchants anxiously awaited cargoes that never arrived. Mediterranean storms could come quickly: one of them sank 100 small ships filled with grain.

The Structure of Society

Medieval society was roughly divided into three social groups: the clergy who prayed and cared for souls; nobles who governed and fought; and peasants, the vast proportion of the population, who labored. Burghers, town residents whose entrepreneurial activity made possible the economic dynamism of medieval Europe, were, despite their increasing importance, outside this classical typology.

The clergy were technically the first estate in France. Everywhere, they had many roles, serving as priests, teachers, judges, nurses, landlords, and chaplains. But they could only be tried in ecclesiastical (Church) courts and, in the evolution of the modern state, their status as a class apart would come into question. The secular clergy ministered to the population as a whole. Most of the lower clergy were as poor as their parishioners, but bishops generally were from noble families. The regular clergy included hundreds of thousands of monks and nuns living in monasteries and convents according to strict religious rules, in principle cut off from the outside world by their vows (and in many places legally considered dead!).

Nobles owned most of the land, with their status and income stemming from this land ownership, as well as from their military function. Noble titles connoted superiority of birth, and noble families usually intermarried. Nobles were in principle not to work, but rather to stand ready to defend their monarch, their own interests, or family honor.

Peasants, who made up about 85 percent of the population of Europe in 1500, lived in villages or in small settlements on the lands of the lords, dependent on the latter for protection in exchange for labor. Peasants had no legal status, with the exception of those (for the most part in Western Europe) who owned some land. In some places, they were considered barely better than animals by the lords who oppressed them and the clergy who told them their lot in life was to suffer in anticipation of heavenly rewards.

At least a fifth of the European population lived in extreme poverty. For ordinary laborers, three-quarters of their earnings went to purchase food, mainly bread. Towns and cities were crowded with poor people struggling to get by. Pope Sixtus V complained of vagrants in Rome "who fill with their groans and cries not only public places and private houses but the churches themselves; they provoke alarms and incidents; they roam like brute beasts with no other care than the search for food." The poor also wandered everywhere their feet could carry them, begging and sometimes stealing. Whereas poor beggars from within communities were tolerated, townspeople and villagers alike feared the poor outsider, particularly the gypsy. But acts of charity, encouraged by the Catholic Church, which viewed such acts as essential for salvation, helped many poor people survive.

During the fifteenth century, rebellions—generally protests against new tax impositions—remained small. Such rebels often asked for a return to "ancient rights." But banditry was pervasive. Nobles and urban artisans in medieval times even sometimes placed themselves at the head of bandit bands, particularly in regions where state power was weak (for example,

This early sixteenth-century print shows fishing, plowing, drawing water, the slaughtering of pigs, and beggars begging, all of which made up typical village life.

between Venice and Turkey, or in the Pyrenees, or between the Papal States and the Kingdom of Naples). Wandering minstrels, some of whom were blind, sang the deeds of Balkan bandits. The story of Robin Hood, the English bandit and popular hero, had its counterparts in a good many places.

Feudalism

Feudalism (a term first used by lawyers in Italy in the twelfth century) developed during the ninth and tenth centuries in response to the collapse of the authority of territorial rulers. Between about A.D. 980 and 1030, law and order had broken down in much of Europe, violence becoming the norm. This insecure time (of which contemporaries were keenly aware) had been characterized by warfare between clans and between territorial lords, attended by retinues of armed men, as well as the ravages of predatory bands.

Under feudalism, rulers and powerful lords imposed obligations of loyalty and military service on "vassals," who received, in exchange, use of lands (called fiefs) to which, at least in principle, the lords retained rights, as well as the subsequent protection of heirs under the same conditions, although a vassal had to pay the lord a fee upon inheriting an estate. Vassals also agreed to fight for their lord so many days a year and to ransom the lord if he was captured. For their part, lords adjudicated disputes between vassals. Vassals could join together to oppose a king who failed to meet his obligations; likewise, a king or lord could punish a vassal who neglected his obligations to his lord. Elaborate ceremonies featuring solemn oaths, sworn before God and blessed by churchmen, specified mutual obligations of lord and vassal. "You are mine," said one powerful lord in Aquitaine in what is now southwestern France to a lesser lord, "to do my will."

Despite some decline of royal rights throughout the period, and an increase in the power of great lords, there remained a crucial difference between a king and a prince. Kings received sacred anointment from ecclesiastical authority, and therefore claimed to rule "by the grace of God" even when, as in the case of the early Capetian monarchs of France, they were incapable of coercing the great lords and their families. While swearing to protect vassals and peasants, even the greatest lords avoided using the language associated with kingship. No one was ever anointed duke or count.

Feudalism developed in the context of an overwhelmingly agricultural economy, where great estates were in the possession of rulers or lords. The lord would keep part of the estate for himself (his domain) and would divide the rest among peasants, who would pay for the use of the land with services or in kind (payment in crops, animals, or some other commodity). In return, lords would offer protection. Peasants worked the lands of the lords, giving to the latter not only their labor, but most of what they produced. They were also obligated to mill their grain, brew their beer, and

Peasants at work defer to richly dressed nobles. Note the peasant tipping his hat to his lord.

bake their bread (and pay to do so) on the lord's estates. Thus, feudalism was a system in which the more powerful extracted revenue or services from the weak. Many lords also maintained judicial rights over their vassals and peasants.

Feudalism would finally disappear in the monarchical states in the late fourteenth century with the emergence of stronger state structures and the reimposition of the authority of the Roman Catholic Church in much of Europe. Thus, feudal relationships dissolved as the strength of rulers increased and noble independence declined in the stronger states. The granting of more noble titles by rulers in itself reflects the revived strength of the state. Gradually, royal courts usurped noble judicial authority in some places. Furthermore, economic development contributed to the continued growth of a money economy (payment in specie or in coin minted by rulers), which increasingly made feudalism obsolete. Some of the signs of an emerging money economy, above all, in Western Europe, included the ebbing of military and service obligations to rulers and lords, and the shift to cash payment by peasants to lords, instead of payment in service, crops, or animals.

The Black Death of the mid-fourteenth century itself helped sound the death knell of feudalism in Western Europe by decimating at least a third of the population. As wages rose because of a shortage of labor in the murderous wake of the Black Death, peasants were able to improve their legal status. The plague had also killed many lords. When lords tried to reimpose feudal relationships, some spectacular rebellions occurred, particularly from 1378 to 1382. The resentment of royal troops (along with the imposition of new taxes) contributed to peasant rebellions in Flanders (1323–1328), northern France (the Jacquerie of 1358), and the Peasants' Revolt in England in 1381. There was also unrest among the urban poor (as demonstrated by the revolt of the Ciompi in Florence; see Chapter 2), as ordinary people resisted attempts to return to the *status quo ante.* States took advantage of the chaos by assessing new taxes, such as the hearth tax. By increasing their authority, the monarchies of Western Europe gradually brought to a close the feudal era. Yet, remnants of feudalism (the existence of serfs, who were peasants legally bound to the land that they worked) remained in Eastern Europe and Russia until the nineteenth century.

The Subsistence Economy

Agriculture lay at the base of the European economy. Farming was the principal activity of between 85 to 95 percent of the population. Land was the most prized possession, a principal determinant of status. Wealthy people probably made up 10 to 15 percent of the population. For most, wealth depended on the possession of great estates (known in England as manors).

Peasants were constantly engaged in a protracted and more often than not losing battle against nature. Much land was of poor quality, hilly, rocky, or marshland that could not be farmed. In most of Europe, small plots, poor and exhausted soil, and traditional farming techniques continued to limit yields. Peasants scratched out a living, using horses, cattle, oxen, and mules (where peasants were prosperous enough to own such beasts), or more often, their own hard labor. Steep slopes had to be cleared and terraced by hand (the traces of terracing today provide a glimpse of the struggles of poor peasants in earlier times). Peasants plowed with hand "swing" plows. The "three-field system" left about a third of all land fallow (unplanted) in order that part could replenish itself during the growing

Peasants separating grain from stalks by flailing.

season. This mode of agricultural production itself necessitated sizable landholdings, and could not have worked on small peasant plots. Furthermore, villages held some land in common, probably granted originally by lords. This was economically wasteful, but nonetheless for centuries offered the landless poor a necessary resource for survival. And under the best of circumstances, peasants had to save about one-fifth to one-eighth of their seed for replanting the following year.

Peasants also had to pay part of what meager benefits they managed to extract from the land to lords, by virtue of the latter's status and ownership of land. Lords increasingly found it more advantageous to rent out plots of land, and gradually many commuted labor services to cash, which they spent on goods, including luxuries, available at expanding markets and fairs. These included silk, cotton, and some spices that traders brought from the Levant (countries bordering on the eastern Mediterranean). Peasants (like other social groups) also had to tithe (give 10 percent of their revenue) to the Church. These tithes had traditionally been in kind, but were increasingly monetized during the late Middle Ages. In a fundamentally subsistence economy, this left the rural poor—that is, most families—with little to eat.

Yet, even with the rise in population, lords in the thirteenth century faced frequent shortages of labor, and were forced to grant favorable terms to peasants. In this way, many peasants in Western Europe succeeded in purchasing their freedom, transforming their obligations into rents paid to the lords. Nonetheless, even free peasants still had to pay feudal dues to

Peasants carrying sickles and scythes raise their hands or hats to their lord as they await their orders for the day.

lords and for the right to mill grain, brew beer, or bake bread, monopolies that the lords retained.

Serfdom began to disappear in France and southern England in the twelfth century, and by 1500 serfdom remained only in parts of eastern France. Peasants were free to move about, although they still owed dues and fees to lords, and, in France, remained under the lord's jurisdiction. Rulers had reason to encourage the movement toward a free peasantry in Western Europe, because free peasants could be taxed, whereas serfs (who were legally attached to the land they worked) were entirely dependent on the lords who owned the land. In Western Europe, the free peasantry reflected the growth in the authority of rulers and a relative decline in that of nobles. In the West, most peasant holdings were increasingly protected by custom and by civic law.

In Eastern and Central Europe, by way of contrast, peasants were rapidly losing their freedom during the sixteenth century, becoming serfs as landowners sought to assure themselves of a stable labor supply. This in itself was a sign that nobles were carving out territorial domination virtually independent from that of kings and other rulers.

Many people were constantly on the move in Europe. Peddlers, artisans, and agricultural laborers were obliged to travel in search of work. Shepherds moved distances of up to 500 miles with their sheep from the plains to summer pastures of higher elevations, and back again in the fall ("transhumance"). Hundreds of thousands of rural people migrated seasonally from the Pyrenees, Alps, and other mountainous regions to undertake construction work in towns, or to follow the harvest. Or people moved in the hope of simply staying alive. The roads, particularly during years of dearth, seemed full of vagabonds and beggars.

Most poor families survived by eating bread and not much else. For peasants, meat was something that lords and burghers ate, fruit was rare, vegetables poor, and bread, soup, and perhaps peas and beans the stuff of life. In southern France, grain made from chestnuts (which were themselves eaten in many forms) served as "the bread of the poor."

Yet, European agriculture was not totally stagnant. Considerable agricultural progress occurred in medieval Europe. Innovations such as three-field rotation, the use of mills, and metal harvesting implements were introduced at that time, although not adopted by all peasants until much later. Once adopted, these methods would remain basically the same until the era of mechanization in the nineteenth century, although a good many refinements contributed to subsequent progress, including the arrival of new crops brought from the New World by Columbus and his successors.

Free peasants contributed to the rise in agricultural production, which, however modest, was sufficient to feed a growing population. Not all peasants were desperately poor. Many could survive (and a minority did quite well) when famine, disease, and war left them alone, selling in the nearest market what produce they had left over after replanting, dues, and other

The medieval innovation of the three-field system allowed for the renewal of one field by leaving it fallow for a season.

obligations were paid up for that year. Many lords became market-oriented farmers in response to increased population. This in itself increased agricultural production.

The growth in the European population during the medieval period depended on these modest increases in agricultural yields. In England, Flanders, northern France, and Sicily (as well as North Africa), grain was intensively cultivated for the market. Urban growth encouraged cash-crop farming, enriching larger landlords, merchants, and wealthy peasants. There were, to be sure, areas of prosperous agriculture, such as the rich valley of the Po River in central Italy, and the plains of Valencia near the southern coast of Spain. Landowners brought more land under cultivation, cleared forests, drained marshes and swamps, and where possible, irrigated arid fields. Free peasants moved toward the eastern frontiers of Europe in search of land, which they brought under cultivation. Agricultural growth, which had been steady until the beginning of the fourteenth century, slowed down until the mid-fifteenth century because of the population losses due to the bubonic plague. But once the population began to grow again, plots that had been abandoned during the Black Death now were plowed once more. In general, too, farming techniques and tools improved during the fifteenth century. The Mediterranean lands, in particular, produced olives and wine, as well as wheat. Beer (made from cereal grains and hops) was a drink limited to Northern Europe, particularly the German states, England, and Scandinavia.

Religion and Popular Culture

Religion maintained a great hold over the lives of most Europeans in 1500, permeating everyday life. The Church, its faith and learning preserved during the so-called Dark Ages, viewed itself as an institution necessary for the salvation of souls and a unifying force in Europe. This gave the clergy great importance as counselors and distributors of the sacraments (above all, penance, the forgiveness of sins), without which Christians believed that salvation could not be achieved. Western Christendom was interlocked with Western civilization, although Muslim and Jewish heritages remained strong in Spain and Turkish-controlled areas. One of Europe's major and most traveled routes took pilgrims from many countries to the shrine of Santiago de Compostella in northwestern Castile.

In many parts of Europe, Jews, some of whom were moneylenders and peddlers, remained outcasts, although in general they did not live apart from the Christian population until the fifteenth century, when they were forced to do so by civil and ecclesiastical authorities. The popes forced Jews in Rome to wear distinctive badges; Venice established the first "ghetto" in 1516. Many Jews, forbidden to enter certain trades, were forced to wander in search of towns "where their weary feet could rest."

Religious themes and subjects permeated virtually all medieval art and much of its music. In the twelfth century, the magnificent Gothic cathedrals, houses of God reaching toward Heaven, began to be built. The construction of these churches often lasted as long as a century, absorbing enormous resources, and were paid for by gifts, large and small, from people of all walks of life. Church bells tolled the hours (clocks would remain novelties until the end of the sixteenth century).

Christianity shaped a general system of belief and values that defined the way most people viewed themselves and the world in which they lived. Thus, the Church blessed oaths of fealty sworn by vassals to lords and rulers, and took an important role in the rites of passage (birth, marriage, death) that marked the lives of peasants and nobles alike. The Italian Renaissance (see Chapter 2), to be sure, rediscovered the dignity of humanity, but it did so within the context of Christian belief.

The clergy had enormous moral authority in village life. When preachers passed through villages, peasants and penitents waited long into the night to have them hear their confessions. Most people believed that saints could intercede with God on behalf of people who prayed to them.

Religious holidays interspersed the calendar year. Thus, popular religious festivals played an important part in daily life in Europe. While ordinary people did not participate in elite culture, elites participated in popular culture, which, to a great extent, had been shaped by Christianity. Likewise, Jewish popular culture reflected a cultural interchange between ordinary people and elites.

Storytellers, whether amateur or professional, kept oral traditions of popular culture alive at a time when most people were illiterate. The most accomplished storytellers passed on their tales during evening gatherings, when villagers, principally women, gathered together to darn, tell stories, and keep warm. Many of these stories and tales reflected the fatalism of societies in which most people died relatively young.

There was much of which to be afraid. Most people believed in magic and the presence of the supernatural on earth. By such views, sorcerers or saints could intervene between people and the bad luck that might befall them. Primitive healers were believed to stand between disease and survival. They could maintain an equilibrium in the community. People believed that rubbing certain saints' images could bring good fortune. When the wine harvest failed in some parts of France, villagers whipped the statue saints that had failed them. People believed that it was a good sign to encounter a wolf, deer, or bear, that a stork landing on a house assured its occupants of wealth and longevity, that meeting a white-robed monk in the morning was a bad omen, a black-robed one a good one, that a crow cawing over the house of someone sick meant death was on its way, and that a magpie announced a cure. Such beliefs helped peasants cope with a world in which droughts, harvest failures, accidents, as well as a myriad of fatal illnesses, could bring personal and family catastrophe.

The belief in the supernatural translated into a belief that conjurers, "cunning folk" and witches could determine earthly events. Many people in need turned to sorcerers before they turned to God. Later, particularly in the seventeenth century, tens of thousands of people were executed for sorcery. Magic might, it was commonly believed, help expectant parents determine the sex of their child. Likewise, a cunning man might discover the identity of a thief by placing papers with names inside little clay balls; the guilty party's name would be the first to unravel inside a bucket of water. If an accused murderer were forced to touch the body of the victim, it was believed that blood would rush from the corpse if he or she were guilty.

Festivals marked the cycles of the year, with time still largely governed by the agricultural calendar. At the beginning of Lent, young men in some places in Western Europe carried brands of blazing straw and frolicked to ensure the village of agricultural and sexual fertility. Carnival was the highlight of the year for most people in early modern Europe, particularly in the Mediterranean region where it can be sunny and relatively warm even in February. There was more to Carnival than simply fun, as people ate and drank as at no other time, tossing flour, eggs, and fruit at each other and playing games, and much more (a disproportionate number of babies were conceived during that magic time). Carnival also stood the world on its head, if only briefly. The poor acted out the misdeeds of the wealthy in elaborate plays that were both ritualized and spontaneous. Ordinary people could poke fun at the powerful in elaborately staged farces

A peasant village carnival.

and parades by dressing up as and spoofing the behavior of judges, nobles, and clergymen. Liberated, however briefly, from their station in life by festivity and disguise, they crowned their own "kings" and "queens" of Carnival.

THE EMERGENCE OF EARLY MODERN EUROPE

The late Middle Ages brought some significant economic, social and political changes that helped shape the emergence of early modern Europe. Following the devastation of the Black Death, Europe's population slowly revived and then grew. More land was brought into cultivation, providing a somewhat greater supply of food. However, the balance between life and death was precarious indeed; famine, disease, and war still intervened frequently and murderously to check population growth.

At the same time, the continent's trade and manufacturing developed rapidly, particularly that in the Mediterranean region and in Northwestern Europe. Prosperous banking families provided capital for traders and manufacturers, as they did for states, and basic mechanisms for the transfer of credit evolved. The Mediterranean region, particularly the Italian city-states, was the center of commerce; trade with Asia and the Middle East developed at a rapid pace. At the same time, towns grew in size, and their merchants became more prosperous, especially in northern and central Italy and in the Low Countries, reflecting the importance of trade and textile manufacturing on urban growth. The growing prosperity of the entrepreneurial elite of many towns, more numerous and larger in Western

Europe than in Eastern Europe and Russia, reflected their relative independence from territorial rulers. One of the characteristics of this relatively favored status was the proliferation of guilds and other organizations that reflected the dynamism of medieval urban, economic, social, and political life.

Yet, at the same time, much of the modern state system was already in place. During the 1350–1450 period, the kingdoms of France, Spain, England, Scotland, Denmark, Norway, Sweden, and Hungary emerged, as rulers consolidated and extended their authority over their territories, eroding the independence of feudal lords and ecclesiastical authorities. Most of the small territorial units were in the German states or in Italy. France and England were sovereign states. The Iberian Peninsula was divided between Castile and Aragon—joined through the marriage of Queen Isabella and King Ferdinand in 1469, forming contemporary Spain—and Portugal. The basic layout of three Scandinavian states already existed. And important states of Central Europe (Poland-Lithuania, Hungary, and Bohemia) were already reasonably well defined. Even the Swiss cantonal federation had emerged.

A Rising Population

Europe's population had almost doubled between 1000 and 1300, rising from about 40 million to perhaps 75 million people. But early in the fourteenth century, the population began to decline, probably because of rampant disease. Then, in the middle of the century, the Black Death ravaged Europe, killing between a third and half of the European population. A bacillus spread by fleas carried by black rats, the plague reached Constantinople from Asia in 1347. It then tore through the Italian peninsula, Spain, and France in 1348, Austria, Switzerland, the German states, the Netherlands, and England in 1349, and Scandinavia and Poland in 1350. Victims died horrible deaths, some in a few days, others lingering in agony, but not for long. Some villages were completely abandoned, as people tried to flee its path. In vain, states and cities tried frantically to prevent the arrival of travelers, fearful that they were carriers of the dread disease.

For the next century, births and deaths remained balanced (with higher mortality rates in cities wiping out increased births in the countryside). Europe only began to recover during the second half of the fifteenth century, thanks to a lull in epidemics and the absence of destructive wars. However, the population did not reach the level it had been at in 1300 until about 1550, or somewhat earlier, when it began to rise rapidly, particularly in towns and in Northern Europe (see Table 1-1).

Europeans remained perpetually vulnerable to disaster and death. Epidemics almost routinely took huge tolls in Europe. Plague was the worst of these, but influenza, typhus, malaria, typhoid, and smallpox also carried off many people, particularly the poor, who invariably suffered from in-

TABLE 1-1. THE EUROPEAN POPULATION IN THE SIXTEENTH AND
SEVENTEENTH CENTURIES (IN MILLIONS)

	1500	1600
Spain and Portugal	9.3	11.3
Italian states	10.5	13.3
France	16.4	18.5
Low countries*	1.9	2.9
British Isles	4.4	6.8
Scandinavia	1.5	2.4
German states	12.0	15.0
Switzerland	0.8	1.0
Balkans	7.0	8.0
Poland	3.5	5.0
Russia	9.0	15.5

*Currently Belgium, the Netherlands, and Luxembourg.
Source: Richard Mackenney, *Sixteenth-Century Europe: Expansion and Conflict* (New York: Macmillan 1993), p. 51.

adequate nutrition. Moreover, Europeans looked to the heavens not only in prayer but also to watch for the bad weather that could ruin harvests, including rainy periods that brought flooding. Famine still killed regularly, a natural disaster that checked population growth, killing off infants, children, and old people in the greatest numbers. "Nothing new here," a Roman wrote in the mid-sixteenth century, "except that people are dying of hunger."

Life, for most people, was short. Life expectancy was about twenty years and, once one had made it out of infancy and childhood alive, perhaps forty years. Infants born in Paris could expect to live to only twenty-three years of age (a figure that includes infant mortality, and that therefore underestimates the average span of life for those surviving infancy). About a fifth of all babies born died before they reached their first birthday. In France, only about half of the children lived past the age of ten. Women lived longer than men, but many died during childbirth. Of 100 children born, less than half lived to age twenty and only about a fifth celebrated a fortieth birthday. Christ, who died at age thirty-three, was not considered to have died young.

The balance between life and death was precarious. In most towns, deaths outnumbered births almost every year. Prosperous families had more children than the poor (the opposite pattern of today). The exposure and abandonment of newly born infants was common. Furthermore, couples may have been practicing birth control, with careful sexual abstention one possible reason for relatively low rates of reproductivity. The fact that one partner often died prematurely also served as a check on population. So, too, did the fact that most couples married relatively late. In Shakespeare's great play *Romeo and Juliet*, Juliet, who marries at the age of fourteen, was not at all representative of most brides. Most English men married at between twenty-six and twenty-nine years of age, women between twenty-four and twenty-six years.

The choice of a marriage partner was important for economic reasons (although in parts of Western Europe, up to a fifth of women never married). In any social stratum, marriages were often arranged—that is, parents played a major and often determining role in choosing partners for their children. For families of means, particularly nobles, the promise of a sizable dowry counted for much. Yet, some evidence suggests that by the end of the sixteenth century the inclinations of bride and groom among English families were sometimes difficult to ignore. For the poor, marriage could increase the chances of improving one's situation or even just getting by. Thus, a young woman whose family could provide a dowry, however modest, or who had a skill, was an attractive prospective spouse, as was a young man with a trade.

Wives remained legally subservient to their husbands, although in what has been called the poor household "economy of makeshifts" their role as managers of income and as workers gave them some degree of equality. Sexual infidelity, while common, also ran against the grain of a popular sense of justice, which placed a premium on loyalty and mutual obligation between marriage partners and between parents and children. Such liaisons might also jeopardize the system of inheritance and the protection of family property by leading to the appearance of unanticipated offspring, in an age when contraceptive techniques were rudimentary and not well known. Still, about a fifth of English brides were pregnant at the time of their wedding, as sexual relations between couples expecting to marry were very common.

Kinship and neighborhood solidarities defined the lives of ordinary people. In some places—for example, the south of France—extended families were common, that is, parents and sometimes other relatives lived with couples. In England, however, the nuclear family (a couple and their children) was the most common household. When children of the lower classes began their working lives—usually at the age of fourteen or fifteen, or earlier for some apprentices—their obligations to their parents did not cease. Often, however, they left home in search of work, rarely, if ever, to return. The poor turned to family and neighbors for help in bad times, as well as for help with harvests, if they owned some land.

One of the consequences of the rise in Europe's population was the inflation that characterized the sixteenth century, particularly its last decades. It seemed to one Spaniard that "a pound of mutton now costs as much as a whole sheep used to." Between 1500 and 1600, the price of wheat rose by 425 percent in England, 650 percent in France, and 400 percent in Poland. The expanding population brought price rises before the arrival of silver from Latin America, a cause of continued inflation during the second half of the century. An English author at mid-century insisted that "the principal cause is the engrossing of things into a few men's hands." A larger population also put pressure on the value of land. The rapid rise in rents led a mid-fifteenth-century Englishman to denounce rich landlords as "men without conscience, men utterly devoid of God's fear, yea men that live as though there were no God at all. . . . They take our houses over our heads, they buy our grounds out of our hands, they raise our rents. . . ."

An Expanding Economy

One of the hallmarks of medieval society had been the marked expansion of trade and manufacture that began in the eleventh century. This occurred after several centuries in which commerce was at a standstill, when virtually all wealth was closely tied to the land and outside markets were extremely limited. During the twelfth and thirteenth centuries, merchants greatly increased the amount of products carried on land routes and in the low galley-ships that hugged the Mediterranean coastline, more confident than ever before that their goods would find purchasers. Rivers like the Rhône and Rhine were essential trade arteries. In the markets of Flanders and northern France, olive oil, fruit, and wine from the Mediterranean region were exchanged for timber, cereals, and salted fish from the Baltic region.

With the expansion in commercial activity, a money economy slowly developed. Yet, trade and barter remained important, particularly for peasants, most of whom were part of a subsistence economy. Currency still did not penetrate some mountainous regions.

The late Middle Ages brought a significant rise in the availability of credit to states and entrepreneurs. In particular, Italian merchants advanced capitalist techniques during the thirteenth century in their trade with the Near East. Some merchants were no longer itinerant travelers, but rather sedentary entrepreneurs able to raise capital and extend (and obtain) credit. They also developed bills of exchange (see Chapter 5), an order drawn upon an agent to pay another merchant money at a future date, perhaps in another country and in another currency.

To raise capital, merchants borrowed from banking families, other merchants (or merchant-banking families who did both), moneylenders, or formed temporary partnerships. Here and there, then, businesses began to work on a commission basis, and some entrepreneurs specialized in transporting goods. They began to keep registers of profits and losses, using double-entry bookkeeping.

Banking families in Venice and other Italian city-states were already well established in the thirteenth century. The powerful merchant-banking families influenced rulers by loaning kings and popes alike vast sums. On a smaller scale, moneylenders still played an important part in rural economies. Territorial rulers and great lords increasingly required a healthy treasury or at least good credit.

Bankers sitting behind their *banco* (counter) doing business.

The greater availability of credit facilitated a commercial boom in the sixteenth century. By 1500, with new mechanisms of credit, coin or money no longer necessarily had to be carried from place to place in order to purchase goods. At the same time, merchants and manufacturers were able to control the distribution of more products, and merchant-manufacturers could put various stages of production under their control. Yet, the multiplicity of states hindered commerce. Even within France, on the Loire River and its tributaries more than 200 tolls were collected in 120 different spots.

The sixteenth century also brought a marked increase in manufacturing, which in some regions may have multiplied by 500 percent. The extraction of iron, copper, and silver quadrupled, for example in Central Europe. Large-scale manufacturing was limited to mining and textiles, as well as to arms manufacturing and shipbuilding.

The production of textiles, whether for large, distant markets or only for local consumption, dominated the manufacturing economy. The manufacture of silk, techniques for which had been imported from China into Europe by Arabs in the tenth century, centered in the Italian states. It spread during the second half of the fifteenth century across the Alps to the German states, France, and Spain, which produced raw silk and no longer depended on imports from Asia and Persia.

The manufacture of cloth spread rapidly in Tuscany, northern France, Flanders, and the Netherlands. The woolens industry of Flanders, which had developed during the medieval period, boomed, centered in the towns of Ypres, Ghent, and Bruges. England, which continued to export wool to the continent, became a major producer of woolen goods in the fourteenth century, forming a base for English industrialization and for London's prosperity as an exporter of manufactured goods. However, Antwerp first emerged as Europe's most important center of trade.

Urban merchants and artisans were organized into guilds, which regulated production and distribution, thus protecting, at least in principle, guild members and consumers. The structure of craft production was organized hierarchically. Apprentices who learned their craft became journeymen and, if all went well, could eventually become masters, joining a masters' guild, and employing journeymen and training apprentices. Most cloth was finished in towns by craft artisans. Through the guilds, masters could preserve the quality of work within their particular trades and, at the same time, the reputations of their town.

During the sixteenth century, a period of great economic dynamism, the gap between rich and poor probably grew, particularly as the massive inflation of that period, pushed by population increase, reduced the value of wages. During the fourteenth and fifteenth centuries, it had become increasingly difficult for journeymen to become independent master craftsmen. Early in the sixteenth century, some German journeymen refused to work for masters who paid them less than they desired or had been used to receiving. Tensions between employers and workers probably intensified during the sixteenth century as a whole.

Many craftsmen avoided restrictions on their work by working outside the walls of cities or in the countryside. In this way, they avoided guild monopolies and guild specifications on wages and piece rates. Likewise, merchant-capitalists who owned raw materials put out spinning, weaving (sometimes renting out looms), and other work into the countryside, where labor was even cheaper. Rural production spread rapidly in northern Italy, the Netherlands, northern France, and England between 1450 and 1550. Hundreds of thousands of peasants produced woolen or linen yarn or wove it into cloth; then urban workers dyed, bleached, or shrunk the cloth, which merchants then sold. This "cottage industry" (also sometimes called "domestic industry") would remain an important part of the manufacturing process well into the nineteenth century.

Merchant-capitalists put out spinning, weaving, and other work into the countryside in cottage (domestic) industry. Here a woman is spinning in her home.

As they grew richer, some merchant families purchased land and noble titles. Merchants therefore became important figures in every state. Many nobles resented the ennoblement of commoners, following the old saying, "the king could make a nobleman, but not a gentleman." In the mid-sixteenth century, a French noble heaped scorn on "the infinity of false noblemen, whose fathers and ancestors wielded arms and performed acts of chivalry in grain-shops, wine-shops, draperies, mills and farmsteads; and yet when they speak of their lineage they are descended from the crown, their roots spring from Charlemagne, Pompey, and Caesar." The rising importance of merchants reflected the fact that, with continued economic growth, the possession of money, the ability to acquire credit, to draw up a bill of exchange, and entrepreneurial skill were gradually becoming more important than the military might and distinguished birth of nobles.

The Growth of Towns

The growth of towns, particularly during the twelfth and thirteenth centuries, reflected and accentuated increased economic development and security in medieval Europe. Fortified stone ramparts, gates, and towers gave each town visible characteristics. A "bourgeois" or "burgher" was technically someone who lived in a town. Towns were the residence of most courts (including municipal courts), hospitals, and fraternal associations, such as religious confraternities, as well as guilds. Administrative and religious buildings were the cornerstones of the medieval towns. Most towns had a relatively large number of clergy living within their walls, ministering to the needs of the population, or, in the case of some convents or monasteries, living a cloistered existence.

Most major towns in Europe were founded before 1300, although new ones were added. The physical development of towns still followed the outlines of original Roman settlements (for example, Leicester in northern England, the German town of Trier, and Narbonne in southern France). In Poland, about 200 new towns were created between 1450 and 1550, adding to the 450 already in existence.

In Italy, Venice, Florence, Genoa, Milan, and Pisa became independent city-states in about 1100, free to establish their domination over surrounding towns and villages. The decline of the Byzantine Empire and the inability of the Holy Roman Empire to establish its authority throughout Italy prevented the development of large territorial states. The prosperity of the city-states, too, impeded the creation of a single Italian state, or even a peninsula divided into two or three major political units. Freed of feudal overlords, the dynamism of these city-states underlay the Renaissance (see Chapter 2). Venetian and Genoese merchants sent trading fleets carrying goods to and from the Levant and beyond, as well as along the spice routes to China (visited by the Italian adventurer Marco Polo during his long voyage from 1275 to 1292), India, and Central Asia.

In Northern Europe, as well, the growth of cities and towns was linked to the expansion of commerce and long-distance trade. In northern Germany, independent trading cities were enriched by the Baltic grain trade, as Polish landowners, like their Hungarian and Bohemian counterparts, concentrated agricultural development on the production of grain for export to the Dutch Netherlands and other Western countries. Lübeck and Hamburg, among other northern German trading cities, formed the Hanseatic League, which at first was a federation against banditry. Its towns began to thrive in the mid-twelfth century, establishing networks of trade that reached from London all the way to Novgorod. The Polish port of Gdansk had its own currency, fleet, army, and diplomats. Likewise, some towns in southern Germany formed leagues to resist territorial lords and protect trade routes. The fairs held outside the towns of Champagne in northern France, as well as Lyon at the confluence of the Saône and Rhône Rivers, and Beaucaire on the Rhône in Provence, served as trading points between Northern Europe and Mediterranean merchants. The market function of trading towns swelled their populations; merchants and small manufacturers catered to the needs of the local population. Market towns also reflected the fact that the European economy remained closely tied to the land, as landowners, particularly in regions of commercialized agriculture, marketed their produce.

Medieval Europe boasted major urban centers of learning, dominated by Church teaching. Paris (theology), Montpellier (medicine), and Bologna (Roman law) were major university centers. Oxford and Cambridge Universities were founded in the thirteenth century. Universities existed not in the sense that we know them today. Rather, the term referred to a common, corporately organized body of students or masters in one town. By 1500, dozens of towns had universities. And, in turn, literacy (limited to a small proportion of the population in the best of circumstances) rose faster in towns than in the countryside, as the equivalent of secondary education shifted from rural monasteries to urban church or grammar schools.

Northern Italy and the Low Countries had the densest networks of towns. However, town dwellers remained a relatively small minority of the population, no more than about 15 percent of the population. Only about 2 percent of the European population lived in towns larger than 40,000. In 1500, only about 6 percent of Europeans lived in towns of more than 10,000 people. Most towns were small: in the German states, only about 200 of 3,000 towns had more than 10,000 residents. Only Constantinople, Naples, Milan, Paris, and Venice had more than 100,000 inhabitants.

Town governments were dominated by oligarchies of rich merchants, guild masters, and property owners (in Italian towns, nobles were part of these oligarchies). Despite the fact that many peasants still lived in towns ("agro-towns"), working fields outside town walls during the day and returning home before the gates slammed shut at nightfall, town and country seemed in some ways worlds apart.

Municipal Liberties

A contemporary saying went "town air makes free" (for example, no town person in Western Europe could be a serf). Towns formed a type of corporation, with residents purchasing freedom from taxes and paying rulers and lords dues as necessary. To some extent, then, towns within the feudal context stood as zones of freedom, because their residents were in most cases not bound by service obligations to landowners. These towns were independent or semi-autonomous because of their purchase of exemptions from the authority of the rulers of territorial states. In such cases, councils, not territorial lords or rulers, made decisions that affected the lives of residents. Towns could also loan money to kings waging war against recalcitrant vassals or other rulers, including popes.

Urban freedoms had to be won and maintained from lords. Urban oligarchs jealously guarded pretensions of municipal independence against noble and monarchical claims. Cities and towns felt pressure from rulers who tried to expand to attain revenue and political consolidation. Towns purchased charters of exemption from taxes in exchange for the payment of lump sums. In some cases, rulers actively sought alliances with towns against nobles, sworn enemies of towns. Where territorial rulers were weak, as in Italy and the German states, towns obtained the greatest degree of freedom. By contrast, towns developed less rapidly in areas where rulers and nobles exercised strong authority.

Traditions of municipal liberties would leave a significant heritage in Western Europe, ultimately shaping the emergence of constitutional forms of government. Whereas social relationships in the countryside were largely defined by personal obligations, in towns these were replaced by collective rights through guilds and other associations. In England, northern France, the Netherlands, Flanders, and Switzerland, urban medieval confraternities and other voluntary associations would spur a democratizing impulse within trading towns as they struggled to maintain their independence from rulers and rural nobles. Lacking the associational infrastructure of many towns in Western Europe, however, Eastern European towns were not able to stem the tide of the increasing power of nobles and, in the case of Russia, the state. As the Muscovite state expanded its authority, the tsars ran roughshod over urban pretensions. Towns in the East extracted none of the special charters of rights that characterized towns in the West. Russian rulers considered towns their personal property, and the residents of towns owed service to their territorial lords.

The Emergence of Sovereign States

Although hardly anyone used the term "state" to denote a political entity, by 1500 the largest monarchical states (see Map 1.1) were taking on some of the characteristics of the modern state, despite significant limits on the

MAP 1.1 EUROPE IN 1500 Europe in 1500 was a maze of fragmented states although sovereign monarchical states were beginning to emerge.

authority of their rulers. During the sixteenth century, France, Spain, and England would evolve into "new monarchies." What was "new" about them was their growing reach, an evolution begun in the late medieval era. While monarchies grew stronger in Western Europe, however, they were actually weakened in Eastern Europe during the late Middle Ages. Struggles for power, civil war, and the growing domination of lords hindered the emergence of strong states there at least until the late sixteenth century.

Sovereign states emerged in Europe during the medieval period as rulers moved toward greater authority and independence. Yet, to be sure, these states were not "nation-states" in the modern sense, in which citizens feel that they belong to a nation by being, for example, Spanish, French, or Italian. Such "imagined national communities," defined by ethnic bonds and cultural and linguistic traditions, would only develop beginning in the late eighteenth century and the nineteenth century. In medieval Europe, rulers governed a complex of territories, semi-independent towns, feudal vassals, and corporate institutions such as guilds that were largely independent of the crown, exchanging personal and or corporate privileges for loyalty.

Yet, between the tenth and fifteenth centuries, the kingdoms of France, England, and Spain grew into sovereign states, as their rulers consolidated their states by establishing their primacy over rivals. Rulers made laws and imposed administrative unity to a degree that was unprecedented. They asserted their authority, but not domination, over the nobles of the territories they claimed. Royal authority directly touched more subjects than ever before. Rulers could raise and command armies, mint money, impose taxes, summon advisers, and appoint officials to represent their will.

The French kings, their territories clustered around Paris, had little real power during the medieval period. Until the mid-fifteenth century, the kings of England held Normandy, Brittany, Maine, Anjou, and Aquitaine, and the counts of Flanders held wealthy lands in what is now northern France and southern Belgium. During the Hundred Years' War, French kings raised the funds and armies necessary to expel the English from France (with the exception of the Channel port of Calais). During the last half of the fifteenth century, the French kings ended the *de facto* independence of the large, prosperous provinces, which were technically fiefs of the crown. In 1482, the crown of France absorbed Burgundy, whose powerful dukes were related to the kings of France, and a decade later the regent for Charles VIII (ruled 1483–1498) invaded Brittany, adding it to France. Through timely royal marriages and warfare, the French monarchs established the foundations for a stronger, more centralized monarchy.

England, too, emerged as a stronger monarchical state during the late medieval period, but with significant differences from its continental counterparts. The vassals of King John (ruled 1199–1216) and the people of London had rebelled against more taxes to finance his attempt to recover continental territories lost to France. In 1215, they forced him to sign the Magna Carta, the "great Charter of Liberties." John agreed to impose major taxes only with the permission of a "great council," representative of the barons and to cease hiring mercenaries when his barons refused to fight. Later in the century, King Edward I (ruled 1272–1307) summoned barons, bishops, and representatives from England's major towns in the hope of obtaining their agreement to provide funds for another war against the king of France. From that "parley," or "parliament," came the tradition in England of consultation with leading subjects and the origins of an English constitutional government that constrained royal authority.

In Central Europe, the Holy Roman Empire was not really a sovereign state. It dated from 962, when German nobles had elected a ruler. By the end of the thirteenth century, the principle that the Holy Roman emperor would be elected, and not designated by the principle of hereditary, had been established. Considering themselves the successors of the Roman Empire, the Holy Roman emperors saw themselves as the protectors of the papacy and of all of Christendom, which involved the emperor in the stormy world of Italian politics.

The Holy Roman Empire encompassed 300 semi-autonomous states, ranging from several large territories to a whole host of smaller states, principalities, and free cities that carried out their own foreign policy and fought wars. The emperor could not levy taxes or raise armies outside of his own hereditary estates. German princes consolidated their own power into many independent and semi-independent territorial states, in what became known as "German particularism." The Holy Roman emperors were unable to consolidate their authority and were increasingly unable to enforce their will outside of the boundaries of their hereditary estates.

The Austrian Habsburgs, the ruling house in the German Alpine hereditary lands, had gradually extended their territories in the fourteenth and fifteenth centuries between the Danube River, the Adriatic Sea, and the Little Carpathian Mountains. Beginning in 1438, when the first Habsburg was elected Holy Roman emperor, until 1740 (when the male line was extinguished), only Habsburgs held the ruling title of Holy Roman emperor. Smaller states, such as the thirteen cantons of Switzerland, struggled to maintain their autonomy against rising Austrian power.

Developing State Structures

The growth of bureaucracies was one means by which rulers consolidated more effective power. Rulers had always had some kind of council, but the importance of their advisers grew in the fourteenth and fifteenth centuries. Chanceries, treasuries, and courts of law represented bureaucratization. Serving as royal officials, some humble men of talent began to reach positions of influence within states.

Rulers still earned revenue from their own lands. But in order to meet the expenses of their states, rulers drew income from taxation, sale of offices (posts in the service of the monarch that were often both lucrative and prestigious), government bonds, and confiscation of land from recalcitrant nobles. (Like other rulers, popes also centralized administration and finances, virtually selling posts.) Rulers also imposed taxes on salt, wine, and other goods, impositions from which nobles and churchmen were exempt. States themselves in the sixteenth century became the great collectors and distributors of revenue. Moreover, the gradual growth of public debt was another sign of the increased power of states. Royal dependency on the loans of merchant-bankers enriched the latter, providing more capital for their ventures.

As they consolidated their realms in the fifteenth century, rulers could offer lords noble titles and offices (lucrative positions within their households or as officials). Thus, with the strengthening of sovereign states, which in part entailed the loss of some noble judicial rights and the right to have armies of retainers, nobles depended more on monarchies for power and honor. More of them came to court and served as royal officials. Furthermore, the sale of offices, especially in France and Spain, ultimately encouraged loyalty to the throne.

Royal courts now adjudicated property disputes, although kings now less frequently dispensed justice themselves. Royal courts gradually eroded noble jurisdiction over the king's subjects. Yet, in France and many of the German states, nobles retained rights of justice over peasants.

Rulers, surrounded by courtiers and councils, became more grand. One of the signs of the ascension of monarchical power was that thrones became hereditary, as rulers worked to consolidate their authority and territories. As people were quite apt to die young, such arrangements, which varied throughout Europe, mattered a great deal.

In the fifteenth century, regular channels for diplomacy emerged among the states of Europe. The Italian city-states were the first to exchange permanent resident ambassadors. By the middle of the fifteenth century, Florence, Milan, Venice, and the kingdom of Naples all routinely exchanged ambassadors, who provided news and other information but also represented the interests of their states. States sent diplomatic representatives to the courts of friend and rival alike.

Limits to State Authority

Significant constraints, however, still limited the authority of rulers. We have seen that the privileges of towns, established through the purchase of royal charters of financial immunity, tempered royal power. Some regions (for example, Navarre in Spain), nominally incorporated into realms, nonetheless maintained autonomy through representative institutions. And, to be sure, distance and physical impediments such as mountains and vast plains also prevented the effective extension of royal authority.

Even more important, there existed the tradition that assemblies of notable subjects who counseled the king had rights, and had to be consulted. In the thirteenth century, rulers had convoked assemblies of notable subjects to explain their policies and to ask for their help and, in doing so, had strengthened and publicized their rule. Because they depended on those whom they convoked to provide military assistance when they required it, they also heard grievances. From this, parliaments, assemblies, diets, and estates developed, representing (depending on the place) nobles, clergy, towns, and, in several cases, everyone else.

Early in the sixteenth century, an Italian exile told the king of France what the monarch would need to attack the duchy of Milan: "three things are necessary: money; more money; and still more money." The most powerful states—France, Habsburg Austria, and Spain—could raise sizable armies with relative ease. But, to meet the extraordinary expenses of wartime, they increasingly borrowed money from wealthy banking families. Rulers also utilized subsidies from friendly powers, imposed special taxes and forced loans, and, especially in Spain and France, sold offices. Sixteenth-century inflation would make wars even more expensive.

Royal levies to finance warfare through direct taxation could only be imposed with the consent of those taxed. The dialogue between rulers and assemblies, and the strength and weakness of such representative bodies, would define the emergence and nature of modern government in the European states.

The princes of the German states had to ask assemblies of nobles for the right to collect excise taxes. Estates dominated entirely or predominantly by nobles in Poland-Lithuania, Bohemia, and Hungary balanced royal authority. In Bohemia, the rights of towns partially balanced noble prerogatives. Rulers could suspend decisions of those "sovereign" bodies, yet such assemblies could not be completely ignored.

The prerogatives of nobles and churchmen also impeded royal authority. Nobles and churchmen successfully resisted royal taxes, which fell on the poor (the vast majority of the population), whom no one represented. Nobles still had to be convinced or coerced to provide armies. Kings became, at least in principle, supreme judges (though not for the clergy, as ecclesiastics were generally tried in Church courts), royal courts offering litigants and petitioners a final appeal.

The struggle between rulers and the popes dated to the late eleventh century, when the popes and Holy Roman emperors had struggled for primacy, particularly over the contested right of lay rulers to appoint bishops and invest them with signs of spiritual authority (the lay investiture crisis, *c.* 1060–1122). Yet, the clergy generally taught obedience to secular as well as ecclesiastical rulers. Furthermore, in the late medieval period, kings were able to further consolidate their power when popes granted the rulers of France, Spain, and some German towns certain rights over the clergy, including that of naming bishops.

TRANSFORMING DISCOVERIES

The use of gunpowder would transform warfare from "chiefly a matter of violent housekeeping" between lords and vassals to sometimes massive struggles between dynastic rivals. Warfare would became more pervasive in the early modern period because of dynastic quarrels between rulers as they sought to consolidate their territories. The enhanced ability of the rulers of the largest sovereign states to command resources would swell the size of armies, whose ranks would be increasingly filled by mercenaries. Yet, despite so much fighting, there would be surprisingly few major changes in national boundaries between 1450 and the beginning of the Thirty Years' War in 1618.

The invention of printing also led to major change in the late Middle Ages. Common religious texts, most notably the Bible, could be printed in large quantities and could reach more people than ever before. Other texts, religious and nonreligious in nature, helped expand the horizons of Europeans.

European horizons expanded in another significant way, as well. Beginning in the late fifteenth century, explorers sailed across the oceans, conquering colonies, above all, in the Americas. After being on the defensive

Theodore Galle's *Nova reperta* ("new discoveries") celebrates the discovery of the New World and forms of the new technology (gunpowder, the compass, the clock, the saddle with stirrups).

The Printing Press and the Power of the Printed Word

The invention and spread of printing in the fifteenth century in some ways marked the end of the medieval period (see Map 1.2). Before its invention, monks and scribes had copied books on parchment sheets; one copy of the Bible required about 170 calfskins or 300 sheepskins. The development of woodblock printing and paper had occurred in China in the eighth century; both reached Europe from the Arab world via Spain in the thirteenth century. The manufacture of paper facilitated the copying of manuscripts by replacing parchment, which was very expensive. Paper more readily accommodated merchants, officials, and scholars. But the process of copying itself remained slow. Cosimo de' Medici, the Florentine banker and patron of Renaissance art, hired 200 scribes who filled his library by copying 200 volumes (most of which had religious themes) in two years' time.

All this changed in the fifteenth century when Flemish craftsmen invented a kind of oil-based ink. This and the innovation of a wooden hand-press made possible the invention of movable metal type in the German

MAP 1.2 SPREAD OF PRINTING THROUGH EUROPE, 1450–1508   Towns and dates at which printing shops were established throughout Europe, increasing the number of books produced and read.

Cathedral town of Mainz in about 1450 by, among several others, Johann Gutenberg (c. 1395–1468), whose printed Latin Bibles of stunning beauty are treasured today.

Printing shops began to spread in the 1460s to other German towns, reaching the Italian states, Bohemia, France, and the Netherlands by the end of the decade, and Spain and England in the 1470s (see Map 1.2). By the beginning of the sixteenth century, more than 6 million books had been printed, with the average edition running between 200 to 1,000 copies—the latter figure about the average printing of a scholarly publication in the United States today.

Books provided scholars with identical ancient and medieval texts to discuss and critique. Accounts of discoveries and adventures in the New World filtered across Europe from Spain, England, and France. The number of scholarly libraries—which were really just private collections—grew rapidly. New professions developed: the librarian, the bookseller, the publisher, to say nothing of the various trades involved with the printing and publishing process, from typesetters to editors. Moreover, with the greater dissemination of knowledge came an increase in the number of universities, rising from twenty in 1300 to about seventy in 1500.

More people learned how to read, although literate individuals remained far in the minority. In Florence and other prosperous cities, the rate of literacy may have been relatively high, although in the Italian city-states as a whole it is unlikely that more than 1 percent of workers and peasants could read and write. The literate population of the German states in 1500 was about 3 or 4 percent. But among the upper classes many more people developed the habit of reading, as the Bible and other books and even dictionaries could be purchased, discussed, and debated.

Printing made censorship considerably more difficult. Furthermore, not all that was published pleased lay and ecclesiastic leaders. No longer could destroying one or two manuscripts suffice to root out an idea. Thus, Pope Alexander VI warned in a bull in 1501: "The art of printing is very useful insofar as it furthers the circulation of useful and tested books; but it can be very harmful if it is permitted to widen the influence of pernicious works. It will therefore be necessary to maintain full control over the printers so that they may be prevented from bringing into print writings which are antagonistic to the Catholic faith or which are likely to cause trouble to believers."

Exploration and Conquest of the New World

By the last decade of the fifteenth century, the inhabitants of the Iberian Peninsula already had several centuries of navigational and sailing accomplishments behind them. The Portuguese had captured a foothold on the Moroccan coast in 1415, beginning two centuries of expansion. Early in the fifteenth century, they began to explore the west coast of Africa and had taken Madeira and the Azores islands in the Atlantic. Their goal was to break Muslim and Venetian control of European access to Asian spices and silk.

King Ferdinand and Queen Isabella of Spain had initially rejected the request of the Genoese cartographer and merchant Christopher Columbus (1451–1506), who sought financial backing for an ocean voyage to reach the Indies. Columbus, the son of a weaver, wanted to carry the word of God to Asia. In 1492, he convinced the Spanish sovereigns to give him their full support; the royal couple feared that Portuguese vessels might be the first to cross the oceans to reach the great wealth of Asia.

Late in 1492, Columbus set sail with three ships. He believed the earth was a perfect sphere, and since Africa stood in the way of a voyage sailing to the East, he thought it possible to reach the Orient by sailing west across the Atlantic Ocean, which he believed to be quite narrow. His small fleet reached not Asia but rather the small Caribbean island of San Salvador in the Americas. He then also reached Cuba and finally Hispaniola (now the Dominican Republic and Haiti) in the Americas. "What on earth have you come seeking so far away?" he was asked. "Christians and spices," he replied, but he also probably believed that he would find gold, and asked the Indians he encountered on the shore in sign language if

The Portuguese arrive in Japan in 1542.

they knew where some could be found. Columbus was impressed with the beauty of Hispaniola (although he remained convinced that he had discovered islands near India) and the "docility" of the indigenous people. Yet, in the absence of gold, he suggested that the crown could make Hispaniola profitable by selling its people as slaves. Columbus, whose greatest contribution was to find a way across the sea using the trade winds, made three subsequent voyages of discovery, the last in 1502, when his mind was deteriorating.

Portugal, a much poorer state than Spain, struggled to defend its fledgling empire and trade routes against Spanish encroachments. In 1498, Vasco da Gama (c. 1469–1524) reached India; the cargo of spices he brought back to Lisbon paid for his costly expedition sixty times over. The Portuguese maritime route stretched around the coast of Africa across the Indian Ocean to the South China Sea. This route could now compete with overland spice and silk routes that had long linked Europe to the markets of the East. An Indonesian ruler remarked of the Portuguese adventurers, "The fact that these people journey so far from home to conquer territory indicates clearly that there must be very little justice and a great deal of greed among them." This had made them "fly all over the waters in order to acquire possessions that God did not give them."

In 1493, Pope Alexander VI divided the non-Christian world into zones for Spanish and Portuguese exploration and exploitation (see Map 1.3). He awarded Portugal all of sub-Saharan Africa and Asia; Spain, the pope's ally, received most of the Americas, although Portugal claimed Brazil, which became the largest colony in the Americas. But the practical problems of drawing boundaries down the middle of oceans with primitive navigational instruments resulted in zones of contested territory. No one asked the indigenous populations what they thought.

Soon more and more Spanish explorers reached the Americas. Vasco Núñez de Balboa (c. 1475–1519) established Spanish sovereignty over what is now Panama. The island of Cuba, in turn, fell to the Spanish, and then served as a staging point for the conquest of Mexico by Hernando Cortés (1485–1547), which opened a new chapter in European expansion. Cortés, after landing on the coast of Mexico in 1519, went to see the Aztec emperor, Montezuma, who sent him away, although he later sent him gifts of gold and silver. Determined to conquer Mexico, Cortés formed alliances with Montezuma's non-Aztec peoples, who naively hoped that Cortés might help them achieve their independence. The Spanish adventurer then conquered Mexico with no more than sixteen horses and six hundred soldiers, but with 100,000 native American allies. Further south, Francisco Pizarro (c. 1476–1541) led his men in the conquest of the Inca Empire in Peru. Although the Incas were a culturally rich people, they had never seen iron or steel weapons before, nor did they have draft animals. When Pizarro's horses lost their shoes in Peru and there was no iron available to replace them, he had them shod in silver.

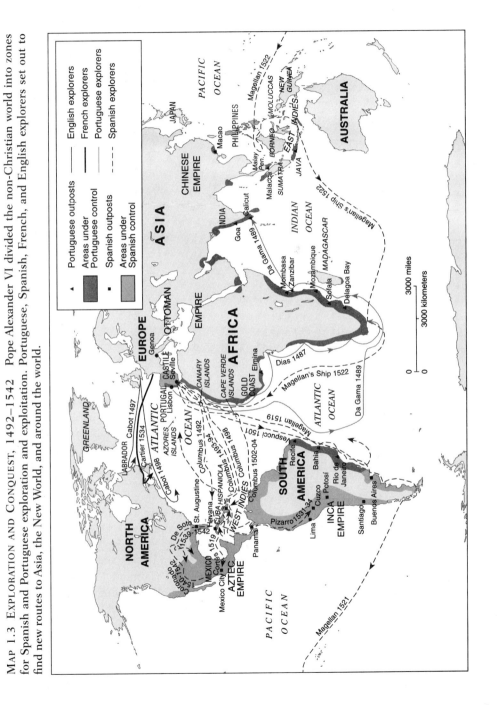

MAP 1.3 EXPLORATION AND CONQUEST, 1492–1542   Pope Alexander VI divided the non-Christian world into zones for Spanish and Portuguese exploration and exploitation. Portuguese, Spanish, French, and English explorers set out to find new routes to Asia, the New World, and around the world.

The first meeting between Hernando Cortés and Aztec Emperor Montezuma in 1519.

The victory of the conquistadors (conquerors) was the victory of steel over stone-bladed wooden swords. Moreover, the surprise element of cannon and guns also contributed to their victory in the Americas as in Southeast Asia, where a witness to a Portuguese attack in 1511 reported, "the noise of the cannon was as the noise of thunder in the heavens and the flashes of fire of their guns were like flashes of lightning in the sky: and the noise of their matchlocks was like that of ground-nuts popping in the frying-pan." In addition to their ability to kill, guns had a shock effect, except in China, where gunpowder had been discovered.

Steeped in tales of crusading chivalry and conquest, the conquerors who followed Columbus to the Americas set out looking for adventure and wealth. Cortés, for example, was the son of a poor Castilian noble family. "We came here to serve God and the king," said one, "but also to get rich." Unlike Columbus, most conquerors died young, far from home, their dreams of wealth shattered by the harsh realities of life in what seemed to them a strange and often inhospitable world. Ferdinand Magellan (c. 1480–1521), the Portuguese-born explorer, was killed by angry islanders on a Pacific beach. His crew nonetheless circumnavigated the globe, having proven that a southwest passage to India did exist and returning in 1522 to Seville.

Not only did many of the conquistadors die in the Americas, many times more of the native people they encountered also died as a result of contact with the Europeans. At one point during his conquests, Cortés and his small army had to fight their way out of the Mexican city of Tenochtitlán, then larger than any other European city except Constantinople. But as the Spanish departed temporarily, the smallpox they had brought with them began to decimate the Indians, bringing massive death on the heels of military conquest. The indigenous population of Mexico fell from about 25 million—or more—in 1520 to perhaps as little as 1 million in 1600. The native population of Peru fell from about 7 million in 1500 to half a million little more than a century later. Other European diseases, including measles, typhus, smallpox, and bubonic plague, also decimated the native population. In Guatemala, a Mayan Indian kept a chronicle of the ravages of European disease among his people: "Great was the stench of the dead. After our fathers and grandfathers succumbed, half of the people fled to the fields. The dogs and vultures devoured the bodies. The mortality was terrible. Your grandfather died, and with him died the sons of the king and his brothers and kinsmen. So it was that we became orphans, oh my sons! So we became when we were young. All of us were thus. We were born to die."

In turn, the Indians gave syphilis, a much less deadly disease (which may have originated in Asia) to the Spanish. It spread with Spanish mercenaries who had fought in Naples two years after Columbus' voyage to America (the French called syphilis "the Neapolitan disease," while the Neapolitans referred to it as "the French disease").

There were other, more beneficial exchanges between the Old and New World. Before the arrival of Europeans, there were no domesticated animals larger than the llama and alpaca in the Americas, and little animal protein in the Indian diet. Spaniards brought horses and cattle with them, as well as cats and dogs. Sheep had accompanied Columbus in 1493 on his second journey. Pigs also were carried on the relatively small ships of discovery and conquest. Taking up little room on board ship, they not only could be eaten but provided the additional benefit of manure for farming once the explorers had gone ashore. The 350 pigs brought to Cuba by Columbus had multiplied to over 30,000 by 1514. But they ate their way through much forest land and also eroded the indigenous agricultural terrace system, upsetting the ecological balance of conquered lands.

Every year the Spanish galleons returned with more riches, as if "the hand of God was guiding them." The Spaniards returned home with tobacco, potatoes, new varieties of beans, chocolate, chili peppers, potatoes, and tomatoes (not until the early eighteenth century, however, could the first European recipes with tomato sauce be found in Italy). They brought back to Europe Indian maize, which they planted and which provided feed for farm animals. These crops had significant, positive effects on European demography, leading to the availability of more food and accompanying population increase. In turn, the Spaniards planted wheat, barley, rice, oats, fruit trees, and bananas in their colonies. By 1600, most of the important food plants of Eurasia and Africa were cultivated in the Spanish Americas.

In 1565, a Spanish galleon completed global transoceanic trade by sailing across the Pacific Ocean from Manila to unload cinnamon on the coast of Mexico. Thereafter, Spanish ships returned with silver, which could purchase silks, porcelain, spices, jade, and mother-of-pearl, which Chinese junks carried to the Philippines, and which oceangoing ships carried to Acápulco. Shipping routes led from Seville, which had been part of Moorish Andalusia until the Castilian reconquest, to the Caribbean Sea and to the ports of Vera Cruz in Mexico and Cartagena in Colombia. They supplied the American colonists with European goods, and on the return route carried Mexican and Peruvian silver that replenished the coffers of European princes and merchants. Saluting Acápulco in 1604, Spanish poet Bernardo de Balbueña wrote, "In thee Spain is joined with China, Italy with Japan, and ultimately a whole world in disciplined commerce." All four continents, Europe, Asia, Africa, and America, moved closer together in reciprocal economic relationships that represented the beginnings of a globalization of trade.

Not only did the Europeans seek to trade with the people in the New World, they also sought to acquire permanent territories as well. Thus, Spanish legal documents affecting the new colonies, drawn up in Spain, declared that Indians would keep all lands they already held, but that all other territories henceforth belonged either to the crowns of Spain or were to be divided up among the conquerors as booty. The conquistadors built new towns, placing the church, town hall, and prison around a central marketplace (*plaza*).

In return for the pope's blessing of the colonial enterprise, missionaries began to arrive hoping to convert the Indians to Christianity. The harsh reality of the colonial experience for the natives, however, was largely untempered by the good intentions of some of the missionaries. "For this kind of people," snapped a Portuguese priest in Brazil in 1563, "there is no better way of preaching than the sword and the rod of iron." However, at least in principle, the missionary impulse remained strong: one monk argued that souls being lost to Satan by Martin Luther's Reformation (see Chapter 3) were being balanced by conversions in the Americas.

An early sixteenth-century Spaniard humanist wrote of Columbus that he "sailed from Spain . . . to mix the world together and give to those strange lands the form of our own." Europeans sought to impose their culture on the peoples they conquered, although Christian teaching made only limited headway in India and virtually none in China. Unlike its view of Muslims, the Church did not consider Indians infidels, but rather as childlike innocents. "Are these Indians not men?," asked a Dominican priest in Santo Domingo in a sermon to shocked colonists in 1511, "Do they not have rational souls? Are you not obliged to love them as you love yourselves?" A papal pronouncement depicted the Indians as "true men . . . capable not only of understanding the Catholic faith, but also, according to our information, desirous of receiving it." In the 1590s, a Franciscan friar boasted that he had built over 200 churches and baptized more than 70,000 Indians. Where Christianity was successful, as it ultimately was in much of Latin America, Christian belief sometimes merged with local religious deities, customs, and shrines to create a distinctive form of Christianity.

Obligatory labor service, enforced more than occasionally by brutality, at first formed the relationship between rulers and the ruled. The Church and the crown periodically tried to protect the Indians against the harsh treatment accorded them by many of their Spanish countrymen in the name of profit. Bishop Bartolomé de Las Casas (1474–1566), whose father had accompanied Columbus on his second voyage to the Americas and who had himself been a conquistador before becoming a priest, spoke out against the treatment of Indians. He saluted the "marvelous government, laws, and good customs" of the Mayas, whom he wanted placed under the authority of the Church.

As the Indian population was depleted through disease, overwork, and brutality, the Spanish looked for new sources of labor. By the fifteenth century, Portuguese traders along the coast of West Africa had begun to make profits selling Africans as domestic servants in Lisbon or as sugar plantation workers in the Portuguese Atlantic islands. The slave-trading network was based on chieftains and traders in African kingdoms, merchants in Seville and Lisbon, settlers in Mexico and Peru, and Brazilian sugar growers. Domestic slavery still existed in Italy, Spain, and Muscovy in the sixteenth century, as well as in the Arab world, and some Indians in the New World also had slaves. The Spaniards believed that Africans could better survive the brutally difficult work and hot climate of America. By 1600, 275,000 black slaves had been transported to Europe and America, and five times that many would be shipped in the next century.

Gradually, more Spanish settlers arrived to populate the American colonies, including small traders, shoemakers, blacksmiths, swordsmiths, and masons. In Paraguay, the governor asked that no lawyers be allowed to emigrate, "because in newly settled countries they encourage dissension and litigation." In Mexico, Spaniards asked that "his Majesty be pleased not to suffer any scholars or men of letters to come into this country, to throw us into confusion with their learning, quibbling and books." By the mid-sixteenth century, about 150,000 Spaniards had crossed to America and by the end of the century, about 240,000 Spaniards had migrated there, and about the same number of Portuguese had gone to Asia. Most of these emigrants never returned to the Old World.

In 1552, a Spanish official wrote Charles V that the discovery of the East and West Indies was "the greatest event since the creation of the world, apart from the incarnation and death of Him who created it." But Michel de Montaigne (1533–1592), a French writer who had met Indians brought back from Brazil, offered another view in 1588, when he observed that "So many goodly cities ransacked and razed; so many nations destroyed and made desolate; so infinite millions of harmless peoples of all sexes, states, and ages, massacred, ravaged and put to the sword; and the richest, the fairest and the best part of the world topsiturvied, ruined and defaced for the traffic of pearls and pepper."

CONCLUSION

The economic and political structures of early modern Europe drew on the dynamism of the medieval period. Demographic vitality finally overcame the catastrophic losses brought by the Black Death. Within Europe, commerce and artisanal manufacturing expanded. Mediterranean traders roamed as far as the Middle East and even Asia. And, although much of Central Europe and the Italian peninsula remained a hodgepodge of small states, rulers in France, England, and Spain had consolidated their authority, as sovereign monarchical states began to emerge.

Above all, three salient movements of change brought the Middle Ages to an end. The first was the Renaissance, or cultural rebirth, engendered by the rediscovery of classical texts, which began in the mid-fourteenth century in the Italian city-states (see Chapter 2). The commercial prosperity of Florence, above all, but also of Venice and other independent city-states made possible this period of extraordinary accomplishment in literature and painting. Significantly, the High Renaissance ended with an invasion of Italy by the king of France, a fact that itself reflects the domination of the emerging monarchies. Thus began a period of warfare in Italy, much of it fought on the peninsula, between Spain and France, both states considerably stronger than the Italian city-states that tried to resist them. Second, as we have seen, was the exploration and colonization of the New World, which would ultimately help end the Mediterranean Sea's role as the center of European prosperity, and which also followed Spain's emergence as a power (see Chapters 5 and 6). The third was the Reformation (see Chapter 3), which, beginning in the second decade of the sixteenth century, challenged the unity of the Roman Catholic Church. Reflecting the influence of Renaissance humanism in Northern Europe, reformers rejected both the pope's authority and Church doctrine itself. Whereas at the beginning of the sixteenth century there was one Christian religion in Western and Central Europe, by 1600 several Protestant religions had established themselves in parts of Europe. Thus, by 1500, in the waning years of the Renaissance, the stage had been set for the trends that would shape early modern Europe.

CHAPTER 2

THE RENAISSANCE

In 1508, Pope Julius II called Michelangelo from Florence to the papal city of Rome. His intention was that the artist paint frescoes on the ceiling of the new Sistine Chapel, a ceremonial chapel next to the papal residence in the Vatican. With some reluctance (since he considered himself primarily a sculptor), Michelangelo agreed to undertake the work. He signed a contract that would pay him 3,000 ducats and began work that very day in May.

During long, difficult years of intense creativity, Michelangelo often lay on his back, staring at the ceiling (still the best position from which to study his masterpieces), before climbing up the scaffolding to work. His frescoes, depicting Creation, Original Sin, the Flood, and the ancestors of Christ, are a triumph of religious painting. Nonetheless, Pope Julius II—perhaps alone—was so dissatisfied with Michelangelo's work on the Sistine Chapel ceiling that he ordered painters to cover with fig leaves certain parts of the nude figures in *The Last Judgment* frescoes. As a result, Michelangelo left Rome in disgust. He left behind him what is arguably the most beautiful pictorial ensemble in Western painting.

Michelangelo's work represents the epitome of art during the Renaissance, a time of cultural rebirth. From about 1330 to 1530, the city-states of the Italian peninsula emerged as the intellectual and artistic centers of Europe. It was a period during which classical texts were rediscovered, thereby reviving the ideas, architecture, arts, and values of ancient Greece and Rome. By celebrating the beauty of nature and the dignity of mankind, Renaissance artists and scholars helped shape the intellectual and cultural history of the modern world. During the fifteenth century, Michelangelo, as well as Leonardo da Vinci and many other Renaissance sculptors and painters, enjoyed the patronage of wealthy families and produced some of the immortal works of the European experience. From about 1490 to 1530, Rome was the center of a final period of artistic innovation, the High Renaissance, during which time the popes, including Julius II, commissioned paintings, sculptures, and churches.

Yet, weakened by internal political turmoil, the Italian city-states were ravaged by foreign invaders beginning in 1494. Unable to resist French in-

The city-states of Renaissance Europe were the most urbanized part of the Western world. Pictured here is the Loggia dei Lanzi, the principal gathering place in Florence.

vasion and then Spanish domination, after 1530 the city-states were no longer able to support artistic glories, and the Renaissance ended in a mood of discouragement.

THE CITY-STATES OF THE ITALIAN PENINSULA

The city-states were the fundamental political unit of the Italian peninsula, the most urbanized part of the Western world. However the vast majority of the population of the Italian peninsula still lived in the countryside. In 1200, there were several hundred independent city-states on the Italian peninsula; gradually, however, that number was reduced, as many were absorbed as subject territories by more powerful city-states. A century later, at least twenty-three cities in the northern and central parts of the peninsula had populations of more than 20,000. It was within these city-states that the achievements of the Renaissance took place.

Thriving Economies

The economic prosperity and social dynamism of the city-states made the cultural achievements of the Renaissance possible. The city-states had become independent and prosperous because of the expansion of commerce during the eleventh and twelfth centuries. The Italian peninsula formed a natural point of exchange between East and West. The vibrant, prosperous, cosmopolitan traders of the city-states used their situation well.

The survival of Roman law and roads were significant legacies from the Roman Empire. Intensively studied in the twelfth and thirteenth centuries, Roman law provided a framework for order and the development of political life within the Italian city-states. Moreover, the Roman Empire had depended on a network of largely autonomous cities and towns, particularly in the plains of the northern part of the peninsula. These had been linked by a system of roads, unrivaled in Europe, all of which, as the saying goes, did indeed eventually lead to Rome.

Although the people of the Italian peninsula had suffered the ravages of the Black Death and the other epidemics of the fourteenth and fifteenth centuries, the ensuing economic recession of the fourteenth century, which led to declines in manufacturing and population in the central Italian region of Tuscany, did not affect much of the northern part of the peninsula as severely, and it still prospered. Drawing its wool from England and Spain, Florence's textile industry employed about 30,000 workers. The finished Florentine cloth and woolen goods were then traded throughout the lands of the Mediterranean, Burgundy, Flanders, England, and as far as Asia. Agriculture thrived in the broad river valleys of Tuscany and Lombardy. The production of grains, vegetables, and wine, aided by the drainage of swamps and marshes and by irrigation, not only fed the urban population, but also provided an agricultural surplus that could be invested in commerce and manufacturing. Aided by the proximity of Mediterranean trade routes, international trade and small-scale manufacturing brought prosperity to ambitious Italian merchants.

The development of banking during the early fourteenth century helped finance internal trade and international commerce. By the first years of the fifteenth century, the Church's condemnation of usury no longer was taken to apply to banking, as long as the rates of interest were not considered excessive. Florence's gold florin became a standard currency in European trading centers, and the bankers of that city, with agents in Avignon and many other cities throughout the trading network, were central to European commerce and monarchical and papal finances. Unlike traders elsewhere in Europe, Florentine merchants had broad experience with bills of exchange and deposit, which provided credit to purchasers. There were, however, risks to such loans. In the fifteenth century, the king of England forced Florentine merchants to loan him money, or else be ex-

A view of the Republic of Venice, major Adriatic port.

pelled from his realm and lose all their assets there. But he defaulted on the loans after his invasion of France failed during the Hundred Years' War, and several major merchant Florentine companies went into bankruptcy.

Venice and Genoa were also major trading and banking cities, as well as centers of shipbuilding and insurance. Each city had long traded with the East Indies and the Far East. Merchants hedged their bets on whether their shipments would fall victim to the sudden Mediterranean storms, to roving pirates, or to some other mishap on the overland route through Central Asia. The merchants carried fine woolens and linen from the Italian peninsula and Northern Europe, as well as metals, to the East. They returned with cotton, silk, and, above all, spices, including pepper, cinnamon, nutmeg, ginger, and sugar, which arrived via Alexandria or Constantinople from the East Indies to awaken the palates of Europeans of means. Both commercial powers used towns in Crimea as intermediary points for trade from Muscovy, Persia, India, and China (see Map 2.1).

Merchant capitalism eroded the power of the nobility by expanding the ranks and influence of townsmen. The wealth and status of urban merchants—although nobles also engaged in trade—allowed them to dominate the oligarchies that ruled the city-states. Prosperity increased the strong sense of municipal identity and pride; the political theorist Niccolò Machiavelli insisted, "I love my native city more than my own soul."

Social Structure

The social structure of the Italian city-states resembled that of other urban centers of trade and manufacturing in England, France, Flanders, and

MAP 2.1 REACH OF TRADE DURING THE FIFTEENTH CENTURY Major trade routes, both by land and sea led from the Italian city-states of Venice, Genoa, and Florence, as well as from the North and Baltic areas. The Italian city-states formed a natural point of exchange between East and West. Products that were traded are shown at their source.

The *popolo grasso,* or fat people, are shown here lining the streets to view a horse that has returned from winning a race at the Palio.

Holland. In the city-states, the *popolo grasso,* or "fat people," were the elite, including nobles, wealthy merchants, and manufacturers. The *mediocri* were the middling sort, including smaller merchants and master artisans. The *popolo minuto,* or "little people," made up the bulk of the urban population. In cities, artisans and laborers were burdened by high taxes on consumption. Urban elites owned much of the richest land of the hinterland, which was worked by tenant farmers, sharecroppers, and agricultural laborers, as well as by peasant landowners. In the northern and central part of the Italian peninsula, most peasants were free to be miserably poor, while in the southern part many still owed obligations to their lords.

The "fat people" of the city-states comprised no more than 5 percent of the population. The great patricians assumed the status of princes of their cities, whether as dukes, cardinals, or, in the case of Rome, as the pope himself. Although social differences remained sharp in Italian city-states, as everywhere, commercial wealth made possible some degree of social mobility, above all in Florence, the wealthiest city. New families, enriched by commerce, rose into the ruling elite, although opportunities to do so had declined noticeably by the end of the fifteenth century.

An elaborate and highly ritualized etiquette based upon mutual flattery maintained social distance. The wealthiest families became even richer despite the recession that extended throughout much of the fourteenth and fifteenth centuries; their prosperity made them even more eager not to be taken for anyone else of more modest station. Thus, one of the powerful dukes of Milan insisted that his wife be called *Illustrissima*, or the "Illustrious One." Flattery and subservience could be found in every greeting, and in every letter penned to a prince: "Nothing in the world pleases me more than your commands," and the ominous "I live only insofar as I am in your excellency's graces," which was sometimes true enough.

Urban patriarchs dominated their cities through power and patronage. They dispensed titles, privileges, and cash as they pleased. The duke of Ferrara affirmed his power by going door to door once a year to "beg" on behalf of the poor, an inversion of reality that served to define his authority and the subordination of everyone else. But princes and patriarchs also ruled through intimidation, occasionally eliminating enemies with astonishing cruelty.

Renaissance Political Life

The originality of the Italian city-states during the Renaissance lay not only in their remarkable artistic accomplishments but also in their precociously innovative forms of political structure. The organization of some of the city-states into constitutional republics was closely linked to the cultural achievements of the Renaissance. Nonetheless, there was nothing democratic about the city-states of Renaissance Italy, for the elites had brutally crushed the popular uprisings of artisans and shopkeepers that occurred in Siena and a number of other towns during the fourteenth century.

Fourteenth- and fifteenth-century republics were constitutional oligarchies dominated by the most powerful families who filled the executive bodies, legislative or advisory councils, and special commissions that governed each city-state. The percentage of male citizens enjoying the right to vote ranged from about 2 percent in fifteenth-century Venice to 12 percent in fourteenth-century Bologna, the former percentage seeming most representative of the restricted nature of political rights in Renaissance Italy. Venice, Siena, Lucca, and Florence (at least until the waning days of domination by the powerful Medici family) were the most stable oligarchic republics of Renaissance Italy; Genoa, Bologna, and Perugia

MAP 2.2 CITY-STATES IN RENAISSANCE ITALY, 1494   The city-states were the fundamental political unit of the Italian peninsula; their number was reduced as many of them were absorbed by the more powerful city-states.

went back and forth between republican and despotic governments (see Map 2.2).

Some of the other city-states became outright hereditary despotisms (*signori*) run by a single family. Milan, a despotism under the control of the Visconti family, had grown prosperous from metallurgy and textile manufacturing. Francesco Sforza, a *condottieri* (mercenary of common origins), who had married the illegitimate daughter of the last Visconti duke in 1447, helped overthrow the republic less than three years later. Sforza imposed his family's rule with the support of Milanese nobles. The

Sforza family thereafter skillfully played off rivalries between other powerful families, sometimes sanctioning their will with sheer force. The duke of Milan tolerated a council of 900 men drawn from the city's leading citizens, but he appointed magistrates and officials—and in general ruled—as he pleased. Likewise, princely families, such as the Este family of Ferrara and the Gonzaga of Mantua, ran the smaller city-states.

By contrast, Venice, an energetic, prosperous Adriatic port city of lagoons and canals built on a number of small islands, remained a republic. Its constitution offered a balance of political interests: the doge, an official elected for life by the Senate, served as an executive authority whose prerogatives were not that far from those of a monarch. The Great Council, consisting of about 2,500 enfranchised patricians, elected the Senate, which represented the nobility, an increasing number of whom were ennobled merchants living in elegantly decorated houses facing the canals. No one represented the poor, more than half the population of Venice.

Like the monarchies beyond the Alps, the Italian city-states developed small, efficient state bureaucracies, as the despots or oligarchs (a few men or families running the government) of each city improved the effectiveness of state administration. Thus, Florence and Venice had special committees responsible for foreign affairs and commerce. Many offices were sold or filled by members of the leading families linked by marriages. Personal relations between powerful families, for example, between the Medicis and the Sforza, facilitated diplomacy. The Medici engaged financial specialists for the management of the fiscal policies of their city and their family, although the latter, to the detriment of Florence, almost always took precedence ("Better a city ruined," said Cosimo de' Medici, "than lost.").

The *condottieri* were central to the political and military situation in Italy. A military ethos permeated the courts of the Italian princes. The young prince learned military exercises, including jousting (horseback combat with long lances that could occasionally be deadly) and began to hunt, often using falcons. Some dukes hired themselves and their private armies out to the highest bidders, such as powerful Italian princes, the king of France, or the Holy Roman emperor.

Renaissance princes and oligarchs surrounded themselves with an imposing retinue of attendants. The court of Urbino, not particularly wealthy compared to some of the others, employed a staff of 355 people. This number included 45 counts of the duchy, 17 noblemen of various pedigrees, 22 pages, 5 secretaries, 19 chamber grooms, 5 cooks, 19 waiters, 50 stable hands, and 125 servants and jacks-of-all-trades, including the *galoppini,* who galloped around on a variety of errands.

Florence, Milan, Venice, Naples, and the Papal States were as aggressive as France and the other monarchies beyond the Alps, dominating weaker neighbors through force, intimidation, and alliances, picking them off one by one, as in checkers. When they were not battling each other, Florence and Venice combined to limit Milanese control to Lombardy, while establishing their own authority over their respective regions. Venice controlled territory from the Alps to the Po River. Genoa, bitterly divided between merchant factions and nobles living in the hills above the Mediterranean port, struggled to maintain its autonomy because it lay physically exposed to more powerful Milan and the kingdom of France.

The Papal States, which bordered Tuscany east of the Apennines and to their south, functioned like any other city-state. The pope, too, was a temporal, as well as a spiritual, prince. He was elected for life by cardinals, the highest bishops of the Church, who were, in turn, appointed by the pope. Like monarchs and urban oligarchs, popes had to contend with the ambitious nobles of the Papal States. They, too, conspired and sought alliances against other city-states. But despite the prediction of the Tuscan poet Dante Alighieri (1265–1321) that a new imperial civilization would arise on the Italian peninsula, the eternal city was only the peninsula's eighth largest city in the late fourteenth century, ruled by a beleaguered papacy amid distant echoes of past temporal glories. The city-states were increasingly freed from the authority and interference of the papacy. This began with the "Babylonian Captivity" (1309–1378), when the popes lived in Avignon under the direct influence of the king of France and, for a time, a rival pontiff claimed authority from Rome (see Chapter 3). The declining role of the papacy in temporal Italian affairs further aided the rise of Florence, Milan, and Venice.

Florence: Anatomy of a Renaissance City

Florence was the cradle of the Italian Renaissance, fulfilling Dante's dream that it become a great civilizing city. Indeed, early in the Renaissance, the language of the region, Tuscan, emerged as the "courtly language" used by an increasing number of educated Italians beyond Tuscany.

The walled city dominated its rich hinterland of gentle hills and prosperous plain. The Arno River, which flows through Florence, though occasionally turbulent after heavy spring rain, was navigable from the Mediterranean port of Pisa except during the summer months. In 1406, Florence conquered Pisa, another center of textile production, once a worthy challenger of Genoa for maritime trade but now divided into quarreling factions. This window on the sea aided Florentine commerce, enabling the city to become a maritime power.

Several other factors contributed to Florence's success in becoming the center of the revival of classical learning. Roman law and Latin remained the foundation of training of Florentine ecclesiastics, lawyers, and notaries. Although the influence of the Church remained strong, the Medici rulers encouraged a cultural movement that had strong secular elements. Both Christian and secular traditions, then, infused Florentine civic life.

The combination of a dynamic craft tradition and an economy closely tied to the production of luxury goods made Florence receptive to artistic

A drawing of Florence in about 1490. Note the Duomo in the center.

innovation. The city honored the accomplishments of its citizens—including cultural achievements. Lastly, Florence's reputation as a relatively educated city helped attract talented newcomers from rural Tuscany and other regions. It had many schools, including a university, and boasted a rate of literacy probably unmatched in Europe. In the fifteenth century, at least 8,000 children in a population of 100,000 attended church and civic schools, as well as private academies. It was also said that even laborers could recite Dante's verses by heart.

The bell tower of the Palazzo Vecchio, the government building completed early in the fourteenth century, watched over the dynamic center of international banking, commerce, and the manufacture of cloth, woolens, silk, and jewelry. By the middle of the fourteenth century, Florence had become the fifth largest city in Europe. Before the plagues of the 1340s, about 100,000 people lived there. After falling by half, Florence's population revived during the next half-century, equaling that of London and Seville, but not its rivals, Venice and Naples, each of which then had at least 100,000 inhabitants.

Most Florentine neighborhoods remained relatively heterogeneous in social composition. But increasingly grand patrician palaces were physically set off and protected from the crowded street and the anonymity of medieval buildings that stretched along in rows. Fancy, flamboyant dress also distinguished the wealthy people from those of lesser means. So did the unprecedented quest by patrician families for elegant crafted furnishings, such as chimney pieces, chests, and sideboards, and other objects, including candlesticks and bird cages. Covered balconies and top-floor terraces opened onto the streets. More modest and poor families lived not far away, yet a world apart, piled into small, sparsely furnished rooms in buildings up to five stories tall, some standing next to small cottages, lining winding streets and narrow lanes.

A Florentine council in session.

Wealthy merchants, the *grandi*, governed Florence with the support of merchants, lawyers, and craftsmen of more modest means. Organized into seven major guilds, the merchants and manufacturers, particularly the cloth merchants, kept the fourteen lesser guilds (whose members included artisans and shopkeepers) in a subordinate position. The guilds elected the nine members of government, the *Signoria,* which administered the city. The *Signoria* proposed laws and conducted foreign affairs. Its members led the processions through the narrow streets during the various religious holidays. Two assemblies, the Council of the People and the Council of the Commune, served as a legislature. Citizens wealthy enough to pay taxes elected the 600 to 700 members of these councils, which met as needed to approve the decisions of the *Signoria.*

During the fifteenth century, while Florence maintained its leading role in shaping the culture of the Renaissance, the business of government went on in the palaces of the wealthiest citizens of Florence. The elite feared that the poor would revolt as they had in 1378 in the revolt known as the Ciompi, or "the wooden shoes," because many of the laborers could only afford wooden shoes. Suffering from economic hardship and aided by disgruntled members of the lower guilds, the cloth workers had risen up in a bloody insurrection in the hope of expanding the guild system already in power. The possibility of another uprising of the poor thereafter remained in the memory of the "fat people," causing them to keep the workers in a position of resentful subservience.

Timely marriages, and thus alliances, between wealthy families reinforced status and power. A poor choice of allies could bring disaster. New families, some of which had moved to Florence from other parts of Tuscany, managed to enter the ranks of the wealthy ruling families. Families enriched by good economic fortune replaced those for whom recent years had not been so good.

The renewal, then, of the Florentine elite with new families provided continuity within change, despite no small degree of political turbulence in the fifteenth century. The crowning cultural achievements of the Renaissance were not only rooted in Florence's prosperity but also in the relative social and political stability within that innovative city-state.

In 1434, Cosimo de' Medici (1389–1464) and his family seized control of Florentine political life. The family drew its great wealth from banking and the manufacture and commerce of textiles. Supported by a few patrician families, Cosimo banished prominent members of the most powerful rival clans. The Medici now controlled the offices of government. They manipulated the electoral process masterfully, using their wealth to curry support. Cosimo reflected the marketplace toughness of his family.

Florentine nobles generally accepted Medici mastery because stability contributed to prosperity. Wealthy families continued to conspire against each other, even as Florence warred against Venice, but the powerful families remained staunchly patriotic, devoted to their city. Nonetheless, some Florentine nobles continued to oppose the Medici. In the Pazzi conspiracy of 1479, Lorenzo the Magnificent (1449–1492), Cosimo's grandson, sur-

Lorenzo de' Medici (the Magnificent).

vived an assassination attempt during Mass in the cathedral. Several hours later, four of the enemies of the Medici were hanging upside down from a government building, including the archbishop of Pisa. Lorenzo composed verses to be placed under their heads and commissioned Sandro Botticelli (c. 1445–1510) to paint them as they swung. Renaissance culture and the often violent political world of the city-states here converged.

The establishment of a Council of Seventy, which elected committees assigned responsibility for domestic and foreign affairs, helped the Medici tighten their grip on the reins of the Florentine republic. Lorenzo extended the family's banking interests and its influence with the pope in Rome. Among the many honors bestowed on the Medici family, Lorenzo considered the papal nomination of his thirteen-year-old son to the rank of Church cardinal "the greatest achievement of our house."

A DYNAMIC CULTURE

Economically and intellectually dynamic, Florence emerged as the center of the Renaissance. As Florence solidified its leading position on the Italian peninsula, its people rediscovered and celebrated classical learning. While glorifying antiquity, Renaissance poetry, prose, and painting emphasized the dignity of the individual, made in the image and likeness of God. It gradually moved civilized concepts like beauty and virtue away from theological constraints.

The Rediscovery of Classical Learning

The Tuscan poet Petrarch (Francesco Petrarcha, 1304–1374) was among the earliest and most influential of those who rediscovered and celebrated the classics of Latin antiquity. Petrarch, the son of a Florentine notary, learned Latin from a monk who inspired the boy to pursue his fascination with the classical world, which he came to view as a lost age. As a young man, Petrarch lived in Avignon, an international community of lawyers and churchmen at the papal court. There he copied ancient works from the manuscripts and books these men had brought with them. Petrarch and his friends searched far and wide for more classical manuscripts. They uncovered the *Letters to Athens* of the Roman orator and moralist Marcus Tullius Cicero (106–43 B.C.), among other texts, stored in the cathedral of Verona. The study of Cicero led Petrarch to see in classical philosophy a guide to life based on experience.

Petrarch's successors found and copied other classical manuscripts. Among them were classical literary commentaries, which provided humanists with a body of information about the authors in which they were interested. Scholars brought works of classical Greek authors, including the playwright Sophocles, from Constantinople and from the libraries of

Agnese world map.

Detail from Benozzo Gozzoli's *Procession of the Magi* (1459–1460).

Raphael's *Madonna di Foligno* (1512).

Leonardo da Vinci's *Mona Lisa* (1503–1507).

Giovanni Bellini's *Doge Leonardo Loredano* (1502).

Sandro Botticelli's *The Birth of Venus* (c. 1482).

Titian's *Bacchus and Ariadne* (1522).

Michelangelo's *Fall of Man*, from the ceiling of the Sistine Chapel.

Albrecht Dürer's *Self-Portrait* (1500).

Gaulli's *The Triumph of the Name of Jesus*, fresco painted on the ceiling of the Gesú Church of the Jesuits in Rome.

Pieter Bruegel the Elder's *The Peasants' Wedding* (1568).

Mount Athos. Knowledge of Greek texts (as well as certain Arabic and Hebrew texts) spread slowly through Italy after the arrival of a number of Greek teachers from Constantinople.

The development of printing (see Chapter 1), following its invention by a German, Johann Gutenberg, permitted the diffusion of a variety of histories, treatises, biographies, autobiographies, and poems. Printing increased the knowledge of classical texts and the development of textual criticism itself. Many Renaissance scholars considered Cicero to represent the model of the purest classical prose (although others considered him too long-winded), and by 1500 more than 200 editions of his works had been printed in Italy, including his influential *On Oratory* and his letters. Libraries were established in many of the city-states, including Florence, Naples, and Venice, the last major city-state to turn toward antiquity, and provided scholars with common texts for study.

From Scholasticism to Humanism

The Romans had used the concept of *humanitas* to describe the combination of wisdom and virtue that they revered. The term came to refer to studies that were intellectually liberating, the seven liberal arts of antiquity: grammar, logic, arithmetic, geometry, music, astronomy, and rhetoric (the art of expressive and persuasive speech or discourse). Medieval scholasticism was a system of thought in which clerics applied reason to philosophical and theological questions. Those teachers and students who shifted their focus from the scholastic curriculum—law, medicine, and theology—to the curriculum of Latin grammar, rhetoric, and metaphysics became known as "humanists." They considered the study of the "humanities" to be essential for educating a good citizen.

Renaissance humanists believed that they were reviving the glory of the classical age. They considered their era greater than any since the Roman

(*Left*) Petrarch. (*Right*) Humanist educator and his charges.

Empire. They believed the Italian peninsula, although divided by political units, dialects, and by the Apennine Mountains, shared a common, special culture.

Venerating classical civilization, the humanists turned their backs on medieval scholasticism, which they believed was composed of irrelevant theological debates on revealed religion and encouraged the ascetic withdrawal of men and women from the world. Scholastics celebrated the authority of Church texts and revered the saint, the monk, and the knight. Petrarch rejected idle philosophic speculation or even knowledge that seemed irrelevant to mankind. He mocked scholastics: they can tell you "how many hairs there are in the lion's mane . . . with how many arms the squid binds a shipwrecked sailor. . . . All these things or the greater part of it is wrong. . . . And even if they were true, they would not contribute anything to the blessed life. What is the use, I pray you, of knowing the nature of beasts, birds, fishes and serpents, and not knowing, or spurning the nature of man, to what end we are born, and from where and whither we pilgrimage."

The humanists proclaimed the writers of antiquity to be heroes worthy of emulation. Although virtually all humanists accepted Christianity, and clerical religious culture persisted intact, humanism stood as an alternative approach to knowledge and culture. Humanists believed that a knowledge of the humanities could civilize mankind, teaching the "art of living." Petrarch insisted that the study of classical poetry and rhetoric could infuse daily life with ethical values.

Unlike the scholastics, humanists believed that it was not enough to withdraw into philosophy. Petrarch rediscovered the classical ideal that the philosopher, or humanist, was a wise man who could govern. Cicero had written that what made an individual great was not the gifts of good fortune, but the use to which he put them. The poet and orator had been a prominent figure in the political life of the Roman Republic, which had confronted threats to its survival. The active life, including participation in public affairs, had formed part of his definition of true wisdom. From the literature of the Greek and Roman past, humanists looked for guides to public life in their own city-states. The first half of the fifteenth century is often referred to as the period of "civic humanism" because of the influence of humanists and artists on the city-states themselves. Like the classic writers of ancient Rome, Renaissance writers were concerned with wisdom, virtue, and morality within the context of the political community. Humanists wrote boastful histories of the city-states, philosophical essays, stirring orations, and flattering biographies, as well as poetry, eagerly imitating classical styles.

The Renaissance and Religion

In rediscovering classic texts and motifs, the Renaissance remained closely linked to religion. Dante's *Divine Comedy* (1321), an allegorical poem, provides the quintessential expression of medieval thought by its demonstration of the extraordinary power that theology exerted on educated thought and literature. In his voyage through Hell, Purgatory, and Heaven, Dante encounters historical figures respectively suffering terrible agonies for their sins, waiting expectantly for admission into Heaven, or reaping the benefits of having lived a good life. Renaissance humanists could reject medieval scholasticism without turning their backs on the Church. Indeed, they claimed that they were searching for the origins of Christianity in the classical world from which it had emerged.

Although not the first to do so, humanists took classic texts, which were pagan, and ascribed to them meanings prophetic of Christianity. For example, the long epic *Aeneid*, written by Virgil (70–19 B.C.), had been commissioned by the Roman Emperor Augustus in the hope that it would offer the most favorable image of himself and of the empire, that is, of fulfilling the divine mandate to bring peace and civilization to the world. The hero of the *Aeneid*, Aeneas, personifies the ideal qualities of a Roman citizen, wanting to fulfill his patriotic duties, seeking glory for the empire but never for himself. The humanists transformed Aeneas's journey into an allegory for the itinerary of the Christian soul, appropriating antiquity into theology by viewing it as a foreshadowing of the true religion.

The place of the Church in Italian life therefore remained strong during the Renaissance, the relative decline in the papacy's temporal power notwithstanding. There was thus considerable continuity between the medieval period and the Renaissance in matters of religion. There were at least 264 bishops in Italy, as many as in the rest of the Christian world. In 1427, Florence had more than 1,400 clerics out of a population of 38,000 living in ecclesiastical institutions. Religious festivals dotted the calendar. The colorful Venetian water processions of elaborately decorated gondolas, jousting, boat races, and the annual horse race *(palio)* sponsored by rival neighborhoods in Siena still bear witness to the playful but intense festivity of the Renaissance city-states, a festivity that gave ritualized religious expression to civic and political life.

The Renaissance Man and Woman

Renaissance literature and poetry, preoccupied with nature, beauty, and reason, placed the individual at the forefront of attention. Renaissance writers praised mankind as "heroic" and "divine," rational and prudent, rather than intrinsically unworthy by virtue of being stained by original sin, as Church theologians held. This, too, represented a revival of the classic vision of the moral greatness of the individual and his or her ability to discover truth and wisdom.

By this view, the lay person could interpret morality through the ancient texts themselves, without the assistance of the clergy. Once someone had learned to read Latin and Greek, neither ecclesiastical guidance nor formalized school settings were necessary for the accumulation of wisdom.

Universities in general remained under the influence of the theological debates of scholasticism, although the universities of Florence, Bologna, and Padua gradually added humanist subjects to their curricula. Relatively few humanists emerged from the universities, which remained training grounds for jurists, doctors, and clerics.

"These studies are called liberal because they make man free," a humanist wrote; they are humane "because they perfect man . . . those studies by which we attain and practice virtue and wisdom; that education which calls forth, trains and develops those highest gifts of body and of mind, which ennoble man." The young Giovanni Pico della Mirandola (1463–1494) exclaimed, "O highest and most marvelous felicity of man! To him it is granted to have whatever he chooses, to be whatever he wills." Pico described the individual as an independent and autonomous being who could make his own moral choices and become, within the context of Christianity, "the molder and sculptor of himself."

Niccolò Machiavelli (1469–1527), too, found personal fulfillment in the study of the classics. He had been employed in the Florentine chancery, serving as a diplomat. Purged when the Medici overthrew the republic in 1512, he took up residence in the countryside. Machiavelli complained that his days consisted of mundane exchanges with rustics. But "when evening comes I return home and go into my study. On the threshold I strip off my muddy, sweaty, workday clothes, and put on the robes of court and palace, and in this graver dress I enter the antique courts of the ancients and am welcomed by them, and there again I taste the food that alone is mine, and for which I was born. And I make bold to speak to them and ask the motives of their actions, and they, in their humanity, reply to me. And for the space of four hours I forget the world, remember no vexation, fear poverty no more, tremble no more at death: I pass indeed into their world." Machiavelli evoked the exhilaration of the individual discovering the joys of antiquity.

The development of the autobiography in literature reflected the celebration of the individual, however much the genre was limited to public people and the image that they sought to present of themselves, revealing virtually nothing of private life. In the first half of the fifteenth century, the portrait and the self-portrait emerged as artistic genres; princes, oligarchs, courtiers and other people of wealth joined Christ, the Virgin Mary, and popular saints as subjects of painting.

A growing sense of what it meant to be "civilized" arose in the Italian city-states and highlighted the place of the individual in society. The Italian patrician may have been cleaner and more perfumed than people elsewhere in Europe, and certainly claimed to be so. Books on good conduct and manners emerged. The writer Baldassare Castiglione (1478–1529) urged the person of taste to show that "whatever is said or done has been done without pains and virtually without thought" as if correct behavior had become part of his or her very being. Women, he contended, should obtain a "knowledge of letters, of music, of painting, and . . . how to dance and be festive."

Castiglione's *The Courtier* (1528) described the ideal courtier, or attendant at a court, as someone who had mastered the classics and several languages, and who could paint, sing, write poetry, advise and console his prince, as well as run, jump, swim, and wrestle. The idea of a "universal person" had existed for some time, although, of course, not everyone had the leisure or resources to study and learn about so many subjects. One example of such a "universal person" was Leon Battista Alberti (1402–1472), a humanist, architect, mathematician, athlete, and papal secretary. But, to be sure, only the scholar who benefited from sufficient patronage, or someone with considerable financial means could become a "Renaissance man."

Some Renaissance humanists were actively hostile to science because as a form of knowledge it did not necessarily focus on mankind. Yet, although he was not a humanist and could not read Latin, Leonardo da Vinci (1452–1519), painter, scientist, architect, military engineer, and philosopher became the epitome of the "Renaissance man" in the view of later ages. The illegitimate son of a notary from a Tuscan village, he was apprenticed to a Florentine painter at the age of twelve. Following acceptance into the master's guild in Florence, he remained in the workshop of his master until moving in 1482 to Milan, where he enjoyed the patronage of the Sforza family. Taking the title "Painter and Engineer of the Duke of Milan," Leonardo taught students in his workshop and undertook scientific studies of anatomy in which he depicted, among other things,

Drawings by Leonardo da Vinci.

bird wings. His drawings were the first modern scientific illustrations. Leonardo began compiling his prodigious notebooks, in which he jotted down his ideas, perceptions, and experiences. He also sculpted an equestrian monument, designed costumes for theatrical performances, worked as a military engineer, and decorated palaces. In 1500, Leonardo returned to Florence, then went back to Milan six years later, beckoned by the governor of Francis I, king of France. When the Milanese freed themselves from French hegemony, he went south to Rome, where Pope Leo X (pope 1513–1521) provided him with a salary. In 1516, the French king brought Leonardo to his château on the Loire at Amboise, where he sketched court festivals, and served as something of a Renaissance jack-of-all-trades before his death in 1519.

If the Renaissance is often said to have "discovered" mankind in general, this meant, for the most part, men. The Church considered women to be sinful daughters of Eve. Legally, women remained subject to men; they could own property, and make their wills, but could not sell property without their husbands' permission. Both rich and poor families continued to value boys more than girls; poor families were far more likely to abandon female babies or to place them in the care of a distant wet nurse. Many families viewed girls as a liability because of the necessity of providing a dowry, however large or small, for their marriage. Some families of means pushed daughters off into convents. Because of the strict gender division within the Church, women there could aspire not only to holiness and sainthood, but also to leadership in a world of women. Life in a convent left them free to study.

Yet, some patricians educated their girls as well as boys in the humanities. Some girls studied letters, orations, and poems with tutors. But only a small number of women went on to write because they could not enter learned professions. Three alone were well known to contemporaries, including Isotta Nogarola, a fifteenth-century humanist from Verona who abandoned secular life for quiet religious contemplation and scholarship. She apologized for the weakness of women's nature in explaining the fall of mankind in the Garden of Eden, modestly believing that she fell short of "the whole and perfect virtue that men attain."

The Renaissance did not bring about any significant loosening in the restrictions placed on women. In the Italian city-states, women had less of a role in public life than they had enjoyed in the courts of medieval Europe. Women presided over social gatherings, but for the most part in a ritualized, decorative role. Overall, the Renaissance era may even have reduced women's social and personal options. If Renaissance authors idealized love and women, chastity and submission to one's husband remained the reality. If the education of young women clashed with a father's plans for his daughter to marry, the latter won out without discussion. The role of women continued to be to serve their husbands or, in some cases, their lovers. Men's feelings were the focus of considerable attention by Renaissance writers, women's usually were assumed to be unimportant. To be sure, women in large, powerful families like the Sforza, Este, and Gonzaga exerted influence and were patrons to artists. Yet, the subjects they commissioned artists and sculptors to portray were essentially the same as those of their male counterparts and, in patriarchal households, their husbands made the decisions.

RENAISSANCE ART

When the German painter Albrecht Dürer (1471–1528) visited Venice on one of his two trips to the northern Italian peninsula, he was surprised and delighted by the fact that there artists enjoyed considerably more status than in his native Nuremburg: "Here," he wrote, "I am a gentleman, at home a sponger."

Just as the prestige of the artist soared during the Renaissance, remarkable artistic accomplishments mark that special period's place in history. These have endured. Great works of Renaissance architecture, painting, and sculpture are still studied with awe by specialists and appreciated by millions of people each year.

Architecture

Despite the Renaissance concept of the "ideal city" of architectural harmony, reflected in the first treatises on architecture, Florence, Siena, Perugia, and other Italian cities retained their medieval cores, which had developed around their markets and around which stood the town hall

The Pitti Palace in Florence in both the palace and surrounding gardens.

and other public buildings. But during the fifteenth century, their narrow streets and alleyways became interspersed with splendid buildings and dotted with works of art commissioned by wealthy families.

Florence, for example, underwent a building boom during the fifteenth century. Construction of its elegant residences stimulated the economy, providing employment to skilled artisans—brickmakers, masons, roofers, tilers, carpenters, sculptors, cabinetmakers, joiners, and decorative artists, including the talented goldsmiths of Tuscany, sculptors, and painters, as well as day laborers. Renaissance architecture emphasized elegant simplicity, an expansion of the simple rustic fronts that had characterized medieval building. Renaissance architects combined plain white walls with colorful, intricate arches, doors, and window frames. In the fifteenth century, expensive palaces of monumental proportions with columns, arches, and magnificent stairways were considered sensible investments, because they could, if necessary, later be sold at a profit.

Like writers and painters, Renaissance architects looked to antiquity for models. Filippo Brunelleschi (1377–1446) first applied theories of classical architecture to the Foundling Hospital in Florence, the earliest building constructed in Renaissance style. Fourteenth-century architects planned churches in the form of circles, the shape they thought was in the image of God, with no beginning and no end. But they may also have drawn on Rome's Pantheon temple, classical and round. After going to the papal city to study the ruins of classical architecture, Brunelleschi solved daunting technical problems to construct the vast dome, or cupola, of that city's cathedral (Duomo). The magnificent structure, completed in 1413 after work lasting more than a century, reflects the architect's rejection of northern Gothic architectural style, with its pointed arches, vaulting, and flying buttresses that counterbalanced slender vertical columns. Inspired by excavations of classical ruins and the rebuilding of Rome in the late fifteenth century, architects began to copy classical styles closely, adding Corinthian columns, which were tall with ornate capitals and great sweeping arches.

Patronage and the Arts

Renaissance art could not have flourished without the patronage of wealthy, powerful families, though commissions by guilds and religious confraternities were not uncommon. Artists, as well as poets and musicians, were eager, like Leonardo, to be invited into a patrician's household, where there were few or no expenses, and there was time to work. Lesser artists painted coats of arms, tapestries, the prince's pets—dogs and falcons—and even the faces of playing cards.

Some humanists not fortunate enough to be given the run of the palace of a powerful patrician found posts as state secretaries, because they could draft impressive official correspondence, and they tutored the children

Pope Leo X brought to his court artists and musicians. This portrait was done by Raphael.

of patrician families. A few worked as papal courtiers. Such humanists penned orations, scrupulously imitating Cicero, for formal state receptions, clamorous festivals, and funerals, written to awe listeners of all classes. The Medici Pope Leo X, who composed and played music himself, brought to his court a number of distinguished artists and musicians, as well as humanists whom he employed as officials and envoys. At the same time, the genres of wit and satire developed and became part of the ribald and "sharp-tongued" life of the political and social world of the city-state. "Rest be granted by the devil to Pope Sixtus," went one "eulogy" upon the latter's death in 1484, "Friend to Satan, enemy to Christ." The biting, somewhat pornographic satires and lampoons of Pietro Aretino (1492–1556), who enjoyed in succession the patronage of a banker, a cardinal, the duke of Mantua, the Medici of Florence, and then a Venetian doge and nobleman, spared neither secular nor ecclesiastical leaders from mocking jokes and rhymes. Aretino attacked social climbers and the venality of offices in the city-states with particular venom. He spared the one person he referred to as divine—himself.

As the classical texts posited the ideal that the active life included playing a salutary role in one's community, families of means held that they should demonstrate wisdom by making good use of their riches, as they developed their knowledge of the humanities. Commissioning works of art seemed to confirm moral leadership, and therefore the right to govern; in the words of a prosperous Florentine merchant, they "serve the glory of God, the honor of the city, and commemorate myself." Wealthy families also used art to reflect the image that they wished to give of themselves, for example, commissioning portraits to impress the family of a prospective spouse. Portraiture glorified the subject who sat before the artist.

The Medici of Florence, the greatest of the secular patrons of the arts, commissioned buildings, paid for the elaborate decoration of chapels and altarpieces, and restored monasteries. Although wags suggested that he may have been more interested in the expensive bindings of books he purchased than in their contents, Cosimo de' Medici, though himself not a scholar, collected manuscripts and even read some of them. The wealthy banker spent much of his time overseeing the construction of fine palaces and churches. Michelangelo (1475–1564), who designed the Medici tombs in the church of Saint Lorenzo in Florence, was but one sculptor who enjoyed the favor of the Medici. In 1504, he began work on a mural in the city hall commissioned for the city, alongside another undertaken by Leonardo da Vinci.

The long economic recession of the fifteenth century may have actually contributed to the arts. Finding insufficient profits in commerce and manufacturing for their money, patrician families spent considerable sums on paintings and sculpture. This may, in turn, have accentuated the recession by turning productive capital away from economic investments. At the same time, so the argument goes, the recession offered families of means more time to devote to the life of the mind and to culture.

The ruling families of some smaller states were especially lavish in their patronage of the arts. The Gonzaga family of Mantua, for example, carried their enthusiasm for a self-referential courtly life to an extreme that probably was unmatched. To emphasize their might, the Gonzaga brought dwarfs to their court, which was greater in pretension than in might.

The Gonzagas of Mantua. Note the dwarf in the foreground.

Venetian envoys arrived to find the syphilitic marquis in 1515 lying on a couch in his favorite room, attended by his favorite dwarf, who was attired in gold brocade. Nearby stood three pages, and three greyhounds as well, while the walls were covered with paintings of favorite pets and favorite people, and of the duke himself.

Patrons of the arts often specified not only the subject of the work commissioned but certain details as well, requiring, for example, that specific saints be depicted. The size of the work of art and its price of course had to be specified, including the cost of blue pigment or gold for paintings and bronze or marble for sculptures. Cherubs cost more. Although one of the dukes of Ferrara paid for his paintings by the square foot, increasingly patrons paid the artist for his time—and thus his skill—as well as for the materials he used. The contract for a work of art might specify whether it was to be completed by the artist himself, or if assistants from the master's workshop could be employed for certain parts. Patrons sometimes appeared on the canvas, as in the case of *The Adoration of the Magi* (1426), by Tommaso di Giovanni Masaccio (1401–1428), which includes portraits of the notary who commissioned the painting and his son. Conversely, patricians occasionally commissioned artists to humiliate their enemies, as when a painter in Verona was paid to sneak up to the walls of a rival palace and paint obscene pictures.

Renaissance Artists

Because of its basis in the craft tradition, in the medieval world painting had been considered a "mechanical" art. This made the status of the artist ambiguous, because he sold his own works and lacked the humanist's education. Michelangelo's father tried to discourage his son from becoming a sculptor, an art that he identified with stone cutting. Michelangelo himself sometimes signed his paintings "Michelangelo, sculptor," as if to differentiate himself from a mere painter. Yet, in his treatise on painting (1435), Alberti, irritated by contemporary insistence that painting was a "mechanical art," insisted that the artist was no longer a craftsman but a practitioner of a "high art."

Of the artists whose social origins are known, the majority had fathers who were urban shopkeepers or artisans, most often in the luxury trades. Next—surprisingly—in number came the sons of nobles, perhaps reflecting the relative decline in noble fortunes during the Renaissance. Next came the children of merchants and educated professionals such as notaries, lawyers, and officials. Some artists, like Raphael (1483–1520), were sons of artists. A good many others had been apprentice artisans. Only a handful were the sons of peasants.

The contemporary association between craftsmen and painters was appropriate, because, like the former, artists entered a period of apprenticeship. But in contrast, architects and composers lacked such formal training. The architect Brunelleschi belonged to the guild of silk manufacturers and goldsmiths. Composers were usually trained to be musical performers and simply began to write music on their own.

The painters' guild of Venice seems typical of the way in which artists learned their skills. The guild required five years of apprenticeship, followed by two years of journeyman status, requirements similar to those by which silversmiths, shoemakers, cabinetmakers, and other craftsmen were trained. The painters' guilds resembled other craft guilds in that the members were considered brothers in work who passed through life's great hurdles together. They shared not only varying degrees of skill and training but the solidarity of craftsmen as well. Some masters had sizable workshops, where apprentices trained and often lived together, sometimes working on the same paintings (which is one reason it is difficult to authenticate some canvases). If there were no prominent female artists during the Renaissance, at least until well into the sixteenth century, it was because women could neither become apprentices nor attend universities.

By the beginning of the sixteenth century, the artist's status in general had risen so much that a Venetian painter dared propose that only those "noble both by birth and money" be allowed to paint. Michelangelo, Leonardo, Raphael, and Titian (Tiziano Vecellio, c. 1490–1576) lived as gentlemen, the last knighted by Charles V, Holy Roman emperor. Some artists were crowned with laurels—thus the designation of "poet laureate"—by their adoring city-states.

Indeed, artists claimed that they deserved more esteem than a craftsman. Leonardo praised the painter, sitting "at his ease in front of his work, dressed as he pleases, and moves his light brush with the beautiful colors . . . often accompanied by musicians or readers of various beautiful works." In addition to a degree of self-promotion, the artist's quest for beauty and God helps explain the rise of some artists of the Renaissance period from practitioners of a "mechanical art," to the description of Michelangelo offered by a Portuguese painter, "In Italy, one does not care for the renown of great princes: it's a painter only that they call divine." Of course, not all painters ascended to such heights. Yet, for all the ambiguity of the artist's position, less than that of the humanist and still sometimes considered a craftsman, during the Renaissance the status of the artist rose.

Painting and Sculpture

The rediscovery of antiquity, nature, and mankind transformed European painting. Renaissance artists reflected the influence of the Neo-Platonists. In the late fifteenth and early sixteenth centuries, the Neo-Platonists appropriated Plato's belief that eternal ideas—such as beauty, truth, and goodness—existed beyond the realm of everyday life. Humanists believed that the mind could transcend human nature and come to understand these eternal ideas. The artist could reproduce the beauty of the soul through imagination and in doing so reach out to God. To Dante, art was "the grandchild of God." For Michelangelo, beauty "lifts to heaven hearts that truly know."

Artists sought to achieve the representation of beauty in a realistic way by using the proportions created by God in the universe. It was the supreme compliment to say of a Renaissance painter that his work had surpassed nature in beauty. Leonardo put it this way: "Painting . . . compels the mind of the painter to transform itself into the mind of nature itself and to translate between nature and art."

During the Renaissance, nature ceased to be mere background. Painters now faithfully depicted the beauty of mountains, rocks, and gardens for their own sake. Naturalism was heightened by the removal of the kind of pretty detail that embellished medieval art. It can first be seen in the memorable figures of the frescoes (paintings on plaster) of Giotto di Bondone (c. 1266–1337) in the chapels of Holy Cross Church in Florence. These figures, particularly their facial expressions, reflect humanity, deeply personal emotion, and naturalism, unseen since the classical age. The fame of Giotto, who is usually considered the first great painter of the Renaissance, spread rapidly throughout much of Italy and his style greatly influenced his successors.

Objects of everyday life, reflecting a greater preoccupation with realistic depiction, increasingly appeared in paintings. Take, for example, Raphael's painting of the pudgy Pope Leo X, staring off into space while fiddling with a magnifying glass with which he has been examining a book (see p. 69).

Beauty could be portrayed with extraordinary richness, as in the work of Botticelli, or it could be depicted simply. Raphael, who admired and learned from Michelangelo, eight years his senior, wrote of trying to paint a beautiful woman, "I use as my guide a certain idea of the beautiful that I carry in my mind." Raphael's figures reflect a softness and inner beauty that contrast with the powerful, stirring subjects of the tempestuous Michelangelo. Reflecting Neo-Platonist influence, Titian early in the sixteenth century strove to bring the viewers of his paintings closer to the idea of the eternal form of female beauty that he sought to represent with his depictions of Venus.

The Greeks and Romans believed that the painter and sculptor understood and portrayed the soul in reproducing the human face. Leonardo's famous *Mona Lisa* (1503–1507), with its mysterious, confident half-smile, is a compelling illustration of this undertaking. "Movements of the soul," wrote Alberti early in the fifteenth century, "are recognized in movements of the body." Leonardo contended that the depiction of certain gestures indicated the soul or the character of the artist's subject. The painter had to be able to reveal the emotions and passions of the figures he depicted.

Renaissance artists used a large repertoire of stylized portrayals of emotion, the meaning of which was immediately recognized by virtually all viewers of painting. The Florentine Masaccio intended his extraordinary fresco *The Expulsion of Adam and Eve from Eden* (c. 1427) to represent the tortured souls, as well as bodies, of those biblical figures. We see Adam covering his eyes with his fingers in anguish, a truly gripping rendition of Adam and Eve's crushing sense of loss and grief as they leave the Garden of Eden. Likewise, certain colors symbolized status, or hierarchy, even if some of the routine associations of the medieval period (gold for piety, for example) had passed. Violet was often a color of reverence, white that of charity, red of fire, and gray of earth. Clear colors, intense light and splendid proportion were combined in representations of Christ. Deep coloring, more subtle and natural than the blues and golds of medieval painting, enriched the canvas.

Medieval and Byzantine painters offered unlifelike images on a flat space; linear forms were arranged in order of importance, accompanied by symbols easily identifiable to the viewer. The Renaissance development of perspective, through which parallel lines recede from the surface and seem to converge on the vanishing point, facilitated the realistic presentation of figures and movement. Renaissance artists believed that naturalism

Masaccio *(Left) The Expulsion of Adam and Eve from Eden* (c. 1427). *(Right)* Masaccio's *Trinity* (1425).

Andrea Mantegna's *The Dead Christ* (c. 1506).

could only be achieved through the use of perspective. Masaccio first applied the mathematical laws of perspective to painting in his revolutionary *Trinity* (1425), which makes a two-dimensional surface seem to be three-dimensional. The mastery of light contributed to innovative uses of space; for example, through the technique of foreshortening, proportionally contracting depth so as to give the viewer the illusion of projection or extension into space. In his realistic *The Dead Christ* (c. 1506), Andrea Mantegna (c. 1430–1506) utilized this technique, pioneered by Masaccio. This shortcut allowed the artist to create the visual impression of a three-dimensional body on a flat surface. Here one sees Christ's legs receding into space, drawing the viewer toward the physical presence of Christ's body. Florentine artists, in particular, used perspective to develop high relief and silhouette, presenting rounded figures on the canvas surface by effective use of tones and shades.

This mastery of perspective by the naturalist painter Masaccio and, above all, the sculptor Donatello (c. 1386–1466), who lived much longer and produced much more, helped Renaissance painters choose difficult, complicated themes and treat them with a more complex realism. Donatello utilized perspective to achieve dramatic action through gradations of relief. In *The Feast of Herod* (c. 1417), sculpted in bronze for the stone basin in the Siena Baptistery, Donatello captures the shocked reaction of the king and guests as John the Baptist's head is presented to Herod, proportioning unaware musicians in the background through relief and cen-

Donatello's *The Feast of Herod* (c. 1417).

tral perspective. In Leonardo's painting *The Last Supper* (c. 1495–1498), the disciples crowd along the table. The perspective of the ceiling and the sight of Christ centered on the canvas by his presence before the window immediately attracts the viewer's eye, which then falls on the apostles gathered along the table. Here Leonardo identifies Judas, not by leaving him without a halo nor by placing him alone on the other side of the table from Christ, but by painting him as the only figure in shadow.

To Leonardo, painting was the highest form of science and was based on "what has passed through our senses." He asserted "The scientific and true principles of painting first determine" the components of painting: "darkness, light, color, body, figure, position, distance, nearness, motion, and rest." The work of Michelangelo, who attended Latin grammar school, reflects a mastery of mathematics, anatomy, and optics. Animals, birds, and inanimate objects also took on a lifelike quality based upon the discovery of proper proportions.

The quest for the natural representation of beauty led some artists to depict the human body in nude form, which some took to be a more natural and expressive form borrowed from classical paganism. Botticelli's *The Birth of Venus* (c. 1482) represents this trend. Michelangelo believed that the depiction of the human body in sculpture was the ultimate test of human expression. He stripped the body so that its beauty could be better appreciated in its realism, as in his *David* (c. 1501–1504).

Religious, public, and private life overlapped, as the people of Renaissance Italy sought religious meanings in everything they saw. Art with religious subjects also served a teaching function for the Church. In many

Leonardo da Vinci's *The Last Supper* (c. 1495–1498).

patrician houses, a religious image could be found in every room. Devotional images, known as *ex votos*, were often erected in public spaces to fulfill a vow made to a saint in times of danger or illness. Patricians commissioned paintings with religious themes to realize similar vows. Moreover, the splendid tombs sculpted for patricians and popes may have reflected a preoccupation with glorifying the individual, but they nonetheless also emphasized eternal salvation.

Religious themes continued to dominate painting, accounting for perhaps nine of every ten paintings; the Virgin Mary was the most popular figure, followed by Christ and the saints (above all, Saint John the Baptist, the patron saint of Florence). The visualization of certain episodes in the life of Christ or of the martyrdom of Saint Sebastian were intended to stimulate piety and encourage morality. Thus, artists took on a role similar to preachers, whose orations evoked a powerful emotional response.

Classical symbolism abounded in Renaissance painting and influenced the depiction of religious themes, incorporating images drawn from pagan Rome. Artists used details about history or mythology that patrons insisted grace their canvases. Some of the classical gods stood as Renaissance symbols of moral or physical qualities. Michelangelo modeled his Christ in *The Last Judgment* (1536–1541) on a classical portrayal of the god Apollo. Mantegna, then the premier painter of northern Italy, drew upon his meticulous study of Roman archaeology.

Yet, along with scenes from classical mythology, paintings with secular themes increased in number, notably portraits of famous men or of wealthy patricians, but also of more ordinary people as well. Aretino, who

Detail from Michelangelo's *The Last Judgment* (1536–1541).

criticized everything, found fault with the democratization of the portrait, despite the fact that he was the son of a shoemaker, saying, "It is the disgrace of our age that it tolerates the portraits even of tailors and butchers." The growing popularity of secular subjects may have reflected a reaction against the power and venality of the clergy. Her well-heeled friends winked and joined in the laughter when Isabella of Mantua dressed one of her dwarfs as a bishop to greet a visiting dignitary; she ordered another to parody the Mass for the amusement of the audience.

High Renaissance Style

During the period of the High Renaissance (1490–1530), the prestige of artists reached its highest level, and the greatest were revered as geniuses. At the same time, the city-states of Italy lost much of their economic and political vitality and faced French invasion and then Spanish domination. In the midst of economic decline as well as internecine political warfare, artists no longer enjoyed the lavish patronage of wealthy patrician families. Instead, the Church became their patron.

The papacy inspired the monumentalism of the High Renaissance. Besieged in the first two decades of the sixteenth century by denunciations of the sale of indulgences—the purchase of the remission of some punishment in Purgatory for one's sins or for those of some family member—the papacy sought to assert forcefully its authority and image. Papal commissions in Rome were one attempt to recover public confidence and made possible the artistic achievements of the High Renaissance. Following excavations beginning in the 1470s that heightened interest in the ancient Roman Empire, Raphael himself oversaw the reconstruction of ancient Rome and personally supervised excavations of the Roman Forum. Influenced by and more dependent on the Church, the canvases of the painters of the High Renaissance became even larger as they became less concerned with rational order and more with achieving a powerful visual response in their viewers through large canvases.

Some humanists now began to claim that the papacy was the heir to the glories of classical Rome. Popes took names that echoed the Roman Empire. Julius II (pope 1503–1513) ordered a medal struck that read "Julius Caeser Pont[ifex]. II," a term that meant "high priest" in classical Rome. Wide boulevards and spaces were forged to accommodate waves of pilgrims descending upon the city.

Leonardo's *Last Supper* is perhaps the first example of the style of the High Renaissance, or what is sometimes called the Grand Manner. Mannerism (a term from the Italian word for style), which particularly characterized the 1520s, is marked by heightened scale, exaggerated drama, and the submersion of detail to a total emotional effect, reflecting the climate of the times. Donato Bramante (1444–1514), who rebuilt St. Peter's Basilica in Rome, in the "grand manner" of the High Renaissance, capped it with a grand dome in the style of Byzantium.

Painters of the High Renaissance increasingly presented large, ambitious, complex, and sometimes even bizarre canvases. Mannerism's imaginative distortions and sense of restlessness offered an unsettling vision in tune with new uncertainties. Mannerism marked something of a reaction against the Renaissance ideal of attaining classical perfection. Thus, some painters ignored the rules of perspective and rationalism, perhaps reflecting the frightening instability of the time. Nature faded into the background again; emotionalism, as well as mysticism and illusionism, won out over classicism. Toward the end of his career, Michelangelo's work reflected this influence. His majestic marble *Moses* (1515), sculpted for the tomb of Pope Julius II, has an immensely prominent head, with an exaggerated facial expression. It reflects Michelangelo's tragic vision of human limitations, including his own. Raphael and Titian presented human figures who seem almost empowered by divine attributes but who nonetheless retain their humanity. Moreover, Titian's mannerist paintings are known for their intense coloring, as in the unsettling *Bacchus and Ariadne* (1522). Raphael's *Madonna di Foligno* (1512) shows the Virgin sitting triumphantly on a cloud, surrounded by adoring saints.

THE END OF THE RENAISSANCE

Late in the fifteenth century, the Italian city-states entered a period of economic and political decline, making the peninsula more vulnerable to foreign invasion. Subsequently, some of the battles between Spain and France, Europe's two dominant powers, were fought on the Italian peninsula. The exploration and gradual colonization of the Americas, first by Spain, and the increase in trade and manufacturing in Northwestern Europe, helped move the economic and cultural vigor toward the Atlantic

Ocean, to Spain and Northwestern Europe, most notably, England, France, and the Dutch Netherlands (see Chapter 6).

Economic Decline

The economic decline of the northern Italian city-states during the second half of the fifteenth century undermined the material base of Renaissance prosperity, indeed the economic primacy of the Mediterranean region. The Italian city-states lost most of their trading routes with Asia. The Turks conquered Genoese trading posts in the Black Sea, the traditional merchant route to Asia, and the Aegean Sea. Turkish domination reduced Genoa's once mighty commercial network to trade centered on the Aegean island of Chios. Of the Italian city-states, Venice alone continued to prosper. After the Ottoman conquest of Constantinople in 1453, merchants in Venice concluded a deal with the Turks by which they received a monopoly on trade with the East, leaving the other city-states without access to their traditional Asian markets. Venice's economy soon diversified with small-scale manufacturing, however, particularly as the Turkish threat to its interests mounted in the eastern Mediterranean and Venetian galleys no longer could venture into the Black Sea.

Merchants of the Italian city-states sought alternatives. The Genoese established a trading post in the Muslim city of Málaga on the south coast of the Iberian Peninsula, although this made them dependent on local Muslim middlemen. Castile's conquest of Gibraltar and Málaga at the end of the century made transport between the Mediterranean and Atlantic ports safer for Christian vessels. Genoese and Florentine merchants undertook exploratory voyages down the west coast of Africa in search of a new route to Asia. But most such vessels never returned. The Portuguese thereafter took up the quest for a southern route to Asia, after acquiring the Atlantic Ocean islands of Madeira, Cape Verdes, and the Azores, which could be used as bases. Portuguese fleets began to monopolize the spice trade with India and beyond after Bartholomew Dias (c. 1450–1500) in 1487 first rounded the Cape of Good Hope, the southern tip of Africa. From then on, Portuguese crews knew how to reach the Indian Ocean, and then Calcutta, on the southwest coast of India.

The Florentine silk and woolen industries, long prosperous, now faced stiff competition from French and Dutch producers and merchants in Northwestern Europe. The dazzling prosperity of the great Italian merchant families ebbed. The economy of Europe and world commerce itself was changing. Portuguese, Spanish, English, and Dutch traders looked to the New World for new products and significant profits. Christopher Columbus, the Genoese explorer, asked an Italian duke to risk funds for his voyages of exploration in 1492, but he refused. Columbus then gained the support of King Ferdinand and Queen Isabella of Spain (see Chapter 1). The rapid growth of Portuguese and then Spanish trade, first down the coast of Africa and then, after 1492, across the Atlantic Ocean to the New World, accentuated the rise of the Atlantic economy. Competition from the larger sailing ships of England, Holland, and Portugal overwhelmed Florence and Genoa and then, more gradually, Venice.

Foreign Invasion

As long as the Italian peninsula remained free from the intervention of France and Spain or other powers, the city-states could continue to prosper while fighting each other and casting wary glances toward the Ottoman Empire as it expanded its influence in the Mediterranean. But the city-states, divided by economic interests and with a long tradition of quarreling among themselves, became increasingly vulnerable to the expansion of French interests.

Threats to the Italian peninsula mounted from France and the Turks. France had adhered to an alliance of Milan and Florence against Venice, signed in 1451. But the three city-states recognized the threat the aggressive French monarchy posed to the peninsula. Furthermore, following the capture of Constantinople in 1453, Turkish ships now appeared more frequently in the Adriatic Sea. It seemed imperative to end the wars between two leagues of city-states. The Peace of Lodi (1454), signed by Florence, Milan, and Venice, established a new political order. Helping discourage Turkish or French aggrandizement, the peace brought four decades of relative peace, which saw some of the crowning artistic glories of the Renaissance.

The establishment of this Italian League formalized this balance of power—it was already called that—between the strongest city-states. Whenever one or two of the states became aggressive—as when Venice and the Papal States attacked Ferrara—the others joined together to restore the status quo. Such wars were fought for the most part by mercenaries, imported and organized by *condottieri* paid for the task. For the moment, Milan's strong army served as a barricade against French invasion.

Perhaps accentuated by the ebbing of prosperity, political life within the city-states deteriorated. In Florence, the Medici despotism faced opposition from republicans. In the 1480s, Perugia had become a warring camp, torn between two rival families. In 1491, 130 members of one faction were executed on a main square and hanged from poles for all to see. Then, in repentance, the oligarchs erected thirty-five altars on that same square, and ordered priests to say Mass for three days in atonement. In a number of the city-states, some patrician families tried to outdo each other in their violence, crushing their opponents within their cities with brutality, then praying over the bodies. Vengeance, like corruption, seemed endemic. The leading Florentine families faithfully attended church, even as they undertook murders of vengeance in defense of family honor. Considerable tension, then, remained between two parallel codes of conduct, one religious, the other defined by family loyalties.

The Italian peninsula became a battleground for the dynastic ambitions and rivalries of the French kings and the Holy Roman emperors, powerful rulers who could mobilize considerably larger armies than those of the city-states. The absorption of the wealthy and strategically important Duchy of Burgundy into the Holy Roman Empire accentuated the struggle between the Habsburg dynasty and Charles VIII (ruled 1483–1498) of France. The latter decided to press his dubious claim to the throne of Naples, encouraged by the Sforza family of Milan, the enemy of Naples. In response, Naples allied with Florence and Pope Alexander VI (pope 1492–1503), himself a Florentine member of the Borgia family, against Milan.

In 1494, Charles VIII invaded the Italian peninsula with an army of 30,000 men. His French cavalry, Swiss mercenary infantry, and Scottish bowmen tore through northern Italy. In Florence, the Medici ruler offered Charles some Florentine possessions in exchange for leaving. This angered Florentine republicans, who drove the Medici from power in 1494 (after sixty years of rule), backed by the army of France. The new government, establishing the Great Council as a legislative assembly, contributed to the city's artistic splendors by commissioning works of art that symbolized republican independence and ideals. Leonardo and Michelangelo painted scenes of Florentine military victories for the meeting hall of the Great Council. Seven years later, the city government commissioned Michelangelo's great statue *David*. Michelangelo's conscious imitation of a Donatello bust of the same name from early in the fifteenth century referred back to the republic's successful resistance to challenges at that time.

Meantime, Charles' army moved toward Naples, devastating everything in its path. It marched into the city to cheers from Neapolitans who opposed the harsh taxes to which they had been subject by their rulers. But an anti-French coalition that included King Ferdinand of Aragon—whose dynastic territories included Sicily, Venice, the Papal States—and the Holy Roman emperor rallied to defeat the French force. Although the French army left the Italian peninsula, the city-states' troubles had only just begun.

In Florence, Girolamo Savonarola (1452–1498), a charismatic Dominican monk who had predicted the French invasion, opposed both the Medici in Florence and the papacy on grounds that both were worldly and corrupt. He had welcomed Charles VIII of France as "an instrument in the hands of the Lord who has sent you to cure the ills of Italy," including the sinfulness of the Florentines. With the Medici driven from power, Savonarola took virtual control of the Florentine republic. His denunciation of abuses within the Church led to his excommunication by Pope Alexander VI. Savonarola also incurred the enmity of patrician families by appealing for support to all ranks of Florentine society. With the pope's blessing, his enemies first hanged and then burned him—the penalty for heresy—in 1498.

The burning of Girolamo Savonarola in Florence.

The next year, Louis XII (ruled 1498–1515), the new French king, invaded the Italian peninsula, intent on making good his claim on the duchy of Milan. He did so with the support of the corrupt Pope Alexander VI, who wanted French assistance as he tried to solidify papal territorial claims, as well as to look after the extended interests of his children. To encourage the French king, the pope annulled Louis' marriage, so that he could marry his predecessor's widow, thereby keeping Brittany within his domains. When Julius II, who had been a bitter enemy of his predecessor, became pope in 1503, he drove the powerful Borgia family from Rome. Then the dissolute pope set about trying to restore temporal holdings taken from the Papal States by Venice and its allies, constructing an alliance against the Venetians and becoming the last pope to lead his troops into the field of battle. That year the Spanish army defeated the French army and the Habsburgs absorbed the kingdom of Naples. Milan remained a fief of Louis XII until French forces were forced from the city in 1512. Three years later, French troops overwhelmed Swiss mercenaries and returned, until the Lombardy city became a Spanish possession in 1535.

Machiavelli

A mood of vulnerability and insecurity spread through the Italian peninsula as the city-states battled each other. Peasants, crushed by taxes and hunger, ever more deeply resented the rich. In turn, wealthy people were increasingly suspicious of the poor, viewing them as dangerous monsters capable of threatening social order.

The devoted Florentine Machiavelli was among those people seeking to understand why the once proud independent city-states of Italy now seemed virtually helpless before the invasion of foreign powers. The son of a lawyer and educated in the classics, Machiavelli found a position as a diplomat and chancery official of the republican government of Florence. The turmoil in Florence led him to write his *Histories* in 1494, which described the decline of the city-states.

Machiavelli's view of politics reflects his experience living in Florence during these tumultuous decades. Influenced by his experience in government, Machiavelli, who had served as a Florentine diplomat at the court of the king of France and in Rome, believed himself to be a realist. He considered war a natural outlet for human aggression. But he also preferred the resolution of disputes by diplomacy. Machiavelli believed that the absence of "civic virtue" accounted for the factionalism within and rivalries between the city-states. By civic virtue (not the same thing as Christian virtue in the sense of distinguishing between and acting on the difference between right and wrong), Machiavelli meant the effective use of military force.

In 1512, the Medicis overthrew the Florentine Republic, returning to power with the help of the papal army and that of Spain. Following the discovery of a plot, of which he was innocent, against the Medici patriarchs, Machiavelli was forced into exile on his country estate outside of the city. Florence had changed. A Medici supporter wrote one of the family heads: "Your forefathers, in maintaining their rule, employed skill rather than force; you must use force rather than skill." The Medici commissioned works of art which suggested that the "golden age" had returned once again.

A year later, Machiavelli wrote *The Prince* (1513). In it he reflected on the recent history of the Italian peninsula and offered a pessimistic assessment of human nature, marked by his belief that a strong leader—the prince—could arise out of strife. By making his subjects afraid of him, the prince could end political instability and bring about a moral regeneration that Machiavelli believed had characterized antiquity. Drawing on Cicero, he studied the cities of the Roman Republic and the Roman Empire. Machiavelli can be considered the first political scientist, because his works reflect a systematic attempt to draw general, realistic conclusions from his understanding of the recent history of the Italian city-states. This preoccupation with the past in itself reveals the influence of the Renaissance.

Machiavelli put his faith in political leadership. Regardless of whether the form was monarchical or republican, Machiavelli believed that the goal of government should be to bring stability to the city. A sense of civic responsibility could only be re-established through "good laws and insti-

The pensive Niccolò Machiavelli.

tutions," but these, for Machiavelli, depended completely on military strength. He called on the Medici to drive away the new barbarians. Machiavelli's *The Art of War* (1521) expressed hope that the brutish mercenaries who had devastated the Italian peninsula would give way to soldier-citizens who would restore virtue. But for the Italian city-states, it was too late.

Machiavelli's invocation of "reasons of state" as sufficient justification for political action and as a political principle in itself, and his open admiration of ruthless rulers, would leave a chilling legacy. While it is unlikely that Machiavelli had a sense of the state in the impersonal, modern sense of the term, he did hold that "good arms make good laws."

The Decline of the City-States

Thus, for much of the first thirty years of the sixteenth century foreign armies battled each other and alliances formed by the city-states. The army of France in Italy reached 32,000 men by 1525, that of Spain 100,000 soldiers. Only Venice could resist the two great powers. In 1521, the first war between King Francis I of France and Holy Roman Emperor Charles V broke out. The latter's armies decimated the French at Pavia in 1525, carting the French king off to Madrid, where he remained until his family paid a ransom. In 1527, Charles V's mercenary army, angry for lack of pay, sacked Rome. By the Peace of Cambrai (1529), France gave up claims to Naples and Milan. But with the exception of Venice, the Italian city-states were in one way or another dependent upon Charles V, Holy Roman emperor, as the Spanish army repulsed new French invasions.

The long wars drained the city-states of financial resources and men, devastating some of the countryside. Nobles, whose political power had been diminished by the wealthy merchants of the fourteenth and fifteenth centuries, took advantage of the chaos to return to prominence in some cities. Patrician families struggled to maintain their authority against newcomers, including wealthy merchants who had married into poorer noble lines and who began to ape the styles of nobles. The Medici, after having once again been expelled by republicans, reconquered their city in 1530 after a siege of ten months. But in Florence, too, the Renaissance was over.

Changing artistic style had already begun to reflect the loss of Renaissance self-confidence that accompanied the devastating impact of the French invasion. For example, Botticelli seemed to abandon the serenity and cheerful optimism that characterized the Renaissance. To his painting *Mystical Nativity,* completed in 1500, Botticelli added an anxious inscription: "I Sandro painted this picture at the end of the year 1500 in the troubles of Italy . . . after the time according to the eleventh chapter of St. John in the second woe of the Apocalypse in the loosing of the devil for three and a half years. Then he will be chained in the twelfth chapter and we will see him trodden down as in this picture." Botticelli thereafter became preoccupied with suffering and the Passion of Christ, reflecting the fact that the High Renaissance was more closely tied to ecclesiastical influence. The deteriorating political situation, combined with the expansion of Spanish influence after 1530, made it more difficult for artists to find patronage in the Italian city-states.

Soon in Italy only Venice, the city of Titian, remained a center of artistic life. Machiavelli, who died in 1527, the year Charles V's troops pillaged Rome, sensed that the humiliation of the Italian city-states by foreign armies brought to a close a truly unique period in not only the history of Italy but in Western civilization. Of the great figures of the High Renaissance, only Michelangelo and Titian lived past 1530.

Impulses Elsewhere

The cultural glories of the Renaissance ebbed even as different kinds of discoveries by Europeans opened up wider appreciation of new possibilities for mankind. Columbus' cross-Atlantic voyages were signs that the economic and cultural vitality of Europe was shifting away from the Mediterranean to Spain and, to a lesser extent, England. The economic interests of these states would increasingly be across the Atlantic Ocean. The mood of optimism associated with the Renaissance seemed to have moved to Central and Northern Europe as Italy lapsed into a considerably less happy period. Many humanists and artists began to emigrate north of the Alps to lands considered by most cultured Italians to have been barbarian only in the last century. Now new universities in Northern Europe beckoned them.

Other dramatic changes had already begun to occur across the Alps. Relentless calls for reform led to a schism within the Church: the Reformation. In Northern Europe, the Dutch monk and humanist Erasmus expressed the exhilaration many men of learning felt when he wrote, "the world is coming to its senses as if awakening out of a deep Sleep."

CHAPTER **3**

THE TWO
REFORMATIONS

After paying a handsome sum to Pope Leo X in 1515, Albert of Hohenzollern received a papal dispensation (exemption from canon law) that enabled him to become archbishop of Mainz, a lucrative and prestigious ecclesiastical post. Otherwise, under canon law, the twenty-three-year-old Albert would have been ineligible due to his age (archbishops were supposed to be at least thirty years old) and because he already drew income from two other ecclesiastical posts. As part of his payment to the pope and in order to repay the large sum of money loaned to him by the Fugger banking family, the new archbishop authorized the sale of the St. Peter's indulgence, which would release a sinner from punishment for his sins. John Tetzel, a Dominican friar who was in charge of the sale of papal indulgences in the archbishopric of Mainz, was commissioned to preach the indulgence. Half of the proceeds were to go to the papacy, and half to Albert and the Fuggers. In his tour of parishes, Tetzel emotionally depicted the wailing of dead parents in Purgatory, pleading with their children to put coins in the box so that they could be released from their suffering.

The sale of indulgences, particularly their commercial use to allow clergymen to obtain multiple posts, had drawn increasing criticism in some of the German states. Indeed, no other ecclesiastical financial abuse drew as much passionate opposition as did indulgences. More than this, the Roman papacy itself faced considerable opposition in the German states, as the pope had appointed foreigners to many key ecclesiastical posts and had attempted to force the German states to provide him with money for a war against the Turks. The young German monk Martin Luther was among those denouncing Tetzel, the sale of indulgences, and the role of the Roman papacy in the German states.

This opposition to the papacy created a schism that tore Christendom apart beginning in the second decade of the sixteenth century. Originating in the German states and Switzerland, a movement for religious reform

(Left) A criticism of the sale of indulgences using the analogy of Christ driving the money changers out of the Temple. *(Right)* The pope selling indulgences in the Temple.

began to spread across much of Europe, in part reflecting the influence of Renaissance humanism in Northern Europe. Reformers rejected the pope's authority and Church doctrine itself. The movement for reform, or of "protest," came to be called the "Reformation." It led to the establishment of many "Protestant" denominations within Christianity. The followers of the German priest Martin Luther became Lutherans, while those of the Frenchman Jean Calvin in Switzerland became known as Calvinists. King Henry VIII established the Protestant Church of England. Under attack from many sides, the Roman Catholic Church undertook a Counter-Reformation, also known as the Catholic Reformation, which sought to reform some aspects of ecclesiastic life, while reaffirming the basic tenets of Catholic theology and belief in the authority of the pope.

By 1600, the pattern of religious adherence had largely been established for the future in Europe. Catholicism remained the religion of the vast majority of people living in Spain, France, Austria, Poland, the Italian states, Bavaria, and other parts of the southern German states. Protestants dominated England and much of Switzerland, the Dutch Netherlands, Scandinavia, and the northern German states. Wars fought in the name of religion broke out within and between European states, beginning in the late sixteenth century and culminating in the Thirty Years' War (1618–1648). These conflicts shaped the next century of European history, with religious divisions affecting the lives of millions of people.

The Northern Renaissance

Until the middle of the fifteenth century, the Renaissance had been limited to the Italian peninsula. Northern Europe enjoyed very little of the economic and cultural vitality of the Italian city-states. The country estates of noble families were rarely centers of learning. The future Pope Pius II claimed in the mid-fifteenth century that "Literature flourishes in Italy and princes there are not ashamed to listen to, and themselves to know, poetry. But in Germany princes pay more attention to horses and dogs than to poets—and thus neglecting the arts they die unremembered like their own beasts." France and the German states also lacked the Italian peninsula's network of city-states, whose wealthy merchant and banking families patronized humanists and artists.

But in about 1460, Renaissance humanism began to influence scholars in Northern Europe. As in Italy, humanism changed the way many people thought about the world. Humanists were interested in morality and ethics, as well as in subjecting texts to critical scrutiny. Therefore, debates over religion, and the Bible itself, attracted their attention. Humanists began to criticize Church venality and corruption, and the seeming idleness of monastic life. They also called into question scholasticism and its influence on religious theology, as well as criticizing parts of religious practice that they considered illogical and therefore superstitious. The spread of humanism in Northern Europe was gradual, often influencing isolated scholars. In the beginning, it posed no immediate threat to the Church; humanists could not imagine organized religion beyond Roman Catholicism. But the cumulative effect of the Northern Renaissance, and humanism in particular, helped engender a critical spirit that by the first decades of the sixteenth century directly began to challenge Church practices and then doctrine.

Northern Art and Humanism

The Northern Renaissance, which began in the late fifteenth century, reflected considerable Italian influence. Italian ambassadors, envoys, and humanists brought Renaissance art and humanistic thought to Northern Europe. Yet, much of the artistic creativity in Northern Europe, particularly Flanders, emerged independent of Italian influence. Like the Italian city-states, the Dutch Netherlands, which had a well-developed network of trading towns, had wealthy urban families who patronized the arts. Lacking the patronage of the Church, which so benefited Florentine and other Italian painters, Flemish painters did few church frescoes (which a generally wet climate also discouraged). They emphasized decorative detail, such as that found in illuminated manuscripts, more than the spatial harmonies of Italian art. Dutch and Flemish painters favored realism more

Dürer's *Four Horsemen of the Apocalypse* (c. 1497– 1498).

than Italian Renaissance idealism in their portrayal of the human body. They began to break away from religious subject matter and Gothic use of dark, gloomy colors and tones. In contrast to Italian painting, intense religiosity remained an important element in Flemish and German painting, and it was relatively rare to see a depiction of nudes.

Albrecht Dürer's visits to Italy reflect the dissemination and influence of the Italian Renaissance beyond the Alps. Born the son of a Nuremberg goldsmith, Dürer was apprenticed to a book engraver. As a young man, Dürer seemed irresistibly drawn to Italy as he wrestled with how to depict the human form. During two visits to Venice—in 1494 and 1505–1506— he sought out Italian painters, studying their use of mathematics in determining and representing proportion.

Many of the Italian envoys to Northern Europe had studied the classics and carried on diplomacy with oratorical and writing skills learned by reading Cicero and other Roman authors. Literary societies, academies, and universities contributed to the diffusion of Renaissance ideals in Northern Europe. Some nobles now sent their children to humanist schools or employed humanists as tutors, as did a number of wealthy urban bourgeois. Italian artists and scholars found employment in northern courts. Leonardo da Vinci, Renaissance artist and scientist, was employed by King Francis I of France and died in the château of Amboise on the

Loire River. Kings and princes hired humanists to serve as secretaries and diplomats.

Latin gradually became the language of scholarship beyond the Alps. A German scholar emphatically asserted that the German language was "the noblest, most distinguished, most humane of tongues," but he expressed his view in Latin. German, French, Spanish, and English historians borrowed from the style of the Roman historians to celebrate their own medieval past. Unlike Italian historians, they viewed the medieval period not as a sad interlude between two glorious epochs but as a time when their own political institutions and customs had been established.

In England, Latin became the language of high culture, arguably as important as English until William Shakespeare's time at the end of the sixteenth century. There Machiavelli's *The Prince* was widely read and debated in Latin. When continental scholars went to England, they could discuss common texts with their English counterparts. Sir Thomas More (1478–1535), English lawyer and statesman, reflected the influence of Renaissance humanism, writing poetry in Latin. In his *Utopia* (1516), a satire of contemporary political and social life, More asked readers to consider their own values in the context of their expanding knowledge of other societies, including those of the New World.

In France, Francis I established the Collège de France in 1530, which soon had chairs in Greek, Hebrew, and classical Latin. Northern universities became centers of humanistic study, gradually taking over the role royal and noble households had played in the diffusion of education. But some universities were quite slow to include humanists; only one humanist taught at Cambridge University early in the sixteenth century.

The spread of the cultural values of Renaissance humanism across the Alps into the German states and Northern Europe helped prepare the way for the Reformation. For, like the Renaissance, the Reformation was in some ways the work of humanists moving beyond what they considered the constraints of Church theology. Humanists, who had always been concerned with ethics, attacked not only the failings of some clerics but also some of the Church's teachings, especially its claim to be immune to criticism. They also condemned superstition in the guise of religiosity. Northern Renaissance humanists were the sworn enemies of scholasticism, the medieval system of ecclesiastical inquiry in which Church scholars used reason to prove the truths of Christian doctrine within the context of assumed theological truths. By suggesting that individuals who were not priests could interpret the Bible for themselves, they threatened the monopoly of Church theologians over biblical interpretation.

Erasmus' Humanistic Critique of the Church

An energetic Dutch cleric contributed more than any other person to the growth of Renaissance humanism in Northern Europe. Born to unmarried parents and orphaned in Rotterdam, Desiderius Erasmus (c. 1469–1536) spent seven years in a monastery. Ordained a priest in 1492, he taught at the universities of Cambridge and Louvain, then worked as a tutor in Paris and in Italy. As a young man, Erasmus may have suffered some sort of trauma—perhaps a romantic attachment unreciprocated or inopportunely discovered. Thereafter compulsively obsessed with cleanliness, he was determined to infuse the Church with a new moral purity influenced by the Renaissance.

The patronage of Holy Roman Emperor Charles V and several other statesmen permitted Erasmus to apply the scholarly techniques of humanism to biblical study. Erasmus' *In Praise of Folly* (1509) is a satirical survey of the world as he saw it but also a clear call for a pure Christian morality shorn of the corruption he beheld in the monastic system. Thus, he wrote that priests claimed "that they've properly performed their duty if they reel off perfunctorily their feeble prayers which I'd be greatly surprised if any god could hear or understand." He believed that the scholastics of the Middle Ages had, like the barbarians, overwhelmed the Church with empty, lifeless theology.

Erasmus' attacks on those who believed in the curing power of relics (remains of saints venerated by the faithful) reflected his Renaissance sense of the dignity of the individual. His *Handbook of the Christian Soldier* (1503), which called for a theology that de-emphasized the sacraments, was Erasmus' guide to living a moral life. The little book went through twenty Latin editions and was translated into ten other languages. He wrote at length on how a prince ought to be educated and how children should be raised. The most well-known intellectual figure of his time in Europe, Erasmus greatly expanded the knowledge and appreciation of the classics in Northern Europe. Erasmus and other major Northern Renaissance figures forged a Christian humanism focused on the early Christian past. Following his lead, Northern humanists turned their skills in editing texts in Greek and Latin to the large body of early Christian writings. "All the scholars are Erasmians," a humanist had asserted in 1518, "except for a few skulking monks and petty theologians."

THE ROOTS OF THE REFORMATION

In principle, the pope governed the Church in all of Western Christendom. But in reality, the emergence of the monarchical states of France, England, and the kingdoms of Spain in the late Middle Ages had eroded papal authority. Gradually these rulers assumed more prerogatives over the Church in their states. This expansion of monarchical authority itself provided impetus toward the development of churches that gradually took on a national character as monarchs bargained for authority over religious appointments and worked to bring ecclesiastical property under their fiscal control by imposing taxation.

Portrait of Desiderius Erasmus by Hans Holbein the Younger.

In the Italian and German states and in Switzerland, where many smaller, independent states ruled by princes, urban oligarchies, or even bishops survived, the very complexity of territorial political arrangements served to limit the direct authority of the pope. For in these smaller states, too, the ability of the pope and his appointees to manage their own affairs depended on the cooperation of lay rulers. Furthermore, the very territorial expanse of Western Christendom and daunting problems of transportation and communication made it difficult for the papal bureaucracy to reform blatant financial abuses. That the papacy itself increasingly appeared to condone or even encourage corruption added to the calls for reform.

Yet, although Erasmus and other northern humanists were among those criticizing the Church, they were unwilling to challenge papal authority. The papacy, however, had other, more vociferous critics. First, the monarchs of Europe's strongest states claimed even greater authority in religious affairs. Second, religious movements deemed heretical by the Church rejected papal authority. Some people sought refuge from the turmoil in spiritualism. Others based their idea of religion on personal study of the Bible, turning away from not only papal authority but also the entire formal hierarchy of the Church. Third, within the Church, a reform movement known as conciliarism sought to subject the authority of the popes to councils of cardinals and other Church dignitaries. Fourth, as the Church seemed determined to protect its authority, it also seemed more venal, even corrupt, than ever before. More and more calls echoed for the reform of clerical abuses. By questioning fundamental Church doctrine and the nature of religious faith, the resulting reform movement, culminating in the Reformation, shattered the unity of Western Christendom.

The Great Schism (1378–1417)

The growing reach of monarchical authority undercut the influence of the papacy. The monarchs of France, Spain, and England had repudiated the interference of the pope in temporal affairs and reduced his effective authority within their own states by creating what were, for all intents and purposes, national churches.

In the fourteenth century, the struggle between the king of France and the pope put the authority of the papacy in jeopardy. The French and English kings had imposed taxes on ecclesiastical property. In response, Pope Boniface VIII's bull *Unam Sanctum* (1302) threw down the gauntlet to lay rulers. It asserted "it is absolutely necessary for salvation for everyone to be subject to the Roman pontiff." King Philip IV of France ordered Boniface's arrest, and he died in 1303, shortly after his release from captivity. Philip then arranged the election of a pliant pope, Clement V (pope 1305–1314). In 1309, he installed him in the papal enclave of Avignon, a town on the Rhône River. During the "Avignon Papacy" (1309–1378), the popes remained under the influence of the king of France. At the same time, they continued to build up their bureaucracies and, like the monarchs whose authority they sometimes contested, to extract ever greater revenues from the faithful.

In 1377, Pope Gregory XI (pope 1370–1378) returned to Rome, in the hope that his presence there might calm the political situation in the Italian states. When Gregory XI died a year later, a group of cardinals in Rome, most of whom were French, elected Pope Urban VI (pope 1378–1389), popularly believed to be faithful to the Avignon Papacy. After a Roman mob invaded the proceedings, most of the cardinals fled. Upon their return several months later, a smaller group of thirteen cardinals was vexed by the new pope's denunciation of their wealth and privileges. Furthermore, they now viewed him as temperamentally unstable, unfit to be pope. They elected Clement VII, who claimed to be pope between 1378 and 1394. He returned to set up shop in Avignon, leaving his rival in Rome. The Great Schism (1378–1417) began with two men now claiming authority over the Church.

The two popes and their successors thereafter sought to win the allegiance of rulers. The Avignon popes, like their pre-Schism predecessors, were under the close scrutiny of the king of France, and the Roman pope was caught up in the morass of Italian and Roman politics. France, Castile, Navarre, and Scotland supported the Avignon popes; most of the Italian states, Portugal, the Holy Roman Empire, and England obeyed the

Roman popes. In 1409, Church dignitaries gathered at the Council of Pisa to resolve the conflict and elected a third pope. However, neither of the other two would agree to resign. And, in the meantime, secular rulers forced the popes to make agreements that increased the authority of the former over the Church in their states. The Great Schism enabled lay rulers to construct virtual national churches at the expense of papal power.

Heretical and Spiritual Movements

The chaos of two and then three popes claiming authority over the Church, along with the ruthlessness and greed of the claimants, greatly increased dissatisfaction with the organization of the Church. For many people loyal to the Church, the Great Schism cast disrepute on papal authority itself. From time to time heresies (movements based on beliefs deemed contrary to the teaching of the Church) had denied the authority of the papacy and demanded reform. In the twelfth century, the Waldensians in the Alps and the Albigensians in the south of France had defied the papacy by withdrawing into strictly organized communities that, unlike monasteries and convents, recognized neither Church doctrine nor authority.

An undercurrent of mysticism persisted in Europe, based on a belief in the supremacy of individual piety in the quest for a knowledge of God and eternal salvation. William of Occam (*c.* 1290–1349), an English monk and another critic of the papacy, rejected scholastic rationalism. Scholasticism had become increasingly linked to the theology of Thomas Aquinas, who had deduced the existence of God from rational proofs that moved from one premise to the next. Occam, in contrast, posited that the gulf between God and man was so great that scholastic proofs of His existence, such as those of Aquinas, were pointless because mankind could not understand God through reason. "Nominalists," as Occam and his followers were known, believed that individual piety should be the cornerstone of religious life. Nominalists rejected papal authority and the hierarchical structure of the Church. Their views reflected and accentuated the turn of more clergy and laymen toward the Scriptures as a guide for the individual's relationship with God, emphasizing the importance of leading a good, simple life. The Great Schism may have increased the yearning for spirituality as well as for the institutional reform of the Church.

The English cleric and scholar John Wyclif (*c.* 1328–1384) also questioned the pope's authority and claimed that an unworthy pope did not have to be obeyed, views that drew papal censorship. For Wyclif, the Church consisted of the body of those God had chosen to be saved, and no more. Stressing the role of faith in reaching eternal salvation, he insisted that reading the Scriptures formed the basis of faith and the individual's relationship with God. Reflecting tension between faith and an internal

conception of religion and Church ritual, Wyclif rejected transubstantiation (the doctrine that holds that during Mass the priest transforms ordinary bread and wine into the body and blood of Christ). This in itself
reduced the significance of the Mass, while putting him at odds with
Church theology.

Wyclif's de-emphasis of rituals and advocacy of a religion based on faith
suggested the significantly reduced importance of the Church as intermediary between man and God. Wyclif, who had powerful English noble and
clerical protectors, called for Church reform. But the Peasants' Revolt of
1381 in England, in which wealthy churchmen were targets of popular
wrath, gave even Wyclif's powerful protectors pause by raising the specter
of future social unrest. An English Church synod condemned Wyclif, but
he was allowed to live out his remaining years in a monastery. Some of his
English followers, poor folk known as the Lollards, carried on Wyclif's
work after his death. They criticized the Church's landed wealth and espoused a simpler religion. Led by gentry known as "Lollard knights," the
Lollards rose up in rebellion in 1414, before being crushed.

In Bohemia in Central Europe, Jan Hus (c. 1369–1415), a theologian,
had learned of Wyclif's teaching. He, too, loudly criticized the worldliness
of some clerics, and called for a return to a more unadorned religion.
Rejecting the authority of the papacy and denouncing popes as "anti-
Christs," Hus held that ordinary people could reform the Church.

The Challenge of Conciliarism to Papal Authority

The doctrine of conciliarism arose not only in response to the Great
Schism, but also to growing demands from many churchmen that the
Church must undertake reform. The Council of Constance (1414–1418)
was called to resolve the Great Schism and to undertake a reform of the
Church. Many of the ecclesiastical dignitaries who attended also wanted
to limit and define the authority of the papacy.

There were at least four significant parties to conciliarism: the popes
themselves; bishops supporting councils as a way of resolving Church
problems; secular rulers, particularly French kings, but also Holy Roman
emperors, intervening in the Great Schism; and finally heretics condemned at Constance, who were far more radical than the mainstream
conciliarists in their challenge to papal authority.

The Council of Constance first turned its attention to Jan Hus. Holding
a safe-conduct pass given him by the king of Bohemia, Hus travelled to the
Council of Constance in 1414, but was arrested and put on trial for
heresy. Hus refused to recant Wyclif's views, defending his own belief that
the faithful, like the priest saying Mass, ought to be able to receive communion, the Church's rite of unity, in the two forms of bread and wine.
The council condemned Hus, turning him over to the Holy Roman emperor, who ordered him burned at the stake as a heretic. The Hussites, the
only major fifteenth-century dissidents within the Church, fought off sev-

eral papal armies. They finally won special papal dispensation for the faithful to take communion in both bread and wine; their "Utraquist" ("in both kinds") church lasted until 1620.

The council resolved the ongoing conflicting claims to papal authority by deposing two of the claimants and accepting the resignation of the third. In 1417, the council elected Martin V (pope 1417–1431). But the Great Schism, with its multiple papal claimants, by delaying any serious attempts at reform, had reinforced the insistence of some prelates that councils of Church bishops ought to have more authority than the pope.

In principle convoked by the pope, councils brought together from throughout Europe leading ecclesiastical dignitaries who deliberated on matters of faith, as well as on the organization of the Church. But some councils began to come together in defiance of papal authority. Those holding a "conciliar" view of the Church conceived of it as a corporation of cardinals that could override papal authority. William of Occam had argued a century earlier that, when confronted by a heretical pope, a general council of the Church could stand as the repository of truth and authority. Some reformers wanted to impose a written constitution on the Church, as the papacy moved to reassert its authority. At the Council of Basel, which began in 1431, exponents of unlimited papal authority and their counterparts favoring conciliarist positions both presented their views. A break occurred in 1437, when the pope ordered the council moved to Ferrara, and then to Florence in 1438. At that time and until 1445, some of the participants, mostly conciliarists, continued to meet in Basel, although the pope declared that council schismatic. Fifteen years later, Pope Pius II (pope 1458–1464), who had earlier been active in the conciliar movement, turned against it, declaring it a heresy and reestablishing the absolute authority of the pope.

The assertion by some churchmen that councils had authority over the papacy merged easily with those who called for the reform of blatant abuses within the Church. Some monasteries were mocked as hypocritical institutions no more saintly than the supposedly profane world monks and nuns sought to leave behind. Several new religious orders had been founded at least partially out of impatience if not disgust with ecclesiastical worldliness.

Clerical Abuses and Indulgences

Critics of the papacy attacked with particular energy what they considered ecclesiastical financial and moral abuses. Those critics particularly concerned about the former claimed that the papacy seemed to have become an investment trust run by the priests who administered the papacy's temporal affairs. No clerical financial abuse was more attacked than indulgences. Indulgences were based on the idea of transferable merit. Through granting indulgences, the Church supposedly reduced the time a soul would have to suffer punishment in Purgatory (that halfway house between Hell and Heaven that had emerged in Church belief early in the Middle Ages) for sins committed on earth. The practice of selling indulgences began during the Crusades as a means of raising revenue for churches and hospitals. Those seeking the salvation of their souls did not purchase God's forgiveness (which could only be received in the confessional) but rather cancelled or reduced the temporal punishment (such as the pilgrimages, prayers, or charity) required to atone for their sins. In 1457, the pope had announced that indulgences could be applied to the souls of family members or friends suffering in Purgatory. Some people had the impression that purchasing indulgences rather than real repentence was an immediate entry to Heaven for oneself or one's relatives. "The moment the money tinkles in the collecting box, a soul flies out of Purgatory," went one contemporary ditty. The implication was that wealthy families had a greater chance of opening the doors of Heaven for their loved ones than poor people. One papal critic interpreted all of this to mean that "The Lord desireth not the death of a sinner but rather that he may live and pay." In his *Praise of Folly*, Erasmus wrote, "What should I say of them that hug themselves with their counterfeit pardons; that have measured Purgatory by the hourglass, and can without the least mistake demonstrate its ages, years, months, days, hours, minutes, and seconds, as it were in a mathematical table? And now suppose some Merchant, Soldier, or Judge, parts with some small piece of ill-gotten money. He at once conceives . . . his whole life quite cleansed . . . so bought off that [he] may begin a new score."

Another clerical practice that was much criticized was that of the sale of Church offices (positions). Despite a deluge of indignant criticism, in 1487 the pope put twenty-four posts up for sale. More than ever before, those who participated—and benefited from—this trust were Italian clerics. Most popes appointed Italians as cardinals, many of whom lived in Rome while accumulating great wealth from ecclesiastical sees they rarely if ever visited. One powerful French archbishop entered his cathedral for the first time feet first in his casket at his funeral. Some prominent families looked to the Church to provide lucrative sinecures (offices that generated income but that required little or no work) for their children. Reformers decried the appointment of unqualified bishops who had purchased their offices.

Many priests were resented because they charged exorbitant fees for burial. Resentment also mounted, particularly in the German states, because clerics were immune from civil justice and paid no taxes. It seemed symbolic that Pope Leo X allegedly effused to his brother, "God has given us the papacy—let us enjoy it!" Indulgences and pardons were swapped for gold or services; since about 1300, they had become a papal monopoly. Commenting on Leo's death, one wag remarked "his last moments come, he couldn't even have the [Last] Sacraments. By God, he's sold them!"

The papacy also came under attack for moral abuses. In the diocese of Trent in the early sixteenth century, a fifth of all priests kept concubines. Nepotism, the awarding of posts to relatives or friends, seemed to reign supreme. In the fifteenth century, Paul II was mocked as the "happy father," not revered as the Holy Father. Alexander VI (pope 1492–1503) looked after his own children with the care of any other father. Paul III (pope 1534–1549) made two of his grandsons cardinals. (Their expensive hats were far bigger than the young heads upon which they occasionally sat.)

Finally, the sacrament of penance generated some degree of popular resentment against the clergy. Since 1215, the faithful were required to confess their sins each year to a priest. This sacrament originated in the context of instruction to encourage good behavior—the Ten Commandments gradually replacing the Seven Deadly Sins as the foundation of Christian ethics. But for many people, penance had become the priest's interrogation of the faithful in the confessional, during which the confessor sought out details of misdeeds in order to determine one of the sixteen stated degrees of transgression. Specific confessional questions found in priests' manuals included, "Have you dressed proudly, sung and danced lustily, committed adultery, girl-watched, or exchanged adulterous glances in church or while walking on Sundays?" The contrast between the Church's call for sinners to repent seemed ironic in view of popularly perceived ecclesiastical abuses.

Given a boost by the conciliar movement, calls for reform echoed louder and louder. The representatives of the clergy who had gathered at the Estates-General of France in 1484 criticized simony, the sale of Church offices. In 1510, the Augsburg Diet, an imperial institution of the Holy Roman Empire, refused to grant money to the pope for a war against the Turks unless he first ordered an end to financial abuses. The imperial representative Assembly (Reichstag) had increasingly served as a forum for denunciations against the papacy. In 1511, King Louis XII of France, whose armies had backed up his territorial ambitions in northern Italy, called a council with the goal of reasserting the conciliar doctrine and ordered reforms in the monastic houses of his realm. The Fifth Lateran Council, which met from 1512–1517, urged more education for the clergy, sought to end some monastic financial abuses, and insisted that occupants of religious houses keep their vows of chastity. The council also suggested missions to carry the Church's influence into the Americas. Pope Leo, however, emphatically insisted that he alone could convoke Church councils, and the council itself forbade sermons denouncing the moral state of the Church.

Martin Luther

Martin Luther (1483–1546) was born in the small town of Eisleben in central Germany. He was the second son (of eight children) of a miner whose family had been prosperous peasants for several generations. His

The young Martin Luther by Lucas Cranach.

peasant background could be seen in the coarseness of his language, song, and humor. The pious, determined, stocky Luther went off to a nearby town to attend school. It was there that he may have been punished for speaking German and not Latin. In 1501, he began his studies at the University of Erfurt, where he took courses in philosophy and then began the study of law.

In July 1505, Luther was engulfed in a violent storm as he returned to Erfurt after a visit home. As a bolt of lightning struck not far from where he stood in terror, the young student cried out to the patron saint of travelers, "Help me, Saint Anne, I will become a monk." Returning safely to Erfurt, he gathered his friends together, treated them to a nice meal, and told them, "Today you see me, henceforth, never more." They escorted him to the nearby monastery of the Augustinian monks, which he entered against his father's wishes. Luther prayed, fasted, and, outside the monastery, begged for charity. In 1507, he was ordained a priest and soon became a doctor of theology, administrator of eleven Augustinian monasteries, and dean of the theological seminary in the town of Wittenberg.

Luther had, for some time, been wracked with gnawing doubt concerning his personal unworthiness. Was he not a sinner? He had been saved from the storm, but would he be saved from damnation on Judgment Day? Was there really any connection between good works effected on earth and salvation? Even if he confessed all of the sins on his conscience, were there not sins omitted unintentionally that blotted his soul? If mankind was so corrupted by sin, how could charity, fasting, or constant prayer and self-flagellation in the monastery earn one entry to Heaven? He later recalled, "I tried hard . . . to be contrite, and make a list of my sins. I confessed them again and again. I scrupulously carried out the penances that were allotted to me. And yet my conscience kept telling me: 'You fell short there.' 'You were not sorry enough.' 'You left that sin off your list.' I was trying to cure the doubts and scruples of the conscience with human remedies. . . . The more I tried these remedies, the more troubled and uneasy my conscience grew."

Luther's lonely study of theology in the tower library of the monastery did not resolve his doubts. Like other Augustinians, he had been influenced by the nominalism of the followers of William of Occam. This led Luther closer to his contention that faith, not good works, was the key to salvation. Indeed, the teachings of Saint Augustine himself also suggested to him that each person could be saved by faith alone through the grace of God. Believing man is saved "not by pieces, but in a heap," Luther became obsessed with a phrase from the Bible (Romans I:17), "The just shall live by faith." Such a conclusion broke with the accepted teachings of the Church as defined by medieval scholasticism. But more than faith was troubling Luther. He was also especially troubled by the abuse of the ecclesiastical sale of indulgences.

On October 31, 1517, Luther tacked up on the door of the castle church of Wittenberg "Ninety-five Theses or Disputations on the Power and Efficacy of Indulgences." Other critics before him had denounced the

An allegorical painting of the dream of Frederick the Wise wherein Martin Luther uses an enormous quill to tack his Ninety-five Theses to the door of the castle church at Wittenberg.

sale of indulgences, but Luther attacked the theoretical underpinnings of the papal granting of indulgences out of the "treasury of merits" accumulated by Christ and the saints. "The true treasure of the Church," Luther declared, "is the holy gospel of the glory and the grace of God." He had his theses printed and distributed in the region and invited those who might want to dispute his theses to present themselves to debate with him, as was the custom. In February 1518, Pope Leo X demanded that Luther's monastic superior order him to cease his small crusade. Luther refused, citing his right as a professor of theology to dispute formally the charges now leveled against him. And he found a protector, Frederick III, Elector of Saxony.

In April, as denunciations against Luther poured into Rome, he successfully defended his theses before his Augustinian superiors. Pope Leo was trying to remain on good terms with the Elector Frederick, a strong candidate for election as Holy Roman emperor. Instead of immediately summoning Luther to Rome, he therefore proposed that a papal legate travel to Augsburg to hear Luther out. At their meeting, the legate warned Luther to desist or face the consequences. Luther's friends, suspecting that the pope had authorized his arrest, whisked him away to safety.

Luther sought a negotiated solution. He agreed to write a treatise calling on the German people to honor the Church, and promised neither to preach nor publish anything else if his opponents would also keep silent. At this point Luther did not seek to create a new church, but merely to reform the old one. A papal representative sent to meet with Luther in Leipzig in June 1519 accused him of being a Hussite, that is, of denying the pope's authority. There Luther admitted that he did not believe the pope to be infallible.

Luther crossed his Rubicon, but unlike Caesar moved not toward Rome but away from it. "Farewell, unhappy, hopeless, blasphemous Rome! The wrath of God come upon thee, as you deserve" he wrote a friend, "We have cared for Babylon and she is not healed; let us then leave her. . . ." Luther would not be silenced. "I am hot-blooded by temperament and my pen gets irritated easily," he proclaimed, pouring out vigorous tract after tract, each more adamant than the one before.

Three treatises published in 1520 marked Luther's final break with Rome. Here Luther developed his theology of reform, one that went far beyond the prohibition of indulgences and the sale of ecclesiastical offices. He argued his view that faith alone could bring salvation, that good works follow faith but do not in themselves save the soul. Nor does the absence of good works condemn man to eternal damnation, he claimed. Upon reading one of these tracts, Erasmus, loyal critic of the Church, stated emphatically, "the breech is irreparable."

Developing the theological concept of "freedom of a Christian," Luther's immediate goal was to free German communities from the strictures of religious beliefs and institutions that seemed increasingly foreign to their faith. He called on the princes of the German states to reform the Church in their states. In doing so, he argued that the Scriptures declared the Church itself to be a priestly body that was not subject to the pope's interpretation. Luther acknowledged only two of the seven sacraments, those instituted by Christ, not the papacy: baptism and communion. After first retaining penance, he dropped it, arguing that faith was sufficient to bring about a sinner's reconciliation with God. If this was true, the monastic life no longer seemed to Luther to provide any advantage in the quest for salvation. And he rejected what he called the "unnatural" demands of poverty, chastity, and obedience.

On June 15, 1520, Pope Leo X excommunicated Luther from the Church, accusing him of forty-one heresies, "offensive, erroneous, objectionable to pious ears, misleading to simple minds, and contrary to Catholic teaching." The papal bull called Luther "the wild boar who has invaded the Lord's vineyard." In Wittenberg, a crowd burned papal bulls and documents. Luther defiantly tossed the writ of excommunication into the flames.

Luther's bold challenge to the papacy became a matter of state. Charles V had been elected Holy Roman emperor following his father's death in 1519. He had promised before his election that no one would be excommunicated within the empire without a proper hearing. Through the influence of Frederick of Saxony, Charles summoned Luther to the town of Worms in April 1521 to confront the imperial Diet (assembly).

Before the assembled Diet, Luther was asked if he had written the imposing number of treatises and books placed on the table. Acknowledging them all, Luther told the Diet: "I am bound by the Scriptures I have quoted and my conscience is captive to the Word of God. I cannot and I will not retract anything, since it is neither safe nor right to go against conscience. I cannot do otherwise, here I stand, may God help me. Amen." The Diet condemned Luther's beliefs. Charles V, in agreement with the pope, signed the Edict of Worms in May 1521, placing Luther under the "ban of the empire." This forbade him from preaching and declared him a heretic, thus promising to stamp out his influence. In the meantime, Luther had left Worms. Several men loyal to Frederick of Saxony, Luther's protector, kidnapped him, escorting him to safety. In Wartburg Castle, the reformer took shelter from the storms of controversy, translating, despite moods of depression, Erasmus' critical edition and retranslation of the Bible into German.

By declaring Luther an outlaw and forbidding any changes in religion in the Holy Roman Empire, the Edict of Worms made religious reform an issue of state. But Luther could not have survived the ban of the empire if his influence had not already spread, convincing many that through Luther they had now discovered the true Gospel.

SOCIAL BACKGROUND OF THE REFORMATION IN THE GERMAN STATES

Challenging the ways people in Central Europe had thought about religion for centuries, the movement for reform, spread by preachers, found converts in the German states. During the early 1520s, the proponents of Martin Luther's reform convinced many clergy and lay people to reconsider their religious beliefs and restructure their communities. During this crucial period, clergy and urban people of some means convinced German townspeople to accept reform. Then, in 1525–1526, perhaps encouraged by the quest for religious reform, peasants in the central and southern German states rose up against their lords. These events, roundly condemned by Luther, left no doubt that the Reformation would shake the political foundations of the German states.

Urban Centers of Reform

At first the Reformation was overwhelmingly an urban phenomenon in the German states and then Switzerland. The decentralized political structure of the Holy Roman Empire and traditions of popular participation in urban government aided the movement for reform. There were free cities in the northern German states, such as the still powerful Baltic trading city of Lübeck, leader of the Hanseatic League, and self-governing towns in the southern German states. Some towns were under pressure from princely neighbors who wanted them to contribute to the cost of imperial government. But even towns that had not maintained their independence enjoyed municipal privileges (such as autonomous administration or exemption from certain forms of taxation) that had already been eroded or disappeared in France and Spain as monarchies consolidated and extended their authority. Each German town had its own elite of prosperous burghers. Reformers found these communities fertile ground for Luther's ideas. Complaining of incompetent or lazy priests, some towns had endowed posts for preachers in order to attract vigorous, effective priests, a good many of whom now followed Luther.

German towns had a particularly well-developed sense of civic solidarity that included a sense that all citizens of the town shared a common fate in the material world—vulnerability to bad times, and a certain degree of prosperity in good times—and that salvation itself was something of a group enterprise. Erasmus had asked, "What else is the city but a great monastery?" Many German townspeople, then, tended to see their community as a miniature of Christendom. Luther sought to spark a more personal religion that would make people not only better Christians, but better citizens of their communities as well. In many towns, urban leaders and ordinary people may also have accepted reform because it appeared more promising than unreformed Catholicism for the maintenance of local order.

No simple formula could predict how the Reformation would fare in specific parts of the German states. In some towns in the southern German states, wealthy town leaders such as urban nobles, merchants, and bankers remained staunchly Catholic. These property-owning groups were more conservative by instinct and often had a vested interest in the survival of, for example, stained-glass windows financed by their ancestors. Here, also, the role of personality and the configuration of local social and political life came into play; so did pure chance, including such factors as whether preachers and reform literature arrived, how both were received, and by whom.

The Process of Reform

Social and political factors thus helped shape religious outcomes. While the embrace of the Reformation did not constitute a social revolution, in many cases clergy supporting religious reform were drawn from the middle and lower middle classes, groups with some possibility of social mobility. The "middling sort," in turn, brought reform to the lower classes. This process might be marked by the spontaneous singing of Lutheran hymns by those sitting in Mass, or by some other signs of a turn to reform. While archbishops and bishops in general opposed Luther, the lower clergy, particularly those of recent ordination, became influential converts in their towns. Communities accepted reformers by consensus, as local governments began to bow to the wishes of townspeople.

Thus, a crowd cheered in Basel when a priest carried the Bible instead of the communion host during the feast of Corpus Christi. Priests began to wear simpler clothes instead of rich robes. They attempted to change the liturgy of the Mass, for the first time saying some of it in German. Some began to give the faithful both bread and wine during communion. Some crowds mocked Church rituals in angry ways: ringing cow bells outside churches to disrupt Mass; heckling priests trying to deliver sermons; smashing stained-glass windows, crucifixes, statues, and other images of the saints, and occasionally destroying relics considered sacred. Such largely spontaneous actions bewildered Luther, who remained in most ways a very conservative man.

Luther and his followers denied the special status of the clergy as a group marked off from the rest of the population. In the early days of the Reformation, in some places reformers undertook expeditions to "rescue" nuns from convents. A number of former priests began to take wives, which also first shocked Luther, since this represented the end of clerical celibacy, which the Church had proclaimed in the eleventh century. Luther asserted in 1521, "Good Lord! Will our people at Wittenberg give wives even to monks? They will not push a wife on me!" But by 1525 he changed his mind, and married a former nun. The marriage of clerics further broke down the barrier between the priest and the people, symbolizing the "priesthood of all believers" by eliminating the clerical distinction of celibacy. Nonetheless, Luther limited the task of interpreting the Scriptures to professors of theology.

The Peasants' Revolt

The gap between rich and poor seemed particularly great at the beginning of the sixteenth century. In the southern German states, some burghers worried that law and order would collapse, that the poor might rise up. News of several strange and alarming prophecies circulated. A preacher in Strasbourg reminded magistrates and teachers that the Bible should serve as "a vital, certain, unerring guide against false doctrine, divisions and sects, and how one can survive dangerous times." Some people expressed concern that the people might "turn Swiss," referring to the Swiss towns that lived without lords and were self-governing and independent.

In 1524–1525, peasants rose up against their lords in parts of the central and southern German states (see Map 3.1). They demanded the re-

MAP 3.1 THE PEASANTS' REVOLT, 1525–1526   Sites of peasant uprisings in parts of the central and southern German states. The revolt began in Waldshut and Stühlingen in the southern German states and spread west to the Tyrol and Salzburg in Austria, and north to Thuringia and Saxony.

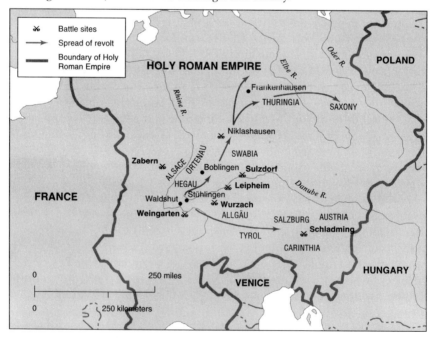

turn of rights (such as to hunt freely and to pasture their animals on the common lands) that the lords had usurped. They also asked for the abolition of serfdom and the tithe, which they declared to be against God's will. Bands of poor people burned castles and monasteries.

The peasants' revolt spread into Austria and Carinthia, and up into Thuringia and Saxony. Pamphlets called for social as well as religious reform. Thomas Münzer (c. 1491–1525), a priest and theologian, merged religious reform with social revolution. He preached against the Church and Luther with equal fury, for he believed that both the Church and Luther had humbled themselves to lay authorities. Münzer led a peasant army in Thuringia, where Luther's reform movement had made many converts.

In the northwestern German states, also in 1525, some towns that had been won over to religious reform rose up against Catholic princes. Swabian peasants promulgated twelve articles against their lords, princes, and bishops, requesting that communities have the right to choose their own pastors. But here, too, the demands of these poor rebels had a social content. They asked for an end to double taxation by both lay and ecclesiastical lords and the "death tax" by which heirs had to give up the deceased's finest horse, cow, or garment. They demanded the end of serfdom, the return of common lands to their use, and free access to forests and streams.

Luther had some sympathy with the plight of the poor. But he rejected the idea that his central theological idea of "Christian freedom," which he believed applied only to the spiritual realm, could be extended into the relationship between lord and peasant. As nobles and churchmen began to accuse him of fomenting insurrection, he denounced the peasants in extravagant language. In *Against the Murdering, Thieving Hordes of Peasants,* he advised the German princes to "brandish their swords. . . . You cannot meet a rebel with reason. Your best answer is to punch him in the face until he has a bloody nose." Catholic and reformed princes put aside their differences to crush the revolt, in which more than 100,000 peasants perished. Münzer was defeated, captured, tortured, and beheaded.

Yet, some of Luther's followers began to see in his teaching a means of resistance against the powerful. Luther asked lords to "act rationally" and "try kindness" when confronted by peasant demands. He asked Christian rulers to "offer the mad peasants an opportunity to come to terms, even though they are unworthy of it." But, when all was said and done, Luther was "opposed to those who rise in insurrection, no matter how just their cause."

THE SPREAD OF THE REFORMATION

Because of the intertwining of religion and politics, what began as a movement for Church reform became entangled in princely rivalries in the

German states. As the breech between Catholic and reformed princes widened, religion became a source of division rather than unity. Although Luther had never intended to bring about a permanent division within Christianity, his followers gradually created a new church in many of the German states. The Reformation then spread beyond the German states.

Divisions within Christendom

The Augsburg Confession, presented by Luther's friends to the Diet that gathered in that city in 1530, became the doctrinal basis of the Lutheran Church. It was implemented by princes and prelates in the reformed states and towns, and in some places by a council, known as a consistory, of ministers and lawyers.

Luther's writing, translated into Latin, then followed trade routes beyond the German states to the west and east. The reformers easily revived the anti-papal Hussite traditions of Bohemia and Moravia and that of the Waldensians in the southwestern Alps. Turkish military victories over Habsburg armies in Hungary left Lutheran missionaries an open field. German merchants carried reform not only to the Baltic states but also north to Scandinavia. In Denmark, King Christian II adopted Lutheranism for his state. In Sweden, the king's conversion and his break with Rome led to a similar reform. When Lutheranism was declared its official religion in 1527, Sweden and its territory of Finland had the first national reformed church.

Some humanists influenced by the Renaissance were attracted by Luther's writing. Erasmus appreciated Luther's call for simple piety and

The Augsburg Confession read before Charles V in 1530.

his denunciation of superstition and corruption within the Church. Furthermore, some humanists, in the tradition of their predecessors who had rediscovered the classics, admired Luther's return to the Scriptures as an original source of knowledge. One of Luther's converts later wrote that his own excitement at the new teaching was so great that he studied the Bible at night with sand in his mouth so that he would not fall asleep. Humanists transformed some monasteries into schools. The first reformed university began in the German town of Marburg in 1527.

But as the gap between reformers and the Church grew larger, Erasmus was caught in the middle. His own criticism of the Church did not go far enough for reformers, but it went too far for churchmen. Erasmus, who had condemned ecclesiastical abuses, remained loyal to Church doctrine. Similarly, Luther and the humanists parted ways by 1525. For the latter, humanistic knowledge was an end in itself; for the reformers, rhetoric was a method for teaching the Scriptures and for arguing in favor of ecclesiastical reform. Many reformers were less committed than humanists to the belief that man is a rational and autonomous being. Luther himself did not share the humanists' Renaissance optimism about mankind. On the contrary, he was not interested in rediscovering mankind, but was preoccupied with an individual's relationship to God, arguing that people depend on grace alone to obtain salvation. Furthermore, Luther opposed attempts by philosophers to intrude in theological questions. Nonetheless, a humanist curriculum continued to influence the training of reform ministers.

Luther's followers gained their first martyrs in 1523, when two former monks were executed in Brussels. German princes requested from the Holy Roman emperor Charles V that a "free general council or at least a national council" consider the growing religious division within the Holy Roman Empire. The Diet of Speyer (1526) proclaimed that each German prince was "to live, govern, and bear himself as he hopes and trusts to answer to God and his imperial majesty." This truce gave reformers time to win even more converts. In 1529, German princes again gathered in Speyer. Some of them prepared a "protest" against the policies of Charles V and the Catholic princes, who had declared themselves against Luther. The followers of Luther became known as "Protestants."

Charles V and the Protestants

Holy Roman Emperor Charles V, the pope's most powerful potential advocate, was a pious man who first denounced Luther with passion. But extensive Habsburg imperial interests kept him fighting a war in Western Europe against King Francis I of France, which prevented him from acting against those who supported Luther. The French king, for his part, was pleased that religion was dividing the German princes, thereby weakening the imperial crown that he had coveted and failed to gain. Charles was away from his German states between 1521 and 1530, for the most part in Italy. These were the crucial years during which the Reformation spread within the Holy Roman Empire; as early as 1524, the first Protestant leagues were formed between states in which reform had won wide appeal.

The Christian crusade against the Turks in Eastern Europe and the Mediterranean also preoccupied Charles and other Catholic princes as well. In 1526, the Turks defeated the king of Hungary at Mohács in Hungary. A subsequent Turkish advance forced Charles to offer concessions to Lutheran princes in exchange for assistance against the Turks. (Luther's hymn "A Mighty Fortress Is Our God" began as a martial song to inspire soldiers against the Ottoman forces.)

For a time, Charles V held out hope for conciliation with the Protestants. In 1531, however, the princes of Hesse, Saxony, and other states and cities that had adopted religious reform formed the Schmalkaldic League. Although first and foremost a defensive alliance, the princes intended that the league would replace the Holy Roman Empire as the source of their political allegiance. Up until this time, Charles had accepted temporary truces, and thus toleration of Protestants. He had suspended the Edict of Worms, until a general council of the Church could be held. When the pope announced that it would be held in the Alpine town of Trent (see p. 127), the stage was set for confrontation with the Protestants. Meanwhile, however, Charles was still preoccupied by hostilities with Francis I of France, who shocked many Christians by allying with the Turks against the Habsburgs. After Charles forced an end to the wars by launching an invasion of France from the Netherlands, he was finally ready to move against Protestants, routing the Schmalkaldic League in battle in 1547, and subsequently forcing reconversion on the people in about thirty German cities. By that time, however, Protestantism had established itself definitively in much of Central Europe.

The Peace of Augsburg

With his attention no longer distracted by war against the Turks and French, Charles tried to bring back more of the German princes and their people into the Catholic fold. He tried without success to impose in Central Europe moderate Catholic reform in order to answer some of the criticism of the reformers. But some of the Catholic princes who had been allied with Charles now left the fold, and three of them took up arms against him in a short war in 1551. The political complexity of the myriad German states mitigated against a general settlement. The Holy Roman emperor gave up the idea of restoring Catholicism in all of the German states.

The Peace of Augsburg of 1555 was a compromise. It was agreed upon by the imperial representative assembly after Charles, worn down by the complexity of imperial politics, refused to participate. It stipulated that the religion of the ruler of each of the empire's states would be the religion of the state (*cuius regio, eius religio*) (see Map 3.2). Although it excluded

MAP 3.2 THE RELIGIOUS SITUATION IN EUROPE AFTER THE PEACE OF AUGSBURG, 1555 The Peace of Augsburg stipulated that the religion of the ruler of each of the Holy Roman Empire's states would be the religion of the state. The map indicates areas that were Roman Catholic, Anglican, Calvinist, Zwinglian, Anabaptist, Lutheran, and Eastern Orthodox.

Religious Situation in Europe

- Roman Catholic
- Anglican
- *C* Calvinist or Zwinglian
- Lutheran
- *E* Eastern Orthodox
- *A* Anabaptists

reformed groups other than Lutherans, Protestants living in states with a Catholic ruler were free to emigrate, as were Catholics in the same situation. The Peace of Augsburg thus recognized that the institutions of the Holy Roman Empire could not provide a solution to what now appeared to be lasting religious divisions in Central Europe. It acknowledged that the Reformation in the German states was an accomplished fact, leaving a religious division in Germany that has lasted until this day. Thus, what had begun as a "squabble among monks" shaped the territorial and political history of Germany. Through the compromise that allowed each prince to determine the religion of his state, the Peace of Augsburg reaffirmed the independence of many German states, or what became known as German particularism.

THE REFORMATION IN SWITZERLAND AND FRANCE

The next stage of the Reformation occurred in Switzerland, a land of rugged peasants, craftsmen, and mercenary soldiers. The sparsely populated (then about a million people) cantons of Switzerland were loosely joined in a federal Diet. In some ways, the thirteen fiercely independent Swiss cantons were closer in organization and in spirit to the Italian city-states than to the German states. Unlike in the German states, where the conversion of a powerful prince could sway an entire state, there were no such territorial rulers in Switzerland. The reformers in Switzerland, then, would be even more closely tied to privileged residents of towns of relatively small size. The Swiss reformers believed that it was imperative to establish the kingdom of God on earth. Their movement would also soon spread to parts of France.

Zwingli and Reform

In Zurich, a town of about 6,000, Huldrych Zwingli (1484–1531) preached salvation through faith alone. Drawing on his strong humanist training, he began preaching from Erasmus' edition of the Greek New Testament. In 1522, several citizens of Zurich publicly munched sausages during Lent in defiance of the Lentan ban on eating meat. Zwingli published two tracts on their behalf in which he insisted that the Scriptures alone should be the basis of religious practice, and that as there was nothing in the Bible about sausages, they could be eaten at any time. This negative scriptural test also led him and his followers to iconoclasm (the stripping of images and altar decorations from churches because nothing about them could be found in the Bible). The Zurich municipal council then embraced reform. It ordered the canton's priests to preach only from the Bible, and two years later forbade the saying of Mass. Zwingli con-

(Left) Woodcut of Huldrych Zwingli. *(Right)* Burning church ornaments and religious statues in Zurich.

vinced the town's magistrates that tithes should be used to aid the poor, whom he believed represented the real image of God.

A doctrinal conflict among reformers helped define the character of the Swiss Reformation. Luther maintained that communion represented the physical presence of Christ. In this he had not diverged far from the Catholic Church, which insisted that through the miracle of transubstantiation (which the pope originally formulated in 1215), the priest transformed bread and wine into the actual body and blood of Christ. But to Luther, who condemned Catholic worship of the Eucharist, the bodily presence of Christ in the Eucharist came from the fact that Christ and God were universally present. Zwingli, by contrast, believed that communion was a *symbol* of Christ's real presence in the Eucharist and that Luther's refusal to abandon this idea demonstrated that he still stood with one foot in Rome. Luther accused Zwingli of reducing Christ's presence to a mere symbol. The "Sacramentarian Controversy" emerged as the first major doctrinal dispute among Protestants. The Augsburg Confession of 1530 sealed the rift by excluding reformers who rejected Lutheranism, including Zwingli and his followers.

Between 1525 and 1530, some German-speaking parts of Switzerland and regions of the southern German states accepted Zwingli's reforms. In 1531, Catholic forces attacked Protestant cantons. Zwingli, the "godly warrior," led the Protestant forces into the Battle of Kappel carrying a sword and a Bible and was killed in the fighting. Both Catholics and Lutherans claimed Zwingli's death to be divine judgment against his religious positions. The peace that followed, however, specified that each canton could choose its own religion, which amounted to a victory for Protestantism.

Radical Reformers

Some Zurich reformers had even more radical changes in mind. Believing that neither Luther nor Zwingli had sufficiently transformed religious morality and communal life, several radical groups, some of whose members were quite poor, formed communities in which they sought to implement "godly living" (see Map 3.3).

Millenarian groups, whose members believed that the end of the world was near, began to spring up. One group of radical reformers who had broken with Zwingli became known as Anabaptists. They rejected the baptism

MAP 3.3 RADICAL RELIGIOUS MOVEMENTS   Areas in which there were Hussites, Utraquists, Anabaptists, and Mennonites.

of infants because no reference to it could be found in the Bible. They believed that only adults could manifest true faith and therefore be worthy of baptism. Starting their own church in 1525, Anabaptists began to rebaptize adults—"anabaptism" means rebaptism in Greek. The Anabaptists also rejected the notion of the Trinity and were therefore sometimes called "Anti-Trinitarians."

The Anabaptists were sectarians, because for them membership was through free will or voluntary self-selection, rather than through territorial organization of churches as was true for Catholics, Lutherans, and Zwinglians. Anabaptists formed communities of believers in Switzerland and southern Germany, seeking isolation—"separation from iniquity," as they put it—from the struggles and temptations of the secular, sinful world. They would not participate in political life and did not believe in having ties with temporal governments. They rejected secular agreements and refused to take civil oaths, pay taxes, hold public office, or serve in the army.

Catholic and Protestant states moved to crush these dissidents who rejected state authority. At the Diet of Speyer in 1529, Charles V made Anabaptism punishable by death, usually by—with intentional irony—drowning, "the third baptism." Many of these groups of radical reformers sought refuge in the mountains of the Tyrol and Moravia, and in Poland. Persecution increased the number of millenarians. Following the Peasants' Revolt of 1525, unsuccessful insurrections in Frankfurt, Cologne, and several other German towns merged social and political goals with opposition to the Catholic Church.

In 1532, a radical group of Anabaptists, millenarians who believed the second coming of Christ was close at hand, took over the town government of Münster by election. The old patrician families left town. The Anabaptists established a council of twelve that expropriated Catholic Church property, then abolished private property and banned the use of money, establishing a system of barter and communally held property.

Their prophet, John of Leyden, convinced the ministers and elders of Münster to allow polygamy (the taking of more than one wife) in the town, ostensibly to solidify the basis of the new theocracy based on endless links of kinship, but perhaps also because there were four times more women than men in the city. John led the way by taking sixteen wives. Under his orders, all books in Münster were burned except the Bible. The Münster Anabaptists then began to kill Catholics and Lutherans. The Anabaptist kingdom of the "new Jerusalem" lasted but sixteen months. Troops sent by Lutheran and Catholic princes alike stormed the town and then tortured to death the leaders, including a number of women, placing their mutilated corpses in an iron cage that still hangs in the church steeple.

Dutch Anabaptists included a group representing the pacifist strand of Anabaptism, which was largely a reaction to the events in Münster. They became known as Mennonites, after their leader, Menno Simons (1492–1559). Some of them emigrated to the Americas in search of religious toleration more than a century later. Likewise, the Unitarian religion has roots in this period, deriving from Anti-Trinitarian views of God as being one, not three.

Jean Calvin and Reform

France, too, provided fertile ground for attacks upon the Catholic Church. In 1520, a Swiss visitor wrote from Paris that "No books are more eagerly bought up than those of Luther. . . . One book shop has sold 1,400 copies. . . . Everywhere people speak highly of Luther. But the chains of the monks are long."

The French monarchy had traditionally maintained a forceful independence from Rome. Pope Leo X had signed the Concordat of Bologna (1516) with King Francis I, giving the king the right to appoint bishops and abbots in France. Initially the Valois ruler was far more preoccupied with his wars against Charles V and the Habsburgs than with the stormy tracts of an obscure German monk. The threat of heresy, however, convinced him in 1521 to order Luther's writings confiscated and burned. Yet, despite the best efforts of the king's expanded bureaucracy, Protestant propaganda arrived in France from Germany through Strasbourg and evangelical attitudes spread during the next several years. In 1534, reformers affixed placards against the Mass in Paris and on the king's bedroom door in his château on the Loire River at Amboise. The "affair of the placards" convinced the king to combat reform in earnest.

Jean Calvin (1509–1564) embodied the second major current of the Reformation. He was born in the small town of Noyon in northern France, where his father worked as a secretary to the local bishop. Calvin's mother

(*Left*) Jean Calvin. (*Right*) A Calvinist service. Note the austerity of the church.

died when he was about five years old, and his father sent him to Paris to be trained as a priest. He then decided that his son should become a lawyer, because he might earn more money.

Late-Renaissance humanism and particularly the teachings of Erasmus helped stimulate in the pious young Calvin an interest in religious reform during the legal studies that helped to make him a systematic thinker. In 1534, the Catholic hierarchy and the king himself moved to crush this movement. Finding exile in the Swiss town of Basel, Calvin probably still considered himself a follower of Erasmus within the Catholic Church. In Basel, he penned tracts denouncing the papacy and calling on the king of France to end religious persecution.

Throughout his life, Calvin was overwhelmed by anxiety and self-doubt, compounded by his virtual abandonment by his father and forced exile. He was also terror-struck by the power of nature and, in particular, by storms as manifestations of God's power—rather like Luther who made his vow to become a monk in a thunderstorm. Humanity seemed to Calvin to be poised before an abyss, a metaphor he frequently used. He feared that oceans might rise and sweep humankind away. Around him Calvin saw only the absence of order. The world was such that "we cannot be otherwise than constantly anxious and confused."

Like other thinkers of the early sixteenth century, Calvin believed that he lived in a time of extraordinary moral crisis. He assessed the world around him pessimistically: "luxury increases daily, lawless passions are inflamed, and human beings continue in their crimes and profligacy more shameless than ever." It seemed to Calvin that the sense of community that ought to bind people together was dissolving.

Calvin argued that the Catholic Church had made the faithful anxious by emphasizing the necessity of good works in achieving salvation: the anxiety came from never knowing how many good works were enough. This had, Calvin insisted, turned Catholics to seek the intercession of saints. He attacked the sacrament of penance with particular vehemence:

> The souls of those who have been affected with some awareness of God are most cruelly torn by this butchery . . . the sky and sea were on every side, there was no port of anchorage. The more they had crossed over, the greater was the mass ever looming before their eyes, indeed it rose up like high mountains; nor did any hope of escape appear. . . . And at last no other outcome but despair was found.

Calvin rejected the increasingly human-like images given God and Christ over the previous century. Unlike Luther, Calvin emphasized not reconciliation with God through faith, but obedience to his will. The reformer sought to provide a doctrine that would reassure the faithful of God's grace and of their own salvation. There was hope in Calvin's thought, faith that the labyrinth—another of his frequent images—of life could be successfully navigated. The imposition of order, based upon the morality dictated by the Bible, would put an end to some of life's haunting uncertainties.

With this in mind, Calvin developed in his *Institutes of the Christian Religion* (begun in 1536, finished 1559) the doctrine of election or pre-destination: "God's eternal decree. . . . For all are not created in equal condition; rather, eternal life is foreordained for some, eternal damnation for others." The belief in predestination called into question the efficacy of good works. If one's fate is predestined and if good works in themselves (as the Catholic Church claimed) did not bring eternal salvation, why lead a righteous life? Calvin believed that good works were signs of having been chosen by God for eternal salvation, though they did not in themselves guarantee Heaven.

Calvinist anxiety over predestination and the question of whether a given individual had been chosen for salvation led to the controversial thesis of the nineteenth-century German sociologist Max Weber that Cal-vinist self-discipline created a "Protestant ethic." Whereas medieval the-ologians had condemned lending money for profit, Calvin, unlike Luther, distinguished between usury and productive loans that would raise capital and increase the well-being of the entire community. Replacing penance as a means of imposing individual discipline, Calvin preached collective, communal discipline in the pursuit of holiness. Validating economic activ-ity, later Calvinists came to view prosperity, along with "sober living," as a sign of election by God.

Late in 1536, Calvin went to the Swiss lakeside city of Geneva, a town of about 13,000 people. With the first successes of the Reformation, word of which had originally been carried there by German merchants, Geneva broke away from the domination of the Catholic House of Savoy. Earlier that year, troops of the Swiss canton of Bern to the northeast, which had embraced Zwinglian reform, occupied the city. Bern established a protec-torate, with Geneva retaining its nominal independence. Citizens elected magistrates and members of two representative councils.

Calvin had become, like Zwingli, convinced that reform must transform not only the individual but society as well. In 1537, he convinced the smaller and most powerful of the two councils to adopt a Confession of Faith, swearing that the people of Geneva "live according to the holy evan-gelical law and the Word of God." Residency in Geneva would be contin-gent on formal adherence to the document. The Mass was banned, and priests were informed that they had to convert to reformed religion or leave the city.

Calvin's plans for Geneva were far-reaching. He hoped to impose Chris-tian discipline, or worldly asceticism, on the city in order to construct a righteous society. His "Ecclesiastical Ordinances" would provide for the organization of religious life in reformed Geneva, but threatened the pow-ers of the councils. Calvin insisted that the Consistory, the judiciary of the reformed church made up of lay elders (called presbyters), would have the right to discipline all citizens and to dispense harsh penalties against those who transgressed Geneva's religious laws. These penalties would include excommunication from the church and exile, imprisonment, and even execution (the councils wanted to reserve such authority for themselves, not the Consistory, however, and the issue would only be resolved a decade later in favor of Calvin). Pastors were to "admonish, exhort, deprecate"; citizens were to "listen to them as to God Himself," and in doing so, lead better lives. Calvin wanted municipal supervisors to monitor the religious behavior of the people, but the councils hesitated to surrender their authority to Calvin—who, like most of the proponents of radical reform, was French—or to assume such a supervisory role. In 1538, the councils asked Calvin to leave Geneva.

In 1540, the majority of citizens of Geneva, believing that the town's ties to Bern limited its sovereignty, elected new magistrates, who executed the leaders of the pro-Bern faction. The councils then invited Calvin to return to oversee reform in Geneva and adopted his "Ecclesiastical Ordinances." Feeling himself called by God to undertake the reform of the city he had called "a place so grossly immoral," Calvin returned. He insisted that "the church cannot stand firm unless a government is constituted as prescribed to us by the Word of God and observed." He created separate, autonomous ecclesiastical institutions that, unlike those of Luther and Zwingli, did not depend on governmental institutions. Although he did not become a citizen of Geneva until many years later, Calvin played a determining role in structuring religious life and simplifying the liturgy in his adopted city.

To John Knox, the Scottish reformer, Geneva seemed "the most perfect school of Christ that ever was on earth since the days of the Apostles." But many citizens of Geneva resisted the close scrutiny of the Consistory. A man named his dog "Calvin" in protest. Always on the alert for the "many ambushes and clandestine intrigues Satan daily directs against us," Calvin forced one man who had publicly criticized him to wear a hair shirt and walk slowly through town, stopping at street corners to pray and acknowledge Calvin's authority. Calvin took it upon himself to decide whether future bridegrooms were free from venereal disease and could marry in Geneva. He determined the punishment of merchants who cheated their clients, and he banned taverns, although cafés were tolerated if no lewd songs were sung or cards played, a Bible was always available, and grace was said before meals. The Consistory imposed penalties for laughing during a sermon, having one's fortune told, or praising the pope.

Calvin's uncompromising nature could be seen in his dispute with the Spanish humanist and physician Michael Servetus, who publicly rejected the concept of the Holy Trinity. The stern reformer warned that if Servetus ever appeared in Geneva, "I will not suffer him to get out alive." He made good on his promise when Servetus foolishly turned up in disguise to hear Calvin preach and was recognized. During his trial in 1553, Servetus at one point so irritated Calvin that the latter blurted out: "May little chickens dig out his eyes a hundred thousand times!" Servetus' death at the stake probably proved to be at least as painful as this. Calvin also cautioned, however, that some pastors were too strict, "pretending zeal . . . terrifying sinners so inhumanely, without any sign of anguish or sympathy, they make God's Word seem insulting and distasteful." Calvin's death in 1564 was brought on by a variety of illnesses that were probably compounded by his chronic state of exhaustion and his fretful anxiety about the possibility of reforming a fallen and sinful world.

Calvinist Conversions

Calvinism proved the most aggressive, expansionist version of the reformed religions. It confronted Catholicism more systematically and over a longer period of time than did Lutheranism. In France, Calvinism made some inroads among all social classes during the 1530s, following the flow of reform literature coming from Switzerland and the German states. People who could not read could nonetheless listen to the Bible being read aloud. Clergy who converted to Calvinism found eager followers, some of whom, distraught by hard times, may have been attracted by Calvinist sermons offering the assurance of the predestination of eternal salvation. In Lyon, a prosperous banking and commercial center, printers were prominent among Calvinists and used their ability to read to convert others.

Henry II, who came to the throne of France in 1547, denounced the "common malady of this contagious pestilence which has infected many noble towns." The Parlement of Paris created a special chamber to hear heresy cases—"the Burning Chamber"—and tried about 500 people. The king, a sadist, attended many of the executions himself. A magistrate from Bordeaux described the courage of the Protestant martyrs:

> Fires were being kindled everywhere . . . the stubborn resolution of those who were carried off to the gallows . . . stupefied many people. Because when they saw innocent, weak women submit to torture so as to bear witness to their faith, facing death calling out only to Christ . . . young virgins heading more joyfully for the gallows than they would have gone to the bridal bed; men exulting upon seeing the dreadful and frightful preparations for and implements of death that were readied for them, and half charred and roasted, they looked down from the stakes with invincible courage and the blows incurred from the hot pincers, bearing a brave mien; and sustaining themselves joyfully between the bayonets of the hangmen, they were like rocks standing against waves of sorrow. In short, they died smiling.

The judicial system could try some heresy cases, but it could not keep up with the rapid pace of conversion, including the conversion of many nobles. By 1560, there were more than 2,000 Protestant, or Huguenot (so named after a leading French reformer in Geneva, Besançon Hugues), congregations in France.

Calvinism became the dominant religion of reform in the Netherlands. There Protestant conversions set the stage for an inevitable clash with the ruling Catholic Habsburg dynasty. Philip II ordered the Spanish Inquisition (which had been set up by the Spanish crown after the expulsion of the Moors and Jews from Spain in 1492 and later extended to the Spanish Empire in the Americas) established in the Dutch Netherlands to root out Protestants. When the Dutch declared independence from Spain in 1581, Calvinism quickly became part of the Dutch national movement during the long war of independence that followed (see Chapter 6).

THE REFORMATION IN ENGLAND

Unlike continental reform, the English Reformation began with a struggle between the king and the Church. But this dispute must be placed in the context of discontentment with ecclesiastical venality and the distant rule of Rome. Lollard influence persisted among the middle and lower classes, which resented the wealth of the high clergy and papal authority. Merchants and travelers returned to England from the continent with Lutheran tracts. John Colet's espousal of a literal interpretation of the Bible placed him close to the thought of Martin Luther. Among Luther's small group of followers at Cambridge University was William Tyndale, who published the first English translation of the New Testament. Burned at the stake as a heretic in 1536, his last words were "Lord, open the eyes of the king of England."

Henry VIII and the Break with Rome

King Henry VIII (ruled 1509–1547), was a religious conservative who published a book (1521) defending the Catholic view of the sacraments against Martin Luther, prompting the pope to grant him the title of "defender of the faith." The Catholic Church in England already enjoyed considerable autonomy, granted by the pope in the fourteenth century, and the king had the authority to appoint bishops.

The issue of royal divorce led to the English break with Rome. Henry's wife, Catherine of Aragon (1485–1536), had given birth five times, but only an extremely frail girl, Mary Tudor, survived. Henry not only urgently desired a male heir for the prestige of the dynasty, he also desired Anne Boleyn (1507–1536), a lady-in-waiting of Irish descent who had long black hair and flashing dark eyes.

Henry had obtained a special papal dispensation to marry Catherine, who was his brother's widow, and now sought the annulment of this same marriage. Obtaining an annulment—which meant, from the point of view of the Church, that the marriage had never taken place—was not uncommon in sixteenth-century Europe and was an escape clause for those of great wealth. Henry justified his efforts by invoking an Old Testament passage that placed the curse of childlessness on any man who married his brother's widow. He furthermore claimed that English ecclesiastical authorities, not the pope, had the authority to grant an annulment. Pope Clement VII (pope 1523–1534), the second Medici pope, was at this time a prisoner of Charles V, the Holy Roman emperor, whose armies had occupied Rome, and who happened to be Catherine of Aragon's nephew. In addition to these political circumstances, the pope opposed the annulment as a matter of conscience. At Henry's insistence, Cardinal Thomas Wolsey (1475– 1530), who had been named at the king's demand as archbishop of Canterbury and hence head of the Church in England, opened a formal church proceeding in London in 1529 to hear the king's case. But Pope Clement ordered the case transferred to Rome, where the English king had no chance of winning.

Furious, Henry blamed Wolsey for this defeat. Stripped of his post, Wolsey died a shattered man in 1530 on the way to his trial for treason and certain execution. The king had named Thomas More to be his lord

(*Left*) Henry VIII. (*Right*) Anne Boleyn.

Sir Thomas More, painting by Hans Holbein the Younger. More, who is here shown as lord chancellor, was later executed for his beliefs.

chancellor in 1529. But More, a lawyer and a humanist man of letters, was a vigorous opponent of the reform movement. Although a layman, each Friday More whipped himself in memory of Christ's suffering at the hands of Roman soldiers.

As a committed Catholic, More balked at Henry's plan to have his marriage to Catherine of Aragon annulled. In 1533, Henry secretly married the pregnant Anne Boleyn. He then convoked Parliament, which dutifully passed a series of acts that cut the ties between the English church and Rome. The Act in Restraint of Appeals (1533) denied the pope's authority. Thomas Cranmer (1489–1556), who succeeded Wolsey as archbishop of Canterbury, showed himself a loyal servant of the throne by mobilizing opinion against Rome and simply declaring Henry's marriage to Catherine, who was sent to a convent, annulled. The Act of Succession in 1534 required all of the king's subjects to take an oath of loyalty to the king as head of the Church of England. Thomas More refused to do so, and Henry ordered his execution. In Henry's eyes, More was a traitor, but he was a martyr and saint to the Catholic Church. When Pope Clement named another cleric languishing in the Tower of London a cardinal, Henry scoffed, "Let the pope send him a [cardinal's] hat when he will, but I will provide that whensoever it cometh, he shall wear it on his shoulders, for his head he shall have none to set it on."

The Act of Supremacy, also passed in 1534, proclaimed the king "supreme head of the Church of England." Another law made possible the execution of anyone who denied the king's authority over the clergy, or who supported "the bishop of Rome or his pretended power." Parliament limited fees that the clergy could assess for burials and forbade bishops from living away from their sees. Reforms brought the clergy under civil law and enhanced the rights and prestige of Parliament. The lack of resistance to Henry's usurpation of ecclesiastical authority reflected the pope's unpopularity, as well as the growing strength of the English monarchy.

After the Break with Rome

Henry's nascent Church of England remained doctrinely conservative in contrast to some of the continental reform churches. Several dozen people were burned at the stake for heresy in the 1530s after Henry broke with Rome, including twenty-five Anabaptists. In 1536, in the Church of England's first doctrinal pronouncement, Ten Articles affirmed the essential tenets of Lutheran reform: salvation by faith alone (although good works were still advised), three sacraments, and rejection of the concept of Purgatory and the cult of saints. However, six more articles promulgated two years later reaffirmed some aspects of orthodox Catholic doctrine, including transubstantiation and clerical celibacy.

Thomas Cromwell (1485–1540), Wolsey's ambitious protégé, oversaw the dissolution of England's 600 monasteries, which was completed in 1538 despite a northern insurrection (the "Pilgrimage of Grace") in defense of the Roman Catholic Church. The members of the clergy dispossessed by the dissolution of the monasteries were pensioned off. Two-thirds of the monasteries were sold within ten years, the largest transfer of land in England since the Norman Conquest of 1066. The appropriation of Church lands doubled royal revenue, allowing the construction of forts along the troublesome border with Scotland and on the Channel coast, as well as paying for new ships of war. Nobles, particularly those living in the more prosperous south, were the chief purchasers of monastic lands. Many turned their acquisitions into pastureland for sheep, or undertook more intensive agricultural production.

A few months after she married Henry, Anne Boleyn gave birth to a daughter, Elizabeth, future Queen of England. But Henry then had Anne tried on charges of adultery with one of his courtiers, claiming that she had coyly dropped her handkerchief in order to attract him. Anne was executed in 1536, but she insisted to the end about Henry that, "a gentler nor a more merciful prince was there never." Next the king married Jane Seymour, who died shortly after giving birth to a son. Another Anne, this one from a small German state, was next in line, as Henry sought allies against Spain and the other Catholic powers. But this Anne did not please Henry—he claimed he had never consummated his marriage to this woman he disparaged as a "Flemish mare," and he divorced her, too. The king ordered the execution of Cromwell, who had the bad judgment in 1540 to boast that if Henry wavered on the path to religious reform, he would take up his sword against him. Catherine Howard became Henry's fifth wife, but in 1542 he ordered her dispatched for "treasonable un-chastity." Catherine Parr would have been excused had she felt some trepidation in becoming Henry's sixth wife, but this pious older woman managed to outlive her husband.

THE CATHOLIC REFORMATION

By 1540, the Reformation had carved out large zones of allegiance in Cen-tral and Northern Europe, as well as parts of France and most of England. It reached into Scotland, where, following the efforts of the fiery reformer John Knox, the Scottish Parliament accepted Calvinism in 1560 as the na-tional religion. More than 90 percent of Protestants were Lutheran, Calvinist, or Anglicans, the remainder scattered among smaller sects.

The Catholic Church responded to the schism within Christendom by reasserting the pope's authority and strengthening its own organization. The Catholic Reformation (sometimes called the Counter-Reformation) was both a defensive response by the Church to the success of Protes-tantism and an aggressive attempt to undertake reform within the limits dictated by Catholic theology.

Retreat to Dogmatism

In 1536, Pope Paul III (pope 1534–1549) designated a commission to re-port on possible reforms in the Church. This commission documented the lack of education of many clergy and scandalous cases of bishops and priests earning benefices from sees and parishes they never visited. At least eighty bishops resided in Rome, most far from their sees.

But the papacy held firm on matters of Catholic Church doctrine. Paul III rejected a last-ditch attempt in 1541 by one of his cardinals and several German bishops to reach agreement on the thorny theological issue of sal-vation by faith alone. Luther, too, also vehemently refused to accept com-promise. The papacy then went on the offensive. The next year, the pope ordered Cardinal Gian Pietro Carafa to establish an Inquisition in Rome to root out Protestantism in Italy. Carafa went so far as to build jail cells in his private residence.

Carafa became Pope Paul IV (pope 1555–1559) despite the veto of Holy Roman Emperor Charles V. He once declared, "If our own father were a heretic, we would gladly carry the wood to burn him!" Recognizing that the break with the reformed denominations was definitive, the new pope retreated into doctrinal orthodoxy and aggressive repression. He formal-ized pre-publication censorship, establishing a list—the Index—of forbidden books in 1559. Censors ordered other books altered, and refused to authorize the printing of publications they deemed controversial.

As part of the Catholic Reformation's efforts to combat, contain, and eliminate "error" in all forms, Paul IV invented the "ghetto," ordering Jews living in the Papal States to reside in specific neighborhoods, which they could leave only at certain times. In a 1555 bull, he stated that the Jews were guilty of killing Christ, and therefore ought to be slaves. In much of Catholic Europe, Jews had to wear yellow caps to identify themselves, could not own land, and were excluded from most professions.

Ignatius of Loyola and the Jesuits

Ignatius of Loyola (1491–1556), a dashing Basque noble, became one of the leading figures of the Catholic Reformation. While recovering from a grave injury suffered in battle, Loyola read an account of the life of Christ and a book on the lives of saints. He vowed to help rekindle Catholic orthodoxy throughout Europe. Loyola made a pilgrimage to a Spanish monastery, left his sword in a chapel, gave his rich robe to a poor man, put on a sackcloth, and travelled through Spain and Italy.

Gradually Loyola attracted followers. The Inquisition came to suspect him because his claims to help people through "spiritual conversion" seemed dangerously close to heresy. He defended himself ably, however, receiving only a short prison sentence.

Ignatius wanted to establish a new order that could inculcate the same kind of intense religious experience that he had undergone while lying wounded. He travelled to Rome, offered his services to the pope, and organized the Society of Jesus, which was officially approved by the pope in 1540. Under Loyola's military-style leadership, the Jesuits, as the order's members became known, grew rapidly in number and influence as aggressive crusaders for the Catholic Reformation.

The Jesuit order provided a model for Church organization, orthodoxy, and discipline. Jesuits underwent a program of rigorous training and took a special oath of allegiance to the pope. They combined the study of Thomas à Kempis' mystical *Imitation of Christ* (1418) and Ignatius' own intense devotional reflections, examination of conscience, and prayers intended to shape the will of the individual to the service of the Church.

"I can find God whenever I will," became the motto of the charismatic Loyola. When he died in 1556, there were more than a thousand Jesuits. Counselors to kings and princes and educators of the Catholic elite, the Jesuit religious order contributed greatly to the success of the Catholic Reformation in Austria, Bavaria, and the Rhineland. Jesuits also contributed to the Church's reconquest of Poland, where some landowners had converted to Lutheranism. In the service of the Catholic Reformation, Jesuits travelled to North America, Latin America, and Asia. They led "missions," delivering fire-and-brimstone sermons, which were aimed at

The Council of Trent.

rekindling loyalty to the Church. The resourceful German Jesuit Peter Canisius (1521–1597) carried the new Catholic crusade to some of the German states, wrote a triple catechism for different age levels, taught at universities there, and established Jesuit communities.

The Council of Trent

In 1545, at the insistence of Holy Roman Emperor Charles V, Paul III convoked the Council of Trent (1545–1563) to assess the condition of the Catholic Church and to define its doctrines. While such an internal reckoning had seemed inevitable for some time, the papacy had long viewed conciliarism as a potential threat to its authority and invoked every possible reason for delay. Once convened, the Council of Trent, which met off and on for eighteen years, made the split within Western Christendom irreparable. Most of the prelates who came to the Alpine town of Trent believed the central goal of the council was a blanket condemnation of what the Church viewed as heresy, as well as the reaffirmation of theological doctrine. Although the pope himself never went to Trent, the Italian delegates dominated the proceedings, coughing and sneezing during speeches with which they disagreed.

The council rejected point after point of reformed doctrine, declaring these positions "to be anathema." It reaffirmed the authority of the pope and of the bishops, the seven sacraments, and the presence of Christ in the Eucharist. It also unequivocally opposed the marriage of clerics and reaffirmed belief in Purgatory and in the redeeming power of indulgences, although the practice of selling them was abolished.

In 1562, Pope Pius IV (pope 1559–1565), who had fathered three children as a young man before becoming the inquisitor general in Rome, convoked the last session of the Council of Trent. The council ordained the creation of seminaries in each diocese in order to increase the number and quality of priests. The priests were henceforth to keep parish registers listing the births, baptisms, and deaths of the faithful, which in recent times have provided historians with extraordinarily useful demographic information. Some monastic houses undertook reforms. The infusion of better educated clergy in the southern German states and Austria aided the Church's efforts to maintain its influence.

The papacy emerged from the Council of Trent much more centralized, better organized and administered, and more aggressive, like the most powerful European states themselves. Gradually a series of more able popes helped restore the prestige of the papacy within the Church.

Putting Its House in Order

"The best way," one churchman advised, "to fight the heretics is not to deserve their criticisms." Some leaders within the Catholic Church now reasoned that the Church should put its own house in order and seek to reconvert people who had joined the reformed religions. Pius V (pope 1566–1572) declared war on venality, luxury, and ostentation in Rome. But abuses still seemed rampant. In 1569, the Venetian ambassador to France reported that the French "deal in bishoprics and abbeys as merchants trade in pepper and cinnamon." But Pius sent some bishops living in Roman luxury packing to their sees, putting those who refused to leave in prison.

Reformers wanted to bring order and discipline to members of religious orders and the secular clergy. "No wonder the Church is as it is, when the religious live as they do [in monasteries and convents]," Teresa of Avila (1515–1582) exclaimed in response to the demeaning battles between religious houses in Spain, struggles that she tried to end. Some churchmen, however, now rejected monastic life as irrelevant to the activist missionary tasks of the Church, another sign of the influence of Protestant reform. New orders, such as the Capuchins—an offshoot of the Franciscans—and the female order of the Ursulines, worked to bring faith to the poor and the sick. Seeing the success Reformation preachers had with mass-produced pamphlets, the Catholic Church also produced catechisms that spread Church teachings. Thus, catechisms, devotional books (including those by the Jesuits), and lives of the saints circulated widely for popular consumption. Jesuits used drama to renew faith by portraying episodes from Church history and the lives of saints. The Catholic Reformation encouraged other new devotional confraternities (religious brotherhoods of people who heard Mass together), some bringing together laymen of various social classes, begun under the direction of local Catholic elites and clergy. The missionary work of Vincent de Paul (1581–1660) helped restore faith among the poor.

The Reformation had emphasized the religious life of the individual and the development of his or her personal piety through Bible study and personal reflection. The Catholic Reformation, too, now encouraged individual forms of devotion and spirituality. In Spain, where reform had made few inroads, there was a deep spiritual revival, one that extended throughout Spanish society. Nobles, artisans, and peasants joined religious confraternities. A spirit of idealism and contemplative self-reflection merged with the intensely emotional religious devotion and piety that had characterized medieval monasticism in its purest form. Teresa of Avila, later canonized as a saint, believed that in order for spiritual values to survive, "mystical theology," a belief that the individual could have direct access to God through prayer and contemplation, had to be restored, and that monasteries and convents had to be reformed.

CULTURE DURING THE TWO REFORMATIONS

The Reformation began as a religious reaction against established abuses within the Church. But it also reflected profound changes in European society. The Reformation followed the expansion of commerce, the arteries of which became the conduits of reform. Both the Protestant and Catholic Reformations affected art, architecture, print culture, education, popular culture, and family life.

The Baroque Style

The monumentalism, flamboyance, and theatrical religiosity of the baroque style complemented the Catholic Reformation. "Baroque" refers to a style of extravagant and irregularly shaped ornamentation (the term itself comes from Old French for "irregularly shaped pear"). As an architectural, artistic, and decorative style, the baroque triumphed in southern Germany, Austria, Flanders, and other Catholic regions during the first decades of the seventeenth century (but was also popular in Protestant England, where it merged with the classical style).

As in the Renaissance, in Rome the Church remained a major patron of the arts, expressing religious themes through visual representation. Its goal was to impress, indeed to overwhelm, the emotions through awe-inspiring dimensions, opulence, movement and, in painting, lurid color. Baroque style emphasized the metaphysical side of humanity, seeking to express the experience of the soul. Baroque palaces and churches featured exuberant curves and ornate decoration and were cluttered with lustrous marble altars, ornate statues, golden cherubs, and intensely colorful murals and ceiling paintings. The baroque merged easily with neo-classicism—the revival of an architectural design dominated by Greek and Roman forms. The Gesú Church of the Jesuits in Rome is a masterpiece of baroque style. With its vast ceilings and enormous paintings of the ascen-

Bernini's *Ecstasy of Saint Theresa.*

sion of Christ and the assumption of the Virgin Mary, it symbolizes the spirit of the Catholic Reformation. The baroque style used optical illusions such as Gesú's false cupola to achieve the impression that the viewer was reaching for Heaven.

The work of Venetian sculptor Gianlorenzo Bernini (1598–1680) best represents the period of high baroque of the Catholic Reformation. His monumental fountains were spread throughout Rome. He planned the piazza outside the entrance to St. Peter's Basilica and sculpted the magnificent canopy over the high altar of St. Peter's. Bernini sought to communicate the intensity of religious experience. In the altarpiece *The Ecstasy of Saint Theresa* (1645–1652), Bernini depicted the saint's convulsions of joy when an angel stabs her with a spear as beams of sunlight engulf the scene. Bernini wrote, "It pleased the Lord that I should see this angel in [this] way. . . . In his hands I saw a long golden spear and at the end of the iron tip I seemed to see a point of fire. With this he seemed to pierce my heart several times so that it penetrated to my entrails." This highly sexual description stands in marked contrast with the puritanical impulse that had seen Renaissance popes order the painting of fig leaves on nudes.

Print Culture

The printing press helped expand the Reformation without causing it. There was, to be sure, nothing about the rapid increase in print culture that would help the cause of religious reform and not the Roman Catholic Church. But a rapid expansion in the publication of pamphlets, books, and other printed material occurred at a time when reformers were challenging Church doctrine and papal authority. The printing of Luther's works facilitated their rapid diffusion, with perhaps a million copies circulating through the German states by the mid-1520s. In 1521, a papal ambassador wrote that "daily there is a veritable downpour of Lutheran tracts in German and in Latin . . . nothing is sold here except the tracts of Luther." The German reformer called the printing press "God's highest and ultimate gift of grace by which He would have His Gospel carried forward." Luther's Wartburg translation of the Bible went through fifty printings in two years. He wrote 450 treatises and delivered more than 3,000 sermons, in addition to thousands of letters; his collected works fill more than 100 volumes and 60,000 pages. Catechisms became his major instrument of religious education. Luther directed many of his dialogues, poems, and sermons to ordinary Germans, and even to children, adopting popular religious themes and images. Luther's book *A Simple Way to Pray, Written for a Friend* was intended for his barber.

Since about 1480, the diffusion of printing had contributed to the expansion of a lay culture in the German states. Much of what was printed was published in the vernacular, that is, German, as opposed to Latin. Although religious literature was the greatest output of early printing presses, other favored themes of books and pamphlets included nature (which fascinated sixteenth-century people), the discoveries of the explorers, the acquisition of technical skills (such as medical skills from self-help medical handbooks), manuals of self-instruction (such as how to defend yourself in court, or how to make beer and wine), and everyday morality.

Visual, often satirical images such as woodcut illustrations and broad-

Satirical images of the pope as a genie and as a donkey playing the bagpipes.

sheets, directed at those who could not read, probably reached far more people than did printed tracts, however. Luther also published a hymnal containing many hymns that are still sung today. Caricatures and cartoons portrayed the reformer as Hercules, as an evangelical saint doing battle with wretched animals representing the Church, as a new Moses, as a miracle worker (and in one popular legend, as the inventor of bratwurst sausage).

Lay Education and Reading

The Reformation, drawing on printing, also profited from increased lay education in Europe, which engendered a critical spirit among students and scholars. The number of universities rose steadily during the last half of the fifteenth century. More people could read than ever before—although in most places this still amounted to no more than 5 to 10 percent of the population. They could read the Scriptures themselves, as Luther, Calvin, and Zwingli encouraged them to do, and they could read them to other people. Lutherans and Calvinists stressed the importance of education as essential to individual and critical study of the Scriptures, and de-emphasized the clergy's role in religious instruction.

During the Reformation, princes and ecclesiastical leaders intensified their efforts to secure religious conformity by controlling what people read. The "blue library" (so called because they were wrapped in blue paper) helped diffuse orthodoxy through pamphlets deemed acceptable and sold at a low price by itinerant peddlers. Each Western European country had such a "literature of bits and pieces." Didactic stories were meant to

Private devotion: An old woman reading the Bible.

instruct people about religious events, saints, and ideals approved by the Church, and to distance them from the "superstitions" of popular culture. Yet, many people living in England probably still knew far more about Robin Hood than they did about the Bible. A chapbook (a small book of popular literature) published in Augsburg in 1621 told the story of St. George slaying the dragon. The Catholic hierarchy removed the dragon from the story, while Protestants left out Saint George.

Popular Rituals and Festivals

Protestant ministers, like their Catholic counterparts, tried to root out such rituals as placing the wedding ring on every finger of the hand and baptizing a child by dunking her three times for good luck. Songs rife with pagan imagery had survived virtually unchanged since medieval times. Religion and magic remained closely intertwined; the Catholic Church had been unable to eradicate the difference in the popular mind between prayer and good luck charms, for example. Archbishops and papal legates undercut the cult of some popular saints.

Many a village became the site of an elaborate tug-of-war between state and ecclesiastical authorities and ordinary people, with the local priest caught in the middle. The clergy, often previously active participants in festive occasions, moved away from what they considered "profane" amusements.

The Catholic hierarchy also tried to suppress some popular festivals and rein in others, returning them to the control of the clergy by imposing a religious purpose that seemed to have been lost in all the fun. The struggle between regulation and tradition began first in the towns and then spread to the countryside. Dances known as the "twirl" in southern France were banned in 1666 because boys tossed girls into the air "in such an infamous manner that what shame obliges us to hide most of all is uncovered naked to the eyes of those taking part and those passing by."

Ecclesiastical and lay hierarchies, Catholic and Protestant, came to view popular festivity as immoral, or at least licentious. *Combat between Carnival and Lent* (1559), a painting by Pieter Bruegel, the Elder, depicts Carnival as a fat man and Lent as a thin woman. Under the twin assault of absolutism and ecclesiastic hierarchy, Lent won. The prominent role of women and youth in festivity drew special condemnation. The clergy also condemned the role in Carnival and other festivals of the lay confraternities. These pious brotherhoods had had their origins in religious devotion, but they now were often fiercely independent and more like festive clubs. The clergy began a long—and often unsuccessful—struggle for control over these lay confraternities. Carnival was largely eradicated in Protestant countries, but it survived in some Catholic ones, although often much transformed. Moreover, local variations in popular culture waned, and cults such as that of Mary became more popular.

Pieter Bruegel, the Elder's *Combat between Carnival and Lent* (1559).

Social and political elites contrasted the "civility" of their beliefs, conduct, and manners with the "barbarity" or "savagery" of popular beliefs and customs. Didactic literature stressing polite comportment and etiquette became popular among people of wealth, further separating them from those less favored. The Church tried to impose more strict sexual mores on ordinary people, while encouraging gestures of deference toward social superiors.

The Role of Women

With convents and nunneries abolished in Protestant states, reformers nonetheless encouraged women to take a more active role in the religious process of being saved. Protestant women, like men, were encouraged to read the Bible themselves, or, as most could not read, to have it read to them. In the case of Anabaptists, women appear to have made decisions about not baptizing their children; most Anabaptist martyrs were female. More women than men seem to have converted to Calvinism in France, perhaps because their legal position was deteriorating—for example, with regard to their dowries and possessions. Perhaps they were attracted by special catechism classes, or by the fact that in Calvinist services, men and women sang psalms together.

Yet, Protestant reformers, too, believed women were subordinate to men. Although a few women published religious pamphlets in the early

1520s and others undertook devotional writing and publishing later, women could not be ministers nor could they hold offices within the new churches. Calvin himself believed that the subjugation of women to their husbands was crucial for the maintenance of moral order. Protestant denominations provided a domestic vision of women, emphasizing their role in the Christian household. The rights of women to manage their own property and undertake legal transactions in their own name were gradually withdrawn.

The fact that a Protestant minister could now marry, however, reflected a more positive view not only of women but of the family as a foundation of organized religion. One pamphleteer admonished husbands that their wives were "no dish-clouts . . . nor no drudges, but fellow-heirs with them of everlasting life, and so dear to God as the men."

Because they no longer considered marriage a sacrament, Protestants also reluctantly accepted divorce in limited cases. Luther viewed adultery, impotence, and abandonment as reasons for divorce, but he counseled bigamy over divorce in the case of Philip of Hesse, and condemned Henry VIII's effort to divorce Catherine of Aragon. Divorce remained quite rare and occurred only after a long, expensive legal process.

In Catholic areas, women could still rise to positions of importance in convents, or in the new charitable orders. But the Council of Trent reaffirmed the Catholic Church's ideal of female chastity, reinforced by the widespread cult of Mary. The chapbooks of the Catholic Reformation still taught that the female body was a source of sin, and therefore had to be controlled.

Witches came to symbolize superstitious aspects of popular religion. Catholic and Protestant churchmen identified and persecuted witches as part of the campaign to acculturate the masses with "acceptable" beliefs. Witch hunts peaked during the first half of the seventeenth century. In the southwestern states of the Holy Roman Empire alone, more than 300 separate witch trials resulted in the execution of 2,500 people between 1570 and 1630, almost all women (in itself not surprising, as Church authorities and priests were all male).

Theologians and judges sought to demonstrate that accused witches embodied the kingdom of the devil. To some extent, the Catholic Reformation wanted to create the idea of a satanic kingdom of evil on earth with which to juxtapose orthodoxy. "Witches," identified by common reputation, sometimes stood accused of saying Latin prayers backward, or performing "black masses" while standing facing their "congregations," instead of facing the altar, defiantly inverting the kingdom of God. One woman was accused of "consuming" several husbands. Often "witches" were blamed for evil that had befallen villagers: a fire, the unexplained death of a cow, a male suddenly smitten with impotence.

Most of those accused of being witches were rural, poor, and single women who confronted the hostility of other villagers, particularly small town officials and wealthy peasants (it was the opposite in 1692 in Salem, Massachusetts, where a good many of the women accused of witchcraft had just inherited property, and therefore were resented by the community). Some "witches" confessed under pain of torture, such as one woman in southern France, who was "scorched like a pig" and cooked alive, having been accused of spreading an evil powder while committing crimes.

Women were targets for repression because they were transmitters of the collective memory of popular culture. They were genealogists, storytellers, and healers, but almost always without formal education. Women were in many ways the guardians of tradition. But they were also regarded by the Catholic hierarchy as the source of sin. The social exorcisms of women had a social value for those in power, affirming authorities' position and role as interpreters of beliefs and customs deemed appropriate.

After the persecution of witches virtually ended, some lay authorities then turned their attention to outcasts, the socially marginal. In the Austrian Netherlands, a sign "useless to the world" was hung above the head of a beggar. Monarchies increasingly demonstrated their authority in carrying out sentences of royal justice and, therefore, the justice of God. Those found guilty of capital crimes—at least those of the lower classes— were tortured and then executed in public, often before throngs, their mutilated bodies exhibited for some time for all to see.

THE LEGACY OF THE TWO REFORMATIONS

In 1600, considerably more than half of Europe remained primarily Catholic, including Spain, France, and Habsburg Austria, three of the four most powerful states in Europe. The fourth was England, and it was overwhelmingly Protestant. The Dutch Netherlands, at war with its Spanish overlords, was largely Protestant as well. Yet, of all of the European states, the Reformation failed to influence directly only Ireland. It generated a strong missionary impulse among Protestants and Catholics alike. With the gradual opening up of the world to European commerce and colonization, the Jesuits, particularly, ranged far and wide. Some made converts, and a few found martyrdom in Asia and Latin America.

In Central Europe, the complexity of the state system facilitated reform. The Peace of Augsburg of 1555 reinforced German particularism, that is, the persistence of a myriad of small, independent states in Central Europe. In contrast, the larger, centralized, and more powerful states like Spain and France most successfully resisted the reform movement. That France and Spain already were large states with relatively strong monarchies helped the Catholic Church remain the dominant religion there, despite the inroads of reform and subsequent wars of religion in the former. Yet, in both states, the Catholic Church remained subordinate to the monarchy, with both the French and Spanish kings retaining considerable authority over ecclesiastical appointments.

The Protestant reformers accepted a separation of functions within the community, what Luther called the "realm of the spirit" and the "realm of the world." Henceforth, the political institutions of the Protestant states remained relatively secularized. In German states and in Scandinavia, Lutheranism was introduced as a state church, in part because reformers originally needed the protection of princes against Catholic rulers, notably Charles V. In England, Anglicanism also took on the status of a state religion. Both Lutheran and Anglican reforms rigorously subordinated the church to the state, separating the spiritual and temporal realms. Whereas Zwingli had called for the complete fusion of church and state, Calvinism alone provided for the institutional separation of both, although in practice the magistrates of Geneva restricted the church's autonomy. Anabaptist sectarians, in contrast, wanted their communities to have nothing at all to do with the state. All reformers called on their rulers to do God's work on earth, arguing that the papacy and the Catholic monarchs had failed to do so.

The Lutheran and Calvinist states were thus not necessarily any more tolerant of religious dissent than those that remained Catholic. Following the Peace of Augsburg in 1555, German princes used their control of the reformed churches to consolidate their political authority. Lutheranism remained wedded to a patriarchal structure of society, which appealed to property owners at all social levels. Yet, the extent to which the princes succeeded in obtaining religious adherence is, of course, almost impossible to know, despite some attempts to make church attendance mandatory and to punish those who were absent.

Nonetheless, compelling people to attend Sunday services did not guarantee what or even if they believed. One can never know how typical were the thoughts of one girl who related that the sermon she had just sat through was "such a deale of bible babble that I am weary to heare yt and I can then sitt downe in my seat and take a good napp." In one English parish in 1547, it was reported that "when the vicar goeth into the pulpit to read what [he] himself hath written, then the multitude of the parish goeth straight out of the church, home to drink."

Finally, the Peace of Augsburg and the Council of Trent did not end the rivalry between Catholics and Protestants, nor, for that matter, the rivalry between different Protestant denominations. Religious conflict would, to a great extent, help define the first half of the seventeenth century, the age of the wars of religion.

CHAPTER 4

THE WARS OF RELIGION

On May 23, 1618, a crowd of protesters carried a petition to Prague's Hradcany Palace, where representatives of the royal government were gathered. The crowd stormed into the council chamber, engaged Catholic officials in a heated debate, organized an impromptu trial, and hurled two royal delegates from the window. The crowd below roared its approval of this "defenestration" (an elegant term for throwing someone out a window), angered only that neither man was killed by the fall. Catholic partisans construed their good fortune as a miracle, as the rumor spread that guardian angels had swooped down to pluck the falling dignitaries from the air. The Protestants liked to claim that the men had been saved because they fell on large dungheaps in the moat below.

The different reactions to the Defenestration of Prague illustrate how the Reformation left some of Europe, particularly the German states, a veritable patchwork of religious allegiances. Religious affiliation, like ethnicity, frequently did not correspond to the borders of states. The Peace of Augsburg in 1555 ended the fighting between German Protestant and Catholic princes. It stated that the religion of each state would henceforth be that of its ruler. Hundreds of thousands of families left home and crossed frontiers in order to relocate to a state where the prince was of their religious denomination.

By contrast, in France in 1572, the Huguenots (the popular name for the French Protestants) rebelled against Catholic domination. This set off a civil war that led to great instability in France. Moreover, after years of mounting religious and political tension, Dutch Protestants led the revolt against Spanish Catholic authority in 1572, beginning a bitter struggle that lasted until the middle of the next century.

From 1555 until 1618, the German states were for the most part at peace. But religious wars then broke out again with unparalleled intensity. The Thirty Years' War (1618–1648) devastated Central Europe, bringing into the conflict, in one way or another, almost all of the powers of Europe. Armies reached unprecedented size, and fought with a cruelty that

Peter Brueghel the Elder's *The Massacre of the Innocents* (1564).

may also have been unprecedented. The Four Horsemen of the Apocalypse seemed to ride back and forth across Central Europe with impunity.

The wars of religion in France and the Thirty Years' War began because of religious antagonisms, but the dynastic ambitions of French princes lay not far behind the rivalry between Protestants and Catholics. In the Thirty Years' War, the dynastic rivalry between the Bourbons of France and the Habsburgs of Austria—both Catholic dynasties—came to the fore, eventually dominating religious considerations.

The wars of religion resulted in the strengthening of the monarchies of France, Austria, and the smaller German states as well. Kings and princes further extended their administrative, judicial, and fiscal reach over their subjects in the interest of maintaining control over their populations and waging war. In France, particularly, a stronger monarchy emerged out of the trauma of religious struggles and competing claimants to the throne. Germany, in contrast, remained divided into several strong states and many smaller ones. Competing religious allegiances reinforced German particularism, that is, the multiplicity of independent German states and strong regional loyalties.

THE WARS OF RELIGION IN SIXTEENTH-CENTURY FRANCE

Early in the sixteenth century, France was divided by law, customs, languages, and traditions. Under King Francis I (ruled 1515–1547), the Valois monarchy effectively extended its authority. Of Francis I, it was said, "If the king endures bodily fatigues unflinchingly, he finds mental preoccupations more difficult to bear." The French monarch ruled with an authority unequaled in Europe, however much it was still dependent on the good will of nobles, above all in time of war. When the king sought loans to continue a war, a Parisian noble assured him that "we do not wish to dispute or minimize your power; that would be a sacrilege, and we know very well that you are above the law."

When the Reformation reached France in the 1540s and 1550s, Calvinism won many converts. At a time when nobles were resisting the expansion of the king's judicial prerogatives and the proliferation of his officials, religious division precipitated a crisis of the French state and brought civil war.

A Strengthened Monarchy

Francis I and his successors became more insistent on their authority to assess taxes on the towns of the kingdom, many of which had held privileged exemptions granted in exchange for loyalty. Kings had asked for tax levies to help out the monarchy in exceptional circumstances, above all, in time of war. Like his medieval forebears, Francis did not automatically command the allegiance of a large standing army with which he could enforce his will. Raising an army or royal revenue depended on the willingness of the most powerful nobles to answer the king's call. The monarchs

Francis I, painted by Jean Clouet.

had justified such requests with an appeal to the common good in tactful language that also held out the possibility of the use of force. Now the French king wished to tax the towns even when there was no war.

Francis reduced the authority of the Catholic Church in France. The Concordat of Bologna (1516), signed between Francis and Pope Leo X, despite the resistance of the French clergy, established royal control over ecclesiastical appointments. Many more royal officials now represented and enforced the royal will in the provinces than ever before. At the time of the concordat, France had about 1 official of some kind for every 115 square kilometers and 1,000 people; forty years later, there was 1 for every 10 square kilometers and 75 people. Francis confirmed and enhanced Paris' identity as the seat and emerging symbol of royal power. The sale of offices originated in Francis' desire for the allegiance of nobles and for the revenue they could provide the monarchy. His successors would depend increasingly on the sale of offices and titles for raising revenue.

The political and religious crises in the middle decades of the sixteenth century threatened monarchical stability. They pushed the country into a period of chaos brought by the lengthy, savage war of religion during which the four Valois kings who succeeded Francis I proved unable to rule effectively.

Economic Crisis

The end of a period of economic expansion provided a backdrop for the political struggles of the French monarchy. The population of France had risen rapidly between the late fifteenth century and about 1570, reversing the decline in population resulting from plagues and natural disasters. Land under cultivation increased during that time, particularly near the Mediterranean, where landowners planted olive trees on hills and terraces. But by 1570, the increase in cultivable land slowed down in much of France. The European population, which had risen from about 2.5 to 4.1 million during the sixteenth century, outstripped available resources. Prices rose rapidly in France, as in most of Europe, pushed upward relentlessly by population increase. Beginning in the late 1550s, the purchasing power of the wage worker declined dramatically, whereas that of landowners remained stable, fed by high prices. As agricultural income fell, nobles demanded vexing services from peasants, such as repairing roads and paths on their estates. Many wealthy nobles rented out land to tenant farmers, then took the proceeds back to their luxurious urban residences. Nobles of lesser means, however, did not do as well as the owners of great estates, because the rents they drew from their land failed to keep pace with rising prices.

One sign of the growing power of the monarchy was that nobles lost some privileges of local jurisdiction to the royal law courts. Finding nobles unwilling to provide all the funds the king desired, the monarchy, in turn, put the squeeze on peasants, extracting more resources through taxation.

As the price of profitable land soared, peasant families tried to protect their children by subdividing land among male offspring. Many peasants with small parcels of land became sharecroppers at highly disadvantageous terms—working someone else's land for a return of roughly half of what was produced. Both trends worked against increased agricultural efficiency, reducing land yields. Landless laborers were barely able to sustain themselves.

Taxes and tithes (payments owed the Catholic Church) weighed heavily on the poor. Peasants, particularly in the southwest, sporadically revolted against taxes, and against their landlords, during the period 1560–1660. The popular nicknames of some of the groups of rebels reflect their abject poverty and desperation: the "poor wretches," who rose against the nobles in central and southern France in 1594–1595 (they first took the name of the Hunters of Thieves as they battled nobles who had impounded their cattle and horses in time of war), and the "bare feet." Many of the rebels espoused the popular belief that their violence might restore an imagined world of social justice in which wise rulers looked after the needs of their people.

French Calvinists and the Crisis of the French State

Protestantism first found a smattering of French converts during the two decades following Luther's posting of his theses on the church door in Wittenberg in 1517. Followers of John Calvin arriving in France from nearby Geneva attracted converts in the 1540s and 1550s. Henry II (ruled 1547–1559), who succeeded his father Francis I, began a religious repression that created Calvinist martyrs, perhaps further encouraging Protestant dissent. The spread of Calvinism led the king to sign the Treaty of Cateau-Cambrésis in 1559, ending the long struggle between France and Spain. After decades of reckless invasions, Henry II agreed to respect Habsburg primacy in Italy and control over Flanders. King Philip II (ruled 1556–1598) of Spain, in return, promised that Spain would desist in its attempts to weaken the Valois kings. These two most powerful kings in Europe ended their struggle for supremacy not only because their resources were nearly exhausted but because as pious Catholic rulers they viewed with alarm the spread of Calvinism in Western Europe, both within the Netherlands (a rich territory of the Spanish Habsburgs) and within France itself. After signing the treaty, Henry II and Philip II could now turn their attention to combating Protestantism.

Some nobles in France, wary of the extending reach of the Valois monarchy and tired of providing funds for the war against Spain, had resisted the monarchy, which had vigorously embraced the Catholic Reformation. Perhaps as many as 40 percent of French nobles had converted to Calvinism, some of them nobles of relatively modest means squeezed by economic setbacks. The conflict between the monarchy and the nobil-

Catherine de Medici, widow of Henry II, served as regent to Francis II.

ity thus compounded religious divisions in the last half of the sixteenth century.

King Henry II, accidentally killed by an errant lance during a jousting tournament celebrating peace with Spain, was succeeded by his fifteen-year-old son, who became Francis II (ruled 1559–1560). Catherine de Medici (1519–1589), Henry II's talented, manipulative, and domineering widow, served as regent to the first of her three sickly and incapable sons. Catherine was reviled as a "shopkeeper's daughter," as her Florentine ancestors had been merchants, bankers, and money changers, all things incompatible with the French concept of nobility (but not with the Italian one). That she was the daughter of the man to whom Machiavelli had dedicated *The Prince* added to the "legend of the wicked Italian queen" in France.

The throne immediately faced the challenge to its authority of three powerful noble families, each dominating large parts of France. Religious differences sharpened the rivalry between them for influence. The Catholic Guise family, the strongest, concentrated its influence in northern and eastern France. In the southwest the Catholic Montmorency family, one of the oldest and wealthiest in the kingdom, held the allegiance of some of the population there. And the influence of the Huguenot Bourbon family extended throughout the far southwest corner and center of France.

In 1560, Louis, prince of Condé (1530–1569), a member of the Bourbon family, conspired to kidnap Francis II and remove him from the clutches of the House of Guise, who were related to Francis' wife, Mary Stuart, queen of Scotland. The Guise clan, who discovered the plot, killed some of the Bourbon conspirators, which understandably damaged relations between these powerful families. Francis died after a stormy reign of only eighteen months, succeeded by his ten-year-old brother Charles IX (ruled 1560–1574), under the regency of their mother, who remained influential throughout Charles' brief reign.

The rivalry between the Guise, Montmorency, and Bourbon families undermined royal authority. Henry II's lengthy war with Spain had drained the royal coffers, and the economic downturn made it almost impossible to fill them again. Catherine's efforts to bring some of the nobles who had converted to Protestantism to the royal court and to effect a rapprochement between the two denominations failed utterly. Such attempts only infuriated the House of Guise, several of whose members held important positions within the Catholic Church hierarchy. For their part, Philip II of Spain and the Jesuit religious order backed the Guise family. The political crisis of France, then, became increasingly tied to the struggle of the Church with the Huguenots.

Taking advantage of the confusion surrounding the throne, French Calvinists had become bolder in practicing their religion. Religious festivals occasioned brawls between Catholics and Huguenots. Calvinists seized control of Lyon in 1562, forcing the rest of the population to attend services. Where they were a majority, Calvinists desecrated Catholic cemeteries, smashed stained-glass windows and shattered altar rails of churches, mocked Catholic ceremonies, and covered statues of saints with mud. Catholics replied by slaughtering Calvinists, more than once forcing them to wear crowns of thorns, like Christ, to their death. Both sides burned the "heretical" books of the other denomination. The violence of a holy war was accentuated by rumors that the Huguenots indulged in orgies, while Protestants accused Catholics of idolatry and of doing the devil's work.

In 1562, the first full-scale religious war broke out in France. It began when Francis, the duke of Guise (1519–1563), ordered the execution of Huguenots whom he and his men had found worshipping on his land. More than 3,000 people were killed in fighting in Toulouse; the bodies of Protestants were tossed into the river, and their neighborhoods were burned as part of a ritual "purification." Members of the Catholic lay confraternities took oaths to protect France against "heresy" and erected crosses in public places as a sign of religious commitment. Catholics won back control of several major cities.

This first stage of the war, during which a Huguenot assassinated the duke of Guise, ended in 1563. A royal edict granted Huguenots the right to worship in one designated town in each region, as well as in places where Calvinist congregations had already been established. Intensifying the eagerness of the powerful quarreling noble families to impose their will on the monarchy was the fact that young King Charles IX and his two brothers were all childless. There was no clear heir to the throne of France.

In 1567, war between French Protestants and Catholics broke out again. It dragged on to an inconclusive halt three years later in a peace settlement that pleased neither side. In 1572, Catherine and Charles, though Catholics, first agreed to provide military support to the Dutch Protestants rebelling against Spanish authority. The goal was to help weaken France's principal rival. This convinced the duke of Guise even more that Protestants slowly but surely were taking control of France. Pressured by his mother, Charles then renounced aiding the Dutch and agreed to accept instead the guidance of the Catholic House of Guise. With or without the king's knowledge or connivance, the Guise family tried but failed to assassinate the Protestant leader Admiral Gaspard de Coligny (1519–1572), a Montmorency who had converted to Protestantism and whom they blamed for the earlier murder of the Catholic duke of Guise.

The marriage between Charles' sister, Margaret, a Catholic Valois, and Henry of Navarre, a Bourbon Huguenot, which took place on August 18, was to be, in principle, one of religious reconciliation. The negotiations for the wedding had specified that the Huguenots in Paris come unarmed. But the king's Guise advisers, and perhaps his mother as well, convinced him that the only way of preventing a Protestant uprising against the throne was to strike brutally against the Huguenots in Paris. Therefore, early in the morning on August 24, 1572, Catholic assassins hunted down and murdered Huguenot leaders. During what became known as the Saint Bartholomew's Day Massacre, the duke of Guise himself killed Coligny, whose battered corpse was thrown through the window, castrated, and then dragged through the dusty streets of Paris by children. For six days Catholic mobs stormed through the streets, killing more than 2,000 Protestants. The Parlement of Toulouse, one of the twelve judicial courts of medieval origin that combined judicial and administrative functions, made

The Saint Bartholomew's Day Massacre, 1572, in which more than 2,000 Huguenots perished in Paris.

it legal to kill any "heretic." Outside of Paris, another 10,000 Protestants perished. The pope had a special Mass sung in celebration, and Protestants claimed that he danced for joy when he heard the news, rewarding the messenger with a large sum of money. Thousands of Huguenots emigrated or moved to safer places, including fortified towns they still held in the southwest.

Charles IX died in 1574 and was succeeded by his ailing brother, Henry III (ruled 1574–1589). At his coronation, the crown twice slipped from Henry's head, a bad omen in a superstitious age. The new king was a picture of contradictions. He seemed pious, undertook pilgrimages, and hoped to bring about a revival of faith in his kingdom. He also enjoyed dressing up as a woman, while lavishing every attention on the handsome young men he gathered around him, and spent money with abandon.

Along with the bitter religious factionalism that had been exacerbated by the massacre, Henry III also had to confront a worsening fiscal crisis compounded by a series of meager harvests. But when he asked the provincial estates (assemblies dominated by nobles) for more taxes, the king found that his promises of financial reform and of an end to fiscal abuses by royal revenue agents were not enough. The estates deeply resented the influence of Italian financiers at court, the luxurious life of the court itself, and the nobles who had bought royal favor.

The Catholic forces around the king themselves were not united. A group of moderates, known as the *politiques,* pushed for conciliation. Tired of anarchy and bloodshed, they were ready to put politics ahead of religion. The *politiques* therefore sought to win the support of the moderate Huguenots, and thereby to bring religious toleration and peace to France.

In 1576, Henry signed an agreement that liberalized the conditions under which Protestants could practice their religion. Concessions, however, only further infuriated the intransigent Catholics, who became known as the "fanatics" (*dévots*). Angered by these concessions to Huguenots, a nobleman in the northern province of Picardy organized a Catholic League. More extensive than smaller local anti-Protestant organizations that had sprung up in the 1560s, the Catholic League (despite an insincere oath of loyalty taken to the king) posed a threat not only to Huguenots but to the monarchy. It was led by the dashing Henry, duke of Guise (1550–1588), who was subsidized by Philip II of Spain, and vowed to fight until Protestantism was completely driven from France. But another military campaign against Protestants led to nothing more than a restatement of the conditions under which they could worship.

Henry III's reconciliation with the House of Guise did not last long. The death of the last of the king's brothers in 1584 made Henry of Navarre, a Protestant, heir to the throne. This was the Catholics' worst nightmare. The Catholic League threw its full support behind the aged, ambitious Catholic Cardinal de Bourbon, who was next in line after Henry of Navarre.

Henry of Navarre, later King Henry IV.

Henry of Navarre

Henry of Navarre (1553–1610) was born in the town of Pau on the edge of the Pyrenees Mountains, the son of Antoine of Bourbon, patriarch of the powerful Bourbon family. Henry inherited the keen intelligence of his mother, Jeanne d'Albret, and his father's indecisiveness. His mother was a committed Huguenot and raised Henry in that faith. When his father, who was notoriously unfaithful to his wife, sent her back to the southwest in 1562, Henry converted to Catholicism, his father's nominal religion. After his father's death in battle, Henry re-embraced Protestantism. Taken to the royal court as a hostage by Catherine de Medici, he was permitted to have Huguenot tutors. Among his friends at court were the future Henry III and Henry, duke of Guise.

Henry consulted a fortune teller, who predicted that he would one day be king of France. A member of the Parlement of Bordeaux described the precocious boy: "We have here the prince of Béarn . . . a charming youth. At thirteen years of age, he has all the riper qualities of eighteen or nineteen; he is agreeable, polite, obliging and behaves to everyone with an air so easy and engaging that wherever he is there is always a crowd. He mixes in conversation like a wise and prudent man, speaks always to the purpose . . . and never says more nor less than he ought." It was after Henry's wedding in Paris in August 1572 to Margaret, Catherine de Medici's daughter, that the Saint Bartholomew's Day Massacre occurred. Henry then was given the choice of embracing Catholicism or being executed. He chose the former. When the fighting temporarily ended, Henry had more time for his favorite pursuits—hunting and pursuing women.

The Huguenots had every reason to be wary of a young man who seemed to change faiths with the ease of someone ordering dinner not long after lunch. Furthermore, he seemed to have reconciled himself to the Saint Bartholomew's Day Massacre, counted the "fanatic" duke of Guise among his friends, had accompanied the Catholic army, albeit under guard, to the siege of La Rochelle, and had written the pope begging forgiveness for past misdeeds.

But having left Paris and the watchful eye of the Catholic dukes, Henry formally abjured Catholicism and took up residence as royal governor in the southwest, where Protestantism was strong. There he tried to steer a path between militant Catholics and Huguenots, and his endorsement of mutual religious toleration won wide approval. When Henry of Navarre became heir to the throne in 1584, an English diplomat reported optimistically that "all the good Frenchmen begin to cast their eyes upon him, and to try more and more to gain his favor."

The Catholic League rallied its forces, drawing its muscle from the artisans of Paris and other northern towns. In defiance of the king, it forced the Parlement of Paris to withdraw the toleration afforded the Huguenots. The Catholic League's goal was to put the Cardinal de Bourbon on the throne, although the duke of Guise wanted it for himself.

The struggle between the "three Henrys" now began in earnest. Henry (Valois) III first allied with Henry (Bourbon) of Navarre and with the duke of Montmorency against Henry, duke of Guise. The Guise family provocatively accused the king in 1585 of destroying the kingdom through inept rule and called for a rebellion that would bring the duke of Guise to the throne and drive Protestantism from the kingdom.

Henry III then switched partners, joining the duke of Guise against Henry of Navarre. The Treaty of Nemours (1585) between Catherine de Medici and Henry, duke of Guise, abrogated all edicts of religious toleration and turned over a number of towns to the Catholic League. Now the odd man out, Henry of Navarre prepared for a new war. He denounced Spanish meddling and in a quintessentially *politique* statement, promised "to rally around me . . . all true Frenchmen without regard to religion." Although he himself increasingly depended on German and Swiss mercenaries for his army and benefited from the intervention of a German Protestant force, Henry's denunciation of foreign influence was a shrewd piece of political propaganda aimed at moderate Catholics—the *politiques*—and the Catholic clergy. The Catholic League replied with a warning that French Catholics would suffer the fate of martyred English Catholics should Henry win.

In 1587, Henry of Navarre defeated the combined forces of the king and the Catholic League at Coutras, near Bordeaux. Here his defensive position and use of artillery and cavalry proved decisive. But instead of following up his surprising victory by pursuing the Catholic army, Henry hesitated and went back to hunting and making love. As a contemporary put it, "all the advantage of so famous a victory floated away like smoke in the wind."

That year, Queen Elizabeth I of England put to death Mary Stuart, the Catholic queen of Scots and the niece of the duke of Guise (see Chapter 5). Angered by Henry III's inability to prevent the execution of his niece, Guise, at the urging of the king of Spain, marched to Paris in 1588, where he and the Catholic League enjoyed great support. The Spanish king hoped to keep the French king from contemplating any possible assistance to England as the Spanish Armada sailed toward the English Channel. When Henry III sent troops to Paris to oppose Guise, the Parisian population rose in rebellion on May 12, 1588, stretching barricades throughout the city center. The king ordered his troops to withdraw. The "Day of Barricades" marked the victory of a council led by clergymen known as the *Seize,* or Sixteen, the number of neighborhoods in Paris.

For several years, the Sixteen had been energetically supporting the League, while denouncing the king, the Catholic *politiques,* and Huguenots with equal fervor. The hostility of the population of Paris convinced the king to accept Cardinal de Bourbon as his heir, Guise as his lieutenant-general, and to convoke the Estates-General (representatives of the provincial estates, which the monarch could summon in times of great crisis).

Later, in 1588, the delegates to the Estates-General, many of them members of the Catholic League, gathered in the Loire Valley town of Blois. Some of the written grievances (*cahiers des doléances*) submitted set the tone for what followed, that of Paris referring to the king as a "cancer . . . filled with filth and infectious putrefaction" and calling for "all heretics, whatever their quality, condition or estate, [to] be imprisoned and punished by being burned alive." By now, however, the English fleet had defeated Philip II's Armada in the Channel (see Chapter 5), and the nobles found Henry III less intimidated than they had anticipated. When Guise heard a rumor that the king was planning his assassination, he replied, "He does not dare." But Henry's bodyguards cut down Henry, duke of Guise, shortly before Christmas 1588 in the Château of Blois, as Catherine de Medici lay dying in a room underneath the bloody struggle that resulted in Guise's death. The Valois king had the Cardinal de Bourbon and other prominent members of the Catholic League arrested.

Guise's assassination drove the Catholic League to full-fledged revolt. The theologians at the Sorbonne declared that the people were no longer obliged to obey the Valois monarch, who had become a "tyrant." More than 300 towns, most of them in the north, now joined the "Holy Union" against the king. As Catholics prepared to fight Catholics, the—again—

Assassination of Henry, duke of Guise.

Protestant Henry of Navarre appealed for peace: "We have been mad, senseless and furious for four years. Is that not enough?"

Henry III was now forced to make an alliance of convenience with Henry of Navarre against the Catholic League. As their combined armies besieged Paris, a monk assassinated Henry III. The king's Swiss guards, who had not done a terribly good job protecting their king, threw themselves at the feet of Henry of Navarre, telling him, "Sire, you are now our king and master."

The Catholic League, however, had proclaimed Cardinal de Bourbon, whom Henry was holding in custody, to be king. Henry's forces defeated Catholic League armies twice in Normandy, in 1589 and in 1590. His able artillery and fearless cavalry carried the day against an army swollen by Spanish reinforcements. But once again Henry failed to take advantage of the situation his shrewd generalship had made possible. He dawdled before finally laying siege to starving Paris.

The arrival of a Spanish army from Flanders to provision Paris helped win Henry further support from moderate Catholics, who resented Spanish intervention that might prolong the siege. Fatigue began to overcome religious conviction. Henry also played on resentment at the involvement of the pope, too, in French affairs (Henry had been excommunicated in 1585 and, for good measure, a second time six years later). As Henry's army besieged Paris, Spanish troops defeated forces loyal to him in several provinces. Henry captured Chartres in April 1591, more for reasons of the heart—the family connections of one of his lovers—than for strategic reasons. The death of Cardinal de Bourbon led Philip II to proclaim the candidacy of the late Henry II's Spanish granddaughter as heir to the throne, and then to suggest that he might claim it himself. In the meantime, Henry's continued successes on the battlefield and conciliatory proclamations furthered his popularity.

Henry of Navarre, a man of changing colors, had another major surprise up his sleeve. In 1593, Henry astonished friend and foe alike by announcing that he would now abjure Protestantism. This move, however, more reflected his shrewd sense of politics than indecisiveness. Paris, as he put it, was worth a Mass, the price of the capital's obedience. Following his coronation as Henry IV at Chartres the following year, Paris surrendered after very little fighting. Henry's entry into his capital was a carefully orchestrated series of ceremonies that included the "cure" of hundreds of people afflicted with scrofula (a tuberculous condition) by the royal touch, a monarchical tradition in France and England that went back centuries. Henry nodded enthusiastically to the women who came to their windows to catch a glimpse of the first Bourbon king of France.

Catholic League forces gradually dispersed, one town after another pledging its loyalty to Henry, usually in return for payments. Henry's declaration of war on Spain in 1595 helped rally people to the monarchy. The

The entry of Henry IV into Paris, 1594.

pope lifted Henry's excommunication from the Church. Henry invaded Philip's territory of Burgundy, defeating his army. In 1598, the last Catholic League army capitulated. Henry, having secured the frontiers of his kingdom, signed the Treaty of Vervins with Philip II to end the war that neither side could afford to continue.

Restoring Stability to France

Henry IV reasoned that after years of civil war, "France and I both need to catch our breath." But bringing stability to France would be no easy matter. The wars of religion had worsened the plight of the poor. Disastrous harvests and epidemics in the 1590s compounded the misery. The wars of the Catholic League caused great damage and dislocated the economy in many parts of France. That both sides had indiscriminately minted coins compounded inflation.

Henry's emissaries gradually restored order by promising that "the Well-Loved," as he became known, would end injustices. Henry once said that he hoped to live long enough to see "a chicken in every pot." He did slightly reduce the direct tax, of which the peasants bore the brunt. Henry also rooted out some of the corruption in the farming of taxes, whereby government officials allowed ambitious middlemen to collect taxes in exchange for a share. But he shifted even more of the tax burden to the poor by raising indirect taxes.

Gradually Henry succeeded in putting the finances of the monarchy on firmer footing. In 1596, he convinced an Assembly of Notables to approve a supplementary tax. A new imposition (the *paulette*) permitted officeholders, through an annual payment to the throne, to assure that their office would remain in the hands of their heirs. The *paulette* gave the wealthiest nobles of the realm a greater stake in the monarchy. But while increasing royal revenue, it intensified the phenomenon of the venality of office (the purchase of offices and the noble titles that went with them).

Henry could rarely rest at ease. In 1602 and again in 1604, he uncovered plots against him formed by nobles in connivance with the Spanish monarchy. He survived nine assassination attempts and at least twenty-three assorted other plots against him. The first followed his expulsion of the Jesuits, whose pamphleteers had called for his assassination. Small wonder that he carried two loaded pistols in his belt and that some nervous soul tasted his food and drink before he did.

Henry restored monarchical prestige and authority. The "new monarchy," strengthened by Francis I, now stood on more solid ground. Much of Henry's success in achieving the political reconstruction of France can be credited to his arrogant minister of finance, Maximilien de Béthune, the baron and, as of 1604, the duke of Sully (1560–1641). Sully was the son of a prosperous Protestant family whose great wealth had earned ennoblement. His influence, deeply resented by many nobles, was such that he was the only male admitted to the king's bedchamber, where he received the day's instructions.

Sully established budgets and systematic bookkeeping, which helped him eliminate some needless expenses. The monarchy gradually began to pay off some international debts, including those owed to the English crown and the Swiss cantons, whose good will Henry needed to counter Spanish influence in the Alps. These repayments allowed Henry to contrast his honor in the realm of finances with that of the Spanish monarchy, whose periodic declarations of bankruptcy left creditors grasping at air.

In 1598, Henry's Edict of Nantes made Catholicism the official religion of France. But it also granted the nation's 2 million Protestants (in a population of about 18.5 million) freedom of conscience. Huguenots now had the right to worship at home, to hold religious services and establish schools in specified towns—almost all in the southwest and west—and to maintain a number of fortified towns, with garrisons and ministers paid by the state. The Edict of Nantes also established chambers in the provincial parlements, or law courts dominated by nobles, to judge the cases of Protestants (see Map 4.1).

MAP 4.1 WARS OF RELIGION IN FRANCE IN THE SIXTEENTH CENTURY France at the time of the Edict of Nantes, 1598. The map indicates Catholic League provinces, Huguenot provinces, and neutral provinces during the wars of religion, as well as Huguenot and Catholic League towns and battle sites during the wars.

But careful to placate powerful sources of Catholic opposition, a series of secret decrees also promised Paris, Toulouse, and other staunchly Catholic towns that Protestant worship would be forbidden within their walls. The Edict of Nantes thus left the Protestants as something of a separate estate with specified privileges and rights, but still on the margin of French life. "What I have done is for the sake of peace," Henry stated emphatically. The former Catholic Leaguers howled in protest. By registering royal edicts, the parlements gave them the status of law. In this case, they only gradually and grudgingly registered the edict, which provided the Huguenots with more secure status than any other religious minority in Europe.

Many Huguenots, however, who found the Edict of Nantes unduly restrictive, distrusted the king who had abjured their religion on several occasions. Henry's foreign policy, which appeared pro-Protestant, supporting the Dutch rebels against Spain and certain German states against the Catholic Habsburgs, was, in fact, based on dynastic interests. But this support of Protestant rebels and princes made it impossible for Henry to consider further concessions to the Huguenots. Yet, the fact that Sully, a Protestant, rose to become the second most powerful man in France reassured some of them.

At the same time, the Catholic Reformation bore fruit in France. The Church benefited from a revival in organizational zeal and popularity. Henry allowed the Jesuits to return to France in 1604, a sign that religious tensions were ebbing, and he admitted several Italian religious orders.

With various would-be assassins trying to stab him, Henry had to think about an heir. He sought a papal annulment of his marriage to Margaret of Valois, whom he had not seen in eighteen years. While waiting, he prepared to marry one of his mistresses, but she died miscarrying their child. With the blessing of the Church, he then arranged to marry Marie de Medici (1573–1642), a distant relative of Catherine de Medici. This second marriage of convenience brought a sizable dowry that Henry used, in part, to pay off more international debts.

Henry's charismatic and somewhat contradictory personality has always attracted considerable interest. In contrast to the portraits he encouraged depicting him as Hercules or Apollo, or arrayed in a splendid white plume and a warrior's helmet, the king of France was extremely slovenly, sometimes wearing torn or ragged clothes. Henry gave off an odor as powerful as the air of his authority. He became renowned for his physical vigor on the battlefield and in his travels. He gambled large sums, with a notorious lack of success.

Although he knew nothing of music or poetry, and regularly fell asleep at the theater, Henry IV nonetheless was a patron of new architectural projects that added to the beauty of the city of Paris and imprinted his rule upon it. He oversaw the construction of the Great Gallery joining his residence in the Louvre Palace to the Tuileries in Paris. He ordered the construction of four quays facilitating the docking of boats along the Seine. He initiated the splendid Place Dauphine, ringed by buildings of elegant architecture on the west end of the island of Cité, at the point of which his equestrian statue now stands. And he orchestrated the construction of the Place Royale, with pavilions of symmetrical arcades, brick construction, and steeply inclining roofs in the northern architectural style. The new square lay close to the eastern edge of Paris, which was then near many noble residences.

Intelligent and well organized, Henry kept abreast of events throughout his vast kingdom. But he had little sense of protocol, often rushing out of the Louvre by himself as his guards scurried to catch up, once knocking down a messenger as he rushed out a side entrance. His wit was well known: when formally welcomed by a long-winded representative of the town of Amiens, who began "O most benign, greatest and most clement of kings," Henry interjected, "Add as well, the most tired of kings!" When a second spokesman began his official greeting, "Agesilaus, king of Sparta, Sire," Henry cut him short, "I too have heard of that Agesilaus, but he had eaten, and I have not."

Marie de Medici bore the constant burden of her husband's various infidelities and occasional bouts with gonorrhea. Henry produced six illegitimate children by three mistresses, to go with the three born to the queen. His nine offspring made up what he proudly referred to as his "herd." His ease was such that he formally introduced one of his mistresses to his wife, demanding that the latter repeat her curtsy so that she bow a bit lower, and the three dined together in what must have been an uncomfortable meal.

Statemaking

Henry IV laid the foundations for what would become the strongest power in seventeenth-century Europe. His reign was an exercise in early modern European statemaking as he reimposed royal authority throughout the realm. He made the monarchy more powerful by dispensing privilege, favors and, above all, money with a judiciousness that earned loyalty. Provincial governors represented the interests of the monarchy in the face of the privileges and resistance to taxes maintained by the provincial parlements and estates. The difficulties of extracting resources for the state were complicated by the division of the provinces into more peripheral "state provinces" (*pays d'état*) like Languedoc, Burgundy, and Provence, which had been recently added to the realm and retained more of their traditional privileges, and the "election provinces" (*pays d'élection*). In the former, the noble estates assessed and collected taxation; in the latter, royal officials assumed these functions. Henry was suspicious of any representative institutions, which he considered as threatening the exercise of royal authority. He never convoked the Estates-General after having done so in 1593.

Meanwhile, the nobles reaffirmed their own economic and social domination over their provinces. In 1609, Charles Loyseau, a lawyer, published a *Treatise on Orders and Simple Dignities* that portrayed French society as a hierarchy of orders, or three estates: the clergy, the nobility, and, lastly, everyone else. He portrayed the king as the guarantor of this organic society. Henry restored the hierarchy of social orders based upon rank and privilege while imposing his rule. But the boundaries between and within these estates were fairly fluid. A few newcomers even ascended into the highest rank of dukes and peers who stood above even the "nobles of the sword," the oldest and most powerful nobles traditionally called on by the monarchy to provide military support. The "nobles of the robe," while not a coherent or self-conscious group, were men who claimed noble status on the basis of high administrative and judicial office, for example in the parlements. Henry strengthened the social hierarchy by bolstering established institutions, including the parlements, the treasury, and universities, as well as, ultimately, the Catholic Church.

Conciliatory royal language began to disappear when it came to asking for money, however. Royal governors, whose influence had grown during the wars of the Catholic League, strengthened the monarchy at the expense of towns that prided themselves on their ancient privileges, further eroding their fiscal independence.

The royal privy council, some of whose members were chosen, like Sully, from the ranks of lesser nobles known for their competence and dedication, strengthened the effectiveness of state administration and foreign relations. The king personally oversaw this council, excluding troublesome nobles. Henry monitored the activities of his ambassadors and his court, whose 1,500 residents included the purveyors of perfume, of whom he might have made greater use.

Henry also took an intermittent interest in encouraging French manufacturing, particularly of silk and tapestries. To promote internal trade, the king encouraged investment in the construction of several canals linking navigable rivers. He was the first king to take an active interest in supporting a permanent French settlement in the New World, thereby increasing the prospects of French fishermen and trappers following Jacques Cartier's exploration of the St. Lawrence River in 1534. Samuel de Champlain founded the colony of Québec in 1608. This settlement became a base for further explorations by Champlain and those who followed him. Two years later, the first two French Jesuit missionaries arrived in what became known as New France.

On May 14, 1610, Henry set out from the Louvre in a carriage for Sully's residence, accompanied by horsemen and guards. The carriage became ensnared in traffic in central Paris. When some of the guards dashed forward to try to clear the way, a crazed monk named François Ravaillac jumped up to take revenge for the king's protection of Protestants. He stabbed the king three times, as Henry sat listening to a letter being read to him. Henry IV died before the carriage reached the Louvre.

Louis XIII and the Origins of Absolute Rule

Henry's sudden death left Marie de Medici, his widow, as regent for his young son, Louis XIII (ruled 1610–1643), who was eight years old at the time. Neither Philip III of Spain nor James I of England, nor any of the princes of the German states, were in a position to try to intervene in France on behalf of either Huguenots or Catholics. Marie put aside Henry's planned campaign against the Habsburgs and adopted a policy that considered Catholic powers to be friends.

Marie foiled several plots by nobles prepared against her in 1614–1616. The convocation of the Estates-General accentuated the eagerness of noble rivals to gain influence with the young king. One of them, Charles d'Albert, duke of Luynes, an expert falconer and flatterer who shared his passion for training hawks with the young king while using his position to enhance his family's fortune, convinced Louis to impose his own rule. The king ordered the murder of one of his mother's confidants; Louis then exiled his unpopular mother, hoping to restore calm. When a group of nobles took this as occasion to raise the standard of revolt, the king's army defeated them at Ponts-de-Cé near Angers in 1620. The royal army then defeated a revolt by Huguenot nobles in the southwest and west.

Emotionally, the stubborn, ill-tempered, and high-strung boy-king Louis XIII never really grew up. Throughout his life, he demonstrated the psychological burdens of having been regularly whipped as punishment, on his father's orders, on occasions when he was "stubborn or does something bad." His father's murder when he was young also marked him. As his father's body was carried up the stairs of the Louvre, the chubby eight-year-old had shouted, "Ha! If I had been there with my sword, I would have killed [the assassin]." Louis XIII's marriage to an Austrian princess began with a wedding-night fiasco that, whatever happened between the precocious young couple, led to a six-month period in which they did not even share a meal. Finally, things went better. After suffering several miscarriages, the queen produced an heir in 1638, but the royal couple was otherwise unhappy.

Louis XIII was intelligent, though not particularly interested in ideas. He preferred sketching and music, the latter calming him when he fell into a rage. He enjoyed hunting and winning at chess, once hurling the offending pieces at the head of a courtier who had the bad grace to checkmate him.

Louis could be modest and timid, a pious man who attended church every day. But he was invariably willful, ruthless, and cruel, lashing out savagely at his enemies; indeed, no other ruler of France had as many men

Cardinal Richelieu before the Sorbonne, which he founded.

executed as Louis XIII, including a number of nobles convicted of dueling, a practice that the king detested as symbolizing a possible threat to the royal monopoly on force and the possibility that nobles could raise private armies against the throne.

During Louis XIII's reign, Cardinal Armand Jean du Plessis de Richelieu (1585–1642) further centralized royal power, expanding the administrative authority and fiscal reach of the crown, dramatically increasing tax revenues. Richelieu's family, solidly entrenched in the west of France, had long served the monarchy in court, army, and church. Ordained bishop of Luçon, near the Protestant stronghold of La Rochelle, the gaunt, clever Richelieu staked his future on and won the patronage of the queen mother. He perfected the art of political survival during the court struggles of the next few years. Richelieu was a realist. His foreign and domestic policies reflected his *politique* approach to both. Although he was made a cardinal in 1622, he nonetheless always put reasons of state ahead of any consideration of religious principles.

In 1629, Richelieu prepared a long memorandum for his king. "If the King wants to make himself the most powerful monarch and the most highly esteemed prince in the world," he wrote, "he must consider before God, and examine carefully and secretly, with his faithful servants, what is needed in himself, and for the reform of the State. . . . [The Estates and the Parlements] which oppose the welfare of the kingdom by their pretended sovereignty must be humbled and disciplined. Absolute obedience to the King must be enforced upon great and small alike." Richelieu divided France into thirty-two districts (*généralités*), organizing and extending the king's authority. Officials called intendants governed each district, overseen by the king's council and ultimately responsible to the king himself.

In order to enhance the authority of the monarchy and the church, Richelieu turned his attention to the Huguenots. After forcing the surrender of insurgent Protestant forces at La Rochelle in 1628, he ordered the destruction of the Huguenot fortresses in the south and southwest, as well as the châteaux of other nobles whose loyalty he had reason to doubt.

During the Thirty Years' War (1618–1648), Louis XIII, influenced by Richelieu, reversed his mother's pro-Spanish foreign policy, returning to the traditional French position of opposition to the Habsburgs. The dynastic rivalry between the two powers proved greater than the fact that both kings were Catholic. Louis XIII thus surprised and outraged the Spanish king by joining England and the Dutch Republic, both Protestant powers, against the powerful Catholic Austrian Habsburgs during the Thirty Years' War. And in 1635, France declared war against Spain itself.

Richelieu's successes, however, did not stand well with his resentful enemies. His toleration of Huguenot worship drew the wrath of some Catholic nobles, as did continuing costly wars against the Catholic Habsburgs, which included French subsidies to Protestant Sweden. Revolts occurred in Dijon and Aix, both seats of provincial parlements, where local notables resented having to bow to the authority of royal officials.

One of the most conservative Catholic nobles, a royal minister, briefly turned the king against Richelieu. Marie de Medici, returned from brief disgrace, tried to convince her son to dismiss the cagey cardinal. The "Day of Dupes" (November 10, 1630) followed, which amounted to little more than a high-stakes family shouting match between Marie de Medici, Louis XIII, and Richelieu. Marie left thinking she had won the day, but awoke the next morning to find that the king had ordered her exile. The king's own brother led a second plot against Richelieu from 1641 to 1642, backed by the king of Spain.

After decades of religious wars, the assassination of Henry IV, and a fragile, temperamental young monarch around whom plots swirled, the monarchy of France had nonetheless been greatly strengthened. Louis XIII's sometimes decisive and brutal actions enhanced the reputation of the king who was known to many of his subjects as "The Just," whether fitting or not. A hypochondriac whose health was even worse than he feared, Louis XIII died of tuberculosis in 1643 at the age of forty-two. Philippe de Champagne's portrait of the king preserves his sad eyes and premature aging. But the man-child monarch had, with Richelieu, laid the foundations for absolute monarchical rule in France.

THE THIRTY YEARS' WAR (1618–1648)

In Central Europe, religious divisions led to the Thirty Years' War, a brutal conflict between the largely mercenary armies of Catholic and Protestant states that laid waste to the German states. Dynastic rivalries were never far from the stage, bringing the continental Great Powers into the fray.

When the war finally ended, the Treaty of Westphalia (1648) established a territorial and religious settlement that lasted until the French Revolution.

Factionalism in the Holy Roman Empire

The Holy Roman Empire was a loose confederation of approximately 1,000 German autonomous or semi-autonomous states. These states ranged in size from powerful Habsburg Austria to Hamburg, Lübeck, and other free cities in the north, and even smaller territories no more than a few square kilometers in size run by princes or bishops. It would have been almost impossible for a traveler to determine where one state stopped and another began had it not been for the frequent toll stations, which provided much of the revenue for each. The southwest German state of Swabia, for example, was divided between sixty-eight secular and forty ecclesiastical lords and included thirty-two free cities.

Geographic factors further complicated the political life of the German states. A few of the largest states included territories that were not contiguous. The Upper Palatinate lay squeezed between Bohemia and Bavaria; the Lower Palatinate lay far away in the Rhineland. The former was predominantly Lutheran, the latter Calvinist.

Since 1356, when the constitutional law of the Holy Roman Empire had been established, seven electors (four electoral princes and three archbishops) selected each new Holy Roman emperor. The empire's loose federal structure had a chancery to carry out foreign policy and negotiations with the various German princes. But only in confronting the threat of the Turks from the southeast did the German princes mount a consistent and relatively unified foreign policy.

Other institutions of the Holy Roman Empire also reflected the political complexity of Central Europe. An imperial Diet brought princes, nobles, and representatives of the town together when the emperor summoned them. An Imperial Court of Justice ruled on matters of importance to the empire. The Holy Roman Empire, once the most powerful force in Europe, had been weakened by its battles with the papacy in the thirteenth century. Yet, for some states the empire offered a balance between the desire for a figure of authority who could maintain law and order and continued political independence.

The Peace of Augsburg (1555), which ended the war between the Holy Roman Emperor Charles V and the Protestant German states, had stated that, with the exception of ecclesiastical states and the free cities, the religion of the ruler would be the religion of the land (cuius regio, eius religio). This formula, however, did not end religious rivalries, or the demands of religious minorities that rulers tolerate their beliefs. The Peace of Augsburg, in fact, reinforced German particularism. It also helped secularize the institutions of the Holy Roman emperor by recognizing the right of the German princes to determine the religion of their states.

The Origins of the Thirty Years' War

Rudolf II (1557–1612), king of Bohemia and Holy Roman emperor (he succeeded his father Maximilian II as Holy Roman emperor in 1576), wanted to launch a religious crusade against Protestantism. With that in mind, he closed Lutheran churches in 1578, reneging on an earlier promise to Bohemian nobles that he would tolerate the religion to which a good many of them had converted. Moreover, Rudolf's brother Archduke Ferdinand II (1578–1637) withdrew the religious toleration his father Maximilian II had granted in Inner Austria.

Rudolf's imperial army, which had been fighting the Turks on and off since 1593, had annexed Transylvania. The emperor moved against Protestants both there and in Hungary. But in 1605, when Rudolf's army undertook a campaign against the Turks in the Balkans, Protestants rebelled in both places. A Protestant army invaded Moravia, which lies east of Bohemia and north of Austria, close to the Habsburg capital of Vienna. In the meantime, Emperor Rudolf, only marginally competent on his best days (he was subject to depression and later to fits of insanity), lived as a recluse in his castle in Prague. His family convinced his brother Matthias (1557–1619) to act on Rudolf's behalf by making peace with the Hungarian and Transylvanian Protestants and with the Turks. This Peace of Vienna (1606) guaranteed religious freedom in Hungary. Matthias was then recognized as head of the Habsburgs and heir to Rudolf.

Rudolf II, Holy Roman emperor, surrounded by six electors. As king of Bohemia, he was the seventh elector.

Most everyone seemed pleased with the peace except poor Rudolf, who concluded that a murderous plague that was ravaging Bohemia was proof that God was displeased with the concessions he had been forced to grant Protestants. He denounced Matthias and Ferdinand for their accommodation with Protestants and with the Turkish "infidels." Matthias allied with the Protestant Hungarian noble Estates and marched against Rudolf, who surrendered. Rudolf ceded Hungary, Austria, and Moravia to Matthias in 1608, and Bohemia to him in 1611. Rudolf was forced to sign a "Letter of Majesty" in 1609 that granted Bohemians the right to choose between Catholicism, Lutheranism, or one of two groups of Hussites (see Chapter 3). Protestant churches, schools, and cemeteries were to be tolerated.

The decline in the effective authority of the Holy Roman emperor, after four centuries of power, contributed to the end of a period of relative peace in the German states. In the last decades of the sixteenth century, these states had become increasingly quarrelsome and militarized. "The dear old Holy Roman Empire," went one song, "How does it stay together?" Rulers of some member states began to undermine imperial political institutions by refusing to accept rulings by the Imperial Supreme Court and even to attend the occasional convocations of the Diet. "Imperial Military Circles," which were inter-state alliances responsible for defense of a number of states within the empire, had become moribund because of religious antagonisms between the member states.

For a time, the Catholic Reformation profited from acrimonious debates and even small wars between Lutherans and Calvinists. But increasingly Protestants put aside their differences, however substantial, in the face of Catholic determination to win back territories lost to Protestantism.

Acts of intolerance heated up religious rivalries. In 1606, in Donauwörth, a south German imperial free city in which Lutherans held the upper hand and Catholics enjoyed toleration, a riot began when Protestants tried to prevent Catholics from holding a procession. The following year, Duke Maximilian of Bavaria sent troops to assure Catholic domination. This angered Calvinist princes in the region, as well as some Lutheran sovereigns. The imperial Diet, convoked two years later, broke up in chaos when Holy Roman Emperor Rudolf II refused to increase Protestant representation in the Diet. The political crisis now spread further when some of the German Catholic states sought Spanish intervention in a dispute over princely succession in the small Catholic territories of Cleves-Jülich, which Henry IV of France threatened to invade. In 1609, Catholic German princes organized a Catholic League, headed by Maximilian of Bavaria. Six Protestant princes then signed a defensive alliance, the Protestant Union, against the Catholic League.

Matthias, who had been elected Holy Roman emperor in 1612, wanted to make the Catholic League an institution of Habsburg will. He also hoped to woo Lutherans from the Protestant Union, which was dominated by the Calvinists. But Matthias' obsession with Habsburg dynastic ambitions, his history of having fought with the Protestant Dutch rebels against Spain, and his opportunistic toleration of Lutheranism cost him the confidence of some Catholic princes. Archduke Ferdinand, ruler of Inner Austria, waited in the wings to lead a Catholic crusade against Protestantism. Ferdinand, who had inherited the throne of Hungary in 1617 and that of Bohemia in 1618, became Holy Roman emperor upon Matthias' death in 1619. Ferdinand was a pious man who had been educated by the Jesuits and whose every decision followed consultation with his confessor, who convinced him that he could save his soul only by launching a war of religion. In the meantime, Protestant resistance in Bohemia mobilized, seeking Protestant assistance from Transylvania and the Palatinate.

Conflict in Bohemia

In Bohemia, Ferdinand, backed by many nobles, imposed significant limitations on Protestant worship. In Prague, Calvinists and Lutherans, including university professors and students and members of literary societies, began to look outside of Bohemia for potential support from Protestant princes. Protestant leaders convoked an assembly of the Estates of Bohemia, citing rights specified by Rudolf's "Letter of Majesty" of 1609, and petitioned Emperor Matthias to order the withdrawal of the repressive dictates. Ferdinand ordered the assembly to disband.

Following the Defenestration of Prague in 1618, Protestant leaders established a provisional government in Bohemia. "This business of Bohemia is likely to put all Christendom in combustion," predicted the English ambassador to the Dutch capital of Amsterdam. It began a destructive war between Catholic and Protestant forces that would last thirty years, lay waste to many of the German states, and finally bring a religious and territorial settlement that would last for two centuries.

Bohemia rose in full revolt against not only the Church but the Habsburg dynasty as well. With almost no assistance from the nobles, the rebels turned to the Protestant Union, promising the Bohemian crown to Frederick, the young Calvinist elector of the Palatinate and the most important Protestant prince in Central Europe. But in their desperate quest for support, the Bohemian Protestants attempted to woo three other rulers with exactly the same promise. In 1619, the Estates offered Frederick the crown. He accepted, saying this was "a divine calling which I must not disobey."

The Protestant cause, like that of the Catholics, became increasingly internationalized and tied to dynastic considerations (see Map 4.2). After his brother died in 1619, the Catholic Archduke Ferdinand received enough votes from electors to become Holy Roman Emperor Ferdinand II. He then learned that Protestant rebels had refused to recognize his authority in Bohemia and had offered his throne to Frederick. Even more deter-

MAP 4.2 THE THIRTY YEARS' WAR, 1618–1648   Protestant and Catholic armies clashed in battles that ranged back and forth across Europe.

mined to drive Protestants from his realm but lacking an army, Ferdinand turned to outside help. The Catholic king of Spain agreed to send troops he could ill afford; the price of his intervention was the promise of the cession of the Rhineland state of the Lower Palatinate to Spain. The Catholic Maximilian I of Bavaria also sent an army, expecting to be rewarded for his trouble with the Upper Palatinate and with Frederick's title of elector in the Holy Roman Empire.

The Expansion of the Conflict

In the meantime, Protestant armies marched on Vienna, the Habsburg capital, and laid siege to it. The Catholic armies lifted this siege in 1619. Had news of this not been so slow to reach Spain, Philip III of Spain might have changed his mind about intervention. But with Spanish armies and monies already on the way, the internationalization of the Bohemian crisis had reached the point of no return. The Dutch could not provide assistance, as they were fighting for independence from Spain. Several of the German Protestant states also declined, fearing Catholic rebellions in their own lands.

During a short-lived truce brought about by the arrival of a seemingly neutral French army in 1620, the Catholic League raised a largely Bavarian army of 30,000 troops. Count Johannes von Tilly (1559–1632) commanded the Catholic forces. The depressed, indecisive count from Flanders managed to subdue Upper Austria and then defeated the main Protestant Union army at the brief but significant Battle of White Mountain, near Prague in November 1620. With the Catholic forces now holding Bohemia, Tilly's army then overran Silesia, Moravia, Austria, and part of the Upper Palatinate. The extent of the Catholic victory expanded the war, increasing the determination of the Catholic League to crush all Protestant resistance and, at the same time, of the Protestant forces to resist at all costs.

Frederick fought on, counting on help from France and other states who had reason to fear an expansion of Habsburg power in Central Europe. He also hoped to convince James I of England that a victory of the Catholic League would threaten Protestantism. But the English king had placed his hopes on the marriage of his son, Charles, to the sister of Philip IV of Spain (who had succeeded Philip III in 1621), an alliance that might bring about a diplomatic settlement to the complicated crisis (see Chapter 6). Again dynastic rivalries outweighed those of religion.

The war went on, with Tilly's army winning a series of small victories and a Spanish victory in 1622 over the Dutch at Jülich in the Rhineland eliminating any possibility of English armed assistance to Frederick through Holland. For the moment, Frederick's only effective force was a plundering mercenary horde in northeastern Germany. Tilly's victory over a Protestant army in 1623 and conquest of most of the Palatinate forced Frederick to abandon his claims to Bohemia's throne after having been king for all of one winter. But encouraged by the renewed possibility of English assistance, after James' plans for the marriage of his son to the Spanish princess fell through, Frederick turned north to Scandinavia for assistance.

The Danish Period

Christian IV (ruled 1588–1648), Protestant king of Denmark, had ambition and money, but not a great deal of sense. Also duke of the northern German state of Holstein, the gambling, hard-drinking Dane wanted to extend his influence and perhaps even territories in the northern German states. Frederick's difficulties seemed to offer the Danish sovereign the opportunity of a lifetime. In 1625, he led his troops into the northern German states, confident that the English and the Dutch, and perhaps the French as well, would rush to follow his leadership against the Habsburgs.

But King James I of England had died, succeeded by Charles I, who was even more beset than his father by opposition to his policies. Moreover, Louis XIII of France, who was besieging Protestants at La Rochelle in France, provided the Danes with only a modest subsidy to aid the fight against the Habsburgs. England and the Netherlands did no more than send some money and a few thousand soldiers to help the Danish king. Christian, essentially left to his own devices, was unaware of the approach of a large imperial army commanded by one of the most intriguing figures of the age of religious wars.

Albert Wallenstein (1583–1634) was a tall, gaunt Bohemian noble who, after marrying a wealthy widow, had risen to even greater fortune as a supplier of armies. Raised a Lutheran, he converted to Catholicism at age twenty and became the most powerful of the Catholic generals. The fact that a convert could rise to such a powerful position again reveals how a religious war evolved into not only a dynastic struggle between the rulers of France, Spain, and Austria, as well as Sweden and Denmark, but also into an unprincipled free-for-all in which mercenary soldiers of fortune played a major part. Wallenstein, an ardent student of astrology, was ambitious, ruthless, and possessed a violent temper. His abhorrence of noise was obsessive, and odd, for a military person. Because he detested the sound of barking or meowing, he sometimes ordered all dogs and cats killed upon arriving in a town, and forbade the townspeople and his soldiers from wearing heavy boots or spurs or anything else that would make noise. He alternated between extreme generosity and horrible cruelty, and was always accompanied by an executioner awaiting his master's command. Wallenstein, entrusted by Ferdinand with raising and commanding as army drawn from myriad nationalities fighting for the Catholic cause, marched north with 30,000 men.

Tilly defeated the Danes in 1626, aided by some of Wallenstein's mercenaries and King Christian's inept generalship. The Catholic army then marched to the Baltic coast and crossed into Denmark, devastating Jutland. But Wallenstein's successes engendered opposition within the Catholic states. Furthermore, his troops devastated the lands of friend and foe alike, extracting money and food, plundering, selling military commands to any buyer, including criminals.

Christian, who had spent much of his personal fortune and bankrupted his kingdom during this ill-fated excursion, signed a peace treaty in 1629 (the Treaty of Lübeck) whereby he withdrew from the war and gave up his claims in northern Germany. The treaty was less draconian than it might have been because the seemingly endless war was wearing heavily on some of the Catholic German states. They feared an expansion of Habsburg power, and some of them did not want to add Protestants to their domains.

The Danish king lost no territory in Denmark (although he did surrender his claims to several northern German bishoprics), but he agreed that he would never again interfere in the affairs of the Holy Roman emperor.

Ferdinand II now implemented measures against Protestants without convoking the imperial Diet. He expelled from Bohemia Calvinist and Lutheran ministers and nobles who refused to convert to Catholicism and ennobled anyone he wanted, including foreigners, as a means of assuring Catholic domination. He confiscated the property of nobles suspected of participating in any phase of the Protestant rebellion. With Frederick's Palatinate electorship now transferred to Maximilian I of Bavaria, the Habsburgs could count on the fact that a majority of the electors were Catholic princes. Captured Habsburg dispatches in 1628 made clear that Ferdinand sought to destroy the freedom of the Protestant Hanseatic cities in the north in the interest of expanding the Habsburg domains. These revelations alarmed Louis XIII of France.

Ferdinand found that it was not easy to impose Catholicism in territories where it had not been practiced for decades. In the Upper Palatinate, the first priests who came to celebrate Mass there were unable to find a chalice. Until the 1640s, half of the parishes in Bohemia were without clergy. Italian priests brought to Upper Austria could not be understood by their parishioners, some of whom rebelled against their authority and were executed on the emperor's command. The Edict of Restitution (1629) allowed Lutherans—but not Calvinists, who were few in number in the German states except in the Palatinate—to practice their religion in certain cities, but ordered them to return all monasteries and convents acquired

Protestant caricature showing two devils vomiting parish priests and Jesuits into Augsburg, which was forcibly converted to Catholicism in 1629.

after 1552, when signatories of the Peace of Augsburg had first gathered. Because the Edict of Restitution also gave rulers the right to enforce the practice of their religion within their territories, the war went on.

The Swedish Interlude

In the meantime, England, the Dutch Republic, the northern German state of Brandenburg, and the Palatinate asked the Lutheran King Gustavus Adolphus (ruled 1611–1632) of Sweden, a kingdom of barely a million inhabitants, to intervene on the Protestant side. The possibility of expanding Swedish territory was more than Gustavus, who had an adventurer's disposition, could resist.

Gustavus, the "Lion of the North," who survived shipwreck at the age of five, had been tutored in the art of war by mercenary soldiers. He also played the flute, composed poetry, and conversed in ten languages. The Dutch ambassador described him as "slender of figure, well set up, with rather a pale complexion, a long-shaped face, fair hair, and a pointed beard which here and there runs into a tawny color." Gustavus retained, as did a disproportionate number of rulers in his century, a violent temper. Once, coming upon two stolen cows outside an officer's tent, he dragged the thief by the ear to the executioner. His courage was legendary; he barely paused as cannonballs exploded nearby and as his horses were shot out from under him or fell through the ice.

Gustavus, influenced by an appreciation of Roman military tactics, formed his battle lines thinner—about six men deep—than those of rival commanders. This allowed battle lines to be more widely spread out; the king personally demonstrated to his men the proper way of firing in such a formation. Gustavus organized his army into brigades of four squadrons with nine cannon to protect them, sending the unit into battle in an arrow-shaped formation. Superior artillery served his cause well, hurling larger shot further and more accurately than that of his enemies.

The dashing young Swedish king subdued Catholic Poland with his army of about 70,000 men. Swedish intervention and the continuing woes of Spain, at war in the Alps, Italy, and the Netherlands, now gave Protestants reason for hope. After defeating a combined Polish and Habsburg army in 1629, Swedish troops occupied Pomerania along the Baltic Sea.

In 1630, sure of a Catholic majority, Emperor Ferdinand convoked the imperial electors to recognize his son as his heir. He also wanted them to support his promise to aid Spain against the Dutch in exchange for Spanish assistance against the Protestant armies. But the electors of Saxony and Brandenburg, both Protestants, refused even to attend the gathering. Catholic electors demanded that the powerful Wallenstein be dismissed; even the king of Spain feared the general's powerful ragtag army. Ferdinand thereby dismissed the one man whose accomplishments and influence might have enabled the Habsburg monarchy to master all of the German states.

King Gustavus Adolphus of Sweden in battle.

Despite a sizable subsidy from the king of France, Gustavus Adolphus enjoyed only the support of several tiny Protestant states. Some Lutheran German states still hoped to receive territorial concessions from the Habsburgs. The Catholic dynasty preferred Lutherans to Calvinists, viewing the latter as more radical reformers. Ferdinand now sent Tilly to stop the invading Swedes. He besieged the Protestant city of Magdeburg in Brandenburg, forcing its surrender in 1631. The subsequent massacre of the population and accompanying pillage had a similar effect as the Defenestration of Prague; the story of the atrocities spread across Europe. Protestant Brandenburg and Saxony now allied with Sweden.

That same year, the combined Protestant forces under Gustavus Adolphus defeated Tilly's imperial Catholic army at Breitenfeld near Leipzig. The Swedish army, swollen by German mercenaries, then marched through the northern German states, easily reversing Habsburg gains over the previous twelve years.

The expansion of Swedish power generated anxiety among both Protestant and Catholic states. Louis XIII now worried about the further expansion of Swedish power, which it had helped finance. In Bavaria, the Swedes defeated Tilly, who was killed in battle (1632). The rout of the Catholic imperial forces seemed complete. Spain, its interests spread too far afield in Europe and the Americas, could not then afford to help. The plague prevented another Catholic army from being raised in Italy; even the pope begged off a request for help by complaining that the eruption of Mount Vesuvius was preventing the collection of taxes. Upon learning that the Swedes had taken yet another city, an imperial official wrote, "We cry 'Help, Help!', but there is nobody there!"

In April 1632, Ferdinand turned once again to Wallenstein to save the Catholic cause, the latter agreeing to raise a new imperial army in return for almost unlimited authority over it. Wallenstein reconquered Silesia and Bohemia. Against him, Gustavus led the largest army (175,000) that had ever been under a single command in Europe. Although reason dictated that the Swedish army should dig in for the winter of 1632, Gustavus took a chance by attacking Wallenstein in the fog at Lützen in Saxony in November. The two sides fought to a bloody draw, but a draw amounted to a Catholic victory. Gustavus fell dead in the battle, facedown in the mud, shot in the arm, back, and head.

Wallenstein's days also were numbered. His new army had accomplished little, and was now living off the land in Central Europe, engendering peasant resistance. Furthermore, Wallenstein, who was ill, demanded command of a Spanish army that had subsequently arrived to help the Catholic forces. In the meantime, it became known that Wallenstein had considered joining Gustavus after the Battle of Breitenfeld in 1631, and that he was offering his services to both France and the German Protestants. Ferdinand dismissed Wallenstein for the final time, and then ordered his murder. In February 1634, an Irish mercenary crept into Wallenstein's room, speared him, wrapped his body in a rug, and hauled it down the stairs for all to see.

With the aid of the remnants of Wallenstein's forces, the Spanish army defeated the combined Swedish and German Protestant army in 1634 in the southern German state of Swabia. The elector of Saxony abandoned the Protestant struggle, making peace in 1635 with Ferdinand. One by

The assassination of Wallenstein, 1634.

one, other Protestant princes also left the war. The Catholic forces now held the upper hand.

The Armies of the Thirty Years' War

The Thirty Years' War was certainly one of the cruelest episodes in the history of warfare. A contemporary described the horror of the seemingly endless brutalities that afflicted Central Europe: "[The soldiers] stretched out a hired man flat on the ground, stuck a wooden wedge in his mouth to keep it open, and emptied a milk bucket full of stinking manure droppings down his throat—they called it a Swedish cocktail. . . . Then they used thumb-screws, which they cleverly made out of their pistols, to torture the peasants. . . . They put one of the captured hayseeds in the bakeoven and lighted a fire in it. . . . I can't say much about the captured wives, hired girls, and daughters because the soldiers did not let me watch their doings. But I do remember hearing pitiful screams in various dark corners."

Several factors may have contributed to the barbarity of soldiers during the Thirty Years' War. Mercenaries and volunteers were usually fighting far from home, knowing they had to live off the land to survive. Strident propaganda against other religions may have contributed to the brutality. In response, Gustavus Adolphus and other leaders, however, imposed harsh penalties, including execution, for atrocities, not wanting to so frighten the local population that ordinary channels of provisioning the army would disappear.

During the Thirty Years' War, at least a million men took arms. The size of the armies was enormous for the time. Even Sweden, where there was no fighting, felt the impact of the death of at least 50,000 soldiers between 1621 and 1632 from battle wounds and, more often, disease. Yet, considering the number of troops engaged in the long war, relatively few soldiers perished in battle, particularly when compared to those who succumbed to illness and to civilians who died at the hands of marauding troops. Armies came and went through the German states, Catholic and Protestant, speaking many languages, taking what they wanted, burning and looting. Marburg was occupied eleven different times. Atrocity followed atrocity.

The armies themselves remained ragtag forces, lacking discipline and accompanied by, in some cases, the families of soldiers. Given the practice of armies living off the land, the safest place was in the train of an army. The presence of large numbers of women (including many prostitutes) and children as camp followers may have contributed to the length of the war, making life in the army seem more normal for soldiers.

Although Gustavus ordered that troops "provide themselves with proper attire instead of their long smocks and peasant attire" so that people would judge them well, the reality was quite the opposite. Soldiers, for the most part, wore what they could find. Some, if they were lucky, had leather clothes, carried rain cloaks against the damp German climate, and wore

Soldiers pillaging a farmhouse during the Thirty Years' War. Note the farmer being tortured over his hearth to reveal where he has hidden money, while other soldiers rape the women and steal the food.

felt hats. Some Habsburg troops sported uniforms of pale gray, at least at the beginning of a campaign. As the months passed, and uniforms disintegrated, soldiers were forced to disrobe the dead, friend and foe alike, or to steal from civilians. At best, soldiers wore symbols indicating their regiment and fought behind banners bearing the colors of the army—thus the expression "show your colors." The Swedes wore a yellow band around their hats. The imperial forces placed red symbols in their hats, plumes, or sashes if they could find them.

Drawn from a bewildering number of nationalities, most armies also lacked a common language. The Habsburg army included Saxons, Bavarians, Westphalians, Austrians; Maximilian's Bavarian army counted Germans, Italians, Poles, Slovenes, Croats, Greeks, Hungarians, Burgundians, French, Czechs, Spaniards, Scots, Irish, and Turks.

Some soldiers may have joined regiments because they were searching for adventure; others joined out of religious conviction. Yet, a multitude of soldiers fought against armies of their own religion. Some states and armies changed sides when a better opportunity arose. Army recruiters gave religion not the slightest thought in their search for soldiers to fill quotas for which they were being handsomely paid. In any case, recruits on both sides were attracted by the strong possibility that they would be better clothed and fed—bread, meat, lots of beer, and occasionally some butter and cheese—than they were at the time they joined up.

The Wars of Religion and Dynastic Struggles (1635–1648)

Between 1635 and 1648, what had begun as a religious war became a dynastic struggle between two Catholic states, France and Habsburg Austria, the former allied with Sweden, the latter with Spain. France declared war on Philip IV of Spain in 1635. Richelieu had planned for the struggle for some time, hoping to force Habsburg armies away from the borders of France. He took as a pretext the Spanish arrest of a French ally, the elector of Trier. Alliances with the Dutch Republic and Sweden had prepared the way, as did reassurances given by neighboring Savoy and Lorraine, and by French protectorates in Alsace.

The French incursions into the Netherlands and the southern German states did not go well. Louis XIII's army found itself short on capable commanders and battle-experienced troops, largely because France was already fighting in Italy, the Pyrenees, the Netherlands, and the northern German states. But France's involvement, like that of Sweden before it, did provide the Protestant states with some breathing room. French forces joined the Swedish army, helping defeat the imperial army in Saxony.

The wars went on. When the pope called for representatives of the Catholic and Protestant states to assemble in Cologne for a peace congress in 1636, no one showed up. Four years later, another combined French and Swedish force defeated the Habsburg army. Maximilian I of Bavaria then sought a separate peace with France. Devastating Spanish defeats in northern France in 1643, as well as in the Netherlands and the Pyrenees, and the outbreak of rebellions inside Spain, left the Austrian Habsburgs with no choice but to make peace.

At the same time, unrest in France, including plots against Richelieu, and the English Civil War, which began in 1642, served to warn other rulers of the dangers that continued instability could bring. The Swedish population was tiring of distant battles that brought home nothing but news of casualties. In the German states, calls for peace echoed in music, plays, marketplace, and song. Lutheran ministers, in particular, began to inveigh against the war from the pulpit. Among the rulers of the great powers, only Louis XIII, hoping to help further diminish his Habsburg rival's power, wanted the war to go on. He helped subsidize an invasion of Hungary by Transylvanian Protestants in 1644. As Swedish and Transylvanian forces prepared to besiege the imperial capital of Vienna, Ferdinand III (ruled 1637–1657), who had succeeded his father, concluded a peace treaty with the prince of Transylvania. The Holy Roman emperor promised to tolerate Protestantism in Hungary. After Habsburg armies suffered further defeats in 1645, Ferdinand realized that he had to make peace and offered an amnesty to princes within the empire who had fought against him.

The preliminaries for a general peace agreement had begun in 1643 and dragged on even as a Franco-Swedish army drove the imperial army out of the Rhineland and Bavaria in 1647. Following another French victory early in 1648, only the outbreak of the Fronde, a rebellion of nobles against the king's authority in France, forced the young Louis XIV to seek peace.

The Treaty of Westphalia (1648)

The Treaty of Westphalia was unlike any previous peace settlement in history, which had invariably been between two or three states, rarely more. Its framers believed that they could restore international stability and diplomatic process in a Europe torn by anarchy by eliminating religious divisions as a cause of conflict. The treaty proved almost as complicated as the Thirty Years' War itself. Two hundred heads of state converged in Westphalia. Thousands of diplomats and other officials shuttled back and forth between two towns. Letters took ten to twelve days to reach the courts of Paris and Vienna, at least twenty to Stockholm, and a month to arrive in Madrid. In the meantime, the French tried to delay any treaty, hoping to force Spain to surrender. In the summer of 1648, the Swedes reoccupied Bohemia, hoping to win a larger indemnity and toleration for the Lutherans. When by the separate Treaty of Münster Spain finally formally recognized the *fait accompli* of Dutch independence, the Spanish Army of Flanders fought against France in a last-ditch effort to help Ferdinand III. In August 1648, a French army defeated a Spanish force a month after the Swedes had captured part of Prague. His back to the wall, Ferdinand signed the peace treaty, finally concluded on October 24, 1648.

The Treaty of Westphalia did not end the war between Spain and France, but it did end the wars of the German states. Sweden absorbed West Pomerania and the bishoprics of Verden and Bremen on the North Sea (see Map 4.3). France, by an agreement signed two years earlier, annexed the frontier towns of Metz, Toul, and Verdun, and parts of Alsace. Maximilian I of Bavaria kept the Upper Palatinate, and therefore the status of elector. Frederick's Protestant son ended up with the Lower, or Rhine Palatinate, and was restored to the status of elector. With this addition of an elector, eight votes would now be necessary to elect the Holy Roman emperor.

With minor exceptions, the territorial settlement reached in Westphalia remained in place until the French Revolution. For the most part, the treaty ended wars of religion in early modern Europe. The Treaty of Westphalia reinforced the strong autonomous traditions of the German states, which emerged from the long nightmare with more independence from the Holy Roman Empire, which was considerably weakened. Member states thereafter could carry out their own foreign policy, though they could not form alliances against the empire. The Habsburg dynasty's dream of forging a centralized empire of states fully obedient to the emperor's will had failed, although the emperor emerged from the wars with more control over most of Austria. Bohemia lost its independence. Bohemian Protestant landowners recovered neither their lands nor their religious freedom.

By the Treaty of Westphalia, German Calvinists gained the same rights as those previously granted to Lutherans. The settlement granted religious

MAP 4.3 EUROPE AFTER THE TREATY OF WESTPHALIA, 1648   The treaty ended the Thirty Years' War.

toleration where it had existed in 1624. But it also confirmed the Peace of Augsburg's establishment of territorial churches—Catholic, Lutheran, or Calvinist—still to be determined by the religion of the ruler. Sects were often forbidden, and their followers were persecuted. Generally speaking, Lutheranism remained dominant in the northern half of the Holy Roman Empire, Catholicism in the southern half, with many Calvinists in the Rhineland.

Before his death in battle, Gustavus Adolphus noted "all the wars of Europe are now blended into one." More than 200 states of varying sizes had fought in the war. The devastation brought by thirty years of war is simply incalculable. Catholic Mainz, occupied by the Swedes, lost 25 percent of its buildings and 40 percent of its population. In four years, the predominantly Protestant duchy of Württemberg lost three-quarters of its population while occupied by imperial troops. Almost 90 percent of the farms of Mecklenburg were abandoned during the course of the war. Many villages in Central Europe were now uninhabited. Although devastation varied from region to region, German cities lost a third and the countryside two-fifths of their population during the Thirty Years' War. Central Europe, like the rest of the continent, may have already been suffering from the economic and social crisis that had begun in the 1590s. But the wars contributed to the huge decline of the population of the states of the Holy Roman Empire from 20 to 16 million people during the ghastly period of the wars of religion.

A year before the Treaty of Westphalia, a Swabian family reflected on the Thirty Years' War when one of them wrote in their Bible: "They say that the terrible war is now over. But there is still no sign of peace. Everywhere there is envy, hatred and greed; that's what the war has taught us. . . . We live like animals, eating bark and grass. No one could have imagined that anything like this would happen to us. Many people say there is no God . . . but we still believe that God has not abandoned us."

War was not alone in taking lives: epidemics, the worst of which was the bubonic plague, and other diseases, including influenza and typhus, also took fearsome tolls. This was chiefly so in towns, which were often clogged with starving and therefore more vulnerable refugees from the fighting and marauding. The flight of many peasants from their land reduced agricultural productivity. Relatively little fighting took place in the northwestern German states, so there, at least, less devastation occurred. On the other hand, Mecklenburg and Pomerania, among other states that endured considerable fighting and the coming and going of armies, lost about half of their populations. It would be decades before the German states recovered from the Thirty Years' War.

If much of the religious settlement of the Treaty of Westphalia and the reinforcement of German particularism would prove enduring, dynastic rivalries were hardly at an end. France had emerged from its religious wars with a stronger monarchy; Louis XIII had made his state more centralized

Seventeenth-century Dutch allegory of peasant impoverishment. His home ravished by war and weighed down by the needs of his family, this man wandered the countryside, seeking only to survive.

and powerful. France's rivals, too, would extend their authority within their own states. In the mid-seventeeth century, Europe would enter the era of monarchical absolutism. The most powerful European states, above all Louis XIV's France, would enter a period of aggressive territorial expansion. Dynastic wars would help shape the European experience from the mid-seventeenth century to the French Revolution of 1789.

PART TWO
STATEMAKING

During the last half of the fifteenth century, the balance of economic and political power in Europe began to shift away from the Mediterranean region and the Italian city-states. The discovery and then colonization of the Americas contributed greatly to the development of the Atlantic economy, adding to the strength of Spain and England, transporting their rivalry across the Atlantic Ocean. The surprising English naval victory over the Spanish Armada in 1588 symbolized the subsequent shift in power from Southern to Northern Europe.

In the seventeenth century, when aggressive European monarchs were running roughshod over noble prerogatives and town privileges, England and the Dutch Republic maintained representative government. The English Civil War led to the defeat and execution of the king in 1649, the fall of the monarchy, and in 1688, to the "Glorious Revolution," which affirmed the civil liberties of English people and the rights of Parliament. In the largely Protestant Netherlands, which earned its independence after a protracted struggle against Catholic Spain, the prosperous merchants retained a republican form of government and helped generate the golden age of Dutch culture. In contrast, many European rulers relentlessly extended their power between 1650 and 1750, becoming absolute rulers. In principle, they were above all challenge from within the state itself, affecting the lives of more people than ever before through taxation, military service, and the royal quest for religious orthodoxy.

CHAPTER 5

THE RISE OF THE ATLANTIC ECONOMY: SPAIN AND ENGLAND

Protestant England and Catholic Spain, opposed in religion, commerce, and alliances, drifted toward a war neither could afford. In 1585, England went to war with Spain. In July 1588, after three years of preparation, the Spanish Armada, 130 ships and 30,000 men strong, sailed through the English Channel. King Philip II of Spain had ordered the duke of Medina Sidonia, the king's Captain-General of the Ocean Sea, to meet up with Spanish forces waiting in Flanders for a planned invasion of England. The Armada's commander was an austere aristocrat of great wealth and good sense but with no experience in battle and little idea of how his enormous fleet might meet up with the Spanish army.

On July 30, English watchers on the cliffs above the English Channel first caught sight of the supposedly invincible Spanish fleet. On the night of August 7, the English fleet attacked Philip II's Armada in battles along the English coast. After the Armada anchored near Calais, the English sent ships set on fire against the Armada, which caused the Spanish ships to break their tight tactical formation. With the help of strong winds, the English then pinned the Spanish ships against the shore, and destroyed six Spanish ships in the longest and most intense artillery battle that had yet occurred at sea, much of it at such close range that the sailors could hurl insults at each other. Superior English cannon, shot, and gunners took their toll on the Armada. More than 1,000 Spaniards died during the long battle that day. The captain of one ship that had failed to answer the flag-ship's call for help was hanged from a yardarm, and his body was hauled from ship to ship to reestablish discipline.

The English ships failed to follow up their advantage, however, letting the fighting Spanish galleons escape. The rough winds of the Channel carried the Spanish ships away from the dangerous Flemish shoals toward the

The English defeat of the Spanish Armada, 1588.

North Sea and a long, northern voyage up to the straits between the Orkney and Shetland Islands, in order to head back to the safety of Spanish ports. More than 30 Spanish ships sank in gales off the western coasts of Scotland and Ireland. When some of the ships of the Armada limped into port in Spain, Medina Sidonia wrote King Philip II, "I am unable to describe to Your Majesty the misfortunes and miseries that have befallen us, because they are the worst that have been known on any voyage; and some of the ships that put into this port have spent the last fourteen days without a single drop of water." Of the 130 ships that had sailed against England, only 60 could now be accounted for. At least a third had been sunk or wrecked, and many others were severely damaged.

Victory over the Spanish Armada accentuated England's rise to international dominance, enormously boosting English self-confidence. With English armies crushing an Irish rebellion in 1595, fears of an effective Irish alliance with Catholic Spain ended. Despite the defeat of the Spanish Armada, however, Philip did not make peace with England, and the war between the two nations dragged on until 1604. The surprising English naval victory over the Spanish Armada symbolized a shift in power from Southern to Northern Europe, although Spain remained militarily stronger until the 1630s.

ECONOMIC EXPANSION

The rise of England and Spain must be seen in the context of the sixteenth-century expansion of the European economy. By 1450, the European population had begun to recover slowly from the Black Death, the murderous plague that had swept the continent a century earlier. In general, the population continued to rise until the mid-seventeenth century, when religious and dynastic wars and new plagues led to such devastation that the period has become known as "the age of crisis." These cataclysms particularly struck Central Europe. But the Mediterranean region, too, suffered population decline.

During the 1600s, the commercial and manufacturing center of Europe shifted from the Mediterranean to Northwestern Europe. By 1700, Venice which alone among the Italian city-states had managed to retain significant trade links with Asia, had become a virtual backwater because it had failed to adapt to the global economy that was expanding across the Atlantic Ocean to the Americas. Spain, then France, England, and (after its long, successful war of independence from Spain) the Dutch United Provinces emerged as powers in the late sixteenth century as they explored new trade routes to Asia.

Spain's preeminence did not survive the end of the seventeenth-century economic crisis, however. Its merchants lacked the flexibility shown by the English and Dutch to adjust to varying demand for colonial products such as pepper and to create new trading opportunities. Furthermore, merchants in Amsterdam and London, not those in the Spanish city of Seville, expanded trade by using innovative commercial techniques. Spanish merchants proved less able than their northern rivals to lower costs of transportation from the New World. In contrast, English textile merchants found new markets in Spain and the Mediterranean for their cloth, which they could produce less expensively.

Increased Agricultural Productivity

Populations cannot grow unless the rural economy can produce enough additional food to feed more people. During the sixteenth century, farmers brought more land into cultivation at the expense of forests and fens (marsh lands) in order to supply a growing population. Moreover, Dutch land reclamation in the Netherlands in the sixteenth and seventeenth centuries provides the most spectacular example of the expansion of farm land; the Dutch reclaimed more than 36,000 acres between 1590 and 1615 alone. Modest agricultural progress was, however, limited to Western Europe. In Russia and Eastern Europe, hundreds of thousands of serfs who were legally bound to the land labored to produce enough grain to feed the masses of population and to generate a surplus that their lords could sell to Western European traders.

Much of the potential for European economic development lay in what at first glance would seem to have been only sleepy villages. Such villages, however, generally lay in regions of relatively advanced agricultural production, permitting not only the survival of peasants but the accumulation of an agricultural surplus for investment. They had access to urban merchants, markets, and trade routes.

Rural industry was an intrinsic part of the expansion of industry. Although at the end of the seventeenth century one textile enterprise in France brought some 1,700 workers together in the same place, woolens and textile manufacturers, in particular, utilized rural cottage (domestic) production, which took advantage of cheap and plentiful rural labor. In the German states, the ravages of the Thirty Years' War further moved textile production into the countryside. Members of poor peasant families spun or wove cloth and linens at home for scant remuneration in an attempt to supplement meager family income. Organizational change within industry remained far more important than technological innovation in the growth of manufacturing. This was also true in the growth of state-sponsored industry—for example, arms production and naval shipbuilding.

Expansion of Trade

More extended trading networks helped develop Europe's economy. English and Dutch ships carrying rye from the Baltic states reached England, the Netherlands, Spain, and Portugal. Population growth generated an expansion of small-scale manufacturing, particularly handicrafts, textiles, and metallurgy in England, Flanders, parts of northern Italy, the southwestern German states, and in some of Spain. Only iron smelting and mining required marshaling a significant amount of capital.

The development of banking and other financial services contributed to the expansion of trade. By the middle of the sixteenth century, financiers and traders commonly accepted bills of exchange in place of gold or silver or other goods. Bills of exchange, which had their origins in medieval Italy, were promissory notes that could be sold to third parties. In this way, they provided credit. At mid-century, an Antwerp financier only slightly exaggerated when he claimed, "One can no more trade without bills of exchange than sail without water." Merchants no longer had to carry gold and silver over long, and in many places, dangerous journeys, nor did they have to identify and assess the approximate value of a variety of coins issued by mints here and there. Thus, an Amsterdam merchant who purchased soap from a counterpart in Marseille could go to an exchanger and pay him the equivalent sum in guilders, the Dutch currency. The exchanger would then send a bill of exchange to a colleague in Marseille, authorizing him to pay the Marseille merchant in his own currency after the actual exchange of goods had taken place.

Bills of exchange contributed to the development of banks, as men dealing in bills and currency began to provide loans, profiting from the interest attached to them. Not until the eighteenth century, however, did banks such as the Bank of Amsterdam and the Bank of England begin to provide capital for business investment. Their principal function was to provide funds for the state.

The money changer's office.

The rapid expansion in international trade increased the role of merchant capitalists, particularly in Northern Europe, in the emerging global economy. The infusion of capital stemmed largely from gold and silver brought by Spanish vessels from the Americas. This capital financed the production of goods, storage, trade, and even credit across Europe and overseas. Moreover, an increased credit supply was generated by investments and loans by bankers and wealthy merchants to states and by joint-stock partnerships, an English innovation (the first major company beginning in 1600). Unlike short-term financial cooperation between investors for a single commercial undertaking, joint-stock companies provided a permanent funding of capital by drawing on the investments of merchants and other investors who purchased shares in the company.

Amsterdam and then London emerged as the banking and trading centers of Europe, although Italian banking houses in Genoa retained their financial role in trading cities like Lyon and Liège. Merchant towns in Castile, Catalonia, Italy, Holland, and England, as well as the Hanseatic cities of northern Germany, each had their own merchant dynasties.

The Global Economy

Trade with the Americas and Asia provided new outlets for European goods, as well as bringing from the New World products such as tomatoes, corn, bell peppers, rum, and spices to those who could afford them. The construction of larger ships, weighing as much as eighty tons, a size that would not be surpassed until the middle of the nineteenth century, facilitated oceangoing trade. From seaports, trade continued along the major rivers—principally the Rhine, which flows from Switzerland to the Baltic Sea; the Danube in Central Europe; the Seine, which links Paris to the English Channel; and the Rhône, which carries boat traffic from Lyon to the Mediterranean. The Scheldt River estuary led from the North Sea to the powerful trading and manufacturing city of Antwerp, which had a population of more than 100,000 people. There, vast quantities of English and Flemish goods were traded for goods from the German and Italian states. Land trade routes also remained important—for example, the route from Marseille to northern France and the Netherlands, that from Valencia on the Mediterranean to Madrid and Toledo in the heart of Castile, and that from Piedmont to the western German states and Holland.

England and the Dutch Netherlands, as well as France, benefited from a new and more complex colonial trading system. In each case, specially chartered East Indian trading companies helped mobilize investment capital and, enjoying monopolies issued to them by each state, set out to make money. When Hugo Grotius published his treatise on the freedom of the seas, he subtitled it *The Right which Belongs to the Dutch to Take Part in the East India Trade* (1609). By the end of the seventeenth century, the Dutch East India Company employed 12,000 people. These companies helped link the dynamism of entrepreneurs eager to make windfall profits and willing to take speculative risks to the political strategies of each state. For, although officially independent of each government, each represented the interests of the state. Yet, only in England did colonial trade play a major role in the development of the national economy, principally because English manufactured goods increasingly found markets in its bustling settlement colony of North America.

Overseas trading remained a risky business; storms, wars, and pirates all posed considerable risks. Appropriately enough, the first English company to receive royal authorization for a monopoly on colonial trade was called the London Merchant Adventurers, which exported wool to Antwerp. Spanish kings, in particular, were notorious for declaring bankruptcy and thus repudiating all debts after borrowing money from wealthy subjects based on the expectation—sometimes in vain—of the arrival of valued colonial goods or bullion.

Price Revolution and Depression

The rise in population and the economic boom of the sixteenth century brought a considerable rise in prices. During this "price revolution," the cost of living badly outdistanced wage increases. Real income thus fell for ordinary people. Those who suffered included small landholders in England, many of whom fell into the ranks of landless laborers; relatively poor nobles in France and Italy, whose tenants had long-term leases; and landless laborers and wage earners in city and country alike.

Those affected adversely by the price revolution were quick to blame rapacious landlords, greedy merchants, hoarders of grain, selfish masters, usurers, and the spirit of acquisition engendered, some people believed, by the Reformation. Basic long-term causes included the infusion of gold and particularly silver brought principally by the Spanish from the New World, currency debasement undertaken by monarchs to help fund their dynastic wars, and the population increase itself, which placed more pressure on scarce resources.

A long depression followed the economic expansion of the sixteenth century. This in itself reflected the relative decline of Mediterranean trade, symbolized by the end of Venetian supremacy in about 1600. The Thirty Years' War (1618–1648) also disrupted trade and manufacturing. International trade fell off dramatically, and manufacturing suffered. Furthermore, Spaniards had begun to exhaust the gold and silver mines of Latin America, disrupting the money supply. But, in all, the leveling off of the population probably compounded the fact that European markets were saturated. Urban growth slowed down, although ports such as Amsterdam, Hamburg, and Liverpool continued to grow with the expansion of the Atlantic trading system. By contrast, many of Europe's old ecclesiastical, administrative, and commercial centers stagnated.

THE RISE OF SPAIN

Sixteenth-century Spain, the most powerful state of its time, was not one kingdom but two: Castile and Aragon. Castile was by far the larger and wealthier; its vast stretch of mountainous land across much of the center of the Iberian Peninsula contained a population of 6 or 7 million, five-sixths of that of Spain as a whole. Aragon, lying in northern Spain, had prospered during the Middle Ages because of its flourishing Mediterranean trade. It became a federation of dominions, including Catalonia and Valencia, and was greatly influenced by Mediterranean peoples and cultures (see Map 5.1). In contrast, Portugal was a poor Atlantic state of mariners lying on the western edge of Iberia. It had a population of about 1 million people (roughly equivalent to that of Aragon) and was merged into the Spanish kingdom during the period 1580–1640. Following the death of the Portuguese king without a male heir, Philip II of Spain had claimed the Portuguese throne by virtue of being the only son of Isabella, daughter of King Manuel I of Portugal.

MAP 5.1 SPAIN IN THE AGE OF FERDINAND AND ISABELLA IN THE LATE FIF-
TEENTH CENTURY

Centralization and the Spanish Monarchy

In 1469, Isabella of Castile had married Ferdinand, heir to the throne of
Aragon. But even a happy royal marriage could not in itself forge a unified
kingdom. Royal policies in Castile, but not in Catalonia, Valencia, or
Aragon, were successfully implemented to create a relatively centralized
monarchy. In Castile, the crown centralized the system of justice and
made the municipalities more subservient. The Castilian dialect gradually
emerged as the language of Spain, giving some truth to the old saying that
"a language is a dialect with an army."

Ferdinand and Isabella and their successors were known as the Catholic
kings because of their devotion to the Church. But like other monarchs,
they brought the Church, its privileges, and some of its income from tithes
and the sale of indulgences under royal control. While the Reformation
shook the foundations of the Church in much of Europe, it barely challenged Spanish religious orthodoxy. The Spanish Inquisition, whose origi-

nal purpose had been to enforce the conversion of Moors and Jews in the late fifteenth century, served the Catholic Reformation in the late sixteenth century. Its tribunal interrogated and punished those accused of questioning Church doctrine. Housed in Castile, the Inquisition became a respected agent of royal as well as Church authority in some parts of Spain. Elsewhere, above all in Sicily and the Dutch Netherlands, local people considered the Inquisition another aspect of Spanish/Castilian domination and resisted it.

In Castile, Ferdinand and Isabella stripped the Castilian nobles of some of their privileges and power while dispensing titles and positions. In Catalonia and Valencia, on the other hand, nobles resisted any attempts by the monarchy to reduce their privileges (for example, the power of baronial courts), and therefore most of their noble prerogatives were left intact. Nonetheless, because they feared a revolt of the lower classes against them, the Catalan and Valencian nobles did become willing allies with the crown in maintaining social hierarchy and order.

Parliamentary traditions in the Spanish principalities limited the reach of the Castilian monarchy. The rulers of Spain were not able to tamper with Catalonia's traditionally less centralized constitutional traditions, which dated from the late thirteenth and fourteenth centuries, when Catalonia itself had been a Mediterranean power. Thus, the territories of Catalonia and Valencia maintained their political institutions, principally their Cortes (assembly), which continued to limit the authority of the

Ferdinand of Aragon and Isabella of Castile.

monarchy and which had to be consulted in order to achieve compliance with royal edicts. The Spanish monarchy therefore was less a "new monarchy"—at least outside of Castile—than that of France, because particularly strong institutional limits on its effective authority remained.

Disagreements between the monarchy and the Castilian Cortes were frequent during the middle decades of the sixteenth century. The Cortes excluded nobles and had representatives from only the governments of the eighteen most important cities and towns of Castile (forty-four towns had been represented in the Cortes during the Middle Ages). The Castilian Cortes, which maintained the right to approve extraordinary taxes, continued to refuse special taxes to subsidize the monarchy for thirty-five years (1541–1575). Despite the crown's efforts, this battle between monarchy and Cortes over taxes led to an inefficient royal fiscal apparatus. But Philip II, whose reign began (1556) and ended (1598) in royal bankruptcy, had to abide by the Roman law adage that described the medieval customs of his domains: "What touches all must be approved by all."

The Spanish Economy

Spain's colonial empire in the Americas contributed to its expanding economy. Although income drawn from the colonies never accounted for more than about 10 percent of the crown's income, during the first years of the Spanish colonial period Mexican gold helped finance the next wave of conquests. In 1545, Spaniards discovered the rich silver mines of Potosí in Peru, and a year later they uncovered more deposits in Mexico. A new refining process utilizing an amalgam of mercury helped Spain triple the silver resources of Europe at its own profit. Mules carried silver extracted at Potosí on a fifteen-day journey down 12,000 feet and many miles to the port of Arica; then the sea voyage of several months by convoy began. The Spanish empire contributed considerably to the sixteenth-century European trading boom. Spain shipped colonial products and Spanish woolens to France and the Italian city-states. Spanish ships supplied the colonies with wine, oil, European grain, shoes, and clothing.

The Castilian economy developed rapidly. The mountain ranges and central plateaus of Castile were divided between land for agricultural production, areas for raising sheep for the woolens industry, and rocky outcrops. The wool trade formed the basis of the Castilian export economy. The mining of silver, lead, iron, and mercury also developed in sixteenth-century Castile. Agricultural production was closely linked to manufacturing, as were sheep to the production of woolen goods. Nonetheless, 85 percent of the land of Spain could not be plowed because it consisted of mountains or lay on rocky slopes or at high elevations, with no possibility of irrigation.

Spanish royal revenue came from peasant obligations owed on royal domains as well as from taxes on commerce and manufacturing, import and export taxes, levies on sheep owned by nobles, farmers, monasteries, or textile manufacturers as they crossed specific mountain passes, and from the Church as payment for collecting tithes (an ecclesiastical tax of 10 percent of revenue). The crown imposed protectionist measures against foreign goods, banned the export of gold and silver, and attracted Italian and Flemish craftsmen to Spain.

In northern Spain, the rainy Cantabrian coast and mountains and valleys were populated by small farmers and fishermen. To the south, the Castilian provinces of Andalusia and Granada benefited from relatively rich land, producing wheat, olives, and wine. Castilian farmers expanded production by terracing hillsides and planting them in perennials, including grapevines and olive trees. Demand for textiles increased, and farmers planted flax, hemp, and, in Andalusia, mulberry trees. Farm towns built irrigation works and processing facilities such as wine and olive presses, flax-soaking ponds, and grist and fulling mills to turn these crops into market commodities. Wealthier farmers were able to purchase their neighbors' surplus and used their plow animals to transport these goods to the most attractive markets, where they sold them to wholesale merchants. Some of the latter were nobles who collected dues or obligations owed them in wheat, barley, wine, olive oil, cheese, chickens, or other farm products.

Spanish nobles incurred no stigma by engaging in wholesale or international commerce until the eighteenth century. Some of them, like merchants, processed the agricultural surplus and sold it to the rest of Europe. Many nobles capitalized on their revenues from farm products by building facilities to store and process the products—including flour mills, tanneries, and wine cellars, which often doubled as taverns—in the towns where they lived. Several wealthy dukes became shipping magnates. They earned fortunes because they owned the tuna fishing rights on Castile's Mediterranean shore, exporting fish preserved in salt or olive oil all over Europe.

The Expansion of the Spanish Empire

Through marriage and inheritance, Spain's territorial interests reached far and wide. The Spanish throne passed to the Austrian branch of the Habsburg dynasty in 1496, with Ferdinand and Isabella's daughter, Princess Joanna, marrying Philip the Fair, the Habsburg duke of Burgundy, who was the son of Maximilian, the Holy Roman emperor. A year after Isabella's death in 1504, Ferdinand, hoping to produce an heir to the Spanish throne, married a niece of King Louis XII of France. But three years later, their infant son died; royal families, as well as ordinary people, were subject to the harsh demographic realities of the age. In 1516, the Flanders-born son of Joanna and Philip the Fair inherited the throne of Castile and Aragon as Charles I of Spain. In 1519, he became Holy Roman Emperor Charles V (ruled 1519–1558) upon the death of his grandfather, Maximil-

Charles V was the grandson of Ferdinand and Isabella. This portrait is by Titian.

ian I. Along with his Spanish possessions, including Spain's American territories, he also inherited Aragon's Italian possessions. The emperor only briefly resided in Catalonia and rarely visited Castile. But with far-flung dynastic interests, he demanded extraordinary taxes from his Spanish subjects to pay for his wars abroad, including defending the Spanish Italian possessions of Naples, Sicily, and Sardinia against France during the 1520s.

The king's departure from Spain in 1520 was followed by open revolt against royal taxation. The revolt of the *Comuneros* (urban communities) began in Toledo and spread to other towns of northern Castile. Bourgeois and artisans opposed the royal officials Charles had imported from Flanders, but the revolt was also directed against Castilian nobles. After royal forces burned the arsenal and commercial town of Medina del Campo in north-central Castile in August 1520, Charles' regent suddenly switched tactics. He suspended supplementary tax collections and agreed not to appoint any more foreigners to office in Spain. When uprisings continued, Charles' army gradually restored order. One of the leaders of the revolt, the bishop of Zamora, was later tortured and garroted (slowly strangled with a wire) and his body hung from a tower as a warning to those who would challenge royal authority.

With an eye toward his succession, Charles V arranged the marriage of his son, Philip, to the English princess Mary Tudor of England in 1554. Charles formally abdicated as Holy Roman emperor in 1558, dividing the

Habsburg domains between his son Philip and his brother Ferdinand (see Map 5.2). Philip II (ruled 1556–1598) inherited Spain, the Netherlands, the Spanish colonies in the Americas, and parts of Italy. Ferdinand I (ruled 1558–1564), who was elected Holy Roman emperor, inherited the Habsburg ancestral domains, including Austria. This ended the period when one ruler held all Habsburg territories and any remote possibility that a single Catholic monarch would rule all of Europe, but it did not end the cooperation and strong family ties between the two branches of the Habsburg dynasty. Mary Tudor's death in 1558 eliminated the intriguing prospect that England might have become part of the Spanish Empire.

Despite the separation of the Habsburg domains, Philip II inherited the problem of ruling a vast empire. The royal bureaucracy handled the day-to-day operations of the state. Charles V had once asked for a pen and paper in one of the palaces of his various realms and was informed that none could be found. In contrast, his son's reign generated a mountain of paperwork each month. Thus, like its rivals France and England, the Spanish state developed a larger, more centralized bureaucracy, including royal councils, essential to the operations of the empire. The council of state and the council of war offered the king advice on matters of internal and colonial policy. Royal secretaries handled correspondence and busied

MAP 5.2. HABSBURG LANDS AT THE ABDICATION OF CHARLES V, 1558 The division of the Habsburg lands between Philip II (who had already begun to rule Spain in 1556) and Ferdinand I.

Philip II of Spain.

themselves with the operations of the royal household. Most such officials were commoners, for whom such positions provided financial and social advantages. Many of them were extremely able and devoted to the daunting task of maintaining the Spanish Empire.

The monarchy sent officials, many trained in law, from Spain to represent its interests in America. The growing bureaucracy was such that one judge sent from Spain in 1590 used 50,000 sheets of paper by the time he left thirteen years later. But it could take two years for administrative instructions or correspondence to reach distant officials in Latin America and for their response to arrive in Spain. Another official awaiting instructions put it this way, "If death came from Madrid, we should all live to a very old age."

The Age of Philip II

Spanish power peaked during the reign of Philip II. He chose as his capital the centrally located Castilian town of Madrid, which became a capital city of nobles and bureaucrats, many of whom, in one way or another, lived off the court. The city grew from a town of about 30,000 people in the 1540s to well over 150,000 inhabitants in the 1620s. Madrid survived through a "command economy"; royal commissioners paid government-fixed prices for what they wanted from the capital's hinterland. As Spain's capital grew, it had to be supplied from distant regions by overland transport provided by countless mule trains over mountain ranges and through deep valleys.

Like Francis I of France several decades before him, Philip decided that he needed a permanent royal residence that would provide an elegant symbol of his authority and power. Outside of Madrid, Philip built the magnificent Escorial Palace between 1563 and 1584. Virtually the king's only public appearances after he became crippled by gout were elaborate religious ceremonies at the palace. These were carefully orchestrated to uphold the sanctity of the throne.

Complex rituals of court etiquette affirmed a sense of power, social hierarchy, and order that were supposed to radiate from the Escorial through Spain and to the far reaches of the empire. Once the king had ridden a horse, it could never be ridden again by anyone else except the king. The king received visitors in a room determined by the status of the visitor. The primacy of court ritual and etiquette was such that Philip III (ruled 1598–1621), Philip's son and successor, contracted a fatal fever from a portable coal heater that had been placed too close to him. The duke of Alba, powerful adviser and military commander, recognized the danger, real or imagined, but refrained from moving it, or even saying anything, because the noble in charge of such things was not in the room.

Philip II led a tragic life marred by the premature death of four wives and a number of children. Perhaps because of sadness, he wore only black. The king himself may have contributed to the misfortunes of his offspring.

The Escorial Palace built by Philip II between 1563 and 1584.

In 1568, he ordered Don Carlos, his bad-tempered and irresponsible twenty-three-year-old son by his first marriage, placed under lock and key. Don Carlos seemed unfit to rule; furthermore, detesting his father, he may have even entered into contact with Dutch leaders who had begun to denounce Spanish policies in their land. Don Carlos' death six months later haunted Philip, inevitably generating stories that he had ordered him murdered. The introverted, sometimes indecisive king thereafter lived among the whispers of intrigue and storms of aristocratic rivalries of the noble families and factions.

With Habsburg domination of Italy secured by the 1559 Peace of Cateau-Cambrésis with France, Philip turned his attention to fighting the Turks. The Ottoman Empire had expanded into Europe following the conquest of Constantinople in 1453. Suleiman the Magnificent (ruled 1520–1566) took advantage of the dynastic and religious rivalries of the European states to expand his domain in the Balkans, where the Ottoman cultural heritage endures today, and into the rich plains of Hungary. The Turks also became bolder in their attacks on Spanish ships in the central and western Mediterranean. When the Turks took the Venetian island of Cyprus in 1571, the pope helped initiate the Holy League, an alliance with Venice and Spain. The long naval war against the Ottoman Empire,

The Battle of Lepanto, 1571.

during which Turkish ships raided the coast of Spain, lasted from 1559 to 1577. With southern Spain virtually undefended and with the Moriscos (Moors who had been forced to convert to Christianity) rebelling (1568–1570) against taxes, the Turks might well have captured Grenada. But a Spanish-Austrian Habsburg fleet defeated the sultan's larger navy in the Adriatic at the Battle of Lepanto (1571), a monumental struggle in which more than 200 galleys fought, taking the lives of 15,000 Christians and 30,000 Turks. The Turkish threat in the western Mediterranean ended. Yet, overexpansion had already planted the seeds of Spanish imperial decline.

THE RISE OF ENGLAND

The consolidation and then the extension of the authority of the Tudor monarchy made possible England's emergence as a power late in the sixteenth century. From the reign of Henry VII to that of Elizabeth I, the Tudor monarchs held in check the great landed magnates, putting down rebellions and extending the reach and prestige of royal government. During the same period, the English state expanded its control over Wales and Ireland while holding at bay Scottish threats to the Tudor dynasty.

The House of Tudor

On August 22, 1485, at the Battle of Bosworth Field, King Richard III lost his kingdom for the lack of the proverbial horse, and his life as well. Victorious in the long War of the Roses, Henry VII (ruled 1485–1509) became the first Tudor monarch. In 1487, he crushed a last-ditch uprising by his enemies, the Yorkists. And ten years later, he put down a tax rebellion that began in Cornwall and reached the gates of London. Like Isabella of Castile and Ferdinand of Aragon, the ambitious Henry VII set out to make the Tudor state so powerful that it could resist any challenge from noble factions, the "overmighty subjects," some of whom had been killed at Bosworth Field.

Thomas Wolsey, who was archbishop of York and adviser to the king, brought to the King's Council loyal officials drawn from the ranks of the nobility and high clergy. These men met at Westminster in the Star Chamber, so called because its blue ceiling, like the skies, was spangled with stars. The Star Chamber became one of the highest courts in the land, generating revenue for the crown by assessing fines and other monetary penalties.

Henry strengthened royal authority in England. At the expense of Parliament, which enacted the laws of the land and attempted to restrict monarchical authority, Henry imposed tariffs protecting the cloth and wool industries, decreed acts unifying weights and measures, and put forth edicts punishing vagabondage and begging. He reduced expenses by disbanding his army, while filling royal coffers by selling monopolies (the exclusive right to import and market foodstuffs or commodities). Monopolies were extremely unpopular, however, among the middle and lower classes because they kept the prices of some products artificially high.

The king won the loyalty of most nobles. When selling offices failed, he resorted to the sheer coercive power of the throne. The Star Chamber enforced compliance, exacting fines and sometimes arresting the recalcitrant for real or imagined offenses. Henry obtained from Parliament writs of attainder and forfeiture, by which he could declare anyone guilty of treason, execute them, and seize their property.

Henry VII depended not only upon the personal loyalty of local elites but also on the efficiency and prestige of six or seven hundred unpaid justices of the peace. These unsalaried men, largely drawn from prosperous landed families, dispensed justice, collected taxes, enforced troop levies, and maintained local order. Their judicial authority covered every criminal offense except treason. While maintaining a strong tradition of decentralized government in England, the justices of the peace also strengthened the efficiency and prestige of the monarchy. Gradually, the royal Assize Courts took responsibility for felony cases. Charged with enforcing parliamentary statutes and the orders of the Privy Council, which administered the Tudor state, they also helped extend the state's effective authority.

Henry VIII became king upon his father's death in 1509 and married Catherine of Aragon, who was Ferdinand and Isabella's daughter, as well as his brother's widow. Beneath Henry's proud and impetuous character lay a deep-seated inferiority complex that he tried to overcome with grand deeds. The single-minded Henry dreamed of standing at the head of an empire. The new king spent vast sums fighting against France for more than a decade, beginning in 1512. Cardinal Wolsey, who had been his father's trusted adviser, sought to restrain Henry's ambition. But when the House of Commons refused to provide the king with more funds, Henry simply debased the currency, giving the state more spending power at the cost of higher inflation.

Foreign wars had devastated royal finances. To raise money, the spendthrift monarch heaped more financial obligations on the backs of the poor. Wolsey utilized the cynically named "Amicable Grant," a royal assessment first imposed in 1525 on lay and ecclesiastical revenues. Peasants in southeastern England, sometimes led by local gentry (the rural elite whose status came from its ownership of land and who dominated the House of Commons), rebelled against these new levies. Henry responded to the threat by forcing landowners to loan money to the crown, imprisoning some of the wealthiest, confiscating their estates, selling off property that had belonged to the Roman Catholic Church on unfavorable terms, and further debasing the currency, adding to inflation.

Henry wanted to make his monarchy more efficient. Royal government, including control of the state's finances, passed from the royal household of the king's servants to a small but able bureaucracy of officials and their clerks, who were loyal to both the king and Parliament. He reduced the size of the king's advisory council and formalized its structure. The Privy Council assumed oversight functions and routinized communication with the local justices of the peace. The king appointed new administrative officials and established new revenue courts. At the same time, the general acceptance of the "king's law"—common law—gradually helped generate a sense of national unity.

Henry VIII extended the power of his monarchy by breaking with Rome in the 1530s over his divorce of Catherine of Aragon. He established the Church of England (see Chapter 3), which kept some of the ritual and doctrine of the Catholic Church. Henry became head of the Church of England, dissolving monasteries and confiscating and selling ecclesiastical lands. But while leading the break with Rome, Henry planted the seeds for conflicts between Protestants and Catholics in England.

Fearing the possibility of Welsh or Irish assistance to Holy Roman Emperor Charles V should he attempt to invade England to restore Catholicism, Henry established English domination over Wales and direct rule over Ireland, extending English control on the periphery of the British Isles. Since the late twelfth century, English lords had gradually increased their military colonization of Ireland, pushing back the Gaelic tribes and claiming the finest land by virtue of ancient titles. The English kings delegated authority to English nobles. Yet, effective English authority had remained fragile in Ireland as long as the crown's continental interests took precedence and disorders in Ireland did not compromise English authority. After the English Reformation, the crown selected English Protestants for all posts in Ireland. And after a minor rebellion against royal authority, which was put down with great cruelty, in 1541 Henry proclaimed himself king of Ireland and head of the Irish Church. In exchange for the Gaelic chieftains' recognition of Henry as their king and acceptance of English law, the crown recognized them as Irish lords. Thereafter, however, the costs of administering Ireland increased rapidly, requiring more troops, as the Irish continued to chafe at English rule.

Scotland also proved to be a thorny problem for England. Although in 1503 James IV had married Henry VII's daughter, Margaret Tudor, relations between Scotland and England deteriorated when Henry VIII became king. When James invaded England in 1513 in support of the French, Henry responded by ordering a major military campaign against the Scots. This ended with the wounding or death of more than 10,000 Scots at the battle of Flodden (where James IV was killed). Nonetheless, Catholic Scotland remained an ally of Catholic France. The new Scottish king, James V, first married the daughter of Francis I of France and, after her death, he married a member of the powerful French Catholic family of

Guise. In 1542, an English army again invaded Scotland, defeating the Scots at Solway Moss. Following James V's sudden death a month after the battle, Mary Stuart (James' six-day-old daughter and the granddaughter of Henry VII of England) became queen of the Scots. In 1546, after Henry's war with France dragged to a halt, another English army laid waste to Scotland, sacking the capital and university town of Edinburgh.

Henry VIII died in 1547. On his deathbed, the originator of the English Reformation hedged his bets, leaving money to pay for Catholic Masses to be said for the eternal repose of his soul. The nine-year-old son of Henry and Jane Seymour became King Edward VI (ruled 1547–1553) under the tutelage of his uncle, the duke of Somerset, who governed as Lord Protector. Again, rebellions sparked by economic hardship broke out. While seeking accommodation with Protestant dissenters, the young Edward (who ruled from age nine to fifteen under the influence of advisers) brought theologians from Geneva and Strasbourg to undertake an aggressive campaign on behalf of the Reformed Church of England.

Wars against Catholic Scotland and France continued. The Lord Protector was intent on destroying Catholicism in Scotland. After English troops defeated a French force sent to help the Catholic cause, the young Catholic queen of Scots fled to safety, marrying Francis, the son of Henry II, the king of France.

(*Left*) Lady Jane Grey, queen of England for 9 days. (*Right*) Mary Tudor, later queen of England.

In England, tensions between Protestants and Catholics accentuated anti-Catholicism. Landowners began to resist paying more taxes to finance new wars. Allied with fearful Catholic nobles, the duke of Warwick became the new Lord Protector in 1549, taking the title of duke of Northumberland.

Northumberland quickly betrayed the Catholic lords who had supported him. He tightened the crown's control over the Church of England and undertook a repressive campaign against Catholicism. Northumberland's influence over the sickly young king whetted his desire for power. He plotted for Lady Jane Grey (1537–1554; niece of Henry, she stood third in line to the monarchy) to ascend the throne after she married his son. After Edward's death, Northumberland proclaimed his daughter-in-law queen of England. But most nobles rallied to the cause of Mary Tudor (ruled 1553–1558), the daughter of Henry VIII and Catherine of Aragon. She seemed to them the rightful heir to the throne, despite the fact that she was Catholic.

Mary Tudor succeeded her half-brother and attempted to return England to Catholicism. Mary restored all rituals and doctrines of the Catholic Church, and she acknowledged the primacy of the pope over the Church of England. The queen abrogated Henry VIII's reforms and began to persecute Protestants, some of whom fled to France. "Bloody Mary" embellished the macabre heritage of the Tower of London with the heads of Northumberland, his son, and Lady Jane Grey, who ruled for only nine days. Mary married Philip II, who ascended the Spanish throne in 1556. England joined Spain in its war against France; Calais, the last English outpost in France, was soon lost. Sparked by widespread opposition to her Catholicism, which was popularly identified with England's Catholic rivals, France and Spain, a rebellion broke out against the queen. When Mary died in 1558, few in England grieved.

Elizabeth I (ruled 1558–1603), Anne Boleyn's daughter, became queen at age twenty-five, succeeding Mary, her half-sister. Elizabeth's throne was threatened by religious division, compounded by antagonism with the Catholic powers, France and Spain. Not many people could have expected the young queen to succeed.

Elizabeth was a woman of intelligence, vanity, sporadic fickleness, and an occasional flash of temper. She enjoyed music, dancing, hunting, and the company of men. Tall, with reddish hair and an olive complexion, she was cautious, even suspicious, having been raised in a world of conspiracy. The queen preferred to wait out many pressing problems in the hope that they would go away. Educated in the tradition of Italian humanism, Elizabeth learned French, German, and Italian, as well as Latin, and enjoyed translating texts from these languages into English.

Elizabeth never married. It was not uncommon for women to remain unmarried in early modern Europe—in England, about 10 percent of all women remained single throughout their lives—but it was unusual for a

Queen Elizabeth dancing with Robert Dudley.

monarch to remain single. The question of whether Elizabeth would ever marry preoccupied the other rulers of Europe, as well as her subjects.

In response to a parliamentary petition that she marry and produce a direct heir, Elizabeth responded that she trusted God to ensure that "the realm shall not remain destitute of an heir." As for her, it would be enough that at the end of her life "a marble stone shall declare that a queen, having reigned such a time, lived and died a virgin." Elizabeth had rejected one continental hopeful after another, beginning with the handsome but dull Philip II of Spain, Catholic widower of Mary Tudor. Nor was marriage the outcome of a two-year romance with the handsome Lord Robert Dudley, the death of whose wife in 1560 from a suspicious fall down a flight of stairs understandably fueled rumors for some years.

Elizabeth was an able administrator who chose capable people to serve the crown. She appointed as her principal adviser the clever, loyal Sir William Cecil (Lord Burghley, 1520–1598). A Protestant, Cecil served as royal secretary for nearly as many years as Elizabeth was queen. Nonetheless, in the later years of her reign, bitter battles for influence and power within Elizabeth's inner circle did belie the appearance of relative harmony. In the 1590s, two powerful men battled for power: the ambitious Robert Devereux, the earl of Essex, a soldier who had the ear of the queen, and Robert Cecil, son of William Cecil. From Ireland, where he had failed to crush Irish resistance to English control, the ambitious Essex returned to London without orders to do so in order to destroy his rival. This time, in 1599, Elizabeth forgave him. But two years later, Essex's small private army of followers rose in rebellion; failure led to his execution and that of his most powerful friends.

Religious Settlement and Conflict under Elizabeth I

When Elizabeth took the throne, she was determined to find a means to resolve religious conflict within England, for she recognized that unless the conflict was resolved, it might one day threaten her reign. Elizabeth had been raised a Protestant, but she did not hold particularly strong religious convictions and rarely attended church services. Although she was thought to be favorable to some Catholic rituals, when she first encountered a procession of monks with candles and incense at Westminster Abbey, she cried out, "Away with these torches, we see very well." In the quest for unity, she dismissed many Catholic advisers.

Queen Elizabeth oversaw the religious settlement, which at first aimed to please a wide spectrum of religious beliefs without resorting to heresy hunting or persecution. In 1559, Parliament passed the Act of Uniformity and the Act of Supremacy, which established the lasting foundations of the Church of England, reorganizing it to have Protestant dogma but essentially Catholic structure. The Uniformity Bill imposed the *Book of Common Prayer* (1550) on religious services of the Church of England and required attendance at public worship and imposed fines for not attending services. The bill barely passed the House of Lords (which was primarily composed of Catholics), and probably would not have passed at all had two bishops not been imprisoned in the Tower of London and thus unable to vote. The Act of Supremacy required all officials, clergy, and candidates for university degrees to take an oath acknowledging the queen as "governor" of the English Church. This title replaced that of "head" of the Church and suggested that the queen would not interfere in matters of doctrine.

Thirty-Nine Articles, enacted in 1563, provided an institutional framework for subsequent relations between state and church in England. The landed elite, strengthening its control of Parliament during Elizabeth's reign, generally supported the Church of England. Protestant preachers combed the countryside, seeking to win back people who had converted to Roman Catholicism.

Some English Protestants wanted to carry the anti-Roman reforms further than Elizabeth's religious settlement. They sought to eliminate from the Church of England what some members considered vestiges of elaborate Catholic ceremonies, such as baptismal crosses, altar rails before which Catholics knelt while receiving communion, elaborate priestly garb, and stained-glass windows that they associated with Catholicism.

Puritanism, the English version of Calvinism, first took hold among English exiles on the continent during Queen Mary's reign. It emerged in the late 1550s as a dissident force within the English, or Anglican Church. Puritans could be found in every social stratum, but they were drawn primarily from the middle and lower classes. They drew hostility by insisting on a simplified but more intense religion based on individual conscience, the direct authority of the Holy Scriptures, and a community of belief in which preaching played a preeminent role. Although a few Puritans served as bishops in the Church of England and some fiercely defended Elizabeth's royal supremacy, other Puritans wanted the Church of England to be separate from the English monarchy. The Tudor monarchy, on the other hand, wanted to make the Church serve its secular goals of national glory, prosperity, and public order.

A modest Catholic revival, aided by the arrival of Catholic Jesuit missionaries from the continent, accentuated religious divisions in England. Royal religious policies became more harsh. Dissident Protestants suffered persecution along with Catholics. A Jesuit missionary was tortured to death on the rack in 1581, and six years later the first Puritan was executed for having spoken in Parliament on behalf of free speech in the name of his religion.

Since Elizabeth had no heirs, the Catholic Mary Stuart, niece of Henry VIII, stood next in line for succession to the English throne. After her husband King Francis II of France died in 1560, Mary returned to her native Scotland to assume the power that her mother wielded as regent until her death that same year. The Scottish Reformation had begun in earnest

Mary, queen of Scots.

when the theologian John Knox (c. 1505–1572) returned home from Geneva to preach reform. Soon after coming to the throne of England, Elizabeth had made peace with Scotland and France. But Elizabeth and Protestants worried that if Mary became queen of England, she would restore Catholicism to England. When Protestants forced Mary to abdicate the Scottish throne in 1568, she fled to England. There Elizabeth kept her potential rival under virtual house arrest.

In 1569, Catholics in the moors and bogs of the isolated English north rebelled in the hope of putting Mary Stuart on the English throne, precipitating Elizabeth's order for her rival's imprisonment. The Catholic force marched southward, but hastily retreated upon learning that sizable English forces loyal to Elizabeth awaited them. English troops defeated a second Scottish army gathered near the border between the two countries. Elizabeth ordered the execution of over 500 of the rebels. This "Northern Rising" ended in complete failure, and the Catholic Church's hopes for a successful Counter-Reformation in England were finally dashed. Pope Pius V excommunicated Elizabeth in 1570 from the Church to which she did not wish to belong, removing the queen's Catholic subjects from the obligation of obedience to her and encouraging several further plots against her. Two years later, French Catholics undertook the Saint Bartholomew's Day Massacre of Protestants in Paris (see Chapter 4), the horror of which firmed Elizabeth's resolve to resist Mary's claims to the throne at all costs. She then vowed to support the Dutch, most of whom were Protestant, in their rebellion against Catholic Spain. In 1583, she foiled a plot, which involved the Spanish and French embassies, to depose her in favor of Mary Stuart. Four years later, under pressure from Parliament and fearing new Catholic plots against her, Elizabeth ordered Mary Stuart's execution.

Tudor Statemaking

The reach and efficiency of the English state increased under Elizabeth's guidance. Lords and other wealthy gentlemen served on the Privy Council, which consisted of between twelve and eighteen members drawn from the nobility, gentry, and officers in the royal household. It oversaw the lord-lieutenants, a new office that gave noblemen control of local militia. Patronage flowed downward from the monarch. England's queen, like her predecessors, used patronage to foster loyalty to the crown. The most desirable posts were at court, including those in the royal household. Some of these carried life tenures; a few were hereditary. More than 500 men were employed in government departments. The most powerful officials at court, such as the Lord Chancellor, also dispensed patronage by selecting officials and filling local positions in the counties. Closely tied to the satisfaction of the private interests of the landed elite, the office of the Exchequer resembled similar offices created by continental monarchs who did not have to contend with a representative body as powerful as the English Parliament. Although it met during only three of the forty-five years of Elizabeth's reign, Parliament retained an important role in government because the crown needed its assent for new laws and new taxes.

Upon ascending the throne, Elizabeth found the crown's financial situation bleak. Revenues raised through taxation and customs dues were inadequate to finance the war against Spain and the Irish campaigns. The sale of some royal lands, forced loans, the occasional seizure of a Spanish ship laden with silver or gold, and purveyance (the right of agents of the monarchy to buy food at below-market prices) could only be temporary expedients. The collection of "ship money" (a tax on ports, which the crown with dubious logic extended to inland towns as well) was extremely unpopular and generated resistance during the hard times of the 1590s. But by exercising frugality in the expenses of government and increasing taxation, the crown managed to replenish its coffers, another sign of a stronger and more efficient state, despite a decade and a half of expensive warfare against Spain.

The English monarchy in the Elizabethan Age was in some ways relatively more centralized and efficient than that of Spain or France. This was so despite the fact that the French monarchy employed about ten times more officials than did the English crown (taking the difference in population into consideration). In Elizabethan England, unlike in France, churchmen did not serve in the highest offices of the realm. Although English nobles still had retainers, by the 1590s they no longer had full-fledged private armies that could threaten the throne's monopoly on force. This contrasted with the situation in France during the same period, when the Guise and Bourbon families, among others, sent their own armies to fight in the wars of religion. English noble violence was instead channeled into service to the crown, and into dueling.

Foreign wars also served to increase the reach of central government in England. The second half of the sixteenth century brought regular training for the militia, which provided the bulk of troops as needed, along with gentlemen volunteers and cavalrymen still recruited by summons. But in the last eighteen years of Elizabeth's reign, more than 100,000 soldiers were impressed into service for wars on the continent and to maintain English hegemony in Ireland. Lord-lieutenants assumed responsibility for troop levies in the counties. The vast majority who were conscripted as soldiers were the poorest of the poor, unfortunate men who happened to be at the wrong place at the wrong time when the press-gangs turned up to roll them out of taverns or out of church and into the queen's service.

The monarchy imposed English law on northern England, Ireland, and Wales, which Henry VIII had absorbed into England. The emergence of a national market economy that was increasingly tied to London also played an important part in the nationalization of English political institutions. Within England, the sense of belonging to a nationality was certainly more

Queen Elizabeth greeting the Dutch ambassadors.

advanced than anywhere on the continent. With the exception of part of Cornwall in southwestern England (where the Cornish language was spoken by many), the people of England spoke English, however great the variation in dialect and accents. A somewhat Anglicized Welsh gentry had even begun to send their sons to Oxford and Cambridge Universities.

The fact that Britain is an island may have made the English more xenophobic and precociously nationalistic than their continental counterparts. The Venetian ambassador commented in 1555 on the "strange fancies [that] prevail amongst this people, and how much their ideas differ from those of other nations." Indeed, the English seemed "most hostile by their nature to foreigners . . . naturally the enemies of all aliens, but they hate the French and Spaniards most of all." Such sentiments reinforced the strong current of English anti-Catholicism.

Strong traditions of local government and loyalties persisted in England, however, fueled by social differences and the overwhelming influence of wealthy local landed families. The county and parish remained the economic, social, and political universe of most people in England. The state remained an abstraction until the tax collector or the press-gang came to intrude in an individual's life.

Demographic and Economic Expansion

In the last half of the sixteenth century, England emerged as a commercial and manufacturing power. The population of England and Wales—its vassal—grew rapidly, from about 2.5 million in the 1520s to more than 3.5

million in 1580, reaching about 4.5 million in 1610. Reduced mortality rates and increased fertility, the latter probably generated by expanding work opportunities in manufacturing and farming (leading to earlier marriage and more children), help explain this rapid rise in population. While epidemics and plague occasionally took their toll, the people in England still suffered less than did those on the continent. Furthermore, despite the somewhat wrenching effects of the English Reformation, the country had been spared the protracted wars of religion that occurred in France and Central Europe during the same period.

England provides the primary example of the expansion of agricultural production well before the "agricultural revolution" of the eighteenth and nineteenth centuries. A larger population stimulated increased demand for food, as well as for manufactured goods, particularly woolens. English agriculture became more efficient and market oriented through crop specialization than almost anywhere on the continent. Between 1450 and 1650, the yield of grain per acre increased by at least 30 percent. In sharp contrast with farming in Spain, English landowners brought more dense marshes and woodlands into cultivation.

The great estates of the English nobility largely remained intact, and many wealthy landowners aggressively increased the size of their holdings, a precondition for increased productivity. Marriages between the children of landowners also increased the size of landed estates. Primogeniture (the full inheritance of land by the eldest son) helped keep land from being subdivided. Younger sons of independent landowners left behind the family land to find other respectable occupations, often in the church or in urban trades. Larger farms were conducive to more commercialized farming at a time when an expanding population pushed up demand and prices. Some landowners turned a part of their land into pastureland for sheep in order to supply the developing woolens trade.

Some of the great landlords, as well as yeomen (farmers whose holdings and security of land tenure guaranteed their prosperity and status) reorganized their holdings in the interest of efficiency. Open-field farmers selected crops in response to the growing London market. In their quest for greater profits, many landlords put the squeeze on their tenants. Between 1580 and 1620, many landlords raised rents and altered conditions of land tenure in their favor, preferring shorter leases and forcing tenants to pay an "entry fee" before they would agree to rent them land. Landowners evicted those who could not afford their new, more onerous terms. They also pushed tenants toward more productive farming methods, including crop rotation. Many peasants had difficulty competing with their wealthier neighbors. During bad years, the peasants might be forced to sell their land, while wealthy neighbors could survive with relative ease.

Many landowners utilized "enclosure" to expand their holdings. Enclosure included the buying up and hedging of wastelands, the enclosure of one's own land by fences, consolidating arable strips of land and enclosing them, and dividing common lands and pasture areas. The enclosure of common lands, sold by villages to the highest bidders and entailing the end of the common rights of villagers—rich or poor—to use the land, and the removal of tenants in order to consolidate estates, marked a push toward "agrarian individualism." Enclosure in this sense drew considerable resistance, for it left many of the rural poor fenced out of common land on which they had depended for firewood, gleaning, and pasturing. Thomas More's *Utopia* (1516), inspired by news of explorations of the Americas, described an imaginary island where all people lived in peace and harmony and blamed England's economic inequities on enclosure. Riots against enclosure were widespread in the 1590s, a decade in which popular tax rebellions shook France, Spain, Austria, and Ukraine, among other places, and again in the 1620s and 1630s. They were particularly prominent in regions where open fields were being enclosed for pasture or in the fens and forests where drainage and deforestation projects authorized by Parliament eliminated extensive common lands.

England's precocious economic development also drew upon the country's natural resources, including iron, timber and, above all, coal, extracted in far greater quantities than anywhere on the continent. New industrial methods, including furnaces for separating silver from copper ore and for using coal in the making of glass, expanded the production of iron, brass, and pewter in and around Birmingham.

But, above all, textile manufacturing transformed the English economy. Here, too, new industrial methods, such as the stocking knitting frame, increased productivity. Woolens (which accounted for about 80 percent of exports), worsteds (sturdy yarn spun from combed wool fibers), and cloth found eager buyers in England as well as on the continent. Moreover, late in the sixteenth century, as English merchants began making forays across the Atlantic, these textiles were also sold in the New World. Cloth manufacturers undercut production by urban craftsmen by "putting out" work to the villages and farms of the countryside. In such domestic industry, poor rural women and their daughters could do spinning and carding (combing fibers in preparation for spinning) of wool in their homes.

The English textile trade was closely tied to Antwerp, in the Spanish Netherlands, where workers dyed English cloth. Sir Thomas Gresham, a sixteenth-century entrepreneur, became England's representative in the bustling river port. Wining and dining the city's merchants and serving as a royal ambassador, he so enhanced the reputation of English business that English merchants could operate on credit, no small achievement in the sixteenth century. At home, he convinced the government to end special privileges accorded the Hanseatic cities of northern Germany and helped convince the state to authorize lucrative English trading monopolies. Gresham's shrewd sense of finance saved the relatively meager royal coffers from bankruptcy on several occasions through the negotiation of timely loans.

Gresham advised the crown to explore the economic possibilities of the Americas. This led to the first concerted English efforts at colonization. Even more than Spanish colonialism, English overseas ventures were undertaken with commercial profits in mind. When the Spanish, hoping to crush the Dutch rebellion that began against their rule in 1566, closed the Scheldt River, which leads from the North Sea to Antwerp, English merchants responded by seeking new, more distant outlets for trade. From 1577 to 1580, Sir Francis Drake (1540–1596), explorer and privateer who stole treasures brought back by Spanish galleons, sailed around Cape Horn in his search for a passage that would permit commercial ties with Asia. Sir Walter Raleigh (1554–1618; a Renaissance scholar, poet, historian, and explorer) said of Drake, "A single purpose animates all his exploits and the chart of his movements is like a cord laced and knotted round the throat of the Spanish monarchy."

London came to replace Antwerp as Europe's leading center of trade. London's Merchant Adventurers competed with Spanish and Portuguese rivals for spices and other products that fetched increasingly handsome prices at home. They traded textiles and other manufactured goods for slaves, gold, and ivory from the African and Brazilian coasts. West Indian sugar and Virginia tobacco entered the English domestic market in lucrative quantities. English merchants traded in India and Indonesia. In 1600, Queen Elizabeth chartered the East India Company with the goal of competing with Dutch traders. To compete with the Spanish, who already had a colonial empire that stretched several thousand miles from what is now the southern United States to Terra del Fuego at the southern tip of South America, Raleigh sought to establish a colony in Virginia between 1584 and 1587. After a first settlement failed, a settlement colony succeeded in

View of seventeenth-century London, Europe's leading center of trade.

Longeat at Wiltshire, one of the great early Elizabethan manor houses.

Virginia, largely because of the popularity of tobacco, which began to reach England in the first decades of the seventeenth century.

The developing economy produced a marked rise in the number of people working in manufacturing. English towns grew as migrants arrived in sufficient numbers to overcome high mortality rates caused by catastrophic health conditions stemming from poor sanitation. London grew into the largest city in the world, its population rising from about 50,000 in the 1520s to 200,000 in 1600, and jumping its walls to 375,000 in 1650. The next biggest towns in England lagged far behind: Norwich, Newcastle, and Bristol boasted only about 25,000 people each, followed by Exeter and York. On the average, about 6,000 people moved to London each year. Including its developing industrial suburbs, about 8 percent of the population of England lived in London by the mid-seventeenth century.

English Society in the Tudor Period

English society under the Tudors reflected what William Harrison, writing in 1577, called "degrees of people," that is, sharply defined social differences. Contemporaries sometimes simplified English social structure by dividing people into the ranks of "gentlemen," "the middling sort," and "the poor." Ownership of land in the form of estates—inherited or acquired—conferred status, or "gentility," in England. All nobles were gentry, but the vast majority of gentry were not nobles. In order to administer the realm and maintain public order in every corner of the country, the crown required the allegiance and the assistance of the landed elite.

Titles were granted by the crown, originally in exchange for military service, and were inherited by the eldest son. The nobility and gentry had social and political influence and constituted the elite that dominated England for more than the next three centuries. Country manors literally commanded the surrounding countryside. One contemporary exuded, "Nobility is a precious gift, which so glittereth in the eyes of all men that there is no one corporal thing in this world, whereof we make a greater account."

The lord and his family dominated regional economic, social, and political life through ties of kinship and patronage. Ordinary people addressed the nobleman as "your lordship," and the wealthy gentleman as "sir"; poor women curtsied to them as a mark of respect. Village bells were rung in their honor when they passed through. Wealthy landowners mediated in village disputes and provided some charity in exchange for deference. (One man of means chatted with "his people" in the street: "I asked a poor woman how many children she had. She answered 'Six.' 'Here,' I said, 'is a sixpence for them.' 'No, sir,' she said proudly, not realizing the gentleman was offering a gift, 'I will not sell my children.' ")

The Privy Council and Elizabeth's court were remarkably homogeneous from the early 1570s, with few newcomers breaking into the inner circle of like-minded aristocrats. The borders between public and private life within this upper circle of relatives, friends, enemies, and acquaintances were hard to distinguish. The education of gentlemen at Oxford and Cambridge Universities or through private tutoring helped shape common cultural values and social homogeneity among what was increasingly becoming a national elite.

Yeomen stood beneath the gentry on the social ladder, but they could move up if they were able to purchase and maintain large estates. In any case, they possessed, in Harrison's words, "a certain preeminence and more estimation" among the common people. They had political rights and could vote in the parliamentary elections. They improved their houses, bought or built solid furniture, purchased silver and pewter accoutrements, wore nice clothes on Sunday and holidays, and were able to assure the education of their children.

Within the upper reaches of the "middling sort" were men considered "of sufficiency," even if they were not lords or gentlemen. They were believed by virtue of steady income to be worthy of assuming some kind of public responsibility. England's precocious commercial and manufacturing boom in the sixteenth century increased the wealth and status of merchants and manufacturers. Wealthy merchants and artisans served on town councils, perpetuating their influence from generation to generation. Members of these councils led the way in the pageant-like processions during municipal and national celebrations, such as that of

Midsummer Eve, followed by guild members, each wearing the decorative costume of their various trades. Most craftsmen were much better off than the urban and rural poor.

Originally intended to maintain the highest standards in the training of craftsmen and in production, the guilds' influence waned as towns became larger and more complex. Yet, some guilds, particularly in London, held monopolies over specific trades. They could control production and therefore the prices of certain commodities. Since guild regulations and ordinances had to be approved by the civic authorities, disagreements between guilds and municipal governments were frequent.

Lower on the social scale were smallholders, farmers who owned just enough land to get by ("husbandmen"), poor clergymen depending for survival upon small fees rendered for their services, and ordinary craftsmen. The majority of the population owned neither land nor skills, and thus lay at the bottom of the social hierarchy. Most laboring families lived in rented one-room cottages and owned little—if any—furniture. Cottagers, employed as farmhands but also often employed as spinners, weavers, carders, or nailmakers, lived on bread, cheese, lard, soup, beer, and garden greens, occasionally supplemented by harvest-time feasts provided by their employers. Farm servants lived in Spartan accommodations provided by landlords. In London and smaller towns, the urban poor struggled to survive as common laborers, porters, sweepers, and in other menial occupations, living in squalor in whatever pitiful lodgings they could afford, or, for many, living without shelter.

Social divisions in English society were reflected in how people lived, dressed, and even spoke. During the sixteenth century, the rich got richer—and lived that way, dressing and eating differently from those who were poor. Responding to complaints that "a Babylon of confusion" might blur class lines because anyone with money could purchase the most elegant clothing, Parliament had earlier in the century decreed that only dukes, earls, and barons could wear sable cloth woven of gold and embroidered with gold and silver. So could their horses. But no one, not even wealthy merchants—or horses, for that matter—of a lesser rank, even if they could afford to do so, was permitted to wear gold and silver. Gentlemen with land bringing an income of 100 pounds a year could wear velvet in their doublets but not in their gowns and coats. Ben Jonson (1572–1637), author of scurrilous satires on London life, wrote that to become recognized as a gentleman, a man had to go to London, "where at your first appearance 'twere good you turned four or five hundred acres of your best land into two or three trunks of apparel."

Cardinal Wolsey had earlier attempted to moderate the dietary excesses of wealthy people, including the high clergy. Copying sumptuary regulations that could be found throughout Europe since the Middle Ages, he specified the number of separate dinner courses that people of various ranks might consume, with the largest number—nine—reserved for cardinals like himself. But to no avail. A critical commentator wrote toward the end of the century, "Nowadays, if the table be not covered from the one end to the other as thick as a dish can stand by another . . . and to every dish a several sauce appropriate to his kind, it is thought unworthy of the name of dinner." The poor ate no such meals. The condition of life of some artisans, landless cottagers, rural laborers, and unskilled and under-employed workers declined; soaring food and lodging costs sapped their meager earnings. Their lives became even more insecure.

There was, to be sure, some degree of social mobility in Tudor England: new economic opportunities brought greater prosperity to gentry, yeoman, merchants, and manufacturers. By the end of the century, the economic gap between nobles and wealthy gentry landowners had been reduced. Some yeomen achieved gentry status, and merchants and manufacturers made money. The interests and lifestyles of the middling sort gradually moved closer to those of gentlemen and their families as English society became more polarized. And, to be sure, some farm servants were able to save enough money to become husbandmen, or even yeomen; likewise, some apprentices became independent masters within their trades. But social advancement remained relatively rare among the poor, whose num-bers were rapidly expanding along with their impoverishment.

The Quest for Public Order

After almost a century of inflation accentuated by a rising population, har-vest failures in the 1590s brought the period of economic expansion to an abrupt halt in England. Never had there seemed to be so many poor and hungry people on the roads, dressed in rags, sleeping in fields, searching for wild berries or edible roots, and begging, just trying to get by. "They lie in the streets," came a report, "in the dirt as commonly is seen . . . and are permitted to die like dogs or beasts without any mercy or compassion showed them at all." Shakespeare's *Midsummer Night's Dream* refers to contemporary harvest failure and food shortages.

Ordinary people sometimes took matters into their own hands. Food ri-ots spread through much of England, as the poor seized grain and sold it at what they considered a reasonable price. Women usually made up the ma-jority of participants in the food riots because it fell to them to try to make ends meet at the market. Such disturbances increased the resolve of the state to maintain order at all costs. Riots against enclosure also reflected the fact that the poor assumed that they had a right to subsistence and be-lieved there had been better times when elites and ordinary people lived in harmony and the rights of both were respected.

The prosecution of serious crimes increased rapidly during Elizabeth's reign, peaking between 1590 and 1620. Vagrancy, considered a serious of-fense, was the most prevalent of these as people took to the road in search of food. Vagrants were arrested, and placed in stocks for three days, before

Whipping a man arrested for vagrancy and expelling him from town. In view of what's happened to his friend in the upper left corner, he's lucky to have escaped with his life.

being sent home. Untold thousands of poor people did not get that far and died before being arrested, such as the person buried in 1592, "a poor woman which died in a barne at the parsonage whose name we could not learne." Thefts rose rapidly. A contemporary estimated that there were twenty-three different categories of thieves and swindlers, including "hookers," who snatched linen and clothes with a long pole from windows, "priggers of prancers" (horse thieves), and "Abraham men," who "feign themselves to have been mad." But most thieves lacked such colorful names and specializations; they stole what they could in order to survive. Robert Whitehead, a poor man, was typical of those arrested for theft, having stolen a sheep, "beinge a verie poore man and havinge a wiefe and seaven smale children and being most hungery." The theft of goods worth more than twelve shillings could bring the death penalty, but more often offenders were publicly whipped and branded, or perhaps mutilated by having an ear extracted, and perhaps sent to serve as oarsmen in the galley ships. Women were often treated more harshly than men, unless they were pregnant. After 1572, individuals over age fourteen caught begging without a license were to be whipped and also "burned through the grisle of the right ear with a hot iron of the compass of an inch about, manifesting his or her roguish kind of life." Although only about 10 percent of those convicted of capital crimes were actually executed, such punishment was particularly brutal, including hanging by slow strangulation and being slowly crushed to death by weights.

The English upper classes, convinced that most crime went unpunished, became obsessed with maintaining order, a fact reflected in several of Shakespeare's plays, in which ordinary people appear as potential threats to social order. To some people, society stood on the verge of being overwhelmed by lawlessness and sin. At a time when the monarchy was extending its reach, many Elizabethans believed that social order depended on the maintenance of social hierarchy and the securing of obedience to the moral authority of government. Thus, the Tudors formulated a doctrine of obedience to authority, basing their arguments on religious teaching. As early as 1547, one of the first homilies on obedience had instructed that on earth God "hath assigned kings, princes, with other governors under them, all in good and necessary order." Such homilies, which were read in church from the pulpit, warned the English of the consequences of challenging social hierarchy:

> There reigneth all abuse, carnal liberty, enormity, sin and Babylonical confusion. Take away kings, princes, rulers, magistrates, judges, and such estates of God's order, no man shall ride to go by the highway untroubled, no man shall sleep in his own house or bed unkilled, no man shall keep his wife, children or possessions in quietness, all things shall be common; and there needs must follow all mischief and utter destruction both of souls, bodies, goods and commonwealths.

Elizabethan literature and drama constantly returned to the theme of a place for everyone and everyone in his or her place—or moral law based upon the necessity of social order. In Shakespeare's *The History of Troilus and Cressida,* Ulysses proclaims:

> The heavens themselves, the planets, and
>   this centre
> Observe degree, priority, and place,
> Insisture, course, proportion, season, form;
> Office, and custom, in all line of order; . . .
> But when the planets
> In evil mixture to disorder wander,
> What plagues and what portents, what mutiny!
> What raging of the sea, shaking of earth! . . .
> take but degree away, untune that string,
> And hark what discord follows. . . .

Many wealthy English men and women believed that the slightest offense against the monarchy contained the seeds of rebellion; in 1576, a woman was burned at the stake for saying that Elizabeth was "baseborn and not born to the crown." Fear of disturbances and challenges to authority contributed to the development of a sense of national consciousness of England's elite, just as the defeat of Spain's Armada in 1588 led to pride in being both Protestant and English.

In 1598, Parliament passed the first poor law, followed by another in 1601. These laws recognized for the first time the principle that the needy ought to receive some sort of assistance from their communities. Justices of the peace, under the supervision of the clergy, were to oversee the distribution of assistance to the poor in the local communities in which they resided. The poor laws also specified the establishment of poor houses for the incarceration of the poor who could not or would not work (including the aged, sick, and insane).

The poor laws, then, reflected a combination of concern for and fear of the wandering poor. Ministers denounced the poor from the pulpit as sources of disorder, while trumpeting the virtues of sobriety, submission, obedience, and social deference. Orders were sent from London detailing measures to be taken in the interest of social order by the justices of the peace, who only had recourse to troops in dire circumstances. Local elites took a more active role in enforcing ordinances against begging and vagrancy. Landed gentlemen and the merchants and manufacturers of the towns found that they now had more in common than wealth—a fear of the poor.

The Elizabethan Theater

The arts reflected the prosperity of the upper and middle classes in England. Protestant censors were more lax in censoring theatrical performances than had been their Catholic counterparts. In 1576, two professional theaters opened in London, followed by others in a number of provincial towns. Putting aside the repertory of religious allegories and miracle and morality plays that had been staged in royal castles, country manor houses, or entire towns, they staked their survival on their ability to attract audiences that would pay to see the actors perform. The more than 2,000 different plays staged in London between 1580 and 1640 consisted mostly of romances and dramas. During that period, more than 300 playwrights produced enough work to keep 100 acting companies working in London or touring provincial towns.

William Shakespeare (1564–1616) wrote plays that reflected uncertainty, ambivalence, and even disillusionment about contemporary English society. Historians know little about his life, despite the fact that he is perhaps the most revered Western author of all time. He was born in Stratford-on-Avon, where his father made gloves and was able to provide him with a primary school education. Shakespeare moved to London with his young wife to become an actor and in the late 1580s began to write plays. He found first patronage and then unparalleled success, angering rivals, one of whom referred to him as "an upstart crow beautified with our feathers." He became part owner and actor in the Lord Chamberlain's Company of the Globe Theater, which seated 3,000 viewers and hence

(*Left*) William Shakespeare. (*Right*) The Swan Theater, an Elizabethan playhouse that closely resembled Shakespeare's Globe Theater.

was the largest of London's six private theaters. Seats at such private theaters cost at least six times more than the cheapest tickets at the public theaters, which included places for the so-called "penny stinkards" who stood in the uncovered pit below the stage.

Audiences shouted for what they liked and hooted at what they did not. Fights were not infrequent, both inside and outside of the theater. The playwright Christopher Marlowe (1564–1593) died in a brawl in an inn under mysterious circumstances; the actor and playwright Ben Jonson killed another actor in a duel. Because of their rowdy reputations, most London theaters stood outside the city walls. London officials tried to close down the public theaters because they thought that disease spread easily among assembled crowds and because of complaints about profanity and lewdness on stage. Some great landowners found public crowds too socially mixed for their taste and helped revive private theaters.

Elizabethan drama reflected contemporary awareness and disapproval of the machinations of the powerful. In his dramatic, sometimes violent plays, as well as his comedies, Marlowe evoked the Elizabethan elite's unabashed struggle for position and power. Edmund Spenser's complex *Faerie Queen* used the legend of King Arthur to skirt censorship, presenting a thinly veiled criticism of the greed and corruption of contemporary political life. Spenser (1552–1599), a melancholy, frustrated man who never ascended to the heights of influence that he had sought, placed his "kingdom in Fairy land" in uncorrupted Ireland.

Despite the problems of religious division, warfare, and the struggles for influence that were reflected in the drama of the times, England under the

Tudors became a power that would influence the world. Elizabeth died in peace on March 24, 1603, in the forty-fifth year of her reign. She left England a substantially more unified, effectively ruled, and powerful state—despite the social disturbances engendered by harder times—than that she had inherited.

The Decline of Spain

In 1600, the word "decline" was first used to describe the overstretched Spanish Empire. Had the Spain of the Catholic kings fallen from God's favor? Castilians themselves still regarded Spain as a haven of peace and prosperity compared to the rest of Europe, which was wracked by religious wars. Responses from more than 500 towns and villages to a survey that Philip II sent around Castile in 1575 reflected Spanish self-confidence.

The Dutch Revolt

The decline of Spanish power began with the Dutch revolt. In the Netherlands, the Dutch nobles and officials resented higher taxes imposed by the Spanish crown. Above all, many of the Dutch were angered by the Spanish king's attempt to promote the Catholic Reformation by imposing the Inquisition in a land where most people were Calvinists. In the early 1560s, resistance first began against the presence of Spanish border garrisons and then against the unpopular governor.

In 1567, Philip II appointed the arrogant duke of Alba (1507–1582) to restore order in the north with 10,000 Spanish troops. The ruthless Castilian executed prominent Calvinist nobles on the central square of Brussels in the Southern Netherlands, established military courts, imposed heavy new taxes, and virtually destroyed self-government in the Netherlands. But Alba's reign of terror as governor also helped transform the resistance of Dutch nobles and officials, led by William of Orange (1533–1584), into a national revolt.

Alba believed that "Everyone must be made to live in constant fear of the roof breaking down over his head" and warned "I am resolved not to leave a creature alive, but to put them all to the sword." Alba's Council of Troubles, known to the Dutch as the "Council of Blood," executed thousands of people from 1567 to 1573, leading a Catholic bishop to claim later that in six years Alba had hurt the Church more than Luther and Calvin combined.

In 1572, rebellion became full-fledged insurrection. Spanish troops dominated on land, but the Dutch controlled the sea. When a Spanish army undertook a siege of Leiden, southwest of Amsterdam, the people of the town opened the dikes, and Dutch ships sailed over the rushing waters to drive the Spaniards away. But Alba's successor earned victories in the

The rescue of Leiden by the Dutch sea beggars, who arrive over the flooded low-lands after the breaching of the dikes.

Southern Netherlands. There Catholic nobles began to have second thoughts about continuing a struggle launched by Dutch Protestants. They detached the southern provinces from the rebellious federation. In 1579, the Dutch provinces formed the Union of Utrecht, and two years later they declared their independence from Spain as the Dutch United Provinces.

For the moment, Spain could supply its armies because Alba's armies had recaptured some of the Southern Netherlands, while Philip maintained peace with England. As the Dutch revolt wore on, however, the problems of fighting a war a thousand miles away plagued the Spanish king. Military contractors or entrepreneurs recruited mercenaries, and Italians, Burgundians, Germans, and Walloons made up much of the Spanish army.

Spanish routes for troops, supplies, and bullion to the Netherlands had to be maintained through a combination of diplomatic charm, cunning, and coercion. As allegiances and the fortunes of war eliminated first the Palatinate, then Alsace and Lorraine as routes through which armies could pass, the Spanish forged the "Spanish Road" as a military corridor (see Map 5.3). It began in Genoa, went overland across the Alps, and then passed through Lombardy and Piedmont, Geneva, Franche-Comté, Lorraine and, finally, the Duchy of Liège, with Spanish agents assuring supplies along the way.

MAP 5.3 THE SPANISH ROAD   The route taken by the Spanish armies, supplies, and money from Spain to the Netherlands was long and difficult, as it passed through mountainous terrain and many states.

Spanish officers compounded problems of recruiting and supply, however, by trying to save money. They charged sharpshooters for powder and shot, a dubious strategy at best. Compared to other armies fighting in Europe at the same time, the Spanish army seemed better only in terms of medical attention. The army's guarantee before battle to carry out the written wills made by soldiers seems to have been, on the other hand, a curiously self-defeating approach to inspiring confidence. Mutinies, the largest involving non-Spanish troops, occurred with ever more frequency as troops demanded payment of back wages, better and more regular food, and decent hospital conditions. Soldiers deserted, encouraged and aided by Dutch agents, as well as by those of France, against whom Spain was also warring. By 1577, the Spanish army in the Netherlands, unpaid for months, had dwindled in size from 60,000 to no more than 8,000 men.

Throughout the long war, the superior Dutch fleet kept the Spanish ships in port, while the English navy, allied with the Dutch in 1586, controlled the Channel. When the Spanish fleet sailed north in 1588, the result was the disastrous defeat of the Armada. The ships of "sea beggars," as they were called, fighting under William of Orange (until his assassination in 1584), then harassed Spanish ships.

At the beginning of the seventeenth century, the Dutch gradually fell back behind the protective town fortifications and natural barriers formed by rivers. The war became a series of long Spanish sieges against frontier towns defended by brick fortifications, bastions, and moats—a defensive system that had its origins with the Italian city-states. With the defense having a marked advantage, towns could be conquered only by being starved out.

France withdrew from the war in 1598, and England withdrew six years later. But a truce between Spain and the Dutch, signed in 1609, ended in 1621. In Holland the "war party" led by Maurice of Nassau (1567–1625), who was the son of William of Orange, won the upper hand, appealing for Calvinist religious orthodoxy and calling for a crusade against Catholicism that would also free the Southern Netherlands from Spanish rule. Army officers and merchant traders wanted to keep the struggle against Spain going as long as possible. It dragged on, an expensive drain on the Spanish economy.

Economic Decline

Economic decline—above all that of Castile in the middle decades of the seventeenth century—underlay Spain's fall from a position of European domination. But decline is, of course, relative. Spain remained an important state although its population, which had risen to 8.5 million people between 1541 and 1591, fell by almost a quarter to 6.5 million by the middle of the seventeenth century, as harvest failures, plague, smallpox, and emigration took their toll.

The "price revolution," the sharp rise in the level of inflation during the sixteenth century in Europe, may well have affected Spain less than some parts of Northern Europe, but it still had adverse effects on the Spanish monarchy. Gold and silver from the Americas accelerated inflation, to which royal monetary policies of currency debasement contributed. The monarchy, which had declared bankruptcy in 1557, suspended payments in 1575, and again in 1596, renegotiating loans at more favorable rates. But during the period 1568–1598, Spain had five times the military expenditures of the Dutch, English, and French combined, at least partially because it had to reconstitute the Armada. One of the results of so many expensive wars was that Spain lost its margin of safety when it experienced a series of epidemics, plagues, and harvest failures beginning in 1576 and continuing for most of the last quarter of the century. The economy

The expulsion of the Moriscos from Spain.

slipped into stagnation. To one noble it already seemed that "the ship is sinking."

Forced to take out large loans from foreign bankers at disadvantageous interest rates, the state attempted to find new sources of revenue. To raise funds, the crown imposed a tithe, or assessment of a tenth of the most valuable piece of real estate in each parish, and in 1590 the Castilian Cortes agreed to an extraordinary tax assessed on towns. An excise (sales) tax was imposed on consumption. This undermined the economy by encouraging the middle class to abandon business in favor of the acquisition of perpetual privileges—and thus tax exemptions—as they obtained noble status. The monarchy's massive expulsion of the Moriscos in 1609 (about 300,000 people, a third of the population of Valencia and a fifth of Aragon) proved counterproductive. The king succumbed to pressure from the Catholic Church and from wealthy families eager to seize Moorish land. The region of Valencia lost one-third of its population, including many skilled craftsmen and some of the most able and advanced farmers.

Castile, in particular, suffered a reduction in agricultural output because of twenty-five years of bad weather and crop failure. The rain pattern in Castile, with its annual summer drought, meant that Spanish farmers could not adopt the double-cropping innovations—for example, the summer planting of a nitrogen-fixing forage crop such as alfalfa—that brought agricultural expansion in England and the Netherlands.

Nobles added the lands of indebted peasants to their large estates (lati-fundia), but they showed little interest in increasing the productivity of their land, in contrast to their English counterparts. They turned fields into pastureland or simply left them untended. Royal policies may also have damaged the agricultural economy. In part because royal policies favored sheepherding over farming—because it was easier to collect taxes on sheep than on agricultural produce—many landowners converted marginal land into pasture for sheep and expanded their home textile manufacturing (as occurred in the Netherlands at the same time). But fine woolens manufacturing suffered from foreign textile imports, especially the importing of lighter cloth from France and the Netherlands. Furthermore, the stagnation of the population further reduced demand for Spanish woolens. Despite all those sheep, the production of wool fell by three-quarters in Toledo during the first two-thirds of the seventeenth century, and textile manufacturing completely disappeared from some cities.

At the same time, farmers were hampered by a state-imposed fixed maximum for grain prices, which discouraged ambitious agricultural initiatives. Toward the end of the sixteenth century, Spain had become dependent on imported grain. Its decline in demographic vitality generated less demand for food. This further reduced tax revenue. Many peasants simply abandoned their farms, moving to towns.

"Conquered by you, the New World has conquered you in turn, and has weakened and exhausted your ancient vigor," a Flemish scholar wrote a friend in Spain. The Spanish colonies, too, became something of a financial drain on the crown because of the cost of administering and defending them. The flow of Latin American silver, which had paid less than a quarter of the crown's colonial and military expenses, slowed to a trickle beginning in the 1620s. The colonial market for Spanish goods shrank with a precipitous decline in the Indian population (caused, above all, by disease; see Chapter 1), undermining Spanish commerce and industry. Furthermore, the colonies had also developed their own basic agricultural and artisanal production and relied far less on Spanish goods. The Atlantic ports of northern Castile endured competition in shipbuilding and commerce not only from Seville and Cádiz, but from Spain's own colonies, and above all, from England and the Netherlands.

The monarchy lost its financial autonomy within Spain. The intransigence of the Cortes of Aragon put more pressure on the crown to raise money in Castile. But the Castilian Cortes by 1600 had clearly affirmed its right to supervise state expenditures and was influential in establishing a system of state finance, with the Council of Castile serving as a court of final appeal.

Although the burden of taxes in Castile increased by four times between 1570 and 1670, the Spanish crown proved less efficient in collecting taxes than the monarchs of France and England. More than this, increased taxes on the poor generated more discontent than income. Spain's Italian subjects resisted contributing money for distant wars that did not concern them. Charles V had largely financed his wars through fiscal impositions on the Netherlands, his wealthiest province. But the Dutch revolt, in addition to dramatically raising royal expenses, stopped the flow of money from the Dutch subjects to the crown and thus drastically reduced royal revenue.

During the early years of the seventeenth century, officials, academics, military men, merchants, and clergy flooded the passive Philip III with well-intentioned critiques addressing the question of Spain's decline. Some of these critics (*arbitristas*) offered practical suggestions, such as reducing taxes and digging navigable canals, that they hoped would end Spain's economic malaise.

Other countries, notably France, may have had similar discouraging demographic and economic trends, but their natural resources were greater and their economic structure more solid. Money in Spain that might have gone into economic development often ended up being loaned to the crown at usurious interest, or exchanged for honorific privileges.

There were many families claiming noble titles in Spain, perhaps 10 percent of the population. Although some nobles served as officials and military commanders, others transformed indolence into a high art. One of the king's advisers, for example, was described as having "spent all

The painting *A Soldier's Dream* allegorizes Spanish feelings of morose despair and fatalism as the Spanish Empire begins to crumble.

his life in Madrid in total idleness, almost exclusively shared between eating and sleeping." A doctor gravely urged his aristocratic patients to
limit themselves to six courses per meal. The wealthiest aristocrats—the
"grandees," a small elite established by Charles V in 1525—spent wildly
and ostentatiously, flocking to court to curry favor. They did little besides
hunt, gamble, and conspire against their enemies. Many nobles were unwilling to serve as officers in the army. Furthermore, most of the clergy, in
a country dotted with monasteries and convents, contributed little to the
economy.

Contemporary Spaniards, particularly Castilians, lapsed into a morose
acceptance of decline. The novelist Miguel de Cervantes (1547–1616)
had fought with the king's armies at the Battle of Lepanto (1571), where
he received a wound that permanently crippled his left arm. Several years
later, he was captured by Turkish pirates. After five years as a slave, he
managed to return to Spain. The first part of Don Quixote was published
in 1605, the second in 1615. It is more than the tale of a zany noble intent
on bringing true chivalry back to Spain, accompanied by his sensible, subservient squire, Sancho Panza. Don Quixote is the story of national disillusionment in the face of perceived national decline. Cervantes blamed the
nobles, who lamented the end of heroic noble ideals. Among the next generation of great Spanish writers, the dramatist Pedro Calderón de la Barca
(1600–1681) tragically portrayed in his plays the floundering Spanish
aristocracy struggling to preserve its honor. Nobles and churchmen, the
two pillars of Spain, purchased the work of the increasingly gloomy Greek-
born artist El Greco (1541–1614). His The Burial of the Count Orgaz
(1581) shows figures looking up at a vision of celestial glory, while on
earth things already did not seem to be going very well.

An Empire Spread Too Thin

Spain's mounting economic problems were exacerbated by the fact that
the empire's interests, some of which were defended in costly wars, were
spread so widely, not only in Europe, but across the seas. Philip IV
(1605–1665), who succeeded to the throne in 1621, was intelligent,
strong-willed, lazy, and had a keen interest in the arts. He chose as his
chief adviser and the person who handled the affairs of state Gaspar de
Guzmán, the duke of Olivares (1587–1645), an Andalusian noble whose
family had, like Spain itself, suffered reverses. The short, increasingly
obese, and fiery Olivares sketched ambitious plans to shape the rebirth of
Spanish might. Confronted with the growing economic strength of the
Dutch rebels, as well as that of the English, Olivares sensed that Spain
could not remain a power without a marked economic resurgence. "We
must devote all our efforts," he had written, "to turning Spaniards into
merchants." The Count Duke, as he was called, mastered his master, convincing the lazy king that only hard work and reform could restore the glo-

(*Left*) King Philip IV. (*Right*) The Count Duke Olivares.

ries of the not-so-distant past. He would tutor his king, whose chamber pot he once ceremoniously kissed, in the fine art of monarchy.

The Count Duke espoused the growth of monarchical power and state centralization. His motto "one king, one law, one money" generated resistance, in the latter case because of the by then notorious instability of the Castilian currency. At a time when complaints mounted against the extraordinary excise taxes, Olivares sought to subject all of Spain to the laws and royal administration of Castile. In 1624 he told the king, "The most important thing in Your Majesty's Monarchy is for you to become King of Spain. By this I mean, Sir, that your Majesty should not be content with being king of Portugal, of Aragon, of Valencia and count of Barcelona, but should secretly plan to and work to reduce these kingdoms of which Spain is composed to the style and laws of Castile, with no difference whatsoever. And if Your Majesty achieves this, you will be the most powerful prince in the world."

Olivares wanted to force Dutch capitulation to restore the monarchy's reputation, fearing defeat as dishonorable, anxious that it might begin a chain reaction that would destroy the empire. He persuaded the king to allow the truce with the Dutch to lapse in 1621, thus necessitating massive expenses for land and sea warfare. Olivares concluded from the Dutch surrender of the fortress town of Breda in 1625 that it was God's will that the fight against the Protestant rebels in the north continue. To preserve the "Spanish Road," Olivares sought to bolster Spanish interests in northern Italy and in Austria, the same expensive strategy employed earlier by

Philip II. But France cut the Spanish supply routes in Savoy in 1622 and then in Alsace nine years later. Furthermore, Olivares embroiled Spain in a war in northern Italy when Spanish armies intervened in the hope of preventing the succession of a Frenchman as duke of Mantua, fearing that this might compromise Spanish control of Milan and northern Italy. Intermittent hostilities with France lasted from 1628 to 1631, and made more likely a full-scale conflict between the two powers.

Spain could ill afford such conflicts. In 1628, Dutch pirates captured a Spanish fleet loaded with silver. This enormous loss made it imperative that the crown find new resources with which to wage war. But for the first time, Castile's monarchs could not establish credit with foreign investors to finance Spain's foreign wars. Increased taxation, the floating of short-term loans through bonds, the sale of yet more privileges, and the imposition of new financial obligations on Aragon and the Italian territories all proved inadequate to the task of financing an expensive, distant war. The monarchy was finally able to override the opposition of the towns represented in the Castilian Cortes. But unable to overcome opposition to the centralization of the fiscal apparatus, Philip IV was forced to convoke the Cortes in 1632 to seek another extraordinary tax.

Its interests gravely overextended, Spain's position weakened. English ships began to nip at its imperial interests in the Americas. Dutch ships fought the proud Spanish galleons in the West Indies. Three decades of intermittent warfare with France began in 1635, as the Thirty Years' War (see Chapter 4) became a struggle between competing dynasties. As more and more bullion from the Americas had to be diverted to pay military expenses in the Netherlands and Italy, the monarchy demanded new contributions from Catalonia and Portugal, as Spain had assumed the expensive and ultimately extremely damaging responsibility for protecting Portuguese shipping around the world. Tumultuous tax riots, beneath which lay resentment against Castilian domination, broke out in the Portuguese town of Evora in 1637. The Portuguese upper classes began to resist Spanish authority.

Olivares' decision to demand more taxes from Catalonia proved fateful. Faced with resistance, he ordered the arrest of several Catalan leaders, amid riots in the countryside. Catalan nobles put aside their differences, and a full-scale revolt against Castilian rule began in 1640. Catalan and French forces together defeated the Spanish army. A year later, Andalusian nobles were foiled in a plot to create an independent kingdom there. Nobles in Madrid hatched plots against Olivares. When Portugal proclaimed its independence, there were few Spanish troops there to protest. The vigorous assertion of localism reflected the disillusionment of provincial elites with Castilian power. Philip sent the despondent Olivares into exile in 1643.

However, the illusion of Don Quixote was maintained—that the restoration of traditional aristocratic and ecclesiastical values would restore

Spanish might. Olivares established two court academies intended to train young nobles in the art of government. Heeding the advice of churchmen, he also attempted to ban prostitution and take other such measures in what he considered the interest of traditional morals, censoring the theater and books, prohibiting certain kinds of fancy clothing and long hair. It would not be enough.

By the 1660s, the Cortes was no longer an impediment to monarchical authority in Castile, and thereafter it was convoked only on ceremonial occasions. But, at the same time, the Spanish monarchy may in the long run have been damaged by its inability to reform its financial apparatus. The crown extended its reach and solidified its authority against possible provincial rebellions. Over the long run, Spanish rulers weakened parliamentary traditions. Yet, enhanced centralization was not matched by more efficient tax collection.

Ironically, amid such signs of decline, the last years of Philip IV and the reign of his pathetic successor, Charles II (ruled 1665–1700), sustained a period of considerable cultural accomplishment in the arts and in literature. But this, too, may have been generated by the prevailing mood of introspection. Olivares put dramatists and a small host of other writers to work in the name of glorifying the monarchy and imparting a sense of purpose that he hoped would revive Spain.

King Philip IV added more than 2,000 canvases to what already was a rich royal collection, including many by Italian masters. He covered the palace walls with grandiose paintings of battle scenes. Diego de Velázquez (1599–1660), the court painter, undertook forty portraits of the vain king. Their sharp realism stands as a commentary on the Spanish monarchy's fading glory and disillusionment. Velázquez also commemorated the badly needed—but ultimately fruitless—victory over the Dutch in *The Surrender of Breda* (1634–1635).

In the meantime, the Dutch rebels, aided by increased commercial prosperity, had fought the Spanish armies to a draw. The Treaty of Münster, which was part of the Westphalia settlement of 1648 that ended the Thirty Years' War, officially recognized Dutch independence after a struggle that had lasted three-quarters of a century. The provinces of the Southern Netherlands, that is, modern-day Belgium, which were overwhelmingly Catholic, remained a Habsburg possession. In Catalonia, Barcelona surrendered to royal troops in 1652. Catalan nobles accepted the supremacy of the crown in exchange for an affirmation of social hierarchy and royal protection against ordinary Catalans who resented their privileges. The Aragonese nobles, too, accepted this compromise.

The Spanish monarchy never learned that it could not fight effectively on a variety of fronts. In contrast, the French monarchy, concentrating its efforts in Italy, for the moment realized the wisdom of fighting on one front at a time. Thus, subsequent Spanish victories in the north against French armies were not enough, for when the French turned their atten-

Diego de Velázquez's *Surrender of Breda* (painted 1634–1635).

tion to the Spanish front they easily held their own. The Treaty of the Pyrenees, signed between France and Spain in 1659, established the border between these countries that has lasted, with only a few minor changes, until this day. Spain also gave up Milan to Austria, and Naples and Sicily to the Italian Bourbon dynasty. The Portuguese, aided by the English, turned back several half-hearted invasions by Spanish armies, and in 1668 Spain recognized Portugal's independence. Ten years later, France occupied the Franche Comté, the last major Spanish holding in Northern Europe.

By 1680, when the depression that had lasted almost a century ended, Spain had become a second-rate power. This was because of agricultural and manufacturing decline, to be sure, but, above all, it was because the Spanish crown had overreached.

CONCLUSION

The development of trade across the Atlantic Ocean to the Americas was part of European economic expansion during the sixteenth century. Following the union of the crowns of Castile and Aragon, Spain grew into a great power. Philip II expanded the Spanish Empire, which, in the Americas stretched from what is now the southern United States to the southern tip of Latin America, and in Europe included the Netherlands and several Italian states. The Tudor monarchy in England overcame the country's religious divisions in the wake of the English Reformation to strengthen its authority. In this, it resembled the ruling Valois dynasty of France, another "new monarchy" in that it enhanced its reach, efficiency, and prestige. The burgeoning of English trade, manufacturing, and agriculture in the Elizabethan Age underlay England's relative prosperity, even as social polarization, reflected in the crises of the 1590s, became more apparent.

The surprising English naval defeat of the Spanish Armada in 1588 symbolized not only the rise of England but in some ways anticipated the decline of Spanish power. Spain's rulers had expanded their vast empire and imperial interests beyond the ability of the state to sustain them. When silver from the Americas slowed to a trickle, Spain's own limited natural resources, combined with demographic stagnation that began early in the seventeenth century, undercut Spanish Habsburg power. The inability of the Spanish monarchy to impose fully its authority on Aragon and Catalonia, or to collect taxes efficiently, prevented a revival of Spanish preeminence. The long revolt of the Netherlands ended with recognition of Dutch independence in 1648. That the Dutch Republic and England, two trading nations, had emerged as European powers reflected the shift of economic primacy to Northwestern Europe.

CHAPTER **6**

ENGLAND AND THE DUTCH REPUBLIC IN THE SEVENTEENTH CENTURY

England and the Dutch Republic were anomalies in the seventeenth century. At a time when aggressive European monarchs were forging absolute states by overwhelming noble prerogatives, the privileges of towns, and other impediments to an extension of royal authority, these two seafaring, trading nations maintained representative government. It was not always easy, and might well have been otherwise.

The Stuart monarchs' flirtation with absolutism in England brought bitter discord, resistance, and civil war. In the Dutch Republic, which had earned its independence in 1648 after a long war against Spanish absolute rule, the prosperous merchants who dominated the economic and political life of the country brushed aside the absolutist challenge of the House of Orange, which wanted to establish a hereditary monarchy.

In both England and the Netherlands, religious divisions accentuated the struggle between absolutism and constitutionalism. Both the protracted revolt of the largely Protestant Dutch against Catholic Spain and the English Civil War echoed the religious struggles between Catholics and Protestants during the Thirty Years' War (1618–1648) in Central Europe (see Chapter 4). The Dutch had risen up in open rebellion in 1566 in part because the Spanish Habsburgs attempted to impose the Catholic Inquisition on what had become a Protestant country. In England, the attempt of Kings James I and Charles I to return the English Church to elaborate rituals associated by many people with Catholicism pitted the monarchy against Parliament. This constitutional crisis led to the defeat and execution of Charles I in 1649, the fall of the monarchy, and in 1688,

The bustling harbor of Middelburg in the province of Zeeland, southwestern Netherlands, in the early seventeenth century.

to the "Glorious Revolution," which brought King William III and Queen Mary to the throne. Parliament, which historically represented landed interests, succeeded in balancing and constraining royal authority. By virtue of Parliament's victory in the Civil War, England remained a constitutional monarchy. England's new monarchs agreed to a Bill of Rights, which affirmed the civil liberties of English people and the rights of Parliament.

That the two new powers of Northern Europe, England and the Dutch Republic, were largely Protestant has led some historians to associate their success with the "Calvinist ethic" of hard work. Yet, the emergence of England and the Dutch Republic as Great Powers was largely because of their social structure, especially the vitality of the "middling sort" in both nations, the relative unity of the two states, and the location of both rising powers on the Atlantic. Aided by governments quick to realize the benefits to their states of an expansion of international trade, the Dutch Netherlands and England mobilized the resources of its middle classes. England's international commerce rapidly developed. And as Amsterdam emerged as a banking center and first port of call for international trade, the Dutch Republic enjoyed the golden age of its culture.

CONFLICTS IN STUART ENGLAND

Conflicts between the Stuart kings and Parliament, as well as religious conflicts, led to the English Civil War, which helped define the constitutional and political institutions of modern Britain. The monarchy tried to enhance its authority at the expense of Parliament by attempting to impose extralegal taxes without the consent of Parliament. But the English gentry, whose status and influence came from ownership of land, emerged from the period with their parliamentary prerogatives intact. The nature and extent of royal prerogatives were at issue, as well as religious, social, and ideological divisions. These were played out through the English Civil War and its aftermath.

Conflicts between James I and Parliament

King James I (1566–1625) succeeded his cousin Queen Elizabeth to the English throne in 1603. As King James VI of Scotland, he had overcome court factionalism and challenges from dissident Presbyterians. The two countries were joined in a personal union because he ruled both. The first Stuart king of England was lazy, slovenly, and frivolous, particularly enjoying hurling jelly at his courtiers. But there was more to him than that. He was an intelligent and well-read blunderer, once described as "the wisest fool in Christendom." Before coming to the throne, James had sketched out a theory of divine right monarchy. And in a speech to Parliament in 1609 the king had called "The state of MONARCHIE . . . the supremest thing upon earth: for Kings are not only GOD'S Lieutenants upon earth, and sit upon throne, but even by God himselfe they are called Gods." James described Parliament as nothing "but cries, shouts, and confusion." Relations between the monarch and Parliament degenerated rapidly.

The English monarchy was in a precarious financial position. Queen Elizabeth's war debts were at least partially to blame. But the financial weakness of the English crown also resulted from the monarch's growing inability to tax efficiently. (Tax increases helped contribute to the major political crises of the sixteenth century, including the Fronde in France; see Chapter 7.) For the moment, James increased royal revenues by selling the right to monopolies on such essential products as coal and soap. Parliament traditionally had to approve extraordinary expenditures. When the Stuart kings tried to assert the monarchy's authority to raise money in ways many people believed unprecedented and thus unconstitutional, opposition grew in Parliament.

James brought to court like-minded dandies, most of whom proved not only unpopular with Parliament but incompetent and provocative as well. In the last years of his reign, James became increasingly dependent on his young, handsome favorite, George Villiers, the duke of Buckingham (1592–1628). A relative newcomer to court circles, Buckingham convinced the king to sell peerages and titles, offices, monopolies, and other privileges to the highest bidder. Opposition to such attempts to raise money mounted within Parliament.

Although it met sporadically and at the king's pleasure, Parliament transformed itself from something more than a debating society into an institution that saw itself as defending the rights of the English people. The House of Commons, lashing out at the beneficiaries of royal monopolies, impeached on charges of bribery Lord Chancellor Francis Bacon (1561–1626), philosopher of science and once the king's friend. Here, too, there was a principle at stake: the accountability of ministers, if not responsibility, to Parliament.

English foreign policy contributed both to the monarchy's mounting debt and the emerging political crisis. Queen Elizabeth had denied that Parliament had the right to discuss matters of foreign policy unless invited by the monarch to do so. Parliament, however, still insisted on that right. Thus, for example, James favored peace with Spain, but Parliament clamored for war because Bavaria, an ally of Habsburg Spain, had invaded the Protestant Upper Palatinate. And in 1621, asserting its right to influence foreign policy, Parliament refused to provide more funds for the conflict, setting the stage for the greatest constitutional crisis in English history.

Parliament also denounced the monarch's attempt to arrange a marriage between his son, Charles, the heir to the throne, and the daughter of Philip IV of Spain. As dynastic marriages were an essential part of foreign policy, cementing or building alliances, members of Parliament objected to what appeared to be a sudden royal espousal of a foreign policy that seemed pro-Spanish and therefore pro-Catholic. Parliament declared its right to discuss the proposed marriage, and thus foreign affairs. But James defied Parliament by stating that it could not discuss matters of foreign policy, denying that the privileges of Parliament were "your ancient and undoubted birthright and inheritance." Rather he described them as "derived from the grace and permission of our ancestors and us."

James' wedding plans for his son fell through in 1623, however, when the Spanish king refused to allow Charles, who had gone to Madrid with

(*Left*) King James I. (*Right*) The young Charles, heir to the throne and later Charles I.

Buckingham, even to set eyes on his daughter. But two years later, James arranged Charles' marriage to another devout Catholic, Henrietta Maria of France. The secret price of this liaison included the king's promise that he would one day allow English Catholics, who numbered 2 or 3 percent of the population, to practice their religion freely. In a country in which anti-Catholicism had been endemic since the English Reformation of the mid-sixteenth century, James seemed to be taking steps to favor Catholicism.

James was succeeded upon his death by his son, Charles I (ruled 1625–1649). The young king was indecisive and painfully shy, traits compounded by a stammer. Even more than his father, Charles rejected the view that his appointments to ministries and other important offices should represent a wide spectrum of political and religious views. Charles stubbornly refused to oust Buckingham, even as Parliament began impeachment proceedings against the royal favorite.

Religious Divisions

King Charles I once claimed, "People are governed by the pulpit more than the sword in time of peace." In the seventeenth century, no other realm of life so bitterly divided Europeans as religion. In England, religious divisions helped accentuate and define the political crisis. The Established or Anglican Church faced a challenge from the Puritans, a dissident religious group of Calvinists that had emerged during Elizabeth's reign.

It is difficult to define what exactly it meant to be a Puritan in early seventeenth-century England. Many Puritans were more sure of what they were against than what they were for. As Oliver Cromwell, imposing leader of Parliament during the English Civil War, put it, "I can tell you, sir, what I would not have, though I cannot, what I would." Most Puritans were strongly attracted by the Calvinist idea that each individual was predestined by God through His grace to be saved or not to be saved. Puritans emphasized preaching and the individual's personal understanding of the Bible, spiritual devotion, discipline, and sacrifice as the basis of religion. Puritans opposed the role of bishops in the Church of England, in part because they emphasized the personal worth of the individual minister, not the value of an ecclesiastical title. They wanted authority to be taken away from bishops and given to local synods. They de-emphasized the sacraments and wanted worship to be simpler than the contemporary Anglican Church services, which they roundly criticized. Relentlessly hostile to Catholicism, Puritans held that elaborate church accoutrements—such as stained-glass windows and altar rails—smacked of the Roman papacy.

Puritans could be found in all social groups, above all, among the "middling sort"—including merchants, shopkeepers, and artisans—particularly in London, but also among the gentry at one end of the social spectrum and weavers at the other. Puritans did not choose the name by which they came to be known in the late sixteenth century, and which was originally intended as a term of abuse. Considering themselves "the godly," they believed that they represented the true Church of England, and worked for change and moral improvement within it. They remained a minority, probably not more than 10 percent of the population, and perhaps a third of all gentry. As Puritan numbers increased, however, their influence grew. University graduates who had embraced Puritanism formed "a godly preaching ministry" in many parishes, with endowed lectureships providing opportunities for Puritans to preach and win converts.

The Puritans were increasingly hostile to those who espoused a kind of Protestantism known as Arminianism. At first no more than a handful of ecclesiastics with the king's ear, Arminians soon came to wield considerable power. Charles I became an Arminian, and so did Buckingham. English Arminians, like their Dutch counterparts, broke with Calvinists over predestination, which Arminians rejected, but which Puritans accepted, and over the related concept of free will. Arminians accepted free will, while Puritans denied that an individual could achieve salvation through free will.

Puritans and Arminians also clashed over forms of worship. The Arminians accepted rites and rituals that to the Puritans seemed to replicate those of the Catholic Church. Indeed, Charles believed deeply in the traditions and rituals of the High Church, including the ceremonies associated with the Anglican Prayer Book. The Puritans wished to eliminate as much of the ritual as possible. The Arminians emphasized royal authority over the Church of England because they depended on it, and thus at least seemed to be proponents of royal absolutism. Arminians tried to forbid Calvinist preaching on controversial issues. And they emphasized the authority and ceremonial role of bishops, which Puritans opposed with particular vehemence.

The king's aggressive espousal of Arminianism enhanced the influence of William Laud (1573–1645), bishop of London. In 1633, Charles named the Arminian Laud to be the head of the Established Church as Primate of England (archbishop of Canterbury). The pious, hard-working, and stubborn son of a draper, Laud warned Charles that the religious extremes of Catholicism and radical Puritanism both posed threats to the Established Church, that "unless your Majesty look to it, she will be ground to powder." Laud espoused High Church rituals, and because of this, he was viewed with suspicion by the Puritans. Most Puritans also believed that Bishop Laud was secretly working to make Catholicism the established church of England, and therefore feared his influence in government. Under Elizabeth I and James I, Catholics had remained a force in some sectors of English life. Fear of a "popish plot" to restore Catholicism as the religion of the English state existed at all levels of English society. Landowners whose families had purchased ecclesiastical lands during the Reformation now worried that Laud might return them to the Catholic Church. Most people in England identified Catholicism and "popery" with the Spanish Inquisition, the Saint Bartholomew's Day Massacre in France, and the duke of Alba's Council of Blood in the Netherlands (see Chapters 4 and 5). And they viewed with alarm reconversions of some families to Catholicism, including a third of the gentry families of Yorkshire by the first years of the seventeenth century.

Charles I and Parliament Clash

Charles' fiscal policies deepened popular dissatisfaction with his reign. In 1625, the king decreed a forced loan on landowners, demanding that they provide him with subsidies, which he levied without Parliament's consent and which he insisted be paid within three months, an unprecedented short period of time. The next year, he ordered the imprisonment of seventy-six gentlemen, including five extremely prominent knights, who refused to meet the royal demand. Parliament refused to consent to the levies unless Charles met its demands for fiscal reform. The king convoked three Parliaments in four years, but dissolved each when it refused to provide him with funds. Parliament continued to demand that Charles appoint ministers it could trust and began impeachment proceedings against Buckingham. However, Buckingham disappeared as a source of irritation to Parliament when a disgruntled naval officer who had not been paid assassinated him in 1628.

After Buckingham's death, Charles again asked Parliament to provide him with more funds. In response, Parliament promulgated the Petition of Right, which it forced Charles to accept in return for the granting of a tax. This constrained the king to agree that in the future he would not attempt to impose "loans" without Parliament's consent, and that no "gentlemen" who refused to pay up would be arrested—nor would anyone else be imprisoned without a show of just cause. The Petition of Right, which was initially put forward in 1628 by Sir Thomas Wentworth (1593–1641), then an opponent of the crown and one of the men imprisoned for refusing to pay the forced loan, was a significant document in the constitutional evolution of England. It defined the rights of Parliament as inalienable and condemned arbitrary arrest, martial law, and taxes imposed without Parliament's consent.

Angered by the Petition of Right and by Parliament's insistence that his collection of customs duties was a violation of the Petition, Charles ordered Parliament's dissolution in 1629. Members of the Commons, however, physically held in his chair the speaker of the house, whose role was to communicate with the king on behalf of Parliament. They proceeded to declare that anyone who attempted to collect funds not levied with the approval of Parliament should be considered "a capital enemy to the kingdom and commonwealth," as would anyone who sponsored "inno-

Riot in St. Gile's Cathedral, Edinburgh, when the bishop begins to read from the Anglican Book of Common Prayer.

vation of religion," which is what Puritans considered Laud's espousal of elaborate High Church ceremonies. A defiant Parliament then disbanded.

For the next eleven years, Charles ruled without Parliament and tried to raise monies in new and controversial ways. Inflation had increased the royal debt dramatically, as well as greatly increasing the costs of ships and arms for waging war. The monarchy had exhausted its credit. Unlike James, Charles had some scruples about peddling privileges, but none at all about other means of raising funds. He fined gentlemen who did not attend his coronation. Most controversially, Charles ordered that "ship money" (a tax levied on port towns to provide ships for defense in times of emergency) also be imposed on inland towns beginning in 1634. Ship money raised the question of royal prerogatives because the tax seemed an affront to English Common Law and had been imposed without Parliament's consent.

Charles' high-handed royal policies led to a rebellion in Scotland. The king had seized lands from Scottish nobles and, at Laud's instigation, in 1637 he ordered the imposition of the Anglican Book of Common Prayer on the Scottish Presbyterian Church (established as the Scottish national church in the 1560s). The Scots had never been pleased with the union with England that had been weakly forged in 1603 when James VI of Scotland ascended the English throne as James I. They demanded that the prayer book be considered by a general church assembly. In 1638, some Scottish leaders signed the *National Covenant*, attacking the pope and the prayer book and swearing to defend their religion and liberties. Faced with the resolution of Scots to maintain the Presbyterian Church, Charles convoked the church assembly in Scotland, but he also began to prepare for an invasion of Scotland. In the meantime, Scottish nobles and landowners began evicting Anglican bishops and taking over churches, and the Scots rose up in arms.

This was a turning point in the dramatic reign of King Charles I. Desperately needing funds to defeat the Scots, in March 1639 the king demanded that the city of London help pay for the war. After several allocations, insulting in their modesty, London finally consented to lend the crown a large sum, but only on the condition that Charles convene Parliament. Furthermore, London would provide the bulk of the loan only when Charles had proven good faith by permitting Parliament to sit for a sufficient period of time.

Nobles and gentry led resistance to royal policies from the beginning; some were already in touch with the rebellious Scots, who in 1640 captured the northeastern English port of Newcastle without resistance. Running short of cash and facing mutinies in the royal army, in April 1640 the king summoned Parliament for the first time in eleven years. But when it refused to allocate money for the war against Scotland until Charles agreed to consider a list of grievances, the king dissolved this "Short Parliament" after less than two months. Charles I's defiance of Parliament turned political division into a full-fledged constitutional crisis.

THE ENGLISH CIVIL WAR

The political crisis of the Stuart monarchy became a constitutional conflict about how England was to be governed. To the king's opponents, Parliament existed to protect fundamental English liberties that had been established under the Magna Carta in 1215. By this reasoning the king did not have the right to dispense with its counsel and traditional authority to allocate royal finances, nor did he have the right to impose taxes without historical precedent. While Parliament, led by Puritans, was not yet claiming sovereignty, it was clearly asserting its traditional prerogative to balance royal authority.

Defenders of Parliament and local prerogatives were upset at the king's effort to expand his reach. They perceived Laudian religious reforms and the collection of ship money as the work of cynical and power-crazed men perhaps manipulated by the pope. Justices of the peace resented the usurpation of their authority by various decrees of martial law and by royal courts that had impinged on regional courts. Local officials believed that the king's lieutenants were exceeding their traditional authority over military affairs by bypassing established routines of local approval of military levies. Some Londoners felt particularly aggrieved, including those merchants who were not able to export cloth because of royal control over cloth exports through the monopoly of the Merchant Adventurers. The monarchy alienated other Londoners when it allowed some craftsmen to operate outside the structure of the London guilds, tried to regulate construction in London and its growing suburbs, and attempted to force the city to provide sums for the war with Scotland. The sale of the right to collect royal customs generated controversy as well, particularly as the government sold more privileges to pay off those who collected or "farmed" taxes on its behalf.

Many in the country resented the Catholic influences on the king. Charles surrounded himself with confidants, advisers, artists, and musicians whose sense of royal decorum and aesthetic tastes seemed to suggest the influence of continental Catholicism. The queen brought Flemish artists to Court who emphasized the religious themes of the Catholic Reformation, serving to convince critics of royal political policy that a plot was afloat, as a contemporary put it, "to seduce the King himself with Pictures, Antiquities, Images & other vanities brought from *Rome*."

Those who consistently supported Parliament became known as the supporters of "Country," while those who supported virtually unlimited monarchical prerogatives were identified with "Court." While the terms "Court" and "Country" are something of a simplification and virtually disappeared in the 1640s, they do reflect essential political differences during the political crisis.

Titled nobles, of whom there were about 1,200 in the country, generally supported the king. Gentry formed the core of the political opposition to the king. Nonetheless, the gentry did not make up a monolithic social group, and not all of those in the gentry supported Parliament against the king. During the previous century, many in the gentry had extended their landholdings, and men enriched by commerce or service in the law or army had become part of the gentry through the purchase of land. The roots of confrontation may have come from the struggle of these economically dynamic gentry to obtain political power commensurate with their rising station in English life. And their economic success may have affronted the wealthiest nobles, most of whom supported the king. On the other hand, gentry of modest means may not have experienced either an increase or decline in their holdings and may have been happy with the status quo. Some gentry of lesser means who had fallen upon hard times may have blamed the monarchy for their plight and hence supported Parliament. However, gentry in the economically less advanced north of England may have supported the king as a conservative force for stability.

The English Civil War has been called "the Puritan Revolution" even though its causes extended beyond the question of religion, and Puritans were not alone in resisting the monarchy. There were many Puritans in Parliament, including the body's leader, John Pym (1584–1643). A brilliant speaker and powerful debater, Pym was a zealot, an impetuous and perhaps even paranoid man whose strong convictions were in part defined by an obsession that a "popish plot" existed to restore Catholicism to England. Puritans dominated the ranks of the lesser gentry in the eastern counties, areas that took the side of Parliament during the Civil War. Puri-

(*Left*) John Pym. (*Right*) William Laud, bishop of London and later archbishop of Canterbury.

tan preachers denounced the collection of ship money. Most Puritans believed along with Pym that Laud was trying to restore Catholicism.

As the political crisis grew in the 1630s, the authority of Anglican bishops, their appointment as state officials, and their right to nominate ministers smacked to many of "popery." Charles I echoed the famous statement of his father, James I, "No bishops, no king!," an assertion that would come back to haunt him. Laud expanded the power of ecclesiastical courts, which tried people accused of offenses against the Church of England. This reminded some people of the Spanish Inquisition.

Moving toward Conflict

Having dissolved the "Short Parliament" in May 1640, Charles again convoked a newly elected Parliament the following October. That summer brought religious and social turmoil. Ordinary people smashed altar rails and shattered stained-glass windows. The crown's strengthening of the army with Catholic Irish regiments, commanded by Thomas Wentworth, who was now a supporter and adviser of the king and had been named the earl of Strafford, confirmed to credulous ears that a "popish plot" was in the works. The English army suffered defeat in Scotland, and the war required yet more funds. Led by Pym, Parliament turned its wrath upon Charles' advisers, perpetuating the half-truth that the "eleven years of tyranny" had been the fault of bad advice. It indicted Strafford, who was tried and executed in London before a rejoicing throng. Parliament denounced as illegal the most unpopular royal acts during the previous eleven years (including many of the new taxes introduced by the king) and abolished some of the courts controlled by the monarchy. Parliament proclaimed that it could only dissolve itself, and that in the future the king would have to summon it every three years.

Parliament's session took place at a time when the Irish were rebelling against English rule. Beginning in the summer of 1641, Irish peasants, who were overwhelmingly Catholic, rose up against the English and killed many Protestant landlords. This seemed to many Protestants to confirm their fears of a Catholic conspiracy against English liberties. Furthermore, many believed that the king could not or would not repress the insurgents. The Irish rebellion highlighted crucial questions about the rights of Parliament by making urgent the issue of who controlled the militia.

In November 1641, Parliament passed the Grand Remonstrance. Presenting what Parliament considered a history of royal misdeeds, it denounced "a malignant and pernicious design of subverting the fundamental laws and principles" of English government and called for religious and administrative reforms. Its passage by a narrow margin indicated that Parliament remained divided over how far to carry its opposition to royal policies. Puritans, who narrowly controlled the House of Commons, now wanted to reform both church and state. Wealthy nobles began to form a solid bloc around the cause of the king, fearing that reform might weaken their influence. In November, the high sheriff of Lancashire called upon "gentlemen" to take arms with their tenants and servants on behalf of the king "for the securing of our own lives and estates, which are now ready to be surprised by a heady multitude." In some places, fighting began that month, as both sides fought for control of the militias.

Emboldened by an intransigent Court faction, the king attempted a bold coup against Parliament in January 1642. He personally led several hundred armed soldiers into Parliament and ordered the arrest of Pym and several other leaders. Forewarned, Pym and other leaders had left Commons before Charles arrived, and were protected in London by artisans and craftsmen. All chances of compromise disappeared. Fearing for his safety in London, where people had become more forceful in their support of Parliament and their demands for radical reform, Charles and his family headed north to more friendly country, and his supporters left Parliament. In June, Parliament promulgated "Nineteen Propositions," which denounced confrontational royal policy. In August 1642, Charles responded by mobilizing his forces at Nottingham.

Taking Sides

As civil war spread, Parliament's soldiers came to be known as "Roundheads" for the short, bowl-shaped haircuts many of them wore. The king's "Cavaliers" liked to think of themselves as fighting the good fight for God

and king against those who would shatter social harmony by making "subjects princes and princes slaves." But so far as civil wars go, there was relatively little actual fighting. Relatively short "campaign seasons" were
interrupted by winter. There were only four major battles, only one very far
from London (see Map 6.1). The two sides fought to a draw on October
23, 1642, at Edgehill, near Shakespeare's birthplace of Stratford-on-Avon,
south of Birmingham. When a royal military advance on London was
turned back, Charles set up headquarters in Oxford, fifty miles northwest
of London. In February 1643, the king rejected Parliament's terms for a
settlement. When a second royal march on London failed, both sides intensified massive propaganda campaigns to win support. The war became
a war of words, among the first in history. More than 22,000 newspapers,
newsletters, pamphlets, broadsides, sermons, and speeches were published between 1640 and 1661. At least 2,000 pamphlets were published
in 1642, an average of almost 6 a day.

The war nonetheless took its toll. Life in thousands of villages was disrupted, if not by actual fighting and the death of conscripted or volunteer
soldiers, then by requisitions, plundering, and general hardship. About 10
percent of the English population was forced to leave home during the
war. Many counties—perhaps most—were neutral, as local gentlemen

MAP 6.1 THE ENGLISH CIVIL WAR   Major battles during the English Civil War,
as well as Cavalier and Roundhead strongholds.

struggled to maintain control and keep their counties free of fighting and devastation.

Each side had to organize the pursuit of the war. In regions of royalist allegiance, the Cavaliers utilized existing administrative hierarchies, above all the justices of the peace. Lacking London's credit institutions, Charles financed the war by selling more titles and received gifts and loans from nobles. But fearful of losing further popular support, the king sought approval for forced levies by calling meetings of freeholders or grand juries.

The Roundheads of Parliament at first had to improvise as they governed territories under their control. Parliament, in keeping with its insistence on local prerogatives and resistance to monarchical centralization, kept civil, fiscal, and military authority relatively decentralized in regions under its control. At first its troops, living off the land, were more ruthless than those of the royalists, though later in the war the situation was reversed. Parliament did not hesitate to impose martial law in some troublesome counties. A regional military structure finally developed, based on associations of counties pledging mutual assistance in the parliamentary cause. Gentlemen organized government as best they could, confiscating the property of some prominent families supporting the king's cause. Parliament raised funds through heavy excise and property taxes.

Patterns of allegiance in the English Civil War were influenced by local economic and social considerations. Parliament drew considerable support from the most economically advanced regions—the south and east—while King Charles I retained the allegiance of most of northern and western England.

For example, Parliament found adherents where commercial agriculture had entailed changes in land use. Cultivation for the urban market had flourished in the aftermath of deforestation, the draining of marshlands, and the privatization of common lands through parliamentary acts of enclosure, some of which the monarchy had opposed. Districts in which cloth manufacturing had developed during the previous hundred years were also particularly likely to support Parliament, perhaps because people were no longer totally dependent on wealthy landowners for work. In the dairying, cattle-grazing, and forested areas of the west, dispersed patterns of settlement had been conducive to small-scale cloth manufacturing, particularly cottage industry. But if in some economically dynamic regions the "middling sort" tended to support Parliament, in others they did not. Here no clear pattern is discernible. Regions of rich but traditional agriculture, such as in the west, often supported the king, perhaps because economic and social hierarchies survived intact.

Villages became sites for religious and political struggle. Festivals served a social function, bringing villagers together to celebrate the holidays of the year. Puritans, however, considered such festivals frivolous, disruptive, ungodly. They associated such events with Catholic festivals, above all the perceived licentiousness of Mardi Gras. Puritans particularly disliked

Roundheads destroying altar railings and paintings of saints.

those festivals called "church ales," which were drinking bouts often overseen by gentry and even clergy, raising money for the Anglican Church.
Puritans believed that village festivals eroded social hierarchy and family
life by encouraging all participants to behave as equals in drinking, dancing, and sexual freedom. Wanting ordinary people to toe the line, Puritans
considered bat and ball games, stoolball, and a game resembling football
to be unsightly free-for-alls that defamed the Sabbath. The Puritans sponsored their own festivals, attempting to replace the merrymaking and
pranks of Halloween—the night before All Saints' Day—with less boisterous gatherings. Support for the king remained strong, however, among
villagers in regions where the traditional festive rituals, with the benevolent encouragement of wealthy country gentlemen, had survived the Puritan assault in the decades before the Civil War.

Oliver Cromwell and the New Model Army

In 1643, Parliament allied with the Scots, many of whom were Presbyterians delighted to participate in what they considered a holy war against the
Anglican episcopacy. Pym's sudden death at the end of that year did not
lessen Parliament's resolve to force the king to capitulate. A Scottish army
crossed into England. In July 1644, Parliament's army combined with the
Scots to defeat the Cavaliers at Marston Moor, near York. About 45,000
men fought in this largest battle of the English Civil War. This gave Parliament control of northern England. Scottish participation made an early
end to the war unlikely, adding to the determination of the "war party" faction to whom Charles listened.

Oliver Cromwell (1599–1658), who led the Roundheads to victory at

Marston Moor, emerged as the leader of Parliament. Cromwell was born into a gentry family, "by birth a gentleman living neither in considerable height nor yet in obscurity," as he put it. He never lost what well-heeled gentry considered his rough edges. Several years before being elected to Parliament in 1640, he had undergone—perhaps after serious illness—a deep spiritual conversion. Cromwell became convinced that God had chosen him to be one of the elect and that as such he would gain eternal salvation. Strong Puritan views led him into politics, and he believed that his rise to power was God's will. Cromwell combined idealism with the stubbornness of someone who can easily convince himself that he is right all the time.

Combining three existing armies, Parliament formed the New Model Army in 1645. Cromwell, as second in command, instilled strict discipline. Moreover, Roundhead soldiers' morale improved with regular wage payments. Unlike its predecessors, the New Model Army won grudging good will in the counties by paying for supplies and not plundering. (In contrast, the king's army, which was short on funds, began to plunder the countryside.) Although it included a few more commanders of relatively ordinary birth than before, the New Model Army was not unique in the social origins of either its soldiers or officers, but rather in its single-minded discipline and radical purpose.

Cromwell prevailed on Parliament in 1645 to pass a self-denying ordinance, which forced members of Parliament who held military commands to relinquish them. But the ordinance permitted several exceptions to this rule, one of which was for Cromwell. This angered a minority of moderate Parliamentarians, now wary of Cromwell's rising power.

Oliver Cromwell.

Divisions within Parliament

Two political groups emerged in Parliament. "Presbyterians," a majority within Parliament, were moderates both in political and religious matters. Originally a pro-Scottish group that had rallied behind Pym, most (despite the name "Presbyterians") were Puritans. Opposed to the power of bishops, they wanted an established national Calvinist Church in which lay elders selected ministers, and they were against religious toleration. They had agreed to the execution of Archbishop Laud at the beginning of 1645. But they were ready to accept a negotiated settlement with the king.

The Independents were militant Puritans, more radical than the Presbyterians in that they wanted the church to be a loose alliance of congregations that would choose their own ministers. The Independents were less willing to compromise with the king on the issue of parliamentary prerogatives. They favored state toleration of some religious dissent and opposed an established church. More than this, some of them desired more far-reaching political changes that would protect individual rights. Cromwell's rise to leadership reflected the ascendancy of the Independents in Parliament.

Cromwell began to purge Presbyterian commanders within the New Model Army, replacing them with Independents who were loyal to him. Singing psalms as they rushed fearlessly into battle, Cromwell's "Ironsides," as his troops—"base and mean fellows"—were called, maintained an air of invincibility. In June 1645, the New Model Army routed the royalists. Charles surrendered to the Scots a year later, hoping to obtain a less draconian peace than if he capitulated directly to Parliament. But the Scottish army left England, leaving the king in the custody of Parliament in February 1647.

Radicals

As the war dragged on, England fell into virtual anarchy amid growing resentment over the billeting of soldiers, food shortages, and rising prices. The English Civil War unleashed forces that seemed to challenge the foundation of social and political order. During the siege of royalist Oxford, a hungry sentry called down to the besieging forces, "Roundhead, fling me up half a mutton and I will fling thee down a Lord!" At times the Roundheads appeared to hold back as if wary of the consequences of victory. Even some gentry who had taken the side of Parliament feared that a crushing victory might unleash "turbulent spirits, backed by rude and tumultuous mechanic [i.e., ordinary people] persons" and attacks against property by the mob, "that many headed monster."

In such a climate, new religious groups proliferated, some of them radical. Baptists did not believe that children should be baptized, reasoning that only adults were old enough to choose a congregation and hence be baptized. Baptists institutionalized church discussion and debates, which sometimes led to chaotic gatherings. Some Baptists permitted couples to marry by simply making a declaration before the congregation.

"Levellers" were far more radical, demanding major reforms. A group that had begun to form in the mid-1640s, Levellers accepted the sanctity of private property but demanded new laws that would protect the poor as well as the wealthy. Levellers, many of whom had been Baptists, found adherents among small property owners, including many London artisans, as well as great support in the New Model Army, "wherein there is not one lord." Some Levellers may have begun as staunch Puritans before becoming more radical. Royalists and Presbyterians both held that the Levellers wanted "to raise the servant against the master, the tenant against the landlord, the buyer against the seller, the borrower against the lender, the poor against the rich." Henry Denne defended the Levellers against such accusations: "It hath been . . . mine endeavor . . . to give unto every limb and part not only his due proportion but also his due place, and not to set the head where the foot should be, or the foot where the head. I may . . . seem guilty of the crime . . . [of turning] the world upside down, and to set that in the bottom which others make the top of the building, and to set that upon the roof which others lay for a foundation."

Yet, while the Levellers proposed a new English constitution and demanded sweeping political reforms that would greatly broaden the electoral franchise, they still based these rights on property ownership, which they defined as men having "a permanent fixed interest in this kingdom," excluding wage laborers and servants. Women were also prominent in Leveller petition campaigns. They echoed their husbands' demands, although calls for female enfranchisement were extremely rare.

Smaller groups of radicals soon went even further. Unlike the Levellers, the "Diggers," who called themselves the "True Levellers," denied the claims of Parliament to speak for Englishmen, opposed the private ownership of land, and sought the abolition of wage labor. They espoused agrarian reform and even began a brief colony that began to share wasteland with the poor and the landless. Another group, the "Ranters," rejected the idea of Heaven, Hell, and sin, and postulated that the true salvation could be found only in drink and sex.

To some people in mid-seventeenth-century England, the world indeed seemed "turned upside down." Some radicals opposed not only hierarchical authority within the state, but also paternal authority within the family. The assumption that the king ruled his nation as a husband and father directed his wife and children had been prominent in early modern political theory. The expansion in the number of literate people in southern England, in particular, not only exposed more people to the writings of the New Testament but also to radical ideas propagated in pamphlets. Some of these latter demanded education for women and denounced the subjugation of women to their husbands. Conservatives railed against such claims, echoing what seemed to be a growing anxiety about patriarchal order and increasing concern about "unruly women" defying their husbands.

Parliament's Victory

Pressured by the Presbyterians, who feared the radicals of the New Model Army, Parliament ordered the disbanding of part of it without paying the soldiers. The army, however, refused to disband and set up a general council, some of whose members were drawn from the lower officer corps and the rank and file. This reflected Leveller influence within a body that had been previously loyal only to Cromwell.

The New Model Army considered Parliament's attempts to disband it to be part of a plot against the Independents, and a few regiments mutinied and prepared a political platform, the *Agreement of the People,* written by London Levellers. This text anticipated later theorists by claiming that "freeborn Englishmen," not just property owners, were the source of political authority and that "every man that is to live under a government ought first by his own consent to put himself under that government; and . . . that the poorest man in England is not at all bound in a strict sense to that government that he hath not had a voice to put himself under." Cromwell worked to curb the radicals and ruthlessly restored order in the New Model Army, subduing mutinous Leveller regiments and ordering several leaders shot.

The Council of the New Model Army was formed at the end of the Civil War to air grievances and prepare a political platform after Parliament sought to disband the army without paying the soldiers.

Charles I's execution, January 30, 1649.

In November 1647, King Charles escaped the custody of Parliament and fled to the Isle of Wight. At the beginning of the new year, against the opposition of Presbyterians who hoped that some compromise could still be reached with the king, the House of Commons passed a motion that no further addresses should be made to the king. The implication was that Parliament alone should proceed to establish a new government without Charles' participation or consent, probably indicating that Cromwell and many other members of Parliament had already decided that Charles I should be put to death and a republic declared.

In May 1648, a group of Presbyterian moderates joined Cavalier uprisings in southern Wales and southern England. Charles had been secretly negotiating with the Presbyterian Scots, hoping that they now would join an alliance of Anglicans and members of Parliament who had become disillusioned with Cromwell's radicalism. But the New Model Army turned back a Scottish invasion in August. Besieged royalist forces in Wales surrendered after eight weeks. The king was now being held on the Isle of Wight, "more a Prisoner," as an observer put it, "than ever . . . and could not goe to pisse without a guarde nor to Goffe [to play golf]."

Believing itself the virtuous repository of English liberties, a detachment of the New Model Army, under Colonel Pride, surrounded the Parliament house and refused to let Presbyterians—and some Independents as well—enter. "Pride's Purge," which took place without Cromwell's consent or knowledge (although afterward he said that he approved of it), left a "Rump Parliament" of about a fifth of the members sitting.

The Rump Parliament, dominated by Independents, then appointed a High Court to try the king on charges of high treason. Denying the legality of this court, Charles refused to defend himself. Although the decision was taken by a minority of members and was unpopular, the High Court found Charles guilty as charged. Despite international efforts to stay his sentence, Charles I was executed at Whitehall on January 30, 1649, the first monarch to be tried and executed by his own subjects. Charles' beheading had immediate international repercussions; one power after another severed diplomatic relations with England, and the tsar of Russia ended the exclusive trade privileges of English merchants.

The Puritan Republic and Restoration

The Rump Parliament abolished the monarchy and the House of Lords. It established a Puritan republic, the Commonwealth of England, with Cromwell as its leader. It then sought to consolidate power at its borders.

In 1649, Cromwell brutally put down the Irish uprising, which had gone on since 1641, and conquered Ireland. The Act of Settlement in 1652 expropriated for English colonists the land of two-thirds of the Catholic property owners in Ireland and assured the ascendancy of English Protestants in that strife-torn land for the next 300 years. The Scottish Protestants did not fare any better for having supported Charles, however belatedly, as Cromwell from 1650 to 1651 then conquered Scotland. Having defeated both the Irish and the Scots, Cromwell turned his attention to foreign wars. England fought a naval war against the Dutch from 1652 to 1654, and a war with the Spaniards from 1655 to 1659, with an eye toward reducing the power of both these economic rivals.

The Rump Parliament met until 1653. It would not dissolve itself and so Cromwell, torn between his determination to assure a "godly reformation" in England and a mistrust of political assemblies, dissolved it in a military coup. The Long Parliament (if the Rump session is counted) had lasted since 1640. Cromwell now picked 140 men to serve as a new Parliament. This body came to be called the Barebones Parliament, named after one of its members, a certain "Praise-God Barbon," a leather merchant.

England became a military dictatorship. The army council dissolved the Barebones Parliament six months later and proclaimed a Protectorate under a new constitution, the Instrument of Government. Cromwell took the title "Lord Protector." He had not sought but now held almost unlimited power. Thomas Hobbes' description two years after the execution of Charles I of the natural state of mankind as being one of war, "everyone against everyone," seemed to apply to England. What could save England? To Hobbes, England could be saved only by a powerful state, "that great Leviathan . . . to which we owe . . . our peace and defense."

The Puritan republic had turned out to be as oppressive as the monarchy of the Stuart kings. Cromwell imposed taxes without parliamentary approval and purged Parliament when it disagreed with him. When Parliament produced its own constitution, Cromwell sent its members packing in 1655. But he was obliged to recall Parliament the following year to vote money for the war against Spain.

Although Cromwell granted de facto religious freedom to all Puritan sects (including the Presbyterians, Independents, and Baptists), he continued to deny such freedom to both Anglicans and Catholics. He did, however, allow Jews, who had not been allowed in England since 1290, to return in 1655. The Lord Protector proved to be a better military administrator than a civilian one. Dividing the country into twelve districts, he developed a more efficient civil service. But Cromwell lost support as a result of the seemingly endless financial impositions incurred in his war with the Dutch and through having to supply an army of 50,000 men in England. Cromwell also alienated people through his exhortations that people behave in "godly" Puritan ways, as set forth in a code enforced by the army. He began to wear armor under his clothes and took circuitous routes in order to foil assassins who might be stalking him. He still considered himself a humble caretaker of government who would keep order until godly righteousness prevailed.

In 1657, a newly elected Parliament produced another constitution and offered Cromwell the throne of England. He refused, but dissolved Parliament because republicans in it kept discussing the possibility of a new constitution. A year later, Cromwell died, succeeded by his considerably less able son, Richard, the New Protector (1626–1712). Then several military successors stumbled on, backed by remnants of the New Model Army.

Increasingly, however, it seemed to the upper classes that only restoration of the Stuart monarchy could restore order in England. Charles (1630–1685), the heir to the throne of his executed father, lived in exile in Holland. Armed force played a deciding role in a tumultuous time. General George Monck (1608–1670), who commanded the army in Scotland, had shrewdly kept Scottish tax money to pay his soldiers, and thus commanded the only paid, reliable force in England. He was a conservative who had been a royalist officer during the Civil War before developing a personal loyalty to Cromwell once the war had ended. After Parliament tried to assert control over the army, Monck marched with his forces on London and dissolved Parliament. New elections returned an alliance of royalists and Presbyterians, giving Parliament a moderate majority inclined to accept a restoration. When Charles issued a conciliatory proclamation, Parliament invited him to assume the throne of England. Eleven years after the execution of his father, Charles II crossed the Channel in May 1660 and was crowned king on April 23, 1661.

In restoring the monarchy, the new Parliament, on behalf of the upper classes, reacted to the threat of republicanism, popular politics itself, and the profusion of religious sects that seemed to threaten the established or-

der. The command of local militias was wrested from "persons of no degree or quality" and again handed to "the nobility and principal gentry."

A man of considerable ego preoccupied with protecting his throne
against future challenges, Charles II also manifested considerable charm,
energy, courage, unfailing good humor, and loyalty to those who had remained loyal to him (with the notable exception of the queen, to whom
he was anything but faithful). He could also lash out vindictively when he
believed himself betrayed. Despite a vague interest in art and science,
Charles manifested a lifelong aversion to reading and writing, remaining a
man of many words and few letters who allowed himself to be manipulated
by his advisers. But he earned the affection of most of his subjects because
the return of monarchy seemed also to end the extended period of division
and chaos.

The English Civil War had been a victory for parliamentary rule. Yet, in
some ways the Restoration turned the clock back before the conflict. The
Church of England again became the Established Church; the crown refused other religions official toleration. The Church of England expelled
Presbyterian ministers in 1661–1662. Once again the king was chronically short of money and depended on Parliament for funds. Parliament
paid off and demobilized the New Model Army, the last reminder of
Cromwell's rule.

With the Civil War over and the monarchy restored by a victorious Parliament, the way seemed clear for England to continue to expand its commerce and influence in a climate of social and political peace. Between
1660 and 1688, the tonnage hauled by English ships more than doubled,
as the merchant fleet established trade routes to Newfoundland, Virginia,
and the Caribbean. In 1664, a small English force seized the Dutch colony
of New Amsterdam, which became New York. Although it was retaken by
the Dutch, it became part of England again in 1674. England's colonies
gradually developed in North America, and settlements took hold on the
coasts of India and Africa, where slaves were the principal commodity. Tobacco, calico, furs, sugar, chocolate, and rum began to arrive in England,
changing tastes and habits of consumption. London became a booming
port, the East India Company a powerful force in shaping royal policy.
Lloyd's of London began to insure vessels sailing to the New World in
1688. By 1686, almost half of the English ships were trading with India or
America. Exports and imports increased by a third by 1700.

England's foreign policy entered a new, aggressive period in support of
English manufacture and commerce. To undermine Dutch commercial
competition, Parliament passed a series of Navigation Acts between 1651
and 1673, requiring that all goods brought to England be transported either in English ships or in those belonging to the country of origin. This
led to three brief wars with the Dutch, fought in 1652–1654, 1665–1667,
and 1672–1674.

THE GLORIOUS REVOLUTION

The struggle for sovereignty between Parliament and the Stuart kings, was manifested in parliamentary opposition to new taxes and fears that Arminianism would lead to the restoration of Catholicism in England. This led to another constitutional crisis and planted the seeds for what became known as the Glorious Revolution of 1688, whereby Parliament would summon a new king to rule England. Moreover, Parliament would also pass the Bill of Rights, which would enshrine the rights of Parliament and of property owners.

Stuart Religious Designs

After the return of the Stuarts to power, religion once again surfaced as a divisive issue in England, threatening to shatter the political unity seemingly achieved with the restoration in 1660. Charles II had returned from France if not with strong Catholic sympathies at least with the conviction that he owed toleration to Catholics who had supported his father. Again a Stuart king's seemingly provocative policies generated determined opposition from Parliament, which again asserted its prerogatives.

Charles favored Catholics among his ministers, and tried to appeal to Dissenters in order to build a coalition against the Church of England. In response, Parliament passed a series of laws against Dissenters between 1661 and 1665 known as the Clarendon Code. The Act of Corporation (1661) required all holders of office in incorporated municipalities to receive communion in the Anglican Church. The Act of Uniformity (1662) stated that all ministers had to use the Anglican Book of Common Prayer. By a further act, Nonconformists had to take an oath that they would not try to alter the established order of church and state in England. Hundreds of Quakers, members of a pacifist group formed in 1649 who refused to pay tithes or take oaths, were incarcerated and died in prison.

In 1670, Charles II signed a secret treaty of alliance with Louis XIV. He promised the king of France that he would declare himself a Catholic when the political circumstances in England were favorable. In return, he received subsidies from the French king. Charles ended restrictions on religious worship and laws that had been directed at Catholics and Dissident Protestant groups as well. The hostile reaction to his actions forced the king to reinstate all restrictive measures. In 1673, Parliament passed the Test Act, which largely superseded the Clarendon Code and excluded non-Anglicans from both military and civil office.

Many people in England still abhorred Catholicism and suspected that there were plots afoot to restore that religion to England. Although Charles II's agreement with Louis XIV remained secret, in 1678 a strange man called Titus Oates loudly claimed the existence of a plot by the

A Quaker meeting. Many Quakers were imprisoned for refusing to take oaths after passage of an act requiring Nonconformists to swear that they would not attempt to alter the Established Church or the state.

Catholic Church against England. Oates claimed that the Jesuits, who were popularly identified with Rome, were preparing to assassinate the king and slaughter all English Protestants. They then would proclaim James, Charles' devout Catholic brother, king (James was heir to the throne, as Charles had no legitimate children, although he had a good many who were illegitimate). Oates had made it all up, as the king knew perfectly well. But he could not speak up because of his own secret promise to Louis XIV of France to restore Catholicism to England. Charles was helpless when parliamentary leaders orchestrated another wave of anti-Catholicism.

In the 1670s, two factions had emerged in Parliament that in some ways echoed the split between "Court" and "Country" before the Civil War. Members of Parliament who supported full prerogatives of the monarchy, some of them trumpeting the theories of divine right monarchy, became known as Tories, corresponding to "Court." Those members of Parliament who were critical of the king's policies and who espoused parliamentary supremacy and religious toleration became known as Whigs (corresponding to Country). Whig leaders orchestrated a plan to exclude James from the royal succession because of his Catholicism. During the ensuing Exclusion Crisis (1678–1681), the Tories defended James as the heir to the throne of England. When in 1679 some members of Parliament tried to make Charles' illegitimate son heir to the throne, Charles dissolved Parliament. In three subsequent parliamentary elections, Whigs profited from the mood of anti-Catholicism to win a majority of seats.

Parliament's passage in 1679 of the Habeas Corpus Act reflected Whig ascendancy. This forced the government to provide a quick trial for those who were arrested. By establishing the legal rights of individuals accused of crimes, it further limited monarchical authority. Habeas Corpus thus was part of the House of Commons' century-long successful struggle for the maintenance of its constitutional role in England's governance.

Charles, however, continued to assert monarchical prerogatives. In 1681, he attempted, like his father before him, to rule without Parliament. His agents worked at the local level to undercut Whig influence by, for example, rewriting town charters to allow his supporters greater local control. In 1683, a number of Whigs were charged with plotting to kill both the king and his brother. Charles had them executed. On his deathbed two years later, Charles II proclaimed his Catholicism.

Thus, in 1685, Charles II's brother assumed the throne as James II (1633–1701). Royal armies put down small insurrections in Scotland and in western England in favor of Charles' illegitimate son and executed him. Naive as he was devout, James forgot the lessons of recent history and began to dismiss advisers who were not Catholics.

In 1687, James made Catholics eligible for office. Dissenters, too, benefited from toleration, because the new king needed them as allies. The king did not denounce Louis XIV when he revoked the Edict of Nantes and thereby ended toleration for the Huguenots (see Chapter 7). This made English Protestants even more anxious. In November 1687, when it became apparent that the queen was pregnant, James boldly predicted the birth of a son and Catholic heir to the throne. For the enemies of the king, the timing of the birth of a son, and the fact that the only witnesses were Catholics, inevitably sparked rumors that the newborn was not really the king's son but a surrogate baby.

In this new dispute over religion, royal prerogative remained the central constitutional issue. James may have entertained visions of implanting monarchical absolutism in England, a tide that approached from the continent. Certainly he sought to restore Catholicism as the state religion. Looking as though he had fallen completely under the influence of the pope and Louis XIV, in April 1688 he issued a declaration of toleration and ordered the Anglican clergy to read it from the pulpit. When seven bishops protested, James put them in prison. The tide was against James, however, as most of the country did not support his actions. When the bishops were tried in court, a jury found them to be not guilty.

William, prince of Orange, the future King William III of England.

The "Protestant Wind"

Mary (1662–1694), one of James' Protestant daughters by a previous marriage, had married the Protestant Dutchman William of Orange (1650–1702). A group of Tories and Whigs now worked together to invite William to restore Protestantism and, from their point of view, the English constitution. William prepared to invade England from Holland. His followers flooded England with propaganda favorable to his cause.

The context of European international politics seemed favorable to William. Louis XIV's revocation of the Edict of Nantes had outraged the Dutch. Furthermore, the Dutch worried that James' successful restoration of Catholicism to England might make the Dutch Republic more vulnerable to Catholic France, as they believed that England was an indispensable partner in helping resist Louis XIV's grand ambitions in Europe. The Dutch hoped that a friendly Protestant monarch on the throne of England might even reduce tensions stemming from the trade rivalry between the Dutch Republic and England.

The Catholic continental monarchs failed to come to the aid of James II. Louis XIV's principal interest remained continental territorial expansion, and his aggressive moves against the German states left him without potential allies against William. Despite declaring war on the Dutch Republic, Louis limited his attacks to verbal bluster and the seizure of several Dutch ships in French ports. Emperor Leopold of Austria, another powerful Catholic monarch who might have been interested in rescuing James, was tied up fighting the Turks in the east. King James II now paid for having devoted too little attention to matters of diplomacy.

Despite all evidence that William was planning an invasion of England, James seemed unable to act. The king did little to prepare military defenses except to appoint Catholic officers in his new regiments and to bring more troops from Ireland. He relied on his navy to protect his throne. Hoping for a last-minute compromise, he promised to summon a "free" Parliament. But it was too late.

In a declaration promulgated early in October 1688, William accused James of arbitrary acts against the nation, Parliament, and the Church of England. Aided by a munificent wind—later dubbed the "Protestant wind"—that blew his ships to the southwestern coast of England while keeping James' loyal fleet away in the Channel or in port, William landed at Torbay with a force of 15,000 men on November 5, 1688. William marched cautiously to London, encouraged by defections from James' cause by gentry and soldiers along the way. Uprisings on William's behalf occurred sooner than expected in several northern towns, further isolating the king. After rejecting a petition from a number of peers and bishops calling for compromise, James was in a state of virtual physical and psychological collapse. At the end of November, he promised to summon Parliament and allow William's supporters to sit. But riots broke out in other towns against his rule and against Catholics. In December, James fled to the coast, anticipating reaching France. After being recognized and mistreated by fishermen, however, he returned to London. Several days later, he left England for exile in France. Parliament, victorious again, declared the throne vacant by abdication and invited William and Mary to occupy a double throne.

The Bill of Rights

This "Glorious Revolution" of 1688, less dramatic than the English Civil War, was arguably of more lasting importance in the constitutional evolution of England. Parliament passed a Bill of Rights in 1689 that put an end to decades of constitutional battles. Accepted by William and Mary, it became a milestone in English history. It was passed at a time when the rights and influence of representative bodies lay in shambles throughout much of the continent as absolute monarchs—above all Louis XIV—consolidated their power (see Chapter 7). The Bill of Rights reaffirmed the rights of Parliament, and guaranteed the rights of property owners to self-government and of the accused to the rule of law. In particular, it reasserted Parliament's financial authority over government by enumerating what a monarch should not do and by reducing royal control over the army. The Bill of Rights stipulated that Protestant dissenters could worship in England as they pleased and that they could establish academies of their own. Anglicanism, however, remained the Established Church of England, and only those who were Anglican could hold office. Catholics faced discrimination. They could not occupy the throne and, like Dissenters, they were excluded from government positions.

The English philosopher John Locke (1632–1704), friend of some of the wealthy landowners who sent James II into exile, was specific about the ways in which the power of monarchs ought to be limited. "The end of government," he wrote, should be "the good of mankind," above all, the protection of the right of property. Thomas Hobbes agreed, writing "The greatest and chief end therefore of men uniting into Commonwealths, and putting themselves under Government is the preservation of their property." But whereas Hobbes, who supported Charles I against Parliament, held that individuals should surrender their rights to the absolute state of unlimited sovereignty in exchange for protection from the "state of nature," Locke argued that the rights of individuals, including the ownership of property, found protection when Parliament's rights limited monarchical prerogatives. Remembering the turmoil of the Thirty Years' War on the continent, Locke also advocated religious toleration and espoused the right of subjects to rise up against tyranny as the English had against Charles I.

The Glorious Revolution also reaffirmed the political domination of the gentry, whose interests Parliament represented above all. The monarchs named nobles to hereditary seats in the House of Lords, but wealthy landowners elected members to the House of Commons. The gentry's economic and social position was more secure than during the inflationary years of the first half of the century. Order and social hierarchy reigned, and the fear of popular disorder ebbed. Benefiting from the consensus of 1688, the elite of wealthy landowners, increasingly more open to newcomers than its continental counterparts, would continue to shape British political life in the eighteenth century.

THE GOLDEN AGE OF THE DUTCH REPUBLIC

The Dutch Republic of the United Provinces (usually known today as the Netherlands, or sometimes simply as Holland, its most populated and prosperous province) was the other European power that defied the pattern of absolute and increasingly centralized rule that characterized seventeenth-century Europe. Spain ruled the Netherlands from 1516, when Charles V, who had inherited the territories of the dukes of Burgundy, became king of Spain. After a long, intermittent war that had begun in 1566 against Spanish rule (see Chapter 5), the Dutch Republic officially became independent in 1648 (see Map 6.2). The United Provinces, a confederation of republics, had been federalist in structure since the Union of Utrecht in 1579, when the provinces and cities of the Dutch Netherlands came together to form a defensive alliance against the advancing Spanish army. The federalist republic, from which William of Orange had

MAP 6.2 THE NETHERLANDS, 1648   At the conclusion of
the Thirty Years' War, the Dutch war of independence also
ended, with the northern United Provinces becoming the
Dutch Republic and the southern provinces remaining under
Spain as the Spanish Netherlands.

launched his successful invasion of England, resisted the aspirations of
the House of Orange for a centralized government dominated by a hereditary monarchy. Like their English counterparts, most of the Dutch did not
want absolute rule, which they identified with the arbitrary acts of the
Spanish monarchy.

The Structure of the Dutch State

The States General served as a federal body of delegations from each of
the seven provinces of the Dutch Republic. Each held to traditions of autonomy, provincial sovereignty, and religious pluralism. Nobles received
automatic representation in the States General. But their economic and
political role in the Republic was relatively weak, except in the overwhelmingly agricultural eastern provinces.

The Dutch Republic was in some ways less a republic than an oligarchy of wealthy, influential families who monopolized political power. This political elite remained relatively open to prosperous newcomers. Wealthy merchants and bankers served as regents, the members of the governing oligarchy in the Dutch provinces. They were determined to defend the federalist structure of the Republic.

No republican ideology existed until at least the second half of the seventeenth century. But Dutch citizens enjoyed some basic rights unavailable in the monarchies of the continent. Provincial courts protected the Dutch against both occasional arbitrary acts of the central government and those of town governments. They developed solid fiscal institutions and modern double-entry accounting techniques that generated international confidence, permitting the Republic to raise sizable loans as needed.

The princes of the House of Orange served as stadholders (chief officials) of the Republic. Through patronage, the Orangists also dominated some high federal appointments, naming sons of nobles to important positions in the army and navy. But after the revolt of the Netherlands against Spanish rule, the stadholder had influence, not authority. He was not a ruler, and could not declare war, legislate, or even participate in the important decisions of the Republic. Many of the Orangist stadholders chaffed under the restrictions on their authority, dreaming of establishing a powerful hereditary monarchy. In 1650, William II (1626–1650), stadholder of six of the seven provinces, arrested six leaders of Holland and sent an army to besiege Amsterdam. A compromise reinforced the power of the stadholder. But with William's sudden death two years later, the balance of power swung back to the regents of the provinces, particularly Holland. Any possibility of the Netherlands becoming an absolute state ended. Nonetheless, the House of Orange tried to curry support among the other six provinces against Holland, whose lucrative commercial interests shaped the Republic's foreign policy during the seventeenth century, as it led the resistance against Spain.

Expanding Economy

Despite the war of independence against the Spanish Habsburgs, the Dutch economy developed more rapidly during the first two-thirds of the seventeenth century than did the economies of its competitors, England and France.

In 1609, following the signing of a truce between Spain and the Netherlands, the Amsterdam Public Bank opened its doors, serving as a nexus of Dutch financial operations. The bank's offices were in the town hall, reflecting its conservatism and fiscal solidity. Its principal function was to facilitate Amsterdam's burgeoning foreign trade with other European countries and across the seas by encouraging merchants to make payments in bills drawn on the bank.

The Amsterdam Bourse in the seventeenth century. Merchants had fixed places at the Stock Exchange where they met to arrange various financial matters.

Amsterdam's banking, credit, and warehousing facilities were soon unmatched in Europe. Although an ordinance in 1581 had included bankers among those occupations considered disreputable—along with actors, jugglers, and brothel-keepers—and therefore excluded from receiving communion in the Dutch Reformed Church, bankers came to be respected by the beginning of the seventeenth century. Thanks to the bankers, investors would now raise capital for frequently risky commercial ventures with relative ease and invest at the Bourse (Stock Exchange).

Good credit allowed the United Provinces to raise loans by selling negotiable bonds at low interest rates. Bills of exchange became a type of credit; signed by a merchant, they specified the payment due date. This attracted foreign merchants to Amsterdam, particularly after mid-century, when bills of exchange became acceptable as currency.

The United Provinces, small in territory and population, also expanded its agricultural resources during the first half of the century. Thousands of workers and horses reclaimed much of the country's most fertile land from the sea. Increased productivity generated an agricultural surplus that could be invested in commerce or manufacturing, and a greater food supply sustained a larger population. Commercial livestock raising and capital-intensive farming became lucrative, producing butter and cheese for ever more distant markets.

Canals and rivers expedited internal trade in the Dutch Republic. These boats along the Spaarne at Haarlem carried goods to the port, where they were loaded for distant trade.

The Dutch Republic's population rose by a third between 1550 and 1650, to almost 2 million people, which made it Europe's most densely populated country after several of the Italian states. More than half the population lived in towns. As Amsterdam became a major international port of trade and London's rival, its population rose from about 50,000 in 1600 to about 150,000 by mid-century.

Early in the seventeenth century, Amsterdam began construction of three large canals, which expanded its area by almost four times. These canals permitted boats to dock outside merchants' warehouses, where they were loaded with goods, which they then carried to the large ships of the port. Handsome tall townhouses had narrow and increasingly ornamented facades, dauntingly steep staircases, and drains and sewers. They were built for the bankers, merchants, and manufacturers of Amsterdam and reached skyward above new tree-lined streets along the canals. The city pushed out from the port along the semi-radial canals that spread out from the sea. Thus, the United Provinces benefited not only from relatively good roads, which expedited internal trade, but also from 500 miles of canals dug during the middle decades of the century.

Dutch traders, specializing in bulk goods carried by specially designed long, flat vessels that could be cheaply built and operated, expanded their range and the variety of goods they bartered. This allowed Dutch merchants to undercut rivals. The Dutch Republic's merchant fleet tripled during the first half of the century. Dutch shipbuilding boomed, aided by wind-powered sawmills. The Dutch Republic's 2,500 ships in the 1630s accounted for about half of Europe's shipping. Amsterdam became the principal supplier of grain and fish in Europe as the Dutch dominated the lucrative Baltic trade. Dutch ships carried wheat and rye from Poland and East Prussia, dropping off what was needed for local consumption and then carrying much that was left to France, Spain, and the Mediterranean. Dutch fishing boats ousted their English competitors from the rich North Sea fishing grounds and from the whaling waters of the Arctic Sea. Dutch ships hauled most of the iron produced in Sweden; until mid-century, they also carried much of the coal extracted from the mines of Newcastle in England. Dutch traders exchanged products in Russia, the West Indies, Brazil, Japan, Southeast Asia, and the West African coast, from which they carried slaves. Herring caught by Dutch fishermen and salted for preservation became available in much of Europe, exchanged for salt, wine, and other commodities.

During the 1620s and 1630s, Dutch merchants extended their reach in the East Indies, where cinnamon, nutmeg, and other valuable spices were produced. In 1602, a group of investors had founded a private trading company, to which the government of the Dutch Republic granted a monopoly for trade in East Asia. The Dutch East India Company proved to be stiff competition for the English company of the same name. Increased

A merchant of the Dutch East India Company and his wife view the company's fleet sailing into the Bay of Batavia on Java in the East Indies.

affluence, in turn, helped the Dutch carry on the war against Spain. When fighting in Central Europe during the Thirty Years' War and a Spanish embargo on Dutch commerce reduced some continental trade, Dutch traders successfully developed trade overseas with India, Ceylon, and Indonesia, establishing a vast network of company settlements.

Dutch Religion and Attitudes

In contrast to England, where religious division led to civil war, the Dutch Republic remained a relative haven of toleration in an era of religious hatred. During the last decades of the sixteenth century, perhaps 60,000 Huguenots fled to the Dutch Republic to escape persecution in France and the Spanish Netherlands. In 1631, about a third of the wealthiest residents of Amsterdam had moved there from the Spanish Netherlands. Published works circulated through the Netherlands defending the rights of religious dissidents, including Mennonites, Lutherans, Quakers fleeing England, and Dutch Collegiants (a dissident Protestant group). By 1672, Amsterdam's Jewish community numbered 7,500 in a city of 200,000 people. Most were immigrants from the German states, and they spoke Yiddish among themselves, as well as German and Dutch. Many other Jewish families had come from Spain. The municipal government rejected a request by Christian merchants that their Jewish competitors be restricted, as in many European cities, to a specific neighborhood, or ghetto. The Amsterdam regents built a thousand dwellings for refugees, and the town of Haarlam established a home for widows and daughters of men who had come to the Republic to flee persecution. Refugees from religious persecution in other countries contributed to the prosperity of the Dutch Republic.

Nonetheless, despite the religious toleration generally accorded in the Dutch Republic, the Dutch Reformed Church, a strict Calvinist confession closely tied to the House of Orange, did persecute and discriminate against some religious groups. Dutch Arminians asked for protection from persecution in a Remonstrance (which gave them their most common name, the Remonstrants). Catholics, most of whom lived in the eastern provinces, also faced Calvinist hostility, although many had fought for Dutch independence. Jews were excluded from most guilds, and gypsies were routinely hounded and persecuted. Over all, however, toleration seemed less divisive to the Dutch than intolerance, and seemed to make economic sense as well.

The Dutch Republic blossomed like the famous tulips that were so popular in Holland (which, in fact, had been originally imported from Turkey). A French visitor reported that Amsterdam was "swollen with people, chock-full of goods, and filled with gold and silver." The Dutch in the middle decades of the seventeenth century reached a level of prosperity

Een dwaes en zijn gelt
zijn haeft gheschenden.

(*Left*) The Dutch Republic's famous tulips. (*Right*) Emanuel de Witte's *The Fish Market* (1672).

unmatched in Europe at the time. Real wages rose in the Republic during the last half of the century while falling elsewhere. Dutch families enjoyed a relatively varied diet, consuming more meat and cheese—as well as, of course, fish—than households elsewhere in Europe. The smell of fruit that had ripened on voyages from Southern Europe and of expensive tobacco filled the air of Amsterdam. Europe's finest market offered a plethora of colonial goods, such as coffee, tea, cocoa, ginger and other spices, dried and pickled herring and other fish, a wide range of grains, finished cloth from Antwerp and Florence, Silesian linens, and English woolens. Dutch manufacturers, with windmills providing power, found lucrative outlets for draperies, worsteds, papers, books, and jewels. At the beginning of the century, Amsterdam had almost 200 breweries and more than 500 taverns.

Although prosperity reached far down the social ladder, the Dutch Republic also had its poor, who lived in the narrow streets away from the Stock Exchange, in poor farmhouses in the eastern flatlands, and in the huts of ethnic Frisian fishermen facing the brutal North Sea waves and wind. The urban poor occasionally rioted and sometimes stole in order to survive. The proliferation of charitable institutions demonstrated Dutch compassion but also their desire to confine vagrants and beggars, as well as a capacity to lash out in brutal repression when patience with the poor grew thin. Beatings, floggings, and branding—and even death—remained common forms of punishment, and gallows stood at the main gates of large cities.

Dike breach at Caevarden. Because so much land had been reclaimed from the sea, many of the Dutch lived in chronic fear of flooding.

Yet, despite prosperity, a sense of precariousness and vulnerability permeated the Republic. The armies of the ambitious king of France camped across the low-lying Southern Netherlands. The Republic had almost no natural resources and was subject to sudden calamities brought by weather. A good part of the Dutch Netherlands would thus have been under water were it not for the famous dikes. These occasionally broke with catastrophic consequences long remembered (a flood in 1421 had claimed over 100,000 lives). A sense that disaster might be looming was reflected by the popularity in the Republic of novels and histories about disasters. This may explain the sense of solidarity and duty that brought people of various classes together against Spanish rule. This also contributed to the relative unity of Dutch culture, which prided itself on being distinct from that of the Southern Netherlands, which was under Flemish and French Catholic influence.

The Dutch Republic remained in some ways sternly Calvinist, however. The Dutch made money to make money, not necessarily to enjoy it. With relative abundance came a sense of guilt that could be resolved only by simplicity of life, although contemporary canvases depicted occasional lavish feasts. Many Calvinists believed the Republic was too successful, too affluent. The Reformed Church cautioned against excess, fearing that the Dutch soul might be compromised by self-indulgence. Churchmen reminded the Dutch that they, like the lands taken from the sea, had to be reclaimed from temptation. Authorities were to be vigilant. An occasional banquet was fine, but excess, identified with the Southern Netherlands or, worse, the French, had to be avoided.

Seventeenth-Century Dutch Culture

Dutch painting in the golden age of the seventeenth century reflected not only the Republic's precocious commercial wealth, but also its toleration and openness to secular styles and subject matter. The Dutch press, too, enjoyed relative freedom; books were printed in the Republic that could not have been printed elsewhere. The first English and French newspapers were both published in 1620 not in London and Paris, respectively, but in Amsterdam. Dutch publishers diffused knowledge of the Scientific Revolution (see Chapter 8). Dutch writers and poets discovered their own language, translated Latin authors, and popularized Dutch accounts of the revolt against Spain.

Dutch painting reflected Dutch society, particularly the wealth and taste of the middle class. Like the artists of the Renaissance, Dutch painters depended on the patronage of people of means, particularly wealthy Amsterdam merchants. Although Delft and several other towns each claimed their own style, the great port dominated the art market. Some shopkeepers and craftsmen were prosperous enough to buy a painting or two, and some well-off peasants did so as well.

Holland's regents, in particular, patronized Dutch painting. In contrast, the princes of Orange patronized French and other foreign artists whose work reflected baroque themes associated with the Catholic Reformation. Dutch nobles purchased few paintings, unlike their counterparts in France and in Southern Europe. When they did buy works of art, they favored the classical religious themes of foreign artists.

The relationship between religion and art in the Dutch Republic contrasted sharply with their relationship in the Southern Netherlands, which remained under Spanish and French influence. The Catholic Reformation had adopted the visual arts as one means by which the Church hoped to resist the Protestant tide. Flanders (the western part of what is now Belgium) became a northern outpost of the Catholic Reformation, encouraging religious themes with emotional appeal. By contrast, in the Dutch Republic ecclesiastical artistic patronage was generally absent, and the Dutch Reformed Church ordered the removal of paintings from its churches.

For the most part, Dutch painters looked to their water-swept country for inspiration. The Dutch school retained much of its cultural unity at least through the first half of the century for several reasons. Until 1650, the Republic remained relatively isolated from outside cultural influences, despite the arrival of refugees and immigrants. Very few Dutch artists and writers had the resources to travel as far as Italy or even France; even

Rembrandt's painting *The Syndics of the Cloth Guild* (1662).

those who earned a comfortable living showed little inclination to go abroad. The group paintings of merchants or regents and municipal governments, which were the most expensive canvases, were usually commissioned by the subjects themselves, as in the case of Rembrandt van Rijn's *Syndics of the Cloth Guild* (1662) and his *The Night Watch* (1642), a theatrically staged masterpiece of a group of city officials in uniform.

Rembrandt (1606–1669) was the son of a miller from Leiden and the grandson of a baker. He was one of the handful of Dutch painters who amassed a fortune, allowing him to marry the daughter of a municipal official. Rembrandt's life was one of brilliant achievement. Certainly few artists, if any, have so successfully portrayed the human emotions of his subjects with his use of color, light, and shadow. Despite his posthumous fame, in his own time the brooding Rembrandt was in some ways a tragic figure, a loner isolated from other painters. He bickered with his patrons and squandered most of what he made on his elegant house in Amsterdam. He lost his investments in the Dutch East India Company. Furthermore, he lost some public favor because he was unwilling to cater to the public's taste. He was nearly ruined financially before rebounding when his baroque portraiture and religious themes found more buyers. Rembrandt increasingly became his own favorite subject, and he thereafter undertook little more than self-portraits, of which there are at least eighty. His self-portraits reveal a thinly disguised sadness.

Dutch painters depicted everyday life. The prolific Jacob van Ruisdael (c. 1628–1682) mastered the visual effects of light on figures, trees, and household objects. Within the Dutch school of the seventeenth century, only Rembrandt (who is sometimes considered to be a baroque painter) often turned to the classical biblical themes that were so predominant in Flemish art, but he did so hoping to capture the Catholic market. Although seascapes and naval scenes proliferated, there were few canvases depicting battles, a favorite subject in absolute states, and those that did exist took their place on the large walls of palaces and châteaux, not in the narrow houses of Amsterdam.

Perhaps more than other early modern Europeans, the Dutch considered the household a place of refuge and safety from the struggles of the outside world, as well as the basis of economic, social, and political order, and therefore worthy of artistic representation. The popularity of household scenes in Dutch painting also reflected the Republic's prosperity. Paintings of families at work, at play, or eating were particularly popular. Jan Steen (1626–1679) portrayed boisterous revelers of different means in *The Fat Kitchen* and *The Thin Kitchen*. Still lifes of platters of food became staples for Dutch artists, as in such paintings as *Still Life with Herring* and *Jug Still Life with Lobster*. The banquet became a favorite subject, with all of its accoutrements, such as oak table and chairs, iron cooking pans, elegant plates and drinking vessels, and its rituals, such as the prayer, the careful carving of the meat, and the rounds of toasts.

The relationship between parents and children emerged as another familiar domestic theme. The Dutch painters also frequently portrayed servants, furniture and other household goods, and domestic pets. Women on Dutch canvases appear more equal to men than they were in reality, however. (A Dutch woman was legally subordinate to her husband's authority, and a cuckolded husband had the right to have his adulterous wife executed. Nonetheless, women could sign contracts, and a good many operated businesses after their husband's death.)

Like Renaissance painters, Dutch artists considered themselves craftsmen and were apprenticed to a master and then became members of a guild. The majority were of modest means. Most painters were harried by creditors, haunted by debts, and sometimes sold their works at reduced prices. Some painters managed only by dealing in the work of other painters, others by holding another job, such as Steen, who operated a brewery and inn in Delft when he was not before his easel. Even in the Dutch Republic, painting proved to be a tough way to earn a living.

THE DECLINE OF THE DUTCH REPUBLIC

The relative decline of Dutch power is perhaps not surprising, given the greater economic resources and population of France and England, its chief rivals. England emerged in the second half of the century as the world's dominant commercial power, although the decline of Dutch trade was not complete until the second or third decade of the eighteenth century.

The Dutch Republic tried to steer a course between England (its greatest commercial rival) and France. But this proved impossible. Three wars against England (1652–1654, 1665–1667, and 1672–1674), fought in defense of Dutch commercial interests, drained Dutch resources. Furthermore, Louis XIV of France had designs on the Dutch. "It is impossible," proclaimed Colbert, "that his Majesty should tolerate any longer the insolence and arrogance of that nation." In 1667, France imposed damaging tariffs on Dutch goods and also forced the Dutch out of the cinnamon-producing island of Ceylon in the Indian Ocean. In Brazil, the Dutch West India Company failed to dislodge the Portuguese, although it did establish small settlements on Africa's west coast. Few Dutch, including missionaries, demonstrated much enthusiasm for these distant places, and the Republic's colonial empire lagged behind those of England and Spain, to be sure, but also behind that of France.

With Spain weakened, Louis XIV coveted the Southern Netherlands, the conquest of which would place the Dutch in direct danger. The Dutch Republic therefore had a vested interest in the survival of the Spanish Netherlands as a buffer against the French threat. Should France be able to open the Scheldt River (closed by the Spanish in 1585 with the goal of breaking the Dutch rebellion) to international trade, Antwerp's return to its former prosperity would certainly be at Amsterdam's expense. In 1672, Louis XIV attacked the Dutch Republic, having signed a secret treaty with King Charles II of England. French armies quickly occupied all of the Republic except for Holland and one other province. But the Dutch successfully defended the Republic by land and sea, defeating the English fleet and pushing back the French army.

Taking advantage of the invasion, William III of Orange (who became King William III of England in 1688) forced the States General to name him stadholder in 1672. He ordered the dikes opened, literally flooding the French into retreat. Royalist mobs murdered the leading official of the Republic, several influential regents of Holland who had dedicated themselves to keeping the stadholders in place, and other leaders of the province of Holland. Supporters of the House of Orange eased into important political positions in that province. The Orangists controlled the Republic's foreign policy until the end of the century, but they still could not impose a monarchy on the provinces. With William's death in 1702, the main Orange dynastic line ended.

After the Glorious Revolution in England in 1688, the United Provinces allied with England and Sweden, fearing that Louis XIV of France might invade the Netherlands again. The alliance helped stave off the French threat in the last decades of the century, but at the same time it dragged the small country into a series of wars with France that lasted until the mid-eighteenth century. Military spending on armies and expensive southern fortifications contributed to the decline of the Dutch Republic as a power. It thereafter assumed a secondary role in European events.

Although the Dutch remained successful traders through the first decades of the eighteenth century, the relative decline of Dutch influence in Europe could be first seen by about 1670 or 1680. Some luxury products, such as linen and Delft porcelain, continued to sell abroad, but Holland's textile industry and shipbuilding failed to keep pace with those of its rivals, above all England. Higher wages in the Republic and a lack of technological innovation were at least partially to blame. Furthermore, some Dutch entrepreneurs invested in the colonies, land, government stocks, or even in English manufacturing, not in Dutch industry. Businessmen reduced investment in agriculture and land reclamation as prices fell.

Spain's golden age of art coincided with its decline as a Great Power. In contrast, Dutch painting languished with decline. Painters began looking abroad for inspiration and, in doing so, lost some of the originality that had catapulted them to prominence. In the 1650s, the Amsterdam regents ignored the influence of the Dutch school when planning the construction and decoration of the new town hall, which combined Italian classicism and the Flemish baroque flamboyance. Some Dutch leaders now took pride in speaking French, believing it the language of good taste. French classicism overwhelmed Dutch literature and poetry. Although the French military invasion of 1672 failed, a cultural invasion succeeded, and Dutch artists came to offer pale imitations of French classical work.

The originality of Dutch political life also waned with relative economic decline. The most powerful merchant families maintained increasingly tight control over the position of regent and other influential posts. A form of municipal corruption ("contracts of correspondence") allowed them to divide up or even purchase lucrative government positions. Spectacular cases of social mobility became rarer. More regents were now landowners, who (though many were nobles living in the republic's cities) had little in common with merchants who had vital interests in government policies. After 1650, no major cultural figures emerged from regent families. There were fewer paintings of attentive and hardworking municipal and provincial officials. Their simple style of life disappeared. And, as if to vindicate Calvinist sermons about excess, so did Dutch power.

Government became more rigid, more distant from the Dutch people, and less tolerant, persecuting religious dissenters and undertaking a witch hunt against homosexuals. The Dutch army became increasingly one of mercenaries, not citizens. The Dutch Republic's loss of vitality and economic primacy was accompanied by its decline in international affairs. At the dawn of the eighteenth century, England and the Netherlands remained the only non-absolutist states among the major European states. While the Dutch languished, England became a Great Power.

CHAPTER 7

THE AGE OF
ABSOLUTISM,
1650–1720

~~~

In Louis XIV's France, architects and artists were paid to glorify the monarch. In 1662, the king chose the sun as his emblem; he declared himself *Nec pluribus impar*—without equal. To Louis, the sun embodied virtues that he associated with the ideal monarch: firmness, benevolence, and equity. Henceforth, Louis XIV would frequently be depicted as Apollo, the sun god, especially inside and outside the royal château of Versailles.

The rulers of continental Europe, including Louis XIV, relentlessly extended their power between 1650 and 1750. The sovereigns of France, Prussia, Russia, Austria, and Sweden, in particular, became absolute rulers, that is, in principle above all challenge from within the state itself. Rulers extended their dynastic domains and prestige. They made their personal rule absolute, based on loyalty to them as individuals, not to the state as an abstraction. Absolute rulers asserted their supreme right to proclaim laws and levy taxes, appointing more officials to carry out the details of governance and multiplying fiscal demands on their subjects. They ended most of the long-standing municipal privileges, which had survived longer in Western Europe than in Eastern Europe, such as freedom from taxation, or the right to maintain independent courts. The absolute state affected the lives of more people than ever before through taxation, military service, and the royal quest for religious orthodoxy.

Absolute rule thus impinged directly on the lives of subjects, who felt the extended reach of state power through, for example, more efficient tax collection. A Prussian recalled that in school no child would question "that the king could cut off the noses and ears of all his subjects if he wished to do so, and that we owed it to his goodness and his gentle disposition that he had left us in possession of these necessary organs."

274

Absolutism was, at least in part, an attempt to reassert public order and coercive state authority after almost seventy years of wars that had badly disrupted trade and agricultural production, contributing to social and political chaos. England and Spain had been at war in the last decades of the sixteenth century. Wars of religion had raged through much of Europe on and off for more than a century—above all, the Thirty Years' War (1618–1648). The Dutch war of independence against Spain began in 1572 and did not officially come to an end until 1648. The tumultuous decade of the 1640s was particularly marked by political crises. The wars had led to often dramatic increases in taxes, which multiplied four times in Spain under Philip II, and five times in France between 1609 and the end of the Thirty Years' War in 1648. During the 1640s, the English Civil War led to the execution of King Charles I in 1649 (see Chapter 6). In France, the period of mid-century rebellion known as the Fronde included a noble uprising against the crown and determined, violent peasant resistance against increased taxation. The multiplicity and seemingly interrelated character of these crises engendered considerable anxiety among social elites: "These are days of shaking, and this shaking is universal," a preacher warned the English Parliament.

The illustration for the cover of Thomas Hobbes' *Leviathan* (1651) depicts the absolute state. Note how the ruler's body is made up of the masses over whom he rules.

THEORIES OF ABSOLUTISM

The doctrine of absolutism originated with French jurists at the end of the sixteenth century. Like absolutism itself, this doctrine arose in part as a reaction to the chaos of the sixteenth-century religious wars concluded in the German states with the Peace of Augsburg (1555). This treaty stated that the religion of the ruler would become the religion of the land (*cuius regio, eius religio*).

The emergence of theories of absolutism reflected contemporary attempts to conceptualize the significance of the rise of larger territorial states whose rulers enjoyed more power than their predecessors. France was a prime example of this trend. The legal theorist Jean Bodin (1530–1596) had lived through the wars of religion. "Seeing that nothing upon earth is greater or higher, next unto God, than the majesty of kings and sovereign princes," he wrote in the *Six Books of the Republic* (1576), the "principal point of sovereign majesty and absolute power [was] to consist principally in giving laws unto the subjects in general, without their consent." The ruler became the father, a figure of benevolence. Bodin, who like many other people in France longed for peace and order helped establish the political theory legitimizing French absolute rule.

Almost a century later, the political philosopher Thomas Hobbes (1588–1679) emerged as the thundering theorist of absolutism although he lived in England, the least absolute state in Europe and one of the few nations in which the rule of law was separated from the will of the ruler. Hobbes experienced the turmoil of the English Civil War (see Chapter 6). In *Leviathan* (1651), he argued that absolutism alone could prevent society from lapsing into the "state of nature," a constant "war of every man against every man" that made life "solitary, poor, nasty, brutish, and short." People would only obey, Hobbes insisted, when they were afraid of the consequences of not doing so. Seeking individual security, individuals would enter into a type of contract with their ruler, surrendering their rights in exchange for protection. A ruler's will thus became the almost sacred embodiment of the state. In France, Jacques Bossuet (1627–1704), bishop and tutor to Louis XIV, postulated that kings ruled by "divine right," that is, by virtue of the will of God. Unlike Hobbes' notion of authority based on a social contract, Bossuet held that the ruler's authority stemmed from God alone.

Yet, theorists of absolutism recognized the difference between absolute and arbitrary power. Inherent in their theories was the idea that the absolute ruler was responsible for looking after the needs of his people. As Bossuet wrote: "It is one thing for a government to be absolute, and quite another for it to be arbitrary. It is absolute in that it is not liable to constraint, there being no other power capable of coercing the sovereign, who is in this sense independent of all human authority." But he went on: "it does not follow from this that the government is arbitrary, for besides the fact that all is subject to the judgment of God . . . there are also laws, in states, so that whatever is done contrary to them is null in a legal sense; moreover, there is always an opportunity for redress, either at other times or in other conditions." Thus, according to even the most determined proponents of absolutism, the monarch, whose legitimacy came from God, nonetheless was subject to limits imposed by reason through laws and traditions. Western monarchs recognized at least in theory the necessity of consulting, when the occasion arose, with institutions considered to be representative of interests such as the Church and nobility: parlements, estates, or the Assembly of Notables in France, the Cortes in Spain, and Parliament in non-absolutist England. Theorists thus recognized the difference between absolutism and despotism. Nonetheless, although Bossuet envisioned limits on sovereign authority, he did not sanction armed resistance against that authority, no matter how depraved or evil it might be.

CHARACTERIZING ABSOLUTE RULE

Absolute states were characterized by strong, ambitious dynasties, which through advantageous marriages, inheritance, warfare, and treaties added to their dynastic domains and prestige. They had nobilities that accepted monarchical authority in exchange for a guarantee of their status, ownership of land, and privileges within the state and over the peasantry, whether peasants were legally free, as in Western Europe, or serfs, as in the case of Prussia, Poland, and Russia. Absolute states contained an increasingly centralized and efficient bureaucracy able to extract revenue. And above all, the absolute state was characterized by deployment of a large, standing army capable of maintaining order at home and maintaining or expanding dynastic interests and territories in the context of European power politics.

Although some Western sovereigns were somewhat limited by representative bodies—diets, parlements, estates—absolute monarchies nonetheless created an unprecedented concentration of governing power. Between 1614 and 1788, no king of France convoked the Estates-General, an assembly of representatives from the three estates—clergy, nobility, and commoners—that had been created early in the fourteenth century as an advisory council to the king. The Portuguese assembly of nobles did not meet at all during the eighteenth century.

The absolute states of Central and Eastern Europe—Prussia, Austria, and Russia—shared similar social structures: a strong nobility with ties to rulers who granted concessions and privileges in exchange for cooperation, a subservient peasantry in the process of losing remaining rights to rulers and landlords, including—through progressive enserfment—that of personal freedom, and a relatively weak and politically powerless middle class. Unlike England and the Dutch United Provinces, these states had no representative institutions and few towns of size and importance to stand in the way of absolute rule.

Monarchs and Nobles

Absolute rulers depended on some degree of compliance by nobles. In each absolute state, the relationship between ruler and nobles determined the specific character of absolutism. This delicate balance is reflected in the oath of loyalty sworn to the king of Spain by the Aragonese nobility: "We who are as good as you swear to you who are no better than we to accept you as our king and sovereign lord, provided you observe all our liberties and laws; but if not, not."

Monarchs negotiated compromises with nobles, awarding titles and privileges for obedience, or at least compliance. In some cases, nobles asserted independence vis à vis royal authority. But emphatic assertions of royal authority reduced nobles to the role of junior ruling partners in governance. With some nobles themselves frightened by the social and political turmoil that shook Europe during the first half of the century, they now more willingly served rulers as royal officials and military commanders.

But sovereigns needed to woo nobles to gain their compliance. In exchange for loyalty and in many cases service, rulers confirmed noble privileges and allowed them to continue to dominate state and local government. "Tables of ranks" dividing nobles into distinct grades or ranks were established at the turn of the century by the kings of Sweden, Denmark, Prussia, and Russia, and made it clear that noble privileges were bestowed by monarchs. Louis XIV of France (ruled 1643–1715) asserted the right to monitor the legitimacy of all titles and even to confiscate noble estates. In 1668, he ordered the investigation of "false" nobles holding dubious titles. These measures helped the king maintain the loyalty of nobles,

Dueling Swedish nobles. One of the noble privileges that was confirmed by absolute sovereigns was the right to carry and use swords.

some of whom resented those who held titles they considered suspect. The great noble families thereafter enjoyed an even greater monopoly over the most lucrative and prestigious royal and ecclesiastical posts.

Using the augmented power of the state, rulers also placated nobles by ending a turbulent period of peasant uprisings against taxes, obligations to their lords, and the high price of grain. And they reduced the vagrancy and petty criminality that had increased since the difficult decade of the 1590s. Insurrections occurred less frequently and were savagely repressed by kings.

The gradual centralization of authority in Eastern Europe left nobles with even more autonomy than they had in the West, allowing Russian lords, Polish nobles, and Prussian Junkers the possibility of further increasing their wealth and power through the extension of their estates, which were worked by serfs. Beginning in the late sixteenth century, such seigneurs made fortunes shipping grain to the West, where prices of cereal and food had risen dramatically in response to population growth. Royal decrees in Prussia and Russia and assembly legislation in Poland progressively limited the right of peasants to move from the land they worked, or even to inherit property. Ravaged by hard times, peasant proprietors had to sell their land to nobles. Impoverished and virtually powerless to resist, peasants lost their personal freedom, a process most marked in Russia. Thus, as feudalism gradually disappeared in Western Europe, it became more prevalent in the East as lords dispossessed peasants from their land. In the West, lords increased their power over land; in the East, over both land and persons. The economic crises of the seventeenth century, including the disruptions of the Thirty Years' War and the decline in Western demand for grain imported from the East because of increased production in the West, only made conditions of life harder for serfs.

In the Ottoman Empire, absolutism was even more despotic. All lands were considered the sultan's private imperial possessions. He granted landed estates to those who served him, but because the sultan recognized no rights of property, no hereditary nobility could develop, in sharp contrast to other European states, to challenge his authority. No representative institutions existed. Towns in the overwhelmingly rural empire had neither autonomy nor rights.

Expanding State Structures

Absolute monarchs extended their authority within their territories by expanding the structure of the state. To fill the most prestigious offices, they chose nobles for their influence and wealth more than their competence. But they also began to employ able officials to collect vital information, for example, projected revenues or the anticipated number of soldiers available in times of war.

The Renaissance city-states of Italy had created relatively efficient civil administrations and set up the first permanent diplomatic corps. During the seventeenth century, the apparatus of administration, taxation, and military conscription gradually became part of the structure of the absolute state. The result was that in Europe as a whole, the number of government officials grew about fourfold.

One result of these expanding ranks of officials was the tripling of tax revenues between 1520 and 1670 in France and Spain, and in non-absolutist England as well. To raise money, absolute rulers sold monopolies (which permitted only the holder of the monopoly to produce and sell particular goods) on the production and sale of salt, tobacco, and other commodities, and imposed taxes on the trading towns of their realms. The rulers of France, Spain, and Austria also filled the state coffers by selling hereditary offices. Philip IV of Spain put it this way: "Without reward and punishment no monarchy can be preserved. We have no money, so we have thought it right and necessary to increase the number of honors." James I of England doubled the number of knights during the first four months of his reign. Queen Christina of Sweden doubled the number of noble families in ten years. In addition, as royal power and prestige rose, the monarchs more easily found wealthy families to loan them money, usually in exchange for tax exemptions, titles, or other privileges.

Absolutism and Warfare

The regular collection of taxes and the expansion of sources of revenue increased the capacity of absolute rulers to maintain standing armies, maintain fortifications, and wage war. By the end of the sixteenth century, Philip II of Spain had allocated three-quarters of state expenditures to pay for past wars or to wage new ones. Appropriately enough, the bureau in Prussia that a century later would oversee tax collection itself evolved from the General War Office, making explicit the close connection between the extraction of state revenue and the waging of dynastic wars.

Absolutist statemaking and warfare had direct and indirect consequences for most of the European population. Kings no longer depended on troops provided by nobles or conscripted by military contractors, thereby avoiding the risk that private armies might challenge royal power. Standing armies continued to grow in size during the eighteenth century (see Table 7-1). During the sixteenth century, the peacetime armies of the continental powers had included about 10,000 to 20,000 soldiers; by the 1690s, they reached about 150,000 soldiers. The French army, which stood at about 180,000 men in peacetime, rose to 350,000 soldiers, the largest in Europe, during the War of the Spanish Succession (1701–1714). The Russian army grew from 130,000 in 1731 to 458,000 in 1796. In contrast, England and the Dutch Republic, two non-absolutist states, had relatively small armies and, as sea powers, both depended on their navies.

TABLE 7-1 THE SIZE OF EUROPEAN ARMIES, 1690–1814

	1690	1710	1756/60	1789	1812/14
Britain	70,000	75,000	200,000	40,000*	250,000
France	400,000	350,000	330,000	180,000	600,000
Habsburg Emp.	50,000	100,000	200,000	300,000	250,000
Prussia	30,000	39,000	195,000	190,000	270,000
Spain	na	30,000	na	50,000	na
Sweden	na	110,000	na	na	na
United Prov.	73,000	130,000	40,000*	na	na

*Drop reflects peacetime and non-absolutist character of the state.
na Figures not available.
Source: Paul Kennedy, *The Rise and Fall of the Great Powers* (New York: Vintage, 1989), p. 99.

As absolute monarchs consolidated their power, the reasons for waging international wars changed. The wars of the previous century had been fought, in principle, over the rivalry between the Catholic and Protestant religions, even if dynastic interests were never far from the surface. Now, although religious rivalries still constituted an important factor in international conflict (as in the case of the long struggle between the Muslim Ottoman Empire and the Catholic Habsburg Empire), "reasons of state" became a prevalent justification for the rulers of France, Prussia, and Russia to make war on their neighbors.

The organization and financing of warfare illuminate the early modern state in action. In some countries, road and bridge improvements were undertaken to enhance the rapid movement of armies. Warfare both encouraged and drew upon the development of credit institutions, further expanding the capacity of the state to raise money to wage war. But as the British and Dutch cases demonstrated, a state did not have to be absolutist in order to marshal sufficient resources to fight sustained wars. English colonial trade generated excise and customs taxes, permitting the expansion of the Royal Navy. The crown's reputation for repayment facilitated raising money through loans at home and abroad. Amsterdam's stature as a great banking center contributed to the ability of the Dutch government to fight extended wars. In contrast, the French monarchy lacked the confidence of wary investors, and despite the sale of privileges, found itself in an increasingly dangerous financial situation. Moreover, the French monarchy often had to pay higher rates of interest than private investors because it was a bad credit risk.

Even in peacetime, military expenditures took up almost half of the budget of any European state. In times of war, the percentage rose to 80 percent, or even more. Inevitably, there came a point even in absolute states when noble and other wealthy families upon which monarchies depended for financial support began to grumble. But as Table 7-1 reveals, huge standing armies characterized absolute states even in peacetime, nowhere more so than in France, the model of absolute rule in Europe. For the first time uniforms, colorful signs of the state's influence, became standard equipment for every soldier.

Absolutism and Religion

Absolute monarchs intruded in matters of faith and self-expression by both aiding established churches and limiting ecclesiastical authority within their states. An alliance with established churches helped monarchs achieve and maintain absolute rule. In particular, the Catholic Church's quest for uniformity of belief and practice went hand in hand with the absolutist monarch's desire to eliminate challenges to his authority. Absolute monarchs lent their authority and prestige to the Catholic Church, the support of which, in turn, seemed to legitimize absolute monarchical power. The Church helped create an image of the king as a sacred figure, benevolent but strict, who must be obeyed because he served God's interests on earth. In turn, absolute monarchs obliged the Church by persecuting religious minorities.

At the same time that they supported established churches, however, absolute rulers also reduced ecclesiastical autonomy in their realms. Although the Catholic Church was a significant economic, social, and political force in the Catholic absolutist states—France, Spain, Austria, and Portugal—it lost authority to their absolute monarchs. The Church owned as much as two-thirds of the land of Portugal, and at least 10 percent in Spain, Austria, and France, as well as half the land of Bavaria and Flanders, in addition to considerable holdings in all of the Italian states. The Church claimed the right to the tithe. But absolute monarchs maintained authority over ecclesiastical appointments, in effect creating national churches to the consternation of the papacy in Rome.

Signs of the victory of absolute rulers over the Catholic Church included shackling or eliminating the Inquisition in France and Spain, closing monasteries and expelling religious orders in France and Austria, assuming control over censorship, reducing ecclesiastical authority over marriage, and establishing the principle of state supervision over education.

In France, the very existence of the French, or Gallican Church, defied papal claims to complete authority over the Church. By the Concordat of Bologna in 1516, the pope had given the kings of France virtual control (subject to confirmation by the pope) over the appointment of bishops and other high ecclesiastical officials in France. It also had allowed the French kings to overrule the judgments of ecclesiastical courts. This irritated French "ultramontane" clergy, who rejected the Gallican Church, recognizing only the authority of the pope "beyond the mountains," that is, beyond the Alps in Rome. The provincial noble parlements, or law courts, by contrast, remained defiantly Gallican. The Gallican Church itself was far more likely to remain loyal to the monarchy that defined its prerogatives.

Yet, Gallicans themselves insisted that the pope and bishops retain spiritual authority, with the king having a monopoly only on temporal power.

The Russian Orthodox Church, independent of the Greek Orthodox Church since the fifteenth century, and the tsarist autocratic state closely supported each other. The Church taught the faithful obedience to the tsar. But in 1716, Peter the Great forced bishops to take an oath that they would not interfere in state affairs. And by the end of the century, the Russian clergy lost the right to be tried in their own courts and became subject to those of the state.

Recognizing no distinction between church and state, the Turkish Ottoman Empire was a theocracy. The sultan's subjects believed his despotic authority was divine. The Muslim religious hierarchy, which included judges, theologians, and teachers, provided officials for the imperial administration. Yet, the supreme religious dignitary occasionally invoked religious law, of which he was the main interpreter, to counter some orders of the sultan, although the latter's political authority remained absolute.

The expansion of the Ottoman Empire had been based upon the concept of the crusading "Holy War" against infidels, or non-Muslims. As the Turks destroyed the Byzantine Empire, capturing Constantinople in 1453, they confiscated many of the resources of the Orthodox Church and other Christian denominations. The Ottoman Turks had enslaved prisoners of war, purchased slaves abroad, or imposed a slave levy upon the Christians of the empire. Many Christian children had been trained as officials or

Janissaries crossing the Drove, a branch of the Danube River.

soldiers and had converted to Islam. The empire also depended on the contributions of non-slave Christians, including skilled Greek sailors who made Turkish galleys feared in the Mediterranean. Some joined the "janissary" infantry, a military corps that assumed police duties in periods of peace.

Yet, the Ottoman Empire tolerated religious diversity. As long as non-Muslims did not resist Turkish authority, they were free to practice their religion and to become officials within the empire. In Albania (where alone conversions seemed to have been forced), Bosnia, and Herzegovina, many people, including some nobles, converted to the Muslim faith. Young Christians captured by Turkish fleets could convert to Islam in order to escape a life chained to benches as galley slaves. In contrast, Muslims captured by Christian powers remained galley slaves, even if they converted.

Monumentalism in Architecture and Art

Absolute monarchs embraced the extravagant emotional appeal of monumental architecture. They designed their capitals to reflect the imperatives of monarchical authority. Madrid, Berlin, St. Petersburg, and Versailles outside of Paris were planned, shaped, and invested with symbols of absolute rule. These cities were laid out according to geometric principles. In contrast to the narrow, winding streets of trading cities that had evolved organically from medieval times, straight, wide boulevards were created in one fell swoop. The boulevards that led from arches of triumph were built in a classic style to celebrate the power of rulers. These boulevards' symmetrical panorama symbolized the organized and far-reaching power of absolutism and the growth of the modern state. Royal armies paraded down the boulevards to squares or royal palaces, on or before which stood imposing statues, and around which were grouped government buildings and noble residences. Barracks housing standing armies also became a prominent feature of the new urban landscape.

Monarchs paid artists and architects to combine baroque elements with a more restrained, balanced classicism, influenced by the early sixteenth-century Roman style of the High Renaissance. This became known as the Louis XIV style. Thus, the facade completing the Louvre palace in Paris, the work of Gianlorenzo Bernini (1598–1680), drew on the architectural style of Roman temples, thereby linking Louis to the glories of Julius Caesar and other victorious generals. In fact, with the Royal Academy laying down the classical rules painters were to follow, myriad sculptures and paintings represented the king during the early part of his reign as a Roman commander (such as François Girardon's 1680 bronze equestrian sculpture). Later on, artists were asked to produce historical representations of Louis' own triumphs. In the gardens of Versailles, the identification of Apollo with the king is made clear both by Jean-Baptiste Tuby's basin sculpture of *Apollo Rising from the Sea* (1668–1671) and

Charles LeBrun's painting of Louis XIV as a Roman commander.

specifically by Girardon's *Apollo Attended by Nereids* (1666– 1672), a marble group in which one of the muses, or sea nymphs, carries a vase that shows Louis crossing the Rhine. Inside the château, Charles LeBrun's ceiling paintings also associate Louis' wars with purposeful *Apollo in His Chariot* (Charles De Lafosse, 1670s), a depiction whose lavish frame suggests the sun looking down on all who walk beneath. Instead of being compared to past heroes, the king himself was setting the standard for glory. Hyacinthe Rigaud's full-length portrait of Louis XIV in 1701 shows a supremely confident and powerful king standing in a regal pose wearing luxurious coronation robes, clutching his staff of authority and looking with condescension at the viewer—his subject.

ABSOLUTISM IN FRANCE

Absolutist France became the most powerful state in Europe. Francis I and Henry IV had extended the effective reach of monarchical authority (see Chapter 4). Louis XIII, aided by his invaluable minister Cardinal Richelieu, had crushed Protestant resistance. Richelieu piled new administrative structures on old ones, using provincial "intendants" (noble royal officials) to centralize and further extend monarchical authority. Richelieu's policies led to the doubling of taxes between 1630 and 1650, sparking four major waves of peasant resistance between 1624 and 1645, including one uprising in the southwest in 1636 in which about 60,000 peasants took arms, some shouting "Long live the king without taxes!" At Louis XIII's death, the stage was set for Louis XIV (ruled 1643–1715) to rule as a divine-right king of an absolute state. But before the young Louis could take control of the government, France would first experience the regency of his mother and the revolt known as the Fronde.

The Fronde: Taming "Overmighty Subjects"

Louis XIV was four years old at the time of his accession to the throne in 1643. His mother, Anne of Austria (1601–1666), served as regent. She depended on Cardinal Jules Mazarin (1602–1661) for advice. Mazarin, a worldly, charming, and witty Italian, always dressed in the finest red silk and was well known for his love of money. A master of intrigue who had served as a papal envoy, rumor had it that he and Anne were secretly married.

During the Regency period, Anne and Mazarin kept French armies in the field, prolonging the Thirty Years' War, which had become a struggle pitting the dynastic interests of France against the Austrian and Spanish Habsburgs (see Chapter 4). Most nobles, with much to lose from civil disturbances, remained loyal to the monarchy. But Mazarin's prolongation of the victorious struggle against Spain generated a political crisis. Peasants, already weighed down by payments in cash, kind, and labor owed to nobles (an increasing number of whom were becoming absentee lords) and suffering the effects of poor harvests, resisted the additional wartime financial burdens imposed by the state.

Resistance to royal authority culminated in a revolt that shook the Bourbon monarchy at mid-century. Between 1648 and 1653, powerful "nobles of the sword" (those nobles who held ancient titles and whose forebears had gathered retainers to fight for the king) tried to regain the influence lost during the reign of Louis XIII. Ordinary people entered the fray, demanding lower taxes because of deteriorating economic conditions. The revolt became known as the Fronde—so named from a slingshot the boys of Paris used to hurl rocks.

Mazarin, whom many nobles considered a "foreign plotter" and an outsider like Anne of Austria, had borrowed money for the state from financiers. He did so against expected revenue from new taxes or the sale of offices. Nobles were willing to suffer extraordinary levies in times of war. But now they complained bitterly that supplementary impositions in peacetime were needless. Furthermore, some of the oldest noble families had claimed for some time that they had been excluded systematically from the highest, most lucrative, and most prestigious offices. In fact, there was some truth in this claim, as the king feared the power of disloyal "overmighty subjects," preferring lesser nobles for military offices and skilled bureaucrats for some civil posts. Several offices had been abolished. Cardinal Richelieu had convinced the king to order the execution of noble plotters on three occasions during his reign. Now nobles of the sword denounced Mazarin, his system of patronage, and his financier friends, some of whom had made fortunes supplying the royal armies.

In 1648, Mazarin attempted to secure the Parlement of Paris' approval for increased taxes. The Parlement of Paris was the chief law court in France and was made up of nobles of the robe, who had purchased their positions from the crown. Wanting to safeguard their privileges and power, they defied the Regency by calling for an assembly of the four sovereign courts of Paris to consider the financial crisis. Meeting without royal permission, the assembly proposed that the courts elect delegates to consider financial reforms in the realm. The provincial parlements joined the protest against what seemed to be unchecked royal authority. Financiers who had earlier purchased titles from the crown now refused to loan the state any more money.

When Mazarin ordered the arrest of some of the defiant members of the parlement in August 1648, barricades went up in Paris and ordinary Parisians rioted in support of the parlement. From inside the Louvre palace, Louis XIV, then a boy of nine, heard the angry shouts of the crowds. At one point the mob burst into Louis' bedroom. Popular discon-

(*Left*) Louis, prince of Condé. (*Right*) Jules Mazarin, the Italian cardinal and royal chancellor.

tent forced the court to flee Paris in January 1649. These events would affect the king's later successful consolidation of his power.

The role of the prince of Condé (Louis de Bourbon; 1621–1686), head of the junior branch of the Bourbon family, was crucial in the Fronde. Condé's great victory in 1643 over the Spanish at the battle of Rocroi in northern France, which ended any possibility of a successful Spanish invasion of the country, earned him the name of "the Great Condé." The king himself called the proud Condé, only half in jest, "the most powerful man in France." But as long as Mazarin had met Condé's demands for money and offices, the latter remained loyal to the young king. In 1648, Condé marched to Paris with his army to defend the king. A temporary settlement was bought by minor and short-lived tax reforms. But major uprisings against taxes, which had doubled in two decades as Richelieu and Mazarin had in turn raised money in order to wage war, broke out in several provinces. Relatively poor nobles, who resented that wealthy commoners were able to purchase titles with the proceeds of tax-farming and various services to the court, led other revolts. Condé himself changed sides in 1649 and supported the *frondeurs*.

Fearing Condé's influence, a Spanish invasion, and further insurrections, Anne and Mazarin found noble allies against Condé and early in 1650 ordered him imprisoned. Condé's arrest further mobilized opposition to Mazarin, whose enemies forced the minister to flee the country early the next year. More revolts broke out in the provinces, notably in Bordeaux, where the parlement joined the rebellion, which gained popular support. A year later, Condé was released from prison at the demand of the Parlement of Paris. In September 1651, at the age of thirteen, Louis XIV declared his majority and right to rule. But he faced an immediate challenge from Condé who, controlling Bordeaux and its region, marched to Paris in 1652 with the goals of reestablishing his own and the other great nobles' political influence and of getting rid of Mazarin (who continued to influence royal policy from his exile in Germany). However, finding insufficient support from the parlement, the municipal government, or ordinary Parisians, Condé fled to Spain. King Louis recalled Mazarin to Paris.

The young Louis XIV restored monarchical authority by ending the nobles' rebellion and putting down peasant resistance against taxation. He tamed the men he called his "overmighty subjects." He exiled ten members of the Parlement of Paris who had been disloyal to the crown and agreed to give amnesty to others if they would submit to royal authority. Louis made clear that henceforth the Parlement of Paris could not meddle in the king's business. To make the point, in 1652 the king summoned the parlement to the Louvre for a formal ceremony that confirmed its humiliation. And in 1673 the king deprived the twelve parlements of their right to issue remonstrances (formal objections to the registration of new royal ordinances, edicts, or declarations, which could be overridden by the king) before they registered an edict. Laying claim to a monopoly on violence, the king also disbanded the private armies of headstrong nobles and tightened royal control over the provincial governors.

Even at the height of the revolt, when the *frondeurs* were demanding that the king abolish the posts of intendants except in frontier regions, most of them would have been hard pressed to describe the kind of government they wanted. They were also divided by personal rivalries. Furthermore, only the king himself could confirm the social ascendancy of the nobles of the sword. Unlike the English Parliament's successful rebellion against the crown in defense of constitutional rule (see Chapter 6), French noble resistance to absolute rule was broken by the French crown's defeat of the *frondeurs*. The king's predecessors, particularly Francis I, had frequently consulted with prominent nobles about important matters. Louis XIV felt no obligation to do so. Yet, the Fronde also demonstrated that the crown had to rule more subtly, even as Louis XIV kept the reins of power for himself.

Mercantilism under Louis XIV

Following Mazarin's death in 1661, Louis XIV, now twenty-two years of age, assumed more personal responsibility for the day-to-day running of the monarchy. The state's firmer financial footing owed much to the cool calculations of Jean-Baptiste Colbert (1619–1683), controller-general of the realm, who directed administration, taxation, and public works. The grandson of a provincial merchant of modest standing, Colbert suffered the hostility of the old noble families. His frosty personality led him to be dubbed "the North." He employed surveyors and mapmakers to assess the economic resources of the provinces. Traditionally, taxes were "farmed" by royal agents who collected the tax for the state and kept part of it for themselves. Whereas formerly only about a quarter of these revenues reached royal coffers, now as much as four-fifths of what was collected poured into the royal treasury. Even though the royal tax on land (the *taille*) had been reduced, state revenues doubled, despite abuses and privileged exemptions (nobles and clergy in France did not pay the *taille*).

Mercantilism provided the financial basis for absolutist France. Mercantilists posited that all resources should be put into the service of the state and that a state's wealth was measured by its ability to import more gold and silver than it exported to other countries. Jealous of English and Dutch prosperity, Colbert became the chief proponent of French mercantilist policies, which emphasized economic self-sufficiency. He founded commercial trading companies to which the king granted monopolies on colonial trade, levied high protective tariffs on Dutch and English imports, and reduced or eliminated—where possible—tolls within France itself. He established the royal Gobelins tapestry manufacture on the edge of Paris and encouraged the textile industry and the manufacture of other goods that could be exported. He improved roads and oversaw the exten-

King Louis XIV visiting the royal Gobelins tapestry manufacture on the edge of
Paris.

sion of France's network of canals, including the Languedoc Canal linking the Mediterranean to the Garonne River and thus to the Atlantic
Ocean.

Yet, despite the growth of the French merchant fleet and navy, the
French East India Company, established by Colbert in 1664, could not effectively compete with its more efficient and adventurous Dutch and English rivals. The monarchy had to bail out the company and later took
away its trading monopoly. Trade within France remained hamstrung by a
bewildering variety of restrictions and internal tariffs that in some places
were not much different from those that characterized the hodgepodge of
German states.

While the king was a master of extracting revenue from his subjects, his
greatest talent was for emptying the royal coffers with dizzying speed.
Louis XIV and his successors plunged the monarchy into an ever-deepen-
ing and eventually disastrous financial crisis.

Louis XIV's Absolutism

As Louis XIV grew into manhood, he looked the part of a great king and
played it superbly. Handsome, proud, energetic, and decisive, Louis built
his regime more on ceremony than on intelligence and sense. His love of
gambling, hunting, and women sometimes took precedence over matters
of state. But he also supervised the work of the high council of his prominent officials and, though a spendthrift, he closely monitored the accounts
of his realm.

The king became a shrewd judge of character, surrounding himself with men of talent. He consciously avoided being dependent on any single person, the way Louis XIII had been on Richelieu, or his mother on Cardinal Mazarin. During a visit to the château of Vaux-le-Vicomte, built by the unpopular minister of finance Nicholas Fouquet, Louis was served with solid gold tableware and viewed pools filled with seawater and large saltwater fish. The king, who was ready to get rid of Fouquet anyway, promptly ordered him arrested and took the magnificent château for himself.

Having affirmed his authority over Paris, Louis dissolved any remaining pretensions of autonomy held by the elites in the major provincial towns. One result of the Fronde was that the monarchy expanded the narrow social base on which state power had previously rested. Louis selected governors, intendants, and bishops who would be loyal to him. The king made mayors into officials of the state who had to purchase their titles in exchange for fidelity to the king. Wealthy merchants and other townsmen now preferred to seek ennoblement rather than try to maintain municipal privileges that seemed increasingly archaic. The presence of royal garrisons, which towns once resisted, not only affirmed the sovereign's authority but were welcomed by local elites as protection against plebeian insurrection. By the early eighteenth century, towns practically begged for garrisons because troops were good for local business.

The development of absolutism affected towns in other ways, bringing intendants and lesser royal officials, lawyers, and clerks to reside there. In 1667, Louis took another important step in affirming his authority by appointing a lieutenant-general of police for Paris. He gave him extensive authority over a wide range of policing activities, ranging from powers of

Louis XIV surrounded by loyal nobles.

arrest to responsibility for street cleaning and fire fighting. And thanks to the lieutenant-general of police, Paris soon had street lighting—thousands of glass-enclosed candles—during the early evening hours.

Louis XIV portrayed himself as God's representative on this planet, charged with maintaining earthly order. He may or may not have said, *L'état, c'est moi* ("I am the state"), but during his long reign the monarch was indeed identified with the state itself. The royal propaganda machine provided ideological legitimacy by cranking out images of the king as a glorious monarch. During the military disasters and hard times of the War of the Spanish Succession (1701–1714), the emphasis shifted toward a view of the king as the father of his people, while hammering home the necessity of obedience. At the same time, royal censors suppressed publications (especially after the Fronde) prohibited imported books, and limited the number of printers.

Louis XIV created the first French ministry of war and shaped it into an effective bureaucracy. The king and his ministers brought the noble-dominated officer corps under royal control, making seniority the determinant of rank and charging wealthy nobles handsome sums for the privilege of commanding their own regiments or companies. The ministry of war ordered the construction of military academies, barracks, and drilling grounds, and fortified key border towns.

Louis XIV described himself as first seigneur of the realm. Nobles still insisted more than ever—though more quietly than at the time of the Fronde—that institutionalized noble privileges were necessary to counter the excesses of absolute authority. In exchange for acknowledgment by the nobles of monarchical legitimacy, the king confirmed their privileges, including titles, ownership of land, and seigneurial rights over peasants. Nobles were almost completely immune from royal taxes (basically paying only indirect taxes) until Louis made them subject to two additional taxes (the *capitation*, a head tax, and the *vingtième*, a tax of 5 percent, usually only on land). They benefited from the economic development the monarchy could encourage, such as by building better roads and networks of canals that were largely underwritten by the state. Greater efficiency in the collection of taxes on wealth, too, benefited nobles, since the taxes (to which the nobles were not subject) provided money for the salaries of various royal officers and for the trips of nobles to Versailles to offer homage to the king, and financed the construction of official buildings.

The king awarded ever more titles, ecclesiastical offices, and government and military positions to those who loyally served him. This was the easiest way for the king to raise money, as well as to enhance loyalty. As one minister put it "as soon as the crown creates an office God creates a fool willing to buy it."

Since the time of Henry IV, offices had effectively become forms of hereditary property. Louis XIV's lavish sale of offices and titles—500 sold with a single edict in 1696—expanded the nobility. Few noble families now could trace their titles back more than several generations. This accentuated differences between the nobles of the sword (some of whom could trace their noble lineage back centuries) and the nobles of the robe (many of whom had purchased their offices). The nobles of the sword dominated court life, but the king did not hesitate to dip into the ranks of commoners to find efficient, loyal officials, exempting them from taxation and providing lucrative posts for their offspring. Louis de Rouvroy, the duke of Saint-Simon, a noble of the sword, denounced the "reign of the vile bourgeoisie," that is, nobles of recent title whom he viewed as upstart newcomers unworthy of prominent posts.

Louis XIV at Versailles

Louis XIV never forgot hearing the howling Parisian mob from his room in the royal palace. Resolving to move his court to Versailles, twelve miles west of Paris, he visited Paris only four times during the seventy-two years of his reign. Realizing that an adequately fed population would be less likely to riot, Louis XIV and his successors worked to assure the sufficient provisioning of the capital.

The Sun King followed Colbert's advice: . . . nothing marks the greatness of princes better than the buildings that compel the people to look

The château of Versailles, built by Louis XIV from 1669 to 1686.

on them with awe, and all posterity judges them by the superb palaces they have build during their lifetime." The staging ground for royal ceremonies was the fabulous château of Versailles (constructed 1669–1686), surrounded by geometrically arranged formal gardens, interspersed by 1,400 fountains supplied by the largest hydraulic pumps in the Western world.

The château, with hundreds of splendidly decorated rooms, was monumental in scale. The royal dining room was so far from the kitchen that the king's food often arrived at his table cold and, during one particularly cold winter, the wine froze before Louis could taste it. The château's corridors were so long that some nobles used them as urinals, instead of continuing the lengthy trek to the water closet.

Louis summoned the greatest nobles of the realm to Versailles to share in his glory. There they could be honored, but none could become too powerful. More than 10,000 nobles, officials, and servants lived in or near the château. Intricately detailed etiquette governed royal ceremonies. They began with the elaborate routine of dressing the king in the morning in the company of the richest and most powerful nobles. As in the king of Spain's palace near Madrid, court rituals at Versailles were orchestrated to inspire a sense of the majesty and power of the monarch, but also to maintain differences in rank and privilege. The ultimate reward for a loyal noble was to be named to a post within the royal household. Louis XIV allowed the nobles to form cabals and conspire, but only against each other.

Nobles attended the expensive theatrical and operatic productions put on at royal expense. These included the works of the great Jean-Baptiste Molière (1622–1673) and Jean Racine (1639–1699), both of whom wrote effusive praise for the king into some of their plays. But for nobles at Versailles there was little else to do except eat, drink, hunt—in the company of the king, if they were favored—gamble, and chase each other's wives and mistresses.

Social struggles mark the plays of Molière. The son of an upholsterer, the playwright started a travelling theatrical company before settling in Paris. The lonely, unhappy Molière poked fun at the pretensions of aristocratic and ecclesiastical society, depicting the private, cruel dramas of upper-class family life. But his popular works also helped reaffirm the boundaries between social classes. He ridiculed the bourgeois, whose wealth could purchase titles but not teach them how to behave as nobles. In The Bourgeois Gentilhomme (1670), the parvenu gives himself away with a social gaffe. Molière also detested hypocrisy, which he depicted in Tartuffe (1664), a tale of the unfortunate effects of untempered religious enthusiasm on a family. Tartuffe brought Molière the wrath of the Church, but he had an even more powerful protector, Louis XIV.

Nobles sustained an aristocratic culture tied to notions of civility, or codes governing how nobles and other people of means ought to behave in public. A guide to manners published about twenty years after Louis XIV

Portrait of the young Jean-Baptiste Molière, playwright.

became king advised: "Formerly . . . it was permitted to spit on the ground before people of rank, and was sufficient to put one's foot on the sputum. Today that is an indecency." The same book had good advice on eating, too: "If everyone is eating from the same dish . . . you should always wipe your spoon when, after using it, you want to take something from another dish, there being people so delicate that they would not wish to eat soup into which you had dipped it after putting it into your mouth."

Louis XIV believed that his court stood as the center and apex of civilization. Indeed, French arts and literature had an enormous influence in Europe, particularly during the first thirty years of his reign. Foreign monarchs, nobles, and writers considered French the language of high culture. In 1700, advertisements placed in London newspapers by private teachers promised that their pupils would soon speak the French spoken at the court of Louis XIV. The château of Versailles encouraged imitation. Philip V of Spain and Frederick the Great of Prussia, among others, ordered similar palaces built. The duke of Saxony rebuilt his capital of Dresden along neo-classical lines. The château also served as a model for noble estates and townhouses built in the classical style.

Louis XIV's Persecution of Religious Minorities

One of the most salient results of the victory of absolute rule in Catholic states was the persecution of religious minorities. Such campaigns in part served to placate the papacy and the Church hierarchy in each Catholic

(*Left*) The symbol of the sun used to glorify the absolute ruler, Louis XIV. (*Right*) This caricature shows Louis XIV, the Sun King, as the exterminator of Protestantism.

state. Louis XIV had little interest in theology, although he was relatively pious, for all his eager attention to his mistresses, several of whom bore him children. But as he grew older, the king brought into his inner circle a number of extremely devout advisers, and into his bedroom a fervently religious mistress.

Reversing the tolerant policies of Henry IV and Louis XIII, in the late 1670s Louis XIV launched a vigorous campaign of persecution against Huguenots, closing most Protestant churches and initiating attempts to force conversions to Catholicism. In 1685, Louis XIV revoked the Edict of Nantes, by which Henry IV in 1598 had extended religious tolerance to Protestants. This pleased the provincial estates in regions where Protestants were a forceful minority and memories of the wars of religion were still fresh. But the economic cost to France was in the long run considerable. Although the king forbade Huguenots from leaving France, many merchants and skilled craftsmen were among the 200,000 Huguenots who nonetheless emigrated during the next forty years. Many went to England, South Africa, Prussia, and to the Dutch United Provinces.

With the motto "one king, one law, one faith," Louis XIV also persecuted Jansenists in his quest for religious orthodoxy. Jansenists were followers of Cornelius Jansen, bishop of Ypres in the Southern Netherlands, who had died in 1638. They could be found in France, the Netherlands, Austria, and several Italian states. Seeking reforms within the Church, Jansenists emphasized the role of faith and divine grace in the pursuit of salvation. Believing mankind to be fallen and hapless, incapable of understanding the will of God, Jansenists came close to accepting a Calvinist doctrine of predestination. Their enemies called them "Calvinists who go to Mass." Calvinists had developed the notion of "vocation," whereby one was to throw oneself into secular life and live as a saint, as if one had the certainty of salvation. Jansenists, in contrast, believed that one should completely withdraw from the world, given the certainty of sin and mankind's ignorance of God's will. Jansenists, who were notoriously ascetic and disapproved of the frivolity of Versailles, criticized the Church for encouraging a lax morality by holding out the possibility of repeated penance, indeed deathbed conversion.

The pope had condemned Jansenism in 1653, perhaps at the insistence of the Jesuits, who were the Jansenists' most determined enemy. Louis XIV continued to tolerate them for several decades. But he began to persecute them in the name of "one faith" in 1709 when, influenced by Jesuit advisers, he ordered the Jansenist community at Port-Royal outside of Paris evicted and its abbey burned to the ground. He convinced Pope Clement XI to issue a papal bull, *Unigenitus* (1713), which condemned Jansenism. The Parlement of Paris, however, refused to register the edict. Louis was still trying to force compliance two years later when he died. The king's attempt to impose religious orthodoxy in France fell short, indicating that absolute rule had its limits.

The Limits of French Absolutism

France, like other countries, was far from being a nation-state in which most people thought of themselves as French, as well as or instead of Norman, Breton, or Provençal. More than half the population did not speak

Protestant allegory representing French Huguenots fleeing religious persecution in France.

French. Inadequate roads isolated mountain regions, in particular, limiting the effective reach of absolute rule.

The absolute monarchy stood at the top of a complex network of patronage based on personal ties that reached into every province and every town. But Louis XIV's intendants still had to take local networks of influence into consideration, using intimidation, cajoling, and negotiating to gain their ends in what was Western Europe's most populous state.

The king played off against one another the jurisdictions and interests of the estates, parlements, and other provincial institutions dominated by the nobles. The provincial estates were assemblies of nobles of the *pays d'état* (regions retaining a degree of fiscal autonomy, including Brittany, Provence, Burgundy, and Languedoc), which claimed to represent each province. The estates oversaw the collection of taxes and tended to details of provincial administration and spending. They met annually amid great pageantry and carefully orchestrated ceremony that, like those at Versailles, reaffirmed social hierarchy. In principle, the estates could refuse to provide the crown with the annual "free grant" (a subsidy provided by each region to the monarch), which was hardly "free," since the king informed the estates of the amount of money he wanted. Louis XIV abolished the custom of allowing the estates to express grievances before voting the amount of their "gift" to the monarchy.

The interests of the nobles also prevailed in the parlements, which were sovereign law courts that registered, publicized, and carried out royal laws. The parlements, most of whose members were nobles, claimed to speak for their province in legal matters, asserting the right to issue binding commands in cases of emergencies. But, unlike the English Parliament, no national representative political institution existed in France.

Louis XIV's successor, Louis XV (ruled 1715–1774) held that "sovereign power resides in my person alone. . . . It is from me that my courts of justice derive their existence and their authority. The plenitude of this authority which they exercise only in my name, remains always with me. I alone possess the legislative power without sharing it with, or depending for it on, anyone. . . . The whole system of public order emanates from me."

But even the king of France was not as omnipotent or omniscient as he would have liked to think. Louis XV, bothered by the traffic in Paris, once complained, "If I were lieutenant-general of police, I would ban two-wheel carriages." Bodin, theorist of absolutism, expressed the view that a ruler would be wise to avoid exercising full power, for example by not interfering with his subjects' property. This ambiguity is perhaps best symbolized by the king's phrase to the estates of a province, "We entreat you but we also command you. . . ."

Even the Bourbons were bound by the so-called fundamental laws of the realm, as well as by those they believed God had established. They therefore were responsible for any crimes they might commit. More than this, an absolute monarch could not stem the tide of change. Louis XIII placed markers around the city of Paris, even beyond the city walls, warning that anyone who built beyond would have his house razed and be slapped with a stiff fine. But Louis XIV had to surrender to spontaneous population growth, finally ordering the walls torn down in 1670.

THE HABSBURG MONARCHY

The eighteenth-century French philosophe Voltaire only somewhat exaggerated when he dismissed the Holy Roman Empire, that cumbersome federal structure of Central European states that once served as a powerful protector of the papacy, as having ceased to be holy, Roman, or an empire. The Holy Roman Empire included almost 300 German states, ranging from Austria to archbishoprics barely extending beyond the walls of towns like Mainz and Trier. Until 1648, seven electors (four princes and three archbishops) picked the Holy Roman emperor, invariably the Habsburg ruler (after 1648, there were eight electors). But in a Europe increasingly dominated by absolute monarchs, the Holy Roman Empire seemed an anomaly.

In principle, the Holy Roman emperor still commanded the allegiance of the states of the empire. These included sizable states such as Bavaria and Saxony, whose rulers oversaw elaborate courts modeled after Versailles, maintained standing armies, and paid for all this by levying taxes on their subjects and customs duties and tolls on merchandise being carried through their territories. The Holy Roman Empire also included many small principalities, duchies, and even towns ruled by bishops. But in reality the empire had increasingly only a shadow existence, despite its mystique as the defender of Catholicism. The Treaty of Westphalia (1648), which concluded the Thirty Years' War, reflected the inability of the Holy Roman Empire to enforce its will, conduct foreign policy, or effectively maintain an army. During the long war, some German princes, with powerful allies outside the empire, had gone their own way. Indeed, the Treaty of Westphalia specifically empowered each member state to carry out its own foreign policy. The imperial Assembly, the Reichstag, thus had virtually no authority to conduct foreign policy with other states. The imperial army was too small and difficult to mobilize to be effective. The imperial court of law was powerless to enforce its decisions, depending entirely on the good will of the individual states.

The strongest state within the Holy Roman Empire, the territories of Habsburg Austria, extended beyond the boundaries of the empire itself. The Habsburgs had ruled Austria without interruption since the thirteenth century. The old Habsburg principle was "Let others wage war. You, happy Austria, marry [to prosper]." Advantageous marriages brought the dynasty the wealthy territories of Burgundy and the Netherlands in the fifteenth century. Charles V, who became Holy Roman emperor in 1519, added Hungary and Bohemia. Counting Spain and its far-flung possessions, he reigned over perhaps a quarter of the population of the European continent, as well as the vast Spanish Empire of the Americas.

When Charles V gave up his power in 1556 and formally abdicated as emperor in 1558, he divided the Habsburg domains into two parts. His brother Ferdinand I inherited the Austrian Habsburg lands (including Austria, Hungary, and Bohemia) and succeeded him as the elected Holy Roman emperor. Charles' son Philip II became king of Spain with his empire including the Netherlands, dependencies in Italy, and colonies in the Americas. The Spanish and Austrian branches of the Habsburgs were henceforth two separate dynasties, although the interests of both as Catholic states, but also as rivals of France, sometimes converged.

The Austrian Habsburg monarchy exercised foreign policy and directed the armed forces, but it had less effective authority within its territories than the kings of France had within their realm. Nobles oversaw the court system and police apparatus. When confronted with threats to their traditional prerogatives, nobles put aside differences, such as those between the great landowners and the lower nobility, and formed a common front to preserve their privileges against monarchical erosion.

Austria was the only power able to exercise its influence equally in both Western and Eastern Europe. The Austrian Habsburgs successfully implemented an effective state administration, expanded educational opportunities for the upper classes, and brought resistant or even rebellious nobles under dynastic control. But timely marriages were no longer enough. Throughout the sixteenth century and during the first half of the seventeenth century, the Habsburgs had been almost constantly preoccupied with politics within and between the German states. During the Thirty Years' War, however, the Habsburgs were unable to expand their domination throughout Central Europe. While still seeking a major role in the German states, the Habsburgs remained vulnerable to French expansionism and to Turkish incursions, forcing the monarchy to confront threats on two fronts.

The Habsburg empire's polyglot structure of territories of different nationalities, including fifteen major languages, was a source of weakness. Leopold I, elected Holy Roman emperor in 1658 (ruled 1658–1705; Louis XIV was the opposing candidate), was simultaneously Holy Roman emperor, duke of Upper and Lower Silesia, count of Tyrol, archduke of Upper and Lower Austria, king of Bohemia, prince of Transylvania, king of Hungary, Slavonia, Dalmatia, and Croatia, and titular ruler of Lombardy, Styria, and Moravia (see Map 7.1). The monarch did not rule through a single administration, but rather in each case through local political institutions. The Hungarian and Croatian provincial diets, or noble estates, impeded Habsburg absolutism. Hungarians also resented German-speaking administrators and tax collectors, as well as the Habsburg armies that

MAP 7.1 THE HOLY ROMAN EMPIRE UNDER LEOPOLD I, 1658   The Holy Roman Empire included a polyglot structure of territories of different nationalities.

helped protect them from the Turks. Some Hungarian Catholic prelates were irritated by the close ties between the ruling dynasty and the Roman papacy. In Bohemia, the scars of the religious conflicts between Catholics and Protestants during the Thirty Years' War healed very slowly. Bohemia, and Moravia as well, remained a center of Protestant intellectual ferment. Furthermore, many Bohemian nobles resented the fact that a decree in 1627 had abolished the principle of an elective monarchy and made the Bohemian crown a hereditary Habsburg possession.

Hungary had been part of the Habsburg domains since the sixteenth century. The Hungarian nobles, proud of their defense of the Habsburg empire against Turkish incursions, seized every opportunity to extract concessions from the Habsburgs. Unlike their Austrian counterparts, most of the Hungarian, or Magyar, nobles had become Protestant during the Reformation. Habsburg persecution of Hungarian Protestants helped spark an insurrection in 1679 against Habsburg rule that spread into Moravia, Slavonia, and Silesia. This led Leopold to promise the Hungarian Estates to restore some landowner privileges that had been suppressed. But dissatisfied Protestants then called for Turkish assistance at a time when the

Turks were preparing to attack Habsburg territories. The Ottoman army besieged Vienna, the Habsburg capital, in 1683. It was saved after two months by the arrival of a combined relief army of Austrians, Germans, and Poles under the command of the crusading Catholic Polish King John Sobieski (ruled 1674–1696). Pope Innocent XI succeeded in convincing Leopold I, who had been trained for the priesthood before becoming emperor and who saw himself as a prince of the Catholic Reformation, to lead a "Holy League" in 1684 against the Turks. In the War of the Holy League (1686–1687), and in subsequent fighting, Habsburg armies recaptured most of Hungary and the eastern province of Transylvania from the Turks, as well as much of Croatia. The Peace of Karlowitz (1699) ratified the Habsburg victory over the Turks and provided for further Turkish concessions to Venice and Poland. Although for the moment Ottoman garrisons remained only eighty miles from Vienna and Turkish galleys still roamed the Mediterranean, the Ottoman threat to Central Europe had passed.

The Habsburg victory over the Turks had also been, for all intents and purposes, over Hungary. In 1687, the Hungarian Estates were forced to declare that the Hungarian throne (the crown of Saint Stephen, named after Hungary's patron saint) would henceforth be a hereditary possession of the Habsburgs and no longer elective. Hungary thereby recognized the sovereignty of the Habsburg dynasty in exchange for a promise that the Hungarian Diet would be convened at regular intervals, Hungary would

Leopold I, the Holy Roman emperor.

Turkish siege of Vienna, 1683.

have its own administration, and Magyar nobles would continue to be exempt from royal taxation. While he consolidated Habsburg authority within the dynasty's domains, however, Leopold failed to impose centralized rule on Hungary. Thus, Hungary's special position within the monarchy revealed the limits of Habsburg absolutism and Austrian power.

The Habsburg monarchy, the least absolute of Europe's absolute states, was less successful than France in maintaining its power. In 1700, Austria's Habsburg dynasty lost its long-standing ties to Spain when that country passed from the Habsburg dynasty to the Bourbon dynasty with the death of the childless Charles II (ruled 1665–1700). France's defeat in the War of the Spanish Succession (1701–1714), fought to determine who would inherit the Spanish Habsburg territories, enabled the Austrian Habsburgs to pick up some of the remaining pieces of the decimated Spanish Empire in Europe. A treaty with the Turks in 1718 added parts of Wallachia, Serbia, and Bosnia to Hungarian territories. However, Austria ceded its preeminence in Central Europe to Prussia during the eighteenth century.

THE RISE OF PRUSSIA

The presence of all the essential components of absolutism explain Prussia's rise as a power: a proud, ambitious dynasty, the Hohenzollern family of Brandenburg; privileged but loyal nobles, or Junkers, whose estates formed the base of the economy and who dominated a downtrodden peasantry devoid of rights; an increasingly centralized and efficient bureaucracy; and, above all, the emergence of a large standing army. Austrian defeats in the Thirty Years' War and vulnerability to French and Turkish challenges left the way open for a rival to emerge among the German states. Bavaria and Saxony were weak claimants for primacy among the German states. Both had relatively weak nobilities, and the rulers of both states had failed to develop either a strong bureaucracy or a strong army. The Catholic clergy undermined the authority of the Bavarian dukes. The attention of Saxony, subject to Swedish influence, was often turned away from German affairs toward the volatile world of Polish politics.

The small north-central German state of Brandenburg-Prussia, stretching across the sandy marshes between the Elbe and Oder Rivers, seemed an unlikely candidate to rival Austria and to grow into a powerful absolute state. In 1618, Brandenburg's ruling Hohenzollern dynasty inherited East Prussia, which lay 100 miles to the east of Brandenburg along the Baltic Sea and was bordered by Poland. It then absorbed several smaller territories in the Rhineland, more than 100 miles to the west (see Map 7.2). Consisting of three diverse, noncontiguous realms, Brandenburg-Prussia lacked not only defensible frontiers but also the developed network of prosperous trading towns of other regions in Germany. During the Thirty Years' War, Swedish and Austrian armies took turns ravaging it. But it

MAP 7.2 THE RISE OF PRUSSIA, 1648–1720   Territories acquired by Brandenburg-Prussia.

gained territory with the Treaty of Westphalia (1648), which ended the war and permitted Prussia to absorb much of Pomerania, on the Baltic Sea coast.

Prussian nobles accepted Hohenzollern authority as a guarantee of their privileges, the trade-off that underlay statemaking in early modern Europe. Only nobles could own land, evict peasants from their lands, and were free from taxation. But they needed people to work their estates. During the late fifteenth and the sixteenth centuries, the peasants lost their freedom, including their right to free movement and often to inheritance. They became serfs, legally bound to the lord's estate, and could be sold with the land on which they worked. A burgher in a Prussian town in 1614 described serfdom as "this barbaric and Egyptian servitude . . . in our territory serfdom did not exist fifty or a hundred years ago, but lately, it has been brought in on a large scale, with the help of the authorities." The authority of the Hohenzollerns, however, stopped at the gate of the manor: Junkers retained rights of seigneurial justice over their peasants. The bourgeoisie, which included merchants and skilled craftsmen, also stood powerless before the Junkers, in contrast to the middle class in England and the Dutch United Provinces, where they presented an imposing obstacle to the growth of absolutism. Unlike the Prussian nobles, the middle-class burghers could not export grain freely and had to pay tolls, duties, and taxes.

Frederick William (ruled 1640–1688), the "Great Elector" of Brandenburg (so named because the ruler of Brandenburg had the right to cast a ballot in the election of the Holy Roman emperor), initially had neither a standing army nor the resources to raise one. Prussian nobles at first resisted the creation of a standing army, fearful that it might aid the elector in reducing their privileges. In 1653, Frederick William convinced the Junkers to grant him funds with which to build an army in exchange for royal confirmation of their privileges over the peasantry and their right to import goods without paying duties. Furthermore, the king agreed to consult the nobles on matters of foreign policy.

Then Frederick William turned to the business of augmenting state authority in his three fragmented territories. He extracted concessions from each of them, including more taxes and the right to recruit soldiers. With his permanent standing army, Frederick William was able to wage war in alliance with various states and thereby to acquire more territory, as well as recruiting peasants to serve as soldiers and Junkers as officers. The Great Elector established a centralized administrative bureaucracy, arguably the first modern civil service in Europe. The Hohenzollern family owned more than half of East Prussia, which provided considerable state revenue. A state official supervised military affairs and the collection of taxes in each district, pulling in twice as much revenue as extracted by the king of France at the same time. Elected by local nobles, he was responsible to the king, who gradually expanded his duties as a royal representative. The Prussian bureaucracy, which was coordinated by an office with the suitably imposing name of the "General Directory Over Finance, War, and Royal Domains," reached a degree of efficiency unmatched in eighteenth-century Europe. The remaining prerogatives of the towns disappeared in the expanding state. Prussian towns, most of which were small but compelled to pay a disproportionate percentage of taxes, lost their representation in the provincial estates. In 1701, the Great Elector's son Frederick III (ruled 1688–1713) took the title of King Frederick I in Prussia. This claim to royalty through kingship initiated Prussia's claim to European standing as a power.

Frederick William I (ruled 1713–1740), grandson of the Great Elector, succeeded Frederick III as elector of Brandenburg and king in Prussia. As a boy, Frederick William could not count to ten without his tutor's assistance, but upon his succession he continued the centralizing policies of his grandfather and father. Living modestly, he occupied only several rooms of his palace, with the basement serving as the royal treasury. The bad-tempered "Sergeant-King" wore his officer's uniform around the house and turned the royal gardens into a military training ground. He was known for fits of screaming rage, calling everyone in sight "blockhead," sometimes beating officials with a stick, and knocking out the teeth of several judges whose sentences displeased him. Officials known as "fiscals"

King Frederick William I.

went around to make sure that the king's representatives served him well. But the king was astute enough to break with tradition by employing some commoners; finding state service a means of social mobility, many served with uncommon loyalty and efficiency.

A Prussian official described, with some exaggeration, the feature that defined his country's absolutism and the emergence of Brandenburg-Prussia as a power: "What distinguishes the Prussians from other people is that theirs is not a country with an army. They have an army and a country that serves it." Military expenditures accounted for half of Prussia's state budget. King Frederick William I increased the Prussian army from about 39,000 to 80,000 soldiers. He engaged only tall soldiers for his royal guard, those standing more than six feet in height, virtual giants at the time. One of his first royal acts was to abolish the luxury industries in Berlin, the capital of Brandenburg-Prussia, that catered to court and nobles, and to replace them with workshops that made military uniforms. The king ordered all young men in Prussia to register for military service and organized a procedure by which each regiment was assigned a specific canton from which to recruit or conscript soldiers. Prussia established the first system of military reserves in Europe, soldiers who drilled in the summer for two months. This meant that far more men in Prussia experienced military life than in any other country.

THE RUSSIAN AND SWEDISH EMPIRES

Early in the sixteenth century, Muscovy was a relatively small state. It stood vulnerable to invasions by the Mongols, who had conquered what is now Russia in the thirteenth century, the Tartars of Crimea on the edge of the Black Sea, and to the kingdom of Poland-Lithuania, a kingdom and grand duchy joined in a confederation late in the fourteenth century. Gradually, however, the duchy of Muscovy, where Orthodox Christianity had taken hold, emerged as the strongest of the territories of Russia, absorbing Novgorod and other rival states and principalities late in the fifteenth century. Muscovy's ruler Ivan III (ruled 1462–1505) began using the title "lord of all Russia," a title that offended the far more powerful state of Poland-Lithuania. In 1500 and again twelve years later, Ivan brazenly attacked Poland-Lithuania, capturing the fortress town of Smolensk, which guarded the upper Dnieper River.

The Expansion of Muscovy

The rise of Russia as an absolute state and empire began with the further expansion of the state of Muscovy later in the sixteenth century. Tsar Ivan IV (ruled 1533–1584) absorbed parts of the Mongol states to the east, and

Ivan the Terrible watching the beggars of Novgorod being tortured to death.

drove back the Muslim Tartars, conquered the Don and Volga river basins to the south, and unsuccessfully battled Poland-Lithuania for control of the Baltic territory of Livonia. Peasants and hunters expanded the influence of Muscovy into the cold and sparsely populated reaches of Siberia.

Ivan earned his sobriquet "the Terrible." He was raised in a world of violence marked by the bloody feuds of the Muscovite nobles or *boyars,* some of whom poisoned his mother when he was eight years old. Five years later, Ivan ordered a noble ripped apart by fierce dogs; as an adult, he had an archbishop sewn into a bearskin and thrown to hungry wolves. His goals were to assure himself a reliable military force and sufficient revenue. His means was to create a "service state" in which nobles would serve him while receiving protection against peasant insurrections or other nobles. Allying with a group of military retainers, he decimated noble families he viewed as too powerful or slow to obey. Ivan alternated between moods of religious fervor, drunken passion, and stormy brutality. After being defeated in Lithuania in 1564, Ivan became even more paranoid, subjecting his people to an eight-year reign of terror. He killed his own son with a massive blow to his skull and routinely ordered anyone who displeased him tortured to death.

Ivan's death in 1584 led, almost unimaginably, to an even worse period for Muscovy, the "Time of Troubles," a period of intermittent anarchy. Weak successors allowed nobles to regain control of the sprawling country. In 1613, the Assembly of Nobles elected the first Romanov tsar. The next two tsars restored order, regaining some of the lands lost to Poland-Lithuania and Sweden.

For most peasants, life itself was an endless "time of troubles" in the face of state taxation and brutalization at the hands of their lords. Revolts seemed endemic, some led by men who claimed to be the "true" tsar who would restore justice. One of the latter, Stephen Razin, whose symbol was a horsetail, led a huge force of peasants on a march to the cry of "To Moscow against the landlords." The peasant army captured several cities before being decimated in 1670, its leader tortured in Moscow for all to see.

Serfdom emerged as one of the fundamental characteristics of Russian absolutism. In times of dearth or crisis, many peasants traditionally had fled the region of Moscow to settle on the frontierlands of Siberia in the east or on land in Ukraine, an extensive, thinly populated territory standing between Russia, Poland, and a Tartar state on the Crimean peninsula—the word *Ukraine* itself means "border region." The resulting chronic shortage of rural labor, and the need to provide landed estates to loyal nobles, led the state in 1649 officially to establish serfdom, which had become widespread by the end of the sixteenth century. The chronically indebted peasants gave up their freedom in exchange for loans from the crown and from landlords. The Orthodox Church, a major landowner, also contributed to the expansion of serfdom. Thereafter, 90 percent of the peasants were bound to the land, assuring the state and nobles of a relatively immobile labor supply. In exchange for the tsar's support of this system, Russian nobles, like their counterparts in Prussia, pledged their service to the state.

The Romanov dynasty also enjoyed the good will of the Orthodox Church. By the early sixteenth century, the Russian Orthodox Church had become centered in Moscow, which now claimed the title of the third Rome. But after a mid-seventeenth-century schism, the Orthodox Church faced the hostility of the Old Believers, dissidents who claimed authority over the tsars and disliked changes in Church ritual that reformers had implemented. Old Believers participated in violent peasant uprisings until the end of the eighteenth century.

Several neighbors blocked Muscovy's further expansion. The Commonwealth of Poland and Lithuania (which had been formally united in 1569) stood to the west, and Swedish territories were to the north. The northern port of Archangel on the White Sea, its harbor frozen solid much of the year, offered Muscovy its only access to the sea. Through Archangel passed trade with England and Northern Europe. Turks, Cossacks (a warrior people living in southern Russia), and Crimean Tartars were among the southern peoples resisting incorporation into Muscovy and Poland-Lithuania. Polish territories included much of White Russia (Belarus) and Ukraine. The rest of Ukraine was subject to the influence of Poland, Russia, and Cossacks, and was further divided by religion. Most landowners in

Ukraine were Polish Catholics. Most Ukrainian peasants were, like Russians, Orthodox Christians and spoke a language similar to Russian, but were a separate people. Peasant revolts rocked Ukraine in the late 1640s. A Cossack and former officer in the Polish army launched an uprising, driving back the Polish army, before accepting Russian sovereignty in 1654. Under the Treaty of Andrussovo (1667), which concluded a war with Poland, Russia absorbed Ukraine east of the Dnieper River.

The Swedish Empire

In the 1640s and 1650s, Swedish kings added to their dynastic holdings at the expense of Denmark and Norway, Estonia and Lithuania, and West Pomerania and Bremen in northern Germany. Like the Habsburg empire, that of Sweden offered a babel of languages, including Swedish, Finnish, Latvian, Estonian, and German, the language of administration. Sweden was a relatively poor state, but revenues from lucrative copper mines, the sale of Swedish iron and steel, the finest in Europe, and trade with Muscovy and the West generated enough revenue to finance expansion. But

King Charles XII of Sweden crossing the Dvina River in his war against Peter the Great.

expansion also had its costs: Queen Christina (ruled 1632–1654) raised money by selling almost two-thirds of royal lands, with Swedish nobles becoming the main beneficiaries. Swedish peasants, who had their own estate in the Swedish Diet (or assembly), complained of the "unheard-of state of servitude . . . since private persons took hold of the country." Specifically, they demanded, in vain, the return of all alienated lands to the throne. The lower estates did not dare challenge royal prerogatives. They asserted, "We esteem Your Majesty's royal power as the buttress of our liberties, the one being bound up in the other, and both standing or falling together."

Emboldened by his fledgling empire, King Charles XI (ruled 1660–1697) in the 1680s established absolute rule in Sweden. He overcame the resistance of the wealthiest nobles by winning the support of their jealous colleagues of lesser means, as well as that of the estates of burghers, clergy, and peasants, who sought royal protection against the most powerful nobles. His son Charles XII (ruled 1697–1718) became king at the age of fifteen and refused even to take the coronation oath when he came of age in 1700. Symbolically, he snatched the crown and placed it on his own head, and never convoked the estates. Having been instructed only in warfare as a youth, he remained a headstrong military man who acted by impulse, not reflection. Instead of diplomacy, he relied on warfare to achieve Swedish ends. Charles' unwillingness to ally with Prussia or other states against Russia in the long run cost Sweden dearly. Instead of turning Sweden's full military attention toward Denmark, which sought to recapture lost provinces from Sweden, he spent five years campaigning against Russia (see below), a quest that took him into the Ottoman Empire, where he sought assistance against Russia. But during Charles XII's reign, the crown added to its wealth by reclaiming land that had been sold to nobles in the previous decades. Gradually the Swedish monarchy established a bureaucracy and increased state revenue. But when Charles XII was killed in a war in Norway, leaving no heir, the Swedish nobility succeeded in imposing a parliamentary regime based on the prerogatives of the estates and marked by political struggles among the nobility, clergy, burghers, and peasants. In 1772, however, King Gustavus III (ruled 1771–1792) overthrew the parliamentary system, supported by some nobles, and reimposed absolute rule. By then, however, Sweden's empire was a fading memory.

Peter the Great Turns Westward

In Western Europe so little was known about "barbaric" Russia that Louis XIV sent a letter to a tsar who had been dead for twelve years. Peter the Great (ruled 1682–1725) first imposed order on a state torn by bloody uprisings; then he transformed Muscovy into the Russian Empire.

The young Peter the Great, founder of St. Petersburg.

Impressed with the relative efficiency of Western states, Peter forced a number of significant administrative and military reforms on Russia. Whereas Ivan the Terrible and several of his successors had been turned back by Poland and Turkey, Peter aggressively and successfully moved Russian interests toward Europe. Wars brought territorial acquisitions at the expense of Sweden, Poland, and the Turks.

As a boy growing up in the violent world of Russian court politics, Peter learned far more about guns, ballistics, and fortifications than about Russian grammar. Wearing a military uniform, he became tsar at the age of ten after a bloody struggle, which he witnessed firsthand, between the clans of his father's two widows. Seven years later, Peter killed members of his own family whom he perceived to be a threat to his rule.

The tsar, who wore shabby clothes, worn-out shoes, and his hair very long, stood close to seven feet tall and suffered from chronic back problems compounded by frenetic energy. A nervous tic became most apparent when he was anxious or angry, which seemed to be most of the time, as he lashed out with clubs or fists.

When he was twenty-five, Peter visited Western Europe incognito, encouraged to do so by Europeans he had met living in the foreign quarter on the edge of Moscow. Peter undertook his travels dressed as a humble workman. In the West, he shocked statesmen and nobles with his dress and coarse manners, snatching roasts with his hands from fancy buffets. Four months on the Dutch docks taught him ship carpentry. He always preferred the company of artisans and dockworkers to nobles and state officials. In London, the tsar and his entourage virtually destroyed a rented house with wild parties—the tsar loved to dance and drink—leading a bishop to worry aloud that this "furious man had been raised up to so absolute an authority over so great a part of the world."

Peter was not an uncritical admirer of the West. But impressed with the military strength and administrative efficiency of the Western powers, Peter emulated what he considered to be the more "rational" organization of Western monarchies. He borrowed Western technical knowledge, attaching it to the structures of Russian absolutism. He ordered nobles to become educated and told his guards and officials to shave off their beards—which the Old Believers believed distinguished Russians from Westerners. He encouraged the use of individual glasses, bowls, and napkins at meals, and ordered a Western book of etiquette to be translated into Russian. Furthermore, he ordered nobles to build Western-style palaces and to wear Western-style clothes and for women to wear bonnets, petticoats, and skirts. German and, to a lesser extent, French, became the language of court. Purchasing German and Italian paintings and statues, Peter began the royal collection that would later become the world-renowned Hermitage Museum.

Fearing the military superiority of his rivals, Sweden and Poland, Peter now raised the first Russian standing army, gradually replacing Western mercenary soldiers with Russian troops by implementing military conscription in 1705 to complement Cossack cavalrymen. Thereafter, every twenty peasant households had to provide one recruit, most of whom served for life, and to replace the recruit if he were killed. Peter brought Western commanders to train his army and provided soldiers with uniforms and Western flintlock muskets with socket bayonets.

The docks of Amsterdam and London inspired Peter's interest in building first a river navy and eventually an oceangoing fleet. Skilled workers from Prussia and from the Dutch Republic built warships and taught languages and mathematics. The tsar also sent Russian craftsmen abroad to learn new skills. But Russians gradually replaced Western Europeans as designers, builders, and ship commanders. By the end of the century, Russia had a fleet.

Military might, then, also underlay Russian absolutism. Even in peacetime, at least two-thirds of state revenue went to the army and navy. Peter forced nobles to send their sons to new military and engineering schools by decreeing they could not marry unless they did so. In order to pay for his army, the tsar tripled state revenues, imposing a direct tax on each male serf, or "soul." Landlords became responsible for the collection of these new taxes. He established state monopolies on the production and sale of salt, oil, tobacco, rhubarb, and even dice, used for gambling, awarding the profitable right to collect these revenues to his favorite nobles, or to foreigners. Hoping to expand Russian industry and attract gold and silver payments from abroad, Peter oversaw the exploitation of mines and the establishment of a metal industry in the Ural Mountains. But even absolute authority could not overcome the primitive transportation system, the lack of raw materials and capital, and the absence of a sizable merchant class.

Western travel and Peter's observers in the absolutist courts of Europe inspired the reorganization of the civil administration. While remaining an autocrat, Peter was nonetheless the first tsar to distinguish between his person as ruler and the state itself. Indeed, he made officials take two oaths, one to him and one to the state whose power he enhanced.

Peter divided his domains into fifty administrative districts, appointing a governor for each. He created a Senate, an administrative body charged with ruling in his absence during wartime and with overseeing state administration in time of peace. He experimented with councils whose members could—if they dared—give him advice. The tsar also put towns under the direct control of provincial governors, although they retained a measure of self-government. Peter created a cadre of nobles to fill positions in the bureaucracy. The Table of Ranks (1722) required all male nobles to enter state service, serving in the army, navy, or bureaucracy, and allowed commoners who rose through the bureaucracy or military to assume noble titles. Thus, the nobility became an instrument of the state, instead of, as in the case of other European absolute states, a social institution that could impede the ruler's will. Peter also placed the Orthodox Church fully under state control by first not naming a new patriarch (the head of the Russian Orthodox Church) upon the death of the incumbent in 1700 and later simply abolishing the patriarchate.

The tsar's turn toward the West angered the old noble families of Moscow, traditional Orthodox Church leaders, and Old Believers alike. Peter executed some nobles who refused his order to provide service to the state. Old Believers considered the reforms sacrilegious and contrary to the historical development of Russia. Many churchmen resented that Peter had subordinated the church to his state. Peter overcame four uprisings and several conspiracies directed against him. When his son announced that he would, on becoming tsar, end the Western reforms and restore old Russian customs, Peter ordered him tortured to death for opposing his will.

Peter the Great expanded Russian territory (see Map 7.3). He did so, for the most part, by pushing back the neighbors who had blocked Muscovy's expansion: Sweden, Poland, and the Ottoman Turks. He added territory beyond the Ural Mountains along the Caspian Sea, at the expense of the Turks. Like his successors, Peter dreamed of conquering the Turkish capital of Constantinople, which would give him control over its straits, the crucial passage between Europe and Asia leading to the Black Sea. A Russian army invaded Moldavia. Peter's new fleet sailed down the Don River, conquering the Turkish port of Azov on the Sea of Azov, which gives access to the Black Sea. He later surrendered Azov to the Turks, however, after his army was subsequently surrounded by a large Turkish force.

MAP 7.3 THE EXPANSION OF RUSSIA   The state of Muscovy was expanded through the acquisitions of Ivan III, Ivan IV (the Terrible), and Peter the Great.

Russia's role in European affairs, however, remained minimal, despite its participation, with Habsburg Austria, Poland, and Venice, in the long series of wars against the Turks in the last decades of the seventeenth century. Russia joined Denmark and Saxony in attacking Sweden in the Great Northern War (1700–1721). The Russian ambassador in Vienna reported that once the news of Peter's victory arrived, "people begin to fear the tsar as formerly they feared Sweden." Peter's goal was to win a "window on the Baltic Sea" at Sweden's expense. The Swedes did turn back the assault of a much larger Russian army at Narva (1700) in Estonia. But after Charles XII passed up the opportunity to pursue the Russian army in order to invade Poland and Saxony, the Russian army conquered the mouth of the Neva River in 1703.

There Peter ordered the construction of a new capital city, where he forced nobles and wealthy merchants to build elegant townhouses. St. Petersburg offered a striking contrast to the chaos of tangled streets and shabby wooden buildings of Moscow, then by far the largest city in Russia. Built on coastal marsh lands, St. Petersburg, from its fortifications to its broad boulevards, reflected architectural ideas borrowed from the West, particularly Amsterdam. State offices, including army and military headquarters, occupied the centrally located islands. Symmetrical facades rose along the Neva's south bank, near the shipyards, admiralty, and fortresses. Geometrically arranged boulevards, squares, and gardens completed the tsar's capital.

Russia supplanted Sweden as the Baltic region's dominant power. In 1709 at the Battle of Poltava, Peter's army first turned back an invading Swedish army in Ukraine, and five years later Russian troops raided Sweden for the first time. After losing its German and Polish territories, Sweden then entered its period of constitutional struggles, marked by attempts by the nobility to reassert economic and social prerogatives lost to the monarchy and allowing Russia to solidify its expansion. The Treaty of Nystadt (1721), after which Peter proclaimed Russia an empire, confirmed Russian primacy in the Baltic region. This settlement added Estonia and Livonia (the southeastern part of modern Finland) to Peter's empire, bringing Russia ever closer into European affairs.

By the time of Peter's death in 1725, Russia's expanse had increased sixfold since the time of Ivan the Terrible. The Russian Empire, thirty times bigger than France, had joined the European state system by virtue of its expanded territorial interests. The accession of Catherine the Great (1729–1796) in 1762 ended a long succession crisis, palace plots, and assassinations. The empress oversaw the next stage of Russian expansion, incorporating Ukraine into the empire.

THE BALANCE OF POWER

During the century beginning about 1650, the concept of a balance of power between states gradually took hold in many of the courts of Europe. Like the evolving European state system itself, the emergence of the concept arose in part out of the decline of religious antagonisms as a dominant cause of warfare. The quest of absolute rulers to add to their dynastic territories and the growing global commercial rivalry between the Great Powers increasingly shaped European warfare.

As a diplomatic concept dating from the time of the Renaissance city-states of fifteenth-century Italy, the balance of power held that Great Powers should be in equilibrium, and that one power should not be allowed to become too powerful. The decline of one power could threaten the balance of power if, as a result, another power considerably enhanced its

Diego de Velázquez's *The Maids of Honor.*

El Greco's *The Burial of the Count Orgaz,* 1586.

Antonio Carnicero's *The Ascension of One of the Montgolfiere Brothers, 1792.*

Abraham van Beyeren's *Still Life with Grapes and Fruit*.

Jan Vermeer's *The Painter and His Model as Klio*, 1660.

Rembrandt's, *The Night Watch*, 1662.

Elizabeth I.

Hyacinthe Rigaud's *Louis XIV*, 1701.

Peter Paul Rubens' *The Disembarkment of Marie de Medici at Marseille*, 1622–1625.

François Boucher's *Madame de Pompadour.*

William Hogarth's *The Marriage Contract*, which pokes fun at the signing of a marriage contract by a wealthy merchant, who is marrying his daughter to the son of a nobleman.

Jean Antoine Watteau's *The Sign of Gersaint*.

strength. Now the main threat to peace ceased to be religious "heresy" but rather French expansionism.

The Origins of International Law

Horrified by the Thirty Years' War, two Northern Europeans systematically analyzed questions of international relations, drawing on the recent history of Europe. They helped lay the foundations for the evolution of modern diplomacy. In 1625, the Dutch jurist Hugo Grotius (1583–1645) sought to establish the foundations of international law by arguing that laws to which nations were subject followed from nature and not from God. Samuel von Pufendorf (1632–1694), a German Protestant who tutored the family of a Swedish diplomat in Copenhagen, found himself under arrest for eight months when he was caught up in the war between Sweden and Denmark. Pufendorf's *Of the Law of Nature and Nations* (1672) postulated legal principles for times of peace—which he argued should be the natural state—and for times of war. He claimed that only a defensive war was justified, pending international arbitration to resolve crises. The problem was, of course, that unless there existed some powerful, impartial body to adjudicate disputes between nations, each side in any conflict invariably claimed that its cause was just. But European power politics swept away such theoretical considerations.

Louis XIV's Dynastic Wars

The connection between absolutism and war, as well as the concept of the balance of power, was particularly clear in the dynastic wars of Louis XIV. Some of the wars of the early modern period were fought to prevent France from becoming dominant, as France's rivals formed alliances to preserve the balance of power. The rulers of Russia, Sweden, and Turkey, like France, were seeking to expand their territories. Habsburg Austria was struggling to retain its territories, but needed help against France, as well as against the Turks, from other powers.

Dynastic interests determined a state's choice of allies. Yet, strong states with large standing armies were quite likely to switch sides, in order to gain the most beneficial terms from new allies. For example, in order to expand its influence in Central Europe, France needed an alliance with either Austria or Prussia. But inevitably such a coalition pushed the other German power into opposition, forcing it to look for allies against France. Usually this partner was England (called Great Britain after 1707), France's rival in North America. Following the conclusion of hostilities that reworked borders, alliances frequently shifted, as rulers anticipated the next opportunity to expand their territories. Nowhere was this process clearer than in the case of Louis XIV's France.

Louis XIV was determined that territorial gain and prestige be the measure of his greatness (see Map 7.4). He sought to expand his kingdom's borders to what he considered to be France's "natural" frontiers, that is, the Pyrenees Mountains to the south and the Rhine River to the east. International conditions seemed conducive to the king's grandiose plans. England had been divided by civil war in the 1640s, and its restored monarch, Charles II, faced mounting political opposition at home. To the north, Sweden confronted a Danish threat to its control of the Baltic Sea. In Central Europe, the Austrian Habsburgs faced opposition from other German princes, as well as from the Turks.

MAP 7.4 EXTENSION OF FRANCE'S FRONTIERS UNDER LOUIS XIV   Louis XIV sought to expand his dynastic territories through wars fought between 1643 and 1715.

Louis XIV crossing the Rhine before invading the Dutch Republic in 1672.

Louis XIV's "grand strategy" was to contain the two Habsburg powers, Spain and Austria, by initiating a series of wars. Each conflict followed the king's violation of a previous agreement or formal treaty, and was accompanied by the claim that French aggression was "just." Each war was to pay for itself: French armies would force local populations to offer "contributions." The Treaty of the Pyrenees (1659), ending this round of hostilities with Spain, established the frontier between the two nations that exists today.

France again went to war against Spain in 1667. Louis wanted to annex Spain's French-speaking Franche-Comté to the east and the Spanish Netherlands (Belgium) to the north. When French armies invaded the Spanish Netherlands, England, fearful that Flanders and its Channel ports would fall to France, joined the Dutch Republic, Sweden, and Spain to turn back Louis XIV's armies. By the Treaty of Aix-la-Chapelle (Aachen) in 1668, France extended its frontier further north, annexing Lille and part of Flanders. Four years later, Louis XIV invaded the Dutch Republic after assuring English neutrality by making secret payments to King Charles II. The Dutch fended off the French by opening up the dikes to create a barrier of water. After several more years of indecisive fighting and negotiations, France absorbed Franche-Comté, but only tiny parcels of the Southern Netherlands. Still the king of France was not satisfied. He conquered Alsace and Lorraine beyond his eastern frontier by claiming each in turn and then launching an invasion. He annexed Strasbourg and occupied Luxembourg. Despite the opposition of a wary alliance of Habsburg Austria, Spain, Sweden, and Saxony, he ordered the invasion of the Palatinate, intending to secure the Rhine. This initiated the War of the League of Augsburg (1688–1697). England and the Dutch Republic (an alliance in itself solidified by the fact that William III of Orange now was king of

England) and a number of other German states also joined the alliance against France.

After hesitating in the face of massive opposition, in 1692 Louis made a foolish attempt to invade England. Dutch and English ships drove the French fleet onto rocks off the coast of Normandy; the two sea powers then enforced an economic blockade of France. Louis XIV retaliated by turning French privateers loose on his enemies' ships. French defeats as well as rising opposition in the Dutch Republic and England to the cost of the war forced both sides to negotiate. The Treaty of Ryswick of 1697 confirmed French gains in Alsace, but also made clear that the other European powers would ally again if necessary to keep France from further territorial acquisitions in the Southern Netherlands and the German states.

The question of the succession to the throne of Spain soon presented Louis XIV with the greatest temptation of all. Like a compulsive eater confronted by a table of delicious food, it was more than he could resist. The Habsburg King Charles II of Spain had no direct heir. Louis opposed the candidacy of the Habsburg Archduke Charles of Austria (son of Holy Roman Emperor Leopold I), hoping to end the virtual encirclement of France by Habsburg powers. Then Louis XIV, whose wife was the daughter of the late Philip IV of Spain, put forth his own claim to the throne.

When Charles II died in 1700, he left a will expressing his desire that his diminished empire remain intact, and that Louis XIV's grandson, Philip of Anjou, succeed him, but that Philip renounce all claim to the throne of France. However, on ascending the Spanish throne, the Bourbon Philip V (ruled 1700–1746) made clear that he favored the interests of his imposing grandfather. The Austrian Habsburg ruler Leopold I refused to accept Charles II's will as valid and attacked the Italian territories of the Spanish Habsburgs.

Louis XIV refused to rule Philip out of the line of succession to the French throne, so that if Philip's elder brother, the duc de Bourgogne, died without male issue, Philip would then inherit the throne of France and the kingdoms would be joined. The matter became pressing in 1712, after smallpox struck the French royal family, leaving only Bourgogne's youngest son as heir to the French throne. If the future Louis XV had died then, Philip would have become heir to both kingdoms.

The French king's aggressive action drew Great Britain into the wars of the continent. The Dutch Republic again had reason to fear French occupation of the Spanish Netherlands. If the French opened up the Scheldt River to trade, Antwerp would reemerge as a commercial rival to Amsterdam. This vital link to the English Channel had been closed since the Dutch formally received independence from Spain in 1648, thus preventing ships from reaching Antwerp. The Grand Alliance against France also included Austria, Prussia, and Portugal. The War of the Spanish Succession reflected the fact that European wars were gradually taking on a global dimension (see Chapter 6), as the powers fought for markets as well as prestige. As in the War of the League of Augsburg, British and French forces also battled in North America.

France fought with Bavaria and Spain as allies. The English commander, the duke of Marlborough (1650–1722), raised an army of English, Dutch, and mercenary troops. In 1704, at Blenheim in southern Germany, the allied armies, aided by the Habsburg troops of Prince Eugene of Savoy (1663–1736), crushed a combined French and Bavarian force. Louis XIV's armies retreated behind the Rhine. Winning victories in the Spanish Netherlands in 1708 and 1709, the allied armies also drove the French from the Spanish Netherlands and from the Italian peninsula. The English fleet captured Gibraltar (1704), which guards the entrance to the Mediterranean Sea. During the terrible winter of 1709–1710, France suffered military defeat and famine. The great kingdom of Louis XIV seemed on the verge of collapse.

But the French and Spanish armies revived their fortunes. Dynastic changes, too, helped Louis XIV's cause. In 1711, Archduke Charles of Austria became Holy Roman Emperor Charles VI (ruled 1711–1740). Should France and Philip V of Spain be defeated, the British and Dutch now confronted the possibility that Charles might one day become king of Spain, reviving the dynastic union that had made the Habsburgs Europe's strongest power during the first half of the seventeenth century. It was now in the interests of Great Britain and the Dutch Republic to bring the war to an honorable conclusion. Louis XIV, weakened by age and illness and suffering the financial burdens of the war, agreed to negotiate.

Under the 1713 Treaty of Utrecht (confirmed by that of Rastatt in 1714, when Emperor Charles VI accepted peace), Habsburg Austria received the Southern Netherlands as security against future French ambitions and annexed Lombardy and Naples, replacing Spain as the paramount power on the Italian peninsula (see Map 7.5). Philip V was recognized as king of Spain, but renounced all claims to the throne of France. The decline of Spain, which had now lost all of its European possessions beyond the Pyrenees, continued unabated. In North America, France ceded Newfoundland, Nova Scotia, and Hudson Bay to Great Britain.

Louis XIV had reigned so long that on his death in 1715 the throne passed to his great-grandson, young Louis XV, with affairs of state in the hands of a regent. Philip V kept the throne of Spain, but the futures of the monarchies of Spain and France would be separate. Louis XIV was defeated by more than powerful alliances mounted against him. Britain had proved better able to sustain long wars; its more developed commerce and manufactures provided greater tax revenues. The non-absolutist British state collected taxes more efficiently than the absolute monarchy of France, which turned much of the collection process over to tax farmers who kept part of the take. Britain's interests remained overseas, dominated

MAP 7.5 EUROPE IN 1721 Territorial realignments in Europe after the Treaty of Utrecht (1713), the Treaty of Rastatt (1714), and the Treaty of Nystadt (1721).

by lucrative commercial concerns, protected by the Royal Navy. France's foreign policy led to more costly wars on the continent.

France had been the preeminent power in Europe at the time of the accession of Louis XIV; this was no longer true at his death. The king's reputation had fallen victim to age and untempered ambition. Perhaps a lingering sense of failure explains why Louis XIV tried to burn his memoirs shortly before his death, although they were rescued from the fire by one of his officials. As he lay dying, Louis confessed with uncharacteristic insight that perhaps he had "loved glory too much."

THE MODERN STATE

As they established absolute rule, the sovereigns of continental Europe constructed the modern state. While extending authority over their subjects and expanding their dynastic territories, they developed state bureaucracies and established large standing armies. They broke noble resistance to absolute rule, confirming their privileges in exchange for loyalty to the throne. This relationship between rulers and nobles thus remained essential to the functioning of most European states in the eighteenth century.

Following a period of relative stability and even moderate economic expansion, the structure of Western European society then began to change as the European economy entered a remarkable period of dynamic growth, particularly during the second half of the eighteenth century. This was the case above all in Britain, where the expansion of capital-intensive agriculture techniques, population growth, and a boom in manufacturing combined to begin the Industrial Revolution. The changing structure of society, in turn, would affect the developing state by encouraging demands for political reform. Beginning in the 1760s and 1770s, the monopoly on political power by oligarchies and absolute rule itself came under challenge. Old scientific assumptions had already been shaken and then fallen as scientists expanded their knowledge of the universe. The scientific methodology, discoveries, and culture of the Scientific Revolution helped create modern science.

PART THREE

NEW CULTURAL AND POLITICAL HORIZONS

During the late seventeenth century and the eighteenth century, Europe entered a period of remarkable intellectual and political ferment. Rejecting the weight of tradition, men and women of science developed the scientific method, a means of understanding based on systematic observation of natural phenomena and experimentation regarding their causes and effects. Their successors, the philosophes, the thinkers and writers of the Enlightenment, believed their role was to bring light and progress to the world through the application of reason to their reflections on the nature of mankind. Influenced by growing religious skepticism and drawing on expanded literacy, the philosophes espoused views of nature, mankind, society, government, and the intrinsic value of freedom that challenged some of the fundamental tenets most Europeans shared.

During this exciting period, Europe also entered a remarkable period of economic and social change. Increased agricultural productivity supported a larger population which, in turn, expanded demand for food and permitted the development of large-scale manufacturing in and around northern English towns.

Changes also came in the realm of political life. The public political sphere was transformed by newly created "public opinion" through the emergence of newspapers and societies, which facilitated political interest and discussion. Reform-minded people in increasing numbers denounced unwarranted privilege and "despotism" and celebrated the British model of constitutional monarchy and the successful rising of the American colonists against British rule. In a time of economic and social change, new cultural and political innovations began to transform Europe.

CHAPTER 8

THE NEW PHILOSOPHY OF SCIENCE

In 1633, ecclesiastical authorities summoned Galileo (1564–1642), born Galileo Galilei, to Rome to face the Inquisition. The stakes were high. In the first year of the new century, the Italian Giordano Bruno (1548–1600), a Dominican friar accused of heresy who loudly proclaimed the virtues of scientific investigation, had been burned along with his books in Rome.

Many Church fathers were now eager to put Galileo on trial. Jesuits vehemently objected to his work on physics, for Galileo espoused an atomistic theory of matter that seemed to challenge the Catholic Church's view that during Communion bread and wine become the body and blood of Christ. The papacy's political situation forced the Church's hand. Protestant armies had recaptured some of the lands in which the Catholic Reformation had appeared victorious. The papacy, its influence weakened by the Protestant Reformation and eclipsed by powerful dynastic rulers, could ill afford another defeat.

Urban VIII, who before his elevation to the pontificate had been Galileo's friend, accused the astronomer only of supporting the views of Copernicus, not of heresy. This would save Galileo from death but might also put the pope in a bad light for having protected the scientist. Although Galileo chose not to die for his principles and agreed to renounce these "errors" as heresies, in 1633 he was still sentenced to a lifetime of house arrest. When guards returned him to his house, however, he cast a glance to the heavens and proclaimed of the earth, "See, it's still moving!"

The origins of modern science date to the seventeenth century, a period so marked by innovative thinking that it has been called the "century of genius." In several different corners of Europe, a few people struggled to understand the workings of the cosmos in a new way. Their own observations of the skies, including those of Galileo, seemed to contradict explanations of the universe that had originated with Aristotle in the fourth

Testeleu's tapestry of the establishment of the French Royal Academy of Science, 1666, and the Foundation of the Observatory, 1667.

century, B.C., and, having acquired the authority of the Church, had been passed down for centuries. Rejecting the weight of tradition, these thinkers developed the scientific method, a means of understanding based on systematic observation of natural phenomena and experimentation regarding their causes and effects. But what we now know as the "Scientific Revolution" owed its impact less to new technology and inventions than to new ways of thinking about the universe.

CHANGING VIEWS OF THE UNIVERSE

The thought of the Greek philosopher Aristotle (384–322 B.C.) dominated European science until the sixteenth century. Trying to understand the universe seemed closely linked to explaining motion. Both problems lay at the heart of the Scientific Revolution. Copernicus, a sixteenth-century Polish astronomer, observed the heavens and concluded that ancient and medieval science could not explain what he saw with his own eyes. His successors, above all Galileo later in the century, made systematic mathematical calculations to explain celestial motion. In doing so, they created scientific methodology, which would also be applied to reach an understanding of the workings of the human body.

Ancient and Medieval Science

Aristotle believed that God placed the earth at or near the center of the universe. He envisioned a hierarchical order of the cosmos comprised of a series of spheres that became progressively purer. Aristotle also believed that terrestrial bodies naturally moved toward the earth, the center of the universe, unless they were propelled in another direction. In this view, impetus imparted motion through contact with an object; when the contact ceased, the object simply stopped moving or fell back to earth. The natural tendency of all matter, then, was toward rest, regarded as a nobler state than motion. Because all motion had to be explained, a "mover" therefore had to be found for every motion.

In the second century, the Greek astronomer Clausius Ptolemy (c. 85–165 A.D.) published a massive work that became known as *Almagest* (from the Arabic for "greatest"), which summarized the conclusions of Greek astronomers and presented his own theories and observations. He described instruments such as the quadrant, invented by the Arabs, with which he tried to measure the orbits (which he held to be spherical) of the sun, moon, and planets in the sky. Ptolemy accepted Aristotle's contentions, asserting that the earth was encased by a series of clear spheres—about eighty—revolving around it. The most distant sphere contained the furthest stars, which he believed were fixed points of light. Within those spheres, the moon was closest to the earth; next came the planets Mars, Venus, Jupiter, and Saturn. With minor variations, medieval thinkers still held Ptolemy's views.

Within the context of Christian theology, people of learning in the Middle Ages believed that scientific inquiry should serve theological ends by studying nature and explaining the mysterious ways of God. Church savants never raised the possibility that mankind could, with understanding, alter or even master nature.

Aristotle's belief that the heavens and earth displayed two different kinds of motion—one toward the center of the earth, which seemed the natural state, but also an unnatural violent motion away from it—nicely fit the medieval Church's view that the universe consisted of good and evil. The earth, standing at the center, was heavy, corrupted not only by its weight but by original sin and earthly misdeeds. Angels therefore were placed far off in a weightless existence in Heaven. The goal of human beings was to achieve the lightness of Heaven, God's domain, on the exterior edge of the universe.

The beliefs of the late medieval poet Dante (1265–1321) reflected the prevailing influence of Aristotle's physics and Ptolemy's astronomy. Dante held that the universe comprised ten spheres surrounding the spherical, motionless earth. In his *Inferno*, Dante and the Roman poet Virgil travel to the core of the earth, then climb out to the other side, the Southern Hemisphere, where they find Purgatory. Hell lay at the earth's center, with Heaven the tenth, most distant sphere. Dante and his contemporaries believed that the earth consisted of four elements: earth, water, air, and fire, the first two of which had a natural tendency to fall toward the center of the stationary earth.

Medieval European scholars seemed little interested in astronomy. Yet, to be sure, some medieval thinkers took significant steps toward modern science by embracing the study of natural phenomena and revering the scholar who studied such problems. Medieval scientists made lasting contributions in such fields as optics—inventing eyeglasses—and biology. They classified objects for study and espoused experimentation based on scientific procedures and the use of mathematics to verify theories. But even the contributions of the most brilliant medieval thinkers remained only in the realm of theory.

As the Renaissance drew on the discovery of classical prose and poetry, Italian scholars of the period also turned to classical Greek scientific texts that had been recovered, edited, and printed. The conquest of Greece during the fourteenth century had brought the Arabs into contact with classical learning. Arab scholars, who also made significant original contributions in astronomy, mathematics, and medicine, preserved many ancient Greek and Roman texts, translating them into Arabic. Some of the manuscripts brought by Greek scholars to the West from Constantinople after its conquest by the Turks in 1453 suggested that mathematics could be applied in the quest for knowledge about the universe. Arab scholars had raised troubling questions challenging age-old views of the earth as they observed and even began to measure the heavenly phenomena they beheld. In this way, the texts of Ptolemy became subjects of renewed interest and study.

Ptolemy's view of the cosmos itself reflected the domination of Aristotle's theory of motion. Yet, there had earlier been at least one dissenting voice. Archimedes of Syracuse (c. 287–212 B.C.) had challenged Aristotle's contention that rest was a natural state for all objects and that only the presence of an "active mover" could generate motion. But Ptolemy's view of the cosmos was challenged in the fourteenth century by thinkers at the University of Paris and Oxford University. They observed that falling bodies move at an accelerating speed and that the accompanying presence of a "mover" simply could not be observed. A few scholars also rejected Aristotle's explanation that air itself served as a natural propellant. They observed that an arrow shot from a bow clearly was not continually propelled by air or anything else, but sooner or later simply fell to earth. The gradual development of a theory of motion, based on an understanding of the role of the mass of the moving object, along with the development of mathematics itself, provided the basis for new discoveries in the fields of astronomy and mechanics.

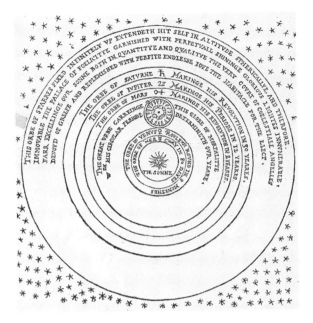

Copernicus's helio-
centric world system.

Copernicus Challenges the Aristotelian View of the Universe

The revolution in scientific thinking moved forward because of a cleric who kept his eyes toward the heavens, but not necessarily in pious contemplation. Nicholas Copernicus (1473–1543) launched the strongest attack yet on the Aristotelian view of the universe. He was born near the Baltic coast in Poland. After the death of his father, Copernicus' uncle (a wealthy bishop) assumed responsibility for his education. From the University of Cracow, Copernicus went to Italy to study medicine and law. After learning Greek, he read medieval scientific and humanist texts. Also trained as a doctor and portrait painter, he devoted his life to observation and discovery.

Copernicus' *Concerning the Revolutions of the Celestial Spheres* was not published until he lay dying in 1543, the same year the work of Archimedes was first translated into Latin. Paradoxically, in view of the intense theological debate it would generate, Copernicus dedicated his study to the pope. Copernicus was troubled by the inability of the Ptolemaic system (itself a refraction of the Aristotelian view of the universe) to account for what his own observations, made with the naked eye, told him: that the planets, the moon, and the stars obviously did not move around the earth at the same speed. Nor did they seem to be in the spherical orbits Ptolemy had assigned them. That Mars seemed to vary in brightness particularly perplexed him. What Copernicus observed, in short, contradicted the fundamental assumptions of the Aristotelian and Ptolemaic universe.

Ptolemy had rejected the idea that the earth might be moving because such a view could not be reconciled with Aristotelian physics. A late medieval thinker, Nicholas of Cusa (1401–1464), a German bishop and theologian who wrote on astronomy, believed the earth might be in motion, but neither he nor anyone else in the period tried to make mathematical calculations that might prove or reject this bold theory. More than this, he had suggested the possibility that the sun stands at the center of the universe and, by implication, that the universe is infinite, and nonhierarchical in nature, unlimited by Aristotelian layers of spheres. The extraordinary Renaissance artist and humanist Leonardo da Vinci, who called wisdom "the daughter of experiment," had also suggested that the earth might move around the sun.

Copernicus concluded that the sun, not the earth, lies at the center of the universe, and that the earth turns on its axis once a day and rotates around the sun once every 365 days. "In the middle of all sits the Sun enthroned," he wrote. "How could we place this luminary in any better position in this most beautiful temple from which to illuminate the whole at once?" Copernicus' postulation was, like his critique of some of Ptolemy's conclusions, not totally original. But his assertions were bold, explicit and, for many, convincing. Furthermore, they suggested that mathematics could verify astronomic theories.

The notion that the earth was but one planet rotating in circular orbit around the sun raised shocking questions about the earth's status. This perplexed and angered Catholic, Protestant, and Jewish theologians by seeming to reduce the standing of mankind. It seemed unbelievable that mere mortals peering into the heavens were themselves moving rapidly through the universe. Martin Luther, himself not given to accepting inherited wisdom without skepticism, said of Copernicus, "This fool wants to turn the whole of astronomy upside down!"

That Copernicus did. Yet, he seemed uninterested in carrying out his own systematic observations and made serious errors in calculations when he did so. He also could not explain why there was no constant wind from the east, which might be expected based on the assumption that the earth moved in that direction around the sun. Copernicus sometimes sought to answer his own doubts by turning to the teachings of the ancients and did not completely abandon the system of celestial spheres postulated by Ptolemy, whom he continued to revere. Copernicus also continued to accept the notion that the spherical universe was finite, and that it perhaps was limited by the stars fixed in the heavens.

The Universal Laws of the Human Body

As scientists began to chart movements in the heavens, some scholars now began to question old assumptions about the human body. They contended that it is subject to the same universal laws that govern celestial and terrestrial motion. The Renaissance had generated interest in human anatomy. Most assumptions about how the body works had been passed down for centuries from the ancient world. Galen (129–c. 210), a Greek contemporary of Ptolemy, was the first person to develop theories about medicine based on scientific experiments. He carried out a number of experiments on apes, assuming that animal and human bodies were essentially the same in the arrangement of bodily organs. Like Aristotle, Galen believed that disease followed from an imbalance in the four bodily humors—blood, phlegm, yellow bile, and black bile. He held that two kinds of blood initiated muscle movement and digestion, respectively: bright red blood, which flowed up and down through the arteries, and dark red blood, which could be found in the veins. Doubting Galen's view of anatomy, Andreas Vesalius (1514–1564) published *On the Fabric of the Human Body* (1543). Arguably the founder of modern biological science, Vesalius rejected old explanations for the circulation of blood and began to dissect and study cadavers—in the Middle Ages, the Church had considered this to be sinful—and was the first to assemble human skeletons.

The English scientist William Harvey (1578–1657) largely solved the riddle of how blood circulates. Like astronomers, he adopted a scientific methodology: "I profess," he wrote, "to learn and teach anatomy not from books but from dissections, not from the tenets of philosophers but from the fabric of nature." Harvey's accomplishment was in the realm of thought and owed virtually nothing to prior inventions. Indeed, he made

(*Left*) Vesalius dissecting a cadaver. (*Right*) A particularly pensive skeleton appears in Vesalius's *Epitome* (1543).

William Harvey demonstrating the circulation of blood.

his discoveries before the invention of the microscope, and he referred only twice in his experiments to a magnifying glass.

Harvey's theory of blood circulation pictured the heart and its valves functioning as a mechanical pump. Yet Harvey, like medieval thinkers, retained a belief that "vital spirits" were to be found in the blood. The long-run consequence of Harvey's work was, as in the case of Vesalius, to undermine further Aristotelian philosophy and medieval science and to help establish a basis for the development of modern biology and medicine in later centuries.

Brahe and Kepler Explore the Heavens

Tycho Brahe (1546–1601), a Danish astronomer, and Johannes Kepler (1571–1630), his German assistant, carried the search for an understanding of the way the universe works to a new stage of scientific knowledge. While studying philosophy at the University of Copenhagen, Brahe became fascinated with the heavens after observing a partial eclipse of the sun. Brahe, an odd-looking nobleman who had lost part of his nose in a duel and replaced it with a construction of silver and gold alloy perched above his handlebar moustache, built an astronomical observatory on a Danish island.

Brahe rejected Copernicus' contention that the earth rotated around the sun. He claimed that if this were true, a cannonball fired from west to east (the direction Copernicus thought the earth moved) would travel farther in that direction, and a weight dropped from a tall tower would strike earth to the west of the tower because of the earth's movement. Brahe came up with a cumbersome, compromise explanation that had the five known planets rotating around the sun, which in turn moved around the stationary earth.

In 1572, Brahe observed a bright exploding star that he called Nova. This and a comet sighted five years later irretrievably compromised the Aristotelian view of the universe as unchanging. Brahe compiled data based upon his own observations, systematically charting what he could see of the planetary orbits, and using mathematics to locate the position of the planets and stars. At the same time, his rejection of the Copernican view that the sun was the center of the universe and the fact that his calculations were often inaccurate remind us that the Scientific Revolution did not develop in a linear fashion. False turns and setbacks were part of the story.

Upon the death of the Danish king, his patron, Brahe had moved to Prague. There he set up an observatory and met Johannes Kepler, who became his assistant in 1600. Kepler was the son of a German mercenary soldier and an herb dealer with an interest in astrology (his mother would later be condemned to be burned at the stake for her dabblings in astrology; Kepler saved her life by undertaking a lengthy legal process). Kepler was a dazzling but strange combination of rigorous astronomer and math-

The Danish observatory in which Tycho Brahe charted the heavens.

(*Left*) Johannes Kepler. (*Right*) Kepler's depiction of the orbits of the planets.

ematician, religious mystic and astrologer, who took credit for predicting not only a particularly harsh winter, but also peasant uprisings in Germany.

Facing persecution from Lutheran theologians in 1596 because of his Copernican beliefs, Kepler briefly found protection from the Jesuits. But four years later, he was forced to leave a teaching position in Austria because he refused to convert from Lutheranism to Catholicism. Kepler moved to Prague and began to work with Brahe. On his deathbed, Brahe implored Kepler to complete his observation tables by charting movements in the heavens. Holy Roman Emperor Rudolph II, whose interest in science outweighed any concern that Kepler was Protestant, appointed him to succeed Brahe as imperial mathematician.

Kepler shared Copernicus' belief that observers on earth were moving while the sun stood still. After carefully plotting the orbit of Mars, Kepler concluded that the orbits of the planets were "imperfect"—not circular, but rather elliptical. He also concluded that the planets were affected by some sort of force emanating from the sun. William Gilbert (1544–1603), an English scientist, had published a book on the magnet in 1600, the first study written by a university scholar and informed by laboratory experimentation. Gilbert's investigations of magnetic force provided a model for the development of a modern theory of gravitation. Kepler now decided that it was perhaps magnetic force that attracted the earth and sun to each other. He also determined that tides were the result of the magnetic attraction of the earth and the moon.

Based upon his mathematical calculations, Kepler postulated three laws of planetary motion, which he assumed were determined by the power, or specific magnetic attraction, of the sun. Kepler used observation and mathematical calculations to demonstrate that the planets were a separate grouping with different properties from those of the fixed stars, and that Aristotle's crystalline spheres simply did not exist.

Kepler's discoveries, blows to Aristotelian and medieval science, suggested that the hand of the prime mover—God—was not required to govern the movement of the planets. Even more than Copernicus' placing of the sun at the center of the universe, Kepler's conclusions challenged the theological assumptions of the Catholic Church. Kepler, who had been proscribed by his own church, learned in 1619 (three years after Copernicus' work was banned) that some of his writings had been placed on the list of books forbidden to Catholics. Nonetheless, the Scientific Revolution still occurred within the system of Christian belief. Kepler himself sought to glorify God by demonstrating the consistency, harmony, and order of divine creation as expressed in the working of the universe.

Francis Bacon and Scientific Method

From England Sir Francis Bacon (1561–1626), lawyer, statesman and philosopher, launched a frontal assault on ancient and medieval metaphysics and science. Calling himself "a bellringer who is first up to call others to church," Bacon helped detach science from philosophy. Medieval scholasticism had focused, he argued, on abstract problems that were without practical consequences, such as the question of how many angels could stand on the head of a pin. So, too, had Renaissance humanism. Bacon rejected outright all arguments based on the weight of traditional authority, calling for "a total reconstruction of sciences, arts and all human knowledge."

Bacon carried out few experiments and made no discoveries that could have been considered significant by his own standards (he died after catching a bad cold while carrying out an experiment of marginal value: stuffing snow into a dead chicken). But Bacon announced the dawn of a new era in which mankind would gradually begin to understand and then perhaps even overcome its physical environment. Through inductive reasoning, that is, proceeding from observation and experimentation to conclusions or generalizations, the truths of the universe would be revealed by discovery and scientific experiment, not by religion. Bacon's renown—he served for three years as King James I of England's Lord Chancellor (before being dismissed for accepting bribes)—helped create, for the first time, interest in science in England, albeit limited to a small number of people.

"Arts and sciences," Bacon wrote in 1620, "should be like mines, where the noise of new works and further advances is heard on every side." Scientists should divide up the toil by specializing and working in cooperation to "overcome the necessities and miseries of humanity."

(*Left*) Francis Bacon at work. (*Right*) The feisty Galileo at age sixty.

Galileo and Science on Trial

On the Italian peninsula, Galileo emerged as the most dominant figure of the early stage of the Scientific Revolution. The scion of a wealthy family, he studied medicine and mathematics. Like Copernicus, he taught at the University of Padua, the leading center of scientific learning in Europe, at a time when virtually every other university showed little interest in scientific observation. That Padua was under the protection of Venice, which was hostile to the pope, facilitated its university's precocious role in the development of scientific methodology. Scholars in Padua hotly debated Aristotelian explanations of motion, and particularly the question of the relationship between the natural sciences and metaphysics, or the nature of being. The latter debate was especially crucial, because on it hinged the question of whether scientific investigation could be independent of the Catholic Church, which considered revealed religion the only source of knowledge.

New ways of thinking about the heavens, systematic observation, and scientific measurement had played a more significant role in the early stages of the Scientific Revolution than did the development of new technology. The invention of the telescope, however, led to a further advance in the Scientific Revolution. Upon learning in 1609 that a man in Holland had invented a "spy glass," as the first telescope was called, that could magnify objects many times, Galileo constructed one of his own. This enabled him to study stars beyond the view of the naked eye, as well as Jupiter's moons, Saturn's spectacular rings, some of the innumerable stars of the Milky Way, and mountains on the moon. His observation of spots that seemed to move on the surface of the sun led Galileo to conclude that the sun, too, rotated. That sunspots seemed to change also challenged the traditional view of the static nature of the universe.

Galileo undermined Aristotelian notions of motion. He demonstrated that the earth was in perpetual rotation and that balls of varying weights will pick up speed at the same rate as they fall, that their speed is not determined by their mass. From such experiments, he developed a theory of inertia: a body moving at a constant speed in a straight line will continue to move until encountering another force. Galileo thus stood Aristotle on his head. Galileo believed that motion, not rest, was a natural state. He demonstrated that air and clouds move with the earth as it rotates around the sun, while appearing immobile to an observer also moving with the earth. The rooms in his house that he set aside for experimentation served as the first university laboratory.

Unlike other scholars, Galileo did not disdain seeking practical information from craftsmen and artisans. He consulted men who built cannons, and the soldiers who fired them, and people who made compasses, astrolabes, quadrants, and other scientific instruments for navigation. He began to investigate pumps and other means of regulating rivers, as well as planning the construction of stronger military fortresses. Nonetheless, he did not care whether or not his discoveries reached ordinary people. More than this, he claimed that "the mobility of the earth is a proposition far beyond the comprehension of the common people." And he believed that the "all-too-numerous vulgar" ought to be kept in darkness, lest they "become confused, obstinate, and contumacious."

At first, Galileo tried to reconcile his findings and those of Copernicus with early Church texts. But the feisty Galileo's insistence that the universe was mathematical in its very structure and subject to laws of mechanics that could be discovered left him open to attacks by ecclesiastical authorities. In 1610, he wrote Kepler, "here at Padua is the principal professor of theology, whom I have repeatedly and urgently requested to look at the moon and planets through my glass, which he obstinately refused to do. Why are you not here? What shouts of laughter we should have at this glorious folly!" In 1616, the pope condemned Galileo's proposition that the sun is the center of the universe and warned him not to teach it. Undaunted, Galileo published his *Dialogue Concerning Two World Systems—Ptolemaic and Copernican,* in which he taunted Aristotelians by presenting a lengthy dialogue between those espousing the respective systems of Ptolemy and Copernicus. A certain Simplicio took the side of Ptolemy in the dialogues; the character's very name outraged the Church by intimating that a farcical character symbolized the pope. This led to Galileo's condemnation by the Inquisition in 1633. But from house arrest in his villa in the hills above Florence, Galileo continued to observe, experiment, and write, publishing his texts in Holland. When he went blind in 1638, the pope refused to allow him to go into Florence to see a doctor. Despite his blindness, he continued his scientific investigations until his death four years later.

DESCARTES AND NEWTON: COMPETING THEORIES OF SCIENTIFIC KNOWLEDGE

Two brilliant thinkers, one French and the other English, both accepted Galileo's rejection of classical and medieval systems of knowledge. But they offered contrasting theories of scientific knowledge. René Descartes sought to discover the truth through deductive reasoning. Across the English Channel, Isaac Newton followed his countryman Bacon's insistence that the way to knowledge was through scientific experiment. One amazing discovery after another added to the foundations of "the new philosophy" of science. Science played a major part in the quest for demonstrable truth and authority during and following the period of intense social and political turmoil that lasted from the 1590s until the mid-seventeenth century.

Descartes and Deductive Reasoning

The reclusive French philosopher René Descartes (1596–1650) shared Bacon's and Galileo's critiques of ancient and medieval learning. But he offered a different methodology for understanding the universe, espousing deductive reasoning, that is, deducing a conclusion from a set of premises, not from scientific observation.

In 1637, Descartes published *Discourse on Method*. In this deeply personal account, he discussed his rejection of the scientific teaching he had encountered as a young man. Too much of what he had learned had been handed down from tradition without critical commentary. He defiantly "resolved no longer to seek any other science than the knowledge of myself, or of the great book of the world." Bacon had spoken of the necessity of "minds washed clean of opinions." Descartes had read Bacon. But instead of beginning with empirical facts in the quest for general principle, Descartes went much further by attempting to create an entire system of knowledge that began with general principles.

Any person, Descartes claimed, has to begin with a blank slate in order to understand the world through deductive reasoning. "I think, therefore I am" (*Cogito, ergo sum*) was his starting point, the postulation of a self-evident truth and the assertion that the ability to think is the basis of human existence. Then each problem has to be separated, he argued, into "as many parts as may be necessary for its adequate solution," moving from the simplest idea to the most difficult, in the same way as a mathematical proof is formulated. Cartesianism (the philosophy of Descartes and his followers) held that the world could be reduced to two substances: mind and matter, "thinking substance" and "extended substance," the latter defined as an infinite number of particles that fill all space, leaving neither void nor vacuum. Matter could be discovered and described mathematically, as could the laws of motion. Beginning with the certainty of his own existence, Descartes argued that the existence of the material universe and God could be deduced. "Begin with the smallest object, the easiest to understand," he insisted, "and gradually move to a knowledge of those that are the most complex."

This materialist approach to knowledge left little or no room for ancient or medieval learning. As a sign of this break, Descartes published his works in French, identifying Latin with ecclesiastical doctrine and scholasticism. Like Kepler, Descartes viewed God as a benevolent, infinitely powerful clockmaker, who created the universe according to rules that the human mind could discover with proper reasoning. God then stepped back, according to this view, forever absent from the actual workings of what He had created.

Mathematics, Descartes argued, demonstrates "the certainty and self-evidence of its reasonings." It therefore stood as the foundation of all science. Eventually a rule for every phenomenon could be discovered. Like the cosmos, the human body could be understood, its composition deduced.

Descartes thus subordinated experimentation to reason in the quest for truth. One of the stream of savants who went to meet Descartes recalled, "many of them would desire him to shew them his Instruments . . . he would drawe out a little Drawer under his Table, and shew them a paire of Compasses with one of the Legges broken; and then, for his Ruler, he used a sheet of paper folded double."

(*Left*) René Descartes. (*Right*) Sir Isaac Newton.

The Newtonian Synthesis

Sir Isaac Newton (1642–1727) built upon the thought of Kepler, Galileo, and Descartes to effect a bold synthesis of the Scientific Revolution, to which he added his own extraordinary discoveries. Newton's *Principia, The Mathematical Principles of Natural Philosophy* (1687) was the first synthesis of scientific principles. Newton synthesized the empiricism of Galileo and others with the theoretical rigor and logic of Descartes, thereby laying the foundations for modern science, which is based on both theory and experimentation.

Newton conducted some of his experiments while living on his prosperous family's farm. There, sitting under a tree ruminating about celestial motion, Newton observed a falling apple, which led him to recognize that the force that caused objects to fall to earth was related to planetary motion. Newton demonstrated that earthly and celestial motion are subject to laws that could be described by mathematical formulas, the science of mechanics. Going beyond Kepler's three laws of planetary motion, Newton postulated a theory of universal gravitation, the existence of forces of attraction and repulsion operating between objects. Newton concluded that Kepler's laws of planetary motion would be correct if the planets were being pulled toward the sun by a force whose strength was in inverse proportion to their distance from it. The moon, too, seemed to be drawn to the earth in the same way, while the pull that it exerted determined the ocean tides. Every particle of matter, Newton concluded, attracts every other particle with a force proportional to the product of the two masses, and inversely proportional to the square of the distance that separates them.

Newton's remarkable range of accomplishments—the fact that he continued to dabble in alchemy was not one of them—combined drawing on the thought of predecessors with his own brilliant insights and discoveries. He correctly calculated that the average density of the earth is about five and a half times that of water, suggested that electrical messages activate the nervous system, and anticipated some of the ideas that two centuries later would form the basis of thermodynamics and quantum theory. Newton was the first to understand that all colors are composed of a mixture of the primary colors of the spectrum. He explained the phenomenon of the rainbow, calculated sound waves, and invented calculus. In the late 1660s, he also constructed the first reflecting telescope. Newton's first paper on optics, published in 1671, proposed that light could be mathematically described and analyzed. Some scientists still consider it to mark the beginning of theoretical physics.

Unlike his predecessors in the development of science, Newton became wealthy and a hero in his own time. He was knighted by the king, and when he died he was given a state funeral and buried in London's Westminster Abbey. He was elected to Parliament in 1689 representing Cambridge University, where he was professor, and became warden of the

Royal Mint seven years later. However, Newton remained a remote, chaste, humorless figure who published his discoveries with reluctance and initially only when it seemed that rivals might first take the credit for a discovery. He brazenly accused those working on similar problems of copying him, and was ungenerous in acknowledging what he had learned from others. His fame marked the victory of the scientific method, however, over ancient and medieval thought. The eighteenth-century English poet Alexander Pope went so far as to compare Newton's accomplishments with those of God on the first day of creation. Pope penned an "Epitaph Intended for Sir Isaac Newton": "Nature and Nature's laws lay hid in night; God said, Let Newton be! and all was light!"

The Newtonian synthesis of scientific thinking and discovery spread rapidly from England to the continent. Newton's followers clashed with Cartesians, the followers of Descartes. Newton rejected Descartes' materialism, at least partially because it seemed to leave open the possibility that the world was made up totally of matter and that God did not exist, although the French philosopher never made such an assertion. For his part, Newton believed that God had to intervene from time to time to keep the great clock of creation running, lest it run down. That Newton continued to produce manuscripts on theological questions reflected his own belief that there seemed to be no necessary contradiction between science and religious faith.

Like Descartes, Newton insisted on the explanatory power of abstract reasoning. But despite his postulation of theories that could not be demonstrated by scientific method, such as his description of gravity as a force that operates between two objects in space, where possible Newton sought to confirm them experimentally. Until at least 1720, some tension remained between the English scientific groups (who insisted on the necessity of experimentation) and their French and German Cartesian counterparts. Yet, this was a creative tension, based on a common acceptance of the primacy of scientific inquiry.

The Cartesians found an ally in the Spanish-born Dutch philosopher and mathematician Baruch Spinoza (1632–1677), who also believed that thought and matter formed the two categories of reality. While making his living grinding lenses for glasses, he found both a philosopher's introspective isolation—arguing in a Cartesian manner that human understanding advances through inner reflection—and stimulation from the new physics. Expelled from the Jewish community of Amsterdam in 1656 for refusing to participate in religious ceremonies, Spinoza, a proponent of human liberation, called for toleration of all beliefs.

The northern German philosopher and mathematician Gottfried Leibniz (1646–1716) agreed with Descartes and rejected as demeaning to the Creator's divinity Newton's suggestion that God had to intervene from time to time in the operations of the universe. For Leibniz, the universe was, like God, infinite in space and time. The bodies of humans and animals ran like clocks, set in motion, like the universe itself, by God. Leibniz's popularity helped perpetuate the Cartesian challenge to Newton, notably in France. His deductive postulation of the infinite nature of the universe and his Cartesian insistence that God created the universe to run without further divine intervention according to the mathematical laws Newton had discovered became the hallmarks of the "new philosophy."

THE CULTURE OF SCIENCE

A "culture of science" developed in Western Europe and very gradually spread eastward. By the 1660s, letters, newsletters, and periodicals linked Europeans interested in science. Gradually a "republic of science" took shape, spawning meetings and lectures, visits by travelling scholars, correspondence and book purchases, personal libraries and public experiments. Above all, the formation of learned associations provided a focal point for the exchange of scientific information and vigorous debates over methodology and findings, expanding the ranks of people interested in science. Only several decades after Galileo's condemnation, Louis XIV of France and Charles II of England granted patronage to institutions founded to propagate scientific learning. Attracted by scientific discoveries, rulers realized that science could be put to use in the interest of their states.

The Diffusion of Scientific Method

Like medieval and Renaissance scholars, savants of science travelled widely seeking to exchange ideas and learn from each other, although most scientific exchange still occurred by correspondence. For example, the Czech scholar Comenius (Jan Komensky; 1592–1670), a member of the Protestant Unity of Czech Brethren, left his native Moravia in the wake of religious persecution during the Thirty Years' War. After more than a decade in Poland, he began to visit scholars in many countries. For seven years, he travelled in the German states, Holland, England, Sweden, and Hungary. Publishing hundreds of works, he proposed that one day scientific knowledge should be brought together in a collaborative form.

Learned associations and scientific societies had already begun to appear in a number of cities, including Rome and Paris in the 1620s. In London, a bequest made possible the establishment of Gresham College, which became a center for scientific discussion and research. In Paris, Martin Mersenne (1588–1637), a monk who had translated Galileo into French, stood at the center of a network of vigorous scientific exchange that cut across national boundaries of states. He organized informal gatherings, attended by, among others, Blaise Pascal (1623–1662), a gloomy young physicist and mathematician who originated the science of probability.

Blaise Pascal's calculating machine.

In England, above all, the culture of science became part of public life during the 1640–1660 period, with the vocabulary of science joining the discourse of the English upper classes. Newton's prestige further spurred interest in scientific method. In several London coffeehouses, Newtonians offered "a course of Philosophical Lectures on Mechanics, Hydrostatis, Pneumatics [and] Opticks." Exchanges, debates, and even acrimonious disputes reached an ever wider scholarly audience. An unprecedented number of pamphlets and books on scientific subjects was published in England.

The Royal Society of London for Improving Natural Knowledge was formed in 1662 under the patronage of Charles II. Its diverse membership, which included merchants, naval officers, and craftsmen, reflected the growing interest in science in England. Members included Edmund Halley (1656–1742), an astronomer who catalogued and discovered the actual movement of the stars as well as discovering the comet that bears his name; the philosopher John Locke (1632–1704), founder of British empiricism, who held that laws of society, like those of science, could be discovered; and Christopher Wren (1632–1723), a versatile architect who rebuilt some of London's churches (including St. Paul's Cathedral) in the wake of the fire of 1666, but who was also a mathematician and professor of astronomy.

The Royal Society, to which Newton dedicated *Principia* and of which he served as president, took its motto from one of the letters of the Roman writer Horace: "The words are the words of a master, but we are not forced to swear by them. Instead we are to be borne wherever experiment drives us." The Royal Society's hundred original members doubled in number by 1670, its weekly meetings attracting visiting scholars. One of the latter, who lived in Paris, reported with some astonishment that "no one is in a hurry to speak, nor tries to speak too long, or to tell all that he knows. [The members] never interrupt the speaker and dissension does not rise to the surface, nor even is a tone heard that could displease. One could not find any more civil, respectful or well-organized gathering than this."

The *Philosophical Transactions of the Royal Society* published some of the most important work of members and foreign correspondents, especially in the field of mathematics. A history of the Royal Society published in 1667 boasted that England had become "a Land of Experimental knowledge. And it is a good sign, that Nature will reveal more of its secrets to the English than to others; because it has already furnished them with a Genius so well proportion'd for the receiving, and retaining of its mysteries."

The natural philosopher Margaret Cavendish, the duchess of Newcastle (1623–1673), participated in debates about matter and motion, the vacuum, magnetism, and the components of color and fire. The author of books on natural philosophy, as well as a number of plays and poems, Cavendish also hosted the "Newcastle circle," an informal gathering of distinguished scientists that received Descartes. But she worked in isolation, which she attributed not only to the fact that she was shy, but to her sex. Despite the evidence of her own achievements, she accepted, at least in her early years, the contemporary assumptions that women had smaller and softer brains than men, and thus were somehow unfit for science and

The Newcastle circle hosted by the duke and duchess of Newcastle. Margaret Cavendish, the duchess, is seated on the far right crowned with laurels.

philosophy. Few men of science would have agreed with the assertion in 1673 by one of Descartes' disciples in France that "the mind has no sex." This bold statement reflected his mentor's belief that thought transcended gender differences—and therefore, having sense organs equal to men's, women should be recognized as their equals. But although she was permitted to attend one session, Cavendish and all other women were formally banned from the Royal Society—this would last until 1945—as they were excluded from the English universities.

In 1666, the French Royal Academy of Science held its first formal meeting in Paris. Like the English Royal Society, the French Academy enjoyed the patronage of the king, but its connection to the monarchy, which provided an astronomical observatory, was much closer. Jean-Baptiste Colbert, Louis XIV's minister of finance, sought to steer the Academy toward the study of what he considered useful subjects that might benefit French commerce and industry. Branches of the Academy began in several provincial cities. Unlike members of its English counterpart, adherents spent much time eating and drinking—one of them complained that too much time was wasted at the fancy dinners that preceded scholarly discussion.

With the gradual ebbing of Latin as the language of science, language barriers became a greater obstacle to the diffusion of ideas and research. (Indeed some writers deliberately had used Latin because they believed that knowledge ought to remain the preserve of the educated few.) Galileo had written in Italian to attract a wider audience among the elite, but also to remove science from Latin, the language of religious discourse. Newton wrote *Principia* in Latin, in part because only then could his work be read by most continental scholars. Newton's *Optics,* by contrast, appeared first in English, then in Latin and French translations. Gradually during the eighteenth century, each country's vernacular became the language of its scientists.

By the end of the seventeenth century, Descartes' ideas had overcome Calvinist opposition to find their way into Dutch university curricula. But the further east one went in Europe, the weaker was the impact of the Scientific Revolution. In part because of the success of the Catholic Reformation, which restricted the free flow of scholarly thought, scientific inquiry lagged in Poland, although several printing houses in Gdansk (Danzig) owned by Protestants began publishing scientific works in the second half of the century. Leibniz enjoyed popularity in the Habsburg domains, at least partially because he served several German rulers in a diplomatic capacity, and perhaps also because his contagious optimism and belief that God had preordained harmony found resonance in a kingdom of many peoples. Nonetheless, theological and devotional literature still dominated the shelves of university, monastic, and imperial libraries. The few publications on science remained strongly Aristotelian, and influenced by clerics.

Some savants in the East did become aware of the debates in the West on scientific method. Some Protestant thinkers in Hungary and Silesia, for example, were gradually exposed to the ideas of Bacon and Descartes by travelling scholars from Western Europe, and a few Hungarians and Silesians learned of the new ideas by visiting Dutch universities. Some Bohemian and Polish nobles began to include books on the new science in their private libraries, one of which eventually comprised over 300,000 volumes and 10,000 manuscripts. Theoretical and practical astronomical work spread in the Habsburg lands, carried on in some cases by Jesuits. Mathematics, optics, and problems of atmospheric pressure, too, were the focus of debate. Holy Roman Emperor Ferdinand III studied military geometry, constructing arithmetic toys for his children. But Copernicus and Kepler notwithstanding, early modern Central Europe would be far more remembered for its music than for its science.

Russia's distant isolation from Western culture—the Renaissance had absolutely no influence there—was compounded by the Orthodox Church's antipathy toward the West and hostility to learning outside Byzantine dogma, and therefore its opposition to scientific experimentation. There was, to be sure, acceptance of some practical knowledge from the West, for example relating to the military, mining, or metallurgy, which largely arrived with foreign merchants and adventurous craftsmen. But seventeenth-century Russia had no gifted scientists and no scientific societies. Foreign books began to appear at court only after about 1650. At that point, however, the Orthodox Church, having suffered a schism, launched another campaign against Western ideas, viewing secular knowledge as heresy, and science as the work of the Anti-Christ. But gradually some nobles began to be exposed to ideas from the natural sciences. These were the nobles who were dissatisfied with Church learning and eager to know more, for example, about the geography of their own expanding state. The literate classes in Russia would thereafter in many ways remain divided between those interested in ideas coming from the West and those who rejected them in the name of preserving what they considered Russia's uniqueness as the most dominant Slavic state.

The Uses of Science

The seventeenth-century Scientific Revolution was above all a revolution in thought. Technological inventions that would change the way people lived lay for the most part in the future. But during the second half of the seventeenth century, scientific experimentation led to the practical application of some discoveries. Thanks to Newton, longitude could now be easily established and ocean tides accurately charted. Voyages of discovery, commerce, and conquest to the Americas increased demand for new navigational instruments. Dutch scientists and craftsmen led the way in producing telescopes, microscopes, binoculars, and other scientific instruments.

But gradually, too, physicians, engineers, mariners, instrument makers, opticians, pharmacists and surveyors, many of them self-educated, began to apply the new discoveries to daily life. Robert Hooke (1635–1703), another member of the Royal Society, improved the barometer, which measures atmospheric pressure, and augmented the power of the microscope by adding multiple lenses. This allowed him to study the cellular structure of plants. Biologists began to collect, categorize, dissect, and describe fossils, birds, and exotic fish, adding to contemporary understanding of the richness and complexity of the world around them.

As Francis Bacon had predicted, governments began to tap science in the service of the state. Absolute monarchs on the continent sought out scientists to produce inventions that would give them commercial and military advantages over their rivals. In France, Colbert called on a Dutch scientist to explain his experiments on "the vacuum, force of [gun]powders, steam, wind, and collision." Colbert ordered the collection of statistics on state finance, commerce, and industry, and he commissioned people to make reliable maps of the provinces and colonies. English government officials also began to apply statistics to administrative and social problems.

Tsar Peter the Great (see Chapter 7) was convinced by his trip to the West that Russia would have to borrow from the West. He corresponded with Leibniz, who convinced him that empirical science, along with the creation of a system of education, would bring progress. The tsar wanted to refute the Western view that "we are barbarians who disregard science." Peter's campaign of westernization, which included opening his country to Western scientific ideas, made Russia a Great Power. The sciences that interested Peter were those that were useful in statemaking: mechanics, chemistry, and mathematics aided in building ships and improving artillery. Here, too, science merged with statemaking.

A seventeenth-century apothecary shop used new scientific discoveries.

Although chemistry was not a subject of university study, al-
chemists pursued knowledge of chemical reactions in their labo-
ratories as depicted here.

Science and Religion

As scientific discoveries led more people to doubt religious authority that
was based on faith alone, points of tension not surprisingly continued
to emerge between science and religion. This was particularly the case
with the Catholic and Orthodox Churches. That there seemed to be a
much closer association between Protestant countries and advances in
science—given the precocious role of England and, to a lesser extent, the
Dutch Netherlands in the emergence of a culture of science—has contributed to the debate over whether Protestantism itself was more conducive to scientific inquiry.

Theological concerns still dominated at most universities, despite the
role of the University of Padua, and of the University of Cambridge, where
by the 1690s both Newton's theories and those of Descartes were taught.
Universities contributed relatively little to the diffusion of the scientific
method. During the century as a whole, their enrollments declined as the
European population stagnated. In Catholic countries, canon law and in
Protestant states civil law predominated in universities, which trained
state and Church officials, respectively. The number of German universities more than doubled to about forty during the seventeenth century. The

impetus for their creation came from Lutheranism and Calvinism, however, not from an interest in science.

Catholic universities continued to be the most traditional. Following Descartes' death in 1650, the University of Paris, which had about 30,000 students and was the largest university on the continent, forbade a funeral oration. Almost three decades later, the archbishop of Paris declared that "in physics it is forbidden to deviate from the principles of the physics of Aristotle . . . and to attach oneself to the new doctrines of Descartes." The University of Paris continued to exclude the new philosophy until the 1730s. Experimental physics as well as botany and chemistry were absent from university study throughout Europe.

The salient role of Protestants in the diffusion of scientific method reflected differences between the theological stance of the Catholic Church and the more liberal ethos of the Protestant Reformation. Catholic theologians held to dogmas of faith and obedience, leaving little room for innovation or experimentation. Protestant belief that the individual should seek truth and salvation in his or her own religious experience through a personal interpretation of the Bible encouraged skepticism about doctrinal theology. The emphasis on individual discovery seemed to lead naturally to empiricism. In Protestant countries, the Reformation had undermined the institutional monopoly on truth effectively maintained in Catholic countries. While Protestant theologians also could be rigid and unyielding, they had no equivalent to the papal Index of Forbidden Ideas or Books, or the mechanism of the Inquisition. Although the Massachusetts Bay Puritans may have forced religious attendance and sought to control what church members read, the English colonies in general accepted the principle of toleration.

Scientists in Catholic states, confronted by ecclesiastical denunciations or by reports of miracles that seemed to fly in the face of logic, found support in Protestant lands. The Protestant Dutch Republic, fighting a long civil war against Spanish rule, emerged as a center of toleration, where most books could be published. When Descartes learned of the condemnation of Galileo's work, he fled France for Holland, where he published *Discourse on Method.* Francis Bacon had been among the first to associate the Scientific Revolution with the Protestant Reformation. Indeed, many Protestants believed that scientific discovery would lead to a better world, and that the wonders of nature were there to be discovered and to give greater glory to God. Yet, Jesuits in Bohemia protected Kepler, who had faced persecution from Protestant theologians, provided he limited himself to speculation about astronomy and mathematics and avoided what they considered theological questions.

The development of a scientific view of the world in England may be better understood in the context of decades of social, intellectual, and political crisis during the mid-seventeenth century. The cause of Parliament and of Puritanism against Charles I's seeming moves toward absolutism

Astronomers using a telescope at the Royal Observatory of London.

and Catholicism attracted political and religious reformers. Many who considered the Catholic Church an obstacle to scientific inquiry opposed Charles I as they sought a climate of freedom. The reformers' triumph in the English Civil War may have emboldened Newton and other proponents of the new philosophy. Moderate Anglicans, like the Puritans before them, insisted that science could bring progress. They encouraged the creation of the Royal Observatory, founded by Charles II at Greenwich in 1675. Newton and other members of the Royal Society almost unanimously supported the exile of the Catholic King James II to France and the Glorious Revolution of 1688. Censorship was relatively rare in England, where political and ecclesiastical authority were not so centralized.

By way of contrast, state censorship, encouraged by the Catholic Church, had formally begun in France in 1623, five years after the sovereign law court of Toulouse had ordered a defrocked monk burned at the stake for denouncing belief in miracles after studying at the University of Padua. Thereafter, each new manuscript had to be submitted to a royal office for authorization to be published. Six years later, separate offices were established for literature, science, and politics, with ecclesiastics having veto power over books treating religious subjects.

Yet, to be sure, not all churchmen in France adamantly waged a war on science. Some French Jesuits became open-minded in pursuing scientific method. Jansenists, forming a dissident movement within the Church early in the eighteenth century, also favored scientific discovery, discussion, and debate, but faced papal and monarchical opposition (see Chapter 11).

CONSEQUENCES OF THE SCIENTIFIC REVOLUTION

The Scientific Revolution seemed to push theology into the background. The idea that mankind might one day master nature shocked many Church officials, although the earliest exponents of scientific method never doubted God's creation of the universe, but rather sought to understand the laws by which the universe operated. Nonetheless, Descartes' materialism seemed to suggest that mankind could live independently of God. His attempt to deduce the existence of God from the laws of motion brought ecclesiastical wrath. For faith in scientific method had distinct philosophical consequences: "If natural Philosophy, in all its parts, by pursuing this method, shall at length be perfected," Newton reasoned, "the bounds of moral philosophy will also be enlarged." The English poet John Donne had already come to the same conclusion in 1612. "The new philosophy," he wrote prophetically, "calls all in doubt."

The men and women of science espoused the application of scientific method to the study of nature and the universe. But it was a short step to subjecting society, government, and political thought to similar critical scrutiny. The English philosopher John Locke claimed that society was, as much as astronomy, a discipline subject to the rigors of scientific method. Moreover, the Scientific Revolution would ultimately help call absolutism into doubt by influencing the philosophes, the thinkers and writers of the eighteenth-century Enlightenment (see Chapter 10). The philosophes' belief in the intrinsic value of freedom and their assertion that people should be ruled by law, not rulers, would challenge the very foundations of absolutism.

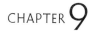

EIGHTEENTH-CENTURY ECONOMIC AND SOCIAL CHANGE

The great English landowners did as they pleased in the eighteenth century. More than one gentleman had an entire village demolished or flooded because it stood in the way of his landscaping plans. Another wrote, "It is a melancholy thing to stand alone in one's own country. I look around, not a single house to be seen but for my own. I am Giant, of Giant's Castle, and have ate up all my neighbors." Fences and servants kept venturesome interlopers far away. Some men of great means gambled fantastic sums on horse races. Sir Robert Walpole's estate guests drank up £1,500 of wine a year, the wages of more than a hundred laborers. English nobles seemed particularly vulnerable to overeating. A certain Parson Woodforde carefully entered in his diary the day of his death, "Very weak this morning, scarce able to put on my clothes and with great difficulty get downstairs with help. Dinner today, roast beef, etc."

At about the same time, a Swiss peasant named Jakob Gujer who was called Kleinjogg (Little Jake) by his friends inherited an indebted small farm and transformed it into something of a model enterprise, where he grew vegetables and new crops and raised cattle. It is said that when the Prince of Württemberg came to see the famous peasant, Kleinjogg told him how flattered he was that a prince should pay a visit to a humble peasant. The prince, teary eyed, replied, "I do not come down to you, I rise up to you, for you are better than I." To which Kleinjogg is alleged to have answered with tactful deference, "We are both good if each of us does what he should. You lords and princes must order us peasants what to do, for you have the time to decide what is best for the state, and it is for we peasants to obey you and work with diligence and loyalty." But there were few peasants with the means and initiative of Kleinjogg on the continent; in England, there were relatively few peasants left at all.

A nobleman and his wife, masters of all they see.

Although in some ways society remained the same as in earlier centuries, economic, social, and political change began to transform parts of Europe during the last half of the eighteenth century. To be sure, these transformations were uneven and regionally specific, above all affecting England and Northwestern Europe, while bypassing most of Central and Eastern Europe. In economically advanced regions, some of the traditional checks on population growth became less imposing. Increased agricultural productivity supported a larger population which, in turn, expanded demand for food. Large-scale manufacturing developed in and around northern English towns, leading to the beginnings of what we know as the "Industrial Revolution."

In a related change, distinctions within the highest social estates or orders were becoming less marked in Western Europe. Moreover, increased wealth generated some fluidity between social groups, contributing, in particular, to the dynamism that made Britain the most powerful state in the world. In France, too, wealth increasingly blurred lines of social class without, however, eliminating them entirely. Distinctions in title no longer necessarily corresponded to patterns of wealth distribution. By contrast, in Central and Eastern Europe social barriers remained much more rigidly defined.

THE SOCIAL ORDER

In early modern Europe, social structure was marked by birth into particular estates, or orders, which conferred collective identities and privileges.

Each order was legally defined, with specific functions and rights conferred to it by virtue of being part of the order, not through individual rights. The nobility was a privileged order, with special rights accorded by law, such as exemption from taxation. Noble titles were hereditary, and stemmed in principle from birth (although in reality many families during the century were able to purchase titles). The clergy was also a privileged order, and, like the nobility, was generally exempt from taxation. The "third estate" in France was simply everyone who was neither noble nor a member of the clergy, and included both peasants and townsmen, all of whom were subject to taxation. Within and between these estates, or orders, some degree of social movement was possible, particularly in Western Europe. The extent of social mobility that existed within the "societies of orders" was debated by contemporaries, as it has been subsequently by historians.

Nobles

"In all states of Europe," a noble remarked in 1770 about his estate, "there are a sort of men who assume from their infancy a preeminence independent of their moral character." In most of the continental European states (with the exception of the Dutch Republic and Switzerland), nobles dominated political life during the eighteenth century, although in most of these states they numbered no more than 2 to 3 percent of the population. They accounted for a much larger percentage in Russia, Spain, Poland, and Hungary, which together may have accounted for almost two-thirds of the nobles in Europe. In Spain's northern provinces, more than 10 percent of the male population, and in Poland perhaps even 15 percent (about 1 million men) claimed noble titles. In Hungary, what may have been the first accurate census in European history in 1784 counted more than 400,000 people claiming to be nobles, about 5 percent of the population. In France, by contrast, there were only somewhere between 25,000 and 55,000 noble families, about 125,000 to 300,000 people claiming noble title. In Britain, there were only about 200 nobles, called peers, whose titles and lands were inherited by only their eldest sons and whose younger sons were thus no longer considered nobles.

The vast majority of nobles drew their wealth from land they owned but that other people worked ("I am idle, therefore I am," went a Hungarian saying about Magyar nobles that spoofed the words of the French philosopher Descartes). Social status came from ownership of land. Noble landlords owned between 15 and 40 percent of the land, depending on the country, and an even higher percentage of productive land. In Prussia, only nobles could own land that was exempt from taxes; in Poland, commoners could not own any land at all. In Russia, non-nobles had lost their right to own property to which serfs were legally bound. Austrian nobles held half of the arable land in the Habsburg domains, hiring agents to col-

(*Left*) Hungarian noblemen in the eighteenth century. (*Right*) A satirical French print calling the nobleman a spider and the peasant a fly. The nobleman built his wealth on his ownership of land and the obligations of money, labor, and kind owed to him by the peasant.

lect what peasants owed them. In the Italian states, the nobility's share of the wealth increased even more than that of the Catholic Church.

Many continental nobles retained specific rights, often called seigneurial rights, over the peasantry. Nobles drew income in rent (cash), kind (crops), and dues (often labor) owed them by virtue of their social status and ownership of land. Some dispensed justice in their own courts. Peasants were obligated to pay to have their grain ground in the lord's mill, to bake bread in his oven, and to squeeze grapes in his press. In the 1770s, enlightened thinkers and economists began to argue that such obligations hindered economic development. The burden of seigneurial dues and debts left peasants with little or sometimes nothing left to pay state taxes, church taxes (tithes), or to feed their families.

Nobles proved remarkably adept at maintaining their privileges while adapting to the challenges and possibilities resulting from the growth of the centralized state. Such privileges included being exempt from virtually all taxation, as were nobles in Prussia, Poland, Hungary, and Russia, or exempt from the direct tax on land. Some French nobles paid the direct tax on land (the *taille*), but most did not. In contrast, British nobles did have to pay property taxes and the only special privileges that peers retained were the right to sit in the House of Lords and, if accused of a crime, to be tried there by a jury of their peers. On the continent, however, other noble privileges included the nobles' right to be judged only by their peers in criminal cases, the right to bear a family coat of arms, to wear certain clothing and jewelry, to occupy special church pews near the altar (in some places Mass could not start until the local nobles had taken their accustomed place), to receive communion before anyone else, and to sit in specially reserved sections at concerts and on special benches at university. To affirm the deference of social inferiors, commoners were expected to bow or tip their hats when a noble walked by, gestures upon which nobles increasingly insisted. The right to duel over family "honor" in some states and the right to wear a sword were honorific privileges that served to distinguish nobles from their social inferiors.

There were significant differences in the wealth and status of European nobles, however. The wealthiest, most powerful nobles considered themselves "aristocrats." They were proud possessors of the most ancient titles (in France, they were the nobles of the sword, whose titles originated in military service to the king), and many of them were members of the court nobility, although "aristocrat" was not a legal category. The *grands seigneurs* in France and the *grandees* in Spain were identified by their great wealth and ownership of very large estates. But the wealthiest nobles may have been the great landed magnates of Eastern Europe. Prince Charles Radziwill of Poland was served by 10,000 retainers and a private army of 6,000 soldiers. Another Polish nobleman's property included 25,000 square kilometers of land, territory about four-fifths the size of today's Belgium. A single Russian prince owned 9,000 peasant households.

On the other hand, in every country there were also nobles of modest means who eagerly, even desperately, sought advantageous marriages for their daughters, and state, military, and church posts to provide a living for their sons. Demographic factors put pressure on poorer nobles, because now more noble children survived birth and childhood. Most Sicilian, Polish, and Spanish nobles owned little more than their titles. About 120,000 Polish nobles were landless, many so poor that they were referred to as the "barefoot nobility." The *hobereaux* were the threadbare nobles of France. Spanish *hidalgos* depended on modest state pensions, and some were so poor that it was said that they "ate black bread under the genealogical tree." In Spain, these impoverished nobles retained such privileges as immunity from taxation, the right to display their coat of arms and to be called "Don" (or sir), and freedom from arrest for debt. But they were not permitted to engage in manual work, and hence they had few ways to emerge from poverty. In 1773, the king changed this when he ordered the poorest of the *hidalgos* to take up manual work.

Nobles tried to maintain an aristocratic lifestyle. Those with great wealth were able to live the life of privilege and excess. They generally maintained large châteaux (manor houses) on their rural estates, as well as often owning elegant townhouses with gardens designed to recreate the illusion of a rural manor. Although some nobles had fallen on hard times

The grandiose palace of Blenheim, whose very stones exude a martial feeling.

and wished their fortunes were the equal of their privileges, they still attempted to have an aristocratic lifestyle, often going into debt as a result. Aristocrats viewed themselves as the epitome of integrity, honor, and personal courage, and the embodiment of elite culture.

The British Landed Elite

Although only nobles could sit in the House of Lords, the British ruling elite of great landowners was considerably broader than the aristocracy. Membership in the elite was consistently augmented by wealthy newcomers since the elite was made up of those who had large land holdings, whether or not they were nobles (see below, p. 389). The ownership of landed estates conferred "gentry" status, which a broad range of families claimed. At the time of the Glorious Revolution of 1688, when the rights of Parliament were reaffirmed by the accession of William III to the throne of England, the landed elite numbered about 4,000 gentry families. British landowners became even more prosperous during the eighteenth century, particularly after about 1750, when they raised rents on their estates and amassed fortunes selling agricultural products. The percentage of English land owned by nobles rose from about 15 to 25 percent, a far larger percentage than in either France or the German states.

Because in Britain only the eldest son inherited his father's title and land, younger sons had to find other sources of income. One such source was the Anglican Church's twenty-six bishoprics, the plums of which were reserved for the younger sons of peers and which offered considerable revenue and prestige. Whereas in the previous century, about a quarter of Anglican bishops had been commoners, by 1760 only a few were not the sons of nobles.

The wives of gentlemen oversaw governesses and domestic servants while instructing them in the responsibilities of family, religion, and social status—to behave politely, but confidently. The young had to learn the prevailing social codes. It was considered poor form to show too much emotion, to be too enthusiastic and, above all, to be overly passionate, sensual or, worse, licentious. One did not seek openly to convert the lower classes to better manners and virtue, but rather to set a good example. The writer Horace Walpole (1717–1797) once claimed he attended church only to set a good example for the servants.

Young gentlemen were tutored at home, or they attended secondary schools, such as Westminster and Eton, boarding schools that characterized the shift to out-of-home education throughout Europe. Oxford and Cambridge Universities then beckoned some for a time, though few actually graduated. Scottish universities, in contrast, offered more dynamic thought and research. Young gentlemen were expected to know something about the classics and contemporary poets. Yet, to many if not most wealthy families, academic knowledge seemed superfluous, even suspect. When Edward Gibbon (1737–1794), the historian of ancient Rome, presented one of his books to a duke, the latter exclaimed, "Another damned thick square book! Scribble, scribble, scribble, eh Mister Gibbon?" A wealthy dowager offered her grandnephew and heir a handsome annual stipend if he would "chuse to travel" and thus forsake "one of the Schools of Vice, the Universities," still blamed by some for causing the Civil War. The goal of the "grand tour" of the continent, servants in tow, was to achieve some knowledge of culture and painting. Such trips further enhanced the popularity of the classical style, so called because it followed the rules of Greek and Roman architecture.

Clergy

Although in France and Prussia the clergy was technically the first order or estate, the clergy did not really form a separate corporate entity, but rather reflected the social divisions between rich and poor that characterized European life in general. Most village priests and ministers shared the poverty of their parishioners. The members of the French clergy were likely to be the most literate, Russian Orthodox priests the least.

The lower clergy, drawn from the lower middle class, from artisans, or from the relatively prosperous peasantry, resented the undisguised ambition, greed, and arrogance of the bishops. Wealth and rank, not piety, usually determined such selections, as in the Italian states, where bishops were overwhelmingly drawn from the families of the great landowners. Many bishops did not take their episcopal responsibilities seriously, though few monarchs were as brazen as King Philip V of Spain, who named his eight-year-old son to be archbishop of Toledo. One French cardinal never visited the diocese from which he drew his income. Moreover, in the 1760s at least forty bishops resided in Paris, only one of whom was, in principle, supposed to live there.

Although some parts of Europe, above all, France, had already become "de-christianized," in that religious practice and presumably belief had declined (see Chapter 10), in most places, religion still played an important part in village life. The clergy baptized children and registered their births, married couples, and buried everybody. Priest and minister supervised charitable activities and provided certificates of good behavior for those leaving in search of work elsewhere. Religion offered consolation to many impoverished people: everyone could go to church, even if the poor were restricted as to where they could sit or stand. In general, the quality of the parish clergy seems to have been quite high in the eighteenth century (when compared to the next century), due in part to efforts to improve clerical training. Nonetheless, many parish priests were still caught between the liturgical demands of Catholic Church law and the persistence of popular superstitions shared by all social groups—for example, the duchess of Alba in Spain tried to cure her son's illness by having him ingest powder from the mummified finger of a saint.

The "Middling Sort"

Most of those people who engaged in commerce, trade, and manufacturing were known as the "middling sort" by the English and the "bourgeoisie" by the French, a term whose complexity makes definition difficult. The term "bourgeois" evolved from the medieval sense of "privileged townsmen" (in earlier times they had been exempt from having to pay taxes to territorial rulers; see Chapter 1).

The middle classes ranged from wealthy entrepreneurs, who had developed the economies of trading and manufacturing cities, to struggling retail merchants and innkeepers who made barely enough to hang on to their businesses. Purchasing land and often titles, the wealthiest commoners "lived nobly." They owned about a quarter of the land in France and most of the cantons of Switzerland. *Rentiers* profited from the urban building boom to force their tenants to pay more, and they increased rural rents as well. The middling sort also included merchants of modest means, small manufacturers, physicians, butchers, bakers, candlestick makers, and craftsmen ranging from jewelers and cabinetmakers (who had catered to the wealthy) to shoemakers and tailors (who had more modest clients).

Triumphant merchants at table. Note that one of the merchants and his servants are smoking tobacco, a new fad. Note also the aristocratic wig on the handsome dog on the right.

Great Britain had already become the proverbial "nation of shopkeepers," with one shop for every thirty or forty people.

In Western Europe, above all, the middle decades of the eighteenth century brought an expansion of the liberal professions, particularly in the number of lawyers, who became closely linked to political life in France. Men trained in law took positions in state bureaucracies and law courts. In England and France, some of the best students, or at least the best connected, became barristers; this gave them the right to plead in court, which their subordinates, attorneys (solicitors), could not do. Distinguished medical schools produced few physicians, not yet a profession viewed with great respect. Beneath them were surgeons, some former barbers who had learned to wield a razor-sharp knife with greater consequences. Military surgeons tended to be a cut above the others, their skills honed in the heat of battle. Despite the fact that some universities taught anatomy, surgical techniques were learned on the job.

To some nobles, "bourgeois" was an expression of contempt, seen in the sense of a seventeenth-century play in which a protagonist is jeered by a young nobleman: "Bourgeois is the insult given by these hooligans to anybody they deem slow-witted or out of touch with the court." In the eighteenth century, the term had not lost the sense provided by a seventeenth-century dictionary: "lacking in court grace, not altogether polite, overfamiliar, insufficiently respectful."

Peasants

If nobles stood at the top of the social hierarchy of early modern Europe, peasants lay at the bottom. In 1787, the peripatetic Englishman Arthur Young was travelling in Champagne in northern France when he encountered a peasant woman who looked to be about sixty or seventy years of age. To his astonishment, she gave her age as twenty-eight, a mother of seven children who survived by virtue of "a morsel of land, one cow and a poor little horse." Each year her husband owed one noble 42 pounds of wheat, and another, 168 pounds of oats, 1 chicken, and a cash payment. He also owed taxes to the state. The woman, old before her time, stated simply that the "taxes and seigneurial obligations" were a crushing burden, one that seemed to be getting worse.

Peasants still formed the vast majority of the population on the continent: from about 75 percent (Prussia and France) to more than 90 percent (Russia). Peasants were the source of the surplus wealth that sustained the incomes of crown, nobility, and church.

Peasants stood at the bottom of society, condemned as "a hybrid between animal and human" in the words of a Bavarian official. A Moldavian called peasants "strangers to any discipline, order, economy or cleanliness . . . thoroughly lazy, mendacious . . . people who are accustomed to do the little work that they do only under invectives or blows." Such cruel images were particularly prevalent in regions where lords dominated peasants of another nationality, as in Bohemia, where German landowners drew on the labor of Czech peasants.

The village was the center of the peasant's universe. Villagers viewed outsiders with suspicion; their solidarities helped them pull through as best they could in hard times, through harvest failures, epidemics, and wars. Folk songs celebrated peasant wisdom and wiliness, as humble rural people outfoxed naive and bumbling outsiders, whose wealth could not impart common sense.

All peasants were vulnerable to powerful outsiders in the overlapping and interdependent systems of domination that characterized early modern Europe. The state, nobles, and churchmen extracted taxes, produce, labor, and cash. A peasant song from Auvergne in central France lamented: "The poor peasant, is always tormented/ Paying the salt tax, and cash to the king./ Always at his door, soldiers and sergeant/ Who shout without pause/ 'Bring some money!'" The proportion of peasant revenue in kind or cash that disappeared into the pockets of nobles, officials, and clergy ranged from about 30 percent (France) to 70 percent (Bohemia). Rulers extracted money, commodities, and labor payments, imposing new taxes when their states were at war.

The peasantry was not, however, a homogeneous mass. In Western Europe, where almost all peasants were free, a peasant's status depended upon the amount of land, if any, owned or controlled through leases. In France, Flanders, southwestern Germany, Switzerland, and Sweden, many peasants owned or rented plots of sufficient size and productivity to do well in most years. Swedish peasants owned about a third of the cultivable land in their country. Recognized formally as a fourth estate, the Swedish peasantry maintained a degree of independence perhaps unique in Europe. Charles XII of Sweden bragged that he would rather be the most miserable Swedish peasant than a Russian noble unprotected by law from the whims of the tsar. Rural industry, for example, linens, provided supplementary income for peasant families in parts of France, Switzerland, and a number of German states. In Zurich's hinterland in the 1780s, about a quarter of the population spun or wove at home for the cotton and silk industries.

Many of the landowning peasants were constantly in debt, borrowing against the often empty hope of the next harvest. Sharecroppers worked land owned by landlords in exchange for a third to a half of what was produced. Landless laborers scraped by, if they were lucky, working on rural estates. All over Europe, some peasants took to the road as peddlers. Seasonal migrants left their homes in the Alps, Pyrenees, and other mountain regions each year for construction work in Milan, Lyon, Barcelona, or other large cities, or to work as laborers on the summer grain and fall vineyard harvests.

Serfdom had largely died out in Western Europe. Yet, many free peasants continued to be subject to some kind of seigneurial justice. In France, thousands of manorial courts still existed in 1789, providing lords with additional income by virtue of legal fees and fines assessed on peasants. Most of these courts, presided over by nobles, occupied themselves with minor offenses such as poaching and trespassing, civil suits for debt, and with family matters such as inheritances and guardianships.

In addition to taxes on land (*taille*) and salt (*gabelle*), peasants also owed obligatory labor service (*corvée*), usually work on roads, in France, Denmark, Sweden, Switzerland, Poland, Russia, and some German states. Obligations varied from only a couple of days in parts of France to as much as 200 days per year in Denmark. In Eastern Europe, peasant children were sometimes required to work in the service of the seigneur. Other obligations included the duty to provide the lord's household with a certain amount of food, for example, a chicken or goose on a holiday, or even just a few eggs, or to provide food for the lord's dogs, or to spin or weave cloth for the lord's household. To these were added mandatory payments to the seigneur upon transfer of land held by peasants with hereditary tenure. When a peasant with such tenure died, the lord claimed both money and the best animals the peasant might have owned.

The conditions of peasant life became worse the further east one travelled. Peasants in Russia and Eastern Europe lived in hovels made of earth, clay mixed with straw, branches, twigs, and sometimes caked manure. Floors were of mud and beds of straw. Only peasants of relative wealth could afford wood as building material.

The further east one went, too, the more authority lords enjoyed over peasants. Most peasants east of the Elbe River were serfs, some of whom had to take an oath of loyalty to their seigneur, as during the Middle Ages. There were some free peasants in the Habsburg domains and in Poland, but very few in Russia. The number of people who lost their freedom by becoming serfs had increased in East Prussia and Brandenburg, such that the German term for serfdom had become the same word for slavery.

Gallows stood near some Prussian manor houses, symbolizing the judicial prerogatives nobles held over serfs, including the right to dispense corporal punishment. In Poland, nobles could have their serfs executed (at least until late in the century). Russian lords could sentence their own serfs to killing labor, and even torture them, as long as they did not die immediately from such treatment, or send them into exile in Siberia. In Poland, a noble convicted of murdering a peasant paid only a small fine.

In Russia, proprietary serfs remained personally bound to the land of the nobles and, after Catherine the Great's Charter of 1785, to the nobles themselves. Some serfs owed landowners or, in the case of state serfs, the state, payments in money or in kind; others, somewhat better off, owed only labor—on the average, about three days a week. Lords could sell serfs, or give them away, for example, as part of a dowry, or lose title to them through gambling. Serfs could be sold individually or as a family to another noble, or be exchanged for animals. Lords could refuse permission for their serfs to marry or to choose a certain occupation. A good number of serfs took their chances in setting out to seek their freedom in the vast expanses on the edge or east of the empire. In Russia, as well as in Central and Eastern Europe, a few serfs managed to put together enough money to purchase their freedom.

Flogging a Russian serf.

A poll tax on males (called "souls" in Russia), from which only nobles were excluded, added to the dependence of the "bonded people" to the state. Villages were collectively responsible for the payment of taxes. Moreover, all peasants could be conscripted into army service for terms of twenty-five years, a life sentence for most soldiers.

Possibilities for peasant resistance were limited; yet the "weapons of the weak" were not insignificant. These ranged from sullen resentment and foot-dragging to arson, open rebellion, or even full-scale insurrection. All nobles in an idle moment—and there were many—pondered the possibility of a massive uprising of "the dark masses." As the legal and material conditions of the serfs deteriorated, rebellions were endemic in eighteenth-century Russia. During the reign of Catherine the Great, the Cossack Emelian Pugachev appeared on the Siberian frontier claiming to be the pretender, "Tsar Peter III" (the real Peter III had spoken of reforms but had been dethroned and then murdered). He led several million peasants against their lords in 1773–1774. Pugachev's followers included Cossacks, Old Believers (dissidents persecuted by the Orthodox Church and doubly taxed), and the miners of the Ural Mountains, as well as desperate serfs. About 3,000 landowners perished in the Pugachev rebellion before it was crushed. Rebel serfs were hanged by having hooks stuck through their ribs.

In Bohemia during the hungry 1770s, 40,000 royal soldiers were required to put down peasant uprisings. And in the middle of the next decade, about 30,000 Transylvanian peasants rose up after a false rumor spread that those enlisting in the Habsburg army would gain freedom from serfdom. They demanded the abolition of the nobility and burned several hundred manor houses to make their point. The uprising ended with the torture of several of their leaders, parts of whose bodies were nailed to the gates of four towns.

THE BEGINNINGS OF THE INDUSTRIAL REVOLUTION

The Industrial Revolution began in England during the eighteenth century. Its early stages brought, above all, an intensification of forms of production that already existed: small workshops and cottage industry (producing goods at home). Technological innovation played a part, but not as large a one as has sometimes been assumed. Yet, ultimately a new source of inanimate power, the steam engine, would replace animal and human power, and increasingly manufacturing would be characterized by factory production.

The growth in manufacturing itself depended on two interrelated factors: agricultural productivity, then the principal source of wealth, and population growth. The two were so closely linked that it is sometimes difficult to know which followed which. An increase in agricultural productivity permitted the European population to increase during the century. At the same time, greater demand for food encouraged capital-intensive farming, including specialization of cash crops (such as vegetables, fruits, olive oil, wine, and raw silk) and the raising of cattle and poultry. Greater profits from agriculture generated a surplus of funds that could be invested in manufacturing. In turn, a larger population, some of the growth concentrated in and around cities and towns, increased the demand for manufactured goods, and provided a labor supply for town-based and rural industry.

Stagnation and Growth in Agriculture

New agricultural methods, first applied in the middle of the seventeenth century, helped raise farm yields in England, aided by the application of natural and artificial fertilizers. Gradually the practice of leaving part of the land fallow every other or every third year gave way to crop rotation. This helped regenerate the soil. Landowners planted fodder and root crops, such as clover and turnips, instead of periodically leaving land fallow. This provided food for animals as well as for human beings, in addition to enriching the soil by retaining nitrogen. The cultivation of potatoes, brought from the Americas, added badly needed nutrition to the diet of the poor.

By 1750, English agricultural yield had increased to the point that almost 15 percent of what was produced could be exported abroad (although about a third of the population still did not have enough to eat). On average, at the end of the century, an acre of agricultural land yielded perhaps 2.5 times more food in England than in France. Agriculture's contribution to the British gross national product reached a peak of 45 percent in 1770, and then only slowly was overtaken by English manufacturing as it rose in remarkable increments. Increased farm profits provided capital not only for further investment in agriculture but also in manufacturing, although most landowners were more likely to invest in government bonds than in speculative ventures.

One of the impediments to the expansion of agricultural production in England had been the widespread existence of open fields or common lands, which made up about half of the arable land in 1700. Beginning in the sixteenth century, on request from landowners, acts of Parliament permitted the "enclosure" of common land, transforming open fields or land that was communally owned into privately owned, fenced-in fields that could be more intensively and profitably farmed by individual owners (see Chapter 5). Over two centuries, enclosure acts forced perhaps half of English small landholders from the land, swelling the ranks of agricultural laborers. Between 1760 and 1815, 3,600 separate parliamentary acts enclosed more than 7 million acres of land, more than one-fourth of the farmland of England. Small tenant farmers, too, suffered, as many could

Measuring land in preparation for enclosure.

not afford to pay rents that rose rapidly after about 1760. The poorest members of the rural community lost their age-old access to lands on which they had gleaned firewood, gathered nuts and berries, and grazed animals. Before enclosure, it had been said, a "cottager" was a laborer with land; after enclosure, he was a laborer without land. Oliver Goldsmith's *Deserted Village* commented with playful, bitter irony:

> The law locks up both man and woman
> Who steals the goose from off the common,
> But lets the greater felon loose
> Who steals the common from the goose.

Agricultural change came far more slowly on the continent and barely at all in much of the Balkans and Russia. Most producers remained at the subsistence level, farming small plots without an agricultural surplus that they might have used to expand their holdings or improve farming techniques. Primitive farming techniques (wooden plows that barely scratched the surface of rocky terrain) characterized the mountainous and arid land of southern Italy and Sicily, the Dalmatian coast, southern France, much of Spain, and the Balkans. Peasants lacked farm and draft animals and therefore fertilizer, meat, and milk. Markets and transportation networks, too, remained inadequate to the task of agricultural modernization.

In Central and Eastern Europe, an old adage went "there is no land without a lord" because in most places only a noble, the crown, or the Church could own land. Serfdom and the absence of independent peasant proprietors left a formidable obstacle to agricultural development in Prussia, much of the Habsburg lands, and Russia.

On the continent, a bewildering variety of land tenures and agricultural practices under which they were held seemed to set rural poverty in stone.

Most continental farmland remained divided into small strips, and each year more than a third of arable land may have lain fallow (unplanted so that the land could replenish itself), with crops rotated between fields. Traditional peasant agricultural methods also blocked a major expansion of production. "Slash and burn" tillage survived in some parts of Europe where peasants simply burned the stubble on their land once the harvest had been taken in, replenishing soil with ash.

The studied attention many English country gentlemen gave to their lands may be contrasted with the approach of many French and Prussian nobles, content to sit back and live from revenue extracted from peasants. While the state had an interest in increasing farm output to generate additional tax revenue, most royal officials, seigneurs, and churchmen looked first to better ways of extracting peasant surpluses, not to improving yields. Nobles resisted occasional royal attempts to reduce seigneurial obligations, or to change them, such as by commuting labor service to payments in cash or in kind. Furthermore, much of what peasants managed to produce they owed to landlords, the state, and to a lesser extent, the Church. "Why should I build a better house" asked a Bavarian peasant, "so that my seigneur can line his pockets with the requisite fees to be paid?" Serfs had even less interest than other peasants in innovation.

Changes on the continent comparable to those taking place in England were largely confined to Northwestern Europe. In northern France, Flanders, the Dutch Republic, and Schleswig-Holstein (and parts of northern Italy as well as Spanish Catalonia), the land was fertile enough and sufficient capital was available to invest in commercial agriculture. Moreover, these were regions generally farmed by people who owned the lands on which they worked, and who therefore had more incentive to augment production. But even in the less densely populated countryside of Eastern and Southern Europe, more land was brought into cultivation, as in Russia where the population pushed into the steppes of the eastern frontier lands.

Other factors, too, contributed to improvements in Western European agriculture. During the eighteenth century, Europe as a whole experienced warmer, drier weather, particularly in the summers, in stark contrast to the unusually cold and damp seventeenth century. This had a salutary effect on population, agricultural yields, and commerce. Land reclamation projects helped expand the amount of land under cultivation. The Dutch reclaimed more land from the sea through ingenuity and hard work. In Schleswig-Holstein, arable lands increased by almost a quarter by the elimination of fens and heaths. Land reclamation added significantly to the amount of land under cultivation in the Southern Netherlands and as well as in Brandenburg. Even in densely settled France, farmers recovered wastelands for pasture, cereal crops, and vines.

Though not to the same extent as in England, the enclosure of separate strips of land and the sale or consolidation of common lands in Northwestern Europe permitted the development of "agricultural individualism," as more land passed to peasant-owners. Beginning in the 1760s, state policies created small farms owned by peasants, helping transform Danish agriculture from the stagnation of serfdom to relative prosperity. Royal decrees abolished serfdom, encouraged enclosure, and forced the commutation of labor obligations to rent payments.

Gradually some techniques that characterized agricultural improvements in England reached the continent. Innovative landowners and tenant farmers began to rotate crops, replacing the old three-field system so that little or no land lay fallow, growing foliage crops to improve the fertility of fields. As in England, turnips, potatoes, and rice enhanced dietary nutrition. Yet, many peasants remained prisoners of tradition, refusing to plant or eat potatoes (Russian peasants called them "apples of the devil"), despite the fact that they can grow almost anywhere under any conditions. Nonetheless, the cultivation of the sugar beet (from which sugar could be made), the tomato (which some peasants held to be poisonous), and chestnuts (the "bread of the poor"), also spread in France.

Animal husbandry also benefited from improved techniques. Oxen, mules, and especially horses could pull plows more easily than peasants. More cattle provided manure for fertilizer, and meat and milk for nutrition. Sheep-raising developed rapidly, providing both food and wool for manufacturing.

From Bilbao to Warsaw, some landowners formed societies to discuss agriculture and a few began model farms. Such groups included nobles, wealthy bourgeois, clergymen, and an occasional university professor. In France, "physiocrats," economic thinkers who believed that land was the source of all wealth, urged landowners to make their property more profitable and encouraged state policies to free the price of grain. Publications on agriculture increased dramatically.

A few rulers took steps to intervene in the interest of agricultural progress. The elector of Bavaria in 1762 offered farmers an exemption from taxes for ten years in the hope that they would plant foliage crops in their fallow fields. Several German Rhineland princes encouraged the selective breeding of cattle. In 1768, Queen Maria Theresa of Austria ordered the division of common pasture lands in some parts of the Habsburg territories and the establishment of agricultural societies.

Population Growth

The European population rose from about 120 million to about 190 million people during the eighteenth century (see Table 9-1). Historians have long debated the causes and consequences of this demographic revolution, studying parish registers of births, marriages, and deaths. Europe's birthrate increased, particularly after about 1740, and the number of deaths each year—the mortality rate—declined even more rapidly. These

TABLE 9-1. EUROPEAN POPULATION, 1700–1800 (MILLIONS)

	1700	1750	1800
Great Britain	9.0	10.5	16.5
France	19.0	21.5	28.0
Habsburg Empire	8.0	18.0	28.0
Prussia	2.0	6.0	9.5
Russia	17.5	20.0	37.0
Spain	6.0	9.0	11.0
Sweden	1.5*	1.7	2.3
United Provinces	1.8	1.9	2.0

*Data for Sweden is from Franklin D. Scott, *Sweden: The Nation's History* (Carbondale, Ill.: University of Southern Illinois Press, 1988), p. 260.
Source: Paul Kennedy, *The Rise and Fall of the Great Powers* (New York: Vintage, 1989), p. 99.

changes came first and foremost in densely settled regions of soaring agricultural productivity: England, the Netherlands, Flanders, northern Italy, and northern France (see Map 9.1). This suggests that an increase in agricultural production was the most important factor in explaining why the European population began to rise.

Plagues and epidemics, as well as chronic malnourishment, still intervened periodically to check population growth. Many monarchs ascended the throne because elder siblings had died, as did Frederick II of Prussia, who came to the throne because his two elder brothers had died before their first birthdays. Moreover, poor people were particularly vulnerable to infection, and rates of infant mortality remained high. Epidemics such as influenza, typhus, smallpox, and the plague occasionally ravaged populations. In 1719, 14,000 people in Paris died of smallpox. Malaria epidemics occurred in Spain in 1784–1787, and then again in 1790–1792. Whooping cough alone killed at least 40,000 children in Sweden during a period of fifteen years in the middle of the century, and more than 100,000 people died of bacillary dysentery in Brittany in one year. Epidemics of all kinds devastated the Balkans with murderous regularity. In Moscow, half the population died of disease early in the 1770s. Some states tried to close their frontiers and ports to prevent the arrival of disease, but usually to no avail. Famine, following several successive harvest failures, accentuated disease, particularly for those at opposite ends of the life cycle, infants and the elderly. Hardship turned into calamity. In 1769 alone, as much as 5 percent of the population of France may have died from hunger. Cities and towns remained unhealthy places where more people died than were born.

Yet, life expectancy gradually rose as diseases and epidemics ravaged the population less often and less murderously. In general, people of means lived longer than poor people, with upper-class Genevans living to almost

MAP 9.1 POPULATION IN 1780   Distribution of the European population in 1780.

Population per sq. km

- 40 or more people
- 20 to 40 people
- Less than 20 people

City populations

- ■ Cities over 500,000
- ⊙ Cities 200,000 to 500,000
- • Cities less than 200,000

forty-two years of age early in the century, and to more than age forty-seven at the end of the century. But the average life expectancy for French men and women during the last half of the century still was only twenty-nine, and in Sweden, a country of relative longevity, it stood at about thirty-three years for men and thirty-six for women during the same period. Vaccinations against smallpox gradually proved effective, at least in Western Europe, although mass inoculations were not yet available. Quinine water helped people survive fevers. Scientific and medical societies encouraged towns to supervise waste removal and to take greater care when burying the dead, forbidding inhumations within town walls. The expansion of the cotton industry provided clothing, especially underwear, that was more easily and effectively washed than wool and other materials.

Warfare, which had checked population growth during the seventeenth century, became less devastating. Most of Western Europe was now spared the long, bloody conflicts (such as the Thirty Years' War) that had taken a toll on civilians. Armies became professionalized, and more under the control of stronger dynastic states. Military discipline and supply improved, sparing civilians much of the rapine of earlier centuries. Eastern Europe and the New World offered new sites for battles between the Great Powers.

Economic opportunity, such as the expansion of rural or cottage industry, encouraged couples to marry earlier—in their early twenties in England—and to have more children. There were fewer single women who never married, although the number of spinsters remained unusually high in some places, notably Ireland and Brittany.

The plague ward in a Hamburg hospital. Note the doctor carrying out a painful amputation on a patient. Both are oblivious to surrounding distractions.

Many contemporaries were aware of the rise in population (although some, especially in France, wrongly believed the population was declining by the end of the century). For the English clergyman Thomas Malthus (1766–1834), the rise of the European population was alarming. Malthus predicted in his *Essay on the Principle of Population* (1798) that natural checks on population growth—plague and disease, famine, war, and infant mortality, what he called "nature's auditing with a red pencil"—would become less significant. But he believed that population would "increase beyond the nourishment prepared for it," that is, food supply would grow only arithmetically (2-3-4-5 and so on), whereas population would henceforth multiply exponentially (2-4-8-16-32 . . .). To be sure, the rise in population put more pressure on the land, particularly in France and other places where most land holdings were small and often too subdivided to be profitably farmed. Yet, Malthus did not take into consideration rising agricultural productivity, nor the fact that some people had already begun to limit the size of their families, although it is extremely difficult to measure the diffusion of birth control. We have only hints of this, such as when the British writer James Boswell referred delicately to his sexual encounters "in armor." In France, coitus interruptus is credited with bringing about a small decline in the birthrate after 1770. But birth control was hit or miss, to say the least.

Manufacturing: Guilds and Domestic Industry

The workshop was the basis of manufacturing in eighteenth-century Europe. In some countries, merchants and artisans were organized into corporate guilds by the product they sold; in Russia, by contrast, a decree in 1775 placed them in guilds according to wealth. Guilds were a type of privilege, because rulers awarded them monopolies over the production or sale of certain products, particularly luxury goods. Masters' guilds and journeymens' associations conferred rights and status on craftsmen; they limited and oversaw the training of boys as apprentices, beginning at the age of twelve or thirteen. In France, journeymen perfected their skills while completing the "tour of France," the origin of the modern bicycle race. A craftsman stopped in a number of cities over a period of several years; he was housed in the craft association's "mother house" before returning home with skills acquired from serving many masters, and with hopes of one day becoming a master himself.

It was, however, becoming increasingly difficult for a journeyman to become a master, particularly if he did not have a father or other relative to smooth the way by putting out some money. By the 1770s, Spanish and French skilled trades, in particular, had become glutted. Moreover, Parisian guilds faced competition from outsiders who escaped corporate controls. "Free" or "illegal" workers lived on the outskirts of the city, beyond the customs tax barrier, where a tax on goods brought into town had

William Hogarth's depiction of a weaver's apprentice.

to be paid. Such craftsmen could produce cabinets and other products more cheaply than their Parisian rivals, whose goods were taxed.

Since at least the sixteenth century in England, partially to circumvent the guilds, some merchant-manufacturers had looked to labor in the countryside to produce goods. This shift to domestic industry (also known as proto-industrialization or the putting-out system) contributed to what would eventually become a worldwide revolution in manufacturing. The early stages of the Industrial Revolution showed an increase in domestic industry rather than a shift to new forms of production. New technology would only gradually lead to the mechanization and the standardization of tasks previously done by hand.

Britain's manufacturing base expanded early in the eighteenth century. In 1720, Daniel Defoe (1680–1731) described the Yorkshire countryside as "one continuous village" with a "manufactory or workhouse" attached to each house or farm. Among the houses of the manufacturers "scattered an infinite number of cottages or small dwellings, in which dwell the workmen which are employed, the women and children of whom are always busy carding and spinning." Hand spinning continued throughout the century to be the largest source of female employment. Many families of home spinners, weavers, glove-makers, and shirt-buttoners also worked the land—theirs or someone else's—part time. Rural industry paused at harvest time.

Master clothiers, or merchant-manufacturers, provided domestic workers with raw materials, such as wool or Indian cotton purchased at one of the cloth halls. Home workers carded, spun, or wove with spinning wheels

Carding and spinning at home.

or looms that they either owned or (in most cases) rented. The master clothier later came around again, paying for the goods that had been completed. He would then carry these goods to the next stage in the production process, for example, to a dyer. Low pay rates in the countryside attracted merchant-manufacturers, encouraging the persistence of rural industry. At the end of the century, hand-knitted stockings produced by rural Scottish families still cost less than those knitted on a power loom.

As the cottage industry was organized by household, women had a major, even determining, role in the organization of the household economy, including training young children. There were both male and female "journeymen" wool spinners. One man, later a successful inventor of textile machinery, recalled, "my mother taught me [while too young to weave] to earn my bread by carding and spinning cotton, winding linen or cotton weft for my father and elder brothers at the loom, until I became of sufficient age and strength for my father to put me into a loom."

Inventions

Technological change also contributed to the Industrial Revolution. Between 1660 and 1760, 210 new inventions were patented in England; during the next twenty-nine years, there were 976. Most of the inventors were artisans or yeoman farmers, although inventors at Scottish universities came up with improvements in dyes and bleaching with chlorine.

But inventions at first had very little to do with increased productivity. They were probably less important than the infusion of investment capital into manufacturing and the expansion of the number of workers in the textile industry. Some inventions were only gradually diffused, or their importance was not recognized until later. No invention was of greater long-term significance than the steam engine, invented by James Watt (1736–1819), a Scot who made musical instruments. Watt added a separate condenser to a primitive steam engine, resulting in a more powerful engine, which he patented in 1769. Yet, like its predecessor, Watt's costly invention was first used only to drain mines, making it possible to dig deeper shafts, and its use was only slowly diffused.

Inventions eventually transformed the production of iron. In 1709, Abraham Darby, a foundryman, came up with a process to smelt iron ore into cast iron by using coke instead of charcoal. But this process spread only slowly; in 1775, there were still only thirty-one blast furnaces in Britain. Moreover, charcoal smelting continued to be important, further depleting Britain's forests. In 1784, Henry Cort (1740–1800), an iron-master, invented the "puddling and rolling" process in iron casting. Molten metal in a furnace was raked to remove carbon and other impurities from the iron, producing wrought iron which was far stronger than cast iron. Iron bridges replaced their flimsy predecessors. Iron made new buildings sturdier and basically fire-resistant. Cast-iron railings and gates began to appear on landed estates and in elegant townhouses. Low-cost iron made possible sturdier plows and other farm implements that, in turn, significantly increased the demand for iron. The export of iron increased by nine times in the course of the eighteenth century, helping British foreign trade triple during its last two decades.

Each major invention was the result of the ingenious application of technology already available to production, rather than of brilliant discoveries by genius-inventors. Improvements in the spinning wheel and basic looms accelerated textile production in the seventeenth and first decades

(*Left*) James Watt. (*Right*) The steam engine.

of the eighteenth century. The stocking frame produced lighter and more fashionable cotton and silk stockings that replaced the heavier woolen hose of the upper classes. John Kay (1704–1764) invented the "flying shuttle" (patented in 1733 but not diffused for more than twenty years), which ultimately made it possible to card and weave at a much greater speed, doubling productivity. But Kay's invention, too, has to be seen in the context of traditional manufacturing: its principal effect was to increase the productivity of hand-loom weavers.

Gradually machines powered by water and then by steam eliminated bottlenecks in textile production. In about 1764, James Hargreaves (c. 1720–1778), a carpenter and weaver, invented an apparatus known as the spinning jenny, which wrapped fibers around a spindle. Drawing on medieval technology, Hargreaves multiplied the number of thread spindles a worker could operate from one to eight, and then soon to eighty spindles. In 1769, Richard Arkwright (1732–1792), a former barber turned entrepreneur, patented a mechanized "water frame," which, combining spindles and rollers, became the first spinning mill. The water frame turned out a strong, coarse yarn that transformed the cotton industry and increased production of wool worsteds (combed wool). With the exception of its water-powered rollers, Arkwright built his power spinning machine out of the same materials as the ordinary spinning wheel that had been found in Europe since medieval times. Using the new technology, Arkwright set up large textile mills and earned half a million pounds in just twenty years. He had his portrait painted with his hand touching his famous spinning machine, as the same painter might have formerly depicted a country gentleman standing with his hand touching a fence, his hunting dogs sitting submissively at his feet. The resourceful manufacturer emerged in Britain as someone considered worthy of emulation. A decade later, a farmer combined features of Hargreaves' jenny and Arkwright's water frame to produce a "spinning mule" that could provide sturdier yarn of consistent quality while further increasing the number of spindles a single spinner could operate.

Cottage industry, artisanal workshops, and factory production often coexisted, not only within the same region, but within industries. With the gradual mechanization of spinning, which in some places probably followed a shortage of cheap rural labor, weaving could only keep pace with the rapid expansion of the number of hand-loom weavers. Even a rudimentary power loom, invented in 1784, was too expensive to compete with domestic industry, which continued to be based on the availability of an inexpensive workforce. Mechanization may first even have increased the demand for production of goods that could best be provided by domestic industry. Hand-loom weavers survived well into the middle decades of the nineteenth century.

In any case, the clever inventions that slowly revolutionized the textile industry did not inevitably lead to factory production. Like framework

Richard Arkwright with his famous invention at his fingertips.

knitting, the first spinning jennys and mules were small enough to be adaptable to workshops and even some houses. Manufacturing remained largely based in small workshops, where skilled workers and their apprentices used stronger, more reliable hand-operated machinery or tools. Many small textile entrepreneurs, who had begun as yeoman farmers, rural artisans, or innkeepers, continued to prosper although they owned little more than a single spinning frame.

The factory, however, slowly became the symbol of the new industrial age in England. One of Arkwright's textile mills in the early 1770s had 200 workers, and ten years later it had four times that number. An ironworks employed more than a thousand workers by 1770, a concentration previously seen only in great shipyards. In 1774, James Watt and Matthew Boulton (1728–1809), a toymaker, went into business in Birmingham producing engines and machine parts in the largest factory in the world. It was not a single structure but rather a number of adjacent workshops, employing about 20,000 men, women, and children in the countryside around Birmingham.

The development of the factory at first had little to do with technological imperatives. Manufacturers preferred bringing workers under one roof so that they could more easily supervise them, imposing the discipline of factory work on people used to having their schedule defined by the rise and fall of the sun and the passing of the seasons. When a defective piece of pottery emerged from the kilns, the pottery manufacturer Josiah Wedgwood would storm over and stomp on it with his wooden leg, chiding his workers. "Thou shalt not be idle" was Wedgwood's eleventh commandment; "Everything gives way to experiment" was his favorite maxim. His goal was to train his workers so thoroughly as "to make such machines of the men as cannot err." Boulton fined workers a part of their wages if they were late. One of his colleagues took deductions from his workers' wages for "being at taverns, alehouses, coffee houses, breakfast, dinner, playing, sleeping, smoking, disputes or anything foreign to my business, or in any way loitering."

By mid-century, factory manufacturing had begun to alter the northern English landscape. "From the Establishment of Manufacturers, we see Hamlets swell into Villages, and Villages into Towns," exclaimed a gentleman in the 1770s. The locus of English manufacturing shifted from the south and southeast to the north and northwest, around cities like "old smoky Sheffield." Yorkshire, which produced 20 percent of England's wool in 1700, accounted for 60 percent at the dawn of the next century; the production of worsteds, too, concentrated there, leaving areas in southeastern England. Northern England's industrial centers, then, lay at the heart of the manufacturing revolution that was transforming Britain and had already affected parts of continental Western Europe.

Expanding British Economy

The production of manufactured goods doubled during the last half of the eighteenth century in Britain. Cotton manufacturing led the way; between 1750 and 1770, British cotton exports doubled. The production of iron followed in importance, along with wool and worsteds, linen, silk, copper, paper, cutlery, and the booming building trades. Coal was substituted for wood as fuel.

Despite its relatively small size, Britain's significant economic advantages over the nations of the continent help explain why the manufacturing revolution first began in Britain. Unlike the German or Italian states, Britain was unified politically. People living in England spoke basically the same language. France and the Italian and German states still had internal tariffs that made trade more costly, whereas in Britain there were no internal tariffs once the union between England and Scotland had been achieved in 1707, creating Great Britain. Moreover, the system of weights and measures in Britain had largely been standardized.

Great Britain was by far the wealthiest nation in the world. Its colonies provided raw materials for manufacturing and markets for goods produced by the mother country. The amount of raw cotton imported from India increased by twenty times between 1750 and 1800. English merchants supplied slaves snatched from the west coast of Africa for the plantations of the West Indies in exchange for cotton. And, beginning in the 1790s, the United States provided Lancashire manufacturers with cotton picked by southern slaves.

England's precocious banking and credit arrangements facilitated the reinvestment of agricultural and commercial profits in manufacturing. London's financial market could provide information twice a week on what investments were worth in Amsterdam and Paris. London's banks, particularly the giant Bank of England, were profitable and respected. Merchants and manufacturers accepted paper money and bills of exchange with confidence. Gentry invested in overseas trade expeditions and in manufacturing without the reticence of continental landowners. Joint-stock companies, which investors had begun to form in the late seventeenth century, offered limited personal liability, which meant that in the case of a company's financial disaster, each investor would be liable only to the extent of his investment.

Expanded demand for manufactured goods led to a dramatic improvement in Britain's roads, which were already well developed. A new process of road surfacing—macadamization—improved travel on the main routes. Turnpikes were extended and improved; investors formed "turnpike trusts," repairing the highways and turning a profit by charging a toll. In 1700, it took fifty hours to travel from Norwich to London by coach; by 1800, the journey could be achieved in nineteen hours; the daunting trek to the Scottish city of Edinburgh had been reduced to a mere sixty hours of travel.

England's water transportation was also unmatched in Europe, a gift of nature. Rich sources of coal and iron ore lay near water transportation. By 1800, Britain was extracting about 90 percent of the world's coal. That extracted in northeastern England could be transported with relative ease along the coast. No part of England stands more than seventy miles from the sea. Navigable rivers facilitated the transportation of raw materials and manufactured goods; so did canals built in the middle decades of the century, including one ninety miles long linking Manchester to the Mersey River and the Irish Sea.

The state offered British businessmen more assistance than any continental rivals could anticipate from their own governments. The powerful Royal Navy protected the merchant fleet, which tripled during the first three-quarters of the century. Navigation Acts forced foreign merchants to ship export goods to Britain in British ships. Bowing to pressure from woolens producers, the British government in 1700 had imposed protective tariffs on imported silk and calico. Agreements with the Dutch Republic and France in the late 1780s reduced trade tariffs with those states, which helped British exports. Other British state strategies were even more imaginative: a law dating from the late seventeenth century required that all corpses be dressed in woolens for burial, a clever way of helping manufacturers. Furthermore, the political influence of businessmen kept taxes low.

Yet, the British government rarely interfered in operations of the economy in ways that businessmen might have considered intrusive. Adam

Smith (1723–1790), a Scottish professor of moral philosophy at the University of Glasgow, emerged as the first economic theorist of capitalism. In his landmark work, *An Inquiry into the Nature and Causes of the Wealth of Nations* (1776), Smith rejected the prevailing theory of mercantilism and extolled economic liberalism. He also observed that the greater division of labor was increasing productivity. Taking a famous example, he argued that a single worker could probably not make a single common pin in one day, but that ten workers, each repeating the same task, such as straightening the wire, or grinding its point, could make hundreds of pins in a workday. Smith's logic anticipated the age of factory manufacturing.

Expanding Continental Economies

On the continent, too, particularly in the West, manufacturing expanded rapidly in the workshops of large cities and small towns. Moreover, spinning, weaving, and the finishing of artisanal products like knives increased in the countryside. Banks provided more capital and credit to manufacturers and merchants. Despite bewildering differences in, for example, weights and measures, currencies (even within some states), and calendars (Russia's was eleven days behind that of the West), European commerce developed rapidly during the eighteenth century. The development of larger-scale commerce within Europe—for example, the Baltic trade—was very important to the growth of European economies. In addition, trade with the wider world brought new products—Chinese silk and porcelain, Indian cotton, West Indian sugar and rum, East Indian tea, South Seas spices, and much more. In the chancy sweepstakes of colonial trade, traders and their investors could make considerable fortunes, but they could also easily be ruined when a sudden storm or pirate attack destroyed a ship and its cargo.

The great successes—and failures—of colonial trade were those in England and the Dutch Republic, but global trade also contributed to the economies of the Italian and German states, and to those of Spain, Portugal, and France (see Map 9.2). France, too, benefited enormously from a dramatic influx of capital, above all profits from the sugar plantations of Haiti.

Bankers, investors, shipbuilders, wholesale and retail merchants, insurance underwriters, transporters, and notaries profited from the marked increase in international trade. Some of the prosperity trickled down to more ordinary folk as well, particularly in port towns: carpenters who built and repaired ships, dockers who unloaded them, public criers who announced their safe return, haulers who carried their products, and artisans who supplied luxuries for wealthy merchants.

Considerable obstacles remained, however, to further economic development on the continent. Traditional suspicion of paper money, the problems of obtaining credit and raising investment capital, and periodic government debasing of currencies created hurdles for those undertaking

MAP 9.2 TRADE FROM COLONIES TO EUROPE, C. 1775 Exports from the colonies to Europe, including the value of the trade.

Exports to Britain
Exports to France
Exports to Spain
Exports to Dutch United Provinces
Exports to Portugal

£2.2 million
£2.4 million
£1.4 million
Value unknown

£1.8 million

£5.6 million
£5.2 million
£4.9 million

ASIA

EUROPE
Glasgow
Liverpool
Amsterdam
Bristol
London
Nantes
La Rochelle
Bordeaux
Lisbon
Cádiz

AFRICA

NORTH
AMERICA

SOUTH
AMERICA

long-distance commerce. London and Amsterdam were alone in having relatively developed banks, credit facilities, relatively low rates of interest, and insurance companies. Even in Western Europe, Britain's South Sea Bubble (see Chapter 11) and the collapse of John Law's bank in France in 1720 scared off investors. Capital remained for the most part in the hands of wealthy families and small groups of associates, who loaned money to states, pushing up the cost of credit. The absence of investment capital led the Prussian and Austrian states to supply capital for some manufacturing enterprises.

France did not lag far behind Britain in the production of manufactured goods, and remained the principal supplier of Spain and its empire. Continental European manufacturing was characterized by small-scale production and cottage industry (taking advantage, particularly in France, of an almost endless supply of laborers). Manufacturing drew upon few technological innovations and very little mechanization. Water, wind, and human and animal motion provided power.

Guild monopolies on the trade and production of certain products, international tariffs and tolls compounded by the vast number of small states in Central Europe, and tariffs within states remained obstacles to more rapid industrial development. Furthermore, as we have seen, relatively few nobles took an active interest in manufacturing, although exceptions were to be found in France, the Austrian Netherlands, and Russia, where they developed coal mines and invested in the iron industry. In the Russian Empire, despite the development of the copper and iron industry of the Ural Mountains, the possibilities for increased manufacturing were limited by monumental distances between population centers and natural resources and an inadequate transportation network that had barely changed since the time of Ivan the Terrible in the sixteenth century.

SOCIAL CHANGES

Economic growth and population increases would ultimately transform Europe into a new industrial world, one in which there would be larger cities and greater social mobility. Urban growth, particularly after 1750, was one of the most visible changes engendered by population growth and the expansion of trade and manufacturing, as well as the continuing centralization of state power. Other changes included the rise of the "middling sort" and the greater vulnerability of the laborer who was displaced by enclosure and forced to move from place to place in search of work.

The Growth of Towns and Cities

Although Europe remained overwhelmingly rural, cities and towns grew faster than the population as a whole, meaning that Europe, particularly

TABLE 9-2. EUROPE'S LARGEST CITIES AT THE END OF THE EIGHTEENTH
CENTURY

City	Population	City	Population
London	950,000	St. Petersburg	270,000
Paris	550,000	Vienna	230,000
Naples	430,000	Amsterdam	220,000
Constantinople	300,000	Lisbon	180,000
Moscow	300,000	Berlin	170,000

the West, urbanized. Cities grew as people moved to areas where there was
work, or for the poorest of the poor, where they might benefit from charity.
New manufacturing centers served as magnets to which those who had no
land or prospects were drawn. By the end of the century, Europe had
twenty-two cities with more than 100,000 people (see Table 9-2).

The British urban population (any settlement of more than 2,500 people qualified as "urban") grew from slightly less than 20 percent of the
population in 1700 to more than 30 percent in 1800, when London's population reached nearly a million people, nearly twice that of Paris. London
was the world's largest port, center of banking, finance, insurance, manufacturing, and exports. In the eighteenth century, fully one-fifth of the
British population spent part of their lives in London. Early in the century,
Norwich, a textile-producing and shoemaking town in East Anglia, was
England's second city, with only 30,000 people, followed by Bristol and
Exeter, each of which had barely 20,000 inhabitants.

Two-thirds of the residents of London had been born outside of the city
and were migrants who had come to the capital in search of opportunity.
But many contemporaries believed that wickedness and crime increased
almost inevitably with growth and prosperity. *Hell Upon Earth, or the
Town in an Uproar* (1729) was subtitled "The Late Horrible Scenes of
Forgery, Perjury, Street-Robbery, Murder, Sodomy, and Other Shocking
Impieties." It denounced "this great, wicked, unwieldy, over-grown Town,
one continued hurry of Vice and Pleasure, where nothing dwells but *Ab-
surdities, Abuses, Accidents, Accusations.*"

London's emerging social geography reflected the paradox that Britain
was both an aristocratic and commercial society. Bloomsbury Square and
Bedford Square, elite districts in West London, near Westminster, the seat
of Parliament, were largely aristocratic creations, as nobles developed
some of the land they owned. At the same time, commercial London also
expanded rapidly in tune with the British Empire. Near the burgeoning
docks of the East End on the River Thames, dilapidated buildings housed
the poor.

As England's economic dynamism began to shift northward with increased manufacturing, Liverpool, teeming port on the Irish Sea, "the em-
porium of the western world," and Manchester, a northern industrial town,
grew rapidly. In the 1720s, Daniel Defoe flattered Manchester, already a

small center of textile manufacturing, as "the greatest mere village in England" and by 1760, 17,000 people lived there. By 1800, Manchester had become the "metropolis of manufactures," with 75,000 inhabitants and growing industrial suburbs as well.

Paris, Rouen, Lille, Bordeaux, and other French cities, too, continued to grow, although in France only about 10 percent of the population lived in towns of more than 5,000 people in 1789 (compared to 25 percent in England). In the German states, there had been but twenty-four cities with more than 10,000 people in 1500; by 1800, there were sixty of them.

After mid-century, the small towns that were centers of regional trade accounted for most urban growth. Royal officials, courtiers and attendants, tax collectors, lawyers, and soldiers swelled the population of state and regional capitals. In Berlin, which tripled in population, these groups and their families accounted for about 40 percent of the Prussian capital's 140,000 inhabitants in 1783.

In southern Italy, Naples was barely able to support its impoverished population of more than 400,000 people. No other town in southern Italy had 10,000 inhabitants. Other towns languished in stagnation, without sufficient trade, manufacturing, or administrative functions to infuse them with dynamism. In Rome, the clergy constituted about half the population of 160,000 people. The Spanish town of Valladolid housed forty-six monasteries among a population of little more than 20,000 people. Eastern Europe and the Balkans had few cities. By mid-century only three cities within the vast Russian Empire had more than 30,000 inhabitants: Moscow, St. Petersburg, and Kiev, each growing at a relatively rapid pace.

A London coffeehouse.

Elegant shops on Capel Street in Dublin.

People with money and leisure time had more to do in cosmopolitan cities. The largest English towns sported theaters and concert halls, gentlemen's clubs, and scientific societies. In 1740, Parliament limited the number of racetracks to two favored by people of means, stating that betting on horses had "contributed very much to the encouragement of idleness, to the Impoverishment of many of the meaner sort of subjects of this Kingdom." Private clubs thrived. Cafés took their name from the coffee served there, a drink only people of some means could afford. In contrast, cabarets and taverns offered cheap alcoholic drink.

Towns took pride in their development. Some began publishing guides for visitors and directories listing the names of shops. Elegant buildings of brick and stone replaced tottering wood-beamed structures dating from medieval times. Streets were widened, paved, and frequently cleaned. Dublin, Boston, and Calcutta offered smaller versions of English urban society, sporting private clubs and municipal pride.

Wealthy merchants and bankers lived in elegant townhouses near the docks in Hamburg, Nantes, Rouen, and Genoa, bustling port cities of international trade. Expanded trade and urban growth engendered consumerism. As the French language spread throughout the courts and upper classes in Europe, Paris became the European capital of luxury goods. French nobles established standards of conspicuous consumption. The sober frugality of the past disappeared in the quest for luxury. Parisians of means purchased fine wines from Burgundy, champagne from Champagne, and sent servants to the market to buy expensive cheeses and oysters from the Norman coast. Some nobles went broke after borrowing vast sums to provide lavishly for themselves and their families.

A wealthy Dutch family living nobly.

Noble and wealthy bourgeois alike insisted on the personal prerogatives of taste, for example, in decoration and food. It became a compliment to say that someone or something reflected "urbanity." Three-cornered hats, along with wigs, which wealthy commoners as well as nobles increasingly favored, and stockings emerged as recognizable symbols of respectability.

Upper-class men and women became concerned as never before with modesty; "water closets" became more common. Social relations became something of an extension of the fenced-in noble château of the countryside, or the walled townhouse with a private garden. A code of conduct served—with income and private space itself—as a barrier between wealthy and ordinary people.

The eighteenth-century consumer revolution extended to the urban poor, as well. The number of ordinary families able to acquire household utensils and even books and cheap prints increased dramatically. For those with a little money or some credit, the tavern and cabaret provided sociability. For people with neither, there was the street.

Social Movement within the Elite

With the growth of manufacturing, trade, and cities came concomitant social changes, including mobility of the "middling sort." In Paris, wealthy merchants purchased elegant townhouses and mingled with nobles. In Barcelona, members of the trading oligarchy earned the right to carry swords like nobles. The Catalan city's sparkling new town hall and aligned, paved streets reflected bourgeois prosperity and urban pride. The bourgeoisie of the Austrian Netherlands demanded privileges granted by the Habsburg rulers to Belgian nobles.

Bankers and wealthy merchants aspired to social distinction and to live the life of the aristocrat. When possible, they would use their wealth to buy their way into the nobility, or to marry a daughter into it. Although in theory a person was born into an estate and remained there for the rest of his life, noble titles could be purchased in most European states. As the rising cost of warfare (larger armies to equip, train, and send into battle, and expensive fortifications to maintain) and reduced tax revenue during hard economic times weighed heavily on royal coffers, the sale of titles and offices swept more men into the nobility. Wealthy commoners en-riched by the expansion of the economy of Western Europe bought titles, thereby acceding to prestigious positions in royal bureaucracies and in the officer corps of the king's standing army. The purchase of noble titles in France (the sale of which began in the fourteenth century), Austria, and Castile provided a relatively easily obtained means of social ascension, without eliminating the distinctions between nobles and commoners. The number of French nobles doubled between 1715 and 1789, and relatively few noble families could trace their origins back more than a couple of generations.

In Britain, on the other hand, it was rare for commoners to move into the nobility. The sale of offices had never been as widespread in England as on the continent, at least not since the Civil War, and the purchase of noble titles was nonexistent. But the crown occasionally elevated spectac-ularly successful, wealthy commoners into the peerage with hereditary no-ble titles (baron, viscount, earl, marquess, and duke), which carried with them a seat in the House of Lords. The monarchy rewarded other landed gentlemen with other titles, including knight (a non-hereditary title), baronet (a hereditary title, granted less frequently), both of which carried the title of "sir." Very few people, however, ever rose from trade into a peerage, or even to the upper gentry.

Entry into the British elite, however, was generally more open than into its continental counterparts. Gradual shifts in social structure in English society, beginning in the seventeenth century, contributed to the nation's social stability. The elite consisted of more than the small number of no-bles; social status and political influence were based on the ownership of large amounts of land, whether by noble or non-noble. Those who were wealthy enough to purchase estates became part of the landed elite and were considered gentry. Hence, membership in the elite consistently reflected the advent of wealthy newcomers. No legal or cultural barriers in Britain prevented bankers, manufacturers, merchants, and urban profes-sionals from acceding through wealth to social and political predominance as "country gentlemen" through the purchase of landed estates. With na-tional and local influence, these country gentlemen dispensed social and political patronage. Furthermore, though nobles dominated Parliament, that body responded to the needs of all property owners, including merchants and other wealthy commoners.

Daniel Defoe, who wrote *Robinson Crusoe* and other novels for an expanding middle-class readership, claimed that "men are every day starting up from obscurity to wealth." Trade and manufacturing in England were honored occupations. Unlike on the continent, where second and third sons often were automatically relegated by their fathers into Church or military posts, many of these sons marched proudly into business. A Manchester cobbler wrote in 1756:

> See, as the Owners of old Family Estates in your Neighborhood are selling off their patrimonies, how your townsmen are constantly purchasing; and thereby laying the Foundation of a new Race of Gentry! Not adorn'd, its true, with Coats of Arms and a long Parchment Pedigree of useless Members of Society, but deck'd with Virtue and Frugality.

In France, Denmark, and Sweden, tensions between the oldest noble families and those more recently ennobled remained strong. The wealthiest nobles were ever more eager to maintain social distance from poorer nobles and those recently ennobled, whom they viewed as boorish newcomers, *parvenu* commoners little better than merchants. This was, to be sure, hardly a new concern in France; during the seventeenth century, the wealthiest noble families, who could trace their nobility and military service to the king back many generations if not centuries, had resented the rush of wealthy commoners into the nobility through the purchase of noble titles. The number of ennobled commoners in the eighteenth century may not have been significantly greater than that in the previous century, but those who were ennobled were wealthier. By the eighteenth century, few noble families could trace their lineage as nobles of the sword back more than a few generations. But those who could still controlled the most important and lucrative offices in the royal bureaucracy, the Church, and the army (although some of the wealthiest families disdained even such lucrative and prestigious service).

The French army began to phase out the purchase of commissions in the late 1770s, and early in the next decade nobles demanded and received royal assurance that their monopoly over the most significant military titles would be respected by the crown. Directed against *parvenu* nobles, the Ségur Law of 1782 asserted that no one could be appointed to a high post in the army who could not demonstrate at least four generations of nobility on his father's side. A year later, the marquis of Ségur quarreled with a recently ennobled secretary of state and threatened to resign from the royal council: "It is war to the death," he insisted, "between the *robe* [nobles who had purchased their titles] and people like us."

However, barriers between the bourgeois and nobles in many places were starting to break down. Wealthy merchants and manufacturers in many states were permitted to purchase titles. In some states, a small number of nobles entered commerce or manufacturing. The expansion of trade and manufacturing led more continental nobles to seek new sources of wealth. French nobles were the principal owners of mines. Swedish nobles contributed to the modest expansion of manufacturing in their country. In eighteenth-century Spain, little stigma was attached to noble commercial ventures, perhaps because there were so many nobles. Russian nobles were particularly noteworthy for undertaking mining projects. In contrast, in Prussia, Poland, and Hungary most nobles still considered participation in commercial activity (above all, retail commerce) or manufacturing to bring derogation, implying a loss of status and honor. Such derogation also, in principle, existed in France, although such was often not the case in reality.

The Changing Condition of the Poor

For millions of people, only a thin line stood between having enough to eat and hunger or starvation, occasional employment and begging, prostitution and petty theft, and between relatively good health and sudden illness and death. Unskilled workers, including male chimney sweeps and market porters, and female domestic servants, seamstresses, embroiderers, braid weavers, and common day laborers, had no protection against the vicissitudes of the market. Such workers lived in rooming houses in the center of cities, or on the edge of town, where rents were cheaper.

If both partners were young, healthy, and could occasionally find work, marriage increased one's odds of survival. But economic crisis often pulled a couple apart, and one partner might be forced to leave to look for work elsewhere. In one village in central France, the priest reported that "in this place there are twenty-four poor families, who have about fifty children begging for the family bread."

At the century's end, almost 30 percent of the British population depended on some sort of poor relief and more than a million people were classified as "paupers" in England and Wales. Laborers, some of whom had been chased from village common lands by parliamentary acts of enclosure, wandered in search of manufacturing work. Thus, the chronically impoverished were constantly on the move, trying to find work. Yet, residents of a given village or neighborhood were far more likely to benefit from local charity than outsiders, who were feared as thieves or worse. Local officials and residents wanted beggars who were not from their community to move on. For this reason, beggars in Austrian law were referred to as "push people," because authorities always sought to push them away.

In France, in particular, many people survived by smuggling, a way of life made possible by the complexity of customs and tax jurisdictions, which made some commodities, above all, salt, much more expensive in one province than another. Prostitution provided a means for some women to get by, practicing their trade until disease or death ended their careers. In one French village, two sisters, unable to survive as seamstresses, admitted their clients as their blind father sat a few feet away. Such was the degradation that the struggle to survive sometimes entailed.

Meager harvests and bitter winters periodically took terrible tolls of the poor (1709–1710, 1739–1740, 1756–1757, 1766, 1775, and 1781–1788), when indigents in France were found frozen to death in church doorways, barns, or fields in the depth of winter. When a severe food shortage occurred or the police expelled beggars from large cities, country roads swarmed with young children who had been abandoned or told by their parents to make their way as best they could. The elderly, particularly widows, were often the poorest of the poor, unable to move elsewhere, depending on neighbors little better off than themselves.

Unlike peasants, who often could find solidarity and some material support in their villages, or upon occasion, from their lords, the urban poor were even more vulnerable to unrelenting misery. In Paris during the 1770s and 1780s, about one person out of six lived—and died—in a state of absolute impoverishment. However, in good times, market "strongmen," or porters, water-carriers, chimney sweeps and ditchdiggers could get by in "the economy of makeshifts."

The urban and rural poor were perpetually undernourished. Bread remained the basis of the diet of the vast majority of Europeans, consuming well more than half the family income—white bread for people of means; black bread (especially in the East), porridge or gruel made from rye, potatoes, or buckwheat (in Brittany and Russia) for everybody else. Vegetables—peas and beans, and cabbage in Central and Eastern Europe—were prized as occasional additions to soup or porridge. The consumption of meat by poor people was rare, except for heavily salted meat that could be preserved. Yet, the orphanage of Amsterdam, a relatively prosperous city, served meat and fish twice a week and vegetables once a week. But dried peas, beans, porridge, or gruel comprised most meals there. Fish and shellfish were common only at the sea's edge for people of ordinary means (especially because they were not allowed to fish in most rivers and ponds). Water, often not very clean, was the drink of necessity; wine and beer were beyond the budget of most people. Swiss peasants prosperous enough to drink coffee and eat chocolate were the exception in Europe. Yet, ordinary people experienced a modest improvement in housing conditions, diet, and health during the century.

Charitable works, however impressive, fell far short of relieving crushing poverty. In France, where about 40 percent of the population lived in poverty, charity could provide less than 5 percent of what was needed. During the Catholic Reformation of the second half of the sixteenth century, the Church had emphasized the importance of charitable works in the quest for eternal salvation. Most Protestants, too, believed in the importance of good works—after all, Christ had washed a beggar's feet. Parishes and, in Catholic countries, monasteries and convents, regularly provided what relief they could afford to the poor, particularly around Christmas and during Lent. Hospices and other charitable institutions cared for the sick, invalids, and the elderly as best they could. But during hard times, the number of abandoned infants increased dramatically, far beyond the capacity of institutions to care for them. Invariably the numbers of the desperately impoverished far exceeded the charitable resources available.

SOCIAL CONTROL

By the middle of the century, many upper-class Europeans believed that they had entered an age of clamoring crowds and even riots. In the 1770s and 1780s, particularly, the lower orders seemed increasingly less deferential. The poor protested the purchase and removal of grain from their markets at prices they could not afford. They stopped wagons, seized grain, and sold it at what they considered to be the "just price," that which would permit even the poor to buy enough to survive.

Artisanal work stoppages, too, became more widespread. Following a London strike by journeymen tailors protesting cuts in their pay, the British Parliament passed the first Combination Act in 1721. The law established wages and working conditions for tailors and allowed the jailing of striking workers without benefit of a trial. Seeing that many craftsmen and skilled workers were leaving Britain, some for the colonies, Parliament passed legislation forbidding their emigration.

Protecting Property

The British Parliament represented the interests of wealthy landowners, who consolidated their property during the eighteenth century. The property franchise ensured that only wealthy landowners could elect members of the House of Commons. The philosopher John Locke summed up the relationship between government and landed property in early modern England: "The great and chief end . . . of men uniting into commonwealths, and putting themselves under government, is the preservation of their property." Thus, in 1723, Parliament passed without discussion a law that added fifty separate offenses against property for which the death penalty could be imposed, although it rarely was.

Hunting was a badge of living nobly. It was a domesticated, non-lethal—at least for the hunters—version of warfare. The exclusive right to hunt was a vigilantly guarded prerogative of any and all who could claim noble status. But acts against poaching were invoked more often to protect the

A gamekeeper snags a poacher.

property of middle-class and even poor landowners. They were not simply measures taken by the rich against the poor.

Wealthy English landowners set brutal mantraps—including trap-guns —and snares that maimed poachers who snuck onto their property, including the "deer parks" established on land that had once been common land. The felonies listed under the Black Act, among them the blackening of one's face as a form of disguise—hence the law's name—included poaching game or fish, or chopping down trees or gleaning branches blown down in storms. Henry Fielding (1707–1754) called attention to such a felony in his novel *The Adventures of Joseph Andrews*: "Jesu!" said the Squire, "would you commit two persons to bridewell [prison] for a twig?" "Yes," said the Lawyer, "and with great leniency too; for if we had called it a young tree they would have been both hanged."

The concern for protecting property could be seen in legislation affecting marriage. The Marriage Act (1753) forbade clandestine marriages. While its central goal was to extend the uniformity of the law, it specifically sought to protect property against ambitious men who might be tempted to try to elope with the daughters of wealthy property owners. Parliament also passed a law permitting divorce by parliamentary act—which none but the very wealthy and well placed could seek—at least partially because gentlemen wanted to be free to divorce wives who shamed them with adultery or who could not produce heirs to inherit their estates.

Subordination and Social Control

During 1724–1733, the French state initiated the "great confinement" of paupers, beggars, and vagrants in workhouses, where they were to learn menial trades under conditions of strict discipline. The subsequent reorganization and expansion of royal efforts at policing the poor during the 1760s represented a marked increase in the reach of the state into rural life, as well as into cities and towns. Police carried out a policy of selective enforcement, in keeping with a current belief in the efficacy of exemplary punishment.

People of means debated strategies of social control with increasing urgency as economic crises in the 1770s and 1780s widened the gap between rich and poor. Some states established temporary programs of poor relief while enhancing the repressive capacity of the police and of hospitals and other institutions that took in vagrants and beggars. Milan's government began locking up beggars. Since the beginning of the seventeenth century, English parishes or townships provided charity to those wearing the requisite "P" for pauper. In order to keep indigents off the road, some towns established workhouses, where the poor would be forced to work in exchange for subsistence. Such places were notoriously unhealthy: of more than 2,300 children taken into London's workhouses during the 1750–1755 period, only 168 were alive at the end of the period (although some might have been discharged). A 1782 English law replaced workhouses with somewhat more humane "poorhouses." In 1795, the Speenhamland system, so called after the parish in which it was conceived, provided for a sliding scale of assistance, determined by the current price of bread and wage rates. But such programs merely scratched the surface as the problem of poverty entered public discourse to an unprecedented degree.

On the continent, the eighteenth century witnessed a largely successful campaign to limit the number of capital crimes to those that threatened life or the state. In contrast, Britain's Parliament added almost two hundred capital offenses to the law between 1688 and 1810, sixty-three of them between 1760 and 1810. About mid-century, two young men were arrested for poaching. Their wives went to the landlord's estate to beg his merciful intercession. The lord, moved to tears, said that their husbands would be returned to them. True to his word, he sent the two corpses to the wives.

But English juries, in particular, hesitated to convict those accused; only about two hundred criminals were executed each year. Executions—including that of a peer who claimed that his marriage had led him to

A public hanging at Tyburn in London.

murder his steward and who had asked to be hanged in his wedding suit—
drew huge throngs at London's Tyburn. Domestics convicted of stealing
from their masters or mistresses or workmen from their employers could
be executed, but corporal punishment, such as branding or being exhibited in stocks to public contempt, was far more common. Children were
worked and punished as adults, though not all as harshly as the seven-
year-old girl who was hanged in Norwich for stealing a petticoat. England
was relatively underpoliced, particularly when compared to France (Paris
had four times more policemen than London, which was twice its size).

The vocabulary adopted by the French police reflected the tendencies of
authorities everywhere to lump the poor into one of two broad categories—"deserving" and "undeserving." Other less general designations
included the poor, the truly poor, the shameful poor, the disabled poor,
the false poor, the indigent, the miserably poor, the beggar of good faith,
the shameful beggar, the professional beggar, and the wandering beggar.
The false beggar simulated horrifying wounds or injuries with the skill of a
makeup artist and, clutching at the clothes of the wealthy passing by, received a few cents as his benefactors scurried away as rapidly as possible.
These categories reflected the belief that many, if not most, of the poor
were destitute because they were lazy and that stiff punishment would be
enough to end begging.

In small bourgs, villages, and the countryside, people feared bands of
thieves, who by setting a fire could intimidate and rob by virtue of their
number, and who could destroy a harvest or a farm in a matter of minutes.
Brigandage was rampant in southern Italy and in Sicily. In France, some of
the most infamous bands were in the grain-rich Beauce region south of

Paris. There some bandits were known as *chauffeurs* because they held their victims' feet to the fire to force the victims to reveal the hiding place of their valuables, a tactic borrowed from marauding soldiers in the Thirty Years' War. Yet, many poor people considered some bandits heroes, Robin Hoods who stole from the rich and gave to the poor. One of the most notorious bands of thieves was organized by a Breton woman, driven to thievery when she could not support her family by peddling haberdashery at fairs. One of her daughters started her own band. It specialized in burglary and held together for ten years, protected by the people of her village, who greeted the police with stony silence and defiant claims that they could not understand the French language. Band members would tear the tongue from the mouth of a beggar who provided the rural police with incriminating information.

A CENTURY OF CONTRASTS

The eighteenth century was a period of contrasts. Musical performances at court and in châteaux and elegant townhouses took place while peasants and day laborers struggled to survive, toiling in fields they rarely owned, in forests belonging to the state or nobles, or working as dock or market porters, chimney sweeps, or common laborers in town. These con-

The capture of the French bandit-hero Cartouche in the early eighteenth century.

trasts were, to be sure, also geographic. The well-heeled financier, whole-sale merchant, manufacturer, or lawyer of Paris, Amsterdam, Barcelona, Vienna, or Milan lived in a vastly more cosmopolitan world, increasingly shaped by consumerism, than did the small middle classes of Prussia, Poland, Russia, and the Balkans, lands in which towns were few and far between. In the northern Italian states and the Austrian Netherlands, prosperous merchants and manufacturers were blurring the lines between nobles and wealthy commoners.

In many ways a century still dominated politically by nobles, the eighteenth century also was a dynamic period of economic and social transformation, beginning with the Industrial Revolution in England, and with the increase in commerce and manufacturing in Northwestern Europe as well. These developments had political consequences during the 1760s and 1770s. The country gentlemen who invariably supported court policies and those who often opposed them began to look and act like political parties. And the domination of political life by an oligarchy of landowners came under challenge from ordinary people without the right to vote. British colonists in North America protested the fact that they were taxed without representation, and then rebelled against British rule.

On the continent, denunciations of unwarranted privilege began to be heard. Calls for reform of the French absolute monarchy came even from one of the ministers of the king, who then tried to abolish guilds and institute free trade. During political crises in the early 1770s, public opinion gradually began to see parlements as blocks against absolute rule and defenders of the rights of the "nation," a term that increasingly came into use. Elsewhere on the continent, too, opposition to entrenched privilege became more insistent in some places. At the same time, the thinkers of the Enlightenment (see Chapter 10) espoused freedom as a good in itself and as a motor of progress. Believing in popular sovereignty and rule by law, they opposed the accumulation of too much power by one or a few people. They, too, called for reform. The French Revolution of 1789 would, at least indirectly, be influenced by these ideals of the Enlightenment.

CHAPTER 10

ENLIGHTENED THOUGHT AND THE REPUBLIC OF LETTERS

"What is the Enlightenment?" wrote the German philosopher Immanuel Kant. His response was *"Dare to know! Have the courage to make use of your own understanding,"* as exciting a challenge today as in the eighteenth century. During that period of contagious intellectual energy and enthusiastic quest for knowledge, the philosophes, the thinkers and writers of the Enlightenment, believed their role was to bring light and progress to the world through the application of reason to their reflections on the nature of mankind. Unlike most scientists of the eighteenth century, they wanted their ideas to reach the general reading public. Education therefore loomed large in this view of their mission. Their approach to education was not limited to formal schooling, but instead took in the development of the individual and the continued application of critical thinking throughout one's life.

The Enlightenment began in Paris but extended to much of Western Europe, including the German states, the Dutch Republic, Great Britain, and as far as North America. The philosophes' writings helped confirm French as the language of high culture in eighteenth-century Europe. Indeed, it was reported from Potsdam that at the court of Frederick the Great of Prussia "the language least spoken is German." But French was hardly the only language of philosophic discourse. In Italy, those influenced by the new thinking used the ideas of the philosophes to attack clerical and particularly papal influence in political life. In Britain the philosopher David Hume and Adam Smith, father of economic liberalism, represented the thought of "the Scottish Enlightenment."

The Enlightenment can be roughly divided into three stages. The first covers the first half of the eighteenth century and most directly reflects the influence of the Scientific Revolution; the second, the "high Enlight-

A metal struck to commemorate the death of John Locke. The two figures symbolize tolerance and justice.

enment," begins with the publication of *The Spirit of the Laws* (1748) by Charles-Louis de Montesquieu and ends in 1778 with the death of Voltaire and Jean-Jacques Rousseau; and the third, the late Enlightenment, influenced by Rousseau's work, marks a shift from an emphasis on human reason to a greater preoccupation with the emotions and passions of mankind. This final stage also features new ideas relating the concept of freedom to the working of economies, best represented by the thought of Adam Smith. At this time, too, several monarchs applied the philosophes' principle that rulers work for the good of their subjects. But these experiments in "enlightened absolutism" were most noted for rulers' organizing their states more effectively, further enhancing their authority. This third period saw popular diffusion of the lesser works of would-be philosophes seeking to capitalize on an expanding literary market. These works, too, were influential in undermining respect for the authority of the monarchy of France and thus indirectly contributed to the French Revolution.

ENLIGHTENED IDEAS

The philosophes espoused views of nature, mankind, society, government, and the intrinsic value of freedom that challenged some of the most fundamental tenets Europeans had held for centuries. Slavery, for example, violated their principle of human freedom. The implications of Enlightenment thought were revolutionary, because the philosophes argued that progress had been constrained by social and political institutions that did not reflect humanity's natural goodness and capacity for material and moral improvement. Although many philosophes saw no or little incompatibility between science and religion, they were skeptical of received truths. Thus, they challenged the doctrinal authority of the established churches and launched a crusade for the secularization of political institutions.

It is to the Enlightenment that we trace the origins of the belief that people should be ruled by law, not rulers, that a separation of powers ought to exist within government in order to prevent the accumulation of too much power in one or a few hands, the concept of popular sovereignty, and the assumption that it is the responsibility of rulers to look after the welfare of the people. The consequences of such modern views of sovereignty, political rights, and the organization of states would be seen in the French Revolution and the era of liberalism in the nineteenth century.

Intellectual Influences on Enlightened Thought

Like all intellectual and cultural movements, the Enlightenment did not emerge spontaneously. Creating what David Hume (1711–1776) called "the science of man," the philosophes reflected the influence of the Scientific Revolution, whose proponents had espoused scientific method in the study of nature and the universe. Sir Isaac Newton, the brilliant English scientist and theoretician (see Chapter 8), emphasized that science—reason and experimentation—holds the key to understanding nature, that mankind discovers knowledge, not through religious teaching, but through "observation, analysis, and experiment."

Two thinkers linked the Scientific Revolution and Enlightenment thought: John Locke and Georges-Louis Buffon. Locke (1632–1704) claimed that philosophy was, as much as astronomy, a discipline subject to the rigors of scientific method and critical inquiry. The son of a landowner and a member of the scientific-minded British Royal Society, Locke maintained a strong interest in medicine. After returning from Holland, where he had gone into self-imposed exile during the political crisis swirling around the throne of King James II, Locke remained close to the government of King William and Queen Mary.

Locke believed that the scientific method could be applied to the study of society. In *An Essay Concerning Human Understanding* (1690), Locke postulated that each individual is a *tabula rasa,* or blank slate at birth. Believing that all knowledge is sensory, Locke denied inherited abilities and rejected the idea that humanity is stained by original sin. He anticipated that the discovery of more laws of nature would be the basis of secular laws on which society should be based. He was confident that mankind might thereby be able to improve social conditions.

Locke had asserted the dignity of the individual in contending that every person has the right to life, liberty, and property (though he excluded slaves in the Americas from such innate rights). He argued that monarchies were based on a social contract between rulers and the ruled. People had to relinquish some of their liberty in exchange for security. But, unlike Thomas Hobbes, Locke insisted that mankind's liberty and rights stemmed from the laws of nature. He became a leading proponent of educational reform, freedom of the press, religious toleration, and the separation of political powers.

Locke's interest in the relationship between nature and the social order led him to consider issues of gender. The assumption that the king ruled his nation as a husband and father ruled his wife and children had been prominent in early modern political theory, only briefly challenged by a handful of radicals during the English Civil War of the 1640s. John Locke argued against the contemporary vision of the state in which "all power on earth is either derived from or usurped from the fatherly power." He denied the appropriateness of the analogy between the family and the state as patriarchal institutions. Rejecting the contemporary view that Adam held supremacy over Eve, he viewed marriage, like government, to be organized by social contract. However, Locke went no further than that, and his espousal of equality within marriage remained only an ideal. In everyday life, he believed that women should defer to men. But Locke's precocious analysis of the family as an institution nonetheless helped stimulate intellectual interest in studying the social role of women.

More than any of his contemporaries, Georges-Louis Buffon (1707–1788) linked the Scientific Revolution to the Enlightenment. Buffon, whose initial presentation to the French Royal Academy of Science was a study of probability theory applied to gambling on hopscotch, became the curator of the Royal Gardens. Surrounded by monkeys and badgers in his laboratory, he carried out many experiments, some of which worked, such as his study of the burning effect of the sun through glass, and some of which did not, including his study of the emotional life of birds. Buffon's experiments with cooling metals led him to build a large forge near his home in Burgundy.

The philosophes acknowledged their debt to the late-seventeenth-century proponents of the scientific method. Voltaire saluted Newton, whose funeral he attended in London's Westminster Abbey, for having called on scientists and philosophers "to examine, weigh, calculate, and measure, but never conjecture." Hume insisted that all knowledge came from reason and experience, that is, from critical inquiry and scientific discovery, and that the ability to reason distinguished mankind from other animals. Many philosophes, reflecting the influence of the Scientific Revolution, considered religion, the origins of which they found not in reason but in faith and custom, to be a social phenomenon, like any other to be studied scientifically. Hume blasted away at the idea of religious truths revealed through the Bible. Montesquieu asked, "Is it possible for those who understand nature and have a reasonable idea of God to believe that matter and created things are only 6,000 years old?"

The very universality of their principles led some of the philosophes to suggest that a sense of morality—of what is right and wrong—might vary across cultures, because it emerged from the nature of mankind, but not from religious teaching. Diderot, influenced by Locke, argued that sensory stimulation, or in the case of people who are blind, deprivation, shapes individual moral responses, and that moral principles for a blind man might be somewhat different from those for someone who could see. He described the so-called "savages" of distant Tahiti as forming a rational social order without the benefit of any ecclesiastical doctrine. Hume called for a "science of morals" to serve the interests of Christians, and found a following among Scottish Presbyterian clergy.

The Republic of Ideas

The philosophes' calls for reform were sometimes subtle, sometimes boldly forceful. Yet, they did not lead insurrections. Their pens and pencils were their only weapons as they sought to change the way people thought. They communicated their ideas in letters, unpublished manuscripts, books, pamphlets, brochures, and through writing novels, poetry, drama, literary and art criticism, and political philosophy.

The philosophes glorified the collegiality and interdependence of writers within the "republic of letters," what the men and women of the Enlightenment sometimes called the informal international community of philosophes. By the mid-eighteenth century, Voltaire could claim with some exaggeration that the professional writer stood at the top of the social summit. He, Montesquieu, and Denis Diderot accepted election to the prestigious French Royal Academy, revealing their ambivalence toward the monarchy that they attacked, however subtly, in their work. The most famous of the philosophes gained money as well as prestige, although Voltaire, Montesquieu, and Holbach were among the few who could support themselves by writing.

The philosophes may have shared the fundamental ideas of the Enlightenment, but significant differences existed among them. They came from different social classes, generations, and nations. And they often disagreed, like people in any republic, arguing in person, by letter, and in their published work. They could not agree, for example, whether the ideal state was an enlightened, benevolent monarchy, a monarchy balanced by a parliamentary body representing the nobility, or a kind of direct democracy. Their views on religion also varied. Montesquieu, Voltaire, and Rousseau were deists. Because scientific inquiry seemed to have demonstrated that the persistent intervention of God was unnecessary to keep the world in motion, they viewed God as a watchmaker who set the world in motion according to the laws of nature and then left knowledge and hu-

Voltaire presiding (with his arm raised) over a dinner gathering of philosophes, including Denis Diderot, who is sitting on the far left.

man progress to the discovery and action of mankind. In contrast, Diderot, one of the principal spokesmen of the Enlightenment, became an atheist.

For all the variety and richness of the republic of letters, four philosophes dominated Enlightenment discourse with what were for the time truly startling ideas about society, religion, and politics: Montesquieu, Voltaire, Diderot, and Rousseau. Each is well worth considering separately.

Montesquieu

Montesquieu (born Charles-Louis de Secondat; 1689–1755) inherited a feudal château near Bordeaux and a small income upon the death of his father. He studied law and later inherited from a wealthy relative more property and the title of baron de Montesquieu, as well as the presidency of the noble parlement, or provincial sovereign law court, seated at Bordeaux.

In 1721, after moving to Paris, Montesquieu published the *Persian Letters*. In the form of reports sent home by two Persian visitors to Paris, his work detailed political and social injustices of life in the West. By casting this critique of eighteenth-century France in the form of a travelogue, Montesquieu was able to dodge royal censorship. The work irritated many people, including ecclesiastics who resented its insinuation that the pope was a "magician." As for the king of France, the Persians reported that he "is the most powerful of European potentates. He has no mines of gold like his neighbor, the king of Spain: but he is much wealthier than that prince, because his riches are drawn from a more inexhaustible source, the vanity of his subjects. He has undertaken and carried on great wars, without any other supplies than those derived from the sale of titles of honors." But beneath the satire of the *Persian Letters,* Montesquieu was arguing the point that nature reveals a universal standard of justice that applies for all people in all places at all times, in Islamic Persia as in Christian France.

Montesquieu's ideas reflected the increased contact between Europeans and much of the rest of the world. Merchants, soldiers, missionaries, and colonists had followed the first European explorers to, among other places, the Americas and Asia. Published accounts of travel stirred the imagination of upper-class Europeans who were interested in their societies and in cultures that lay on the fringes or beyond their continent.

In *Persian Letters,* Montesquieu also offered the first critical examination of the institution of slavery by one of the philosophes. He rejected slavery as an extension of despotism, concluding that "slavery is against natural law, by which all men are born free and independent" because "the liberty of each citizen is part of public liberty." He argued that slavery, in contrast, compromised "the general good of men [and] that of particular societies."

The Spirit of the Laws (1748) inaugurated the high Enlightenment. In it, Montesquieu applied the principles of observation, experimentation, and analysis, which lie at the heart of scientific inquiry, to the social and political foundations of states. He described the relationship between climate, religion, and tradition, and the historical evolution of a nation's political life. Laws, he argued, are subject to critical inquiry and historical study because they develop over time. Historians, freeing themselves from the influence of the Church, could now study "general causes, whether moral or physical."

The British political system fascinated Montesquieu, who went to England in 1729 for two years. He was impressed by the historical role of Parliament, a representative body unlike French parlements, or law courts, despite the similarity of their names. The English Parliament seemed an "intermediate power" that had during the Civil War prevented Britain from becoming either a monarchical despotism or a republic, which he identified with chaos. Montesquieu's point was that each political system and legal tradition evolved differently. He feared that the French monarchy was showing signs of becoming despotic because it lacked the separation of powers found in England. Only constitutionalism, he argued, could combine the guarantees for order (offered by monarchy) with those of freedom. Montesquieu believed that noble rights and the maintenance of municipal privileges that had long been eroded by royal absolutism in France could stave off monarchical depotism. Moreover, Montesquieu ar-

(*Left*) Montesquieu. (*Right*) Voltaire.

gued that the sovereignty of the king came not from God, but from the people.

Voltaire

Brilliant, witty, and sarcastic, Voltaire (born François-Marie Arouet; 1694–1778) was the most widely read, cited, and lionized of the philosophes. He was the son of a notary who had enhanced his family's position through a favorable marriage. Voltaire's parents, who wanted him to be a lawyer, sent him to Paris to be educated by the Jesuits. Instead, the brash, ambitious young man made a name for himself as a dramatist and poet—though many of these early works are quite forgettable. Voltaire developed a pen as quick and cutting as a sword. Some of his early works were banned in France; everything he ever wrote was forbidden in Spain. Imprisoned in the Bastille in Paris for having mocked one of the king's relatives, he took the name "de Voltaire" for unknown reasons. He soon ran into more trouble, beaten by servants while a noble he had insulted watched in silent triumph.

Like Montesquieu, Voltaire reflected the Anglophilia of the thinkers of the early and high Enlightenment. He extolled Britain, its commercial empire, relative religious toleration, and freedom of the press. "The English are the only people on earth," he wrote, "who have been able to prescribe limits to the power of kings by resisting them: and who, by a series of struggles, have at last established that wise Government, where the Prince is all powerful to do good, and at the same time is restrained from committing evil."

Unlike the noble Montesquieu, who hoped the parlements would balance the power of the monarchy, as they did in Britain, Voltaire had little faith in them. Voltaire saw them as representing the narrow and selfish interests of the nobility. He believed that the only representative body that might guarantee the natural rights of the king's subjects in France would be the equivalent of the British House of Commons. Whereas Montesquieu looked to the nobility to protect people from monarchical despotism, Voltaire counted on the enlightened monarchs of centralized states to protect their people against nobles' self-interest.

Voltaire claimed that the political organization of each state was at least partially determined by its specific history and circumstances. As science should study the world of nature, so should the philosophe trace the separate development of nations. This line of reasoning convinced him that Montesquieu was wrong to think that the British political system could be successfully transplanted to France.

Voltaire reserved his most scathing attacks for the Church, an institution, like the parlements, that seemed to him to block the development of freedom in his own country. His impassioned cry for a battle against the teaching of the Church—"*Écrasez l'infâme!*" ("Crush the horrible thing!")—became his motto. Of monks, he once said, "They sing, they eat, they digest." The pope and the Parlement of Paris both condemned his polemical *Philosophical Dictionary* (1764). Voltaire believed that there were times when one has to tear down before one can build. His attacks were clever yet devastating; for example, his pithy description of the Chinese as having "an admirable religion free from superstition and the rage to persecute" was read by virtually everyone as suggesting that in France the opposite was true.

Voltaire, a deist, believed that God created the universe and then let it operate according to scientific laws. He espoused a natural religion based upon reason while repudiating the Church itself. "Almost everything that goes beyond the adoration of a supreme being and of submitting one's heart to his eternal order is superstition . . . the fewer superstitions, the less fanaticism; and the less fanaticism, the fewer calamities," he insisted. At least some of what has often been taken for his anti-Semitism was, in fact, part of Voltaire's unrestrained assault on what he considered another variety of religious dogmatism built not upon reason but on faith alone.

Voltaire intended *Candide* (1759) to be an indictment of fanaticism and superstition. In the short tale, the cheerful optimist Candide bumbles from disaster to disaster. Here Voltaire confronts the seeming contradiction between the goodness of God and the evil in the world. He writes about the earthquake that ravaged Lisbon in 1755, killing thousands of people and destroying much of the Portuguese capital. If God is all good and omniscient, why, Voltaire reasoned, would He allow such an event to occur?

But Voltaire nonetheless believed that religion was beneficial because it offered people hope, and therefore made their lives more bearable. It also kept them in line: "If God did not exist, one would have to invent him. I want my attorney, my tailor, my servants, even my wife to believe in God, and I think that I shall then be robbed and cuckholded less often." Voltaire's belief that religion provided a public service by inducing people to act according to moral principles contrasted with that of Diderot, who believed that mankind's essential goodness made organized religion unnecessary.

Voltaire's fame spread when he took up the cause of a man who seemed wrongly accused of murder. In 1761, Jean Calas, a Protestant from Toulouse, stood accused of murdering his own son, who had been found hanging in the family basement. The young Calas had intended to convert to Catholicism. Convicted by the Parlement of Toulouse, the father was tortured to death, though it seemed likely that his son had committed suicide. Voltaire launched a campaign against the parlement. He began his own investigation, attacking what seemed a preposterous conviction followed by barbaric torture. Several years later, the parlement reversed its earlier decision—too late, however, for Jean Calas. But the Calas Affair helped put the philosophes' critique of religious intolerance into the limelight of public opinion. "Shout everywhere, I beg you, for Calas," thundered Voltaire, "and against fanaticism, for it is *l'infâme* that has caused their misery."

Voltaire's energetic interest in the Calas Affair reflected not only his scathing rejection of the notion that "this is the best of all possible worlds" but also his insistence that progress is somehow inevitable without human action. He concludes *Candide* with the famous, though seemingly ambiguous, advice that "one must cultivate one's own garden," as he did at his rural retreat. But Voltaire was counseling anything but a withdrawal into the sanctuary of introspection. He called for each person to follow the path of light and do battle with those institutions that seemed to stand in the way of humanity's potential. The possibility of human action gave Voltaire confidence and hope. In 1764 he predicted, "Everything I see scatters the seeds of a revolution which will definitely come . . . Enlightenment has gradually spread so widely that it will burst into full light at the first right opportunity, and then there will be a fine uproar. Lucky are the young, for they will see great things."

Denis Diderot

Diderot's monumental *Encyclopedia* best reflected the collaborative nature of the Enlightenment, as well as its wide influence. Denis Diderot (1713–1784), the son of an artisan, was something of a jack of intellectual trades, a man of letters who wrote plays, art criticism, history, theology, and philosophy. Like Voltaire educated by the Jesuits, he flirted with the idea of becoming a priest, and for a time supported himself by writing sermons for bishops. Unlike Montesquieu and Voltaire, Diderot underwent a

An illustration of mining in Denis Diderot's *Encyclopedia.*

rugged apprenticeship in the "republic of letters." He penned a porno-graphic novel to earn enough to indulge the fancies of his mistress. But he also argued that through centuries of male domination, women, despite their capacity for reproduction, had come to be considered inferior to men. Diderot claimed that laws that limited the rights of women were counter to nature.

The *Encyclopedia,* on which Diderot worked for twenty-five years, stands as the greatest monument of the Enlightenment. At the heart of the project lay the philosophes' insistence that knowledge was rational, and therefore ordered, following laws of nature. Social and political institu-tions should be submitted to standards of rationality. All things, as Diderot put it, are equally subject to criticism. By elevating mankind to the center of human inquiry, the authors of the *Encyclopedia* sought to achieve Diderot's goal, "to change the general way of thinking," as well as to bring glory to France.

Voltaire had set a goal for the Enlightenment itself: to educate the liter-ate and intellectually curious of the social elite, and perhaps people fur-ther down the social scale. The *Encyclopedia* at least partially fulfilled that goal. Published over a period of more than twenty years beginning in 1751, it consisted of 60,000 articles and 2,885 illustrations in twenty-eight volumes. Subtitled "A Classified Dictionary of the Sciences, Arts and

Trades," this first such compilation in the West was a bold attempt to organize and classify all knowledge gathered from "over the face of the earth." Its authors insisted that by learning more about the universe, men and women could improve the world. This marked a departure from the assumption that mankind's ability to penetrate the secrets of the universe was limited. Montesquieu contributed sections on taste, Rousseau on music, Voltaire on literature, and Buffon on nature. Diderot gave particular credit to the contributions of everyday artisans by describing how and why ingeniously simple tools and machines could make tasks easier.

The *Encyclopedia* generated sufficient excitement that advance sales alone financed its publication. It earned its publishers a handsome profit. After the first edition, subsequent editions with less expensive paper and fewer illustrations became available at about a sixth of the original price. Lawyers, officials, and rentiers (people living from property income) were more likely to own a copy than merchants or manufacturers, who could afford the volumes but seemed less interested. What began as a luxury product ended up on the shelves of the "middling sort."

The philosophes wanted the *Encyclopedia* to carry the Enlightenment far beyond the borders of France. Although only about one in ten volumes traveled beyond the country, its pattern of distribution in the 1770s and 1780s reflected the success of the enterprise (see Map 10.1). To contemporaries, the *Encyclopedia* seemed to embody Kant's bold challenge, "Dare to know!"

Through Swiss, Dutch, and German booksellers, among others, the *Encyclopedia* reached readers in London, Brussels, Turin, Munich, and St. Petersburg, among other European capitals. The *Encyclopedia*'s prospectus and booksellers' advertisements assured potential buyers that ownership would proclaim one's standing as a person of knowledge, a philosophe. In northern Germany and Scandinavia, customers were described as "sovereign princes" and "Swedish seigneurs." A few copies reached distant African settlements, including the Cape of Good Hope. Thomas Jefferson helped promote the *Encyclopedia* in America, finding several subscribers, among them Benjamin Franklin. There was an Italian edition, despite the opposition of the Church, and a priest was among those taking orders for it. However, in Spain, Inquisition censorship frightened booksellers and buyers alike, and in Portugal only a few copies got by the police.

The *Encyclopedia* did implicitly challenge monarchical authority. It presented ideas that some powerful people did not want in the public domain. Rousseau and Paul-Henri Holbach (1723–1789) wrote enthusiastically about representative government and even popular sovereignty, though only Rousseau came close to espousing a republic.

After initially tolerating the project, French royal censors banned Volume 7 in 1757, after an unsuccessful assassination attempt on Louis XV. Diderot, whose first serious philosophical work had been burned by the

MAP 10.1 DIFFUSION OF DIDEROT'S *ENCYCLOPEDIA* Subscriptions to Diderot's *Encyclopedia* throughout Europe.

public executioner, was briefly imprisoned before being released on a promise of good behavior. Although the philosophes left their skeptical challenge to the Church implicit, disguising the pope in one satire as a figure in Japanese robes, the pope condemned the volumes in 1759.

In the 1770s, the French state again tolerated the *Encyclopedia*, which it now treated more as a commodity than as an ideological threat to monarchy or Church. The small skirmishes fought over the volumes had more to do with rivalries between publishers, between those privileged with official favor and those without. In this way, Diderot's grand project symbolized the ongoing political struggles within the French monarchy itself.

Jean-Jacques Rousseau

The place of Jean-Jacques Rousseau (1712–1778) in the Enlightenment is far more ambiguous than that of Diderot and his *Encyclopedia*. Rousseau embraced human freedom, but more than any other of the philosophes, Rousseau idealized emotion, instinct, and spontaneity, which he believed to be, with reason, essential parts of human nature.

The son of a Geneva watchmaker, Rousseau, a Protestant, went to Paris as a young man in the hope of becoming a composer. The arrogant, self-righteous Rousseau received an introduction into several aristocratic Parisian salons, informal upper-class gatherings hosted by noble women at which ideas were discussed, where he became friendly with Diderot. In 1749, the Academy of Dijon sponsored an essay contest on the question of whether the progress of science had strengthened or weakened morality. Rousseau's essay concluded that primitive or natural humanity had embodied the essential goodness of mankind; and that in order for humanity to be happy, new social and political institutions would be necessary. Young Rousseau won first prize.

Rousseau remained a contentious loner. By 1762, he had quarreled with the other philosophes. Voltaire mocked his insistence that emotion and passion held sway over pure reason. Exiled by the Parlement of Paris because his writings offended monarchy and Church, he moved back to his native Geneva. After being forced to leave Geneva in the early 1770s following the condemnation of his work, he abandoned his children in an orphanage—as his father had abandoned him—and set off to visit England. The rest of Rousseau's life was marked by increasingly quarrelsome and paranoid behavior. He assumed that when his former friends disagreed with his ideas, they knew that he was right but simply refused to admit it. Gradually he became overwhelmed with thoughts of revenge against those whom he considered to have wronged him. In his *Confessions* (the first volume of which appeared in 1782), he appealed to future generations to see how contemporary thinkers had misinterpreted or misrepresented him.

(*Left*) Portrait of Jean-Jacques Rousseau. (*Right*) Rousseau and Voltaire in symbolic battle, a clash of ideas and wills.

In his *Discourse on the Arts and Sciences* (1762), Rousseau argued that civilization had corrupted the natural goodness of man, which he called the "fundamental principle" of political thought. The untempered quest for private property had disrupted the harmony that had once characterized mankind in its primitive state by creating a hierarchy of wealth. Rousseau's idealization of relatively primitive, uncomplicated and, he thought, manageable social and political groupings led him to believe that a republic, such as his own Geneva, alone offered its citizens the possibility of freedom. Its size permitted men wealthy enough to enjoy full political rights to participate directly in decision making. However, Rousseau remained suspicious of representative government, believing that people might ultimately vote themselves into slavery by electing unworthy representatives.

As free people in primitive societies joined together for mutual protection, enlightened people could join together for their mutual development in a kind of direct democracy. This view more than likely reflected his support for artisans' guilds and other small, self-governing groups that characterized Old Regime France. In Rousseau's idealized small state, executive authority would be separate from, yet subordinate to, the legislative power. He was, however, vague on how precisely people were to be organized and governed.

The final period of the Enlightenment prefigured nineteenth-century romanticism by giving emotion more free play, as the sensitive individual is awed by nature. Rousseau's *Émile* (1762) became one of the literary sensations of the century. Beginning "Everything is good as it comes from the hands of the Author of nature, but everything degenerates in the hands of man," the novel describes what he considered to be the ideal natural, secular education of the young Émile, who is gradually exposed by his tutor to nature during walks to explore brooks and mills. Rousseau intended such wonders to stimulate Émile's emotions, which were to be developed before his sense of reason, "the one that develops last," Rousseau claims, "and with the greatest difficulty." Émile's primitive virtue must be preserved against the vices of culture, but also developed as an end in itself so that he becomes a developed, autonomous person. Rousseau assigns Sophie, Émile's chosen "well-born" spouse, an education appropriate to what Rousseau considered a woman's lower status in life. Yet, even Rousseau's insistence on the capacity of women for intellectual development surprised many contemporaries, and was ahead of its time.

Voltaire ridiculed Rousseau's espousal of primitiveness as virtue: "I have received, Monsieur, your new book against the human race, and I thank you. No one has employed so much intelligence turning men into beasts. One starts wanting to walk on all fours after reading your book. However, in more than sixty years I have lost the habit." But, in fact, Rousseau clearly believed in social organization, because it seemed to offer mankind the possibility of achieving freedom from revealed religious truths.

In *The Social Contract* (1762), Rousseau tried to resolve the question of how people could join together in society to find protection and justice for person and property, and yet remain free individuals. Locke had described the relationship between a ruler and his people as a contractual one. Hobbes, in contrast, had argued that individuals could find refuge from the brutality of the state of nature only by surrendering their rights to an absolute ruler in exchange for safety. Rousseau imagined a social contract in which the individual surrenders his or her natural rights to the "general will" in order to find order and security. By general will, Rousseau meant the consensus of a community of citizens with equal political rights. Citizens would live in peace because they would be ruled by other citizens, not by dynastic rulers eager to expand their territorial holdings.

Although *The Social Contract* remained largely unknown until after the French Revolution of 1789, it offered an unparalleled critique of contemporary society. Rousseau summed up his thinking with the stirring assertion that "men are born free yet everywhere they are in chains." Whereas Voltaire and other philosophes hoped that rulers would become enlightened, Rousseau insisted that sovereignty comes not from kings or oligarchies, or even from God. Sovereignty comes, he argued persuasively, through the collective search for freedom.

THE DIFFUSION AND EXPANSION OF THE ENLIGHTENMENT

The groundwork for the Enlightenment lay not only in the realm of ideas—those of the Scientific Revolution and Locke—but also in gradual social changes that affected the climate of opinion. These changes, especially but not exclusively found in France, included the declining role of religion in the eighteenth century, at least in some regions, and the emergence of a more broadly based culture.

Religious Enthusiasm and Skepticism

During the first half of the seventeenth century, the Catholic Reformation seems to have engendered a slow but steady religious revival in France, Spain, and the Habsburg domains, where the founding of new religious orders, monasteries, and the popularity of the cults and shrines of local saints reflected religious intensity. Moreover, the established churches still retained formidable authority and prestige.

The development late in the seventeenth century of Pietism among Protestants in the North German states, emphasizing preaching and the study of the Bible, reflected another dimension of both mounting dissatisfaction with established religions and the existence of considerable religious creativity. Disaffected by abstract theological debates and by the Lutheran Church's hierarchical structure, Pietists wanted to reaffirm the Protestant belief in the primacy of the individual conscience. Like English Puritans and French Jansenists, they called for a more austere religion. They wanted a revival of piety and good works, and asked that laymen take an active role in religious life. For Pietists, Bible-reading and small discussion groups replaced the more elaborate, formal services of the Lutherans, helping to expand interest in German language and culture among the upper classes. But by the last quarter of the century, Pietist influence had waned, reflecting not only the diffusion of Enlightenment thought but also the fact that Lutheranism remained the state religion in the northern German states, maintaining a hold on the universities. Likewise the fact that Jansenists were able to win and maintain a wide following in France, despite official proscription, can be taken as evidence of the strength of religious feeling.

In Britain, religious practice seems to have increased among all social classes. The Anglican Church of England was the Established Church, but Britain also had about half a million non-Anglican Protestants, or Dissenters, at the end of the eighteenth century. As many were middle class, some Presbyterians, Congregationalists, Unitarians, Baptists, and Quakers sent their sons to private academies. Yet, Oxford and Cambridge Universities admitted only Anglicans. Moreover, anti-Catholicism was still prevalent in England, where there were about 70,000 Catholics in 1770, most of them in the lower classes.

Although many Baptists, Congregationalists, and Quakers, among other Dissenters, had traditionally been laborers, there was not a particular religion that held the allegiance of ordinary people in England in the eighteenth century until the ministry of John Wesley (1703–1791). An

Anglican trained in theology at Oxford, the intense, brooding Wesley began to believe that his mission was to infuse ordinary people (who seemed ignored by the Established Church) with religious enthusiasm.

Wesley never formally broke with the Anglican Church nor claimed to be setting up a new denomination. Yet, that was the effect of his lifetime of preaching directly to ordinary people on grassy knolls, in open fields, and on highways, and of writing religious tracts directed at ordinary Britons. Wesley, who is said to have given more than 40,000 sermons, attracted about 100,000 followers to Methodism. Stressing personal conversion, Methodism suggested that all people were equal before God's eyes. This offended some upper-class English men and women, not the least because Methodists shouted out their beliefs and sometimes publicly confessed sins that the upper classes thought best left unnamed. A duchess explained that she hated the Methodists, because "it is monstrous to be told that you have a heart as sinful as the common wretches that crawl on the earth. This is highly offensive and insulting and at variance with high rank and good breeding."

Methodist evangelism was both a dynamic and stabilizing force in British society. There was little or nothing politically or socially radical about Wesley, as shown by his unwillingness to break formally with the Established Church. Far from preaching rebellion or revolution, Wesley encouraged work and self-discipline and abstinence from dancing, drinking, and gambling. Popular protest affronted Wesley's sense of respectability.

The Angelican Church, in turn, began to recruit followers among the lower classes. It established associations like the Society for the Promotion of Christian Knowledge and Anglican Sunday schools, which provided poor children with food and catechism. The evangelical Hannah More (1745–1833), the "bishop in petticoats," abandoned the material comforts of upper-class life for the challenges of bringing religion to the poor. In general, although some evangelicals favored improvements in working conditions, most remained politically conservative.

Yet, by the middle of the eighteenth century, in some of Europe religion seemed to play a significantly smaller role in the lives of people of all classes, particularly in regions with expanding economies and relatively high literacy rates. The number of men and women entering the clergy in France declined, as male and female monastic orders lost a third of their members between 1770 and 1790 alone. Fewer wills requested that Masses be said for the deceased or for souls in Purgatory. A Venetian theologian at mid-century claimed that the people of his state had become "de-christianized." Popular dislike of the exemption of the clergy from taxes increased, although the Church offered the monarchy a sizable yearly contribution from its vast wealth. Thus, the philosophes who challenged the role of the established churches in public life were addressing many readers who had lost interest in organized religion.

Expansion of the Cultural Base

The growing influence of the middle class in England and Northwestern Europe also began slowly to transform cultural life, expanding interest in literature, music, and the arts. The number of literary and other associations reflected this change. Lines between the nobility and the wealthy bourgeoisie became less fixed; culture moved from the closed world of court and château into the public domain.

Increasing literacy expanded the size of the potential audience of the philosophes. By the end of the century, somewhere between half and two-thirds of men in England, France, the Netherlands, and the German states could read. A smaller proportion of women—between a third to a half of the female population of these countries—was literate. A far smaller percentage of people could read in Southern Europe, and few people indeed in Eastern Europe and Russia. Opportunities for women, even those from noble families, to obtain more than a minimal education remained quite rare, although several German states began schools for girls. Even Marie-Antoinette, queen of France and one of the wealthiest people in the world, was so poorly educated that she made frequent grammatical and spelling errors.

Publishers, for example in the northern Italian states of Tuscany and Venice, fed the growing appetites of readers eager to know what events were transpiring in their own and other countries. Newspapers published one or two times a week summarized events transpiring in other countries. The number of English periodicals increased sixfold between 1700 and 1780, reflecting an increasing interest in science and natural history. In the German states, the number of books and magazines published grew threefold during the century's last decades. Novels gained in popularity at the expense of books on theology and popular piety. English female novelists gave women an unprecedented public voice in Britain, presenting their heroines as affectionate companions to their husbands and good mothers. Sentimental novels presented syrupy stories of domestic life and tender love. Nevertheless, traditional literature, such as religious tracts, popular almanacs, and folktales, remained the most widely read literature.

The Enlightenment had a direct influence on the growing popularity of history. Reflecting their interest in understanding human experience, the philosophes helped create history as a modern discipline. Since the classical Greeks, there had been relatively little interest in history in Europe. Church fathers, espousing the primacy of theology and viewing the world as little more than a test to prepare Christians for the afterlife, were generally uninterested in history. But suddenly all human experience, including non-Western cultures, emerged as suitable for historical inquiry. Edward Gibbon (1737–1794) was inspired to undertake his *History of the Decline and Fall of the Roman Empire* (published over a period of twelve years beginning in 1776) by visiting the Colosseum of Rome. Natural science, too, developed a following.

There were also more lending libraries than ever before, at least in Western Europe, as well as reading circles or clubs, some organized by resourceful booksellers. In Paris, London, Milan, Berlin, and other large cities, lending libraries rented books for as short a period as an hour. Household libraries became more common. Reading, which heretofore had largely been a group activity in which a literate person read to others—in the same way that storytellers spun their yarns—became more of a private, individual undertaking.

While some of the most significant works of the Enlightenment were virtually unknown outside the republic of letters, others became the bestsellers of the age. Montesquieu's *Spirit of the Laws* went through twenty-two printings—approximately 35,000 copies—in the first eighteen months after publication in 1748. Buffon's thirty-volume study, *The System of Nature* (1749–1804)—despite its bulk—also enjoyed prodigious success. Voltaire's short novel *Candide* was reprinted eight times in 1759, the year of its publication. Abbé Guillaume Raynal's *The Philosophical and Political History of European Colonies and Commerce in the Two Indies* (1770) was reprinted seventy times. Its descriptions of the colonization of the New World, Asia, and Africa, including the development of the slave trade, which he denounced in no uncertain terms, reached an eager market.

Painting

The philosophes sought the same status and freedom for artists as they demanded for writers. They believed that the arts had to be unfettered by censorship in order to thrive, and subject to critical inquiry. Critics helped shape public taste with reviews of paintings, circulated as pamphlets, which generated strong debate and comment.

Some philosophes worked toward a philosophy of art, but they did not espouse a single theory. The distinguished English portrait painter Joshua Reynolds (1723–1792), president of the Royal Academy, believed that classical rules preserved from antiquity had to be followed. But Hume, among other Enlightenment figures, emphasized the aesthetic appreciation of art, rejecting formal rules or standards for art imposed by royal academies or ecclesiastical influence. Diderot, who wrote two mediocre plays, and the German dramatist and critic Gotthold Lessing (1729–1781) called for the theater to portray the lives and passions of ordinary people, instead of only kings and queens, princes and princesses, saints and sinners.

The secularization of culture could be seen in the development of rococo, a new and generally secular decorative style. It evolved from the highly ornamental baroque style that had characterized the art and architecture of the Catholic Reformation, particularly in Austria and Bavaria.

A room in a nobleman's elegant townhouse, furnished in the rococo style.

Closely tied to noble taste, rococo's popularity in France reflected the fact that many nobles now spent more time away from Versailles, in their own country châteaux or, above all, in elegant Parisian townhouses. However spacious, such urban residences afforded them less room than they enjoyed in the countryside. They therefore lavished more attention on decoration.

The rococo style—sometimes called Louis XV style—began in France but also became quite popular in the German and Italian states. Like the baroque, it featured flowing curves, thus suggesting rocks and shells (*rocailles* and *coquilles*), forming its name. Rococo stresses smallness of scale, reducing baroque forms to elegant decorative style, as in gilded molding for theaters or manor bedrooms. It utilized different materials, including wood, metal, stucco, glass, and porcelain, brought for the first time from China during the century and reflecting the West's growing interest in Asia. It combined texture and color with spirited and even erotic subject matter. Elements drawn from nature, such as birds and flowers, replaced religious objects as decorative elements.

Although Greek mythology and religious themes remained popular, eighteenth-century painters found new sources for artistic inspiration.

The French painter Jean Antoine Watteau (1684–1721) influenced the artistic move away from traditional religious subjects laden with didactic meaning toward lighter, even playful, and more secular themes. Adopting a more realistic style than baroque painting, he often depicted elegantly dressed noble subjects at leisure. Breaking away from the system of direct patronage, Watteau sold his paintings through an art dealer. Painters, like François Boucher (1703–1770), who followed him, adopted the rococo style, emphasizing smallness of scale, as well as elegance and frivolity. As the market for painting widened, scenes of nature and everyday life also became popular.

The expanding middle-class art market and the growing secularization of artistic taste was nowhere more apparent than in Britain. William Hogarth (1697–1764) was the most popular artist of the era. Hogarth portrayed everyday life in London with affection and satire. He was as adept at conveying the elegance of London's parks as the depravation of the city's notorious "Gin Lane." He poked fun at the hearty Englishman putting away pounds of roast beef (it seemed somehow fitting that Hogarth himself died after eating a huge steak), the dishonest lawyer, the clergyman looking for a better post while ignoring his pastoral duties, and the laboring poor drowning their sorrows in cheap gin, a plague that led the government to raise the tax on inexpensive liquor.

In France, the Academy of Painting and Sculpture organized the first public art exhibition in Paris in 1737. A description of one such event

Jean Antoine Watteau's *The Gamut of Love.*

William Hogarth's *Gin Lane* (1751) is a deleterious commentary on the impact of alcohol on the poor of eighteenth-century London.

suggests that such public exhibitions facilitated some degree of social mingling.

> Here the odd-job man rubs shoulders with the great noble . . . the fishwife trades her perfumes with those of a lady of quality, making the latter resort to holding her nose to combat the strong odor of cheap brandy drifting her way; the rough artisan, guided only by natural feeling, comes out with a just observation, at which an inept wit nearly bursts out laughing only because of the comical accent in which it was expressed; while an artist hiding in the crowd unravels the meaning of it all and turns it to his profit.

Music

The taste for music also moved beyond the constraints of court, ecclesiastical, and noble patronage. Opera's great popularity in the seventeenth century had been closely tied to ornate opera houses constructed at European courts. The appeal of composers and their music passed from court to court, sometimes transported by aristocratic diplomats. In the early 1750s, Rousseau penned stinging attacks on French opera. Readers understood his strident language as he intended—he was denouncing court and aristocratic taste itself. Specifically, Rousseau compared the Royal Academy of Music's monopoly on French music to a ruthless inquisition

that stifled imagination. Rousseau's critique generated a storm of controversy because it seemed to be nothing less than a denunciation of the social and cultural foundations of contemporary French society. In harmony
with his philosophical works, Rousseau's operatic compositions extolled
the simple, unpretentious life of rural people.

Court composers were considered the equivalent of favored upper servants. When someone asked Franz Joseph Haydn (1732–1809), who
worked as *kapellmeister* (orchestra director) for the fabulously wealthy Es-
terházy family of Hungary, why he had never written any quintets, he
replied, "Nobody has ordered any." But by the 1790s, Haydn was conducting his symphonies in public concerts in London. The German composer
George Frideric Handel (1685–1759) gratefully accepted the patronage of
several English aristocrats and then King George II.

In England, concerts were held at court or in the homes of wealthy
families; in Italy, they were sponsored by groups of savants and other
educated people who gathered to discuss literature, science, and the arts;
and in Switzerland, concerts were sponsored by societies of music lovers.
The public concert also emerged in Western Europe, in some German
cities, early in the eighteenth century. Gradually public concert halls were
built in the capitals of Europe. Handel began to perform his operas and
concerts in rented theaters, attracting large crowds.

The short life of Wolfgang Amadeus Mozart (1756–1791) reflected the
gradual evolution from dependence on court and aristocratic patronage to
the emergence of the public concert. Mozart began playing the harpsichord

(*Left*) George Frideric Handel composing. (*Right*) Franz Joseph Haydn composing
at the keyboard.

The young Wolfgang Amadeus Mozart about to perform.

at age three and began composing at five. In 1763, his father took him and his sister on a tour of European courts that would last three years, hoping to make the family fortune. The Mozarts were paid handsomely for their time in Paris and at the court of Versailles, but they were disappointed by the fees they received at the German courts and in London. Mozart returned to Paris in 1778 at his father's insistence that he "get a job or at least make some money." The temperamental Mozart failed to make his way in the social world of Paris: "I would wish for his fortune," a contemporary wrote, "that he had half as much talent and twice as much tact."

Thereafter Mozart often lived in his native Salzburg, where he served as unhappy court musician of the unpleasant archbishop. Mozart wrote church music and light music, including a hunting symphony for strings, two horns, dogs and a rifle, before resigning after quarreling with his patron. Mozart spent money as rapidly as he made it, and was constantly in debt, unable to attract the lavish court, noble, or ecclesiastical patronage he desired. But a list of engagements that he sent his father in 1784 revealed that he had very few evenings free. His schedule included public concerts, which had begun only a year or two earlier. Mozart organized a series of subscription concerts of his own that year, but had only mediocre success, perhaps because his music seemed too innovative and complicated. Opera continued to be the preferred form of music. Unlike Handel, who made a good deal of money during the last ten years of his life, Mozart died a poor man at age thirty-five, buried in an unmarked pauper's grave in Vienna.

A prolific genius, Mozart moved away from the melodious regularity of his predecessors to more varied and freely articulated compositions. The operas *The Marriage of Figaro* (1786) and *Don Giovanni* (1787) demonstrated Mozart's capacity to present characters from many walks of life, revealing not only their shared humanity but their personal moods and expectations. *The Magic Flute* (1791) captures yet again the religious underpinning of contemporary culture, even in the century of rational inquiry. Mozart's last opera expressed his belief in the ability of mankind to develop greater virtue and a capacity for love. He thus expressed the confidence of the philosophes.

The Spread of Enlightened Ideas

Salons, academies, and Masonic lodges helped spread Enlightened thought. Salons, which brought together people of means, noble and bourgeois alike, in private homes for sociability and discussion, were concentrated in Paris above all, but they were also found in Berlin, London, and Vienna, as well as in some smaller provincial towns. The English historian Edward Gibbon claimed that in two weeks in Paris he had "heard more conversation worth remembering than I had done in two or three winters in London." The salons of Paris were organized and hosted mainly by women, who selected topics for discussion and presided over conversations. Women thus became mediators of changing culture. In Warsaw, Princess Sophia Czartoryska's salon played an important role in conveying Western ideas to Polish elites. In London, women hosted similar gather-

An actor reading from a work of Voltaire at the salon of Madame Geoffrin. Note the bust of Voltaire, then in exile.

Franz Anton Mesmer magnetizing a distraught patient.

ings, some composed exclusively of women. Sometimes the discussion focused on the place of women in society.

The women of the republic of letters "accustom us to discuss with charm and clarity the driest and thorniest of subject," commented Diderot with admiration but also condescension. Madame Geoffrin in Paris hosted artists on Monday and men of letters on Wednesday. "I well remember seeing all Europe standing three deep around her chair," recalled one of her visitors. Her husband sat silently at the other end of the table while his wife put the philosophes through their paces. One night, a regular guest noted that the place where the silent man usually sat was empty and asked where he was. "He was my husband," came the laconic reply, "and he's dead."

Salon guests could discuss the work of the philosophes without fear of police interference. By the middle of the century, political discussions increasingly captured intellectuals' attention. Not all ideas discussed, of course, were of equal merit. In the 1780s, a crank German scientist, Franz Anton Mesmer (1734–1815), proclaimed the healing properties of electromagnetic treatments. "Mesmerism" attracted considerable interest in the salons of Paris, where discussants debated the nature of the "universal fluid" Mesmer and his disciples believed linked the human body to the universe. Ironically, the very success of science opened the way for such spiritualist healers to step forward, although the French Academy of Science vigorously denounced Mesmerism as nothing more than resourceful charlatanism.

In France (and in some Italian cities as well), academies, which were organizations of local people interested in science and philosophy, fulfilled a similar but more formal role to that of the salons. They were not "academies" in the sense of offering an organized curriculum, but rather formal gatherings taking place about every two weeks of people with similar intellectual interests. Meetings consisted of reading minutes and correspondence, debates and lectures. The academies helped spread Enlightenment ideas by gathering a literate, upper-class audience, including some clergymen, eager to discuss the works of the philosophes. Unlike the salons, however, with several exceptions women were not elected to the academies.

The French academies served two masters: the king and the public. They depended on royal intendants, governors, and other state officials for funding and meeting places. The monarchy believed that the academies served the public interest by bringing together savants to consider questions of contemporary importance. Some of them sponsored essay competitions on topics of contemporary interest (for example, an essay on "wisdom") in the arts and sciences—Rousseau was not the least of the winners—which became an important part of intellectual life in eighteenth-century France; during the decade of the 1780s, more than 600 were held. Some of the topics increasingly reflected Enlightenment influence, such as "religious intolerance and the role of magistrates in the defense of liberty."

Many members of the provincial academies by mid-century began to think of themselves both as representing public opinion, serving as informal counselors to the monarchy, and interpreting the sciences and other erudite subjects to a more general audience. The academies contributed to the development in France of a reforming mood. Moreover, some members became increasingly disenchanted with the Church, viewing it as incapable of reforming itself.

Masonic lodges, another medium for the ideas of the philosophes, had begun in Scotland, perhaps as early as the sixteenth century, as stonemasons' guilds. They now brought together freethinkers and others who opposed the influence of the established churches in public life. Masonic lodges proliferated rapidly in Europe during the middle years of the eighteenth century. Members took vows of secrecy, although in fact their meetings, membership lists (which included women), and rituals were widely known. Members held a variety of political opinions, but they shared a general faith in progress, toleration, and a critical spirit about institutionalized religion. In Scotland, clubs, coffeehouses, and taverns also provided the setting for discussion of the new ideas.

There were at the same time several obstacles to the dissemination of Enlightenment ideas. Books and even pamphlets were expensive. Censorship, although erratic and varying greatly from place to place, also discour-

A gathering of a Masonic lodge in Vienna. Masonic rituals included the use of allegorical symbols, blindfolds, and swords.

aged publication. All books and pamphlets published or sold in France, for example, first had to be approved by the censorship office in Paris. Censored books were burned, and those who published material officially considered blasphemous could be, at least in principle, sentenced to death. Far more frequently, officials closed printers' shops. Even the relatively tolerant Dutch Republic banned Diderot's *Philosophic Thoughts* as an attack on religion. In the face of a spate of publications critical of monarchy, aristocracy, and Church, Louis XV promulgated censorship laws in 1757 that were much harsher than those regulating the book trade in England. The French monarchy also controlled what was published through licensing of printers, booksellers, peddlers, and clandestine publishers. Many of the latter were notoriously unscrupulous, living on an excruciatingly thin margin of survival. Some survived by pirating books, eagerly pushing works by whatever authors were popular.

ENLIGHTENED ABSOLUTISM

The philosophes believed that the success of any state depended on the degree of freedom and happiness it was able to assure its people. As David Hume put it, a state is justified by the good that is done in its name. Voltaire and Diderdot, in particular, believed in "enlightened absolutism."

They wanted enlightened monarchs to impose reforms that would benefit their subjects. Leopold II of Tuscany (1747–1792), the most significant reformer of his era, went so far as to declare that "the sovereign, even if hereditary, is only the delegate of his people." Rousseau, however, warned that absolutism and enlightened thinking were incompatible.

Reform of Jurisprudence

Cesare Bonesana, the marquis of Beccaria (1738–1794), had the greatest influence on his era as a reformer influenced by the Enlightenment. A noble from Milan, Beccaria became professor of political philosophy in Habsburg Austria and ended his career advising the state chancellory on such diverse topics as agriculture, mining, and trade. He made his reputation, however, with his ideas on crime and punishment.

In *On Crimes and Punishment* (1764), Beccaria, who had read Montesquieu, Buffon, Diderot, and Rousseau, among other philosophes, applied their analysis to the issues at hand. He argued that the state's task was to protect society while respecting the dignity of all people. This meant that the rights of those accused of crimes, too, had to be protected. Beccaria wanted standard procedures to govern criminal trials, so that rich and poor would stand equal before the law. The Italian philosophe's assumption that the accused was innocent until proven guilty has remained, along with the tradition of English constitutional law and trial by jury, cornerstones of Western judicial systems.

Beccaria argued that the punishment for a given crime should not be linked to the religious concept of sin, but rather rationally determined by an assessment of the damage done to society. He thus rejected the death penalty except in cases when the state itself is threatened by anarchy. Beccaria argued that offenses against religious orthodoxy were not crimes and therefore should go unpunished. Therefore he argued that "It is better to prevent crimes than to punish them." Beccaria's principles reflected the origins of utilitarianism, an influential social theory of the first decades of the nineteenth century.

Beccaria opposed torture to extract confessions or render punishment. He argued that barbarous punishment, instead of protecting society, only encouraged disrespect for the law and hence more awful crimes. For this reason, he also objected to capital punishment, lamenting the enthusiastic crowds attracted to public executions. Leopold II of Tuscany (an admirer of Beccaria), Gustavus III of Sweden, and Frederick the Great of Prussia banned torture—clear examples of the influence of enlightened thought on contemporary rulers. Joseph II of Austria (1741–1790), Leopold's brother, also banned torture and capital punishment, but he substituted many other brutal penalties that he believed would deter crime.

Instruction in an Austrian schoolroom.

Educational Reform

Education in the widest sense was central to the program of the philosophes. The Empress Catherine the Great of Russia (ruled 1762–1796) admired and read Montesquieu and Voltaire, hosted Diderot, and purchased the latter's library for a handsome price. Born a German princess, she was contemptuous of Russian culture and unwilling to speak either Russian or German, preferring French as the language of learning. She seemed to heed the advice she had received from Diderot: "To instruct a nation is to civilize it." Catherine established a school for the daughters of nobles. Without eliminating censorship, she authorized the first private printing presses and encouraged the publication of more books—on an average only a couple dozen titles were published each year until Catherine's reform, when the annual number increased to almost 400.

A few other monarchs implemented educational reforms. But they did so at least partially in order to assure a supply of able civil servants. In 1774, Joseph II established a structured, centralized system of education from primary school to university, which doubled, for example, the number of elementary schools in Bohemia. Textbooks appeared in the Magyar, German, Croatian, Slovak, Ruthenian, and Romanian languages.

Religious Toleration

Although the eighteenth century was a period of relative religious peace, confessional conflicts could still be intense. For example, English Dissenters and particularly Catholics suffered legal discrimination; they were excluded from public offices and some professions. French Protestants had no civil rights; their births, baptisms, and marriages were considered not to have occurred unless registered by a Catholic priest. Huguenots in southern France rose up in defense of their religion in the ill-fated Camisard rebellion of 1702–1705. Protestants suffered discrimination in Hungary and the Catholic Rhineland. In Austria, in 1728 the bishop of Salzburg gave 20,000 Protestants three days to leave their homes, and royal edicts forced Protestants out of Upper Austria and Styria during the next decade.

Europe's 3 million Jews, in particular, suffered intolerance and often persecution across Europe—above all, in Eastern Europe and Russia. Jews could not take titles of nobility, join guilds, or hold municipal office. In many places, they could own land, although in some of the German states they needed special permission to buy houses. They were excluded from agricultural occupations and certain trades in France, Eastern Europe, and Russia. The Habsburg monarchy required Jews to stay inside until noon on Sundays, and in 1745, it suddenly ordered the thousands of Jews living in Prague to leave. In Vienna and Zurich, Jews were confined to ghettos, and in several German towns, they were not allowed inside the city walls. Although the Swedish government allowed Jews to build synagogues beginning in 1782, they could reside only in certain cities, and were forbidden to marry anyone who was not Jewish, to purchase land, or to produce handicrafts.

The Austrian Habsburgs expelling the Jews from Prague.

Because moneylending had been one of the ways Jews survived, Polish, Russian, and Ukrainian Jews faced resentment and hatred from peasants who often owed them money. In Poland the Catholic Church, which condemned usury, often led the way in persecution; rumors that Jews were ritually sacrificing Christian children during Passover found credulous ears. In 1762, Ukrainian peasants killed at least 20,000 Jews in the bloodiest pogrom of the century.

Yet, by about 1750, Western Europe seemed to be entering a more tolerant age. For one thing, intolerance generated periodic rebellions, which took state funds to put down. But a more humanitarian spirit could also be seen. One of Voltaire's disciples in the 1750s achieved great success for his historical novel that denounced religious persecution.

Some of the rulers who undertook what appeared to be religious reforms were inspired less by a Voltarian critique of ecclesiastical authority than by a desire to strengthen their authority. This was the case in the expulsion of the Jesuits from several countries, which highlighted the struggle between the popes and Catholic monarchs. The Jesuits had been closely identified with the papacy since the inception of the order during the Catholic Reformation. They had gained great influence in the Spanish, French, and Portuguese colonies in the Americas, and as tutors to powerful noble families. Furthermore, the order had begun to undertake colonial commercial activity, with mixed results. These factors combined to make Catholic kings perceive the order as a threat to their authority.

In Portugal, King John V's strong-willed minister, Sebastião, the marquis of Pombal (1699–1782), enhanced the monarchy's authority at the expense of the great noble families and the Church. When Jesuits criticized the regime for, among other things, orchestrating anti-Semitism, Pombal accused them of exploiting the indigenous population of Paraguay, where they virtually ran the colonial state, and of planning to extend their influence throughout the world. After Pombal falsely accused the order of planning the king's assassination, the monarch expelled the Jesuits from Portugal in 1759. Ten years later, Pombal ended the Inquisition's status as an independent tribunal, making it a royal court. Other rulers followed suit, including Louis XV of France in 1764. The expulsion of the Jesuits from some of the most powerful Catholic states reflected the diminishing power of the papacy in the face of absolute monarchs determined to retain control over what they considered to be national churches.

In Spain, Charles III (ruled 1759–1788) ordered universities to include instruction in science and philosophy. He also reduced the feared Spanish Inquisition to a series of legal hurdles governing publishing. In 1781, the last person in Spain was executed after having been accused of heretical religious beliefs. Like the kings of Portugal and France, Charles III in 1776 expelled the Jesuits in part because their near-monopoly on education seemed to pose a threat to the monarchy's control over the Church. Leopold II also reduced the authority of the church in Tuscany, ending the tithe and shackling the Inquisition. Catherine the Great abandoned persecution of Old Believers, a dissident sect within the Orthodox Church, and granted Jews civil equality. And Louis XVI granted French Protestants most civil rights in 1787, formalizing the *de facto* toleration accorded them for some time.

In Britain in 1788, Parliament passed laws reducing restrictions on Catholics—although they still could not hold public office. Nonetheless, London crowds shouting "no popery!" then attacked the property of Catholics during the "Gordon riots." Almost 300 people were killed as the authorities repressed the disturbances. In 1792, however, the first legal Catholic church in England since the sixteenth century opened its doors in London.

Protestant states seemed most receptive to the philosophes' call for religious toleration. In the northern German states and Swiss cantons, the ideals of the philosophes provided support for traditions of religious toleration that had grown out of the sixteenth-century Reformation. The quest for religious tolerance played an important part in German enlightened thought. In *Nathan the Wise* (1779), Lessing argued that people of all religions should be citizens. In Catholic Austria, Joseph II's relaxation of censorship permitted a spate of pamphlets and brochures denouncing ecclesiastical abuses and calling for toleration of Protestants. The king's Edict of Toleration (1781) extended some toleration to non-Catholics. The edict included Jews, who were now "free" to bear the burden of a "toleration tax" and to pay an assessment on kosher meat. Joseph also ennobled several Jews, incurring the wrath of other nobles. Moreover, for the first time, Protestants could enter the Habsburg civil service.

Frederick the Great

The German states appeared to be the most fertile ground for enlightened absolutism. German philosophes remained closely tied to the existing order, looking to the individual states and to the church for reforms. They were less critical of the state than their French counterparts. For Immanuel Kant (1724–1804), the Enlightenment meant the liberation of the individual intellectually and morally, but not politically or socially. The individual should think critically, but also obey.

Frederick II of Prussia (ruled 1740–1786 and known as Frederick the Great), wanted to be remembered as an enlightened ruler. He turned his court into a center of learning for the nobility. Like Catherine the Great, he considered the only worthwhile learning to be French learning. "Sans Souci", his rococo château in Potsdam, had French formal gardens and was considered the height of civility. Frederick, who was a flute-playing "philosopher-king," made Voltaire (with whom he had begun corresponding when he was still heir to the Prussian throne) the centerpiece of his palace for two years. Voltaire praised Frederick for having transformed "a sad Sparta into a brilliant Athens." But he soon became disenchanted with the cynical, manipulative Prussian king, who coolly invaded the Habsburg territory of Silesia in 1740, in the first year of his reign, demonstrating that the needs of his dynastic state would always take precedence over any issue of justice. Voltaire angered Frederick by lampooning a royal favorite and, when the king ordered his hangman to burn the offending tract publicly, Voltaire took the hint and left Potsdam in 1752.

But Frederick again borrowed Enlightenment discourse in 1770 when he claimed that one of his major tasks was "to make people as happy as is compatible with human nature and the means at my disposal." He once claimed somewhat disingenuously that he was nothing more than the "first servant" of his people as king and said that "I well know that the rich have many advocates, but the poor have only one, and that is I." Frederick freed the serfs of the royal domains and ordered the abolition of particularly vexing ties to noble lands, as well as the lords' right to punish their own serfs physically. Judicial reforms ended some flagrant abuses by magistrates. The Prussian king relaxed censorship and abolished capital punishment, except in the army. Despite once stating that "everyone must be allowed to go to heaven in his own way," he refused to emancipate Prussian Jews, asserting that they "injure the business of Christians and are useless to the state," while continuing to depend on their loans. Nonetheless, the Prussian Code, finally completed and promulgated in 1794, eight years after his death, granted "every inhabitant of the state . . . complete freedom of religion and conscience."

Frederick the Great playing the flute at Sans Souci.

Frederick the Great's "enlightened" reforms were, above all, intended to make the Prussian state more powerful, not more just (see Chapter 11). He made Prussia a more efficient absolutist state. Nobles dominated most of the plum positions as military officers and high officials. Yet, because of the needs of the state, some commoners did in fact rise to important posts, including some army officers, who were subsequently ennobled. Frederick improved the state bureaucracy by introducing an examination system to govern entry. In the courts of justice, where candidates had to pass the most complete examinations, the chances of commoners for success were greatest, and in Berlin only a third of all judges were nobles.

Yet, Prussian law reinforced the distinction between noble and commoner. The Prussian Code divided Prussian society into noble, bourgeois, and common estates. Frederick bolstered the position of Prussian nobles because he was determined to prevent any erosion of their status as the landowning class. He refused to ban serfdom on private estates, and he created institutions that would provide credit to nobles having financial difficulties. Marriages between nobles and commoners were not recognized. Even if nobles fell on hard times, they were not permitted to sell their lands to non-nobles. Furthermore, Frederick refused to promote civilian bureaucrats into the nobility.

Frederick intended his law code to enhance the reach of the state rather than to make his people equal before the law. When he freed the serfs of the royal domains (1763), it was because he needed them in the army. The Prussian monarch's *Essay on the Forms of Government* (1781) offered a recipe for enhancing the efficiency of the absolute state. Frederick's view of the world bound the state and the individual subject together. When their mutual interests could not be reconciled, however, the Prussian state always took precedence. As Voltaire had discovered for himself, Frederick the Great's reign reflected the limitations of enlightened absolutism.

Rural Reform

Several Central European monarchs tried to improve conditions of rural life. Following the disastrous decade of the 1770s, marked by hunger and disease, Austrian Queen Maria Theresa banned the mistreatment of peasants by their lords and tried to limit seigneurial obligations. As she put it, sheep must be well fed if they are to yield more wool and milk. Her son Joseph II abolished serfdom in 1781, converting peasant labor obligations into an annual payment to the lord. By restricting labor obligations, the Habsburg monarchs thus increased the potential for imposing more taxes on peasants. Joseph also ended obligations of personal service to the lord; henceforth a peasant could marry and/or leave the land without the permission of the seigneur. Peasants could also turn to the state for support against an oppressive lord; they could even take the lord to court.

Leopold II, who promulgated a new code of his kingdom's laws in 1786 and established a new and more independent judiciary, ended some restrictions on the grain trade, freeing the price of grain. These moves were popular among merchants and wealthy peasants, but not among poor people, who depended upon bread to survive.

Enlightened Statecraft

Some rulers applied Enlightenment rationality to statecraft. Joseph II announced that he wanted the Habsburg state to follow "uniform principles," which included a reorganization of the imperial bureaucracy. He taxed Church property, abolished some monastic orders, and forced a reorganization of the Church within the Habsburg domains. But a more efficient government administration did not mean more freedom for subjects. None of the so-called "enlightened" rulers gave up any of his or her monarchical prerogatives. Absolute rulers harnessed Enlightenment rationality to state actions in order to strengthen their own power rather than to improve the lives of their subjects.

Thus, "enlightened" reforms had little effect on the lives of most peasants. Enlightened absolutism benefited the Russian state and nobility, but brought virtually no change to the Russian masses. Millions of serfs were now bound even more formally to their lords. Nobles retained arbitrary rights of justice over their serfs, and lords alone could own land. Within the Habsburg domains, peasants, though legally free, remained indebted to their lords. Reasons of state lay behind even these seemingly enlightened reforms. Peasants now owed the state even more taxes and were subject to a longer term of military service. In any case, determined noble resistance undermined Joseph's reforms in Austria, Hungary, and the Southern Netherlands. In Tuscany, aristocrats and state officials sabotaged Leopold's reforms.

Catherine the Great, influenced by Montesquieu's *Spirit of the Laws,* wanted the nobility to serve as an "intermediary body" standing between the crown and its subjects. Catherine hoped that by clarifying their rights, nobles might contribute to the functioning and glory of her state. The Charter of the Nobility of 1785 formalized the relationship between the autocratic state and the nobles, recognizing the nobility of blood as equal to that of service. It confirmed their security of property, the right to hold serfs, and immunity from arrest and confiscation of property by the state. For the first time, nobles could travel abroad without the permission of the emperor. Local elective councils of nobles could henceforth send petitions to the tsar or empress, but the autocracy had no obligation to respond. Catherine herself turned against Enlightenment thought, however, fearing that it might become a tool of those opposed to absolute rule. Diderot's confidence in Catherine ended in disappointment when, to his chagrin, he learned that the empress had imprisoned those with whom she disagreed.

CURRENTS OF THE LATE ENLIGHTENMENT

The end of the "high" or "mature" Enlightenment was symbolized by the deaths of Voltaire and Rousseau in 1778. The late Enlightenment was more complex, sharing several currents. British economists applied the concept of freedom for the first time to the workings of the economy. Meanwhile, on the continent, philosophes turned away from the preoccupation with rationality and the laws of nature. The mark of human freedom was no longer the exercise of reason but the expression of the emotions. Rousseau himself had begun this turn toward what he called "reasoned sentimentality" by stressing the importance of emotional development and fulfillment. In a related development, a number of writers began to "discover" and embrace their own national cultures, seeking their origins in medieval poems and songs. And in France, when there were no more Voltaires or Rousseaus, a generation of would-be philosophes, mediocre writers who attacked the institutional structure of the French monarchy, influenced public opinion.

Calls for the freeing of the economy from state control, the emergence of idealism with its implicit promotion of nationalism through the quest for and emotional embrace of the roots of national culture, the development of the concept of public opinion, and the publication, particularly in France, of scathing attacks on the monarchy all served to undermine the established order (see Chapter 11).

Enlightened Thought and Economic Freedom

The philosophes' quest to discover the laws of nature and society led several of them to try to establish a complementary set of laws that could explain the working of the economy. This search led away from mercantilism, which had formed the basis of seventeenth- and early eighteenth-century economic theory, and to the emergence of classical economic liberalism. Mercantilist theory held that states should protect their economies with restrictions and tariffs that would maintain a favorable balance of trade, with more gold and silver flowing into a nation than going out.

A group of economic thinkers known as physiocrats believed that land, not gold and silver, was the source of all wealth. They wanted to end state interference in agriculture and the commerce of farm products. Writing in the *Encyclopedia*, François Quesnay (1694–1774), a French doctor and economist, called on the monarchy to free the grain trade. Quesnay wanted the end of arbitrary controls on prices, which states sometimes imposed in order to preserve public order. He and his friends insisted that the initially higher prices for goods would encourage production, thereby bringing about lower prices in the long run. The physiocrats encouraged wealthy landowners to put science to work to increase farm yields and enlightened rulers to free the agricultural economy from tolls and internal tariffs. In Britain, where commercial agriculture was already well developed, the physiocrats attracted an interested following. English landowners cheered the physiocrats' exuberant proclamation of the value of land and the sanctity of private property.

However, when the oddly named Anne-Robert Turgot (1727–1781), Louis XVI's controller-general, freed France's grain trade from controls in the early 1770s, disastrous shortages accompanied a series of bad harvests (see Chapter 11). Hoarding contributed to much higher prices; grain riots followed, and the experiment soon ended with the old strictures and controls back in place.

Adam Smith (1723–1790), a Scottish professor of moral philosophy at the University of Glasgow, argued against some of the hallmarks of mercantilism. In the name of freeing the economy from restraints, he opposed guild restrictions and other monopolies as well as trade barriers and other forms of protectionism. Such bold proposals flew in the face of contemporary economic thought, which held closely to regulated monopolies and remained suspicious of free market competition. Merchants looked to the state to provide financial, political, and military protection. The Scottish philosopher's optimistic doctrine came to be known universally by its

Adam Smith admiring his book, *The Wealth of Nations.*

French name, *"laissez-faire,"* or "leave alone." Each person, Smith insisted, should be "free to pursue his own interest his own way." If "left alone," Smith argued, the British economy would thrive naturally, generating foreign and domestic markets. The "invisible hand" of the unfettered economy would over time cause the forces of supply and demand to meet, determining the price of a good and clearing markets. By overcoming that "wretched spirit of monopoly," which made people less energetic, the "virtue of the marketplace" would also enhance social happiness and civic virtue. This was a common theme in the Scottish Enlightenment; Scottish philosophes were particularly concerned with how civic virtue and public morality could be inculcated in a society being slowly transformed by commerce and manufacture.

German Idealism

While in England the late Enlightenment brought an emphasis on economic freedom, on the continent it was marked by subjectivism and a greater emphasis on emotion, a shift already reflected by Rousseau's "reasoned sentimentality." The basic tenet of German idealism was that we perceive and understand the world through the medium of our ideas, and not through the direct application of our senses. The foremost proponent of this school was Immanuel Kant, born an artisan's son in the Prussian town of Königsberg. In his *Critique of Pure Reason* (1781), Kant affirmed that rational inquiry into nature leads to knowledge. In his memorable analogy, reason is like a judge who "compels the witness to answer questions which he himself has formulated." But for Kant, reason alone was not the basis for our knowledge of the world. He argued instead that each person understands the world through concepts that cannot be separated from his or her unique experience. This philosophy undermined faith in rational objectivity and universalism that had characterized the high Enlightenment and invited the subjectivity and relativism of early nineteenth-century romanticism.

In the eighteenth century, writers became interested in discovering the roots of national cultures; Sweden, Denmark, Russia, and Poland all discovered their "national" literatures, written in their own languages. The first Czech national theater opened in Prague in 1737. Lessing proudly wrote in German and called for a national theater. Scottish readers eagerly saluted the discovery by the poet James Macpherson (1736–1796) of the work of an imaginary Gaelic bard of the third century, Ossian. Macpherson's publication in the early 1760s of what he claimed were translations of the poet he called the Gaelic Homer set off a bitter debate, one that contributed, despite Macpherson's falsification, to the emergence of Scottish romanticism. Composers began to borrow from popular culture, especially from folk music not necessarily religious in inspiration. The first Jewish periodicals were published in Königsberg in the century's last decades, and the first Jewish school was established in Berlin in 1778. The emotional search for and enthusiastic identification with national cultures contributed, as in the case of Scotland, to the development of romanticism, and though only very gradually, of nationalism. The latter, in particular, helped undermine the established order in several continental states, notably France. In those states, the established order was based on allegiance to a monarchical dynasty and often to established religion as well, and not to national allegiances.

The Enlightenment and Public Opinion

Public opinion, a concept we take for granted, did not always exist. But it began to take shape in French, English, and several other European languages in the eighteenth century (see Chapter 11). During the 1770s, more people in France discussed the pressing political issues of the day than ever before. Barristers helped establish the concept of public opinion when they sought a wide spectrum of support for the parlements. Louis XV had decided to replace these provincial noble law courts in 1768 with more malleable institutions more directly under royal control. Public opinion forced the king to restore the parlements six years later and brought about an end to Turgot's attempt to rationalize the administration. Public opinion, to which opponents of the monarchy and increasingly the court itself now appealed, provided a forum in which political ideas were increasingly discussed. These ideas were largely shaped by Enlightenment discourse on political sovereignty and the limits of absolute rule.

A number of the treatises published during the late Enlightenment dealt with contemporary political issues, in the tradition of Voltaire's broadsides at the time of the Calas Affair, which had exposed the consequences of intolerance and persecution to public opinion. As the financial crisis of the French monarchy worsened during the 1780s, such publications would help make the question of reform an increasingly national issue.

Forbidden Publications and the Undermining of Authority

Some of the fringe members of the republic of letters, whom Voltaire had dismissed as mere "scribblers," also undermined respect for the monarchy and the royal family. Whereas the milieu of the philosophes earlier in the century had been elegant salons, the would-be philosophes of the last period of the Enlightenment hung around cheap cafés, lived in rooms high above the street, and dodged creditors by frequently changing addresses, while insisting that royal censorship blocked their ascent to better things. Some made a modest living peddling forbidden publications. A few kept afloat by spying for the police. A few others turned to petty crime and others, while claiming common cause with the major philosophes against the unenlightened institutions of France, wrote pornography or slandered prominent people, including the royal family. There had been such publications before the 1770s and 1780s, but never so many of them, and never had they been so widely read.

Banned books nevertheless reached France through the efforts of resourceful shipping agents, transporters, bargemen, dockers, and peddlers, who smuggled books published in Switzerland or the Austrian Netherlands to French booksellers willing to circumvent the controls of the booksellers' guild and the state. In 1783, the crown redoubled its efforts to stem the tide of smuggled books and to still the clandestine presses within France. These houses undercut the legitimate Parisian book trade because they could publish banned books and produce cheaper editions of acceptable works. Moreover, royal officials were concerned about the effects of these smuggled satires on public faith in the monarchy.

Was there any connection between the high-minded philosophes and their "successors," who included the authors of *Venus in the Cloister or the Nun in a Nightgown, Christianity Unveiled,* and *Margot the Campfollower?* In fact, the envious and mediocre descendants of the philosophes continued their predecessors' work by undermining respect for the authority of monarchy, aristocracy, and Church, however much their attacks by character assassination and defamation followed from ambition and financial need more than from adherence to Enlightenment ideals.

Moreover, certain themes of the Enlightenment did find their way into their work. They joined their far more illustrious predecessors in attacking the foundations of the French monarchy. Frustrated authors attacked the privileges, for example, of the printing and booksellers' guild, which they blamed for keeping them on Grub Street. Their identification of censorship with despotism, though self-serving, was nonetheless effective. As they denounced the bureaucratic system of state censorship, they argued that only its abolition could permit the free exchange of ideas. Political events and scandals kept the presses of the literary underground turning, fanning popular hostility to monarchy, Church, and nobility.

LEGACY OF THE ENLIGHTENMENT

The Enlightenment philosophes celebrated reason, while acknowledging the passions, and were suspicious of pure faith. Steeped in respect for science and reason, and confident that humanity would discover the truths of nature, they were optimistic about human potential. The philosophes' belief in progress, which Kant insisted was a sign of modernity, separated them sharply from the Catholic Church. Yet, they were not as naive, uncritical, or foolish as Voltaire's Candide, who thought progress inevitable. The philosophes believed that the combination of thought, study, education, and action would lead to a better future. States, they thought, were not ordained by God, but by mankind and, like other phenomena, should be subject to critical scrutiny.

The philosophes' belief in human dignity led them to oppose all forms of despotism. Most spoke out against religious intolerance, torture, and slavery (although an effective campaign against slavery, launched by the English abolitionists of the Society for the Abolition of the Slave Trade in 1787, stood independent of the Enlightenment). Furthermore, some Enlightenment thinkers and writers recognized that contemporary assertions about the inequality of women contradicted their understanding of nature. Diderot, Montesquieu, and Voltaire favored divorce, but they opposed equal status for women.

Some philosophes had strong reservations about the ability of individuals to develop equally. "As for the rabble," Voltaire once said, "I don't concern myself with it; they will always remain rabble." Those with power and influence first must be enlightened, they reasoned, so that eventually everyone could develop through education. And for all their commitment to freedom and insistence on the fundamental goodness of all people, Hume and the other philosophes still considered women inferior to men, reflecting the prejudices of the times in which they lived.

Rejecting what they considered unnatural hierarchies that fettered progress, the philosophes in their commitment to individual freedom influenced the subsequent history of the Western world. Whereas most people in the eighteenth century still considered the monarchy to be the repository of the public good, the philosophes proclaimed that the public had rights of its own and that freedom was a good in itself. Enlightenment thought helped create a discourse of principled opposition to the foundations of absolutism. If the philosophes themselves were not revolutionary, many of their ideas in the context of eighteenth-century Europe were indeed.

CHAPTER 11

EIGHTEENTH-CENTURY DYNASTIC RIVALRIES AND POLITICS

King George III (ruled 1760–1820) proclaimed that he "gloried in the name of Britain." Indeed during his reign, despite his personal failings, a nationalist cult developed around the British monarchy, significantly after the empire suffered its biggest loss, that of the thirteen American colonies.

The king projected the image of an ordinary family man, surrounded by his homely wife and fifteen children. Less interested in goings-on in Hanover, his family's dynastic home, than his predecessors, he won popular affection in Britain. "This young man," wrote Horace Walpole, "don't stand in one spot with his eyes fixed royally on the ground, and dropping bits of German news; he walks about and speaks to everybody." The king's domesticity also made him a target for the gentle spoofs of caricaturists. His nervousness led him to bombard almost everyone he encountered with questions, ending with "hey, hey?" By the last decade of the century, symptoms of a hereditary disease made George III appear to be quite mad.

Early in his reign, King George III had strong ideas about monarchical prerogatives, even within the context of a constitutional monarchy. Yet, during his reign, not only did British nationalism develop precociously, but the idea developed in and beyond Parliament that a party of parliamentary opposition formed an essential part of the parliamentary system of representation.

The nature of the European state system itself also underwent fundamental change in the eighteenth century as the rivalries between Great Britain, France, Spain, and the Dutch Republic (the United Provinces) broadened to a global scale. Whereas Europe in the period of Louis XIV had been marked by frenetic war-making and the pursuit of alliances against France, Europe's dominant power, the wars fought between the

Great Powers in the middle of the eighteenth century reflected a more even distribution of power. This balance of power was increasingly affected not only by events overseas but also by those in Eastern Europe. There, Russia expanded its empire at the expense of the Ottoman Empire, and Russia, Prussia, and Austria dismembered Poland.

The increasingly global nature of Great Power conflict put strains on the structures of states in Europe. They were forced to reorganize themselves to become more efficient, either by granting more power to representative bodies combined with stronger mechanisms for raising money, as in the case of Great Britain, or through some variant of enlightened despotism, as in Prussia. In Britain, where monarchs could not function without Parliament, the role of the House of Commons expanded and political parties emerged. Newspapers and societies for discussing politics created public opinion, which transformed the political sphere as more people demanded political reform. Patriotism, and by extension, a sense of national identity, emerged in Britain. Allegiance was transferred from the ruler to Parliament, which was seen as representing the interests of all Britons (directly or indirectly).

Reform movements and uprisings alarmed rulers and intrigued intellectuals, who in increasing numbers denounced unwarranted privilege and despotism. Reformers celebrated the British model of constitutional monarchy and the successful rising of the American colonists against British rule. Public opinion on the continent challenged absolute rule; in France, the parlements began to defend the "nation" against monarchical despotism.

The role of lawyers in helping constitute public opinion before which acts of authority were to be judged. One of the lawyers, Target, would help draft the first constitution after the French Revolution.

As contemporaries sought explanations for movements that sought to limit monarchical authority, the Bavarian envoy in Vienna went so far as to claim in 1775 that "the spirit of revolt has become universal." Although the diplomat exaggerated, these movements for reform to some degree influenced and encouraged each other.

The Eighteenth-Century State System

Eighteenth-century Europe consisted of states dancing together in temporary partnership until the music changed and old partners were deserted and new ones embraced. The eighteenth-century state system was a pattern of rivalry and alliance in which each state vied for global and dynastic power. Few borders or thrones were secure from challenge by other states and rulers coveting more territory and more power. Rulers sought to expand their power through marriage, inheritance, or warfare. Each state looked out for its own self-interests and forged alliances that would help further those interests. Global and dynastic rivalries led to conflicts and ultimately to wars as states tried to add more territory and other states sought to maintain the balance of power, so that one state did not grow more powerful at the expense of the others. Spain, the Dutch Republic, Sweden, the Holy Roman Empire, and the Ottoman Empire found themselves with far less power than in the seventeenth century, while Britain, Russia, and Prussia continued to expand their power.

The emergence of a global economy increasingly linked to colonial trade engendered rivalries and conflicts between England, France, Spain, and the Dutch Republic, as each battled for commercial and colonial advantage. The wars that resulted were motivated by the hope of economic gain and reflected the primacy of mercantilism, which assumed that there was a finite amount of wealth available in the world, and that the might of any state depended on its success in bringing in more gold than it paid out.

Dynastic rivalries remained a major source of conflict. In England, George I from the German state of Hanover succeeded to the throne in 1714, but his German origins and interests complicated British foreign policy and led to unsuccessful attempts by the Catholic Stuart pretenders to take back the British throne. Meanwhile, on the continent, Frederick the Great of Prussia and Maria Theresa of Austria locked horns in a battle of expansion for the former and survival for the latter. The other Great Powers lined up in alliances on the side of each.

Global Rivalries

As voyages of discovery opened up new horizons to Europeans, the stakes of colonial rivalry between the Great Powers rose. During the seventeenth century, England, the Dutch Republic, France, Spain, and Portugal had gradually expanded their trading routes across the seas. Coffee, tea, molasses, ginger, indigo, calicoes, tobacco, and other colonial products—for the most part luxury goods—fetched high prices. The discovery of gold in Brazil in 1694 and 1719 further whetted the appetites of commercial companies. China also began to fascinate some Europeans. By the end of the seventeenth century, Dutch and French traders began to go there in greater numbers. The land trade routes that stretched through the Middle East and Central Asia still continued to reward the ambition and persistence of merchant-traders, who returned with spices and fine silks. Christian missionaries went out in greater numbers, seeking converts in Asia. Chinese prints, porcelain, gardens, silk, and rugs became popular in Western Europe, particularly during the first half of the century.

In the eighteenth century, the British East India Company carried its trading interests to more distant places, establishing new posts in South India and Bengal. Parliament licensed the company to operate as a military force. British traders exchanged slaves taken from West Africa and textiles and other manufactured goods for colonial products. The British East India Company's ships carried Chinese porcelain, silks, spices, and tea to England in exchange for silver and, increasingly, opium grown in India. An Englishman in the middle of the eighteenth century exclaimed that "the Interests and Commerce of the British Empire are so inseparably united that they may be very well considered as one and the same."

Spain still had the largest empire. It included the largest Caribbean islands, the Philippines in the Pacific, and most of South America except for Brazil, which belonged to Portugal. The Dutch had bases on the coast of South America, West Africa, and South Africa (their colony at the Cape of Good Hope was the only permanent European settlement at the time in Africa), the island of Mauritius in the Indian Ocean, the Indian subcontinent, Indonesia, and Japan.

The British colonies in the New World differed from Spanish colonies and, even more, from French colonies. Many people had migrated to the British colonies seeking economic opportunity, or in the case of Massachusetts Puritans and Maryland Catholics, religious toleration. These settlement colonies also welcomed emigrants from the German states, who hoped to make a living as farmers, artisans, and day laborers. Unlike in the towns and villages they left, men far outnumbered women, although entire families, too, took passage on ships bound for America, where as much as possible they sought to recreate the way of life left behind.

French forts and settlements dotted the North American colony of Nouvelle (New) France, the most important of which was Louisbourg on Cape Breton Island in the Gulf of St. Lawrence. French trappers established posts on the Mississippi River, with the port of New Orleans at its mouth far to the south. The territories claimed by the French, on which they had only scattered military and trading posts, almost tripled in size by mid-century, but by the 1760s the French population of Nouvelle France stood at only about 80,000 people.

Global rivalries led to conflicts between the Great Powers, both on the seas and in the colonies themselves. French and British armies and navies struggled in North America, the West Indies, and India, believing that the gain or loss of Canadian furs, Caribbean spices, or Indian jewels might be a damaging blow to dynastic prosperity and prestige. Spanish colonial rivalry with Britain led to the only war ever fought over an ear. Both Spain and England insisted that their colonies ship goods only on vessels flying their flag. Since 1713 the Spanish had granted the right to Britain to supply its colonies with 4,800 slaves each year; in exchange for this sale, a single English ship each year could call and trade at one Spanish colonial port. Illegal trade, however, continued as before. The Spanish navy sank several English ships, and in 1731 one of its vessels accosted an English frigate suspected of smuggling. A Spanish sword cut off one of the ears of the captain, Jenkins. The incident led to the "War of Jenkins' Ear" in 1939 after a member of Parliament whipped up anti-Spanish sentiment by waving the severed ear in the air during a speech.

The Hanoverians and the Stuarts in Great Britain

In 1702, Queen Anne (1665–1714), Protestant daughter of James II, succeeded her brother-in-law, William III, to the throne of England. Despite eighteen pregnancies and five live births, Anne had no surviving children. The House of Commons had passed the Act of Succession in 1701 to prevent any future restoration of the Catholic Stuart line to the throne. By this act, which broke the strict rules of dynastic succession, the Protestant ruling dynasty of Hanover, related by blood to the English royal family, would become the English royal line upon Anne's death.

In 1707, the Act of Union created the Kingdom of Great Britain, which took the Union Jack as its flag, and linked Scotland to England and Wales. Scotland received seats in the House of Commons, but fewer than its population might have warranted. Parliament's goal in formalizing the existing dynastic union was fear that Scotland might seek to summon Queen Anne's exiled Catholic half-brother (James III) to be king of Scotland, instead of going along with England and Wales' awarding of the throne to the house of Hanover. Ireland, in which English Protestants owned seven-eighths of the land, continued to pay dearly for having supported the Catholic monarch James II after the Glorious Revolution of 1688 had sent him from the throne. Legal restrictions prevented Catholics from being merchants, lawyers, or members of the Irish Parliament, the power of which was strictly limited by the English Privy Council. In England itself, Parliament had not extended the Toleration Act of 1689 to Catholics. British Catholics could not vote, be elected to Parliament, or hold state offices; they also were subject to special taxes, could not possess weapons, be admitted to Oxford or Cambridge Universities, or worship freely, at a time when Protestant Dissenters—that is, Protestants not belonging to the Church of England—were able to rise to respectable positions within the British state.

The Hanoverian George I (1660–1727), a distant cousin of Queen Anne, became king in 1714. He never learned English, brought some of his own advisers from Hanover, was stubborn and obese (many of his subjects referred to their monarch as "King Log"), and may have ordered the murder of his wife's lover in Hanover. All of this was more easily forgiven by wealthy Englishmen than his apparent indifference toward the crown he wore, seemingly demonstrated by the fact that he spent long periods of time in his beloved Hanover.

The Hanoverian dynasty's accession to the throne complicated British foreign policy. The Treaty of Utrecht (1713), the first of two treaties that concluded the War of the Spanish Succession (1701–1714), confirmed Britain's colonial supremacy, adding Newfoundland, Nova Scotia, the Hudson Bay territory, and New Brunswick, as well as Gibraltar and the island of Minorca, and the right to trade in Spanish colonial ports. But George I looked with disfavor on the treaty because it had not furthered the interests of Hanover. Furthermore, many Whigs viewed the compromise treaty as a humiliation for England. It was ratified by the House of Lords only because Queen Anne had created enough new peers to assure passage.

The new Hanoverian dynasty was threatened by remaining support for the Catholic Stuart dynasty. Some conservatives still claimed that James III, the Stuart son of James II, was the legitimate heir to the throne. In 1715, the intransigent supporters (Jacobites) of James III began an uprising in Scotland. Although by the Treaty of Utrecht the king of France had officially renounced support for James, Catholic France still wanted him on the British throne. But troops loyal to George I quickly quelled the rebellion.

George II (1683–1760) became king in 1727. Like his father, he was courageous and had led troops into battle in Germany. But unlike his father, he took the time to learn English (although it remained decidedly his second language). He spoke it with a strong German accent that his subjects mocked ("I hate bainting and boetry!" he once announced). He had a stiff, tedious personality, displaying impatience and a bad temper. On one occasion he bellowed, "I am sick to death of all this foolish stuff, and wish with all my heart that the devil may take all your bishops, ministers, Parliament, and the devil take the whole island—provided I can get out of it and go to Hanover!"

In 1745, the dreamy pretender, Charles Edward Stuart (1720–1788), planned an invasion of England, similar to the one his father had undertaken thirty years earlier. "Bonnie Prince Charlie" landed in Scotland with a small army of enthusiasts, while British troops were engaged on the continent. Adding Scottish clansmen from the Highlands to his force, he then marched southward into England with about 9,000 men. The threat to the

(*Left*) Prince Charles Edward Stuart, "Bonnie Prince Charlie." (*Right*) The Battle of Culloden Moor, 1746, in which hopes for a Stuart restoration were vanquished.

throne was serious enough to give birth to the British anthem "God Save the King," which dates from this time.

But Charles Edward found in England almost no support for his cause. Commercial and manufacturing centers, in particular, rallied against any possibility of a Stuart restoration. The young pretender hesitated a hundred miles from London and then retreated to Scotland. Many highlanders deserted his ranks as English troops ravaged their country. William Augustus (1721– 1765), the duke of Cumberland and third son of George II, overtook and defeated Bonnie Prince Charlie at Culloden Moor near Inverness in April 1746. He earned the nickname of "the butcher" through his ruthless treatment of the defeated rebels. It was the last battle fought on British soil to this day. The pretender hightailed it back to France. The government ordered the execution of two Scottish peers who had thrown their support to the pretender and forbade the wearing of kilts or tartans, symbols of the highlanders. Thereafter, only a handful of Jacobites continued to celebrate Stuart birthdays. They toasted "the king over the water" living in French exile by holding their glasses of spirits over another glass filled with water.

The Prussian-Austrian Dynastic Rivalry in Central Europe

The increased power of Prussia threatened Habsburg interests in Central Europe. Charles VI (ruled 1711–1740), the decent but mediocre Holy Roman emperor, had never recovered from the Habsburg loss of Spain in the War of the Spanish Succession. More than this, he remained obsessed with keeping the remaining Habsburg lands together. As Charles had no son, he spent years during his reign trying to bribe or otherwise convince the other European powers to recognize the integrity of the Habsburg inheritance upon his death. In 1713, he sought to get them to recognize the Pragmatic Sanction, which asserted the indivisibility of the Habsburg domains and recognized the right of female as well as male succession to the monarchy, should Charles have no sons.

When Charles VI died without a male heir, his twenty-three-year-old daughter Maria Theresa (ruled 1740–1780) assumed the Habsburg throne. While Maria Theresa could, as a woman, become empress of Austria, she was barred from becoming Holy Roman empress, thus opening up the question of imperial succession. The young queen had little money, no army, almost no bureaucracy, and bad advisers, and hence was in a poor position to defend her throne against hostile powers. Worse, France and Prussia, despite having pledged to uphold the Pragmatic Sanction, were each preparing to dismember the Habsburg empire.

An immediate threat came from the young Prussian king, Frederick II (ruled 1740–1786). Frederick came to the throne in the same year as Maria Theresa and quickly sought to take advantage of a queen in a world of kings. Confident that the very recent death of the Russian empress would preclude Russian assistance to Austria, Frederick sent his army into Austrian territory.

As a young man, Frederick had little in common with his raging father, Frederick William I (see Chapter 7). The royal son was intelligent, played the flute, enjoyed reading, preferred the French language to his native German, and as a boy expressed little interest in the army. At the age of eighteen, he tried to run off to England to catch a glimpse of his intended

Maria Theresa and her family at the Schönbrunn Palace outside of Vienna. The future Emperor Joseph II stands at her right.

Frederick the Great rides into battle.

English bride. When Frederick's fugue, planned by his best friend—and perhaps his lover—was foiled, the furious king decided to have his son executed. When dissuaded by his officials, Frederick William made the young Frederick watch from a prison cell the decapitation of his friend. Forced by his father to serve in the royal bureaucracy and as an army officer, Frederick became an aggressive absolute monarch.

Frederick, called "the Great" by his subjects, worked twelve hours a day lovingly overseeing minute details of army administration. His own physical courage was legendary—six times in battle horses were killed beneath him. At the same time, he eschewed the extravagant court life of the French Bourbons, allocating a mere 3 percent of state revenue to the court, in contrast to perhaps a third of the budget of the French monarchy.

Frederick the Great's "enlightened" reforms (see Chapter 10) made Prussia a more efficient absolutist state. His intent was to extend the reach of the state rather than to improve the lot of his people. Frederick improved the state bureaucracy by introducing an examination system to govern entry. Through these examinations, talented commoners could be awarded positions in the courts of law; in Berlin, two-thirds of the judges were commoners. Thus, talent as well as birth determined who served the state.

Frederick admired and granted a title of nobility to the rationalist philosopher and theoretician of the absolutist state, Christian Wolff (1679–1754). Wolff contended that the ideal man would follow the dictates of reason and would live to improve the condition of mankind. No one was more suited to this than, he argued, the absolute monarch, whose power, as "first servant of the state," alone could guarantee his subjects' rights and prosperity. In exchange for protection, Wolff argued, like Thomas Hobbes half a century before, the king's subjects would willingly relinquish their freedom. The monarch's absolute, effective rule would replicate the universe as created by God. Frederick saluted Wolff's almost worshipful trust in the state as the source of all rights, taking his ideas to be a blueprint for effective absolutism.

"Old Fritz" strengthened the Prussian economy by establishing state-operated iron- and steelworks, ordering the construction of more canals to haul goods, and encouraging the establishment of workshops in Berlin to produce textiles, glass, clocks, and porcelain. Because he ordered officials to accumulate stocks of grain in good times, Prussia never suffered the desperate periods of dearth that occurred in eighteenth-century France.

With careful budgeting and relative frugality, Frederick the Great managed to pay for his wars. He closely monitored state tax revenues and expenses. He refused to undertake expensive loans, sell noble titles and privileges, or impose ever more crushing levies on the peasantry, policies that were wreaking financial chaos and social havoc in France.

Frederick continued the exemptions of the Junkers (nobles) from many taxes and preserved their domination of the bureaucracy and army. He personally planned educational reforms with an eye to improving the performance of his officials. Nobles oversaw the collection of taxes, and the regional government. Virtually all military officers were nobles. But Frederick also wanted to keep the Junkers in a position of subordination to the crown. Noble army officers could not marry or travel abroad without the king's authority, a constraint that would have been unthinkable in France. Frederick's response to the hint of any disagreement from nobles, officials, officers, or anyone else was "Don't argue!" He tolerated no appeals of royal decisions. In a society with a relatively rigid social structure, aristocratic and military virtues were henceforth inseparable in Prussia, a fact fraught with significance for modern German history.

CONFLICTS BETWEEN THE GREAT POWERS

While the rivalry between Great Britain and France assumed global dimensions, the rise of Prussia and Russia (see Chapter 7) as powers carried European dynastic rivalries and warfare into Central Europe. The War of the Austrian Succession (1740–1748), begun when King Frederick II of Prussia invaded Silesia (a Habsburg territory), revealed the fundamental principle in eighteenth-century power politics: the balance of power. The unchecked success of any one power seeking to expand its territory inevitably brought a combined response from the other powers to maintain a rough balance between the states. The expansion of Prussian power, then, engendered the "Diplomatic Revolution" of 1756, when Austria and France put their long-standing rivalry aside to join forces against Prussia and Britain in the Seven Years' War (1756–1763). The long, costly war between France and Britain was truly global in extent, as both powers battled in North America, the Caribbean, and India. Armies were larger and better drilled than ever before. At the same time, the French and, in particular, the British navy played a greater role in transporting troops and supplies, as well as guarding commercial vessels in the global struggle.

The War of the Austrian Succession

The War of the Austrian Succession reflected naked absolutist aggression. Frederick the Great coveted Silesia (now part of Poland), a Habsburg territory south of Prussia and squeezed between Saxony, Poland, and Austria. With its textile, mining, and metallurgical industries, Silesia was the wealthiest province within the Habsburg domains. In 1740, shortly after succeeding to the throne and without warning, Frederick sent his army into Silesia.

Frederick was the latest in the line of aggressive Prussian kings who identified the interests of the state with a powerful army complemented by a centralized bureaucracy able to raise money through taxes. The Habsburg monarchy embodied, by contrast, the complexity of Central Europe. Austrian Germans dominated the administrative structure of the empire of many different peoples and languages. The multiplicity of privileges (particularly those of Magyar and Croatian nobles), traditions, and cultures undermined the authority, resources, and efficiency of the state. The Habsburg empire also lacked the trading and manufacturing base of Great Britain and the Dutch Republic, foremost among the non-absolutist states, or of France or even Prussia. Mercantilists in Austria hoped that foreign trade would add to the coffers of the state, but the overwhelmingly rural Habsburg lands had little to export, despite the development of manufacturing.

The new empress's troubles were not limited to Silesia. The nobles of Bohemia, the richest province, rebelled against Habsburg rule, offering the throne to the ruler of Bavaria, Austria's rival in southern Germany. Dependent upon the good will of the provincial Diets, no Habsburg monarch could be sure of having either sufficient support from the estates or money with which to raise an effective army.

Now, with Prussian troops occupying Silesia, Maria Theresa travelled to Hungary to ask for the support of the Hungarian Diet, which had agreed to the Pragmatic Sanction in exchange for recognition of Hungary's status as a separate kingdom. Dressed in mourning clothes following the recent death of an infant daughter and clutching one of her sixteen children to her, Maria Theresa convinced the Diet to provide an army of 40,000 men

Aristocratic officers safely above the carnage at the Battle of Fontenoy, 1745.

and cavalry. The Magyar nobles held out their swords to her, shouting their promise to give "life and blood" for her. The gesture could not restore Silesia to the Habsburgs, but it may have saved the Habsburg monarchy. Aided by Hungarian troops, imperial forces put down the Bohemian revolt.

Fearing a disproportionate expansion of Prussian power in Central Europe, other states joined in an alliance against Frederick. Yet, confronted by an alliance of Austria, Russia, Sweden, Denmark, and Saxony, states with a combined population of twenty times its own, Prussia more than held its own, with the help of France as well as Saxony, Spain, and Bavaria, each hoping to help bring about the disintegration of the Habsburg empire. France joined the anti-Austrian coalition because it coveted the Austrian Netherlands, Spain because it wanted to recapture influence in Italy, and the king of Piedmont-Sardinia because he coveted Milan. Frederick, satisfied for the moment with the acquisition of Silesia, withdrew from the war in 1745 after the Peace of Dresden. But Britain was drawn into the conflict by its need to protect the dynastic territory of Hanover from Prussia and France. Indeed, at Dettingen in 1743, King George II became the last British monarch to fight in battle. His horse was spooked and rode off with its frightened royal rider astride. France's army defeated the combined Dutch and British forces in the Battle of Fontenoy in 1745, the bloodiest battle of the century until the French Revolution. Two years later in the United Provinces, with the war going badly, a coup gave William IV of Orange almost monarchical authority as stadholder,

MAP 11.1 THE WAR OF THE AUSTRIAN SUCCESSION, 1740–1748   Major battles and territorial changes at the end of the war.

making the post hereditary. In 1748, the inconclusive Treaty of Aix-la-Chapelle ended the War of the Austrian Succession (see Map 11.1). French forces withdrew from the Austrian Netherlands in return for the English abandoning the fort of Louisbourg on the St. Lawrence River, captured during the fighting. Parma was given to a branch of the Spanish Bourbons, and Piedmont-Sardinia absorbed parts of the Duchy of Milan.

The Seven Years' War

Since the development of absolute states during the seventeenth century, warfare in Europe had been driven by absolutism, specifically the territorial interests of absolute rulers. But previous wars had revealed the limits of absolutism. Wars had dragged to a halt when rulers and states no longer could raise enough money through the sale of offices and titles or by undertaking loans. The Seven Years' War (1756–1763) was remarkable for several reasons. First, it was arguably the first truly global conflict. The commercial interests of France and Britain clashed in North America, the Caribbean, and in India (see Map 11.2). The war intensified the Anglo-French struggle for control of North America. Second, for the first time we can speak of a war not just of kings but self-consciously of nations, at least in the cases of Britain and France. Both states underwent a surge of patriotic enthusiasm, marked, for example, in the case of France by calls for "patriotic gifts" to support the war. In Britain, the sense of being "Britons," as opposed to subjects of the king, developed among all classes, accentuated by an overwhelmingly popular war against Catholic France. In Britain and France, there were calls for the more efficient management of the war, seen as part of pursuing the interests of the country.

Prussia's gains in the War of the Austrian Succession helped engender the Diplomatic Revolution of 1756. This ended more than a century of intermittent warfare between France and the Austrian Habsburgs. Alarmed by the expansion of Prussian power, Austria allied with France, and then Russia, with the goal of recapturing Silesia. The price of France's support would be its future annexation of the Austrian Netherlands (Belgium) and Austrian neutrality in a war between Britain and France (which had effectively already been at war in North America for two years). Frederick the Great now turned to Britain, France's enemy, for an ally. To France and Russia, Britain's sudden and shocking alliance with Prussia seemed a betrayal, even as France reversed its century-old opposition to Habsburg interests. The Great Powers changed partners, then went to war again.

In 1757, Frederick first defeated a large French army and then a Habsburg force. But later a Russian army attacked from the north, occupying Berlin, while more Austrian troops marched on Prussia from the south. Both the French and Russian armies benefited from infantry tactics first implemented by Frederick the Great's army. Prussia's situation seemed desperate, leading the king to compare his state to "a man with many wounds who has lost so much blood that he is on the point of death." But as luck would have it, Peter III became tsar of Russia in 1762, succeeding Empress Elizabeth, Frederick's determined enemy. The new tsar admired the Prussian king and called the Russian troops home. At the cost of perhaps 300,000 soldiers, Prussia had preserved its full independence.

In India, the rivalry took the shape of a struggle between the British and French East India Companies against the background of intrigues and warfare among Indian rulers. In India, where there were only about 5,000 British residents (and 20,000 soldiers), Robert Clive (1725–1774) led an army of British troops and Indian mercenaries into Bengal. There the prince preferred French to British traders and had incarcerated more than

MAP 11.2 THE SEVEN YEARS' WAR, 1756–1763 Areas of conflict, including battle sites, during the Seven Years' War, as well as territorial changes at the end of the war.

a hundred British subjects in a room so small and stuffy that most of them died—the "Black Hole of Calcutta." In 1757, Clive's force defeated the prince's army at Plassey. After putting a pliant puppet on the Bengali throne, Clive continued to use British troops to further his own interests, and that of the British East India Company, defeating several Indian armies. By 1761, the stage was set for British control of most of the Indian subcontinent, with the British navy preventing French traders and soldiers from receiving sufficient supplies.

In what became Canada, there was much more at stake because both powers were fighting for control of a vast territory. In this struggle, France had a decided disadvantage. Even after more than a hundred years as a colony, Nouvelle France had a French population of only about 80,000 people, for the most part clustered in three towns along the St. Lawrence River—Montréal, Québec, and Trois-Rivières—and otherwise scattered over a vast territory. By contrast, the thirteen British colonies already had more than 2 million residents. British incursions into their territory led Indians to ally informally with the French. During what Americans call the French and Indian War (1754–1763), British troops forced over 10,000 French-speaking Acadians (that is, people living in Nova Scotia and New Brunswick) to emigrate. Many of them settled in the French colony of New Orleans, where the word "Cajun" emerged as a corruption of the French "Acadien."

The British navy accentuated its advantage on the seas by seizing 300 French merchant ships and capturing 8,000 sailors even before hostilities formally began. Despite the capture by French troops of several forts in the Great Lakes region, British ships reduced French reinforcements and supplies to a trickle, also defeating a French fleet at Quiberon Bay off the coast of Brittany in 1759.

In 1759, General James Wolfe (1727–1759) led an audacious, successful British attack on the French near Québec, his forces climbing up the cliffs from the St. Lawrence River to surprise their enemy. A year later, the British captured Montréal and then drove the French from the Ohio Valley. In the Caribbean, the British picked off the French islands and their small garrisons one by one.

War left all the combatants exhausted. The British national debt had doubled. The financial crisis of the French monarchy worsened as well, and its capacity to wage war diminished. By the Treaty of Paris of 1763, Austria recognized Prussia's absorption of Silesia in 1740 in exchange for Saxony's retention of independence. The Southern Netherlands, however, would remain an Austrian Habsburg territory. The settlement in North America and the Caribbean was much further-reaching. Canada became British, although France retained fishing rights on the Grand Banks off Newfoundland. But France gave up to Britain all claims to territory east of the Mississippi River, and to Spain territory west of the Mississippi, as well as most of its trading stations in India. It retained the Caribbean islands of Martinique and Guadeloupe, only because English colonists feared com-

General Wolfe's forces scale the heights of the Plains of Abraham in Québec.

petition from sugar produced on those islands if they became British. Spain ceded Florida to Britain (though only, as it turned out, until 1783). Spain also reclaimed the fortress of Havana in Cuba and established control of the enormous Louisiana Territory, which stretched from the almost tropical climate of New Orleans to the freezing plains of central Canada.

Britain then tried to mend fences on the continent, where the balance of power had been preserved. However, Joseph II of Austria wanted to incorporate Bavaria into the Habsburg domains. Austrian troops occupied Bavaria, leading to the brief War of Bavarian Succession (1778–1779). The resistance of Prussia and that of various smaller German states foiled Joseph II's plan. Like Franco-British emnity, Austro-Prussian rivalry continued unabated.

Armies and Their Tactics in the Eighteenth Century

Long after monarchs succeeded in putting an end to private noble armies, warfare remained part of noble culture. Military schools in France, Russia, and several of the German states trained the sons of nobles in the skills of war. In Prussia, Frederick William I believed that any attempt to allow commoners to become officers would be "the first step toward the decline and fall of the army." Noble officers had much more in common with the officers of the enemy than with their own troops, conscripted or impressed from the lower classes. Moreover, the Habsburg state often appointed foreign nobles as officers in its army. Officers captured during a war were treated to a nice glass of wine and a good meal, and then exchanged for their own officers who had fallen into enemy hands. War was fought over territory. In some ways, it seemed like a game of chess played between aristocrats in a manor house parlor. It is said that the French officers at the battle of Fontenoy in 1745 gallantly shouted to their British counterparts, "Fire first, *messieurs les anglais!*"

Recruitment practices differed in the various European states. The Prussian army's military recruitment system was the most comprehensive. Each of its regiments was assigned a district from which to draw recruits, and Prussians were not allowed to serve as mercenaries in other armies. In France, military recruitment was placed directly under the control of the state bureaucracy, which relieved officers of the responsibility for filling a quota of recruits. Villagers now drew lots to see who would be drafted into the reserve force. In Russia, each commune (*mir*) had to provide at least one soldier. Throughout Europe, certain categories of population were exempt from service, including prosperous farmers and the servants of French nobles, Russian merchants, and in many countries, men with families. England was alone among the major powers in not having a standing army, at least partially because in modern times it had not experienced a major foreign invasion. It did not implement mass conscription until World War II.

Yet, mercenaries still sometimes provided the bulk of eighteenth-century European armies, the notable exception being the French army. Military service provided those who joined up with regular meals, shelter, and adventure. The Swiss guards served the French royal family, and their countrymen fought with a variety of armies. The Dutch army included a brigade of Scottish highlanders. However limited the possibilities of social ascension through the army, military service could still provide respectability. Criminals and other men with something unpleasant in their pasts often turned up as soldiers.

Desertion remained widespread, affecting up to 35 percent of an army, despite threats of mutilation for those caught leaving. During the Seven Years' War, about 62,000 soldiers deserted the Habsburg army, 70,000 left the army of France behind, and 80,000 Russians disappeared into the night. Tightly packed formations served to discourage desertions, as they were intended to do, because soldiers were under more constant control. Harsh, even brutal, discipline in camp complemented that in the field. Frederick the Great was not alone in believing that "[the soldier] must be more afraid of his officers than of the dangers to which he is exposed." Although strategies for supplying troops improved during the century, armies rarely moved far from their supply camps. The lack of commitment and unreliability of mercenary and levied troops often helped end fighting.

Military technology had evolved slowly since the invention of gunpowder. The bayonet, a protruding razor-sharp knife first attached to a musket in the previous century, pushed the pikeman, a foot soldier armed with only a spearlike weapon, off the battlefield. The few significant changes in warfare in the seventeenth century included improved flintlock muskets, with cartridges and iron ramrods that permitted riflemen to fire three times per minute, and range increased to 200 meters. Handheld firearms became practical weapons for the first time. Artillery pieces were now also lighter and more mobile, with somewhat greater range. The training of artillery officers, too, improved. Thus, Frederick the Great made exemplary use of artillery to complement infantry during the Seven Years' War.

Soldiers were now far better trained and disciplined than in the previous century; armies were far larger than ever before. Although regular army units in a number of wars were vulnerable to hit and run "guerrilla" attacks by patriots resisting invasion (for example, in the War of the Spanish Succession), the discipline and efficiency of troops in formation won or lost battles. Rifles, inaccurate beyond a short distance, were fired in deadly volleys by rows of soldiers taking turns reloading. Cavalry charges, which generally took place on the flanks with the goal of neutralizing the enemy's cavalry, usually were over quickly.

New tactics had brought great maneuverability in the sixteenth and seventeenth centuries, including linear formations involving coordinated movements that required well-trained and disciplined troops. And in the eighteenth century, even greater troop mobility was achieved by combining line and column formations in a "mixed order." Moreover, the British and Prussian armies were the first to create a light infantry division that could move and engage the enemy more rapidly, often fighting with bayonets, fighting in front of or alongside columns. Yet, defense still dominated in battle, as symbolized by the impregnable fortresses along the northern frontier of France built in the late seventeenth century. Line formation, the basis of contemporary warfare, was more conducive to defense than offense.

Following the unrestrained carnage of the Thirty Years' War (1618–1648), warfare became somewhat more civilized, or at least somewhat more predictable, with fewer civilian casualties. The general acceptance of rules of civility helped reduce the carnage during and after battle. Prisoners of war, even commoners, were kept in relatively decent conditions and were sometimes exchanged for their counterparts. The development of logistical support and professionalized, well-drilled armies meant that soldiers no longer had to "live off the land." The goals of warfare were now generally restrained by traditions of monarchical and aristocratic civility. Once victory was achieved, there seemed no reason to pursue one's enemy to finish him off. Civilians were now generally spared in times of war.

Navies

British statesmen knew that to maintain superiority over France on the seas, their enemy had to be kept busy on the continent, whether by direct military operations or by large subsidies paid to France's enemies among the German states. In the words of the duke of Newcastle, "France will outdo us at sea when they have nothing to fear on land . . . our marine

Siege warfare was still conducted during the eighteenth century. Lines of troops approach and fire on the town.

should protect our alliances on the Continent, and so, by diverting the expense of France, enable us to maintain our superiority at sea." The Royal Navy had begun to grow in size during the second half of the seventeenth century. It ceased to be principally a coastal defense force as it had been under the Tudor monarchs (albeit an able one, as the defeat of the Spanish Armada in the English Channel had demonstrated in 1588; see Chapter 5). As its role in protecting commerce increased, the Royal Navy expanded further, from 105 ships of the line at mid-century to 195 in 1790, while the smaller French navy increased only modestly in size to 81 warships, 9 more than those of the Spanish navy.

Building on earlier improvements in sails and rigging, charts and navigational techniques, the size and quality of ships improved. The British first added copper to hulls, which made their ships more sturdy. Short-barreled cannon of greater caliber proved deadly in close combat. Shipbuilding drew on scientific assistance from experts in mathematics and navigation.

Navies were beset by problems of desertion. Almost one-fourth of the men who joined the British navy between 1776 and 1780, many of whom had been dragged to the docks by press-gangs, deserted. Shipboard disease killed many sailors, despite the use of lemon juice to counter scurvy.

There were few decisive naval confrontations in the eighteenth century. But the British navy did defeat a Spanish fleet in 1718, thereby preventing an invasion of Sicily, and it defeated a French fleet in 1759, making impossible any French plan to assist the rebels against the British monarch. "Do you know what a naval battle is?" asked a French minister. "The fleets manoeuvre, come to grips, fire a few shots, and then each retreats . . . and the sea remains as salty as it was before." Despite the enhanced role of the navies of the Great Powers in defending commercial interests across the seas, such as by guarding merchant and supply ships, it was a century of maritime skirmishes. The cost of full-fledged battles seemed too high; ships were too expensive to build and maintain. Thus, fifteen times more British sailors died of disease between 1774 and 1780 than succumbed to battle wounds.

POLITICAL CHANGE IN GREAT BRITAIN

In England, the Glorious Revolution of 1688 had put an end to fifty years of social and political turmoil. The Bill of Rights of 1689 guaranteed Parliament's right to approve taxation and prohibited the monarch from suspending or dispensing with laws. English monarchs did not consider themselves completely bound by the Bill of Rights, as evidenced by the fact that they maintained standing armies in peacetime in defiance of the 1689 document. But the political struggles of the seventeenth century had demonstrated that the king had to work with Parliament in governing the nation. In turn, the state served as a guarantor of rights of property and patronage. The rights of Parliament and the elective nature of the House of Commons, even if based on an extremely narrow electoral franchise, distinguished British political life from that of its continental rivals. For his part, the English philosopher John Locke had argued that his nation's government should reflect an implicit agreement or contract between the monarchy and the people.

The period of "aristocratic consensus" that followed the Glorious Revolution was not as free from political contention as the term suggests. But it brought major changes in British political life. Thus, beginning in the 1760s, the interests of wealthy property owners were represented in the House of Commons, which gradually became a far more important political forum than the House of Lords, which only represented peers. It also became more difficult for the king to manage the House of Commons. The Whigs reaffirmed the essence of Britain's constitutional monarchy by demonstrating that the king could not rule without Parliament.

Edmund Burke.

Political differences between Tories and Whigs became more consistent. The former were now clearly identified with the prerogatives of the throne, the latter with the rights of Parliament. Whigs believed that the role of Parliament was to defend liberty, property, and the rule of law and thereby preserve the British constitution against possible abuses of power by the throne. In the words of the Irish-born political theoretician Edmund Burke (1729–1797), the British "mixed constitution" (which balanced the institutions of monarchy, the House of Lords, and the House of Commons), stood as an "isthmus between arbitrary power and anarchy." During this period, there emerged a sense that institutionalized opposition within Parliament to government policies was an intrinsic part of a political process in which competing interests were struggling for primacy. Moreover, during the eighteenth century, political life began to spill beyond the narrow confines of the British political elite as ordinary people demanded a voice in political life with increasing insistence. In Britain's North American colonies a similar and in some ways parallel struggle for liberty began, leading to the American War of Independence.

The Growing Powers of Central Government in Britain

During the eighteenth century, Britain, justly famous for its political preoccupation with liberty, saw the powers of central government expand. The increasingly global nature of trade and warfare made greater demands on the state's administrative abilities. The growth, greater centralization, professionalization, and efficiency of military and civilian administration permitted Britain to remain the strongest power on the globe.

Between 1680 and 1780, as the British built and consolidated their empire, their army and navy tripled in size. The power and reach of the Treasury also increased. As the economy grew rapidly, the British state raised taxes and efficiently collected them (the latter in dramatic contrast with the monarchy of France, whose financial plight continued to grow). These included land taxes, as well as excise (taxes on commodities) and customs taxes, which provided an increasing percent of revenue. At the same time, loans to the state greatly raised the national debt. The effective centralization of the British state made it possible for its increasing commercial and manufacturing wealth to be mobilized for the conquest and defense of the empire. The government spent more than three-quarters of its expenditures on the army, navy, or paying back debts from previous wars.

Britain's bureaucracy, though still quite undersized compared to that of France, also grew in size and complexity. A single French province had more officials than the entire government of Britain at the beginning of the century. By the end of the century, this was no longer the case. Limited venality, too, provided Britain with an advantage over its rivals. As the British state increased in size, its officials became more professional (technical expertise became more important), and departments within the bureaucracy became more clearly defined. Posts in the civil service for educated men offered chances for social advancement.

The British government, like its continental rivals, faced the problem of paying off the massive national debt amassed by loans that financed dynastic and trade wars. In 1719, the government had awarded the South Sea Company the right to take over the national debt. The South Sea Company had been founded in 1711 with the backing of a number of Queen Anne's advisers. Two years later, the government had awarded it a monopoly over the slave trade with Latin America and with favorable conditions for European trade. But because of the intermittent fighting with Spain during the War of the Spanish Succession, any profits from such trade seemed in the distant future. Needing a rapid infusion of capital, the directors of the company offered stock for sale on attractive terms. They bribed some potential purchasers and developed ties with high government officials.

With the help of unscrupulous investors, many of whom were holders of part of the national debt who wanted to get their money back, the company converted the debt owed them by the state into company shares. The directors parlayed the price of the stock higher. The scam worked as long as there were more investors whose funds could be used to pay dividends to those who had bought shares earlier. But the profits were all based on the sale of the stock rather than on real commercial gains.

A fever of speculation seized England. Smaller companies started up overnight, most of them insolvent or strangely organized, such as one literally limited to women dressed in calico. One joint-stock company (made

Contemporary lambasting of the South Sea Bubble. "Picture of the very famous Island of Madhead. Situated in Share Sea, and inhabited by a multitude of all kinds of people, to which is given the general name of Shareholders." (Amsterdam, 1720)

up of shareholders who would divide profits according to the amount of their investments) had been set up for "a purpose to be announced." The speculative craze ended with a jolt in 1720. With no gains of any kind forthcoming, the "South Sea Bubble" burst in September of that year. It was the first great financial crash (and coincided with the bursting of smaller speculative "bubbles" in Amsterdam and Paris). Political careers were ruined in the resulting financial chaos.

The financial scandal hung over political life when Robert Walpole (1676–1745) became chancellor of the Exchequer in 1721, a post he would hold for more than twenty years. The son of a landowner of modest means, the short, ruddy-cheeked Walpole was energetic and ambitious. And he was determined to restore political confidence. The king quietly replaced several of his ministers who had been most compromised in the South Sea Bubble. Parliament passed a law that allowed only companies chartered by the government to sell stock shares to the public. Walpole created a sinking fund (intended to "retire" the debt by paying off, or "sinking," part of it each year) to finance the crown's debts, which helped restore confidence.

King George II's lack of interest in matters of government made him as dependent on Walpole as George I had been. Queen Caroline's regard for Walpole contributed to his ability to weather political storms. He survived the wrath of some Members of Parliament (MPs) who disliked his unpopular financial reforms, including greater taxes on imports and on salt, and his goal of keeping Britain out of war.

Walpole perfected the system of political patronage, virtually managing the House of Commons. He used the patronage available to him as the effective head of the government to build unwavering support within Parliament and to place MPs loyal to him—"placemen"—in well-paying governmental positions, some of which were veritable sinecures. In return, they voted with the government.

On the local level, landed magnates doled out and received the plums within the administration: the bigger fish became county lord-lieutenants and the smaller fry became justices of the peace. One tombstone epitaph flaunted the obvious in eulogizing a well-connected lady lying therein, "By means of her alliance with the illustrious family of Stanhope, she had the merit to obtain for her husband and children twelve appointments in church and state," not a bad haul.

However, Walpole's support in Parliament eventually began to crumble. His attempt to reform the excise tax by extending it to wine and tobacco failed in 1733 after generating riots. William Pitt (1708–1778) led a coalition of "boy patriots" against Walpole. Specifically, they objected to his inaction against Spain, whose ships were harassing British ships in the

Sir Robert Walpole, standing at the head of the table, directs a cabinet meeting.

Atlantic. After being forced by public outcry to declare war on Spain in 1739—the perfectly trivial War of Jenkins' Ear—Walpole resigned in 1741.

Lesser lights continued Walpole's policies of building a political coalition based upon patronage. The duke of Newcastle (Thomas Pelham-Holles; 1693–1768), whose notorious incoherence led him to be known as "Hubble-Bubble," succeeded Walpole and ably manipulated the patronage of his position. Then Pitt came to power. The "Great Commoner" Pitt was a lonely, unstable man who alternated between feverish excitement and dark depression. He was demagogic, arrogant, and ruthless, commanding respect through fear.

The Role of the House of Commons

The British monarch could declare war or make peace, call or dissolve Parliament, appoint whomever he or she wanted to serve as cabinet minister, officer, bishop, general, or admiral, and the cabinet and government officials carried out the functions of state. But they did this against the backdrop of ongoing practical compromises between Parliament and the monarch.

During the early decades of the eighteenth century, the House of Commons gradually emerged as an epicenter of political life. Unlike the House of Lords, all of whose members were nobles, members of the House of Commons were elected by Britain's narrow electoral franchise based on landed wealth. Although still dominated by "gentle," or landed interests, the number of merchants elected to the Commons increased, for families that had made fortunes in business, whether they were titled nobles, non-titled gentry, or commoners, invested their money in land. Wealthy MPs could easily control blocs of votes in their counties through patronage. In 1776, only 5,700 men in Britain elected half of the members of Commons, most of whose members were routinely re-elected every seven years. In only three boroughs did more than 4,000 men have the right to vote and in several, fewer than 15 men could cast ballots. Thus, one lord confidently assured his son in 1754, "Your seat in the new Parliament is at last absolutely secured and that without opposition or the least necessity of your personal trouble or appearance." Some MPs were returned from "rotten" and "pocket" boroughs. Rotten boroughs ranged from the infamous "Old Sarum," which had no inhabitants but two representatives in Commons, and another that had been under water for centuries, to those with several hundred voters almost as easily managed. Pocket boroughs were in the pocket of the MP because his election was uncontested.

England's growing industrial towns were barely represented in Parliament. Manchester and Birmingham were not represented at all. Many of those in the urban elites no longer accepted the idea that their interests were "virtually represented" by MPs from districts represented in the House of Commons. Furthermore, emerging political discontent reflected alarm that Commons' role as the defender of the constitution against possible tyrannical abuse was being compromised by institutionalized corruption, symbolized by rotten and pocket boroughs.

The Development of Party Politics in the 1760s: Whigs and Tories

Whigs and Tories had governed in reasonable harmony during the Robert Walpole era. But after Walpole, many Whigs came to believe that ministers ought to be acceptable to Parliament as well as to the king. In contrast, Tories traditionally took the view that the prerogatives of king and church had to be maintained at all costs.

After coming to the throne in 1740, George III gave the impression that he intended to rule without Parliament. When George refused to declare war on Spain in 1761 during the Seven Years' War, William Pitt resigned as chief minister. Subsequently, the king appointed his former tutor, the aristocratic, aloof Scotsman John Stuart, the earl of Bute (1713–1792), as secretary of state and then as chief minister of the government. But Bute was an unpopular choice because he was not a member of Parliament, had little political experience and even less influence, and did not want Britain to undertake hostilities against Spain.

The king's appointment of his "dearest friend" seemed to Whigs to violate the unwritten agreement that the king act with Parliament's consent. Determined opposition merely served to strengthen the king's resolve. The press castigated Bute, and crowds in the street howled against him. Rumor insisted that he owed his controversial appointment to having been the lover of the king's mother. On the verge of a nervous breakdown, Bute resigned in 1763.

Bute's appointment raised the question of ministerial responsibility, dividing the House of Commons along ideological lines. George III sought to diminish the decisive role that the parliamentary Whigs had played during the reigns of his grandfather and great-grandfather. He turned against the Whig country gentlemen who no longer could be counted upon to support him on all matters. The king insisted on the monarchy's independence and particularly on his right to choose whomever he wished as minister.

Members of Parliament representing the interests of the "country gentlemen" began to use the term "party," but without the trappings of formal organization that would come late in the next century. Whigs, to be sure, remained loyal to the throne, although George accused them of being otherwise. But, as in the case of the king's appointment of Bute, they insisted on the rights of Parliament. While the issues dividing Tories and Whigs remained in some ways the same as those that had characterized the Walpole period, or even the Civil War, the emerging notion of political parties was perhaps of more lasting significance than the political groupings themselves.

The young King George III
in saner days.

The term "party" had existed since the time of the Glorious Revolution;
it had the sense of a group of people sharing a belief on a specific matter of
political controversy. It had been somewhat synonymous with "faction,"
which since the 1670s had the negative connotation of a cabal of individuals working for their own interests. With the exception of the Jacobite
Tories, however, the differences between Whigs and Tories were vague and
uncertain during the reign of the first two Georges. George III's seeming
determination to create a government above parties helped the old Whigs
revive their party solidarity. The idea developed that a party of parliamentary opposition formed an essential part of the parliamentary system of
representation.

George III insisted that it was his duty to defeat the forces of "faction."
Edmund Burke, for one, rejected the king's efforts to discredit the concept
of "party." In *Thoughts on the Cause of the Present Discontents* (1770), he
defined a party as "a body of men united for promoting by their joint en-
deavors *the national interest* upon some particular principle in which they
are all agreed." He believed that political parties stood as the basis of
representative government and therefore of political order. A newspaper
article in 1770 went even further: "Opposition, in parliament, to the
measures of government, is so far from being in itself an evil, that it has
been often productive of good to the state." By this description, parties
were to be "a regular and desirable feature of politics, not as a cancer on

the body politic which ought to be removed as swiftly as possible." They alone could ensure the preservation "of responsible government," specifically, the notion that ministers ought to be acceptable to Parliament. This concept of a loyal parliamentary opposition did not exist in France or anywhere else on the continent. Nor, for that matter, did it exist in all constituencies within Britain; in many, politics, dominated by family ties and outright patronage, went on as before.

George III could count on about a third of the members of Commons for unconditional support, at least partially because they held court-appointed posts. Unfailing voters for "court" became increasingly known as "Tories," particularly to the Whig opposition. Supporters of the government rejected the term, as they did all labels, but at the same time they lent credence to the concept by cohesively defending a patriarchal society based on monarchy, titled aristocracy, and the Anglican Church.

In 1766, Pitt returned to power for two years. King George depended on the political leadership of the "Great Commoner," but Pitt lost support even among his political friends by accepting a peerage, becoming duke of Chatham. Vigorous debates among Whigs, principally between the imperious Pitt and the duke of Newcastle and his followers, however, did not diminish the emerging notion of "party" most Whigs now accepted. For Whigs, the most significant issue remained the extent to which Parliament could limit the will of the monarch. Although family connections still loomed large, the significance of such an issue carried the party beyond the sense of a vague coalition.

The Rise of British Nationalism

Although king and Parliament were bitterly divided during the crises that led to the English Civil War and the Glorious Revolution, they were thereafter unified in the quest for British commercial and international predominance. During the eighteenth century, a strong sense of nationalism developed in Great Britain. This included pride in the nation's high degree of freedom and reverence for Parliament as the Protestant institution that had turned back the threat of Catholicism and successfully impeded absolute rule.

The fear of Catholicism, endemic in England since the Reformation, fired British nationalism. During the Anglo-French wars, faced with the threat of French invasion, British patriots across the social spectrum embraced the British Isles as the chosen land of God. British patriots never tired of boasting of Britain's prosperity and social stability while denigrating France, the strongest Catholic power. French support of the American rebels and the French Revolution of 1789 would, of course, bring these feelings to a head.

Many increasingly nationalistic Britons firmly believed that their "privileged island" had been chosen by God for a unique imperial destiny.

William Pitt the Elder, in particular, was an empire builder. Believing that the throne's Hanoverian interests were dominating foreign policy, and having made his reputation attacking Walpole's seeming indifference to British interests abroad, Pitt turned his attention to expanding the colonies. "Who will laugh at sugar, now?" thundered the future prime minister in the House of Commons in 1759 to nobles who had scorned colonial trade. Horace Walpole (1717–1797), Robert Walpole's youngest son, who was a novelist as well as the beneficiary of lucrative posts that left him plenty of time to write, was among the few who had some doubts about all of this. "No man ever went to the East Indies with good intentions," the younger Walpole said, adding sarcastically, "it really looks as if we intended to finish the conquest of the world during the next campaign."

The lure of commercial profit thus helped define British nationalism. A financial community of investors in London closely followed not only the vicissitudes of the economy but the ups and downs of British warfare. A good many financiers had, after all, loaned money to their state and therefore eagerly watched what was done with it. Their foreign and colonial trade often depended on naval protection, further linking their interests to the Union Jack. The state itself depended on expanding commercial activity for tax revenue. Economic interest groups and lobbies developed, learning their way around the London financial community and the corridors of government to represent their views on excise and customs taxes. New patriotic societies, some of them drawing ordinary people into the wave of nationalist enthusiasm, sprang up in many places, with mottoes like "For our country."

The generally harmonious relationship between the landed elite and the commercial community was a source of social and political stability in Britain, and of British nationalism. Nobles and gentry benefited from the expansion of state activity, diversifying their investments with loans to the crown. Unlike the continental powers, in Britain all subjects paid taxes. This afforded all social groups the sense of being Britons. At the same time (in contrast to the case in France), improved communications and the development of a national market aided the process of national integration in Britain.

Their commitment to the nation also enabled the British elite, proud of their freedoms and their country's more decentralized form of government, to accept a stronger state apparatus without complaint about infringements on their liberty. Thus, they did not feel the need for constitutional guarantees (based upon equality before the law) against arbitrary tyranny. The stronger state did not diminish the status of British landowners, and in no way infringed on their personal freedoms within civil society. Monarchy and Parliament joined hands in the pursuit of British empire, with the eager support of London's burgeoning financial community. English peers sought to prove, in Burke's words, that "a true natural aristocracy is not a separate interest in the state, or separable from it."

Anglo-Irish, Scottish, and Welsh gentlemen became more integrated into a national British landed elite, with increasing intermarriage a revealing indication of this process. Many Scots, though hardly all, began to see themselves as British, just as fewer English people considered Scots or Welsh to be outsiders who were potentially disloyal to the crown. The British monarchy became increasingly revered and celebrated as a rallying point for the nation.

Although many property-less Britons had reason to fear impressment gangs sweeping up men unlucky enough to be in the wrong place at the wrong time, and many others objected to having to billet troops, many of the king's subjects began to identify with their nation's increasingly professional armed forces. Moreover, the landed elite embraced military service to the nation.

CHALLENGES TO ESTABLISHED AUTHORITY

In the 1760s and 1770s, movements for reform emerged in several countries. In Britain, "liberty" became the watchword of political opposition to the government. In a parallel struggle on the other side of the Atlantic Ocean, the American colonists of Britain's thirteen colonies demanded "no taxation without representation," and then, when rebuffed, the "patriots" rebelled against British rule in the War of American Independence. Some of the reform movements on the European continent sought to reduce the strength of absolute rule, as in Denmark, or wanted to prevent the imposition of stronger centralized authority, as in the resistance of the parlements in France to Louis XV, or by the provincial estates to the Stadholder William V of Orange,in the case of the Dutch Republic. Other movements for reform challenged what seemed to be unwarranted privileges, again most notably in France, where the most significant attempt came from a reforming minister within the state itself. In every Western country, more information about political events in other states was available through newspapers and gazettes, as well as from merchants, other travelers, and diplomats, who exchanged correspondence in an increasingly literate culture. In Britain and parts of Western Europe, political clubs also reflected greater preoccupation with politics. These reform movements, then, influenced each other, however indirectly.

British Radicals

In the 1760s in Britain, ordinary people (called "the swinish multitude" by Edmund Burke) demanded electoral reform, and some even universal manhood suffrage. Reformers asked that constituencies be redrawn so that rapidly growing industrial regions in the north of England be appropriately represented in Parliament, and that London, which was grossly under-represented, elect more Members of Parliament. Moreover, outside the small, formal political arena defined by the right to vote, shouts for freedom swelled among ordinary people.

John Wilkes (1727–1797), the son of a successful London malt distiller, was an MP of modest means and a Protestant Dissenter. Charming, witty, and reckless, Wilkes leapt into the public eye in 1763 with the publication of his newspaper the *North Briton.* Issue number 45 attacked the government—and the king himself directly—for signing the compromise Treaty of Paris with France that year, ending the Seven Years' War. The king ordered "that Devil Wilkes, a trumpet of sedition" arrested for libel. Wilkes announced that he considered his arrest a blow against liberty and the constitution by the unjust, arbitrary power of government, "a question of such importance," as he put it at his trial, "as to determine at once, whether ENGLISH LIBERTY be a reality or a shadow." The court freed Wilkes after a week in jail on the basis of parliamentary immunity. Wilkes triumphantly boasted that his fate was tied to "that of the middling and inferior set of people" in Britain.

Fearing prosecution for pornography, as the government dug up a bawdy old poem he had written (and the House of Commons lifted parliamentary immunity), Wilkes left for France in 1764. He was arrested, tried, and convicted upon his return to Britain in 1768, and then freed after thou-

The supporters of John Wilkes and liberty take to the streets.

sands of people demonstrated on his behalf. Wilkes then stood for election in Middlesex, the county making up most of Metropolitan London north of the Thames and outside of the "City." With the support of many merchants and small manufacturers wealthy enough to be eligible to vote, Wilkes was re-elected to Parliament. Four times he was elected, and four times Parliament refused to seat him because of his previous conviction.

Wilkes claimed that Parliament's action threatened "the first principle of our constitution," the freedom to stand for election. Cloaking himself in a patriot's garb, he became a rallying symbol for the campaign for the rights of the unrepresented in a time of economic hardship, grain riots, and work stoppages.

"Wilkes and Liberty" echoed in speeches, conversation, and song. In 1769, the Society of the Supporters of the Bill of Rights invoked the name of Wilkes as it called for the government to "restore the constitution." The number 45—the libelous issue of the *North Briton*—became a rallying cry. Wilkes' rather misshapen face appeared on posters, handbills, verses, cartoons, tea mugs and dinner plates. He was elected sheriff of London in 1771, and even lord mayor three years later, though he was not allowed to occupy either position.

Reformers now began to demand greater freedom of the press, specifically a redefinition of libel laws (so that the government could be criticized) and the right to publish parliamentary debates. They further demanded that Parliament meet each year and that MPs be required to live in the districts from which they were returned. However, in general, Whigs disassociated themselves from Wilkes, wary of demonstrations for universal manhood suffrage. Few Whigs were willing to go beyond insisting on the principle of ministerial responsibility within the confines of the existing constitution.

Literary and "philosophical" societies, which had sprung up in most large towns, facilitated the emergence in England of political culture even wider than that which had developed during the political crises of the seventeenth century. Now interest in politics was such that some inns and coffeehouses added special reading rooms to accommodate their clientele. By 1760, London printing presses, the number of which had increased from seventy-five in 1724 to about two hundred at the time of Wilkes' first arrest, churned out eighty-nine newspapers, four of which were dailies. Another thirty-five newspapers were published outside London. By 1790, there were fourteen London daily newspapers (Burke wrote for four of them), and the number of provincial papers printed each day had multiplied by four times.

Political pamphlets, handbills, and caricatures inundated the capital and the larger provincial towns. By the 1760s, artists had stopped omitting the names of the targets of their satirical wit. Like its Whig opponents and the extra-parliamentary radicals, the government found itself obliged to utilize newspapers, pamphlets, brochures, and handbills to argue its case before public opinion.

By the 1780s, two relatively well-defined parties contended for power within the context of a constitutional monarchy. But the changes went further than this because some Whigs demanded political reform and, in doing so, carried political life beyond the narrow limits of the British political arena. Ordinary people, unrepresented in Parliament, began to make their voices heard.

American Revolutionaries

During the 1760s, another challenge to the British crown was smoldering far across the Atlantic Ocean in North America. The thirteen American colonies, many times the geographic size of England, had become ever more difficult for the British government to administer. The population of the colonies, which accounted for about 20 percent of British exports and supplied 30 percent of its imports, had grown by tenfold in just seventy years, from about 250,000 in 1700 to more than 2.5 million in 1775, compared to about 6.4 million in England at the same time. Philadelphia had by that time become the second largest city in the British Empire, with 30,000 residents. Those arriving on the shores of the Americas found a land of opportunity. Many were able to purchase land that would have been beyond their means at home. Artisans and even common laborers commanded relatively high wages because of the shortage of labor in the colonies.

Over the decades, the residents of the colonies had developed a sense of living in a separate society. Merchants, a heterogeneous group that stood atop the social hierarchy, lawyers, and wealthy landowners like the Virginians George Washington (1732–1799) and Thomas Jefferson (1743–1826) led the colonists. They resented the continued presence of the British army—sometimes in their very houses through forced billeting—and the attempt of British officers to try to impose on the colonial forces the same standards of discipline that applied in Britain. They believed that they had the right to resist unjust laws in the name of liberty.

For radicals in Britain, "rotten" boroughs symbolized the threat to liberty; for the American colonists, as expressed by John Adams, "liberty can no more exist without virtue and independence than the body can live and move without a soul." Some British Whigs began to identify themselves with the colonists, who took the name Whigs themselves, claiming that corruption was threatening Britain's constitutional balance between monarchy and Parliament. They saw the two movements as parallel struggles.

The quest of George Grenville (1712–1770), who had succeeded Pitt in 1763 as chief minister, for supplementary revenue aggravated the strained relations between the colonists and the mother country. The king's new favorite also ordered massive efforts to stop smuggling. In 1765, Parliament passed the Stamp Act, which forced Americans to purchase stamps for virtually anything printed. A year later, Benjamin Franklin (1706–1790) of

Philadelphia made the colonists' case to the House of Commons. He argued that the act represented the unfair domination of England over another part of the empire. Commons repealed the Stamp Tax, but the government then initiated other taxes. Furthermore, Parliament proclaimed a Declaratory Act in 1766, which asserted its right to tax the colonies as it pleased. A year later, the Townshend Acts levied duties on colonial imports of paper, tea, and other products.

The American colonists' determined protests encouraged British reformers. The colonists' claim that they were being taxed without having the right to representation played nicely into the hands of political radicals in Britain. The shout "Wilkes and Liberty!" began to echo on both sides of the Atlantic. American political pamphlets and brochures found an eager audience among British merchants, manufacturers, artisans, and other people eager for representation in Parliament. Colonists lobbied in Britain to demonstrate that "the cause of America is the common cause of the realm . . . both countries have the same complaint, and therefore claim the same friends."

The British government was at first divided and uncertain in the face of an upsurge of demonstrations at home and agitation in the colonies. In March 1770 in Boston, British soldiers fired on a crowd that was vociferously protesting the quartering of British troops in that city. The "Boston Massacre," which took five lives, outraged colonists. That year, George III appointed Frederick Lord North (1732–1792) first minister. North, an amiable, sensible man who got along well with the king, was skilled at putting together political coalitions and was a brilliant debater in Commons. He sponsored the Tea Act of 1773. North hoped to aid the East India Company by allowing the company to ship a surplus of tea to the colonies, with the British government collecting its tariff only when the tea arrived in American ports. The move would reduce the price of tea but maintain what the colonists viewed as the unacceptable principle that Britain could tax goods imported into the colonies. It would also threaten the interests of American smuggling, a widespread money-making operation.

On December 16, 1773, colonists dressed as Indians forced their way aboard British merchant ships docked in Boston and dumped the cargo of tea into the harbor. Parliament responded to the Boston Tea Party by passing the repressive "Intolerable Acts." These specified that the port of Boston be blocked until the colonists had reimbursed the merchants and government for the tea dumped into the harbor. In September 1774, representatives from the colonies met in the First Continental Congress. By now, Benjamin Franklin was drawing a distinction between "uncorrupted new states," by which he meant the colonies, and "corrupted old ones," one of which seemed to be waging war on liberty. The British sent more troops. In April 1775, in the first open fighting between colonists and British regulars, the colonial militia held its own against British troops searching for weapons at Concord and Lexington, Massachusetts, and

Paul Revere's depiction of the Boston Massacre.

then in the pitched battle at Bunker Hill in Boston, when 1,500 colonists, holding the higher ground, turned back two British attacks until running out of ammunition.

In *Common Sense* (1776), some 100,000 copies of which circulated in the colonies, Thomas Paine (1737–1809) launched a devastating attack on the king. *Common Sense* reflected the influence of the Enlightenment, particularly Rousseau's notion of the "social contract." Furthermore, it reiterated Locke's argument that governments received "their just powers from the consent of the people." All laws, Paine wrote, "are laws of nature." Paine helped convince delegates to the Second Continental Congress to adopt Thomas Jefferson's Declaration of Independence on July 4, 1776. It declared the equality of all people, based on "inalienable rights" and that the authority of government stems from the consent of the governed. It also asserted that when governments violated the "unalienable rights" to "life, liberty, and the pursuit of happiness" of their people, the latter had the right to rebel.

The war now became a fight for independence. The Continental Congress appointed George Washington to command its troops. The British government hoped to recover the colonies at the lowest possible cost; military campaigns were compromised by halfhearted and often inept leadership by the British commanders. The initial British policy, that of isolating and punishing the rebels, quickly failed. There were too few British troops to fight a war over a considerable territory against an increasingly determined foe. Next, the British undertook conventional military operations. But the colonial troops simply scattered. In 1776, Washington's army managed to cross the Hudson River into New Jersey. Washington captured Trenton that December, wintering with his ragtag army in freezing temperatures at Valley Forge, Pennsylvania.

In contrast to British soldiers, each of whom required the transport of a third of a ton of food across the Atlantic each year, the colonial army was virtually self-sufficient and broadly supported by the colonists. Trained in part by an officer in the army of Frederick the Great, it became far more than what a loyalist (someone who supported the British cause) dismissed as "a vagabond Army of Raggamufins, with Paper Pay, bad Cloathes, and worse Spirits." The most significant battles of the war were fought in the classic European style of confrontations, not as engagements between hit-and-run patriots and British regulars. Some of the colonists fought with an almost evangelical fervor that reflected the fact that many of them saw the struggle as one of good against evil. The brutality of the British soldiers in requisitioning goods and maintaining order in the territories they controlled was self-defeating. By the time General Richard Howe (1726–1799), discouraged by the failure of the British government to send promised reinforcements, tried to negotiate with the rebels at the end of 1776, the colonists refused to listen because they had no reason to negotiate.

France signed an alliance with the American rebels in February 1778, agreeing to provide substantial loans in gold. The French monarchy realized that favorable commercial treaties with an independent United States might more than compensate for the loss of all rights to territory east of the Mississippi. Thereafter, the French navy harassed British supply routes. In 1779, Spain joined the war on the American side, hoping to profit from Britain's colonial war by recapturing Gibraltar and Minorca. Seeking to prevent the North American colonies from purchasing Dutch supplies, the British fought the Dutch Republic. Britain also confronted the refusal of Russia, Sweden, Prussia, Portugal, and Denmark to curtail trade with the rebellious Americans.

Great Britain had overextended its capacity to wage war. Its naval advantage, the basis of its strength in modern times, had been eroded. Despite swelling the army to 190,000 men, campaigns on land went badly. On October 19, 1781, Lord Cornwallis surrendered his outnumbered army at Yorktown, Virginia, to a combined force of American and French troops. "Your armies are captured," George III was informed, "the wonted superiority of your navies is annihilated; your dominions are lost." Two years later, Britain officially recognized the independence of the American colonies. News of the struggle of the colonists for freedom from British rule spread throughout much of Europe, reported in newspapers. As pub-

The British surrender at Yorktown, 1781.

lic opinion became surprisingly well informed about events across the Atlantic Ocean, the American victory encouraged movements for reform in other places.

Britain, which had lost its richest colony, did not want to lose any others. In 1774, as the resistance in the thirteen colonies became more determined, Parliament had passed the Quebec Act, in an effort to prevent tensions between the British Anglican conquerors and the Catholic population of Quebec from boiling over. The Test Act, which required all officials to take communion in the Anglican Church, was abolished in Quebec, and the Catholic Church was given the status of an established church by being permitted to levy tithes. The British government also strengthened its control over its other colonies. The India Act (1784) created a board responsible to Parliament to which the East India Company had to report, while establishing the jurisdiction of British courts in cases of fraud or other transgressions. Another parliamentary act in 1791 created more centralized administration in Canada, with a governor-general exercising far more authority than two colonial assemblies elected by restricted suffrage.

The advent to power in 1784 of William Pitt the Younger (1759–1806) restored political stability. The next year, Pitt introduced a wide-ranging bill for political reform. It proposed to reduce the minimum tax required for the electoral franchise and to abolish thirty-six rotten boroughs,

William Pitt the Younger addressing the House of Commons.

awarding their representation to manufacturing regions and cities. Opposition among the country gentlemen, as well as that of the king himself, however, led to the bill's defeat. But Pitt did manage to eliminate useless offices that had become sinecures, introduced more accurate accounting methods into government, facilitated the collection of excise taxes, and encouraged further foreign trade. Despite the personal failings of George III, Britain, which remained the world's premier commercial and manufacturing power, emerged from the relatively turbulent decades with its constitutional monarchy strengthened.

The Parlements and the French Monarchy

Two interrelated struggles in the early 1770s challenged the nature of absolute rule in France. The first was against what seemed unwarranted privileges held by nobles and other corporate groups. The second opposed royal policies and pretensions that seemed to transcend absolute rule and verge on despotism. In a way, this debate somewhat paralleled political issues in Britain. Despite the fact that the British monarchy was not absolute, the insistence of Whigs that Parliament's prerogatives be in no way compromised by royal authority reminded some contemporaries of French noble claims, made through the parlements, that the French monarchy was overstepping its own constitutional limits. Likewise, challenges to the tangle of economic and social privilege in France replicated, even if in a different context, campaigns for political reform by ordinary British subjects unrepresented in Parliament and therefore outside the political arena.

In France, those seeking reforms that would limit royal authority had a much more daunting task because of the absolute nature of monarchical rule. The kings of France nonetheless depended on the support of the parlements. These were law courts made up primarily of nobles and seated in Paris and more than twelve provincial cities. Their principal function was to give royal edicts the force of law by registering them. By refusing to register them, the parlements could impede the functioning of the absolute state. Thus, when the king's edicts had to do with increased or new taxation, political opposition to royal policies sometimes emerged in the parlements.

The increased centralization of the French state had in itself helped create contact between more people and the officials of the king. The concept of a "public" emerged, before which the monarch was in some sense responsible and before which the layers of privilege in French society no longer seemed acceptable. The crises that embroiled the king and the parlements from the 1750s to the 1780s helped shift public opinion toward the view that the parlements represented the rights of the "nation," threatened by a monarchy that seemed to be lapsing from absolute to despotic rule.

The issue of Jansenism set the parlements against royal absolutism by raising the constitutional issue of the right of the monarch to circumscribe their traditional prerogatives. The Jansenists (see Chapter 7) were a dissident group within the Catholic Church. The pope had condemned Jansenism in 1713 with the papal bull *Unigenitus,* which Louis XV supported. But Jansenists found support within some of the parlements, which identified with Jansenist resistance to what seemed to be the absolute monarch's despotic rule. Louis XV's support of the papal bull angered some nobles and magistrates, who were inclined to resist what they considered the papacy's undue interference in French affairs.

The period of conflict between the parlements and the crown really began in 1749. The controller-general attempted to make the *vingtième* tax (a tax applying to both nobles and commoners) permanent, drawing heated opposition from the parlements. And the Church again sought, without success, to force the French clergy to accept *Unigenitus.* Many bishops threatened that sacraments would be refused to laymen who did not have a certificate signed by a priest attesting that the person had made his or her confession to a priest who had accepted the papal bull. Seven years later, the pope tried to defuse the crisis by banning these certificates.

But this concession did not placate the Parlement of Paris. Many of the parlements were manipulated by a handful of Jansenist magistrates and lawyers who managed to convince their colleagues that French acceptance of the papal edict amounted to an abandonment of French sovereignty over the temporal affairs of the Church. The king, refusing to hear the parlements' grievances, made clear that he considered the parlements nothing more than rubber stamps, a means of promulgating his will. When the Jesuit order continued to crusade against Jansenism, the Parlement of Paris responded by ordering Jesuit schools closed in 1761, citing the fact that members of the order took a vow of obedience to the pope.

The successive crises over Jansenism may have weakened the authority of the French monarchy by allowing the Parlement of Paris, and several provincial parliaments as well, to claim they were defending constitutional liberties and the independence of the Gallican (French) Church—since Jansenists saw themselves as part of it—against royal encroachment and against Rome. By weakening the authority of the Catholic Church in France, the crisis over Jansenism also eroded the prestige of the absolute monarchy. Jansenism ceased being a political issue after 1758, when the Parlement of Paris won judicial authority over many ecclesiastical matters. But the self-proclaimed role of lawyers and magistrates as representatives of public opinion and protectors of the sovereign political will of the nation against abuses of powers was an important legacy from the Jansenist crisis.

The layers of economic privilege in France had proliferated with the extension of state power, as each monarch sought revenues with increased desperation. Despite increasing calls for reform, even critics who vociferously challenged monopolies (for example, those of guilds) did not intend to end privileges per se. Rather, many of them wanted a share of the privileges and wanted to eliminate "unjust" monopolies that seemed to benefit others unfairly. Wealthy commoners, enriched by the economic changes, sought the kind of privileges nobles enjoyed, above all exemption from many kinds of taxation. Thus, the issue of taxation would mobilize some of the parlements against the monarchy because it raised the question of the layers of privilege that underlay the French state and of the limits of absolute authority.

In 1771, Chancellor René-Nicolas de Maupeou (1714–1792) provoked the parlements by again attempting to make the *vingtième* tax permanent. Many nobles feared that general tax increases might lead to dangerous peasant uprisings, in which nobles stood to lose the most. Facing mounting resistance, Louis XV effectively abolished the parlements. He then created new, more docile law courts that would not resist royal authority, staffed by magistrates who did not own their offices.

Both sides in the conflict between the parlements and Chancellor Maupeou appealed to public opinion. A declaration of high-ranking nobles stated that the king had abused "the constitution of the government and the rights of the people" by trying to establish "a despotism without bounds, without limits, and consequently without rights." The nobility asserted its "right of assembly," recalling that "the nation, in its assemblies, had charged the parlements with defending its rights." Influenced by the ideas of the Enlightenment, lawyers called for judicial reform, religious toleration, and the end to the abuse of privilege. When the monarchy tried to silence the lawyers, the latter turned courtrooms into forums for political opposition. Lawyers explored notions of sovereignty of the nation and put forward the case of the parlements against the crown.

As the idea of the nation gradually entered political discourse, the possibility emerged that when the interests of the monarchy and the nation clashed, popular allegiance could pass exclusively to the nation. Some degree of popular identification with parlements as defenders of the nation against despotism would not be effaced. The Maupeou "coup" lasted only three and a half years, but it had far-reaching effects on the nature of the opposition to the monarchy. It demonstrated that the parlements were not powerful enough to protect "the nation" against royal despotism, suggesting that only a body such as the Estates-General, which had not been convoked since 1614, could do so.

Louis XV was no stranger to unpopularity. He was held to be lazy and indifferent, as rumor had him obediently following the orders of his favorite mistress and advisers. The Seven Years' War had exhausted the treasury, and the king seemed incapable of restoring public confidence. Furthermore, France had lost Canada and several Caribbean islands to Britain, its hated rival. This loss of prestige, as well as income, increased the number of the king's critics. The structures of absolute rule seemed inadequate to managing the cumbersome French state; inefficient tax collection and the weight of growing expenses left the state coffers inadequately filled.

Louis XV's death in 1774 did not resolve the crisis. Following popular demonstrations and a spate of publications in support of the parlements, the twenty-year-old Louis XVI (ruled 1774–1793) dismissed Maupeou and recalled the parlements. Public opinion seemed to have helped turn back what was popularly conceived to be a despotic assault on the restraints on absolute rule.

Convinced that the financial difficulties of the monarchy stemmed from the stifling effect of privileges on the economy, a new minister, Anne-Robert Turgot, undertook ambitious reforms. His goal was to cut away some of the web of privileges, making the absolute monarchy more efficient. Turgot convinced the young king to issue royal edicts, despite the opposition of the Parlement of Paris. These ended noble and clerical tax exemptions, abolished the guilds, freed the internal commerce of grain (the price of which had been first set free in the 1760s), and exempted peasants from having to work a certain number of days each year repairing roads. Economic liberalization would, he hoped, increase agricultural production and manufacturing, thereby augmenting tax revenue.

But like Louis XV's attempts to override the traditional role of the parlements, Turgot's reforms aroused vociferous opposition. Nobles—with some significant exceptions—rallied against proposed financial reforms intended to extricate the country from its growing financial morass. The parlements, still smoldering over their treatment by Maupeou and Louis XV several years earlier, refused to register—and thereby give the status of law—the reforms of Turgot, who had supported Maupeou. Grain merchants and guilds, among other privileged groups, voiced strident opposition. Ordinary people rose up in protest, blaming the freeing of the grain trade for the higher prices of flour and bread in a period of dearth. Accusations of hoarding abounded. Grain riots, in which women played the leading roles, swept across the country during the spring "flour war" of 1775. The significance of these events was that an increasing number of the king's subjects lost the habit of obedience to him. Lawyers, once again insisting on the difference between absolute and despotic rule, would emerge as leaders as the political crisis of the monarchy accelerated in 1788.

The king dismissed Turgot in 1776, ending the most significant reform effort on the continent. That same year, the American colonists declared their independence from Britain. France allied with the colonial rebels, forcing Louis XVI to borrow ever more money at high interest rates and to sell more offices and titles to those who could afford to pay for them. This helped shift power within the nobility from the embittered "nobles of the sword" to the "nobles of the robe," who had been ennobled through the purchase of office or title. The unreformed French monarchy then slid into an even deeper financial crisis.

Other Movements for Reform

Although the influence of the Enlightenment varied in different places, the philosophes all put forward the claims of freedom against privilege and absolutism. Some rulers, principally those of Prussia, Tuscany, and Austria, introduced reforms inspired by Enlightenment thought, putting into practice reforms that seemed to reflect the "enlightened absolutism" that Voltaire and other philosophes had expected (see Chapter 10).

In other cases, movements for reform came from below. In the Swiss Republic of Geneva, native-born artisans during 1765–1768 exerted pressure for the right to vote, meeting in assemblies and demanding equality with the citizens possessing political rights. But they were rebuffed by wealthy Genevans, who tried to placate them with reductions in their taxes. An uprising in 1782 unseated the ruling oligarchy before the intervention of France, Sardinia, and the Swiss canton of Bern put an end to it.

There were also insurrections. In 1761, an uprising on the Mediterranean island of Corsica in the name of "fatherland and liberty" ended rule by Genoa, a northern Italian port dominated by bankers and merchants, although the French occupied Corsica seven years later. In 1770, Greeks rose up against Turkish domination. They were assisted by Russia, the Turks' enemy, eager to enter the world of Mediterranean politics with

Emelian Pugachev in his cage after he
was apprehended.

the goal of ultimately conquering Constantinople. Empress Catherine the
Great sent soldiers and a small fleet in the hope that Greek success might
encourage other peoples to rise up against Ottoman rule. Turkish troops
crushed the revolt, but the Greek movement for independence, by virtue
of the special place of classical Greece in the development of Western civilization, helped ignite pan-Hellenism. Yet, to be sure, many who supported the cause of Greek independence had reservations about the role of
Russia, a state as despotic as that of the Ottoman Turks.

In the Russian Empire itself, there was a massive rebellion, largely of
Cossacks, in 1773–1774 (see Chapter 9). It was led by Emelian Pugachev,
who promised to respect "liberty," including that of religion. The rebels
killed thousands of landlords before being crushed. And in Bohemia and
Moravia in 1775, peasants rose up against their lords and the state. Although Habsburg troops put down the rebellions, the uprising led Maria
Theresa and her son Joseph II to enact reforms that gradually abolished
feudal dues. Each of these uprisings was a movement for freedom, but
also a return to traditional privileges that seemed imperiled by the centralized absolute state.

In Denmark, where the king had imposed absolute rule in 1660 by sup-
pressing parliament and refusing to consult with the estates, a current of
reform emerged early in the 1770s. In part, it was the inspiration of Johann Struensee (1737–1772), a German doctor, who convinced the ailing
King Christian VII (ruled 1766–1808) to undertake reforms to strengthen
the state economically so that, with Russian support, Swedish Baltic ambitions could be thwarted. The king abolished censorship and the death

penalty for thieves, extended religious toleration, and promised to undertake more agricultural reforms in the interests of creating a free peasantry.
But the king's widowed mother and nobles conspired against the reforms.
Struensee was tried and convicted of, among other things, living "without
religion or morality," and executed in 1772. But after little more than a
decade of reaction, the reforms Struensee had encouraged became part of
a program for the future, a sign of the times.

In Sweden, the reforms of the 1760s and 1770s were swept away, as in
the case of France and Denmark. A virtual coup d'état by King Gustavus
III (ruled 1771–1792) imposed absolutism. Thus, while presenting himself as a "patriot king" protecting Swedish peasants from the nobility while
reassuring the "intermediary powers," or estates, the king imposed a new
constitution in 1772. It reduced the power of the Senate and the Diet.
The king's cabinet became the principal arm of Swedish government. Yet,
to the secretary of the British embassy in Stockholm, Sweden had not
proven ready for liberal reforms. "Liberty," he wrote, "is not a plant of sudden growth; time only can give it vigor. It will not take roots but in a soil
congenial to it; and, to be rendered flourishing or lasting, it must be cultivated with care and defended with unremitting attention from the dangers
which perpetually surround it."

Political struggles in the Dutch Republic were similar to the struggles
between Whigs and the crown in Britain, followed by the emergence of
extra-parliamentary demands by ordinary people for political reform. The
regents of the Dutch cities, defending the republic's federalism embodied
by the Estates-General, which represented the seven provinces, opposed
the policies of the bumbling Stadholder William V of Orange (in power
1751–1795). The regents declared war on Britain in 1780 in the hope of
weakening their commercial rival. As the war dragged on, they also sought
to weaken the monarchical pretensions of William V, who wanted to augment executive authority at the expense of the provinces.

In 1785, in the midst of political crisis, the Dutch Republic had allied
with France to counter the Austrian plan to reopen the Scheldt River and
restore Antwerp to some of its former commercial glory, which would have
undercut Amsterdam's prosperity. The possibility that France might
achieve its kings' dream of annexing the Southern Netherlands (Belgium)
made the British government anxious, further irritating the pro-British
William V.

In the meantime, a radical "Patriot Party," primarily drawn from the
middle class and artisans, had begun to demand democratic reforms.
Influenced by the success of the American revolutionaries, they demanded
more democratic representation in the Estates and the right to have urban
militias. These Dutch reformers unseated the stadholder. Prussian King
Frederick William II (ruled 1786–1797), whose sister was the stadholder's
wife, sent an imposing army in 1787, occupying Amsterdam and putting
down the challenge to William V's authority as stadholder. Distracted
by mounting political crisis, France backed down against the alliance of

England and Prussia. The balance of power had once again been preserved. Dutch patriot refugees poured into the Austrian Netherlands and
France.

The Austrian Netherlands, too, experienced political turmoil. The powerful estate of nobles opposed Joseph II's enlightened reforms, which
threatened their privileges, and succeeded in driving out Austrian troops
in 1789. There too a movement for democratic reform emerged, calling for
the transformation of the Estates into a representative assembly. The
Dutch mood seemed to be catching. The prince-bishop of Liège stressed
the importance of preventing "the evil schemes of the majority of the Liè-
gois, who would like to become a republic and to join the United
Provinces as other provinces . . . the burgomasters and other men of that
quality wish to see themselves on chairs of velvet and be received with
cannon salutes . . . only troops and fortresses can hold them to obedience." Dutch patriots invaded the Southern Netherlands in October 1789,
driving away the Austrians. But a popular movement appealed to the nobles even less than did Austrian rule. Nobles, backed by the clergy and
with the tacit support of most peasants, wrested control of the short-lived
state from the urban-based reformers. The return of Austrian troops in
1790 occurred without resistance.

FADING POWERS: THE OTTOMAN EMPIRE AND POLAND

The structure of international power in eighteenth-century Europe was
not fundamentally changed by the quest for reform during the 1760s and
1770s. But in the new, more competitive European environment of the
late eighteenth century, two states that did not have access to the fruits of
international trade and that were unwilling to restructure themselves lost
their power in Europe. Thus, the Turkish Ottoman Empire entered a period of long decline, and Poland literally disappeared as an independent
state, at least until after World War I. The Ottoman Empire, its power
overextended and lacking a centralized structure of government, saw its
territories in the Balkans and Caucasus eaten away by Austria and Russia.
Poland, in contrast, had become a power without becoming an absolute
state; weakened by noble domination of the monarchy, it fell prey to its aggressive absolute neighbors: Russia, Prussia, and Austria, which divided up
the state in three partitions.

The Decline of Turkish Power in Europe

In contrast to other absolute sovereigns, Turkish sultans ruled indirectly,
governing through church or village officials. Indirect rule itself may have
hastened the decline of Ottoman absolutism, signs of which were already
apparent late in the seventeenth century. The Turkish economy, army, and
navy could not keep pace with the Western powers. Turkish cavalrymen,

with curved swords and magnificent horses, fell before Western artillery and rifles.

Like the Spanish Empire at its peak, the Ottoman domains were so vast that they defied effective control. Insurrections, including some by the janissaries, challenged the authority of the sultans. Imperial officials, Muslim and Christian alike, became notoriously corrupt. Turkish authority virtually collapsed in mountainous Montenegro and Bosnia, where the Turks battled Habsburg and Venetian forces. The government began to run out of money. Stop-gap measures, such as the debasement of the currency, failed to provide the empire with sufficient revenue.

Incapable sultans, who were unable or unwilling to impose reforms, further weakened the Turkish cause. As boys they lived in virtual isolation in a world of uncertainty among court eunuchs and palace intrigue. No regular pattern of succession had ever been established. Whereas Peter the Great of Russia undertook Western military reforms, the sultans did not. The advice of officials who had been sent to Vienna and Paris to study methods of state went unheeded in Constantinople. There was not a single printing press in the Ottoman capital until well into the eighteenth century. Long wars fought against Persia in the East made it less easy to repress disturbances in the Balkans. In some parts of the empire, a system of land inheritance replaced the old system; new landowners began to force peasants into serfdom. The haphazard and inefficient collection of taxes, often by dishonest tax farmers, engendered peasant resistance. As the system of indirect rule declined in effectiveness, some local Christian and Muslim leaders now commanded their own military forces, virtually independent of the sultan's authority in Constantinople. This was precisely the same phenomenon that the absolute monarchs of France, Prussia, Russia, and Austria had overcome. The long decline of Ottoman power, which began in the last decades of the seventeenth century, during which the empire lost almost all of its European territories, facilitated the rise of Russia.

The Disappearance of Poland

While the Ottoman Empire survived, Poland did not as an independent state (at least until the end of World War I). Poland had been a strong state in the seventeenth century. But during the early decades of the eighteenth century, the kingdom, its population reduced by wars and bubonic plague to only 6 million people, had become increasingly dependent on Russia. Poland's eclipse made possible Russia's gains in Ukraine.

Polish nobles (the *szlachta*) not only maintained their prerogatives, they relegated the king to virtual political impotence. Nobles, who made up 8 percent of the population, elected the king. They considered this period of domination one of "golden liberty," marked by an unworkable political system by which a single vote in the noble assembly (Sejm) would bring about its dissolution (the *liberum* veto). Deputies were forbidden to make speeches in what became known as the "silent Sejm." Furthermore, Poland lacked a standing army and an efficient bureaucracy.

The War of Polish Succession (1733–1735) began when Russia attempted to impose its candidate on the Polish throne over the opposition of the Polish nobles. Because of France's interest in maintaining Sweden, the Ottoman Empire, and Poland as checks against Austrian Habsburg domination of Central Europe, Louis XV proposed a candidate for the throne, his father-in-law, Stanislas Lesczinski, who had reigned as king of Poland from 1704 to 1709 and now had the support of most Polish nobles. But a Russian army forced the election of Augustus III of Saxony (ruled 1733–1763), who was the Austro-Russian candidate.

When the Polish throne again fell vacant in 1763 with the death of the king, Russian influence led the Polish nobles to elect as king the cultured, cosmopolitan Stanislas Poniatowski (ruled 1764–1795), one of the insatiable Russian Empress Catherine the Great's many lovers ("many were called, and many were chosen," as one wag put it). Stanislas was somewhat influenced by Enlightenment thought. Sensing the necessity of reform, he hoped to advance manufacturing in Poland and looked to Britain as a model. He tried to end the *liberum* veto and to curtail the right of seigneurial courts to impose death sentences. He also established a number of schools. Only by such measures, he believed, could Poland escape poverty and backwardness, where killing a peasant was punished only with a fine. Voltaire and Rousseau were among those philosophes who viewed Poland as fertile ground for Enlightenment-based reform of noble prerogatives and ecclesiastical authority, and who concerned themselves with the fate of the "most unhappy realm." But some of the more powerful Polish nobles, who resented Russian influence, now opposed Stanislas and his reforms. They hoped that France or the Ottoman sultan might intervene on their behalf.

Catherine, like the Prussian king, feared that Stanislas' reforms might lead to a stronger, less subservient neighbor. Since 1764, Russia and Prussia had been allies in the attempt to prevent an expansion of French influence in the Baltic, while preventing Poland from reviving its fortunes. Furthermore, Polish nobles had begun to persecute non-Catholics. Catherine, in the interest of the Orthodox Church, demanded that all non-Catholics be granted toleration in Poland. When Polish nobles formed an anti-Russian and anti-Catholic confederation, Catherine sent troops into Poland. Ukrainian peasants took advantage of the chaos to rise up against their Polish lords. When they burned a Turkish town while chasing out Poles, Turkey entered the war against Russia. Catherine annexed Crimea, Wallachia, and several territories along the Black Sea, at Turkish expense.

Alarmed by an expansion of Russian power, Austria and Prussia demanded territorial compensation. Catherine suggested that the three concerned powers might help themselves to parts of beleaguered Poland. The First Partition in 1772 reduced Poland by about a third (see Map 11.3).

MAP 11.3 THE PARTITIONS OF POLAND   Poland at its greatest extent in 1660–1667, and the loss of territory to Austria, Prussia, and Russia during the Partitions of 1772, 1793, and 1795.

Maria Theresa of Austria "wept and then took her share," the large province of Galicia, which lay between Russian Ukraine and the Austrian empire. Prussia absorbed West Prussia, which had formed a corridor separating East Prussia from the rest of the kingdom. Russia snatched large chunks of territory of eastern Poland.

Stanislas proclaimed a liberal constitution in 1791 which, establishing a hereditary monarchy and abolishing the unworkable system of noble veto, proclaimed that all authority stemmed from the nation. This remarkable document reflected the influence of the French Revolution. Poland became a constitutional monarchy, with the king naming ministers but with the parliament and Poland's few major towns retaining privileges.

But Poland's days were numbered. When Poles rose up in 1792 against Russian authority in the part of Poland that had been absorbed by Russia twenty years earlier, Russian troops intervened. They were backed by Polish nobles, the grave diggers of Polish independence, who opposed the liberal constitution. Prussia refused to come to Poland's aid, receiving in exchange for looking the other way its own annexation of more Polish territory in the Second Partition in 1793. With the Third Partition in 1795, Prussia and Russia ended Poland's independence for more than a century. The Constitution of 1791, perhaps the most progressive constitution of the century, was torn to shreds. "Poland was but a breakfast," wrote Edmund Burke, "where will they dine?" Russia's new gains drew its interests further into Central Europe, and it now shared a border with the Habsburg monarchy.

CONCLUSION

Some historians have argued that movements against absolutism and against privilege, particularly those against the latter in Great Britain and the successful rebellion of its North American colonies, constituted a general Western "democratic revolution." But, despite the quest for political change in several Western states, calls for universal manhood suffrage were rare, those for the extension of political rights to women even more so (an exception being Geneva in the early 1780s). Even in Britain, after a contentious decade marked by demonstrations for political reform, the most widespread riots of the 1780s were the anti-Catholic Gordon riots. In France, the assault on the Old Order was less an attack on the nobles, per se, than on privilege. The institutions of the Old Regime in continental Europe demonstrated not only resiliency, but also a capacity to undertake reform.

Nonetheless, denunciations in France against privilege, shaped in part by Enlightenment thought (and which echoed in other countries as well, helping spark the rebellion of Britain's thirteen North American colonies), would be revived in the late 1780s. The Seven Years' War and assistance to the Americans had considerably worsened the financial crisis of the French monarchy, as the increasingly global dynastic rivalries and wars placed further strains on European states. France entered a serious political crisis when critics of the monarchy condemned the king of ruling despotically and attacked in the name of freedom the layers of economic and social privilege that seemed to constrain effective government and constrict freedom. Calls for sweeping reform led to the French Revolution of 1789, which proclaimed the principle of the sovereignty of the nation. Once again, the eyes of Europe turned toward France.

PART FOUR

REVOLUTIONARY EUROPE

The French Revolution of 1789 struck the first telling blow in continental Western Europe against monarchical absolutism on behalf of popular sovereignty. Popular involvement pushed the Revolution to the left, while counter-revolution and foreign intervention led to the dramatic centralization of state authority and the Terror.

In 1799, Napoleon Bonaparte helped overthrow the Directory, the last regime of the revolutionary era in France. An admirer of the Enlightenment, Napoleon claimed that he was the heir of the French Revolution. But while Napoleon saw himself as a savior who carried "liberty, equality, and fraternity" abroad, his conquest of much of Europe before his final defeat left a mixed legacy for the future.

Following Napoleon's defeat in 1815 at the Battle of Waterloo, the Congress of Vienna created the Concert of Europe, the international basis of Restoration Europe. The British, Austrian, Prussian, and Russian rulers, restoring legitimate rulers to their states after the fall of Napoleon, hoped to prevent further liberal and nationalist insurrections in Europe. But liberal and national movements could not so easily be swept away. During the subsequent three decades, "liberty" became the watchword for more and more people, particularly among the middle classes, who came to the forefront of economic, political, and cultural life. Liberal movements were in many places closely tied to the emergence of nationalism, the belief in the primacy of nationality as a source of allegiance and sovereignty. Yet, liberal and nationalist movements shattered the Congress of Vienna as democratic and nationalist revolutions began in

France in 1848 and spread into Central Europe, challenging liberal and conservative monarchies alike.

In the meantime, during the first half of the nineteenth century, the Industrial Revolution slowly but surely transformed the way many Europeans lived. Dramatic improvements in transportation, notably the development of the railroad but also road improvements, expanded the market for manufactured and other goods. Rising agricultural production, increasingly commercialized in Western Europe, fed a larger population. Migrants poured into Europe's cities, which grew as never before. Contemporaries, particularly in Western Europe, sensed profound economic, social, political, and cultural changes.

CHAPTER 12

THE FRENCH REVOLUTION

In 1791, King Louis XVI decided to flee Paris and the French Revolution. A virtual prisoner in the Tuileries Palace by the first months of the year, he had secretly negotiated for possible intervention on his behalf by the Austrian king and other European monarchs. The royal family furtively left the Tuileries Palace late at night on June 20, 1791, disguised as the family and entourage of a Russian baroness riding in a large yellow coach. But in the eastern town of Sainte-Menehould, the postmaster recognized the king, whose image he had seen on a coin. He rode rapidly to Varennes, where the National Guard prevented the king's coach from going on. Three representatives of the National Assembly brought the royal family back to Paris. Near the capital, the crowds became threatening, and National Guardsmen stood by the roadside with their rifles upside down, a sign of contempt or mourning.

The French Revolution mounted the first effective challenge to monarchical absolutism on behalf of popular sovereignty. The creation of a republican government in France and the diffusion of republican ideals in other European countries influenced the evolution of European political life long after the Revolution ended. Issues of the rights of people, the role of the state in society, the values of democratic society, notions of "left" and "right" in political life, the concept of the "nation at arms," the place of religion in modern society and politics, and the question of economic freedom and the sanctity of property came to dominate the political agenda. They occupied the attention of much of France during the revolutionary decade of 1789–1799. The political violence of that decade would also be a legacy for the future.

The revolutionaries sought to make the French state more centralized and efficient, as well as more just. Napoleon Bonaparte, who some historians consider the heir to the Revolution and others its betrayer, continued this process after his ascent to power in 1799.

The arrest of Louis XVI.

Modern nationalism, too, has its roots in the French Revolution. The revolutionaries enthusiastically proclaimed principles they held to be universal. Among these were the sovereignty of the nation and the rights and duties of citizenship. The revolutionaries celebrated the fact that the Revolution had occurred in France. But wars intended to free European peoples from monarchical and noble domination turned into wars of French conquest. The revolutionary wars, pitting France against the other Great Powers, contributed to the emergence or extension of nationalism in other countries as well, ranging from England, where the sense of being British flourished in response to the French threat, to Central and Southern Europe, where some educated Germans and Italians began to espouse nationalism in response to the invading French armies.

THE OLD REGIME IN CRISIS

The French Revolution was not inevitable. Yet, difficult economic conditions in the preceding two decades, combined with the growing popularity of a discourse that stressed freedom in the face of entrenched economic and social privileges, made some sort of change seem possible, perhaps even likely. When a financial crisis occurred in the 1780s and the king was forced to call the Estates-General, the stage was set for the confrontation that would culminate in the French Revolution.

Long-Term Causes of the French Revolution

The increasing prevalence of the language of the Enlightenment, stressing equality before the law and differentiating between absolute and despotic rule, placed the monarchy and its government under the closer scrutiny of public opinion (see Chapter 11). Borrowing Enlightenment discourse, opponents accused Louis XV of acting despotically when he exiled the Parlement of Paris in 1771 and tried to establish new law courts that were likely to be more subservient than the parlements had been. Opponents believed that the king was trying to subvert long-accepted privileges. He was forced to relent and restore the parlements, which maintained their right to register royal edicts.

Enlightenment literature was not in itself revolutionary. But some of its implications would be, as complaints mounted about noble privileges and guild monopolies, as well as arrogant and sometimes corrupt royal officials. In 1774, Controller-General of Finances Anne-Robert Turgot drew up a program to eliminate some monopolies and privileges that fettered the economy (see Chapter 11). However, the decree abolishing the guilds, among other decrees, generated immediate hostility. Two years later, Turgot's experiment ended. But some writers now began to contrast the freedoms Turgot had in mind with the corporate privileges that characterized the economy and society of eighteenth-century France.

The social lines of demarcation between noble and bourgeois had become less fixed over the course of the century; despite increasing opposition from the oldest noble families who believed their ranks were being swamped by newcomers, in the fifteen years before 1789 almost 2,500 families bought their way into the nobility. Yet, many people of means continued to resent noble privileges, above all the noble exemption from most kinds of taxes. Disgruntled bourgeois did not make the French Revolution, but their dissatisfaction helped create a current of demands for reform. The monarchy's worsening financial crisis would accentuate these calls.

France remained a state of overlapping layers of privileges, rights, traditions, and jurisdictions. Nobles and professional groups such as master artisans in guilds and tax farmers (who generally had bought their offices and could pocket some of the taxes they collected) always contested any plan to eliminate privileges.

The sharpest resistance to reform came from the poorer nobility. Among the "nobles of the sword," the oldest noble families whose ancestors had proudly taken arms to serve the king, some had fallen on hard times and clung frantically to any and all privileges as a way of maintaining their status. They resented the fact that the provincial parlements, in particular, had filled up with new nobles who had purchased offices—the so-called "nobles of the robe"—and that power had shifted within the nobility from the oldest noble families to those recently ennobled.

The monarchy depended upon the sale of titles, offices, and economic monopolies for revenue and long-term credit. But by creating more offices—there were more than 50,000 offices in 1789—it risked destroying public confidence and driving down the value of offices and loans already held.

Economic hardship compounded the monarchy's financial problems by decreasing revenue while exacerbating social tensions. High prices, falling wages, and high unemployment darkened the 1770s and 1780s. A series of bad harvests—the worst of which occurred in 1775—made conditions of life even more difficult for poor people. The harvests of 1787 and 1788, which would be key years in the French political drama, were also very poor. Such crises were by no means unusual—indeed, they were cyclical and would continue until the middle of the next century. Meager harvests generated popular resistance to taxation and protests against the high price of grain (and therefore bread), including the seizure of these commodities and their sale at what was considered to be a just, or reasonable, price. A growing population put more pressure on scarce resources.

Many peasants believed that landowners were increasing their hardship. Some historians have argued that a "seigneurial reaction" was underway as smaller agricultural yields diminished noble revenues, while inflation raised the costs of noble life. By this view, noble landowners reacted by hiring estate agents, lawyers, and surveyors to maximize income from their lands, reasserting old rights over common lands, on which many poor peasants depended for pasturing animals and gathering wood for fuel. Landlords raised rents and tried to force sharecropping arrangements on peasants who had previously rented land.

Although the feudal system of the Middle Ages had long since passed, remnants of it remained. Peasants were still vexed by seigneurial dues and cash owed to their lords. Many nobles still held some rights of justice over their peasants, which meant that they could determine guilt and assess penalties for alleged transgressions; seigneurial courts were often used to enforce the landlord's rights over forests, lakes, and streams, and his exclusive rights to hunt and fish on his estate. Hard times made these obligations—such as being assessed higher dues at harvest time than before—seem truly unfair. Forty percent of the *cahiers* (lists of grievances) drawn up in one district before the fateful convocation of the Estates-General noted frustration with the seigneurial regime. The political crisis that led to the French Revolution would provide ordinary people with an opportunity to redress some of these mounting grievances.

The Financial Crisis

The serious financial crisis that confronted the monarchy in the 1780s was the short-term cause of the French Revolution. France had been at war with Britain, as well as with other European powers, off and on for more than a century. The financial support France had provided the rebel colonists in the American War of Independence against Britain had been underwritten by loans arranged by the king's Swiss minister of finance, Jacques Necker (1732–1804). Almost three-fourths of state expenses went to maintaining the army and navy, and to paying off debts accumulated from the War of the Austrian Succession (1740–1748) and the Seven Years' War (1756–1763), as well as from the American Revolution. The monarchy was living beyond its means.

Where were more funds to be found? Nobles had traditionally enjoyed the privilege of being exempt from most, and the clergy from all, taxation. There was a limit to how many taxes could be imposed on peasants, by far the largest social group in France. In short, the financial crisis of the monarchy was closely tied to the very nature of its fiscal system.

The absolute monarchy in France collected taxes far less efficiently than did the British government. In Britain, the Bank of England facilitated the government's borrowing of money at relatively low interest through the national debt. In France, there was no central bank, and the French monarchy depended more than ever on private interests and suffered from a cumbersome assessment of fiscal obligations and inadequate accounting. French public debt already was much higher than Britain's would be a century later, and it continued to rise as the monarchy sought financial expedients. Public confidence rose and fell, as debt charges sometimes absorbed two-thirds of royal revenues. Even when public confidence waned, however, invariably the market for offices and titles bounced back.

The hesitant and naive Louis XVI was still in his twenties when he became king and probably burdened by sexual impotence. He seemed unable to grasp financial details. Louis knew little of his kingdom, venturing beyond the region of Paris and Versailles only once during his reign. He preferred puttering around the palace with the tools of his second favorite hobby, carpentry (hunting, at which he excelled, came first); he particularly enjoyed taking clocks and watches apart and putting them back together.

The unpopularity of Louis' elegant, haughty wife, Marie-Antoinette (1755–1793), accentuated the public's lack of confidence in the throne (whether or not she ever really snarled "Let them eat cake," when told that the people were starving). The daughter of the Austrian queen, Maria Theresa, Marie-Antoinette was married to Louis to strengthen French dynastic ties to Austria. Unhappy in her marriage, Marie-Antoinette lived extravagantly and was embroiled in scandal. Thus, for example, in 1785, she became entangled in a seamy scandal when a cardinal, the former ambassador of France to the Habsburg court in Vienna, gave her a fabulous diamond necklace in the hope of winning favor. The necklace and some of the prelate's money were then deftly stolen by mysterious plotters, a strange scenario that included a prostitute posing as the queen. The "diamond necklace affair," as it was called, increased the public image of the

(*Left*) Louis XVI. (*Right*) Marie-Antoinette.

king as a weak man, a cuckold. The queen's indiscretions and infidelities seemed to undercut the authority of the monarchy itself, and her detractors indelicately dubbed her the "Austrian whore."

In the meantime, Necker continued to float more loans while attempting to sort out the tangled morass of France's financial bureaucracy. But in 1781, some ministers and noble hangers-on convinced the king to dismiss Necker. The following year, Necker produced a naive and —at best—fanciful account of the royal finances that purported to demonstrate that more revenue was coming to the state than was being spent. Necker hoped to reassure French and particularly the foreign creditors who made up his financial network that reform was unnecessary. Bankers, however, did not believe Necker's figures. Some refused to loan the monarchy any more money until the state enacted financial reforms. The new finance minister, Charles-Alexandre de Calonne (1734–1802), demonstrated that Necker's calculations of royal finances were far-fetched. Yet, Calonne spent even more money, purchasing two more châteaux for Louis XVI and putting the royal treasury deeper in debt by borrowing from venal officeholders in order to pay off creditors now gathered at the royal door.

The parlements, or sovereign law courts, were certain to oppose fiscal reform, which they believed would lead to an increase in taxation through a general tax on land. They distrusted Calonne, an old enemy whom they identified with fiscal irresponsibility and governmental arrogance that some believed bordered on despotism.

To sidestep the parlements, Calonne asked the king in February 1787 to convoke an Assembly of Notables consisting of handpicked representatives from each of the three estates: clergy, nobility, and the third estate (everybody else). The crown expected the Assembly to endorse its reform proposals, including new land taxes from which nobles would not be exempt. Believing that the monarchy's policy of borrowing from Peter to pay Paul could not go on, Calonne suggested that France's financial problems were systemic, resulting from a chaotic administrative organization, including the confusing regional differences in tax obligations. The monarchy's practice of selling the lucrative rights to collect, or "farm," taxes worsened the inefficiency. Calonne knew that the crown's contract with the tax farmers would soon have to be renegotiated, and that many short-term loans contracted by the monarchy would soon come due.

Denouncing "the dominance of custom" that had for so long prevented reform and encumbered commerce, Calonne proposed to overhaul the entire financial system. The Assembly of Notables, however, rejected Calonne's proposals for tax reform and refused to countenance the idea that nobles should be assessed land taxes. Moreover, the high clergy of the first estate, some of whom were nobles, also vociferously opposed Calonne's reforms. They, too, feared losing their exemption from taxation. The corporate nature of French society, based upon privilege, was at stake.

Nobles convinced the king to sack Calonne, which he did on April 8, 1788. Louis XVI replaced Calonne with the powerful archbishop of Toulouse, Étienne-Charles de Loménie de Brienne (1727–1794). Like his predecessor, Loménie de Brienne asked the provincial parlements to register—and thus approve—several edicts of financial reform, promising that the government would keep more accurate accounts. But the Parlement of Paris refused to register some of the edicts, including a new land tax and a stamp tax, which evoked the origins of the American Revolution, something Loménie de Brienne had failed to consider.

THE FIRST STAGES OF THE REVOLUTION

Some members of the Assembly of Notables had been willing to accept fiscal reform and to pay more taxes, but only with accompanying institutional reforms that would guarantee their privileges against monarchical despotism. Specifically, they wanted the king to convoke regular assemblies of the Estates-General—made up of representatives of the three estates—which had not been convoked since 1614. They also wanted the monarch to allow the parlements more say in governing France. The king was in a difficult position. He needed to reduce the privileges of the nobles in order to solve the financial crisis, but to do so without their approval would lead to accusations of tyranny. On the other hand, capitulating to the demands of the privileged classes in return for new taxes would compromise his absolute authority and suggest that his word was subject to the approval of the nation, or at least the nobility. The resolution of this dilemma would lead to the events that constituted the first stages of the French Revolution.

Convoking the Estates-General

The "noble revolt" began the French Revolution. In the summer of 1787, the parlements had called on the king to summon the Estates-General to confront the financial crisis. The members of the parlements had expected that the Estates-General would confirm their prerogatives, but they soon found out that they could not control the course of events.

In response to the refusal of the Parlement of Paris to register the land and stamp taxes, in August 1787 Louis XVI exiled its members to Troyes, a town to the southeast of Paris. Nobles and high clergymen protested vigorously. The provincial parlements backed up the Parlement of Paris. The Parlement of Grenoble refused to register the new stamp and land taxes and convoked its provincial Estates (one of the assemblies of nobles which represented the interests of the region) without royal authorization. The "revolt of the nobility" against the monarchy's attempt to force nobles to pay taxes spread. Provincial parlements continued to demand that the Estates-General be convoked. This revolt was not directed against the institution of the monarchy itself, but against what the nobles considered abuses of the rights and privileges of the nation committed by an increasingly despotic crown. In this, the revolt of the nobles recalled the revolt known as the Fronde, vanquished by the young Louis XIV in the mid-seventeenth century (see Chapter 7).

Confronted by mounting opposition, the monarchy sought compromise. Loménie de Brienne agreed to withdraw the new land and stamp taxes in exchange for maintaining the tax on income (the *vingtième* tax), which nobles and other privileged people had first been assessed in the 1750s to pay for the Seven Years' War. He made clear, however, that the crown would be forced to settle its debts in paper money backed by royal decree. Louis recalled the Parlement of Paris from exile in November 1787 and promised to listen to what it had to say. But the king ordered new loan edicts registered without giving the parlement a chance to be heard. When the duke of Orléans, the king's cousin, interjected that such a procedure was illegal, Louis replied, "That is of no importance to me . . . it is legal because I will it." Louis XVI thus seemed to cross the line between absolutism and despotism.

In May 1788, as hostilities between the king's ministries and the Parlement of Paris continued, the king ordered the arrest of two of its most radical members. He then suspended the parlements, establishing new provincial courts to take their place and creating a single plenary court that would register royal edicts. Resistance to the king's acts against the parlements came quickly. The Assembly of the Clergy, which had been summoned to decide on the amount of its annual gift to the crown, protested the abolition of the parlements. Riots in support of the parlements occurred in several towns. In Grenoble, on June 10, 1788, crowds expressed support for their parlement by pelting soldiers with stones and roof tiles.

On August 8, 1788, Louis XVI announced that he would convoke the Estates-General on May 1 of the following year. He hoped that it would avert royal bankruptcy by agreeing to the imposition of the new taxes. Two weeks later, he reappointed Necker as minister of finance, a measure he believed would appease the nobles, investors, and holders of government bonds, who had never objected to his unrestrained borrowing. But the convocation of the Estates-General helped coalesce public opinion against the king. That the nobles forced the crown to convoke the Estates-General became the first act of the French Revolution. Many people believed that the Estates-General, more than the parlements, would represent their interests and check royal despotism.

The question of how voting was to take place when the Estates-General met assumed increasing importance. The issue highlights tensions between conservatives, many of whom were nobles, and reformers, some of whom were bourgeois but whose members also included some liberal nobles. Would each of the three estates—clergy, nobles, and the third estate—have a single vote, which would almost certainly quash any reform since the majority of nobles and clergymen were against reform, or would each member of the estates be entitled to his own vote?

On September 25, 1788, the Parlement of Paris, which had been reinstated amid great celebration, supported the king's insistence that voting within the Estates-General would take place by estate instead of by head. This meant that when the Estates-General met, as in 1614, each of the three estates would have the same number of representatives and be seated separately. Henceforth, the parlements would be seen by many people as defending the prerogatives of their privileged members, losing their claim to defend the nation against the king's despotism.

Popular political writers now began to salute the third estate (which made up 95 percent of the population) as the true representative of liberty and of the nation against royal despotism. Others asked for some sort of representative assembly that would reflect "public opinion." The "patriot party," a coalition of bourgeois and some liberal nobles, began to oppose royal policies, which they contrasted with those of the "nation." "Patriots" denounced the vested interests of the court and the nobles close to it. Political publications began to inundate France, making these debates national political issues. The Society of the Thirty, a group that included liberal nobles from very old families—for example, the Marquis de Lafayette (1757–1834), French hero of the American Revolution—as well as a number of commoner lawyers, met to discuss, debate, and distribute liberal political pamphlets. They proposed that the third estate, which represented everyone not belonging to the first two estates, be entitled to twice as many representatives in the Estates-General as the nobility and clergy. The loose coalition that made up the patriot party increasingly focused its attentions on this issue.

In January 1789, Abbé Emmanuel Joseph Sieyès (1748–1836), an obscure priest, offered the most radical expression of a crucial shift in politi-

(*Left*) The Marquis de Lafayette. (*Right*) The Abbé Sieyès.

cal opinion. "We have three questions to ask and answer," he wrote, "First, What is the Third Estate? Everything. Second, What has it been heretofore in the political order? Nothing. Third, What does it demand? To become something therein." He contrasted the "nation" against royal absolutism and noble prerogative. Sieyès' polemic represented a radical current of opinion that had revolutionary implications. Moved by the question of whether the estates should vote as one, or whether members should vote as individuals, Sieyès demanded a predominant role for the third estate in political life.

The vast majority of the men elected to the Estates-General were residents of cities and towns, two-thirds of whom had some training in the law—indeed, lawyers would dominate the third estate. Two-thirds of those elected to the first estate were parish priests, many of whom were of humble origin and resented the privileges of the bishops and monastic orders. Some of the younger noble representatives elected to the second estate were liberals. They wanted institutional reforms in the organization of the French monarchy that would permit them to check the power of the king, in much the same way as the Parliament in England served as a check on the English crown. Yet, clearly if each estate had but one vote, the reactionary nobles still had a good chance of imposing their will on the third estate, because most people assumed that the clergy (first estate) would, when push came to shove, follow the nobles (second estate). In December 1788, the king agreed to doubling the number of representatives of the third estate, but declined to give all members an individual vote.

The king asked the local electoral assemblies, along with the first two estates, to draw up lists of grievances (*cahiers de doléances*), which the Estates-General would discuss. Thousands of grievances offered the monarchy a wide variety of opinions, ranging from concrete suggestions for reform to the considered opinion that the foul breath of sheep was ruining pasture land in Lorraine. More important, *cahiers* criticized monarchical absolutism and the intransigence of seigneurs, asked for a more consistent and equitable tax structure, and called for the creation of a new national representative body. A few of the *cahiers* denounced as an abuse of royal power the so-called *lettres de cachet*, documents issued in the name of the king that allowed a person to be arrested for any reason and imprisoned indefinitely. They demanded "that no citizen lose his liberty except according to law; that consequently no one be arrested by virtue of special orders, or, if imperative circumstances necessitate such orders, that the prisoner be handed over to the regular courts of justice within forty-eight hours at the latest." But some *cahiers* also reflected continued popular trust and reverence for the king (as the *cahier* of the third estate of one town that wrote "imbued with gratitude prompted by the paternal kindness of the king"), while denouncing the rapacity and bad faith of his advisers and ministers. Unfortunately, the *cahiers* were edited along the way and most never reached the king. Thus, the very process by which the government received the grievances reflected growing disillusionment with the monarchy's response to the crisis.

On May 5, 1789, the nearly 1,000 members of the Estates-General (about 600 of whom represented the third estate) assembled at Versailles. The king greeted the first two estates, but kept the commoners waiting for two hours. When he finished his speech, members of the third estate violated protocol by boldly putting their hats back on, a right reserved for the two privileged orders. When it became apparent that representatives would vote not by head but by estate, the third estate stalled the proceedings for weeks by insisting that all three estates register their delegates together. On June 17, the third estate overwhelmingly approved a motion by Sieyès that declared the third estate to be the "National Assembly" and the true representative of national sovereignty. The third estate now claimed legitimate sovereignty and an authority parallel, if not superior, to that of the king of France.

The first estate now voted to join the third. But on June 20, as rumors circulated that the king might take action against them, representatives of the third estate found that their meeting hall had been locked for "repairs." Led by their president, Jean-Sylvain Bailly (1736–1793), an astronomer, the members of the third estate took the bold step of assembling in a nearby tennis court. There they took an oath "not to separate, and to reassemble wherever circumstances require, until the constitution of the kingdom is established and consolidated upon solid foundations." With principled defiance, the third estate demanded that defined limits be placed on the king's authority.

The king now declared the third estate's deliberations invalid. Yet, on June 23, he announced some substantial reforms, agreeing to convoke periodically the Estates-General, to abolish the *taille* (the tax on land) and the *corvée* (labor tax), to eliminate internal tariffs and tolls that interfered

The Tennis Court Oath, June 20, 1789.

with trade, and to eliminate the *lettres de cachet*. He also agreed that the Estates-General would vote by head, but only on matters that did not concern "the ancient and constitutional rights of the three orders." To the radicalized members of the third estate, the king's concessions were not enough.

Louis XVI dismissed Necker on June 22, but reversed himself after learning that thousands of people in Paris had invaded the courtyard of the Tuileries Palace to demand that Necker, who in December had persuaded the king to double the representatives of the third estate, stay on. After threatening to dissolve the Estates-General by force, on June 27 the king ordered the first two estates to join the third.

Storming of the Bastille

In Paris, ordinary people now began to pay more attention to the ongoing struggle at Versailles. Many now believed that a conspiracy by nobles and hoarders lay behind a shortage of food and high prices. Furthermore, there seemed to be an increase in the number of royal troops around Paris and Versailles. Rumors spread that the National Assembly would be quashed. On July 11, the king once again ordered Necker into exile. The following day, demonstrators carried busts of Necker. Bands of rioters attacked the customs barriers at the gates of Paris, tearing down most of the toll booths. In response to rumors that the king had ordered even more troops to Paris, people began to arm themselves.

On the morning of July 14, 1789, thousands of people—small tradesmen, artisans, and wage earners for the most part—seized weapons stored in the Invalides, a large veterans' hospital. Early that afternoon, the attention of the Paris crowd, now numbering perhaps 80,000 people, turned toward the Bastille, a fortress in the eastern part of the city, where the crowd believed powder and ammunition were stored. For most of the eighteenth century, the Bastille had been a prison, renowned as a symbol of despotism because some prisoners had been sent there by virtue of one of the king's *lettres de cachet*, summarily and without a trial. On that hot summer day, the Bastille's prisoners numbered but seven, a motley crew that included a nobleman imprisoned upon request of his family, a renegade priest, and a demented Irishman, who alternately thought he was Joan of Arc, Saint Louis, and God.

The crowd stormed and captured the Bastille, which was defended by a small garrison. More than 200 of the attackers were killed or wounded. A butcher decapitated the commander of the fortress, and the throng carried his head on a pike in triumph through the streets. The Bastille's fall would be much more significant than it first appeared. Louis XVI responded to

The taking of the Bastille, July 14, 1789.

the news of the fall of the Bastille with "Is it a revolt?" Came the reply, "No, Sire, it is a Revolution." The crowd's uprising probably saved the National Assembly from being dissolved by force. Now unsure of the loyalty of his troops, Louis sent away some of the troops he had summoned to Paris, recognized both the newly elected municipal government, with Bailly serving as mayor of the "Commune of Paris," and a municipal defense force or National Guard (commanded by Lafayette), and capitulated to the popular demand that he recall Necker to office.

On July 17, the king came to Paris to be received by the municipal council at the town hall, accepting and wearing an emblem of three colors, red and blue for the city of Paris, and white for the Bourbons. By doing so, Louis XVI seemed to be recognizing what became the tricolor symbol of the French Revolution.

The Great Fear and the Night of August 4

Now it was the peasants' turn to intervene in the unfolding of revolution. News of the convocation of the Estates-General had brought hope to many rural people that the king would relieve their crushing fiscal burdens. They had expressed their hopes in the grievances they sent with their third estate delegates to Versailles. The past fifteen years had not been good ones for peasants. The cost of renting land rose dramatically in the 1770s and the 1780s, while recent harvest failures brought widespread deprivation and riots against the high price of grain.

Against this background and heightened hopes for reform, news of the Bastille's fall touched off protests in the provinces. Encouraged by the gathering of the Estates-General, between July 19 and August 3 peasants attacked seigneurial châteaux. In some places they burned title deeds specifying obligations owed to lords. These peasant rebellions helped cause a subsequent general panic known as the "Great Fear." Fueled by the rumor of an aristocratic "famine plot" to starve or burn out the people, peasants and townspeople mobilized in many regions of France. To repel the rumored approach of brigands sent to destroy crops, townspeople and peasants formed armed units to defend themselves and save the harvest. In Angoulême in southwestern France, 20,000 people gathered together, anticipating that brigands would soon fall upon them. In towns, new local governments and National Guard units were established to institute reforms and to restore order as the effective authority of the state disintegrated. These events brought to power lawyers, merchants, and other "new men" who had formerly been excluded from political life.

News of peasant violence and the panic engendered by the "famine plot," galvanized members of the National Assembly. Some believed, or half-believed, the rumors that brigands paid by nobles were on the loose in the provinces. A group of liberal representatives from Brittany had formed a "Breton Club" of about 200 men within the patriot party. They came to the conclusion that only radical measures by the Assembly could restore order and give the legislators the time needed to carry through reforms. The Breton Club convinced a very wealthy noble to rise in the Assembly on August 3 and propose the abolition of tax exemptions.

On August 4, in an effort to appease the peasants and to forestall further rural disorders, the National Assembly formally abolished the "feudal regime," including seigneurial rights. This sweeping proclamation was modified in the following week, however, to preserve the sanctity of property rights by providing the nobles with indemnification for their abolished feudal rights. Thus, owners of seigneurial dues attached to land would receive compensation from the peasants (although, in general, such compensation was not forthcoming and was subsequently eliminated). The Assembly abolished personal obligations, which were vestiges of medieval serfdom, without compensation. The members of the National Assembly thus renounced privilege, the fundamental organizing principle of French society during the Old Regime. Other reforms enacted the following week included the guarantee of freedom of worship and the abolition of the sale of offices, seigneurial justice, and even the exclusive right of nobles to hunt. The provinces and cities, too, were required to give up most of their archaic privileges, such as exemption from the hated salt tax granted to the province of Brittany. In these ways, the National Assembly enacted a sweeping agenda that proclaimed the end of the Old Regime.

Consolidating the Revolution

In one remarkable session, on the night of August 4, 1789, the National Assembly had swept away much of the Old Regime. The Assembly's decrees destroyed absolutism by redefining the relationship between subject and king. No longer would the king rule by divine right, or buy allegiance by dispensing privileges to favorites. Instead, the king would be constrained by powers spelled out in a constitution. The Assembly then began to create the new regime. It began by promulgating the Declaration of the Rights of Man and Citizen, a remarkable document based on universal principles. It next established a new relationship between church and state, creating a national church, making Catholic Church property "national property," and compelling the clergy to swear allegiance to the nation. The National Assembly then turned to the long process of framing a constitution for the new regime, and is therefore sometimes also known as the Constituent Assembly.

In the meantime, however, Marie-Antoinette and some of the king's most influential advisers balked at accepting any weakening in royal authority. Louis XVI was denounced when he objected to the loss of an absolute veto over legislation. Fearing the influence of nobles at the court, crowds early in October marched to Versailles, returning to Paris with the king and the royal family. Henceforth, while many nobles, among others, fled France for exile and sought the assistance of the monarchs of Europe against the Revolution, the king himself became vulnerable to the tide of Parisian popular radicalism. As nobles and clergy led resistance to the Revolution, the Parisian radical clubs moved further to the left. The days of Louis and of the monarchy itself were numbered.

The Declaration of the Rights of Man and Citizen

As it set out to create a constitutional monarchy, the Assembly promulgated the Declaration of the Rights of Man and Citizen on August 26. This set forth the general principles of the new order and intended to educate citizens about liberty. It would become the preamble to the new constitution that was being formulated by the Assembly. One of the most significant documents in Western political history, the Declaration reflected some of the ideas that Thomas Jefferson had enshrined in the American Declaration of Independence of 1776. Article One proclaims, "Men are born and remain free and equal in rights." The Enlightenment's influence is apparent in the document's concern for individual freedom, civic equality, and the sense of struggle against corporatism, unjust privilege, and absolute rule, a discourse based upon a belief in the primacy of reason. All people were to stand equally before the law. All men were to be "equally eligible to all honors, places, and employments . . . without any other distinction than that created by their virtues and talents."

Proclaiming universal principles, the Declaration clearly placed sovereignty in the nation. The notion of rights stemming from membership in the "nation," as opposed to that in any corporate group or social estate, was a fundamental change. The assertion of equality of opportunity, however, was not intended to eliminate all social distinctions. The preservation of property rights assured that differences due to wealth, education, and talent would remain and be considered natural and legitimate. The Declaration thus helped make wealth, not birth, blood, or legal privilege, the foundation of social and political order in modern France.

The Declaration invoked "universal man," meaning mankind. But at the same time, its authors excluded women from the Declaration and did not espouse or foresee equality of the sexes. The Declaration did not specify to what extent women shared in universal rights, and to what extent women were citizens. Nonetheless, many men and women now began to greet each other as "citizen." Moreover, some calls for women's rights arose from the beginning of the Revolution. One woman wrote that by leaving women without the right to vote or to be educated, the Assembly "destined them to provide the pleasures of the harem."

The Declaration stated that no person could be persecuted for his or her opinions, including those concerning religion. The law itself, before which all men (but not yet women) were to be equal, was to be the work of legally elected and responsible representatives. It was to reflect the notion of the "general will," which would be expressed by national representatives. And the nation itself, not the monarch alone, was to be "the source of all sovereignty." The abolition of feudalism on August 4 and the proclamation of the Declaration of the Rights of Man and Citizen were such monumental achievements that already in 1790 people were referring to the Old Regime as having been that which existed before the representatives of the Estates-General constituted the National Assembly. It remained, however, for Louis XVI to accept the Assembly's work.

"The Baker, the Baker's Wife, and the Baker's Little Boy"

The political crisis was by no means over. The National Assembly's actions challenged the authority of the crown. On one hand, the king's closest advisers, the "court party," rejected any constitutional arrangement that would leave the monarch without the power of absolute veto. Royal authority was at stake. On the other hand, speaking for the patriot party, Sieyès insisted, "If the king's will is capable of equalling that of twenty-five million people . . . it would be a *lettre de cachet* against the general will." The majority of the Assembly, having defeated a motion that an upper chamber like the British House of Lords be created, offered the king on September 11 the power of a "suspending" veto over legislation. Lacking an "absolute" veto, the king henceforth could only delay a measure passed by the Assembly from becoming law for up to four years.

When the king failed to accept these provisions and the decrees of August 4, a flood of pamphlets and newspapers attacked his resistance. The radical journalist Jean-Paul Marat (1743–1793) quickly found a popular following for his new newspaper, *The Friend of the People*. A physician beset by financial woes, Marat was like one of the ambitious, frustrated "scribblers" whom Voltaire, forty years earlier, had scathingly denounced as hacks. He captured with stirring emotion and the colorful, coarse slang of ordinary Parisians the mood of those for whom he wrote. The rhetoric of popular sovereignty, some of it borrowed from the philosopher Jean-Jacques Rousseau, came alive in the outpouring of political pamphlets that undermined popular respect for Louis XVI and, for the first time, even for the institution of monarchy itself.

By October, some "patriots" were demanding that the king reside in Paris, echoing a number of *cahiers*. Like many of the most important events in the French Revolution, the "march to Versailles" began with a seemingly minor event. The officers of the Flanders Regiment, recently ordered to Paris by the king, insulted the newly adopted tricolor emblem at a reception in their honor attended by the king and queen. According to rumor, they shouted "Down with the National Assembly!" As the rumor spread, popular anger turned against the royal family in Versailles.

On October 5, women from the neighborhoods around the Bastille, having found the market insufficiently provisioned, gathered in front of the town hall. From there, some 10,000 people, mostly women, proceeded to

Women of Paris leaving for Versailles.

walk to Versailles, hoping to convince the king to provide them with bread. Some of them occupied the hall of the National Assembly, where they claimed power in the name of popular sovereignty. Later in the day, a large force of National Guardsmen led by Lafayette also arrived at Versailles, hoping to keep order and to convince the king that he should return with them to Paris. Louis cordially greeted the women in the late afternoon, promising them bread. The king met Lafayette's procession shortly before midnight and announced his acceptance of the Assembly's momentous decrees of the night of August 4.

Nonetheless, violence followed at dawn. When people tried to force their way into the château, royal guards shot a man dead, and the crowds retaliated by killing two guards and sticking their heads on pikes. Lafayette announced that the king had accepted the August decrees, but this failed to restore order. The crowd insisted that the royal family join it on the road to Paris. Some of the women sang that they were returning to Paris with "The Baker, the Baker's Wife, and the Baker's Little Boy," reflecting the popular notion that the king was responsible for providing bread for his people. The National Assembly, too, left Versailles for Paris. By putting the king and the Assembly under the pressure of popular political will, the women's march to Versailles changed the course of the French Revolution.

Reforming the Church and Clergy

In Paris, the National Assembly set about creating a constitution that would limit the authority of the king. The Assembly proclaimed Louis "the king of the French," instead of the king of France, a significant change that suggested that he embodied the sovereignty of his people. Alarmed by such changes, the king's brother, the count of Artois, went into exile and was soon followed by more than 20,000 other émigrés, most of whom were nobles, other people of means, and clergymen.

The Assembly turned its attention to reforming the Church. The decrees of August 4–11 had ended the unpopular tithe payments to the Church, and now the Assembly looked to the Church's wealth to help resolve the state's mounting financial crisis. On October 10, Charles-Maurice de Talleyrand (1754–1838), who had been named bishop while still virtually a boy, proposed that Church property become "national property" (*biens nationaux*). After the Assembly narrowly passed Talleyrand's measure on November 2, some 400 million francs in Church property—roughly 10 percent of the nation's land—was offered for sale at auction. The primary beneficiaries of the sale were urban bourgeois and prosperous peasants who could marshal enough cash to buy the fairly large parcels of land put up for sale.

To raise funds immediately, the Assembly issued paper money known as *assignats* that were backed by the value of the Church lands. Although the law required everyone to accept *assignats* in payment of debts, their value fell due to lack of public confidence, and those who used the *assignats* to purchase Church lands or pay debts received a windfall. Even poor peasants were thus able to reduce their debts with inflated currency worth less and less. Among the consequences of the sale of Church land and later lands owned by nobles who had emigrated out of fear of the Revolution was that in some parts of France more land was brought under cultivation by peasants. The resulting clearing of lands that had not been previously cultivated also put increased pressure on the environment as trees and brush were cleared to make room for planting crops and small-scale farming and wine production replaced the raising of sheep in some parts of France. The environmental history of the Revolution, however, largely remains to be written.

The confiscation of the Church's property was not the only change the French Revolution imposed on the clergy and the Catholic Church in France. The Assembly also proceeded to alter dramatically the status of the Church itself. On February 13, 1790, it decreed the abolition of the religious orders, deemed useless and politically suspect by many reformers. Even more significantly, on July 12, the National Assembly passed the Civil Constitution of the French Clergy. The Assembly applied new political principles to the Church, redefining the relationship between the clergy and the state, creating, in effect, a national church. Bishops would retain authority over their districts, but they were to be selected by departmental assemblies made up of parish priests who were now to be elected by the people. The bishops now could only publish pronouncements with the authorization of the government. Ten days later, the king reluctantly accepted these measures affecting the Church.

Priests and bishops could no longer be supported by rents from Church property or by tithes. Rather, the Church was now essentially a department of the state, which henceforth would pay clerical salaries, the expenses of worship, and poor relief. In November 1790, the National Assembly proclaimed that all priests had to swear an oath of loyalty to the Revolution, and thus accept the Civil Constitution of the French Clergy. His authority directly challenged, Pope Pius VI denounced the Declaration of the Rights of Man and Citizen in March, and in April 1791 he condemned the Civil Constitution.

The Civil Constitution of the French Clergy also altered the course of the Revolution, largely because it was widely resisted and contributed directly to the growth of a counter-revolutionary movement. Between one-half and two-thirds of the parish priests refused the oath, and the Assembly prohibited these disloyal, "non-juring" priests from administering the Church sacraments. Nonetheless, many continued to do so with popular support. The issue of the oath split dioceses, parishes, and some households. In some provinces, violence mounted against "non-juring" priests; in others, such as Brittany, refractory priests received popular support and protection. Generally speaking, the clergy of the west of France (particularly Brittany), the north, Alsace, and parts of the south, refused the Civil Constitution; in the rest of France, the clergy evinced at least formal acceptance of the Revolution. Such issues were no small matter, as many Catholics, Louis XVI among them, believed themselves obliged by faith to refuse to take sacraments from the "juring" clergy, that is, those who had taken the oath.

The Reforms of 1791

The most urgent task of the National Assembly was to prepare France's first constitution. The Constitution of 1791 formalized the break with the Old Regime by substituting a constitutional monarchy for absolute rule. Although the king retained the power of only a suspending veto, he would still direct foreign policy and command the army. Acts of war or peace, however, required the Assembly's approval.

But France was far from becoming a republic. In sweeping away the Old Regime, the Revolution had redefined the relationship between the individual and the state by stripping away corporatism and hereditary legal privileges. All citizens were to be equal before the law, the Assembly having in June 1790 abolished titles of hereditary nobility. However, the Assembly carefully distinguished between "active" and "passive" citizens.

The three estates hammering out the next constitution.

Only "active citizens," men paying the equivalent of three days' wages in direct taxes, had the right to vote in indirect elections—they would vote for electors, who were wealthier men, who in turn would select representatives to a new legislature (see Map 12.1). Critics such as Marat and the populist orator Georges-Jacques Danton (1759–1794) denounced the restrictive franchise, claiming that the Assembly had merely replaced the privileged caste of the Old Regime with another by substituting the ownership of property for noble title as the criterion for political rights. Rousseau himself would have been unable to vote.

The National Assembly enacted other important reforms as well. It granted citizenship and civil rights to Protestants and Jews (January 28, 1790). It ended the monopoly of the guilds over the production and distribution of goods by abolishing them, declaring each person "free to do such business as and to exercise such profession, art or trade as he may choose." It subsequently passed the Le Chapelier law on June 14, 1791, prohibiting workmen from joining together to refuse to work for a master. This law was a victory for proponents of free trade. The Assembly also passed laws affecting the family: establishing civil marriage, lowering the age of consent for marriage, establishing divorce proceedings, and specifying that inheritances be divided equally among children.

The National Assembly abolished slavery in France, but not in the colonies. This exception led to a slave rebellion on the Caribbean island of Hispaniola in October 1790 against the French sugar plantation owners, many of whom were nobles. It was led by Toussaint L'Ouverture (1743–1803), himself a former slave who had fought in the French army. The National Convention abolished slavery in the colonies in 1794, hoping that

MAP 12.1 FRANCE BEFORE AND AFTER 1789 The map on the left indicates the provinces and provincial capitals in France before the Revolution. The map on the right indicates the administrative districts (*départements*) created in France in 1790.

Olympe de Gouges.

the freed slaves would fight against Britain. Half of Hispaniola—modern-day Haiti—became the first free black state.

In 1791, the call for equal rights for women was first made explicit in France when Olympe de Gouges (1755–1793), the daughter of a butcher, published *The Rights of Women*. "The law," she wrote, "must be the expression of the general will; all female and male citizens must contribute either personally or through their representatives to its formation." Encouraging women to demand their natural rights—and thereby evidencing the influence of the Enlightenment—she called on the Assembly to acknowledge women's rights as mothers of citizens of the nation. She insisted on women's right to education and to control property within marriage and to initiate divorce proceedings. She included an appendix, "a social contract of Man and Woman," defining the nation as "the union of Woman and Man." She suggested that men would remain unfree unless women were granted similar rights: "Enslaved man," she wrote, "has multiplied his strength and needs recourse to yours to break his chains." The concept of "republican motherhood" emerged, stopping short of demanding full political rights for women. Many women saw their role in the near future as supporting their husbands and inculcating their children with republican values. "Women: do you want to be republicans?" went one tract, "Love, obey, and teach the laws that remind your husbands and children to exercise their rights."

Resistance and Revolution

On July 14, 1790, the first anniversary of the fall of the Bastille, an imposing Festival of General Federation took place on the Champ de Mars, a

royal parade ground in Paris, to commemorate the unity of the revolutionary settlement. But, in fact, there was no revolutionary consensus in
France. In the south, nobles had already begun to organize resistance
against the Revolution, and militant Catholics attacked Protestants, who
tended to support the Revolution. By the summer of 1791, as the Assembly promulgated its constitution, open resistance to the Revolution had
broken out in parts of the south and west, and in Alsace in the east.

Such resistance prompted further calls for even more radical changes.
Some of the revolutionaries, who did not accept the distinction between
active and passive citizens, called for more democratic participation in political life. They believed that they were constructing a new nation upon
the ruins of the Old Regime. But from where did this democratic thrust
come? We have seen that the monarchical state had rested on an intertwining network of corporate groups—each with a set of privileges—at virtually every level of society. These included judicial, professional,
administrative, and clerical groups, ranging from provincial estates to artisanal guilds. Participatory and sometimes even democratic procedures
within such bodies (or *corps*), may have contributed to help various participatory and democratic practices that affected the course of the Revolution and pushed France toward a republic.

The first clubs were established by political factions among the deputies
to the National Assembly. Some of the Assembly's most radical members
split off to form the Jacobin Club, so-called because it met in the house of

A patriotic club of women.

(*Left*) The male sans-culotte. (*Right*) The female sans-culotte.

the religious order of the Jacobins. The Cordeliers Club brought together the radicals of Paris, while supporters of the cause of constitutional monarchy gathered at the Club of the Feuillants, whose members had broken with the Jacobins in July 1791. The early success of the Cordeliers and Jacobin Clubs in provincial towns often led monarchists to form royalist clubs. Moreover, some women formed their own political clubs, such as the Club of Knitters, or joined the Fraternal Society of Patriots of Both Sexes. By 1793, there were at least 5,000 clubs in France, struggling to help determine the political course of the Revolution in each region.

During the first years of the Revolution, there was little in France that was not political. The political clubs that had formed among the delegates to the Estates-General, like the Breton Club, were not the only place where political debate occurred. There were also meetings of neighborhood "sections," which had first been defined as electoral districts for the convocation of the Estates-General, and these meetings continued to take place in Paris.

Parisian revolutionaries became increasingly known as sans-culottes. They defined themselves by what they were without—the fancy knee britches or golden pants—or *culottes*, in French—associated with the aristocracy. The sans-culottes were shopkeepers, artisans, and laborers who

(*Left*) Louis XVI dons the Phrygian cap. (*Right*) Planting a liberty tree.

were not opposed to private property, but who stood against unearned property, and especially against those people who seemed to have too much property, or who, living from rents, did not work for a living. They demanded that a maximum price be placed on bread, which alone absorbed more than half of the earnings of the average working family. Sans-culottes were for the Revolution, for "the people," as they put it. They were defined by their political behavior. Even aristocrats could be sans-culottes if they supported the Revolution (which, however, was most unusual). Likewise, laborers or peasants could be called "aristocrats" if they seemed to oppose the Revolution. In a world in which symbols played a crucial political role (for example, the tricolor cockade, patriotic altars for newborns, liberty trees in villages), sans-culottes could be identified by the Phrygian cap—a symbol of freedom drawn from the Roman Republic—red in color, with a tricolor emblem—in contrast to the three-cornered hat that had been worn by urban social elites. The language of the sans-culottes also quickly indicated who they were; they called everyone "citizen," and used the familiar ("*tu*" and never "*vous*"), egalitarian form of address. The political ideal of the sans-culottes was that popular sovereignty had to be practiced every day in direct democracy, in revolutionary clubs and in the sections.

The Flight to Varennes

Fearing the growing violence of the Revolution and counting on the support of the other monarchs of Europe, Louis XVI and his family tried to flee France in June 1791. Apprehended by the National Guard in Varennes after being sighted near the French border, however, the royal family was prevented from continuing their journey into exile and freedom.

The king's attempt to flee turned public sentiment further against him, and strengthened support for a republic. The day after his flight, the Cordeliers Club called for the establishment of a republic, but the majority of the Assembly feared civil war. On July 17, at the Champ de Mars in Paris, people came to sign (or put their "X" on) a petition resting on the "Altar of the Fatherland" that called on the National Assembly to replace the king "by all constitutional means." The National Guard opened fire, killing fifty people. Bailly, the moderate mayor of Paris, and Lafayette, the increasingly disenchanted commander of the National Guard in Paris, declared martial law; Marat and Danton went temporarily into hiding. Even Louis' formal acceptance of the Constitution on September 14 could not stem the popular tide against the monarchy.

WAR AND THE SECOND REVOLUTION

After the king's ill-fated attempt to flee France, the Revolution now entered a new, more radical phase. The king's flight seriously weakened the constitutional monarchists within the Assembly. The leaders of the Parisian population—Georges-Jacques Danton, Jean-Paul Marat, and Maximilien Robespierre—were republican Jacobins who had given up on the idea that a constitutional monarchy could adequately guarantee the liberties of the people. The newly elected National Assembly met on Octo-

(*Left*) Georges-Jacques Danton. (*Right*) Maximilien Robespierre.

ber 1, 1791. Republicans—now identified with the "left" as monarchists were with the "right," due to the location of the seats each group occupied in the Assembly—became a majority in March 1792.

In the meantime, French émigrés at the Austrian and Prussian courts were encouraging foreign intervention to restore Louis XVI to full monarchical authority. The republican followers of Jacques-Pierre Brissot (1754–1793), former radical pamphleteer and police spy as well as a flamboyant orator, called for a war to free Europe from the tyranny of monarchy and nobility. The members of this faction became known as the Girondins because many were from the department, or district, of the Gironde in which the Atlantic port of Bordeaux is located. Under Girondin leadership, the Assembly's proclamations took on a more aggressive tone. Monarchists backed a revolutionary war for other reasons: some, like Lafayette, hoped to restore power to the crown. Others, including the king himself, expected that war would lead to French defeat (because of the desertion of so many noble officers) and to the restoration of the Old Regime. The French declaration of war against Austria in April 1792 led to the Second Revolution in June. The monarchy was overthrown, replaced by a republic. Faced with foreign invasion and full-scale counter-revolution inside France, the Jacobin-dominated revolutionary government lapsed into dictatorship, imposing "the Terror" (during which many suspected counter-revolutionaries were arrested and guillotined).

Reactions to the French Revolution in Europe

The French Revolution had a considerable impact on the rest of Europe even before French armies marched into adjoining states proclaiming the dawning of an era of "liberty, equality, and fraternity." The early work of the National Assembly, particularly the abolition of feudal rights and the establishment of a constitutional monarchy, attracted immediate attention and found considerable favor among educated people in Britain, the Netherlands, and some German and Italian states. Some lawyers and merchants in other lands applauded, for example, measures taken to reduce the independence of the Catholic Church. The promulgation of the principles of national sovereignty and self-determination, however, threatened the monarchies of Europe. The European powers had often gone to war against France over the past century, beginning with Louis XIV's relentless war-making in pursuit of dynastic territorial aggrandizement. The next series of wars against France, however, reflected not dynastic rivalries but rather the threat to the other Great Powers by revolutionary France. The threat posed by the French Revolution brought about a rapprochement between Austria and Prussia, old rivals for domination in Central Europe, as well as a wary alliance between Great Britain and Russia.

The Prussian government's first reaction to the Revolution had been to try to subvert the alliance between France and Austria and then to undermine Austrian authority in the Southern Netherlands (Belgium). In Vienna, the Habsburg Emperor Leopold II was initially preoccupied with demands from the Hungarian nobility for more power, and pressure from the Belgians for independence. In 1789, a rebellion forced Austrian forces out of the Southern Netherlands in December and led to the establishment of a republic that survived only until Austrian troops invaded as winter approached in 1790.

In London, some radical Whigs greeted with enthusiasm the news of the fall of the Bastille and the first steps toward constitutional monarchy in France. But in 1790, the British writer Edmund Burke attacked the Revolution in *Reflections on the Revolution in France*. He contended that the abstract rationalism of the Enlightenment threatened the historic evolution of any nation by undermining its monarchy, its established church, and what he considered the "natural" ruling elite.

The Englishman Thomas Paine (1737–1809) wrote pamphlets denouncing monarchical rule and unwarranted privilege. His pamphlet *The Rights of Man* (1791–1792) defended the Revolution against Burke's relentless attack. Political societies supporting the Revolution sprang up in Britain during the early 1790s, composed mainly of artisans. The French Revolution thus helped revive some interest in political reform in Britain. It also contributed enormously to the development of British nationalism (see Chapter 11). During the revolutionary period, popular respect for the British monarchy and probably also for the nobility seems to have soared, reaffirming social hierarchy (and male domination as well) at a time when to many Britons events in France seemed to demonstrate the consequences of social upheaval. There would be no shortage of volunteers from all classes and religions to fight the French when the nation called for them.

A small group of English women also enthusiastically supported the Revolution. Mary Wollstonecraft (1759–1797), a teacher and writer, greeted the Revolution with optimism, travelling to France to view events first hand. She expressed confidence that the Revolution would lead to a republic that would respect the rights of men and women alike. Angered that the Assembly limited the right to education to men only, she published *Vindication of the Rights of Women* (1792), the first book in Britain demanding that women have the right to vote and hold elected office, as well as demanding greater equality in marriage. The book, damned by most Englishmen as another pernicious work influenced by the French Revolution, was an opening salvo in Britain in the struggle for equality of the sexes.

The rulers of the other European states felt threatened by the proclamation of universal principles embodied in the Declaration of the Rights of Man and Citizen. The Revolution also posed the threat of French expansion, no longer in the interest of dynastic territorial aggrandizement, but on behalf of carrying the revolutionary principles of "liberty, equality, and fraternity" to other lands. Besieged by exiles from France eager to tell tales of terror, the rulers of Prussia, Austria, Naples, and Piedmont undertook the suppression of Jacobin sympathizers in their states. In Britain, the seeming threat of foreign invasion helped forge, principally but not exclusively among the upper classes, a sense of British national identity. Anti-French and anti-Catholic feelings came to the fore as scarcity increased fear of revolution. Pitt the Younger's government lashed out at the development of popular politics in Britain, suspending the freedoms of association, assembly, and the press, as well as in 1794 the writ of *habeas corpus*. "Coercion Acts" facilitated the arrest of those working for parliamentary reform.

Louis XVI's virtual imprisonment in the Tuileries Palace in Paris and the thunderous speeches in the Assembly proclaiming the necessity of "a war of peoples against kings" worried the crowned heads of Europe. On August 27, 1791, King Leopold II of Austria (brother of Marie-Antoinette, who had not seen him in twenty-five years) and King Frederick William II of Prussia promulgated the Declaration of Pilnitz. It expressed their concern about the plight of the French monarchy and stated the common interest of both sovereigns in seeing order restored in France. Despite Robespierre's speeches warning the deputies that the Revolution must first deal with its enemies within France before waging war abroad in the name of "liberty, fraternity, and equality," the Assembly, egged on by General Charles François Dumouriez (1739–1823), who was minister of foreign affairs, in April 1792 declared war on Austria. The stated reason was fear that an Austrian invasion from the Southern Netherlands was imminent. The declaration of war soon seemed a rash move, as the army had been devastated by the desertion of two-thirds of its officers (85 percent of its officers had been nobles before the Revolution) and Prussia soon joined with Austria in fighting the French. The early stages of the war produced many French defeats at the hands of Austrian and Prussian armies.

A Second Revolution

The war greatly influenced the course of the Revolution by sealing the fate of the monarchy and the royal family. As France faced the possibility of foreign invasion by Austria and Prussia, eager to restore Louis XVI to an absolute throne, popular fear that aristocrats and clergymen were betraying the Revolution eventually brought down the monarchy. Early defeats on the northern frontier by Austrian troops and soaring bread prices (in part due to the requisitioning of food for the army) compounded popular anxiety and led to a new revolutionary groundswell, particularly in Paris.

In early April 1792, women from the plebeian districts of Paris marched through the capital demanding the right to bear arms. On June 20, a crowd stormed into the Tuileries Palace and threatened the royal family, shouting, "Tremble, tyrants! Here come the sans-culottes!" Strident calls for the end of the monarchy echoed in clubs and sections. (The sections were administrative districts each of which had assemblies of "active" citizens, many of whom were Jacobins who favored radical action.) On July 11, the Assembly officially proclaimed the *patrie*, or nation, to be "in danger," calling on all citizens to rally against the enemies of liberty within as well as outside of France. The Assembly encouraged the sections to admit the "passive" citizens who had previously been excluded because they had failed to meet tax requirements. Troops from Marseille, among federal volunteers called up to defend the front, sang a new revolutionary song, "The Marseillaise," penned by Rouget de Lisle for the Army of the Rhine. It became the anthem of the Revolution. In the meantime, the Jacobins pressed their attack against the monarchy.

After the Brunswick Manifesto (July 1792), Austria and Prussia warned the French that they would be severely punished if the royal family were harmed. All but one of the forty-eight sections of Paris responded by demanding that the king be immediately deposed. Popular discontent and Jacobin agitation came together in August. A radical committee overthrew the city council and established a revolutionary Commune in Paris on August 9, naming Santerre, a brewer, commander of the National Guard. On August 10, sans-culottes from the Paris sections attacked the Tuileries Palace. The invaders killed 600 of the king's Swiss Guards and servants after they had surrendered. The royal family escaped and found protection in the quarters of the National Assembly. The Assembly immediately proclaimed the monarchy deposed and ordered the royal family's imprisonment.

The popular revolution doomed France's first experiment in constitutional monarchy. The defeat of French armies heightened the mood of anxiety, if not outright panic, in Paris. On September 2, 1792, a Prussian

The September Massacre of 1792 in the abbey of Saint-Germain-des-Prés.

army entered French territory and captured the eastern fortress town of Verdun. The proximity of the allied armies and the fear of betrayal at home led to the imprisonment in Paris of many people suspected of plotting against the Revolution. When a rumor circulated that the prisoners were planning to break out of prison and attack the army from the rear, mobs dragged the prisoners from their cells and killed them. During these September Massacres, more than 1,200 people, including 225 priests, perished at the hands of crowds who constituted themselves judges, juries, and executioners.

But just as Paris seemed vulnerable to foreign invasion, a ragtag army of regular soldiers and sans-culottes stopped the Prussian and Austrian advance with effective artillery barrages on September 20, 1792, near the windmill of Valmy, east of Châlons-sur-Marne. The German poet Goethe, amazed by the victory of such ordinary people over a highly trained professional army, wrote "From this time and place a new epoch is beginning." An officer trained under the Old Regime called the resultant warfare of the revolutionary armies a "hellish tactic," which saw "fifty thousand savage beasts foaming at the mouth like cannibals, hurling themselves at top speed upon soldiers whose courage has been excited by no passion."

The Revolution had been saved by the same people who had first made it. The victory at Valmy helped prepare the way for the proclamation of the First French Republic. Delegates to a new assembly called the National Convention were selected by universal male suffrage in sparsely attended elections dominated by Jacobins (perhaps because the radicals had used scare tactics to keep moderates and royalist sympathizers from voting). The delegates arrived in Paris to draft a republican constitution. Their first act was unanimously to abolish the monarchy and proclaim the republic on September 21, 1792.

In the fall of 1792, not only was the monarchy overthrown and the republic proclaimed, but the revolutionary armies of proud, loyal citizen-soldiers routed the invading foreign armies. Despite the maintenance of strict military discipline, the humblest infantryman now had the same rights as officers: They could be judged by other soldiers, and could no longer be beaten or humiliated as had been the case before the Revolution. Commanders made greater efforts to ensure that their citizen-soldiers were adequately fed and lodged. Yet, conditions often mitigated good intentions. Grain shortages could lead to less available food for troops, and sometimes young soldiers were handed only ancient hunting rifles or even pikes with which to defend themselves. Nonetheless, French forces pushed Prussian troops across the Rhine and entered the city of Mainz on October 21. On November 6, Dumouriez defeated the Austrians at Jémappes, north of Mons in the Austrian Netherlands. The stunned Austrians retreated, and the French revolutionary armies soon occupied all of the Austrian Netherlands (see Map 12.2).

Emboldened by these unexpected military successes, the National Convention on November 19, 1792, promised "fraternity and assistance to all

Legend:

- - - - - Border of France 1789
- - - - Border of France 1799
- • Centers of revolution 1789
- → French revolutionary army offensives
- → Foreign anti-revolutionary army offensives

MAP 12.2 EXPANSION OF REVOLUTIONARY FRANCE, 1792–1799   The map indicates French revolutionary army offensives and foreign anti-revolutionary army offensives. It also shows areas annexed by the French, areas occupied by the French, and dependent republics established by revolutionary France.

peoples who want to recover their liberty." French troops captured Frankfurt and occupied much of the Rhineland. The Convention also declared the outright annexation of the Alpine province of Savoy, belonging to the Kingdom of Sardinia, and the small Mediterranean town of Nice, captured at the end of September. They declared them within the "natural frontiers" of France—a claim that contradicted the principles of popular sovereignty and self-determination contained in the annexation decrees themselves.

In the Austrian Netherlands, the imposition of the new French administrative structure and the creation of Jacobin Clubs failed to win much support, despite the fact that an insurrection against Austrian rule had occurred there in 1791. On December 15, 1792, the Convention abolished all feudal dues and tithes in those territories occupied by French armies.

The governments of both Britain and the Dutch Republic viewed the occupation of the Austrian Netherlands, which lay across the Channel from the former and adjacent to the latter, as a great threat to their interests. When it appeared that both states were considering joining Austria and Prussia in taking action against France, the Convention on February 1, 1793, declared war on Britain and the Dutch Republic. Spain and the Kingdoms of Sardinia and Naples joined this First Coalition against France.

When correspondence between the king and the Austrian government was discovered, the trial of Louis XVI became inevitable. Accused of treason, the king defended himself with grace and dignity. He called on the Convention to look after the needs of his family as he had tried to watch over those of France. But with the words "one cannot reign innocently" ringing in the hall, on January 17, 1793, the Convention condemned the king to death. On the morning of January 21, Louis XVI was guillotined on the Place de la Révolution (as the Place de la Concorde was then called). The huge throng roared its approval as the executioner held up the severed royal head, symbol of the Old Regime, for all to see.

The execution of Louis XVI.

As the Convention and the Paris Commune vied for authority, the French Republic, under continuing attack from beyond its borders, began to split apart. In Paris and the provinces, the Girondins and the Jacobins quarreled bitterly. The Girondins were popularly identified with the economic liberalism that characterized the port cities and with the desire to carry the Revolution aggressively beyond the frontiers of France. Opposed to centralizing power in Paris, they wanted a significant degree of local political control. The deputies of the far left, principally the Jacobins and their followers, sat on the raised side of the Tuileries Hall where the Convention met. They thus became known as "the Mountain," or the *Montagnards*. The political center became known as "the Plain." Backed by the Parisian sans-culottes, the Jacobins insisted on the necessity of centralizing authority in the capital to save the Revolution from internal treason and foreign defeat. The Girondins were moderates in contrast to the Jacobins and believed that the Revolution had gone far enough. The Jacobins accused the Girondins of secretly supporting the monarchy and demanded swift punishment for traitors.

In contrast to eighteenth-century Britain, only a very limited sense of a "loyal" opposition to monarchical policy had developed in Old Regime France. The combination of external and internal threats to the Revolution now made such an evolution virtually impossible. From the point of view of the Jacobins, those who were not for them were against the Revolution. Increasingly all opponents and adversaries were labeled as counter-revolutionaries or conspirators.

The sense of vulnerability and insecurity that greeted the French republic was heightened by reverses in the field. The armies of the First Coalition defeated the French in the Austrian Netherlands in March 1793. Dumouriez then betrayed the Revolution, preparing to march his soldiers to Paris to put Louis XVI's son on the throne as Louis XVII. When his army refused to follow him, Dumouriez fled across the border to join the Austrians and other émigrés. In the meantime, the allies recaptured the left bank of the Rhine.

Counter-Revolution

The Counter-Revolution was aristocratic, clerical, and in some places, popular at the same time. Nobles—including those who had already emigrated—retained considerable prestige, as well as economic influence, in much of western France. Even more, the Counter-Revolution to a great extent had been launched in the name of the Church and occurred in regions where religious practice still seemed strong and where the Civil Constitution of the French Clergy had met considerable resistance (see Map 12.3).

A full-scale insurrection against the Revolution began in March 1793. This revolt in the western part of France became known as the Vendée, after the name of one of the most insurrectionary districts. In August, the

MAP 12.3 THE COUNTER-REVOLUTION   The map indicates areas of federalism and counter-revolutionary activity, including major uprisings.

revolutionary government decreed mass conscription, the *levée en masse*, which initiated the concept of the nation in arms: "Young people will go to battle; married men will forge arms and transport supplies; women will make tents, uniforms, and serve in the hospitals; children will pick rags; old men will have themselves carried to public squares, to inspire the courage of the warriors, and to preach hatred of kings and the unity of the Republic." The unpopularity of military conscription in defense of the republic also generated resistance. Both sides fought with a brutality, including mass executions and systematic pillage, that recalled the Thirty Years' War in Central Europe.

South of the Loire River, the counter-revolutionary forces principally emerged from the relatively isolated bocage, or hedgerow country, where the old noble and clerical elites had been relatively unaffected by the economic changes of the past few decades, specifically the expansion of the market economy. Here peasants had remained relatively isolated from the bourgeoisie of the towns along the Loire River to the north. The latter had benefited economically and politically from the Revolution, buying Church lands and serving in municipal offices, and had a vested interest in the survival of the Revolution. But in Brittany, which had enjoyed a relatively light tax burden during the Old Regime, the revolutionary government was hated for having ended that privilege, thereby increasing taxes. Tenant farmers, bearing the burden of increased taxes, also resented the intrusion of revolutionaries in religious life. Under such conditions, the Counter-Revolution won the allegiance of many people.

The Terror

Facing foreign invasion and civil insurgency, the Jacobins further centralized government authority and implemented a Terror against those considered "enemies" of the Revolution. The Convention set aside the recently promulgated Constitution of 1793 (which was to have replaced the Constitution of 1791). The apparatus of the Terror included special laws reducing the rights of the accused, the establishment of special courts, and the prosecution of those considered disloyal. On March 19, 1793, the Convention passed a law permitting the immediate trial of armed insurgents without a jury. A week later, the Convention established a Committee of Public Safety of nine and then twelve members, which gradually

A revolutionary tribunal during the Terror.

Jacques-Louis David's *The Death of Marat.*

assumed more and more power. The Convention also decreed a special war tax, including a forced levy on wealthy people, and imposed a maximum price on grain. These measures of centralization and government interference in the economy led to an irreversible break between the Jacobins, who believed in state controls, and the Girondins, who believed in economic freedom.

Military requisitions of foodstuffs accentuated hardship. The poor rioted over the high price of grain. More Jacobin Clubs sprang up in the provinces. In Paris, the Society of Revolutionary Republican Women took to the streets to demand laws against hoarding. This group, founded in May 1793, put forward impassioned demands that women be granted citizenship. Another group, called the "enraged" (*enragés*), demanded that bakers be penalized if they charged more than the maximum price for bread.

In June, pushed on by crowds from the radical sections of Paris, the Convention expelled twenty-nine Girondin deputies, accusing them of supporting hoarders, and ordering the arrest of some of them. Among those who left Paris to return home, some began to organize opposition in the provinces against the Jacobins. In Paris, Dumouriez's betrayal of the revolutionary cause added to the tension. Insurgents in Toulon turned over half of the French fleet to the British. In July, Charlotte Corday, a noblewoman, stabbed Marat to death in his bathtub. Tax revenue and foreign trade fell by half. *Assignats,* more of which had rolled off the government presses as the financial crisis continued, plunged further in value.

The Terror represented the appropriation of revolutionary violence from the people by a more centralized apparatus of state power. Its proponents justified it by the external and internal threats to the Revolution. But once established, the Terror also became a means of eliminating all perceived political rivals to Jacobin authority.

Louis Antoine Saint-Just (1767–1794), a precocious, icy young deputy whose mother had once had him incarcerated by *lettre de cachet* in Paris for running off with the family silver, emerged as another central figure of the Terror. After being catapulted to prominence by his denunciation of Louis XVI during the king's trial, he had been largely responsible for drawing up the Constitution of 1793. Now he waged war on royalists, hoarders, and Girondins, all of whom he considered enemies of the Revolution. "Those who make revolutions by halves dig their own grave," he warned.

Maximilien Robespierre (1758–1794), who emerged as the leading figure on the Committee of Public Safety, knew that the Mountain drew its support from the sans-culottes, some of whom were demanding the Terror. But he also believed that the popular movement remained a threat to the orderly transformation of political life in France. Historians have offered widely differing interpretations of Robespierre. These range from the view that he was a popular democrat who saved the essence of the Revolution from counter-revolutionaries to one presenting him as the precursor of twentieth-century totalitarianism.

Robespierre was the son and grandson of lawyers from the northern town of Arras. After the death of his irresponsible, largely absent father, Robespierre depended on scholarships for his schooling. At age eleven, he was chosen to read an address in Latin to the royal family as they passed through Reims. It was raining and the royal family, it was said, without acknowledging the young student, ordered their driver onward. The royal coach splashed Robespierre with mud.

After completing his law degree, Robespierre defended a number of poor clients, including a man unjustly accused of stealing from an abbey. Robespierre discovered that the theft had actually been committed by one of the abbey's own monks. After he was elected to the third estate, Robespierre gradually established a reputation in Paris for his well-organized and thoughtful but colorless speeches. Contemporaries noted the prissiness of the impeccably dressed, slight man with very pale skin and chestnut hair always perfectly powdered. A favorite of the Parisian sans-culottes, the man they called "the Incorruptible" called in 1793 for "a single will" of the nation to save the Revolution.

Insurrections against the Jacobins and the authority of the Convention broke out in Lyon, Marseille, Bordeaux, and Caen, where unlike in the counter-revolutionary west, merchants and others in the urban propertied classes and some of the Girondins played prominent roles in "federalist revolts" against centralized revolutionary authority emanating from Paris. Merchants and lawyers viewed the radicalization of the Revolution as a threat to their own control of political life. Lyon, France's second largest city, fell to republican troops on October 9; bloody reprisals followed, and the city's name was changed to "Liberated City."

The "Law of Suspects" in September deprived those accused of crimes against the nation of most of their remaining rights. The Convention specifically banned clubs and popular societies of women. It did so after

Marie-Antoinette awaits her execution.
Sketch by Jacques-Louis David.

listening to a report by a member who contended that women should
not be part of political life and that their participation threatened the stability of the family: "Women are disposed by their constitution to an over-
excitation which would be deadly in public affairs." Olympe de Gouges was
among the Girondins guillotined. Marie-Antoinette, though hardly a femi-
nist, went to the scaffold.

The Jacobins were so intent on destroying the Old Regime and building
a new political world that they instituted a new calendar in October 1793.
The calendar of twelve months and fifty-two weeks of seven days gave way
to a new republican calendar based upon "weeks" or cycles of ten days and
"months" taking their names from more secular notions of the changing of
the seasons (such as "Germinal"—meaning the budding—and "Ventôse"—
windy—and so on). September 22, 1792, the first year of the republic, became, retroactively, day one of "the year I."

Like their more moderate predecessors, the Jacobins put new revolutionary symbols in the service of destroying Old Regime symbolism and
maintaining revolutionary enthusiasm. Following the execution of Louis
XVI, the revolutionaries chose a female image for liberty and the republic,
which was ironic in that they denied political rights to women. They now
proudly called the female image "Marianne," the name opponents of the
Revolution had derisively dubbed liberty. Unlike lusty and even porno-
graphic images of Marie-Antoinette, the female image of the republic appears gentle, not threatening, and virtuous, representing the abstract
virtues of liberty and popular sovereignty, community and nation. Contemporaries contrasted republican virtue with the abuses of power that
seemed to have characterized the Old Regime. They did so even as Jacobin
representatives of the Revolution abused their power by imposing their
will wherever they were resisted in the provinces.

During the "year II" (which began in September 1793), radical revolutionaries undertook an ambitious campaign of "de-christianization," a war on religious institutions and symbols. They closed down churches and removed crosses standing in public places. The campaign failed, unable to overcome centuries of firmly implanted traditions and beliefs, even among many people who supported the Revolution. "De-christianization" also turned many clergy who had accepted the Civil Constitution away from the Revolution, generating further resistance.

In the provinces, "representatives on mission," armed with dictatorial authority in the name of the Convention, tried to maintain order. They worked with local "surveillance committees" and "revolutionary tribunals" of Jacobins. Some of these revolutionary officials sent counter-revolutionaries to the guillotine. "Revolutionary armies" of artisans and day laborers guarded requisitioned provisions for the military and oversaw the melting down of church bells for war use.

Yet, the Terror was never uniformly implemented. The response to the Revolution in the provinces varied widely; so did the abilities and commitment of those sent to represent the Committee of Public Safety. Between

(*Left*) A contemporary seal shows Marianne, the image of the republic. (*Right*) A more aggressive engraving showing "The French people overwhelming the Hydra of Federalism." (August 1793)

11,000 and 18,000 people perished (a fraction, by comparison, of the deaths that had resulted from the Thirty Years' War, or the American Civil War). About 300,000 royalists, Girondins, or other "enemies of the Revolution" were imprisoned for some period during the Terror. About 15 percent of those killed were nobles or clergy. Thus, nobles and clergy suffered disproportionately in terms of their number in the population as a whole (5 to 8 percent). However, artisans and peasants constituted by far the largest number of those dispatched by the revolutionary tribunals. The majority of these were apprehended near the northern and eastern frontiers that had been invaded by foreign armies or in the counter-revolutionary west where civil war raged. During the winter of 1793–1794, perhaps as many as several thousand prisoners—including priests and nuns—captured from the counter-revolutionary armies of the Vendée were taken out into the swirling waters of the Loire River in boats that had holes bored in them and drowned by virtue of the orders of a cruel revolutionary official.

Some significant French victories on the battlefield undercut the argument that the Terror was necessary because of the immediate external threat to the Republic. A French army defeated the Austrians in the Austrian Netherlands in June. Another French force pushed the foreign armies beyond the Vosges Mountains in the east; a third French army recaptured Savoy. The Spanish royalist army retreated across the Pyrenees.

The Terror struck the *enragés* leaders in March 1794 after they demanded even more economic controls and an intensification of the "dechristianization" campaign. They were brought before the Revolutionary Tribunal, condemned, and guillotined. The Committee of Public Safety then went after Danton and his followers, who believed that the Terror was no longer necessary, and thus had been labeled the "Indulgents." They too were condemned and guillotined. Real and imagined conspiracies provided the justification for the Terror, which now seemed without end. "Who will be next?" was whispered among even those loyal to the most radical members of the Committee of Public Safety. In May, Robespierre survived an assassination attempt.

Besides eliminating his enemies both at home and abroad, Robespierre sought to establish a secularized "Cult of the Supreme Being," which he intended to serve as a "constant reminder of justice" that would bind the people to the new values of republicanism. With the elimination of the *enragés* and the Dantonists, he was able to devote his energies to his Republic of Virtue. Thus, early in June, the republic celebrated the "Festival of Reason." The cathedral of Notre Dame in Paris became a "temple of reason." A popular female opera singer, dressed as Liberty—the image of the republic—wearing a Phrygian cap and holding a pike, bowed down before the flame of reason. The painter Jacques-Louis David constructed huge statues of monsters like Anarchy and Atheism made of pasteboard. After Robespierre set fire to them, a statue of Wisdom rose out of the ashes.

The political use of terror alienated many supporters of the Revolution, especially when more heads rolled in late May and June. The Terror seemed to have taken on a momentum of its own. Saint-Just said, "You must punish not merely traitors, but also the indifferent. . . ."

The Jacobins arrested the Marquis de Condorcet (1743–1794) for alleged counter-revolutionary activity and condemned him to death. Condorcet, an influential philosophe of the late Enlightenment, had been elected to the Assembly in 1791. He believed that all people should have a voice in approving acts of government, albeit indirectly, and that all citizens should be equal before the law. He had campaigned against the death penalty and slavery, and he defended political equality and the rights of women because he considered women fully capable of participating in political life. Condorcet died of apoplexy—or committed suicide—in his cell in the spring of 1794, shortly before he was to be executed. The Revolution seemed to have turned on and destroyed the enlightened reason that had arguably helped bring it about.

THE FINAL STAGES

Growing desire for an end to violence and repression enabled the moderates to regain control of the state. Moderate Jacobins and other members of the Convention, fearing that they might be next in line to be purged, overthrew the Jacobin dictatorship. They established a new government called the Directory, which ended the Terror. Caught between staunch Jacobins on the left and monarchists on the right, the period of the Directory was marked by great political instability, shaped by ongoing wars abroad and economic hardship at home. Although the Directory consolidated some of the gains of the Revolution, it too would be overthrown by conspirators led by the Abbé Sieyès and one of the rising stars of the revolutionary army, General Napoleon Bonaparte.

Thermidor

After the Revolutionary Tribunal was given new powers in June 1794 and used them to send 1,300 people to their deaths over a period of six weeks, the enemies of the Committee of Public Safety in the Convention began to plot against Robespierre and his friends. They were led by fearful fellow Jacobins Joseph Fouché (1758–1820) and Paul Barras (1755–1829), followers of Danton and moderates in the Convention who were afraid that they would be next on Robespierre's list.

Robespierre himself seemed remarkably blind to the plot against him. On July 26, 1794 (the 8th of Thermidor), he haltingly addressed the Convention, calling for one more purge. His voice could barely be heard amidst shouts of "Down with the tyrant!" Unable to respond effectively and anticipating his own martyrdom, Robespierre murmured, "I ask for death." During the night of the 9th of Thermidor, Robespierre, his brother Augustine, and Saint-Just were arrested at the virtually unguarded town hall of Paris. In an attempt to kill himself, Robespierre shattered his own jaw with a shot, a conscious emulation of the classical, stoic death of a hero.

The trial later the same day was as swift and pitiless as those endured by the Terror's other victims. The three Jacobin leaders were guillotined the following morning, followed to the scaffold by more than a hundred of their followers. Lazare Carnot (1753–1823), a talented military engineer and brilliant administrator ("the organizer of victory"), and one of the twelve members of the Committee of Public Safety, survived because the war effort desperately required his administrative talent. In the provinces, particularly in the south, the revenge against the Jacobins by their enemies was swift and brutal. In some southern towns, secret societies organized a "White Terror" (after the color of the Bourbon flag) to lash out against supporters of the Convention.

After dismantling the Paris Commune, the victors of Thermidor—the name taken from the period in the revolutionary calendar in which the Committee of Public Safety was overthrown—set about establishing a new national government. Order was only slowly and incompletely restored in the countryside. The Thermidorians greatly reduced the powers of the Committee of Public Safety on July 31 and then abolished it completely. In November 1794, Jacobin Clubs were ordered shut.

The Directory: Politics and Society

The Thermidorians produced a constitution by creating a two-house legislative assembly and a collective executive of five directors, which provided the name "the Directory" for this period of the Revolution. The two assemblies included the Council of the Ancients (250 members), which discussed and voted on legislation proposed by the second assembly, the Council of Five Hundred. Two-thirds of the members of the new councils were elected from among the members of the existing Convention. In turn, the two councils elected the five directors who formed the collective executive authority, or Directorate. Beginning in 1797, one-third of the members of each council and one of the five directors were to be replaced each year.

People of property benefited from the Thermidorian reaction. The new constitution proclaimed in August limited the vote to a smaller group of men than had voted under the radical republic of 1792–1794, or even in the indirect elections of 1789–1791. But although about 2 million men could vote (out of some 7 million men of voting age), electoral power was further restricted by a system of indirect election that favored the selection of the wealthiest citizens to serve in the assemblies.

The period of the Directory was marked by a decided turn against the asceticism associated with Robespierre's "Republic of Virtue." The *jeunesse dorée,* or gilded youth, drawn from the bourgeoisie and old nobility, set the social and cultural tone of the day. Wearing square collars

The return of high society during the Directory.

and fancy clothes, wealthy young men smashed busts of Marat and shut down theatrical performances favorable to the Jacobins. The red-colored symbols of the sans-culottes—such as the Phyrgian cap—quickly disappeared. Women who could afford to do so wore long flowing white robes of opulence and sensuality, with plunging necklines that would have horrified Robespierre. The familiar (*tu*) form of address, identified with section and club meetings, gave way to the more formal *vous* more characteristic of the Old Regime. Crowds in which women played a prominent part demanded that churches be reopened. Boisterous social events amused the middle class; among them was the macabre "Dance of the Victims," a ball to which only those with a relative who had perished in the Terror could be admitted. Some revelers turned up with their hair cut away from the back of their neck, mimicking the final haircut of those about to be sent to the guillotine.

Under the Directory, the comforts of the wealthy, some of whom had made their fortunes during the Revolution (by buying Church lands or supplying the military), contrasted sharply with the deprivations of the poor. The economy lay in shambles. The winter of 1795 was unusually harsh. The abolition of the Maximum spelled the end of cheap bread, and the price of basic commodities soared. A load of firewood that cost 20 francs in 1790 required 500 francs in 1795. The price of bread rose by thirteen times in Paris during the spring of 1795. Near Paris, people scrambled to eat the carcasses of dead army horses, and in mountainous areas people searched for berries and edible roots while trying to stay warm. The military requisition of food supplies weighed heavily on peasants. The Directory may have ended the Terror, but it did not bring stability to France.

Instability

Nor did the Directory bring peace. France remained at war despite the conclusion of peace agreements with Prussia in April 1795, in which the latter tacitly accepted the French annexation of the left bank of the Rhine, the Austrian Netherlands, and the Dutch United Provinces. But even as these agreements ended hostilities with some of France's enemies, French armies continued to press forward against the Austrian armies in Central Europe and Italy. In the meantime, mass desertion and casualties drastically reduced the size of the French army which, after reaching a million men in the summer of 1794, fell to less than 500,000 a year later.

War compounded the Directory's social and political instability during the terrible year of 1795. That spring, the Directory repressed two small popular demonstrations by crowds demanding a return to controls on the price of bread. Encouraged by the Convention's move to the right, royalists also tried to seize power. The king's son had died in a Paris prison in June 1795, and so the count of Provence, Louis XVI's brother, was now heir to the throne. He denounced the Revolution, making clear that he would never compromise with reforms enacted since 1789. An army of nobles supported by the British landed at Quiberon Bay in Brittany on June

The whiff of grape-shot disperses royalist insurgents, October 5, 1795.

27, but French forces turned back the invaders with ease. On October 5, 1795, royalists attempted an insurrection in Paris, where they found support from the sections in the more prosperous districts. The government called in Napoleon Bonaparte (1769–1821), a young Corsican general, who defeated the insurgents with a "whiff of grapeshot."

Instability continued nonetheless. François-Noël Babeuf (1760– 1797), who was called Gracchus, plotted to overthrow the Directory. Influenced by Rousseau and espousing social egalitarianism and the common ownership of land, Babeuf concluded that a small group of committed revolutionaries could seize power if they were tightly organized and had the support of the poor. Some Marxist historians have considered him an early proponent of socialist thought and twentieth-century revolutionary political tactics. Following Thermidor, Babeuf organized the "Conspiracy of the Equals," finding support among a handful of Parisian artisans and small shopkeepers. But the Directory's police were on their trail. In May 1796, Babeuf and his friends were arrested; they were guillotined a year later after a trial. The Directory took advantage of the discovery of this plot to repress the Jacobins once again.

Caught between the intransigent, dogmatic forces promoted by the followers of Robespierre and the Jacobins on the left and the royalists on the right, and lacking effective and charismatic civilian leaders, the Directory's difficult tightrope act grew more precarious. Its leaders were caught in an atmosphere of intrigue and rumors of coup d'états, fraught with tensions between the directors themselves and the councils.

In 1797, elections returned a good many royalists to the Council of Five Hundred. Fearful that they might press for peace with France's enemies in the hope of obtaining a restoration of the monarchy, the Directory government annulled the election results. The coup d'état of the 18th of Fructidor (September 4, 1797) eliminated two of the directors, including the republican Carnot. In May of the next year, the directors refused to allow recently elected deputies to take their seats on the Council of Five Hundred.

The wily Sieyès (who once replied "I survived" to the question of what he had done during the Revolution) emerged as one of the most influential directors. Sieyès believed France needed a government with stronger executive authority. Because one revolutionary government after another had maintained an aggressive foreign policy, it had gradually become clear to Sieyès that the army would emerge as the arbiter of France's political future.

For all of its failures, the Directory did provide France with its second apprenticeship in representative government. The Constitution of 1795 was an important transition between the political system of the Old Regime, based primarily upon monarchical absolutism and noble privilege, and modern representative government grounded in the sanctity of property. It further preserved the centralized administration of the French state and made efforts to centralize education.

The Directory had rejected cautious British suggestions that a workable peace might be forged without the French having to give up either its Rhineland conquests or the absorption of the Austrian Netherlands. Perhaps fearful that a more bellicose ministry in Britain might replace that of William Pitt the Younger if such a peace were signed, the French fought on.

Under the Directory, France's financial situation deteriorated even further. Inflation was rampant, and the collection of taxes was sporadic at best. *Assignats* were now virtually worthless. Many bourgeois were dissatisfied, having lost money when the Directory cancelled more than half of the national debt in 1797.

Napoleon Bonaparte, the victor over the royalist insurrection, now commanded the Army of Italy, checking in with Paris only when it suited him. His armies overwhelmed the Austrian troops in northern Italy. The fighting ended with the Treaty of Campo Formio (October 17, 1797), which left France in the position of having supplanted Austria as the dominant foreign power in Italy. This victory, and Napoleon's boldly independent diplomatic negotiations in the Italian campaigns, made the general the toast of Paris. The Austrians joined the Prussians in recognizing French hegemony on the left bank of the Rhine and in the Austrian Netherlands. Reorganized in July 1797 as the Cisalpine Republic, much of the north of Italy became a feeble pawn of France.

Despite these victories, years of war had exhausted the French nation and damaged the economy. Peace proved short-lived. In May 1798, Napoleon sailed with an army to Egypt, which had allied with Britain; he hoped to strike ultimately at British interests in India. Fearing that France sought to break apart the Ottoman Empire and extend its interests in an area it had always wanted to dominate, Russia allied with Britain. Austria also joined the alliance, which became the Second Coalition (1799–1802). Austria hoped to undo the Treaty of Campo Formio and to prevent further French expansion in Italy, where French forces had sent the pope into exile and established a Roman Republic.

The combined strength of the Coalition powers for the moment proved too much for the overextended French armies in Italy. In Switzerland, a combined Russian and Austrian army defeated the French. The French unsuccessfully tried to join Irish rebels against British authorities by sending an invasion force that failed to reach Ireland—the logical jumping-off point for an invasion of England. In 1798, British troops crushed a series of Irish rebellions in a bloody struggle in which 30,000 people were killed, and British forces captured one of the French ships sent to aid the insurgents, turning back the rest.

Coalition members began to quarrel over strategy and eventual goals. The tsar withdrew from the Second Coalition in October 1799, as he was irritated with the British for insisting that the Royal Navy had the right to stop and search any vessel on the seas. Nonetheless, after repelling an attack by a Russian and British force, French armies still held the Netherlands and the left bank of the Rhine.

The Eighteenth Brumaire

In the face of endemic instability, Sieyès decided in 1799 to overthrow the Directory in a coup d'état, a move that he had contemplated since his election to the Directorate two years earlier. The go-between was Talleyrand, the foreign minister. The career of the former bishop provides another remarkable example of revolutionary survival; a detractor once claimed that Brie cheese was "the only king to whom he has been loyal." Sieyès contacted Bonaparte, whose successes and attention to the needs of his soldiers seemed to assure their support. Napoleon was summoned back to France, arriving in October. On November 9, 1799 (the 18th Brumaire), Bonaparte (who had been appointed military commander of the Paris region) announced to the hastily convened councils that another Jacobin conspiracy had been uncovered and that a new constitution had to be framed to provide France with a stronger executive authority. The deputies were justly dubious. Some demanded his immediate arrest. Napoleon's response was incoherent and ineffective, but the quick thinking of his brother, Lucien, president of the lower assembly, saved Bonaparte from

A contemporary British caricature of the 18th of Brumaire. "The Corsican Crocodile dissolving the Council of Frogs!!!"

one of his few moments of indecision. Lucien rejected the call for a vote to outlaw Napoleon, and he ordered troops to evict members who opposed him. Those who remained delegated complete power to Sieyès and General Bonaparte.

Many people believed that this latest coup would preserve a moderate republic. Others hoped that Bonaparte would provide an authoritarian government that would end the quarreling factions that dominated the political life of the Directory. A contemporary wrote that "The Revolution of the 18th Brumaire . . . appeared as pure and brilliant rays of sunshine after long and disastrous storms. One can even say that it has begun a new era."

PERSPECTIVES ON THE FRENCH REVOLUTION

The French Revolution, which began in Paris, swept across Europe. In France, it marked a significant break with the past, although, to be sure, important continuities from the Old Regime helped shape the modern world. In other countries, too, the Revolution effected major changes. These included in some places the abolition of feudalism, curtailment of clerical privileges, and a more centralized governmental structure. But while some people welcomed the export of the French Revolution, others did not. To the latter, liberation by the French seemed indistinguishable from conquest. The French presence engendered a patriotic response in some of the German and Italian states, contributing to the emergence of nationalist feeling there.

Like contemporaries viewing the Revolution, historians also have had a variety of different interpretations of it. Many of them still disagree as to the causes, effects, and significance of the Revolution, debating the dramatic events with some of the same passion as those who experienced it first hand.

European Responses to the Revolution

Soldiers in the French revolutionary armies liked to think of themselves as liberating the rest of Europe from feudalism and oppression. During 1793–1794, at least, military successes and political propaganda convinced many if not most soldiers that they carried the cause of freedom on their shoulders along with their backpacks. But, at the same time, French soldiers accepted Thermidor with barely a murmur of regret for the end of the Jacobin period.

In other countries, some people at first viewed the French as liberators who would free them from the domination of nobles and the clutches of kings, nobles, and clergy. But, in fact, the line between a "liberator" and a "conqueror" was quite thin. Enthusiastic shouts for "liberty, fraternity, and equality!," echoed in German, Dutch, and Piedmontese, disappeared in a sea of French muskets, military requisitions, and even vandalism.

The revolutionary wave did bring about sweeping changes in some of the "liberated" territories, and would continue to do so as Napoleon consolidated his authority in France (see Chapter 13). Thus, in Piedmont, French control reduced the influence of the nobility and left a heritage of relative administrative efficiency. The abolition of feudalism in some of the conquered German states, northern Italy, and the Kingdom of Naples increased the number of property owners. The French conquerors proclaimed the rule of law and curtailed some of the influence of the clergy.

But the French faced the realities of almost constant warfare and, increasingly, resistance from the local population. As the wars dragged on and the economic situations of the "republics" grew worse, the benefits brought by the French seemed increasingly less important. Ruined merchants and former officials joined nobles and clerics in opposing rule by France or its puppets. As the Civil Constitution of the French Clergy led to a violent reaction against the Revolution in France, anticlerical measures in the occupied territories had the same effect. The peoples of the Rhineland, the Netherlands, and Flanders bitterly resented the revolutionaries' de-christianization campaign. Increasingly, the French presence bred contempt and hatred. Bavarian, Dutch, Piedmontese, Austrian, and Swiss patriots found willing listeners, while French propagandists heaped abuse on the local populations for their apparent disloyalty. Thus did the French occupation give rise to general opposition and a new wave of national feeling among the conquered. Although Great Britain had not been directly threatened by French invasion, the French Revolution also contributed to the accentuation of British nationalism in the face of a perceived threat by its old Catholic enemy in a new guise.

The French conquests in Europe were themselves an exercise in statemaking, largely unanticipated and unwanted by the local populations. Between 1795 and 1799, the Directory established satellite "sister republics" directly administered by France. The Helvetic Republic (Switzerland), the Batavian Republic (the Netherlands), the Cisalpine Republic (Milan), and the Parthenopean Republic (the Kingdom of Naples) were founded with the goal of shoring up alliances against the other Great Powers. But in the Italian states, only the Cisalpine Republic generated any local enthusiasm for the French invaders, and then only briefly. People "liberated" from the rule of kings and princes found themselves governed by a revolutionary bureaucracy controlled in Paris.

The French found support and hired officials principally from the middle class, which had already provided officials in the old state structure. But the French invasions gradually generated a hatred for the revolutionary invaders and in some places a concomitant nationalist response. This was especially true within the German states, where many writers and other people in the upper classes hoped one day that "Germany,"—300 states, 50 free cities, and almost 1,000 territories of imperial knights of the Holy Roman Empire—would one day be politically unified.

Historians' Views of the Revolution

Until recently, Marxist historians dominated the historiography of the French Revolution. They have described the Revolution as the inevitable result of a bourgeois challenge to the Old Regime. Thus, Marxists interpret the Revolution in terms of the rise of the bourgeoisie and its struggle for social and political influence commensurate with its rising economic power during the expansion of capitalism in the eighteenth century. Marxists use an economic analysis and emphasize that the nobility compromised the authority of the absolute monarchy by refusing to be taxed and that the emboldened bourgeoisie then allied with urban artisans and workers to bring down the absolute monarchy. They then go on to explain the abolition of feudalism by the National Assembly after outbreaks of peasant violence and the replacement of the nobility by the bourgeoisie as the dominant social class in France, reflecting its preeminent role in the country's increasingly capitalist economy.

This traditional Marxist economic interpretation of the French Revolution has been widely criticized. Some historians have noted that differences between aristocrats and bourgeois, and within both social groups, had become considerably blurred during the eighteenth century; that most of the "bourgeois" members of the Estates-General were not drawn from commerce and manufacturing but rather from law, and that, in any case, the upper middle class and nobles by the time of the Revolution shared a common obsession with money, not privilege. Thus, one cannot accurately depict the Revolution as having been simply a victory for the bourgeoisie. Moreover, revisionists have argued that the Revolution did not expedite capitalism but even retarded it, by launching France and Europe into a long series of costly wars.

Views critical of the "bourgeois revolution" thesis have also emphasized that within France the complex nature of local political power, divided among provincial estates and parlements, and among various groups enjoying formal privileges or monopolies and municipalities, served to limit the actual prerogatives of absolute monarchy. Many historians now see the Revolution as affirming the victory of men of property—a rubric that included both nobles and bourgeois—over titled nobles born into status and power.

A related interpretation has seen the Revolution as part of an essentially democratic "Atlantic Revolution" stretching across the Atlantic Ocean. By this view, the American War of Independence was the first manifestation of an essentially political quest for popular sovereignty. It influenced, in turn, the French Revolution and subsequent, related movements for political rights in other European countries, lasting until the Revolutions of

1848, and including movements for independence in Spain's Latin American colonies early in the nineteenth century.

More recently, another revisionist school has argued that a new political culture was already in place in the last decades of the Old Regime. An extreme version of this interpretation sees the French monarchy as a state well on the way to reforming itself through the collaboration of liberal nobles before the Revolution interrupted this process. One related view looks to the 1750s and 1760s for the origins of this new, revolutionary political discourse, or culture, seen in the political and ideological opposition to Louis XV and particularly in the rhetorical violence of the Revolution's first year.

None of these varying interpretations, however, diminishes the significance of the French Revolution in transforming the Western world by providing its first modern democratic experience. This is why its origins and nature continue to generate excitement and debate today more than 200 years after the fall of the Bastille.

CHAPTER 13

NAPOLEON AND EUROPE

The royalist, religious writer François-René de Chateaubriand once called Napoleon, his enemy, "the mightiest breath of life which has ever animated human clay." In a rare moment of introspection, Napoleon once said, "It is said that I am an ambitious man but that is not so; or at least my ambition is so closely bound to my being that they are both one and the same."

Yet, far more than his imposing will, Napoleon's career was shaped by and reflected the breath-taking changes brought by the French Revolution. Statemaking and the emergence of nationalism, accompanied by the increased secularization of political institutions, slowly but surely transformed the European continent. Because Napoleon helped overthrow the Directory (1794–1799) and transformed France into an empire, the question of whether Napoleon was the heir or the undertaker of the French Revolution is an important one.

An admirer of the Enlightenment, Napoleon claimed that he was the true son of the French Revolution. He personally supervised the writing of the new constitution, which made wealth, specifically propertied wealth, the determinant of status. Napoleon's reign was also a watershed in French statemaking: he further centralized the French state and extended its reach, making it more efficient by codifying laws and creating new bureaucratic structures and a new social hierarchy based upon state service.

Napoleon saw himself as a savior who carried "liberty, equality, and fraternity" abroad, freeing the European peoples from sovereigns who oppressed them. From final exile on the distant Atlantic island of Saint Helena, Napoleon claimed to have created European unity. But in the process of "liberating" other nations from the stranglehold of the Old Regime, he also conquered them.

NAPOLEON'S RISE TO POWER

Napoleon's rise to power would have been unthinkable had it not been for the Revolution. With the emigration of most of the officer corps during the early stages of the Revolution, a generation of talented generals had risen rapidly through the ranks by virtue of their remarkable battlefield accomplishments during the revolutionary wars that had raged across much of Western and Central Europe since 1792. During the Directory, generals became increasingly powerful arbiters in political life. Napoleon manipulated the consuls and ultimately overthrew the Directory.

The Young Bonaparte

Of the strategically important Mediterranean island of Corsica, Jean-Jacques Rousseau in the *Social Contract* (1762) wrote, "I have a presentiment that one day this small island will astonish Europe." The year before, the Corsican patriot Pascale di Paoli (1725–1807) had managed to evict the Genoese from Corsica. But in 1768 the French took Corsica. Carlo Buonaparte, one of Paoli's followers, remained on the island rather than join Paoli in exile in England.

On August 15, 1769, Buonaparte's wife, whose family could trace its noble origins back to fourteenth-century Lombardy, gave birth to a son, Napoleon, named after a cousin who had been killed by the French. It is one of the strange ironies of history that Napoleon would have been

Antoine-Jean Gros' painting of the young Napoleon in *Bonaparte at Arcole* (1796).

British had his father followed Paoli into exile. In 1770, the French government accepted the Buonaparte family as nobles. The island's governor arranged for the young Buonaparte to receive an appointment to the royal military school at Brienne, in Champagne, which Napoleon entered as a boy in 1779. There he was exposed not only to a rigorous program of study but also to the humiliating condescension of the other students. They mocked his strong Corsican accent and his relatively humble economic situation. He fought back. Even in the winter snowball fights, Napoleon showed a remarkable determination to succeed. Unusually bright, he earned appointment to the artillery section of the national military academy in Paris, passing the examinations in a single year.

Napoleon stood five feet two inches, which (despite contemporary and retrospective impressions that he was quite small) was about the average height for a Frenchman of the era. He was barrel-chested, was increasingly corpulent as the years passed, had gray eyes, chestnut-colored hair, and a pale complexion.

Napoleon and the Revolution

With the outbreak of the Revolution, Napoleon returned in September 1789 to Corsica. There he helped organize the National Guard and drew up a petition to the National Assembly in Paris asking that Corsica formally become part of France, with its people enjoying the rights of citizenship. In this way, Napoleon clearly distanced himself from those Corsicans who wanted independence, thus parting ways with his hero Paoli, who had returned from England and joined the island's royalists. Napoleon favored the Revolution for three reasons: he wanted to see a curtailment of the abuses of the Old Regime; he hoped that the Revolution might end his island's status within France as little more than a conquered territory; and he thought the Revolution might provide him with an opportunity for promotion.

Napoleon became a Jacobin. He commanded a volunteer force that on Easter Sunday 1792 fired on rioters supporting the cause of the Catholic Church. When Paoli's victorious forces turned the island over to the English, the Buonapartes were forced to flee. Sent by the Committee of Public Safety to fight federalist and royalist rebels and their British allies in the south, in December 1793 Napoleon planned the successful artillery siege of the port of Toulon, which was held by British forces.

Useful political connections and the lack of direct involvement in the bitter factional struggles in Paris may have saved Napoleon from execution in the Terror or during Thermidor. The result was that Napoleon's star continued to rise, while some of his Jacobin friends went to the guillotine. In the Paris of Thermidor, Napoleon helped put down a royalist uprising on October 6, 1795, with what he called a "whiff of grape-shot." He attracted the attention of—and soon married—Josephine de Beauharnais, the lover of the corrupt Barras, one of the directors, and the widow of a member of the National Assembly who had been guillotined during the Terror. In 1796, the directors made Napoleon commander of the Army of Italy. It now seemed appropriate to eliminate the Italian spelling of his name; Buonaparte became Napoleon Bonaparte. Spectacular successes against the Austrians and their allies in Italy made him the toast of Paris. He later recalled with characteristic modesty that after victory over Austrian forces at the battle of Lodi, which opened the way to Milan, "I realized I was a superior being and conceived the ambition of performing great things, which hitherto had filled my thoughts only as a fantastic dream. I saw the world flee beneath me, as if I were transported in air."

Napoleon was now conducting military and foreign policy virtually on his own. His forceful and virtually independent pursuit of the war and subsequent peace arranged with Austria at Campo Formio (October 18, 1797) gave France control of the Austrian Netherlands, Venetia, and the satellite Cisalpine Republic in northern and central Italy. For the moment, only Great Britain remained as an enemy. Napoleon turned his attention to the Middle East: "The time is not far distant," he said, "when we shall feel that, in order truly to destroy England, we must occupy Egypt. The approaching death of the vast Ottoman Empire obliges us to think in good time of taking steps to preserve our trade in the Levant."

Napoleon then set off on a spectacular voyage to Egypt, part of the Ottoman Empire, which had allied with Britain, Russia, and Austria against France. He was accompanied by 35,000 soldiers and a shipload of scientists, a few of the latter already dreaming of carving a canal through the Isthmus of Suez that would eventually give the French an overwhelming advantage in trade with the Far East. After pausing en route long enough to capture the island of Malta, Napoleon defeated Egyptian forces at the Battle of the Pyramids in July 1798. But the tiny British admiral Horatio Nelson (1758–1805), who was prematurely white-haired, could see

Horatio Nelson on the *Vanguard* after being wounded during the Battle of the Nile.

out of only one eye, had lost an arm, and had few teeth left, trapped and destroyed the French fleet on August 1, 1798, in the Battle of the Nile. Undaunted, and temporarily stranded in Egypt because of the naval defeat, Napoleon set off to conquer Syria, before being forced back by dwindling supplies and disease. After a final victory over the Turks in Egypt, Napoleon returned to France. Austria and Russia, their respective interests threatened by French campaigns in the east, now joined Britain in the Second Coalition against France.

In Paris, Abbé Emmanuel Sieyès plotted to overthrow the Directory. Such a venture now virtually required the participation of one of the powerful, popular young generals whom the incessant warfare had catapulted to prominence. One of them nodded toward Napoleon when approached by Sieyès about undertaking such a plot, "There is your man, he will make your coup d'état better than I." Napoleon helped piece together a political constituency from among the quarreling factions of the Directory. With the coup d'état of the 18th of Brumaire 1799 (November 9, 1799), Sieyès and Napoleon overthrew the Directory.

CONSOLIDATION OF POWER

After the overthrow of the Directory, the conspirators established a new government, the Consulat, which brought political stability to France. It did so by concentrating strong executive authority in the eager hands of Napoleon, who oversaw the drafting of a constitution and made peace with the Catholic Church. Designated "Consul for Life" in 1802, Napoleon crowned himself emperor two years later. In the meantime, he continued to wage wars against Britain, Austria, and Russia, and then Prussia, four rivals driven into coalitions by French expansion. By 1809, although he had failed in his goal of bringing Britain to its knees, a series of remarkable victories confirmed his brilliance as a military strategist and tactician. Napoleon had forged a great empire, the largest in Europe since that of Rome.

Establishment of the Consulat

With the fall of the Directory in 1799, Napoleon Bonaparte, at the age of thirty, joined Sieyès and Roger Ducos to form a new, stronger executive of three consuls, replacing the five directors. When the new constitution was promulgated in December, Bonaparte became first consul, the most powerful man in France. He named men personally loyal to him to fill the other two posts. The Constitution of 1799 gave lip service to universal suffrage, but reflected the authoritarian character Sieyès intended. Indirect election for each political institution reduced the political body of the nation to a small number of notables. A Senate, appointed by the consuls, chose men from a list of 6,000 "notabilities" to serve in a Tribunate. A Council of State, whose members were appointed by the first consul, would propose legislation. The Tribunate would discuss the proposed legislation, and a Legislative Body would vote on the laws but could not debate them. There was more than a little truth to the oft-repeated story that one man who asked what was in the new constitution received the reply, "Napoleon Bonaparte." The constitution was submitted to voters in a plebiscite (voters could vote either yes or no). More than 99 percent of the all-male electorate approved the document. The plebiscite became a fundamental Napoleonic political institution, embodying his principle of "authority from above, confidence from below."

The Consulate provided political stability by institutionalizing strong executive authority. France's districts (*départements*) each received an appointed prefect, whose powers, delegated by the central government in Paris, far surpassed those of the intendants of the Bourbon monarchs. Napoleon's brother Lucien, as minister of interior, helped extend effective executive authority to the most distant corners of the nation, curtailing royalist and Jacobin opposition. Napoleon ruthlessly suppressed the press, reducing the number of newspapers in Paris from seventy-three to thirteen, cowing survivors with threats, or winning their allegiance with bribes.

The Concordat

Napoleon made peace with the Catholic Church, bringing it under state supervision. The Revolution had deeply divided France over the issue of religion, often pitting royalists against anticlerical republicans. Deep hostility remained between priests who had sworn allegiance to the nation during the Revolution—the "juring" clergy—and those who had refused. Napoleon wanted to bring this dispute to an end. Influenced by Enlightenment secularism, he believed the Church should not have an institutional role in the affairs of state. But he was also a cynical pragmatist. "There is only one way to encourage morality," he once said, "and that is to reestablish religion. Society cannot exist without some being richer than others, and this inequality cannot exist without religion. When one man is dying of hunger next door to another who is stuffing himself with food, the poor man simply cannot accept the disparity unless some authority tells him, 'God wishes it so . . . in heaven things will be different.'" An agreement with the Church would also undercut popular support for the monarchist cause by restoring some of the Church's prerogatives, but not any that would threaten the government's authority. Napoleon thus shrewdly sought to detach the Church from the quest for a restoration of the monarchy.

With the death in 1799 of Pope Pius VI (pope 1775–1799), who had refused any accommodation with the Revolution, his more liberal successor, Pius VII (pope 1800–1823), was eager to end a decade of religious turmoil. In 1801, Napoleon signed a Concordat with the papacy that helped solidify some of the changes brought by the Revolution. While declaring Catholicism "the religion of the majority of citizens" in France, it ended the division between juring and non-juring clergy. All of the non-juring clergy were to resign their posts. Some ecclesiastics were angered by what they saw as Pius VII's capitulation to the Revolution. A majority of bishops refused to accept the Concordat and did not resign. The pope would henceforth appoint new bishops, but on the recommendation of the first consul, that is, Napoleon; the state would pay clerical salaries. The Church also abandoned all claims to those ecclesiastical lands that had been sold as "national property" during the first years of the Revolution. The Concordat helped restore ecclesiastical influence in France, reflected by an increase in religious observance and in the number of people entering the clergy. Napoleon also pleased the Church by abandoning the confusing official calendar put in place in 1793, reestablishing Sundays and religious holidays.

The Organic Articles, which Napoleon promulgated without consulting the pope, regulated the Gallican (French) Church's status in France and reduced the pope's authority. The Church would now be subject to virtually the same administrative organization and policing as any other organization; a "minister of religion" would sit with the other ministers in Paris. No papal bull or other pronouncement could be read in France's churches without permission of the government; the clergy would have to read official government decrees from the pulpit. Under Napoleon, the Church gained the freedom of religious practice and improved its position compared to what it had been under the Terror and the Directory, but at the expense of some of its independence. A new catechism required primary students to memorize:

Question: What are the duties of Christians with respect to the princes who govern them, and what are, in particular, our duties toward Napoleon. . . ?

Answer: . . . Love, respect, obedience, fidelity, military service. . . . We also owe him fervent prayers for his safety and for the spiritual and temporal prosperity of the State.

Napoleon granted Protestants and Jews state protection. An article of the Concordat guaranteed freedom of worship for people in both religions (who together made up less than 5 percent of the population, most being Protestant). One set of Organic Articles supervised Calvinists, another

Lutherans. An imperial decree in 1808 organized Judaism into territorial consistories, although rabbis, unlike priests and Protestant ministers, would not be paid by the state.

Napoleon's settlement with the Church alienated some of his cautious supporters on the left, notably the group known as the Ideologues. They resented the return of the Church to officially recognized institutional respectability. After a solemn ceremony at Notre Dame in Paris celebrating the Concordat, one general put it bluntly to Napoleon—"A fine monkish show. It lacked only the presence of the hundred thousand men who gave their lives to end all that."

Napoleon's Leadership

One of his staff would later describe Napoleon as an "ever-restless spirit." He ate rapidly and could work days on end with very little sleep, dictating more than 80,000 letters in his extraordinary career. He seemed to absorb every bit of information that arrived in his office or field headquarters and rapidly mastered subjects related to military or administrative concerns. But he often ignored matters that did not really interest him, such as economics and naval warfare, in which France lagged behind Britain, as the defeat at Trafalgar (1805) would demonstrate.

Napoleon was more than just an optimist. He believed that his wildest dreams of conquest and empire would inevitably become reality. Everyone feared his rages, although he could be surprisingly understanding and generous toward subordinates when he believed they erred. A man of monumental stubbornness, he sometimes succeeded in reconciling others of opposing temperaments and views. He delegated very little meaningful authority, mistrusting even his closest advisers, but he tolerated opposing viewpoints. Napoleon's style of leadership became ever more tyrannical. He made up his own mind, and that mind invariably chose war.

Wars of Conquest and Empire

Napoleon had brought stability to France, but France was still at war with the Second Coalition: Great Britain, Austria, and Russia. In February 1800, when Austria turned down his overtures for peace on the basis of the Treaty of Campo Formio, Napoleon returned to the battlefield, retaking Milan and defeating an Austrian army in June 1800. With the Treaty of Lunéville (February 1801), Austria reaffirmed the conditions of the Treaty of Campo Formio, accepting French gains in Italy, as well as French control over the Southern Netherlands (Belgium).

With Austria defeated and Russia tied up by a war against the Ottoman Empire, the British government signed the Peace of Amiens in March 1802. France kept all of its significant gains on the continent, and Britain returned all the French colonies it had captured. Great Britain gained only the end of hostilities.

In Central Europe, Napoleon was now free to dismember the Holy Roman Empire and to dictate the territorial reorganization of the small German states. France had absorbed the left bank of the Rhine, fulfilling the nationalistic dreams of a France extending to its "natural frontiers." Since this expansion came at the expense of Prussia and Austria, these two powers had to be compensated. By the oddly named Imperial Recess of 1803, the two most powerful German states absorbed a number of small, independent German states, ecclesiastical territories, and most of the free cities. The rulers of Baden, Bavaria, Hesse-Kassel, and Württemberg, the other largest German states, also added to their domains. They were grateful to Napoleon for having made this possible. France's position in Italy also was solidified. Piedmont remained a French possession, with Napoleon naming himself president of the Italian Cisalpine Republic. After imposing a Federal Constitution on the cantons of Switzerland that transformed it into the Helvetic Republic, Napoleon forced a defensive alliance on that strategically important country. By 1802, France was at peace for the first time in a decade. Napoleon had brought his nation to a position of dominance in Europe not seen since the time of Charlemagne a thousand years earlier.

No longer satisfied with the title "first consul," in 1802 Napoleon became "consul for life," a change approved by plebiscite. Napoleon prepared the establishment of a hereditary empire in France. Although thousands of émigrés took advantage of a declared amnesty to return to France, the "discovery" in 1804 of a conspiracy against Napoleon's life by a group of royalists led him to act against the Bourbons and to expedite his plan to become emperor. Napoleon accused Louis de Bourbon-Condé, the duke of Enghien (1772–1804), a member of the Bourbon family who had emigrated to Baden, of involvement in the conspiracy. French troops moved into Baden to arrest him. The duke was hurriedly tried and executed near Paris, despite the lack of any evidence of his involvement in plans to assassinate Napoleon. Public opinion throughout much of Europe was outraged. The German composer Ludwig van Beethoven crossed out the dedication to Napoleon of his symphony *Eroica*, shouting "So he is also nothing more than an ordinary man? Now he will trample on the rights of mankind and indulge only his own ambition; from now on he will make himself superior to all others and become a tyrant!" Before his own execution, one of the royalist conspirators lamented, "We have done more than we hoped to do; we meant to give France a king, and we have given her an Emperor."

The Tribunate, Senate, and the people (through voting in a plebiscite) quickly approved the change from the Consulate to an empire. On December 2, 1804, Napoleon was anointed emperor by Pius VII. Instead of waiting for the pope to crown him, Napoleon snatched the crown from the

Jacques-Louis David's *Emperor Napoleon Crowning the Empress Josephine in the Cathedral of Notre Dame* (1805–1808).

pontiff and placed it on his own head. A new constitution presented a telling contradiction: "The government of the republic is entrusted to an emperor." An unknown officer who had scraped by with little money amid the spendthrift glitter of Thermidor, Bonaparte began to wear a coat of red velvet that would have been fit for Louis XIV.

Napoleon was no more temperamentally suited to live with peace than with defeat. Jealous of Britain's naval and commercial supremacy in the Mediterranean and the Western Hemisphere, he began to goad Britain into a new war. A government-controlled newspaper boasted that France would conquer the road to India.

Haiti, the western side of the island of Hispaniola, had proclaimed its independence from France in 1801 under the leadership of a former slave, Toussaint L'Ouverture. In 1802, Napoleon restored French control of Haiti and reinstituted slavery in the French colonies, in response to pressure from sugar planters. French troops captured Toussaint L'Ouverture and took him to France, where he soon died. Tropical disease killed most of the French troops occupying Haiti, and the British prevented the arrival of reinforcements. The French army surrendered, and in 1804 Haiti again became independent. With his plans to extend France's empire to the Caribbean having come to naught, Napoleon shouted "Damn sugar, damn coffee, damn colonies!"

Seeking to recoup the financial losses France had incurred from war, Napoleon sold the huge Louisiana Territory to the United States in 1803 for 60 million francs (then about 11 million dollars). In retrospect, this was a paltry sum for territory that virtually doubled the size of what was then the United States. Napoleon's hope that its former colony would emerge as a rival to Britain also lay behind the sale.

In July 1805, Russia and Austria joined Britain to form the Third Coalition against Napoleon. The new tsar, Alexander I (ruled 1801–1825), a religious mystic who believed that God wanted him to destroy Napoleon, had succeeded his assassinated father, Paul. Undaunted, Napoleon readied an army and ships of all sizes at the port of Boulogne on the English Channel for an invasion of Britain. In 1805, a French decoy fleet lured Nelson's fleet into pursuit, hoping to inflict a crushing defeat on the Royal Navy. But the hunted became the hunter. When the French fleet sailed from the Spanish Mediterranean part of Cádiz on October 21, 1805, it sighted the Royal Navy. Turning to sail back to port, the French vessels were left vulnerable to attack by two columns of ships that succeeded in breaking the French line. As Nelson lay dying of a wound (which might have been avoided, had he not refused to cover up his medals and epaulets that attracted a French marksman's eye), his fleet earned one of naval history's most decisive victories at Cape Trafalgar, not far from Gibraltar. Any chance for a French invasion of England evaporated. Great Britain controlled the seas.

The French were more successful on the continent. They defeated the Austrians at Ulm in October 1805, capturing 50,000 troops. Napoleon

The Battle of Trafalgar.

finally coaxed the Russians into open battle when the tsar himself, who took command of his army, followed the bad advice of an aide who told him that the combined Russian and Austrian armies could easily defeat the French. At Austerlitz on December 2, 1805, Napoleon tricked his opponents into an attack on his intentionally weakened right flank. He then divided the two armies with a crushing attack at their vulnerable center. When the dust cleared after the battle, the Russians and their Austrian allies had suffered 30,000 casualties, the French fewer than 9,000. Austria asked for peace, giving up the remnants of imperial territories in Italy and Dalmatia. Napoleon's allies, Bavaria, Baden, and Württemberg, once again gained Habsburg territories. Alexander limped back to Russia with his broken armies.

In the wake of Austerlitz, the hesitant King Frederick William III (ruled 1797–1840) of Prussia abandoned his tentative agreement to join the Third Coalition, instead signing an alliance with France. In July 1806, Napoleon abolished the unwieldy Holy Roman Empire and organized the Confederation of the Rhine, composed of sixteen German states, excluding Prussia and Austria (see Map 13.1). Napoleon named himself "Protector" of the Confederation, whose members agreed to accept French garrisons in southern Germany and to support Napoleon if war broke out again. Prussia now joined the Third Coalition.

Wanting to knock Prussia quickly out of the war, Napoleon's armies humiliated Frederick William's army at Jena near Nuremberg on October 14, 1806, and then occupied his capital, Berlin. In February 1807, the French and Russian armies fought to a bloody draw in a Polish snowstorm. Had Austrian and British troops been sent to support the Russians, Napoleon might well have been soundly defeated. But Austria was still reeling from the defeat at Austerlitz, and the English were preoccupied with defending their commercial interests in the Western Hemisphere. Napoleon sent for fresh troops from France and added 30,000 Polish soldiers, some attracted by speculation that the emperor might create an independent Polish state.

After defeating the Russian army at the Battle of Friedland (June 1807), Napoleon met with Tsar Alexander on a raft in the middle of a river. Frederick William, the king of Prussia, paced anxiously on the shore as he awaited the outcome. The news was the worst. By the Treaty of Tilsit (July 1807), Prussia lost territory in western Germany and in Poland, which became, respectively, the Kingdom of Westphalia and the Grand Duchy of Warsaw, the latter annexed by Napoleon's ally, Saxony. Russia suffered only the loss of its Ionian Islands in the Aegean Sea, but was forced to accept the territorial settlements in Western Europe as definitive. In return, the tsar received a promise of French support in Russia's current quarrel with the Ottoman Empire. France thus tacitly agreed to back Russia's long-standing ambitions in Southeastern Europe. Finally, the tsar agreed to close Russian ports to British ships.

With Prussia discouraged and dismembered, Austria defeated and weak-

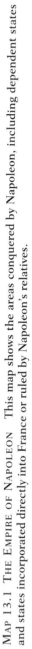

MAP 13.1 THE EMPIRE OF NAPOLEON   This map shows the areas conquered by Napoleon, including dependent states and states incorporated directly into France or ruled by Napoleon's relatives.

States ruled
directly from Paris

States ruled by members
of Napoleon's family

Other dependent states

Battle sites

400 miles

400 kilometers

Moscow 1812

Borodino 1812

Smolensk 1812

Berezina R.

Dnieper R.

Dniester R.

RUSSIAN
EMPIRE

BLACK
SEA

Constantinople

OTTOMAN EMPIRE

AEGEAN SEA

Athens

IONIAN
ISLANDS

SICILY

MEDITERRANEAN SEA

Tunis

Algiers

SARDINIA

CORSICA

ELBA

ADRIATIC SEA

ILLYRIAN PROVINCES

Budapest

AUSTRIAN
EMPIRE

Danube R.

Vienna

Wagram 1809

Austerlitz 1805

Campo Formio

KINGDOM
OF NAPLES

Naples

Rome

KINGDOM
OF
ITALY

Florence

Venice

Milan

PIEDMONT

Antibes

SAVOY

HELVETIC
REPUBLIC

BAVARIA

Ulm 1805

WÜRTTEMBERG

CONFEDERATION
OF THE RHINE

HESSE

BADEN

Jena 1806

Dresden 1813

Leipzig 1813
(Battle of the Nations)

KINGDOM OF
WESTPHALIA

Berlin

PRUSSIA

Elbe R.

Oder R.

GRAND DUCHY
OF
WARSAW

Warsaw

Vistula R.

Niemen R.

Tilsit

Friedland 1807

BALTIC
SEA

Copenhagen

DENMARK

SWEDEN

NORWAY

NORTH
SEA

DUTCH
REPUBLIC

Amsterdam

SOUTHERN
NETHERLANDS

Brussels

Waterloo 1815

Amiens

Lunéville

Seine R.

Paris 1814

Rhine R.

Rhône R.

Grenoble

Marseille

FRANCE

Loire R.

Bordeaux

PYRENEES

Ebro R.

Madrid 1808

SPAIN

Tagus R.

PORTUGAL

Lisbon
1809

Cádiz

Trafalgar
1805

Gibraltar

ATLANTIC OCEAN

UNITED
KINGDOM

Alexander I and Napoleon meet on a raft at Tilsit, on the Niemen River, 1807.

ened, Russia neutralized, and Britain once again left alone to challenge France, Napoleon's position in Europe seemed invincible. Two years later, when Austria challenged Napoleon by invading Bavaria in 1809, Napoleon moved rapidly against Vienna, capturing the Habsburg capital. He then crossed to the left bank of the Danube, and after avoiding being pinned against the river by Austrian forces, earned a great victory in July 1809 at Wagram, smashing through the center of the Austrian army. Defeat forced Austria to surrender Illyria to France and other territory to Bavaria, the Grand Duchy of Warsaw, and Russia, which was still technically but un-easily allied to France. Through conquest, the establishment of satellite states, and alliances with smaller powers, Napoleon had constructed a vast empire.

The Corsican Warrior

Napoleon has been considered one of the most brilliant and successful military leaders in modern history. Yet, his talents lay not in originality but in his stunningly innovative adaption of military strategy and tactics devel-oped in the eighteenth century and during the Revolution. Before mass military conscription, warfare had usually involved relatively limited num-bers of soldiers. Armies had not moved rapidly nor covered much ground. Since the beginnings of the Thirty Years' War (1618–1648), wars had been fought over dynastic honor, commercial rivalry, and disputed territories (see Chapters 7 and 11). Old Regime armies had consisted largely of mercenaries commanded by nobles. Most battles had been fought in precise, drilled ranks, by two relatively small armies in line formation directly facing each other.

In the eighteenth century, technological and tactical improvements in artillery augmented the value of that arm of warfare. Artillery pieces became lighter and therefore could be moved more easily. Improvements in roads also helped expedite the movement of cannon, as well as troops. Properly positioned artillery, launching more powerful shells, could now play a more decisive role against infantry. The artillery became a more respected part of the army; talented officers, Napoleon not the least of them, found a chance for promotion that they would not have had elsewhere.

Warfare changed when armies were no longer made up of mercenaries but rather of "citizen-soldiers" with greater commitment to a cause. Thus, during the French Revolution committed sans-culottes were first mobilized as citizen-soldiers in the *levée en masse* proclaimed in August 1792. They fought to defend the nation, winning the stunning victory over the Austrian army at Valmy (September 1792). The Revolution inaugurated a period of warfare in Europe in which more soldiers entered battle than ever before. Between 1800 and 1815, perhaps as many as 2 million men served in or allied with Napoleon's armies. Napoleon harnessed French nationalism to win the commitment of his armies.

Bonaparte's genius was his ability to organize, oversee, and assure the supplying of and communication between larger armies than had ever before been effectively assembled, and to move them more rapidly than any-

Citizen-soldiers were conscripted to fight in Napoleon's wars. Here the conscripts of 1807 leave their families to defend the nation.

one before him. "Everything is in the execution," as he put it. He built on the French innovation in 1792–1793 of using combat divisions that combined infantry, cavalry, and artillery, and subdivided his armies into corps, each with its own sense of pride and morale.

Napoleon's ability to select and promote able marshals, and to inspire officer and foot soldier alike, drew the admiration of even his most bitter enemies. He founded a military school in 1803 that produced 4,000 officers by 1815—there were lots of vacancies as the relentless fighting took its toll. As in the administration of the empire, however, Napoleon refused to delegate responsibility for crucial strategic and tactical decisions to his subordinates. In the long run, this would cost him dearly.

The infantry remained the heart of Napoleon's armies and his military planning (there were never more than four artillerymen for every 1,000 foot soldiers). Napoleon perfected the "mixed order" formation developed in the eighteenth century, which combined stretching troops across the field in a thin line about three men deep and bunching them in columns not only for marching but also for attack. Napoleon kept some battalions in columns, others in lines, which allowed battlefield flexibility. When he saw the opportunity, he launched an attack by outflanking his opponent and striking against the enemy's lines of communication. When he confronted an army stretched out before him, skilled marksmen threw the opponent's advance forces into disarray. Napoleon then brilliantly assessed the opposing army's weakest point. The concentration of deadly artillery fire—Napoleon once referred to the twelve-pound cannons as his "beautiful daughters"—prepared the way for the assault of the infantry columns. The speed of his army's movements was such that Napoleon could rapidly attack and defeat part of an enemy army before reinforcements could arrive.

Like a master chess player, Napoleon analyzed all possible moves by his opponents and quickly made decisions. At the same time, he remained flexible, believing that in warfare there are no fixed rules. "There is a moment in every battle in which the least move is decisive and results in superiority, as one drop of water causes overflow." When the corner was turned, instead of stopping to celebrate victory, Napoleon sent his troops, particularly the cavalry, to pursue the enemy. Victory became a rout.

Napoleon's armies, unlike the professional armies of the Old Regime, lived off the land. They requisitioned what they needed. This did not make the French troops very popular, even in those lands officially incorporated into the empire. But it did allow the imperial army to travel far afield, in great numbers, marching up to twenty miles a day. Such speed seemed incredible for the period, particularly in that each infantryman carried with him about sixty pounds of equipment.

Finally, Napoleon enjoyed intense loyalty from his officers and troops, even up to the bitter end. He took to the field with his troops and rewarded good work with promotions and decorations, sometimes given on the field

Charles Meynier's *The Return of Napoleon to the Island of Lobau after the Battle of Essling in 1807*, was intended to show the deeply felt loyalty of Napoleon's soldiers, some of whose wounds are being dressed as they stretch their hands toward the emperor.

of battle. The emperor's own courage was also a source of inspiration to his troops. He had the good fortune to be wounded only twice in his long military career (a slight bayonet cut at the siege of Toulon in 1793 and a wound when he was hit by a spent musket ball at Wagram in 1809). During one battle, the Imperial Guard refused to fight until Napoleon had moved to a safer place. Napoleon personally reviewed his troops before and after major engagements. He treated his soldiers with demonstrable respect and even affection because they seemed willing to die for him. At least 400,000 did just that.

The Napoleonic adventure offered even the most humble soldier a chance for glory. Yet, the risks of death and, above all, injury were considerable (only 2 percent of the casualties at the Battle of Austerlitz were deaths). Disease sometimes killed more soldiers than battlefield wounds. Soldiering was a tough life. In good times, soldiers ate reasonably well—bread, vegetables, even some meat, and drank wine or rum. But after defeat, or when they were far inside inhospitable territory, soldiers were fortunate to find enough to eat. As time went on, it became impossible to supply all troops with the basic necessities.

Medical care remained inadequate, despite the improvements brought by a talented and dedicated doctor, Dominique Jean Larrey. He arranged for the wounded to be cared for while the battle was still raging, rather than afterward when it often was too late. Major surgery—the countless amputations occurring after each major battle—was often fatal. Napoleon remained far more concerned with able-bodied soldiers than with the wounded or sick.

Incessant warfare was the most fundamental characteristic of Napoleon's empire. Military genius or not, the emperor's ability to mobilize France through a combination of appeals to nationalism and utilization of the resources of the centralized state dragged his country and much of Europe into a protracted, damaging series of wars. These stretched across Europe, lasting almost from the very beginning of his empire to final defeat.

THE FOUNDATIONS OF THE FRENCH EMPIRE

The Napoleonic empire was a significant episode in the long story of statemaking in Europe. Continuing the tradition of eighteenth-century monarchs, Napoleon sought to make state administration more efficient and uniform. His aggressive conquests brought centrally controlled, bureaucratic government and the Napoleonic Code to much of the continent. For this reason, it is possible to see him as the embodiment of "enlightened absolutism" awaited by the philosophe Voltaire.

Napoleon created a new social hierarchy based not on blood but on service to the state, particularly in the army and bureaucracy. Beyond French borders, the empire was based on an imperial system in which Napoleon made his relatives and marshals heads of state. Thus, he gave the throne of Westphalia to his brother Jérôme, as earlier he had transformed the Cisalpine Republic in northern Italy into a monarchy ruled by his stepson, Eugène de Beauharnais. He made his brother Louis king of Holland. His brother Joseph became king of Naples and later king of Spain. Everywhere that French armies conquered, Napoleon's daunting will imposed change.

Institutional Foundations: Imperial Centralization

Napoleon's Council of State, made up of his chief ministers, the most prestigious and important administrative body of the empire, oversaw finance, interior affairs, and war. Members advised the emperor and drew up laws and regulations for approval by the Legislative Body. Napoleon attached to the council a corps of young, bright, apprentice bureaucrats, trained to assume important administrative posts in the future. In the provinces, prefects orchestrated imperial administration. The Senate, Legislative Body, and Tribunate lost all but their ceremonial roles, and Napoleon completely eliminated the Tribunate in 1808. Even the members of the Council of State found their influence on the emperor increasingly reduced.

Napoleon established the Bank of France in 1800, which facilitated the state's ability to borrow money. He followed the Directory's policy of abandoning the grossly inflated paper money of the Revolution, which stabilized France's currency. He facilitated the assessment and collection of taxes, ordering a land survey of the entire country upon which direct taxes were to be based. And he expanded the number of indirect taxes collected on salt (which had also been a principal source of revenue for the Old Regime monarchy), tobacco, and liquor, as well as on goods brought into any town of over 5,000 inhabitants.

The empire followed the Revolution, and particularly the Directory, in making higher education the responsibility of the state. In a country in which about half the population was illiterate, Napoleon believed that schools could become a means of creating patriotic and obedient citizens through teaching secular values that would ultimately link education to nationalism. Although a national system of primary school education lay far in the future, the emperor could brag that, sitting in Paris, he knew by looking at his clock what every schoolchild in France was studying at that very moment. In 1802, Napoleon established state secondary schools called *lycées*, thirty-seven of which were operating six years later, for the relatively few boys who went beyond primary school. These schools were intended to educate a new generation of technically trained and loyal military officers. Students read only textbooks approved by the emperor. In 1808, Napoleon created France's first public university system, charging it with "direct[ing] political and moral opinions." Education increasingly became seen as a value in itself, and a means of social ascension.

Legal Foundations: The Napoleonic Code

Napoleon wanted to be known to history as the new Justinian, the Roman lawgiver. The Civil Code of 1804, which became known as the Napoleonic Code several years later, may have been the emperor's most lasting legacy. Many of the *cahiers*, or lists of grievances submitted to Louis XVI on the eve of the Revolution, had asked that French laws be uniform. During the constitutional monarchy, the Convention had begun the process of codifying French laws, but it had been interrupted by the vicissitudes of the Revolution. While the fundamental division in French law had been between the written Roman Law in the south and customary law based upon regional and local traditions in the north, there were hundreds of different legal codes in France. Napoleon ordered the Council of State to seek advice from a battery of lawyers to codify the laws of the land. Napoleon personally participated in the most critical discussions and debates. The Napoleonic Code made the rights of property owners sacrosanct: the majority of the articles concerned private property.

The code, over 2,000 articles long, enshrined the equality of all people before the law and the freedom of religion. It also proclaimed the "freedom of work," reaffirming a 1791 law that forbade associations of workers or employers' associations (the latter were extremely rare). The "freedom" guaranteed in relations between employers and workers left workers legally subordinate to their employers and unable to strike. Furthermore, workers were required to carry small passports that had to be handed over to municipal officials, police, or employers when requested.

The Napoleonic Code reflected Napoleon's traditional attitudes toward the family. He considered the family the most important intermediary between the state and the individual, a means of guaranteeing social order. Rejecting scattered demands during the Revolution for the equality of women, the code reaffirmed the patriarchal nature of the traditional family. It made women and children legally dependent on their husbands or fathers. The code granted men control of family property. A woman could not buy or sell property or begin a business without her husband's permission, and any income she earned would pass to his descendants, not hers. A woman worker's wages, too, went to her husband, and women had no control over their children's savings. As during the First Republic, the state recognized divorce, but it was now more difficult to obtain. More articles in the Napoleonic Code established conditions for the sale of cattle than addressed the legal status of women. In cases of adultery, women risked penalties that were far more severe than those for men. Only adult males could officially witness a legal document. The status of women reflected Napoleon's own views. He had complained: "In France women are considered too highly. They should not be regarded as equal to men. In reality they are nothing more than machines for producing children."

The code also formalized the relationship of children to their parents. As in the Old Regime, parents could put their offspring in jail and retained authority over their children's marriages. The code required equal inheritance by all male children (although at least a quarter of the inheritance was reserved for the eldest child), ending primogeniture (inheritance by the eldest son) in northern France, where it still existed. Yet, siblings often found ways to keep the family property together; one brother could buy out his brothers' shares in an inherited property. The end of primogeniture may also have provided an impetus for French couples to have fewer children in an effort to avoid further division of property.

The Napoleonic Code, despite its obvious inequities, imperfections, and the fact that it was sometimes promulgated by a conquering army, served as the basis for the codification of laws and the reorganization of judicial systems in Switzerland, Piedmont-Sardinia, and the Dutch United Provinces. At the end of his life, Napoleon claimed, "My glory is not to have won forty battles . . . but what nothing will destroy, what will live eternally, is my Civil Code."

Social Foundations of the Empire: The Imperial Hierarchy

Napoleon once wrote, "My motto has always been: a career open to all talents." He considered the end of social distinctions by birth to be one of the most lasting accomplishments of the French Revolution. The empire favored the aspirations of the middle class. The elimination of legal barriers to social ascension left wealth, largely defined by the ownership of property and service to the state (rewarded by grants of property, titles, and pensions), as the main determinant of status. Yet, imposing obstacles to social mobility remained. It took wealth to acquire the background, education, and reputation to take one's place in the imperial hierarchy. But even among bourgeois of more modest means, social ascension was sometimes possible.

The army and the bureaucracy were the two pillars of the empire. Napoleon created a new nobility, an elite of "notables," as they were called, rewarding those who served him well with prestigious titles and lucrative positions. At the pinnacle of the new hierarchy were eighteen marshals appointed in 1804 from the ranks of the Senate, including generals who had earned fortunes waging war. Napoleon began to restore titles abolished by the Revolution: prince in 1804, duke two years later, followed by count, baron, and chevalier. But unlike the titles of the Old Regime, these titles were not hereditary. They did not reflect the ownership of a certain estate or château, but rather service to the state.

Napoleon used titles and awards as pillars of the empire. Jacques-Louis David's the *Oath of the Army after the Distribution of Standards* shows the eagerness of the army to defend Napoleon and the empire.

Between 1808 and 1814, Napoleon created 3,600 titles. Yet, Napoleonic notables totaled only one-seventh of the number of the nobles in France on the eve of the Revolution. Some of the new notables had already become rich through purchase of ecclesiastical and émigré lands sold during the Revolution. More than half of all men granted titles by the emperor had rendered service in the military. The civil service was the second most important avenue to a Napoleonic title, with about six of every ten Napoleonic notables coming from the ranks of the bourgeoisie. Some of those who rose to the top of the imperial hierarchy and received appointment to the Senate were Napoleon's old friends and comrades-in-arms. Thus, promotion in the revolutionary army might ultimately culminate in a position in the imperial hierarchy. The emperor often repeated that "in the backpack of each soldier, there is a marshal's baton." Former royalists who now served the imperial cause could also be promoted within the imperial hierarchy. So too could Italians, Dutch, Germans, and others from conquered lands who found that the French Empire offered them dignified and sometimes even lucrative careers.

In May 1802, Napoleon established the Legion of Honor to reward those who served the nation with distinction. It was, predictably enough, organized along military lines, with commanders, officers, and knights. The Legion of Honor drew some early opposition from the Senate and the Council of State because the very idea seemed to fly in the face of the concepts of liberty and equality. A former Jacobin member of the Council of State complained that the award, a decorated cross that could be displayed prominently on one's coat, was nothing more than a "bauble." To which Napoleon replied, "You may call them baubles, but it is by baubles that mankind is governed." The subjects of territories incorporated into the empire were eligible to receive the Legion of Honor. When Rome became part of Napoleon's vast empire, the following parody on the Legion of Honor appeared on the walls of the Eternal City:

> In fierce old times, they balanced loss
> By hanging thieves upon a cross.
> But our more humane age believes
> In hanging crosses on the thieves.

THE TIDE TURNS AGAINST NAPOLEON

Almost inevitably, French rule generated resistance in countries absorbed into Napoleon's empire through conquest. Napoleon manipulated factional splits in some countries, coopted local elites where he could, brushed aside rulers as he pleased, and tried to establish compliant new regimes, some of which he handed over to his brothers. But ultimately French rule over such an extended empire collapsed. Napoleon's failure to force British submission by strangling its economy with his "Continental System," which aimed to cut off Britain from its continental markets, kept his major enemy in the field, or more appropriately, on the high seas. Spanish resistance against French rule became a full-fledged rebellion (the Peninsular War) that, with British assistance, sapped imperial resources. Moreover, French occupation of some of the German states gave rise to German nationalism, solidifying resistance. Prussian and Austrian military reforms led to stronger opponents in the field. And in a final ill-considered expansion of imperial aggression, Napoleon in 1812 decided to invade Russia. The destruction of his "Grand Army" in the snowdrifts and howling winds of Russia was the beginning of the end.

The Continental System

Knowing that the war was costing the British government huge sums (between 60 and 90 percent of the state's annual revenue), the emperor devised a plan he was sure would force his rival to end the conflict. In November 1806, Napoleon announced his Continental System, which prohibited trade with Britain and which he hoped would strangle the British economy by closing all continental ports to British ships. French merchants and manufacturers, as well as the state, would earn fortunes supplying the captive markets of the continent. Increased hardship might cause popular disturbances in Britain.

British Prime Minister William Pitt the Younger and Napoleon carve up the world.

But the blockade of the continental ports was far easier said than done. The continental coastline was vast, the British navy strong (despite the loss of 317 ships between 1803 and 1815), and the merchants and smugglers resourceful. British merchants continued to find American markets for their goods. The banning of British imports did lead to the development of some important innovations in France (for example, the Jacquard loom for silk weaving and the planting of the sugar beet to compensate for the loss of sugar from the West Indies). But France's relative lack of available coal and iron ore, its lack of capital accumulation and investment, and the overwhelming allocation of the nation's material and human resources to war prevented French merchants from taking up the slack left by the absence of British goods in continental markets.

The British government's "Orders in Council" in November and December 1807 demanded that trading ships under all flags purchase a license in a British port. This decision placed Britain at loggerheads with the United States, one of France's principal trading partners. Napoleon retaliated with the Milan Decrees, threatening to seize any ship that had traded with Britain or that had even allowed itself to be searched by British ships. Yet, in 1809, British imports could still be readily found on the continent. The French, suffering a sharp decline in customs revenue, began tolerating violations of the Continental System, even selling special licenses and placing hefty taxes on the importation of British goods to bring in more revenue. The blockade came completely apart in the midst of an economic depression that began in 1811.

Napoleon counted on Britain's deepening crisis with the U.S. government, which opposed the boarding and searching of its vessels by British inspectors, to bring Anglo-American relations to a breaking point. But even the War of 1812 between the British and the United States, which ended with the exhausted British capitulating, could not destroy the British economy. British trade and manufacturing continued to provide the crown with sufficient resources to subsidize continental allies and to defeat Napoleon. French merchants and industrialists began to resent the economic consequences of the blockade, which also seemed to help unify British public opinion against Napoleon and the French at a time when the sense of being British was rapidly taking hold in Britain. The fact that French agents had encouraged an Irish insurrection against British rule in 1798 lingered in the memory of the British upper class. Tory governments, which governed Britain throughout the entire revolutionary and Napoleonic periods, remained committed to defeating Bonaparte (and repressing dissent at home), despite the staggering economic cost of the war.

The Peninsular War

Napoleon's obsession with bringing Britain to its knees led him into the protracted, bloody, and disastrous Peninsular War (1808–1813) in Spain.

In 1807, Napoleon reached an agreement with Charles IV (ruled 1788–1808), the incompetent king of Spain, that permitted French troops to pass through his kingdom to conquer Portugal, Britain's ally. A French army marched on Lisbon, and the Portuguese royal family fled to Brazil. Napoleon started sending more troops to Spain, while a popular insurrection in March 1808 led to the abdication of Charles IV and the succession of his son Ferdinand VII (ruled 1808–1833) to the throne. Believing that the kingdom of Spain was on the verge of falling like an apple into his hands, Napoleon forced Ferdinand to abdicate and summoned his older brother, Joseph Bonaparte (1768–1844), from his wobbly throne in Naples and made him king of Spain.

But Napoleon did not count on the resistance of the Spanish and Portuguese people. Ecclesiastical reforms imposed by Joseph and Napoleon, including ordering a reduction in the number of monastic convents by two-thirds and the abolition of the Inquisition, angered the Church, which remained a powerful force in Spanish life. Napoleon found some allies among the urban middle class, but the Spanish nobility joined their old allies, the clergy, in opposition to the invaders. Local councils organized quick attacks on the French forces, which were easy targets for the small mobile groups of Spanish guerrillas, who attacked and then quickly disap-

Francisco Goya's *The Third of May, 1808,* depicts the execution of citizens of Madrid by French soldiers after the fall of the city during the Peninsular War.

peared into the Spanish landscape. Even after sending fresh troops from Central Europe, victory for Napoleon in Spain seemed ever more distant. British troops led by Arthur Wellesley, later duke of Wellington (1769–1852), arrived to help the Spanish and Portuguese fight the French. By 1810, about 350,000 French troops were tied up in the Iberian Peninsula. Fighting for "church and king," Spaniards sustained what arguably was the first successful guerrilla war in modern Europe. Napoleon's "Spanish ulcer" bled France.

Stirrings of Nationalism in Napoleonic Europe

One of the lasting effects of the Napoleonic period was the quickening of German and, to a lesser extent, Italian national identity. The French revolutionaries had called for a war against the tyrants of Europe. But Napoleon seemed blind to the fact that the exportation of the principles of the French Revolution might encourage resentment and even nationalist feeling against the French in those countries conquered by his armies. Gradually the French discovered that nationalism was a double-edged sword.

In any case, Napoleon's encouragement of nationalist aspirations abroad was little more than a ploy to curry favor in each conquered state in exchange for support against his enemies. Napoleon may indeed have intended that Westphalia, created by the Treaty of Tilsit (1807) out of former Prussian territories and other smaller states that had fought against him, would become a model state. He ended serfdom and gave peasants the right to own land, to move through the kingdom as they pleased, and to send their children to school. But his principal goal was to bolster the Confederation of the Rhine's north flank against possible attacks against his interests.

The subordination of the economic and diplomatic interests of "allied" or "annexed" vassal states to those of France generated understandable resentment. Napoleon considered conquered territories sources for military conscripts and raw materials, or as potential markets for French goods. In Italy, French authorities forbade the importation of textile machinery and imposed disadvantageous tariffs on the local population, fearful of competition with their own industries. With the exception of Jacobin anticlericals, intellectuals, and merchants who stood to profit from the French occupation, most people expressed little enthusiasm for the Napoleonic regime. There was no reason why the people of the Netherlands, where the French occupation had virtually brought the prosperous Dutch trading economy to a standstill, should have welcomed Louis Bonaparte as their sovereign. Poles soon began to doubt Napoleon's promise to reestablish Polish independence; some nobles began to look to the Russian tsar for help, others to the king of Prussia. Yet, among those territories conquered by Napoleon, open insurrections were relatively rare. In the Neapolitan

Republic, where Napoleon had assured his brother Joseph that "all the better people are for you," peasants fighting for church and king overwhelmed the small number of their pro-French countrymen. In the Austrian Tyrol, peasants sang nationalist songs as they fought against the French in 1813.

The impact of the French invasions on nationalism was perhaps clearest in the German states. At first some German intellectuals had praised Napoleon. The philosopher Georg Wilhelm Friedrich Hegel (1770–1831) described the emperor, of whom he caught a glimpse after the Battle of Jena in 1806, as "this world soul . . . dominating the entire world from horseback. . . . It is impossible not to admire him."

But the French invasions carried German nationalism beyond the small ranks of writers and intellectuals. Attacks by German writers against French occupation mounted in 1807. That year, the execution by the French of a Nuremburg bookseller accused of selling anti-French literature prompted Prussia to join the war against Napoleon. Two years later, Napoleon escaped an assassination attempt by a young German student, the son of a Lutheran minister, who shouted "Long Live Germany!" as he was executed.

Gradually German writers discovered, or even invented, the idea of Germany by arguing forcefully that the people of the German states shared a common culture based upon language, tradition, and history. Only in the middle of the eighteenth century had German writers begun to write in their own language; before then, they considered French the language of culture. Like some composers, they began to discover elements of a common culture, drawing on language, literary texts, folk traditions, and other German cultural traditions to express themselves. This emotional quest for cultural and political institutions that would define "Germany" reflected some rejection of the rational tradition of Enlightenment thought identified with France.

German nationalists knew that the multiplicity of states in Central Europe stood in the way of eventual German unification. Hegel, for one, believed that Napoleon had helped the cause of German nationalism by eliminating literally hundreds of tiny states. About 60 percent of the population of the German states passed from one ruler to another during the revolutionary and Napoleonic eras. Still, forty separate German states survived. Among them Baden, Bavaria, and Württemberg, although much smaller and less powerful than Austria and Germany, emerged from the period with their independence and separate traditions for the most part intact.

Even though any possible political unification of Germany seemed distant, if not impossible, German nationalism nonetheless contributed to the determination with which the people of the German states resisted Napoleon. Johann Gottlieb Fichte (1762–1814) called on "the German nation," which he defined as including anyone who spoke German, to discover its spiritual unity. Fichte thundered at a university lecture in February 1813, "This course will be suspended until the close of the [military] campaign, when we will resume it in a free fatherland or reconquer our liberty by death!"

In Spain, people of all classes came to view the French as invaders, not liberators. The constitution proclaimed by the Spanish Cortes in 1812 at Cádiz, which was not under French control, nonetheless reflected the influence of the French Revolution. It proclaimed freedom of the press, established an assembly to be elected by relatively wide suffrage, and abolished the Inquisition. But the constitution, although never implemented because of the eclipse of Spanish liberals in the wake of conservative reaction, was also a self-consciously nationalist document. Some Spaniards, too, were becoming more aware of their own shared linguistic, cultural, and historical traditions, particularly as the French conquerors tried to make their language that of administration.

Military Reforms in Prussia and Austria

Just as the French invasion engendered a nationalist response in some of the Italian and German states, so did the successes of Napoleon's armies lead Prussia and, to a lesser extent, Austria, to enact military reforms. Following the devastating Prussian defeat at Jena in 1806, a minister advised King Frederick William III, "Sire! We must do from above what the French have done from below!" At the instigation of Baron Heinrich Karl vom und zum Stein (1757–1831), a royal decree abolished serfdom and removed class barriers that had served to keep middle-class men from assuming the military rank of officer (it nonetheless also prevented nobles from taking positions considered beneath their status). The Prussian military commander appointed some bourgeois officers and cashiered some of the more inept noble commanders. Stein established a ministry of war, taking away some important decisions from the whims of the king's inner circle and from the monarch himself. The abolition of serfdom improved the loyalty of peasant-soldiers to the state. The elimination of most forms of corporal punishment enhanced troop morale, as did the rewarding of individual soldiers who served well.

Stein also organized a civilian militia, which provided a proud, patriotic reserve of 120,000 part-time soldiers. Napoleon, upon learning of the Prussian reformer's plans, forced the king to dismiss his minister in 1808 (at the time, the Prussians were still bound by the terms of the Treaty of Tilsit, signed the previous year, to limit the size of their army). But henceforth the Prussian army would be much larger and more efficient than the army that Napoleon had previously defeated with ease.

The Empire's Decline and the Russian Invasion

Napoleon now confronted the fact that he still had no legitimate children to inherit his throne. Although he admired his wife Josephine, and may have loved her as well, he was as unfaithful to her during his lengthy absences as she was to him. Napoleon arranged for a bishop in Paris to annul his marriage—the pope having refused to do so—allowing him to remarry with the Church's blessing. Napoleon then considered diplomatically useful spouses. When the tsar would not provide his younger sister, Napoleon arranged a marriage in 1810 with Marie-Louise (1791–1847), the daughter of Austrian Emperor Francis I. She had never even met Napoleon, but that in itself was not as unusual as the fact that the French emperor had his old enemy, the Archduke Charles (brother of Francis I and Napoleon's opponent during the 1809 war with Austria), stand in for him at the wedding ceremony, while he remained in Paris. Napoleon thus entered into a de facto alliance with the Habsburgs, Europe's oldest dynasty. Within a year, Napoleon had a son and heir.

For the first time since Napoleon's remarkable rise to power, dissent also began to be heard openly inside France. Deserters and recalcitrant conscripts dodged authorities in increasing numbers beginning in about 1810. Royalist and Jacobin pamphlets and brochures circulated, despite the censorship of all printed material and theatrical productions. Royalists objected to Napoleon's disdainful treatment of the pope, who excommunicated the emperor after France annexed the Papal States in 1809. Napoleon responded by simply placing Pius VII under house arrest, first near Genoa, and then near Paris in Fontainebleau.

Over the past two years, Napoleon had become increasingly unable to separate options that were feasible or possible from those that were unlikely, or indeed impossible to achieve. One of the emperor's ministers remarked: "It is strange that Napoleon, whose good sense amounted to genius, never discovered the point at which the impossible begins. . . . 'The impossible,' he told me with a smile, 'is the specter of the timid and the refuge of the coward . . . the word is only a confession of impotence' . . . The more I saw of him, the greater was my conviction that he thought only of satisfying his own desires and adding incessantly to his own glory and greatness. The slightest obstacle enraged him . . . death alone could set a limit to his plans and curb his ambition."

Given such megalomania, the emperor's catastrophic decision to invade Russia seems almost inevitable in retrospect. It made almost as little sense as Bonaparte's wild trek into Syria from Egypt fifteen years earlier, though the consequences now would be infinitely greater.

Napoleon's advisers increasingly expressed their doubts about the emperor's endless plans for new conquests. Charles Maurice de Talleyrand, the former bishop who had loyally served as minister for foreign affairs since 1799, had resigned in 1807, after the execution of the duke of Enghien, the member of the Bourbon royal family who had been kidnapped from German exile. Talleyrand now symbolized the "party of peace," which opposed extending the empire past limits that could be effectively administered. In 1809, he began to negotiate secretly with Austria about the possibility of a monarchical restoration in France should Napoleon fall. Members of Napoleon's Council of State began to be increasingly demoralized. Furthermore, as the size of the empire grew, the difficulties of managing it in a period of constant war became even more daunting.

Napoleon's interest in expanding French influence in the eastern Mediterranean and his marriage to a Habsburg princess virtually assured war with Russia. In 1808, he had put the issue succinctly: "Ultimately, the question is always this, who shall have Constantinople?" and thus control access to the Black Sea. For his part, the French emperor was angry that Russia had refused to close its ports to British and neutral vessels carrying English goods. Believing that he could enforce the continental blockade by defeating Russia, Napoleon prepared for war with Russia, forcing vanquished Austria and Prussia to agree to assist him. In the meantime, the tsar signed a peace treaty with the Ottoman Empire, freeing Russia to oppose Napoleon. Alexander I lined up the support of Sweden, whose king was Crown Prince Jean-Baptiste Bernadotte (1763–1844; once one of Napoleon's marshals, he had been elected heir to the Swedish throne in 1810 by the Swedish Estates and would succeed the childless Charles XIII in 1818 as King Charles XIV John). The tsar offered Sweden a free hand in annexing Norway.

In June 1812, Napoleon's "Grand Army," over 600,000 strong, crossed the Niemen River from the Grand Duchy of Warsaw into Russia. Napoleon hoped to lure the Russian armies into battle. The Russians, however, simply retreated, drawing Napoleon ever farther into western Russia in late summer.

The Grand Army may have been the largest army ever raised up to that time, but the quality of Napoleon's army had declined since 1806 through casualties and desertions. Some of his finest troops were tied up dodging guerrilla attacks in Spain. Half of the Grand Army consisted of Prussian, Italian, Austrian, Swiss, or Dutch conscripts. A general complained in 1813, "Some [cavalrymen] had only mounted a horse for the first time in their lives two weeks previously. Most did not know how to handle their horses or their weapons; it was all they could do to hold the reins in one hand and a saber in the other." Officers now were by necessity more hurriedly trained. As the Grand Army was almost constantly at war, there was no chance to rebuild it to Napoleon's satisfaction.

In Russia, disease, heat, and hunger took a far greater toll on Napoleon's army than did the rearguard action of enemy troops. The Grand Army finally reached the city of Smolensk, 200 miles west of Moscow, in the middle of August; there the emperor planned to force the tsar to sign another humiliating peace. The Russian troops continued to retreat deeper into Russia. Napoleon's marshals begged him to stop in Smolensk and wait there. Yet, tempted by the possibility of capturing Moscow, Napoleon pushed on until his army reached Borodino, sixty miles from Moscow. There the two armies fought to a costly draw in the bloodiest battle of the Napoleonic era, with 68,000 killed or wounded, before the Russian army continued its retreat. Napoleon entered Moscow on September 14, 1812. He found it virtually deserted. Fires had broken out, probably set by a few Russian troops left behind for that purpose, and spread quickly through the wooden buildings. Almost three-quarters of the city burned to the ground. There was no enemy left to fight there, nor anywhere else in the region. The tsar and his armies had fled to the east.

Over 1,500 miles from Paris, without sufficient provisions, and with the early signs of the approaching Russian winter already apparent, Napoleon decided to march the Grand Army back to France. The retreat, which began October 19, was a disaster. Russian troops picked off hundreds of the retreating forces, forcing them to take an even longer route to Smolensk, 200 miles away. The Russians were waiting for Napoleon's beleaguered armies at the Berezina River, where they killed thousands of French soldiers. The emperor himself barely escaped capture by the Cossacks. The freezing winter then finished off most of what was left of Napoleon's Grand Army.

The retreat from Moscow was one of the greatest military debacles of any age, and one of the most awful in terms of human suffering and death. A contemporary described some of the French troops: "a mob of tattered ghosts draped in women's cloaks, odd pieces of carpet, or greatcoats burned full of holes, their feet wrapped in all sorts of rags. . . . [We] stared in horror as those skeletons of soldiers went by, their gaunt, gray faces covered with disfiguring beards, without weapons, shameless, marching out of step, with lowered heads, eyes on the ground, in absolute silence. . . ."

The retreat of the Grand Army in Russia, November 1812.

Of the more than 600,000 men who had set out in June from the Grand Duchy of Warsaw, only about 40,000 returned. After racing ahead of the groans of the dying and the frozen corpses, Napoleon issued the famous bulletin sent back to Paris: "The health of the emperor has never been better."

Napoleon arrived at the Tuileries Palace on the night of December 18, 1812. In the wake of a military disaster of such dimensions that press censorship and duplicitous official bulletins (the expression "to lie like a military bulletin" became current) could not gloss over it, the mood of the French people soured.

Undaunted, Napoleon demanded a new levy of 350,000 more troops. This call, coming at a time of great economic hardship, was greeted with massive resentment and resistance. Instead of negotiating a peace that could have left France with the left bank of the Rhine, Napoleon planned new campaigns and further expansion.

The Defeat of Napoleon

Napoleon now faced allies encouraged by his devastating defeat. In February 1813, Russia and Prussia signed an alliance, agreeing to fight Napoleon until the independence of the states of Europe was restored. Napoleon earned two costly victories over Russian and Prussian troops in the spring of 1813, but his casualties were high and opposition to him was growing stronger. Great Britain, still fighting the French in Spain, formally joined the coalition in June. Napoleon rejected Austrian conditions for peace, which included the dissolution of the Confederation of the Rhine, and Austria joined the coalition in August 1813. Napoleon's strategy of winning the temporary allegiance, or at least neutrality, of one of the other four European powers had failed.

In August 1813, Napoleon defeated the allies at Dresden, but then learned that Bavaria had seceded from the Confederation of the Rhine and joined the coalition. In October, his troops outnumbered two to one, Napoleon suffered a major defeat at Leipzig (in the Battle of the Nations) and retreated across the Rhine into France. His armies, ever more filled with reluctant, raw recruits and now lacking adequate supplies, were not the same. Napoleon's military inspiration now seemed less apparent. An insurrection in Holland followed by an allied invasion restored the prince of Orange to authority. Austrian troops defeated a French army in northern Italy. Wellington's English forces drove the French armies from Spain and back across the Pyrenees. Forced to fight on French soil for the first time, Napoleon's discouraged armies were greeted with hostility when they tried to live off the land as they had abroad. Opponents of Napoleon, including some churchmen for whom a Bourbon restoration now seemed a possibility, now spoke more openly in France.

Arthur Wellesley, the duke of Wellington.

Early in 1814, the allies proposed peace (perhaps insincerely, assuming that Napoleon would refuse), if Napoleon would accept France's natural frontiers of the Rhine, the Alps, and the Pyrenees, but Napoleon stalled. An allied army of 200,000 moved into eastern France. In Paris, the Legislative Body approved a document that amounted to a denunciation of the emperor, though it never reached the public. Even Napoleon's normally dutiful older brother Joseph encouraged the members of the Council of State to sign a petition calling for peace. Nonetheless, Napoleon fought on with his 90,000 ill-equipped raw recruits.

Demonstrating that they had learned a key lesson from Napoleon on warfare, the allies were determined not to stop until they had captured Paris. After overcoming stiff French resistance (in February, Napoleon won ten battles in twenty days), the main allied force swept into the French capital in March 1814. Tsar Alexander I of Russia and King Frederick William III of Prussia marched triumphantly into the city. At Fontainebleau, Napoleon's marshals refused to join in his frantic plans for an attack on the allies in Paris and pressured him to abdicate. Talleyrand called the Senate into session; it voted to depose Napoleon. The allies refused to consider Napoleon's abdication in favor of his three-year-old son. Without an army and, perhaps for the first time, without hope, Napoleon tried to kill himself by swallowing poison. That failing, he abdicated on April 6, 1814. The long adventure finally seemed at an end.

MONARCHICAL RESTORATION AND NAPOLEON'S RETURN

The allies sought the restoration of the Bourbon monarchy. In the meantime, Talleyrand had been negotiating with them to obtain the return of the count of Provence to be king of France. The French Senate, too, expressed its wish that Louis XVI's brother return to France as Louis XVIII. By the Treaty of Fontainebleau (April 11, 1814), the allies exiled Napoleon to a Mediterranean island off the coast of Italy. Bonaparte would be emperor of Elba alone. Marie-Louise refused to accompany him, preferring to be duchess of Parma, receiving the title by virtue of being a member of the Austrian royal family. As Napoleon travelled to the Mediterranean to sail to Elba, he heard shouts of "Down with the tyrant!" and "Long live Louis XVIII!" When he saw himself hanged in effigy, he disguised himself in an old blue coat and put on a white Bourbon cockade, later trying to look like an Austrian officer. In the meantime, if in most places the news of the restoration of the monarchy was not greeted with wild outbursts of enthusiasm, there nonetheless seemed to be a palpable sense of relief that the long Napoleonic Wars seemed finally at an end.

The Bourbon Restoration

The count of Provence entered Paris on May 3 as King Louis XVIII (ruled 1814–1815; 1815–1824). With more than a little wishful thinking, he announced that this was the seventeenth year of his reign (counting from the death of the son of Louis XVI, who had died in 1795 in a Paris prison without ever reigning). After the Bourbons were restored to the throne, the allies worked out a surprisingly gracious peace treaty with France, largely thanks to Talleyrand's skilled diplomacy. The Treaty of Paris, signed May 30, 1814, left France with Savoy, and small chunks of land in Germany

Napoleon relegated to the island of Elba after his defeat and abdication.

and the Austrian Netherlands—in other words, the France of November 1, 1792. France could now rejoin the monarchies of Europe.

Despite the opposition of his reactionary brother, the count of Artois, Louis XVIII signed a constitutional "Charter" that granted his people "public liberties," promising that a legislature would be elected, based on a very restricted franchise. This Charter, influenced by the constitution of 1791, distinguished the Restoration monarchy from that of the Old Regime by recognizing the principle of representative government, however much limited to election by a small, wealthy elite. Although the document affirmed monarchical rule by divine right, it confirmed some of the important victories of the Revolution, including equality before the law and freedom of expression and religion, although Catholicism would be the religion of the state. It specified the establishment of a bicameral assembly, which would consent to taxes. Furthermore, the king allowed Napoleon's Code to stand, maintained the centralized reorganization of the state bureaucracy, including the division of the country into "departments," recognized all titles, decorations, and even pensions awarded during previous regimes, and promised that property purchased during the Revolution as "national property" would remain in the hands of the new owners.

A coterie of fanatical nobles and their followers (the Ultra-royalists) convinced the king to enact some measures, however, that were highly unpopular. Many disapproved of the substitution of the white flag of the Bourbon family for the tricolor, the description of the Charter as a "gift" from the king to the French people, the retiring of 14,000 officers at half pay, the restoration of returned émigrés to high positions in the army, and the return to their original owners of national lands that had not been sold.

Napoleon Bonaparte retained the allegiance of a considerable number of Frenchmen, and several attempts to raise local forces to fight the allies occurred. In a good number of towns, crowds attacked customs barriers when the new royalist government reinstituted the collection of indirect taxes. But most of the French were simply exhausted from years of wars and sacrifice, and even Napoleon's most fervent supporters did no more than occasionally shout "Long live the emperor!" and disappear into the night.

The 100 Days

In March 1815, just months after his exile, Napoleon boldly escaped from Elba and landed near Antibes on the French Mediterranean coast. The former emperor knew that he retained considerable popularity in France. Furthermore, so much time had passed and so many dramatic events had occurred since the execution of Louis XVI that one of the monarchy's staunchest supporters claimed, with some exaggeration, "The Bourbons were as unknown in France as the Ptolemies."

Napoleon is acclaimed by the people of Grenoble as he returns from exile.

The word that Napoleon had landed in France and was marching north with a small band of followers stunned everyone. In Grenoble, he won over soldiers, workmen, and peasants by announcing that he had come to save France from the émigrés and uphold the rights won in 1789. Marshal Ney, who had offered his services to the Bourbons, promised to bring Napoleon back to Paris in a cage. But upon seeing Napoleon, Ney fell into his arms. Regiment after regiment went over to Napoleon as he marched north. With Bonaparte nearing Paris, Louis XVIII, his family, and advisers fled for the Austrian Netherlands. Soon Napoleon again paced frenetically through the Tuileries Palace, making plans to raise armies and defend himself against the inevitable allied response, and dreaming of new conquests.

It was not to be. The allies, whose representatives had already gathered in Vienna to create a permanent alliance, declared Napoleon an "outlaw" and quickly raised an enormous army of more than 700,000 troops. Napoleon led an army of 200,000 men into the Austrian Netherlands, engaging Prussian and British forces south of Brussels on June 16, 1815. He forced the Prussians to retreat and ordered one of his generals to pursue them with his army. Napoleon then moved against the British forces commanded by Wellington, his old nemesis. The armies met near the village of Waterloo on June 18, 1815. Wellington had skillfully hidden the extent of his superior infantry behind a ridge. Napoleon watched in horror as a Prussian army arrived to reinforce Wellington. The general sent in pursuit of the Prussians, like all Napoleon's commanders, had been taught to fol-

The Battle of Waterloo, June 18, 1815.

low Napoleon's directives to the letter and not to improvise. He held back, providing no support until it was too late. When the imperial guard broke ranks and retreated, much of the rest of the French army did the same. The defeat was devastating and total.

Napoleon abdicated a second time. The British captured him as he headed toward the Norman coast, hoping to find a way to sail to America. This time the exile would be final. The allies packed Napoleon off to the small island of Saint Helena, in the South Atlantic, 1,000 miles away from any mainland. The closest island of any size was Ascension, a British naval base, some 600 miles distant. Louis XVIII returned to take up the throne of France a second time, 100 days after fleeing Paris.

On Saint Helena, Napoleon's health gradually declined. He died on May 5, 1821, his last words being "France, army, head of the army, Josephine." He died of an ulcer, probably a cancerous one, despite stories that he was poisoned by arsenic.

NAPOLEON'S LEGACY

Napoleon's testament, a masterpiece of political propaganda, tried to create a myth that he saved the Revolution in France. "Every Frenchman could say during my reign,—'I shall be minister, grand officer, duke, count, baron, if I earn it—even king!'" And in some ways, Napoleon was indeed the heir to the French Revolution. He guaranteed the survival of some of its most significant triumphs. Napoleon considered his greatest achievement "that of establishing and consecrating the rule of reason." His Napoleonic Code proclaimed the equality of all people before the law (favoring, however, men over women), personal freedom, and the inviolability of property. Napoleon left the myth, and to some extent the reality, of the "career open to talent," which aided, above all, the middle class, but even peasants in some cases. He consolidated the role of wealth, principally property ownership, as the foundation of the political life of the nation and the measure of one's presumed social value. The result was to increase the number of citizens eligible to participate in political life, however limited by imperial strictures. Furthermore, Napoleon helped turn nationalism into an aggressive secular religion. Bonaparte manipulated this patriotic energy and transformed it into an ideology inculcated by French schools.

Napoleon's reforms, built upon those of the French Revolution, extended into states conquered by his imperial armies. The French imposed constitutions and state control over the appointment of clergy, standardized judicial systems, and abolished ecclesiastical courts. Throughout the empire, Napoleon created new tax structures, standardized weights and measures, ended internal customs barriers, abolished guilds, and established state bureaucracies that were extensions of French rule in the "sister republics" founded by the Directory. In addition to abolishing serfdom in Poland, where the institution was particularly widespread, the French occupation also ended residual peasant seigneurial obligations (such as the requirement to provide labor services to the lord) virtually everywhere, and abolished noble and ecclesiastical courts in northern Italy and the Netherlands. The Napoleonic Code proclaimed freedom of worship, and the French conquest of other European states, including Baden, Bavaria, and the Dutch Republic, helped remove onerous restrictions on Jews. But under pressure from French planters, Napoleon also reestablished slavery in Haiti in 1802, making a mockery of his contention that all men were equal.

Jacques-Louis David's *Bonaparte Leaping the St. Bernard* shows Napoleon crossing the Saint Bernard Pass in the Alps. This painting also shows how Napoleon's myth made him larger than life.

Yet, even Napoleon's success in implementing reforms varied from place to place, depending on existing political structures, the degree of compliance by local elites, and the international situation. In southern Italy, for example, which Napoleon's armies conquered relatively late and where the structures of state authority had always been particularly weak, the French presence had little lasting effect. As the Napoleonic wave subsided, nobles and clerics regained domination over the overwhelmingly rural, impoverished local population.

Napoleon claimed from Saint Helena that he was trying to liberate Europe, but he had actually replaced the old sovereigns with new ones—himself or his brothers. "If I conquered other kingdoms," he admitted, "I did so in order that France would be the beneficiary." Wagons returned from Italy full of art and other treasures, which became the property of Napoleon and his family, his marshals, or the state. French conquests helped awaken nationalist spirit, with the imposition of French administration in the German and Italian states proving especially important for the unification of Germany and Italy later in the nineteenth century. But the effect was, as we have seen, totally unintended and unwanted. Moreover, as the French empire grew in size, it became increasingly difficult to administer effectively.

To the writer Germaine de Staël (1766–1817), the daughter of the Swiss banker Jacques Necker, Louis XVI's minister, Napoleon "regarded a human being as an action or a thing . . . nothing existed but himself. He was an able chess player, and the human race was the opponent to whom he proposed to give checkmate." In the end, his monumental ambition got the best of him. When he could have been satisfied with expanding France's power and place in Europe, he went to war again. About 2 million men served in Napoleon's armies between 1805 and 1814; about 90,000 died in battle and more than three times that number subsequently perished from wounds; over 600,000 were later recorded as prisoners or "disappeared." In all, Napoleon's armies may have suffered as many as 1.5 million casualties. The Napoleonic Wars killed about one in five of all Frenchmen born between 1790 and 1795.

Napoleon's final legacy was his myth. From Saint Helena, Napoleon said, "If I had succeeded, I would have been the greatest man known to history." His career remained the stuff of popular writing throughout Europe for decades. The rise of romanticism helped make the story of Napoleon, the romantic hero, part of the collective memory of Western Europe after his death. Long after Waterloo, peddlers of songs, pamphlets, lithographs and other images glorified Napoleon's life as earlier they had the lives of saints. "I live only for posterity," Napoleon once said. "Death is nothing, but to live defeated and without glory is to die every day." Rumors of his miraculous return to France were persistent long after his death. So powerful was his legend that even the most improbable seemed possible.

FURTHER READINGS

GENERAL

Michael Anderson, *Approaches to the History of the Western Family, 1500–1914* (1980).
Philippe Ariès, *Centuries of Childhood: A Social History of Family Life* (1962).
Philippe Ariès and Georges Duby, eds., *A History of Private Life* (5 vols, 1987–1993).
Geoffrey Barraclough, *The Origins of Modern Germany* (1979).
Jerome Blum, *Lord and Peasant in Russia from the Ninth to the Nineteenth Century* (1961).
Richard Bonney, *The European Dynastic States 1494–1660* (1991).
John Bossy, *Christianity in the West 1400–1700* (1985).
Fernand Braudel, *Capitalism and Material Life, 1400–1800* (1975).
Fernand Braudel, *The Mediterranean World in the Age of Philip II* (New York, 1992).
Robin Briggs, *Early Modern France, 1560–1715* (1977).
Peter Burke, *Popular Culture in Early Modern Europe* (1978).
Carlo Cipolla, *Before the Industrial Revolution: European Society and Economy, 1000–1700* (1980).
Carlo M. Cipolla, ed., *The Fontana Economic History of Europe* (6 vols., 1976–1977).
Eric Cochrane, *Italy, 1530–1630* (1988).
Norman Davies, *A History of Poland: God's Playground* (2 vols, 1981).
Georges Duby and Michelle Perrot, eds., *A History of Women in the West* (5 vols., 1992–1994).
Richard Dunn, *The Age of Religious Wars, 1559–1715* (1979).
Elizabeth Eisenstein, *The Printing Revolution in Early Modern Europe* (1993).
Norbert Elias, *The Civilizing Process* (1994).
R.F. Foster, *Modern Ireland, 1600–1972* (1988).
Jack Goldstone, *Revolution and Rebellion in the Early Modern World* (1991).
Paul Hohenberg and Lynn Lees, *The Making of Urban Europe 1000–1950* (1985).
Lynn Hunt, ed., *The New Cultural History* (1989).
Charles Ingrao, *The Habsburg Monarchy 1618–1815* (1994).
Henry Kamen, *European Society 1500–1700* (London, 1984).
John Keegan, *The Face of Battle* (1976).

John Keegan, *A History of Warfare* (1993).

Paul Kennedy, *The Rise and Fall of the Great Powers* (New York, 1987).

H.G. Koenigsberger, *Early Modern Europe, 1500–1789* (1987).

H.G. Koenigsberger, *The Habsburgs and Europe, 1516–1660* (1971)

Dominick LaCapra and Steven L. Kaplan, eds., *Modern European Intellectual History: Reappraisals and New Perspectives* (1982).

Alec Reginald Meyers, *Parliaments and Estates in Europe to 1789* (1975).

Geoffrey Parker, *The Cambridge Illustrated History of Warfare* (1995).

Geoffrey Parker, *The Military Revolution: Military Innovation and the Rise of the West, 1500–1800* (1988).

Colin Russell, *Science and Social Change in Britain and Europe, 1700–1900* (1983).

Joan W. Scott, *Gender and the Politics of History* (1988).

Quentin Skinner, *Foundations of Modern Political Thought* (1978).

Bonnie G. Smith, *Changing Lives: Women in European History since 1700* (1989).

Charles Tilly, *The Contentious French: Four Centuries of Popular Struggle* (1986).

Charles Tilly, ed., *The Formation of National States in Western Europe* (1975).

Mack Walker, *German Home Towns: Community, State, and General Estate, 1648–1871* (1971).

Piotr Wandycz, *The Price of Freedom: A History of East Central Europe from the Middle Ages to the Present* (1992).

Eric R. Wolf, *Europe and the People without History* (1983).

E.A. Wrigley, *Population and History* (1969).

CHAPTER 1. MEDIEVAL LEGACIES AND TRANSFORMING DISCOVERIES

Kenneth R. Andrews, *Trade, Plunder and Settlement: Maritime Enterprise and the Genesis of the British Empire, 1480–1630* (1984).

Robert Bartlett, *The Making of Europe: Conquest, Colonization and Cultural Change 950–1350* (1993).

M. W. Beresford, *New Towns of the Middle Ages* (1988).

Marc Bloch, *Feudal Society* (2 vols., 1961).

Brenda Bolton, *The Medieval Reformation* (1983).

John Boswell, *Christianity, Social Tolerance, and Homosexuality: Gay People in Western Europe from the Beginnings of the Church Era to the Fourteenth Century* (1980).

John Boswell, *The Kindness of Strangers: The Abandonment of Children in Western Europe from Late Antiquity to the Renaissance* (1988).

Rosalind B. and Christopher Brooke, *Popular Religion in the Middle Ages* (1984).

Alfred W. Crosby, *Ecological Imperialism: The Biological Expansion of Europe, 900–1900* (1986).

R.O. Crummey, *The Formation of Muscovy 1404–1613* (1987).

Georges Duby, *Rural Economy and Country Life in the Medieval West* (1968).

Edith Ennen, *The Medieval Town* (1979).

Edith Ennen, *The Medieval Woman* (1989).

Wallace K. Ferguson, *Europe in Transition 1300–1520* (1962).

Robert Fossier, *Peasant Life in the Medieval West* (1988).

Charles Gibson, *Spain in America* (1966).
Bernard Hamilton, *Religion in the Medieval West* (1986).
Denys Hay, *Europe: The Emergence of an Idea* (1968).
Denys Hay, *Europe in the Fourteenth and Fifteenth Centuries* (1989).
Norman Housley, *The Later Crusades 1274–1580* (1992).
Emmanuel Leroy Ladurie, *Montaillou: The Promised Land of Error* (1979).
Malcolm David Lambert, *Medieval Heresy: Popular Movements from the Bogomils to Hus* (1976).
Robert S. Lopez, *The Commercial Revolution of the Middle Ages, 950–1300* (1971).
Angus MacKay, *Society, Economy and Religion in Late Medieval Castile* (1987).
Richard Mackenney, *Sixteenth-Century Europe: Expansion and Conflict* (1993).
H.E. Mayer, *The Crusades* (1988).
Michel Mollat, *The Poor in the Middle Ages* (1986).
Michel Mollat and Philippe Wolfe, *Popular Revolution in the Late Middle Ages* (1973).
John H. Mundy, *Europe in the High Middle Ages 1150–1309* (1991).
J.H. Parry, *The Age of Reconnaissance: Discovery, Exploration and Settlement, 1450–1650* (1981).
Fritz Rorig, *The Medieval Town* (1967).

CHAPTER 2. THE RENAISSANCE

Michael Baxandall, *Painting and Experience in Fifteenth-Century Italy* (1972).
Judith Brown, *In the Shadow of Florence* (1982).
Eugene Brucker, *Renaissance Florence* (1983).
Peter Burke, *The Italian Renaissance: Culture and Society in Italy* (1987).
Peter Burke, *Popular Culture in Renaissance Europe, 1450–1620* (1986).
A.G. Dickens, *The Age of Humanism and Reformation: Europe in the Fourteenth to Sixteenth Centuries* (1972).
Carlo Ginzburg, *The Cheese and the Worms: The Cosmos of a Sixteenth-Century Miller* (1982).
Carlo Ginzburg, *Night Battles* (1985).
Richard Goldthwaite, *The Building of Renaissance Florence* (1981).
Anthony Grafton and Lisa Jardine, *From Humanism to the Humanities: Education and the Liberal Arts in Fifteenth and Sixteenth Century Europe* (1986).
J.R. Hale, *Renaissance Europe* (1977).
J.R. Hale, *War and Society in Renaissance Europe, 1450–1620* (1986).
Denys Hay and John Law, *Italy in the Age of the Renaissance, 1380–1530* (1989).
Dale Kent, *The Rise of the Medici* (1979).
Margaret King, *Women in the Renaissance* (1991).
Garrett Mattingly, *Renaissance Diplomacy* (1988).
Lauro Martines, *Power and Imagination: City-States in Renaissance Italy* (1988).
Harry A. Miskimin, *The Economy of Early Renaissance Europe, 1300–1460* (1975).

Harry A. Miskimin, *The Economy of Later Renaissance Europe, 1460–1600* (1977).

J.G.A. Pocock, *The Machiavellian Moment: Florentine Political Thought and the Atlantic Republican Tradition* (1975).

John Stephens, *The Italian Renaissance: The Origins of Intellectual and Artistic Change before the Reformation* (1990).

Hugh Thomas, *The Conquest of Mexico* (1993).

CHAPTER 3. THE TWO REFORMATIONS

Cornelis Augustijn, *Erasmus: His Life, Works, and Influence* (1991).

William J. Bouwsma, *John Calvin: A Sixteenth-Century Portrait* (1987).

Euan Cameron, *The European Reformation* (1991).

Anwar Chejne, *Islam and the West: The Moriscos: A Cultural and Social History* (1983).

William A. Christian, Jr., *Local Religion in Sixteenth-Century Spain* (1981).

P.H. Coles, *The Ottoman Impact on Europe* (1968).

A.G. Dickens, *The English Reformation* (1989).

Ronnie Po-Chia Hsia, ed., *The German People and the Reformation* (1988).

Ronnie Po-Chia Hsia, *Social Discipline in the Reformation: Central Europe, 1550–1750* (1989).

Ronnie Po-Chia Hsia, *Society and Religion in Munster, 1535–1618* (1984).

Lisa Jardine, *Erasmus, Man of Letters* (1993).

David Kirby, *Northern Europe in the Early Modern Period: The Baltic World, 1492–1772* (1990).

Sherrin Marshall, ed., *Women in Reformation and Counter-Reformation Europe: Public and Private Worlds* (1989).

Bernard Moeller, *Imperial Cities and the Reformation* (1982).

Steven E. Ozment, *The Reformation in the Cities: The Appeal of Protestantism to Sixteenth-Century Germany and Switzerland* (1975).

Steven E. Ozment, *When Fathers Ruled: Family Life in Reformation Europe* (1983).

Eugene R. Rice, Jr., and Anthony Grafton, *The Foundations of Early Modern Europe 1460–1559* (1994).

Thomas W. Robisheaux, *Rural Society and the Search for Order in Early Modern Germany* (1989).

Robert W. Scribner, *For the Sake of Simple Folk: Popular Propaganda for the German Reformation* (1984).

Lewis Spitz, *The Protestant Reformation* (1987).

Keith Thomas, *Religion and the Decline of Magic* (1971).

Tessa Watt, *Cheap Print and Popular Piety 1550–1640* (1991).

Merry E. Weisner, *Women and Gender in Early Modern Europe* (1993).

CHAPTER 4. THE WARS OF RELIGION

Natalie Zemon Davis, *The Return of Martin de Guerre* (1983).

Natalie Zemon Davis, *Society and Culture in Early Modern France* (1975).

J.H. Elliott, *Europe Divided, 1559–1598* (1968).

Mark Greengrass, *France in the Age of Henry IV: The Struggle for Stability* (1984).

R.J. Knecht, *Francis I* (1992).
Geoffrey Parker, *Europe in Crisis, 1598–1648* (1979).
Geoffrey Parker, ed., *The Thirty Years' War* (1988).
N.M. Sutherland, *The Massacre of St. Bartholomew and the European Conflict, 1559–1572* (1973).

Chapter 5. The Rise of the Atlantic Economy: Spain and England

Ralph Davis, *The Rise of the Atlantic Economies* (1973).
Jan De Vries, *The Economy of Europe in an Age of Crisis, 1600–1750* (1978).
J.H. Elliott, *The Count-Duke of Olivares: The Statesman in an Age of Decline* (1987).
J.H. Elliott, *Imperial Spain, 1469–1714* (1964).
G.R Elton, *England Under the Tutors* (1991).
Felipe Fernández-Armesto, *The Spanish Armada: The Experience of War in 1588* (1989).
John Guy, *Tudor England* (1988).
Henry Kamen, *Spain, 1469–1714: A Society of Conflict* (1991).
John Lynch, *Spain under the Habsburgs, 1516–1700* (2 vols., 1964–1969).
Colin Martin and Geoffrey Parker, *The Spanish Armada* (1988).
Geoffrey Parker, *Philip II* (1978).
Carla Rahn Philips, *Galleons for the King of Spain* (1986).
Peter Pierson, *Philip II of Spain* (1975).
John Salmon, *Society in Crisis: France in the Sixteenth Century* (1975).
Lacey Baldwin Smith, *Elizabeth Tudor* (1975).
Immanuel Wallerstein, *The Modern World System* (1974).
Penry Williams, *The Tudor Regime* (1979).
Joyce Youings, *Sixteenth-Century England* (1984).

Chapter 6. England and the Dutch Republic in the Seventeenth Century

Susan Dwyer Amussen, *An Ordered Society: Gender and Class in Early Modern England* (1988).
Bruce Galloway, *The Union of England and Scotland, 1603–1608* (1986).
Pieter Geyl, *The Revolt of the Netherlands, 1555–1609* (1958).
Christopher Hill, *God's Englishman: Oliver Cromwell and the English Revolution* (1975).
Christopher Hill, *The World Turned Upside Down* (1972).
Derek Hirst, *Authority and Conflict: England, 1603–1658* (1986).
Ronald Hutton, *The British Republic, 1649–1660* (1990).
J.I. Israel, *Dutch Primacy in World Trade, 1585–1740* (1990).
J.R. Jones, *The Revolution of 1688 in England* (1972).
Peter Laslett, *The World We Have Lost: England before the Industrial Age* (1971).
Brian P. Levack, *The Formation of the British State: England, Scotland, and the Union 1603–1707* (1987).
John Morrill, *The Revolt of the Provinces: Conservatism and Revolution in the English Civil War, 1630–1650* (1980).

Geoffrey Parker, *The Army of Flanders and the Spanish Road, 1567–1659* (1972).

J.L. Price, *Culture and Society in the Dutch Republic during the Seventeenth Century* (1974).

Conrad Russell, *The Causes of the English Civil War* (1990).

Simon Schama, *An Embarrassment of Riches: An Interpretation of Dutch Culture in the Golden Age* (1988).

J.A. Sharpe, *Early Modern England: A Social History, 1550–1760* (1990).

Lawrence Stone, *The Causes of the English Revolution, 1629–1642* (1990).

Lawrence Stone, *The Crisis of the Aristocracy, 1558–1641* (1967).

David Underdown, *Fire from Heaven: Life in an English Town in the Seventeenth Century* (1992).

David Underdown, *Revel, Riot, and Rebellion: Popular Politics and Culture in England, 1603–1660* (1985).

Keith Wrightson, *English Society, 1550–1760* (1982).

CHAPTER 7. THE AGE OF ABSOLUTISM, 1650–1720

M.S. Anderson, *Peter the Great* (1978).

Perry Anderson, *Lineages of the Absolutist State* (1974).

William Beik, *Absolutism and Society in Seventeenth-Century France: State Power and Provincial Aristocracy in Languedoc* (1985).

Joseph Bergin, *Cardinal Richelieu: Power and the Pursuit of Wealth* (1985).

J.H. Elliott, *Richelieu and Olivares* (1984).

Richard J. Evans, *The Making of the Habsburg Empire, 1550–1770* (1979).

Pierre Goubert, *Louis XIV and Twenty Million Frenchmen* (1972).

Ragnhild Hatton, *Europe in the Age of Louis XIV* (1979).

Hahil Inalcik, *The Ottoman Empire: The Classical Age, 1300–1600* (1973).

Robert Mandrou, *Introduction to Modern France, 1500–1640* (1975).

Roland Mousnier, *Peasant Uprisings in Seventeenth–Century France, Russia, and China* (1970).

David Parker, *The Making of French Absolutism* (1983).

Theodore Rabb, *The Struggle for Stability in Early Modern Europe* (1975).

Orest Ranum, *The Fronde: A French Revolution* (1993).

Orest Ranum, *Paris in the Age of Absolutism* (1969).

Nicholas Riasanovsky, *The Image of Peter the Great in Russian History and Thought* (1985).

CHAPTER 8. THE NEW PHILOSOPHY OF SCIENCE

Herbert Butterfield, *The Origins of Modern Science, 1300–1800* (1965).

John Fauvel, Raymond Flood, Michael Shortland, and Robin Wilson, eds., *Let Newton Be! A New Perspective on His Life and Works* (1988).

A.R. Hall, *The Revolution in Science, 1500–1750: The Formation of the Modern Scientific Attitude* (1983).

Margaret Jacobs, *The Cultural Meaning of the Scientific Revolution* (1988).

Hugh Kearney, *Science and Change, 1500–1700* (1971).

Alexandre Koyré, *The Formation of the Modern Scientific Attitude* (1983).

T.S. Kuhn, *The Structure of Scientific Revolution* (1989).

Robert K. Merton, *Science, Technology, and Society in Seventeenth-Century England* (1970).

Londa Schiebinger, *The Mind Has No Sex? Women in the Origins of Modern Science* (1990).

R.S. Westfall, *Never at Rest: A Biography of Issac Newton* (1993).

B.H.G. Wormald, *Francis Bacon: History, Politics, and Science, 1561–1626* (1993).

CHAPTER 9. EIGHTEENTH-CENTURY ECONOMIC AND SOCIAL CHANGE

M.S. Anderson, *Europe in the Eighteenth Century, 1713–1783* (1982).

C.A. Bayly, *Imperial Meridan: The British Empire and the World 1780–1830* (1989).

Maxine Berg, *The Age of Manufacturers, 1700–1820: Industry, Innovation, and Work in Britain* (1985).

Peter Borsay, *The English Urban Renaissance: Culture and Society in the Provincial Town, 1660–1770* (1989).

P.J. Corfield, *The Impact of English Towns 1700-1800* (1982).

Douglas Hay et. al., *Albion's Fatal Tree: Crime and Punishment in Eighteenth-Century England* (1975).

Steven L. Kaplan, *Provisioning Paris: Merchants and Millers in the Grain and Flour Trade during the Eighteenth Century* (1984).

Leonard Krieger, *Kings and Philosophers, 1689–1789* (1970).

Paul Langford, *A Polite and Commercial People: England 1727–1783* (1989).

Emmanuel LeRoy Ladurie, *The Peasants of Languedoc* (1974).

G.E. Mingay, *Land and Society in England 1750–1980* (1994).

J.H. Parry, *Trade and Dominion: The European Overseas Empires in the Eighteenth Century* (1971).

Roy Porter, *English Society in the Eighteenth Century* (1986).

Bernard Semmel, *The Methodist Revolution* (1973).

Marc Raeff, *The Origins of the Russian Intelligentsia: The Eighteenth Century Nobility* (1966).

James C. Riley, *The Seven Years War and the Old Regime in France* (1986).

George Rudé, *Paris and London in the Eighteenth Century* (1971).

Lawrence Stone, *The Family, Sex, and Marriage in England, 1500–1800* (1977).

E.P. Thompson, *Whigs and Hunters: The Origins of the Black Act* (1975).

Isser Woloch, *Eighteenth-Century: Tradition and Progress, 1715–1789* (1982).

CHAPTER 10. ENLIGHTENED THOUGHT AND THE REPUBLIC OF LETTERS

Keith Baker, *Condorcet: From Natural Philosophy to Social Mathematics* (1975).

Keith Baker, *Inventing the French Revolution: Essays in the Political Culture of Eighteenth-Century France* (1990).

Roger Chartier, *The Cultural Origins of the French Revolution* (1991).

Maurice Cranston, *The Noble Savage: Jean-Jacques Rousseau, 1754–1762* (1991).

Maurice Cranston, *Philosophers and Pamphleteers: Political Theorists of the Enlightenment* (1986).

Thomas E. Crow, *Painters and Public Life in Eighteenth-Century Paris* (1985).

Robert Darnton, *The Business of Enlightenment* (1979).

Robert Darnton, *The Great Cat Massacre* (1985).

Robert Darnton, *The Literary Underground of the Old Regime* (1985).

Peter Gay, *The Enlightenment: An Interpretation* (2 vols., 1966–1969).

Peter Gay, *Voltaire's Politics: The Poet as Realist* (1988).

Dena Goodman, *The Republic of Letters: A Cultural History of the French Enlightenment* (1984).

Norman Hampson, *A Cultural History of the Enlightenment* (1969).

J.M. McManners, *Death and Enlightenment: Changing Attitudes to Death among Christians and Unbelievers in Eighteenth-Century France* (1982).

Roy Porter and Mikulás Teich, eds., *The Enlightenment in National Context* (1981).

Franco Venturi, *Italy and the Enlightenment: Studies in a Cosmopolitan Century* (1972).

CHAPTER 11. EIGHTEENTH-CENTURY DYNASTIC RIVALRIES AND POLITICS

Paul Avrich, *Russian Rebels, 1600–1800* (1972).

Bernard Bailyn, *The Ideological Origins of the American Revolution* (1992).

C.B.A. Behrens, *The Ancien Regime* (1967).

C.B.A. Behrens, *Society, Government, and the Enlightenment: The Experiences of Eighteenth-Century France and Prussia* (1985).

David Bell, *Lawyers and Citizens: The Making of a Political Elite in Old Regime France* (1994).

John Brewer, *Party Ideology and Popular Politics at the Accession of George III* (1976).

John Brewer, *The Sinews of Power: War, Money, and the English State, 1688–1783* (1989).

J.C.D. Clark, *English Society 1688–1832* (1985).

Linda Colley, *Britons: Forging the Nation, 1707–1837* (1992).

Linda Colley, *In Defiance of Oligarchy: The Tory Party 1714–60* (1982).

Olwen Hufton, *The Poor of Eighteenth-Century France, 1750–1789* (1974).

Isabel de Madariaga, *Catherine the Great: A Short History* (1990).

Sara Maza, *Private Lives and Public Affairs: The Causes Celèbres of Prerevolutionary France* (1993).

Sara Maza, *Servants and Masters in Eighteenth-Century France: The Uses of Loyalty* (1983).

N. McKendrick, J. Brewer, and J.H. Plumb, *The Birth of a Consumer Society: The Commercialization of Eighteenth-Century England* (1982).

Edmund Morgan, *The Birth of the Republic, 1763–1789* (1977).

Daniel Roche, *The People of Paris* (1987).

Robert M. Schwartz, *Policing the Poor in Eighteenth-Century France* (1988).

Franco Venturi, *The End of the Old Regime in Europe, 1776–1789* (2 vols., 1991).

Ernst Wangermann, *The Austrian Achievement 1700–1800* (1973).
Wayne Ph. te. Brake, *Regents and Rebels: The Revolutionary World of an Eighteenth-Century Dutch City* (1989).

CHAPTER 12. THE FRENCH REVOLUTION

Jean-Paul Bertaud, *The Army of the French Revolution: From Citizen-Soldiers to Instrument of Power* (1988).
T.C.W. Blanning, *The Origins of the French Revolutionary Wars* (1989).
John Bosher, *The French Revolution* (1988).
Richard Cobb, *The Police and the People: French Popular Protest, 1789–1820* (1972).
William Doyle, *Origins of the French Revolution* (1988).
Marianne Elliott, *Partners in Revolution: The United Irishmen and France* (1982).
Alan Forrest, *Conscripts and Deserters: The Army and French Society during the Revolution and Empire* (1989).
Alan Forrest, *The French Revolution and the Poor* (1981).
François Furet, *Interpreting the French Revolution* (1992).
A. Goodwin, *The Friends of Liberty: The English Democratic Movement in the Age of the French Revolution* (1979).
Patrice Higonnet, *Sister Republics: The Origins of French and American Republicanism* (1988).
Lynn Hunt, *The Family Romance of the French Revolution* (1992).
Lynn Hunt, *Politics, Culture, and Class in the French Revolution* (1984).
Peter Jones, *The Peasantry in the French Revolution* (1988).
Georges Lefebvre, *The Coming of the French Revolution* (1989).
Darline Gay Levy, Harriet Branson Applewhite, and Mary Durham Johnson, *Women in Revolutionary Paris 1789–1795* (1979).
Colin Lucas, ed., *The Political Culture of the French Revolution* (1989).
Ted W. Margadant, *Urban Rivalries in the French Revolution* (1992).
Sarah E. Meltzer and Leslie W. Rabine, eds., *Rebel Daughters: Women and the French Revolution* (1989).
Mona Ozouf, *Festivals and the French Revolution* (1988).
R.R. Palmer, *The Age of the Democratic Revolution: A Political History of Europe and America, 1760–1800* (2 vols., 1959–1964).
R.R. Palmer, *Twelve Who Ruled: The Year of the Terror in the French Revolution* (1989).
Ronald Paulson, *Representations of Revolution, 1789–1820* (1983).
Jeremy D. Popkin, *Revolutionary News: The Press in France, 1789–1799* (1990).
Georges Rudé, *The Great Fear of 1789* (1973).
William Sewell, Jr., *A Rhetoric of Bourgeois Revolution: The Abbé Sieyès and What Is the Third Estate?* (1994).
Donald Sutherland, *France, 1789–1815: Revolution and Counter-revolution* (1986).
Timothy Tackett, *Religion, Revolution, and Regional Culture in Eighteenth-Century France: The Ecclesiastical Oath of 1791* (1986).

Charles Tilly, *The Vendée* (1964).

Isser Woloch, *The New Regime: Transformations of the French Civic Order, 1789–1820s* (1994).

CHAPTER 13. NAPOLEON AND EUROPE

Louis Bergeron, *France Under Napoleon* (1981).

J. Christopher Herold, *The Age of Napoleon* (1985).

Georges Lefebvre, *Napoleon* (2 vols., 1969).

Felix Markham, *Napoleon* (1963).

Harold T. Parker, *Three Napoleonic Battles* (1983).

Gunther Rothenberg, *The Art of Warfare in the Age of Napoleon* (1978).

Alan Schom, *One Hundred Days: Napoleon's Road to Waterloo* (1992).

Jakob Walter, *The Diary of a Napoleonic Foot Soldier* (1991).

Stuart Wolfe, *Napoleon's Integration of Europe* (1991).

D.G. Wright, *Napoleon and Europe* (1984).

CREDITS

Part One (p. xx): Hans Holbein the Younger, *Jean de Dinteville and Georges de Selve ("The Ambassadors")*, National Gallery, London; Part Two (p. 178): Marcus Gheeraerts the Younger, *Elizabeth I (The Ditchley Portrait)*, 1592 (#2561), By courtesy of the National Portrait Gallery, London; Part Three (p. 324): Engraving after Monsiau, *Frederick the Great and Voltaire at Sans-Souci*, Bibliothèque Nationale, Paris; Part Four (p. 492): *Barricades in the Rue Saint-Antoine*, Bildarchiv Preussischer Kulturbesitz, Berlin.

Color Section 1: p. 1 (top) John Carter Brown Library/Brown University, photograph by Richard Hurley; p. 1 (bottom left) Benozzo Gozzoli, detail from *Procession of the Magi*, Palazzo Medici Riccardi, Florence, Art Resource, NY; p. 1 (bottom right) Raphael, *Madonna di Foligno*, 1512, Vatican Museum, Rome, Scala/Art Resource, NY; p. 2 (top left) Leonardo da Vinci, *Mona Lisa* (1503–1507) Louvre, Art Resource, NY, photograph by Erich Lessing; p. 2 (top right) Giovanni Bellini, *The Doge Leonardo Loredan* (#189), National Gallery, London; p. 2 (bottom) Sandro Botticelli, *Birth of Venus*, Uffizi Gallery, Florence, Alinari/Art Resource, NY; p. 3 (top) Titian, *Bacchus and Ariadne*, 1522, (#35), National Gallery, London; p. 3 (bottom) Michelangelo, Sistine Chapel Ceiling, Scala/Art Resource, NY; p. 4 (top left) Giovanni Battista Gaulli, *Triumph of the Name of Jesus*, Gesù Church, Art Resource, NY; p. 4 (top right) Albrecht Dürer, *Self-Portrait*, 1500, Alte Pinakothek, Munich, Blauel/Gnamm/Artothek; p. 4 (bottom) Pieter Bruegel the Elder, *The Peasants' Wedding*, 1568, Kunsthistorisches Museum, Gemaeldegalerie, Vienna, Art Resource, NY, photograph by Erich Lessing.

Color Section 2: p. 1 (top left) Diego de Silva Velázquez, *Las Meninas*, 1665, Prado Museum, photograph by Erich Lessing, Art Resource, NY; p. 1 (top right) El Greco, *The Burial of Count Orgaz*, 1586, S. Tome, Toledo, Spain, Giraudon/Art Resource, NY; p. 1 (bottom) Antonio Carnicero, *The Ascension of One of the Montgolfiere Brothers on 12 August 1792*, Prado Museum, Giraudon/Art Resource, NY; p. 2 (top left) Abraham van Beyeren, *Still Life with Grapes and Fruit*, Mauritshuis, The Hague, Scala, Art Resource, NY; p. 2 (top right) Jan Vermeer, *The Painter and His Model as Klio*, Kunsthistorisches Museum, Gemaeldegalerie, Vienna, photograph by Erich Lessing, Art Resource, NY; p. 2 (bottom) Rembrandt, *The Nightwatch*, © Rijksmuseum-Stichting, Amsterdam; p. 3 (top left) Unknown artist, *Elizabeth I*, by courtesy of the National Portrait Gallery, London; p. 3 (top right) Hyacinthe Rigaud, *Louis XIV*, Louvre, Paris, Giraudon/Art Resource, NY; p. 3 (bottom left) Peter Paul Rubens, *The Disembarkment of Marie de Medici at the Port of Marseille in 1600*, Louvre, Paris, Giraudon/Art Resource, NY; p. 3 (bottom right) François Boucher, *Madame de Pompadour*, Alte Pinakothek, Munich, Bridgeman Art Library/Art Resource, NY; p. 4 (top) William Hogarth, *The Marriage Contract*, 1743, The National Gallery, London; p. 4 (bottom) Jean-Antoine Watteau, *L'Enseigne de Gersaint Berlino*, Charlottenburg, Scala/Art Resource, NY.

Chapter 1: p. 4 (left) Staatliche Museen Preussischer Kulturbesitz; (right) Ampliaciones y Reproducciones MAS, Barcelona; p. 8 Pieter Dan, *Historie van Barbaryen*, Amsterdam, 1684, Special Collections, New York Public Library, Astor, Lenox, and Tilden Foundations; p. 9 Bibliothèque de l'Ecole des Beaux Arts, Giraudon/Art Resource, NY; p. 10 Hans Sebald

Beham, *Saturn*, 16th C., Warder Collection; **p. 12** Jerusalem Triptych, Polish school, 16th C., National Museum, Warsaw; **p. 13** Miniature from *Heures de Charles d'Angoulême*, late 15th C., Ms. Latin 1173 f.4, Bibliotheque Nationale, Paris; **p. 14** Bibliothèque de l'Arsenal; **p. 16** Hans Wertinger, 1530, Germanisches Nationalmuseum, Nürnberg; **p. 19** From a painting by Bruegel, Metropolitan Museum, New York; **p. 24** Gerini Niccolo' di Pietro, *Storie di S. Matteo* (Banchieri), Scala/Art Resource, NY; **p. 25** Hulton-Deutsch Collection; **p. 34** MEPC Print Collection, Miriam & Ira D. Wallach Div. of Art, Prints, and Photographs, New York Public Library, Astor, Lenox, and Tilden Foundations; **p. 39** Kobe Museum, Japan; **p. 42** Illustration from Lienzo de Tlaxcala, *Antiguedades Mexicanas* (1892), Tozzer Library, Harvard University.

Chapter 2: p. 48 Ghilandaio Domenico, 1485, Sessetti Chapel, Santa Trinita, Scala/Art Resource, NY; **p. 50** Hamburger Kunsthalle, photograph by Elke Walford; **p. 52** Giovanni Maria Butteri, *The Return from the Palio*, National Gallery of Ireland; **p. 57** Pianta della Catena, *Firenze*, 1490, Scala/Art Resource, NY; **p. 58** Giorgio Vasari, *The Signory Discuss the War against Pisa*, Palazzo Vecchio, Florence, Soprintendenza alle Gallerie, Florence; **p. 59** Giorgio Vasari, *Lorenzo de' Medici*, Uffizi Palace, Alinari/Art Resource, NY; **p. 61** (left) Petrarch, Alinari/Art Resource, NY; (right) Ambrosius Holbein, *Aushängeschild eines Schulmeisters*, Oeffentliche Kunstsammlung, Basel, Kunstmuseum Inv. 311; **p. 65** (left) Leonardo da Vinci, *Foetus in the womb*, Her Majesty Queen Elizabeth II/Royal Collection Enterprises Ltd; (right) Leonardo da Vinci, *Divine proportion*, Alinari/Art Resource, NY; **p. 67** Pitti Palace, Alinari/Art Resource, NY; **p. 69** Raphael, *Leo X and His Cardinals*, Uffizi, Florence, Alinari/Art Resource, NY; **p. 70** Andrea Mantegna, fresco, Palazzo Ducale, Mantua, (Sadea-Sansoni) Alinari/Art Resource, NY; **p. 74** (left) Masaccio, *The Expulsion of Adam and Eve from Eden*, Brancacci Chapel, Florence; (right) Masaccio, *The Trinity*, Santa Maria Novella, Florence, Alinari/Art Resource, NY; **p. 75** Andrea Mantegna, *The Dead Christ and Mary*, Brera, Milan, Alinari/Art Resource, NY; **p. 76** Donatello, *The Feast of Herod*, Baptismal Font, Alinari/Art Resource, NY; **p. 77** Leonardo da Vinci, *The Last Supper*, Sta. Maria delle Grazie, Alinari/Art Resource, NY; **p. 78** Michelangelo, detail of *The Last Judgement*, Vatican Palace, Sistine Chapel, Alinari/Art Resource, NY; **p. 83** Unknown artist, *The Burning of Savonarola*, Museo S. Marco, Alinari/Art Resource, NY; **p. 85** Bust of Niccolò Machiavelli from Palazzo Vecchio, Florence, Scala.

Chapter 3: p. 88 Woodcuts from the series *Passional Christi und Antichrist*, Wittenberg, 1521; **p. 90** Albrecht Dürer, *Four Horsemen of the Apocalypse*, Trustees of the British Museum, London; **p. 93** Hans Holbein, *Erasmus*, Louvre, Lauros/Giraudon; **p. 100** Lucas Cranach, *Portrait of Martin Luther as a Young Man*, National Museum, Nuremberg, Scala/Art Resource, NY; **p. 101** Unknown artist, *Dream of Frederick the Wise*, Coll. of Dr. Fritz Schleifenbaum, Huttental-Weidenau, Marburg, Foto Marburg/Art Resource, NY; **p. 108** The Augsburg Confession, 1530, Kunstsammlungen der Veste, Coberg; **p. 113** (left) Zwingli, Bettmann Archive; (right) Illustration from *Chronique de Stumpffen* by Johan Stumf, Zurich, 1548; **p. 116** (left) Jean Calvin from Bibliothèque Publique et Universitaire, Genève, photograph by François Martin; (right) Unknown artist, *Calvinist Service*, 1564, Bibliothèque Publique et Universitaire, Geneve photograph by François Martin; **p. 122** (left) After Holbein, *Portrait of Henry VIII*, by courtesy of the National Portrait Gallery, London; (right) Unknown artist, *Anne Boleyn*, Musée Condé, Chantilly, Lauros-Giraudon/Art Resource, NY; **p. 123** Hans Holbein, *Sir Thomas More*, © The Frick Collection, New York; **p. 127** Council of Trent, Jahurhundert Wien, Haus-, Hof-, und Staatsarchiv; **p. 130** Gian Lorenzo Bernini, *Ecstasy of St. Theresa*, Alinari/Art Resource, NY; **p. 131** Caricatures of the Pope, 1545, The British Library; **p. 132** Gerald Dou, *Old Woman Reading the Bible*, © Rijksmuseum-Stichting, Amsterdam; **p. 134** Pieter Bruegel the Elder, *Battle between Carnival and Lent*, Kunsthistorisches Museum, Vienna, FotoMarburg/Art Resource, NY.

Chapter 4: p. 139 Pieter Bruegel the Elder, *Massacre of the Innocents*, Kunsthistorisches Museum, Vienna, photograph by Erich Lessing/Art Resource, NY; **p. 140** Jean Clouet, Portrait of Francis I, Uffizi Palace, Florence, Alinari/Art Resource, NY; **p. 143** Catherine de Medici, Warder Collection; **p. 145** François Dubois d'Amiens, *St. Batholomew Day's Massacre*, Collection Musée Cantonal des Beaux-Arts, Lausanne, Switzerland; **p. 147** Unknown artist, *Portrait of Henry IV*, Louvre, Photographie Bulloz; **p. 150** Assassination of the duke of

Guise, Bibliothèque Nationale, Paris; **p. 151** *Henry IV Enters Paris*, Bibliothèque Nationale, Paris; **p. 158** Cardinal Richelieu, Warder Collection; **p. 161** Georg Hoefnagel, *Portrait of Rudolf II*, Kunsthistorisches Museum, Vienna; **p. 167** Catholics enter Augsburg, Fotomas Index; **p. 169** Jan Martsen de Jonge, *Gustavus Adolphus in Battle*, Königliches Schloß, Kungl, Husgerlidekammaren, The Royal Collection, Stockholm; **p. 170** Wallenstein assassinated, Fotomas Index; **p. 172** Jacques Callot, *Les Grandes Misères de la Guerre*, 1633, Fotomas Index; **p. 177** Adriaen Pietersz van de Venne, *Allegory of Poverty*, Allen Memorial Art Museum, Oberlin College, Ohio, Mrs. F. F. Prentiss Fund, 1960, © Allen Memorial Art Museum.

Chapter 5: p. 182 Courtesy of the New York Public Library Prints Division, Astor, Lenox, and Tilden Foundations; **p. 185** Jan van Hemessen, *Die Berufung des Matthäus*, Bayer, Staatsgemäldesammlungen; **p. 189** Felipe Bigarny, *Ferdinand the Catholic & Isabella the Catholic*, painted wood, Capilla Real, Granada Cathedral, Francesc Català Roca, Scala/Art Resource, NY; **p. 192** Titian, *Charles V*, Alte Pinakothek, Giraudon/Art Resource, NY; **p. 194** Titian, *Philip II*, Galleria Corsini, Alinari/Art Resource, NY; **p. 195** Ampliaciones y reproducciones MAS, Barcelona; **p. 196** Paolo Veronese, *The Battle of Lepanto*, Accademia, Venice, photograph by Erich Lessing/Art Resource, NY; **p. 200** (left) Master John, *Lady Jane Grey* (#4451), by courtesy of the National Portrait Gallery, London; (right) Antonio Moro, *La Reina Doña Maria de Inglaterra, Segunda Mujer de Felippe II*, 1554, Museo del Prado, Art Resource, NY; **p. 202** Marcus Gheerhaerts the Younger, *Queen Elizabeth Dancing with Robert Dudley, Earl of Leicester*, Viscount del Isle, VC, KG, from his collection at Penhurst Place, Kent, Bridgeman/Art Resource, NY; **p. 206** Follower of François Clouet, miniature of *Mary Queen of Scots*, Victoria & Albert Museum, London, Bridgeman/Art Resource, NY; **p. 207** Artist unknown, *Elizabeth I Greeting the Dutch Ambassadors*, Staatliche Museen, Kassel; **p. 210** Anthony van den Wyngaerde, *Panorama of London*, 1543, Guildhall Library; **p. 211** Jan Siberechts, *A View of Longleat in Wiltshire*, Bridgeman/Art Resource, NY; **p. 215** Fotomas Index; **p. 218** (left) Facsimile of the First Folio edition of 1623, Warder Collection; (right) The Swan Theatre, c. 1596, Warder Collection; **p. 220** Franz Hogenberg, *Engravings of Scenes from The History of the Netherlands, France and Germany*, Cologne, 1620s, Miriam and Ira D. Wallach Division of Art, Prints and Photographs, New York Public Library, Astor, Lenox, and Tilden Foundations; **p. 223** Vicente Carducho, *Expulsion of the "Moriscos" from Spain*, 1609, Prado, Madrid; **p. 225** Antonio Pereda, *Sueño del Caballero (The Soldier's Dream)*, 1640, Accademia de Bellas Artes de San Fernando, Madrid, Art Resource, NY; **p. 227** (left) Velásquez, *Felipe IV*, Museo del Prado, Ampilaciones y Reproducciones MAS; (right) Velásquez, *Gaspar de Guzmán, Duque de Olivares*, Museo del Prado, Ampilaciones y Reproducciones MAS; **p. 230** Velàsquez, *Surrender at Breda*, Museo del Prado, Ampilaciones y Reproducciones MAS.

Chapter 6: p. 233 A. van der Venne, *Harbour at Middelburg*, © Rijksmuseum-Stichting, Amsterdam; **p. 235** (left) James I, by permission of the Trustees of the National Maritime Museum, London; (right) Daniel Mytens, *Charles I when Prince of Wales*, © Her Majesty Queen Elizabeth II/Royal Collection Enterprises, Ltd.; **p. 239** From John Vicar's *Sight of the Transactions of These Latter Years*, etching by Wencelaus Hollar, British Library; **p. 242** (left) John Pym (#1425), by courtesy of the National Portrait Gallery, London; (right) After A. Van Dyck, *William Laud* (#171), by courtesy of the National Portrait Gallery, London; **p. 246** From John Vicar's *Sight of the Transactions of These Latter Years*, etching by Wencelaus Hollar, British Library; **p. 247** Sir Peter Lely, *Oliver Cromwell*, Galleria Palatina, Florence, photo supplied by British Information Services; **p. 250** The New Model Army, Warder Collection; **p. 251** Execution of Charles I, engraving by Sebastian Furck, Hulton-Deutsch Collection; **p. 256** Quaker meeting, engraving by Van Heemsterk the Younger, Trustees of the British Museum, London; **p. 258** Adriaen Key, *William the Silent*, Mauritshuis (Royal Picture Gallery), The Hague, The Netherlands, **p. 263** J. Berckheyde, *The Amsterdam Bourse*, 1668, Amsterdams Historisch Museum; **p. 264** Gerrit Berckheyde, *The Waag and Crane on the Spaarne at Haarlem*, © Rijksmuseum-Stichting, Amsterdam; **p. 265** A. Cuyp, *A Senior Merchant of the Dutch East India Company and His Wife*, © Rijksmuseum-Stichting, Amsterdam; **p. 267** (left) Engraving of tulips by Claes Jansz from *Sinnepoppen*, Amsterdam, 1614, by permission of the Houghton Library, Harvard University; (right) Emanuel de Witte, *The Fish Market*, © Rijksmuseum-Stichting, Amsterdam; **p. 268** Romeyn de Hooghe, *The Dike-break at*

Coevorden, engraving, Bodleian Library, Oxford; **p. 270** Rembrandt, *Syndics of the Cloth Guild,* © Rijksmuseum-Stichting, Amsterdam.

Chapter 7: p. 275 Title page from T. Hobbes, *Leviathan,* 1651, New York Public Library Rare Book Division. Astor, Lenox, and Tilden Foundations; **p. 278** Diederich Porath from the folio *Palaestra Suecena,* Stockholm, 1693, Warder Collection; **p. 283** Janissaries cross the Drave, from *History of Soliman II,* reproduced by kind permission of the Trustees of the Chester Beatty Library, Dublin, photograph from Rex Roberts Studios; **p. 285** Charles Le Brun, Ceiling of the Hall of Mirrors, Versailles Museum, Giraudon/Art Resource, NY; **p. 287** (left) Rousselet, Le Prince de Condé, Empereur des Turcs, from *Courses de Testes et de Bagues faites par le Roy,* 1670, gift of Mrs. Herbert L. Stern, courtesy of the Art Institute of Chicago; (right) Philippe de Champagne, *Portrait of Mazarin,* Chantilly, photographie Bulloz; **p. 290** Gobelins after Le Brun, Louix XIV visiting the Gobelins Factory, Versailles, © R.M.N.; **p. 291** J. B. Martin, The City and the Château of Versailles. Château—Grand Trianon, Giraudon/Art Resource, NY; **p. 293** French school, 17th Century, The Château of Versailles, Photographie Bulloz; **p. 295** C. Coypel, *Portrait of Molière,* Photographie Bulloz; **p. 296** (left) French figurative plaque of the sun, Bibliothèque Nationale, Cabinet des Médailles, Paris; (right) Louis XIV as the Exterminator of Protestantism, Bibliothèque Nationale, Departement des Imprimés, Paris; **p. 297** J. Luyken, © Rijksmuseum-Stichting, Amsterdam; **p. 302** G. Lauch engraving of Leopold I, Trustees of the British Museum; **p. 303** Pierre-Denis Martin, *The Siege of Vienna,* 1683, Alte Pinakothek, Bayerische Staatsgemäldesammlungen; **p. 306** Frederick William I, Warder Collection; **p. 308** Mathieu Merian the Younger, *Ivan the Terrible in Novgorod,* engraving, Bibliothèque Nationale, Paris; **p. 310** T. H. Wedekind, *Charles XII,* Armèmuseum, Stockholm, photograph by Bo Michaëlsson; **p. 312** *Peter the Great,* Versailles, Lauros-Giraudon/Art Resource, NY; **p. 319** Adam Frans Van der Meulen, *Rhine Passage,* 1672, Louvre, Alinari/Art Resource, NY.

Chapter 8: p. 328 Tapestry of Testelin after a cartoon by Le Brun, *Establishment of the Academy of Science,* Musée de Versailles, Giraudon/Art Resource, NY; **p. 331** Copernican heliocentricism, Warder Collection; **p. 333** (left) Jan Stephan van Calcar, title page from Vesalius' *De humani corporis fabricia,* 1543, Kupferstichkabinett, Basel; (right) Skeleton from Vesalius, *Epitome,* Kupferstichkabinett, Basel; **p. 334** Circulation of the blood, *De motu cordis,* 1628, British Library; **p. 335** The Science Museum/Science and Society Picture Library; **p. 336** (left) Kepler, Warder Collection; (right) J. Kepler, *Prodromus Dissertationum,* Tubingen, 1596, Rare Book Collection, New York Public Library, Astor, Lenox, and Tilden Foundations; **p. 338** (left) Francis Bacon, Trustees of the British Museum; (right) Galileo, courtesy Dr. G. B. Pineider, Florence; **p. 341** (left) Unknown artist, *Portrait of Descartes,* Photographie Bulloz; (right) Sir Isaac Newton (#2881), by courtesy of the National Portrait Gallery, London; **p. 345** Pascal's calculating machine, Warder Collection; **p. 346** Frontispiece to *Nature's Pictures Drawn by Fancies Pencil,* 1656, by permission of the Houghton Library, Harvard University; **p. 349** 17th Century French apothecary shop, Bibliothèque Nationale, Paris; **p. 350** *The Alchemist,* engraving after a painting by Teniers, Bettmann Archive; **p. 352** Royal Observatory, London, The Science Museum/Science and Society Picture Library.

Chapter 9: p. 355 Thomas Gainsborough, *Mr. & Mrs. Andrews,* National Gallery, London; **p. 357** (left) Alain M. Mallet, *Description de l'universe,* Paris, 1683, Rare Book Collection, New York Public Library, Astor, Lenox, and Tilden Foundations; (right) Nobleman as spider, Warder Collection; **p. 359** Blenheim Palace, Edwin Smith/Warder Collection; **p. 362** William Hogarth, *Lord George Graham,* by permission of the Trustees of the National Maritime Museum, London; **p. 365** Flogging a serf, Bettmann Archive; **p. 368** John G. Maxwell, *Measuring Land for Enclosure,* 1748, County Records Office, Bedford, Jewell-Harrison; **p. 373** Engraving showing conditions in Hamburg hospital, Germanisches Nationalmuseum, Nürnberg; **p. 375** William Hogarth, *The Weaver's Apprentice,* Trustees of the British Museum; **p. 376** Fotomas Index; **p. 377** (left) C. Wagstaff after Sir W. Beechey, James Watt, Warder Collection; (right) Watt's steam engine, Ironbridge Gorge Museum (Elton Collection); **p. 379** John Raphael Smith, after Joseph Wright of Derby, *Sir Richard Arkwright,* 1801, Derby Museum and Art Gallery; **p. 386** London cafe, Trustees of the British Museum; **p. 387** James Malton, *Shops by Essex Bridge, Capel Street, Dublin* (detail), c. 1790, Victoria & Albert Museum/Art Resource, NY; **p. 388** Cornelius Holsteyn, *Reynier Pauw & His Wife*

Adriana & Their Children (detail), Courtesy Christies, London; **p. 394** *Preserve Us from Gamekeepers,* French engraving, Trustees of the British Museum; **p. 396** William Hogarth, *The Idle 'Prentice Executed by Tyburn,* engraving, 1747, Trustees of the British Museum; **p. 397** Roger-Viollet.

Chapter 10: p. 400 John Locke: commemorative medal, Trustees of the British Museum; **p. 404** The *philosophes,* Bibliothèque Nationale, Paris; **p. 406** (left) Montesquieu, Photographie Bulloz; (right) J.A. Houdon, portrait bust of Voltaire, Louvre, Alinari/Art Resource, NY; **p. 409** Illustration from Diderot's *Encyclopedia,* Warder Collection; **p. 413** (left) Q. de la Tour, *Jean-Jacques Rousseau,* Photographie Bulloz; (right) Rousseau and Voltaire fighting, Bibliothèque Nationale, Paris; **p. 419** Oval Salon, Hôtel de Soubise, Paris, Giraudon/Art Resource, NY; **p. 420** Jean-Antoine Watteau, *La Gamme d'Amour,* National Gallery, London; **p. 421** William Hogarth, *Gin Lane,* 1751, Trustees of the British Museum; **p. 422** (left) Philippe Mercier, *Portrait of Handel,* private collection, photograph courtesy Thames & Hudson, Ltd; (right) Haydn, Warder Collection; **p. 423** *The Young Mozart Performing,* Schönbrunn, Bildarchiv, Österreichisches Nationalbibliothek; **p. 424** *Une soirie chez Madame Geoffrin,* Château Malmaison, Lauros-Giraudon/Art Resource, NY; **p. 425** Mesmer, photo collection of UCLA Bio-Medical Library, History Division; **p. 427** Freemasons, Museen der Stadt Wien; **p. 429** Austrian classroom, Historischen Museums der Stadt Wien, photograph by Rudolf Stepanek; **p. 430** Expulsion of the Jews from Prague, 1745, Warder Collection; **p. 433** Frederick the Great Playing Flute at Sans Souci, Foto Marburg/Art Resource, NY; **p. 437** Adam Smith, Bettmann Archive.

Chapter 11: p. 443 *The Lawyers,* Bibliothèque Nationale, Paris; **p. 448** (left) Louis Gabriel Blanchet, *Prince Charles Edward Stuart,* 1738, by courtesy of the National Portrait Gallery, London; (right) The Battle of Culloden Moor, courtesy of the Director, National Army Museum, London; **p. 449** Marten van Meytens II, *Maria Theresa and Her Family,* 1750, Kunsthistoriches Museum, Wien; **p. 450** Frederick the Great, Warder Collection; **p. 453** Pierre Lenfant, *La bataille de Fontenoy, 11 mai 1745,* Versailles Museum, Giraudon/Art Resource; **p. 458** *The Capture of Quebec,* 1759, engraved after a drawing by Smyth, Wolfe's Aide-de-Camp, Hulton-Deutsch Collection; **p. 461** Siege warfare, courtesy of the Director, National Army Museum, London; **p. 463** Edmund Burke, The Mansell Collection; **p. 465** *Picture of the Very Famous Island of Madhead,* Amsterdam, 1720, Warder Collection; **p. 466** Joseph Coopy, *Robert Walpole and His Cabinet,* Trustees of the British Museum; **p. 469** Benjamin West, *George III,* 1779, © Her Majesty Queen Elizabeth II, Royal Collection Enterprises Ltd.; **p. 473** Wilkes Riots, *c.* 1768, Stock Montage, Chicago; **p. 477** Paul Revere, from *The Boston Gazette,* March 12, 1770, Courtesy of The New York Historical Society, NYC; **p. 479** Louis Nicolas Blarenberghe, *The Siege of Yorktown* (detail), Versailles Museum, Giraudon/Art Resource, NY; **p. 480** Karl Anton Hickel, *House of Commons* (#745), by courtesy of the National Portrait Gallery, London; **p. 485** Pugachev, Warder Collection.

Chapter 12: p. 496 Musée Carnavalet, Photographie Bulloz; **p. 500** (left) Duplessis, *Louis XVI,* Musée Carnavalet, Photographie Bulloz; (right) Vigée-Lebrun, *Marie-Antoinette,* Versailles Museum, Photographie Bulloz; **p. 504** (left) *Lafayette,* Musée Carnavalet, Photographie Bulloz; (right) Jacques-Louis David, *Abbé Sieyès,* Photographie Bulloz; **p. 506** *Tennis Court Oath,* after David, Bibliothèque Nationale, Paris; **p. 507** *The Taking of the Bastille,* Versailles Museum, Giraudon/Art Resource, NY; **p. 512** *Women of Paris March to Versailles,* Bibliothèque Nationale, Paris; **p. 515** *The Three Orders Hammering Out the New Constitution,* Trustees of the British Museum; **p. 517** *Olympe de Gouges,* Musée Carnavalet, Photo Andreani, © Photothèque des Musées de la Ville de Paris by SPADEM; **p. 518** Pierre Etienne Lesueur, *Patriotic Women's Club,* Musée Carnavalet, Photo Ladet/Toumazet, © Photothèque des Musées de la Ville de Paris by SPADEM; **p. 519** Bibliothèque Nationale, Paris; **p. 520** (left) Louis XVI with bonnet rouge, Cabinet des Estampes, Bibliothèque Nationale, Paris; (right) Planting a Liberty Tree, Musée Carnavalet, © Photothèque des Musées de la ville de Paris by SPADEM; **p. 521** (left) Danton, Musée Carnavalet, (right) Robespierre, Musée Carnavalet, Photographie Bulloz; **p. 525** *The Massacres of September,* Photographie Bulloz; **p. 528** Execution of Louis XVI, Bibliothèque Nationale, Paris; **p. 531** Hulton-Deutsch Collection; **p. 532** Jacques-Louis David, *Death of Marat,* Photographie Bulloz; **p. 534** Jacques-Louis David, *Marie Antoinette on Her Way to Her Execution,* Bibliothèque

Nationale, Paris, Photographie Giraudon/Art Resource, NY; **p. 535** (left) Seal of the Republic, Archives Nationales, Paris; (right) The French people overwhelming the hydra of federalism, August 1793. Musée Carnavalet, Photo Briant, © Photothèque des Musées de la Ville de Paris by SPADEM; **p. 539** Debucourt, *The Cafe Frascati*, Bibliothèque Nationale, Paris; **p. 540** *Bonaparte and the Insurrection*. Bibliothèque Nationale, Paris; **p. 543** The Corsican Crocodile dissolving the Council of Frogs!!!, Literature BMC.9427, The Trustees of the British Museum.

Chapter 13: p. 549 Jean-Antoine Gros, *Bonaparte at Arcole*, 1796, Louvre, Photographie Giraudon/Art Resource, NY; **p. 551** *Nelson at Battle of the Nile*, by permission of the Trustees of the National Maritime Museum, London; **p. 557** Jacques-Louis David, *Emperor Napoleon Crowning the Empress Josephine in the Cathedral of Notre Dame*, Louvre, Giraudon/Art Resource, NY; **p. 558** Turner, "The death of Lord Nelson at *The Battle of Trafalgar*," 1805, Tate Gallery; **p. 561** Alexander I and Napoleon, Mansell Collection; **p. 562** Louis-Léopold Boilly, *Le départ des conscrits en 1807 devant la porte Saint-Denis*, Musée Carnavalet, Giraudon/Art Resource, NY; **p. 564** Charles Meynier, *Napoleon on the Island of Lobau*, Versailles Museum, © Photo R.M.N.; **p. 568** Jacques-Louis David, *Oath of the Army after the Distribution of the Standards*, Versailles Museum, Alinari/Art Resource, NY; **p. 570** Gillray cartoon, *The Plumb-pudding in danger*, 1805, Print collection, The New York Public Library, Astor, Lenox, and Tilden Foundations; **p. 572** Francisco José de Goya y Lucientes, *May 3 1808: The Execution of the Defenders of Madrid*, 1814, Museo del Prado, Alinari/Art Resource, NY; **p. 578** Faber Du Faur, *The Last Remnants of the Grand Army en Route to Smolensk*, Bavarian Army Museum, Munich; **p. 580** Francisco José de Goya y Lucientes, *Portrait of Wellington*, National Gallery, London; **p. 581** *Napoleon on Elba*, Trustees of the British Museum; **p. 583** *Acclamation of People of Grenoble at the Return of Napoleon*, Bibliothèque Nationale, Paris; **p. 584** A. A. Alken, *Calvary Charge at Waterloo*, Courtesy of the Director, National Army Museum, London; **p. 585** Jacques-Louis David, *Bonaparte Leaping St. Bernard*, Versailles Museum, Photographie Bulloz.

Text and Tables: pp. xvii–xviii Bertolt Brecht, "A Worker Reads History," H. R. Hays, translator, copyright 1947 by Bertolt Brecht and H. R. Hays, reproduced by permission of Harcourt Brace Jovanovich and the Ann Elmo Agency; **Table 1-1 (p. 21)** European Population in the Sixteenth and Seventeenth Centuries, in Richard MacKenney, *Sixteenth-Century Europe: Expansion and Conflict* (New York: Macmillan, 1993), p. 51, reproduced by permission of the publisher; **Table 7-1 (p. 281)** The Size of European Armies, 1690–1814, in Paul Kennedy, *The Rise and Fall of the Great Powers* (New York: Vintage, 1989), p. 99, reproduced by permission of the publisher; **Table 9-1 (p. 371)** European Population, 1700–1800, in Paul Kennedy, *The Rise and Fall of the Great Powers* (New York: Vintage, 1989), reproduced by permission of the publisher.

INDEX

Page numbers in *italics* refer to illustrations and figures.

Nemours, Treaty of (1585), 148
neo-classicism, 129
Neo-Platonists, 72–73
Netherlands, 299–300, 435
  agriculture in, 183, 223, 263, 369
  American Revolution and, 478
  arts in, 89–90, 269–71, 273
  British wars with, 486, 487
  bubonic plague in, 20
  Catholics in, 266, 268
  censorship in, 427
  colonization by, *see* Dutch Empire
  decline of, 271–73
  dikes in, 268
  economic conditions in, 262–67
  eighteenth-century political reform
    efforts in, 486
  in eighteenth-century rivalries, 442, 444
  English alliance with, 272, 319–20
  English wars with, 252, 253, 254, 272
  Enlightenment in, 399
  financial institutions of, 261–62, 281,
    384
  French Revolution and, 522, 528, 536,
    540, 545
  in French wars of religion, 144
  Glorious Revolution and, 258
  golden age of, 260–71, *261*
  government in, 179, 232, 261–62, 273,
    277
  Huguenots in, 296
  literacy in, 417
  literature of, 273
  Louis XIV's invasion of, 272
  manufacturing in, 384
  middle classes in, 233
  military of, 272, 280, 281, *281*, 459
  Napoleonic wars and, 565, 567, 573, 579,
    585
  nobles of, 219, 356, 384
  Old Regime French wars with, 258, 272,
    319, *319*, 320
  overseas trade of, 80, 81, 183, 184, 185,
    186, 233, 254, 262, 265, 444, 445,
    478
  painting in, 269–71, 273
  population growth in, 264, 371, *371*
  poverty in, 267
  printing in, 38
  Reformation in, 88, 115–16, 121, 136
  religion in, 266–69, 273
  religious freedom in, 266, 273
  representative government of, 179, 232,
    277
  science in, 349
  Spanish control of, 189, 193, 196, 260,
    261
  stadholder's role in, 262
  Swedish alliance with, 272
  taxes in, 219, 225

  textile manufacturing in, 80, 224, 273
  in Thirty Years' War, 159, 166, 168, 173
  towns in, 28
  trade and commerce in, 24, 25, 27, 80,
    209, 262, 264–65, *264*, 267, 271–
    72, 273, 381, 573
  war of independence of, 121, 138, 145,
    154, 163, 164, 165, 168, 174, 179,
    205, 219–22, *220*, *221*, 227, 229,
    232, 262, 275, 351
  and War of the Austrian Succession,
    453–54
  in War of the Spanish Succession, 321
Netherlands, Southern, *see* Belgium
New Amsterdam, 254
New Brunswick, 447
Newcastle, Thomas Pelham-Holles, duke of,
  460–61, 467, 470
Newfoundland, 254, 321, 447
New France, 156
New Model Army, 247, 248, 250, 251, 253
newspapers and magazines, *see* print media
Newton, Sir Isaac, 340, *341*, 342–44, 345,
  347, 348, 349, 351, 352–53, 401,
  402
New York, 254
Ney, Marshal Michel, 583
Nicholas of Cusa, 332
Nightwatch (Rembrandt), 270
Nile, Battle of the (1798), *551*, 552
Nineteen Propositions (England; 1642),
  243
"Ninety-five Theses or Disputations on the
  Power and Efficacy of Indulgences"
  (Luther), 101–2, *101*
nobles:
  absolutism and, 277, 278–79
  in eighteenth century, 356–59
  English monastic lands bought by, 124
  in fifteenth and sixteenth centuries, 5, 9,
    12, *12*, 26, 33, 36
  hunting rights of, 393–94
  in Italian Renaissance, 52–53, 59
  legal privileges of, 357–58, 364, 369,
    434–35, 509, 585
  in Napoleonic France, 568–69
  number of, 356
  as officers, 458, 562, 575
  poorer, 358
  private armies of, 36
  urban growth and, 388
  see also specific countries
Nogarola, Isotta, 66
nominalism, 95–96, 101
non-juring priests, in French Revolution,
  423–424
North, Frederick, Lord, 476
North Africa, Arabs in, 5
North America, *see* Americas
North Briton, (John Wilkes), 473, 474